Encyclopedia of
American
Activism
1960 to the Present

Encyclopedia of
American Activism
1960 to the Present

Margaret B. DiCanio

ABC-CLIO

Santa Barbara, California
Denver, Colorado
Oxford, England

Library of Congress Cataloging-in-Publication Data

DiCanio, Margaret.
    Encyclopedia of American activism, 1960 to the present / Margaret
  DiCanio.
       p.   cm.
    Includes bibliographical references and index.
    ISBN 0-87436-899-5 (alk. paper)
    1. Political participation—United States—Encyclopedias.
2. Political activists—United States—Encyclopedias. 3. New Left—
United States—Encyclopedias. 4. Social
movements—United States—
Encyclopedias. I. Title.
JK1764.D53   1998

323'.04'097309045—dc21

98-39933

03 02 01 00 99 98 10 9 8 7 6 5 4 3 2 1

This book is printed on acid-free paper ⊛ .
Manufactured in the United States of America

ABC-CLIO, Inc.
130 Cremona Drive, P.O. Box 1911
Santa Barbara, California 93116-1911

Contents

A search for social justice during the 1960s and the 1970s aroused controversy and conflict in streets, classrooms, courtrooms, and families throughout the United States and other Western democracies. Boycotts, marches, protests, demonstrations, and suits against the government called for change. Although the causes and the tactics were not new, the theatrics with which the demands were made was new, as was the presence of media that carried the demands into America's living rooms.

Also new was the involvement of a large number of American college students and their faculties. The students brought with them high energy and imagination. Unlike blacks, unionists, veterans, and the poor, who had a history of protest, neither students nor faculty were hampered by fears of losing jobs or homes.

Some historians and the public refer to the events of the 1960s and 1970s as "the movement," as if there had been only one movement. There were many movements. They borrowed strategy and tactics from one another, and members often left their work in one movement to lend a hand in another.

The lifestyle of the bohemian beats, which involved frequent sexual encounters, endless traveling, marijuana, mysticism, jazz, and freedom, appealed to many young people who felt stifled by the conformity of their parents. They adopted symbols of beat freedom—sloppy forms of dress, profanity, and exotic makeup. The beat lifestyle was disseminated by rebels known as the hippies, who hoped to spread a message of love, psychedelic drugs, and rock and roll. The dress styles of the hippies were embraced by participants in other movements. Leather jackets and denims gave way to bell-bottom pants, beads, sideburns and beards, and long hair. Many also adopted the hippies' casual attitude toward drugs and multiple sex partners. In time, sexual freedom came under fire when women from the New Left questioned why they were welcomed as sex partners but never as leaders and policymakers.

Some movements happened simultaneously —pacifists like James Farmer had been working on both the civil rights and antiwar fronts for

Introduction

years—and some movements took place successively, as with the beats' lonely rebellion giving way to the hippies' embrace of the whole world. The nonviolent requests of the civil rights movement were supplanted by Black Power demands. The feminist movement's moderates, who reasoned with men, were eclipsed by the demands and strident ridicule of radical women's liberationists. The antiwar movement came in three varieties—lifelong pacifists bent on ending all wars; students and veterans appalled and wearied by the Vietnam War; and a mixture of clergy, scientists, and many others terrified by the prospect of nuclear war.

The events of the 1960s had their origins in the preceding decades. The fifteen years of the Depression, with its widespread joblessness, followed by World War II and the totalitarian threat of Nazi and Japanese ambition, left that generation with a feeling that combined caution with a sense of great accomplishment. For the next fifteen years, as Europe and Asia rebuilt themselves, having a job and still being alive were pleasures that focused the attention of many on home, family, and getting ahead. In the United States, the 1950s are often pictured as a decade of passivity and conformity. A myriad of factors dampened dissent.

World War II was widely viewed as a struggle between good and evil. Within months after the end of the war, the Cold War began. The Soviet

Union refused to permit democratic elections in the areas of Eastern Europe it had liberated from Nazi Germany and enforced communism as a way of life. Winston Churchill declared in 1946 that an iron curtain was descending across the continent. In 1947, President Harry Truman announced his Truman Doctrine: the United States would grant moral and financial assistance to countries whose political stability was threatened by communism. The United States would defend and rebuild Europe through the Marshall Plan, which would supply allies with economic and military aid. In 1948, Communists seized the government of Czechoslovakia and closed access to Berlin. The United States instituted the Berlin Airlift in response. In Asia, communist forces won the Chinese civil war, and in 1950, a combined force authorized by the United Nations was sent to Korea, with the United States contributing the largest number of troops.

America was once again at war. The big difference from World War II was that the threat of nuclear war had made America vulnerable. Government leaders and newspaper editorials claimed that the Soviet Union was preparing for a nuclear conquest of the United States. The world became divided into good guys (Americans and noncommunists) and bad guys (all communists). The Truman and Eisenhower administrations instituted sweeping inquiries into employee loyalty. From 1947 to 1956, approximately 2,700 federal employees were dismissed. (Some were dismissed because they were perceived as security risks rather than as being actually disloyal.) Another 12,000 resigned rather than be subjected to investigation and dismissal.

The most rigorous advocacy of the search for subversives began in February 1950, when the junior senator from Wisconsin, Joseph McCarthy, announced to the Republican women's club of Wheeling, West Virginia: "I have in my hand a list of 205 that were known to the secretary of state as being members of the Communist Party and are still making and shaping the policy of the State Department." Congress investigated and declared his charges "a hoax and a fraud." But, in June 1950, when the North Koreans attacked the South Koreans, no politician wanted to be perceived as "soft on Communism."

McCarthy launched an era, later named after him, during which no one was safe from suspicion. The Wisconsin senator even denounced the secretary of state, Dean Acheson, as the "Great Red Dean" and charged "those who wear the label Democrat wear it with the stain of historic betrayal." The search for subversives was relentless. American Communist Party leaders were either fined or jailed. Members had to register with the government, and tourists had to sign a declaration that they were not prostitutes, homosexuals, or communists.

McCarthyism stifled debate. To question public policy entailed a risk of being labeled a communist. Colleges and universities, traditional sites for airing dissenting ideas, joined the rush to protect themselves against subversives. Loyalty oaths were instituted, and refusal to sign became grounds for dismissal. An estimated 600 teachers and professors lost their jobs. Outside speakers were seldom invited to campus, lest they be tainted.

While the far right searched for subversives, spies, and communist infiltration everywhere, the far left often dismissed all suspicions as hysteria. But documents that became available after the fall of the Soviet Union revealed that the Soviets' efforts at spying, starting long before World War II, were both more assiduous than many people wanted to believe and generally less effective than American intelligence gathering. In addition, although President Dwight D. Eisenhower, a former general, contributed to the search for subversives in the United States, he also warned against a mindless military buildup. However, a Marxist revolution in Cuba, the Bay of Pigs fiasco, and the Cuban missile crisis buried his warnings under the urge to contain the Soviet threat.

McCarthyism suppressed dissent, but critics of the government and the culture never disappeared entirely, no matter how stifling the social climate became. The beats of the mid- and late 1950s rebelled against the conformity and "dropped out" to pursue personal and literary rebellion. Among other things, they ridiculed the prudishness of the 1950s. One example is the television show *I Love Lucy*. When the star, Lucille Ball, discovered she was expecting a baby, the scriptwriters wrote her delicate condition into the script, but network executives would not permit the word "pregnancy" to be spoken on the air.

Not everyone had a job, and the war to bring democracy to the world had not brought liberation to everyone. Since the end of Reconstruction, little had been done to improve the political and social position of black people. But blacks were not alone in deep poverty; poor whites in Appalachia and migrant farmers who worked America's fields were periodically rediscovered by the media—only to be forgotten again. One of the better-known exposés of migrant farm life was "Harvest of Shame," a television documentary done by Edward R. Murrow on CBS in 1960.

The GI Bill was a source of change. For the first time in the history of the United States, veterans received substantial benefits to reward their risks and sacrifices. Benefits that enabled World War II and Korean War veterans to go to college changed higher education in America. College enrollment soared; colleges were no longer sites to educate only the privileged. The GI Bill brought a substantial segment of the lower-middle class and working class into the world of ideas.

Population growth also became an instrument of change. The dearth of babies born in the 1930s became a boom of babies born from 1946 through 1964. By the 1960s, prosperity brought the first wave of the baby boomers to college campuses. By reason of their numbers, they grew up competing with each other for attention and resources—and ownership of ideas. Everything in life became open to debate—particularly social justice. A need for change was taken for granted. Parents and grandparents who had labored to send their children and grandchildren to college were bewildered by the young rebels' attack on many symbols they held sacred.

A sign of simmering unrest among blacks came as early as the 1947 "Journey of Reconciliation," a trip through the upper South to test compliance with the 1946 Supreme Court decision in *Morgan v. Commonwealth of Virginia* to outlaw

segregation in interstate travel. James Farmer, a member of Chicago's Fellowship of Reconciliation (FOR), a pacifist organization, helped organize it. In 1942 Farmer had helped organize the Congress of Racial Equality (CORE).

A bright spot for blacks was the 1954 *Brown v. Board of Education of Topeka* Supreme Court ruling that eliminated legal segregation in America's schools. In December 1955, black seamstress Rosa Parks refused to give up her seat on a Montgomery, Alabama, bus to a white passenger. Her arrest led to a bus boycott by blacks and the subsequent formation of the Southern Christian Leadership Conference (SCLC), with the Reverend Martin Luther King, Jr., as leader. The Montgomery boycott led to a limited number of local nonviolent actions by blacks in communities in the South, but fear of being beaten or lynched prevented most from taking action. Exposure to outsiders via television and an influx of students engaged in voter registration drives provided blacks immobilized by fear with hope for a better future and encouraged activism.

Broad media coverage of a sit-in on February 1, 1960, supplied a model for many. Four black students sat in at a lunch counter in Greensboro, North Carolina, and persisted until the lunch counter was desegregated. The students' example inspired a generation of young blacks and some whites to become active. Two months later, the Student Nonviolent Coordinating Committee (SNCC) came into being with the goal of linking together southern civil rights groups that advocated nonviolence, while avoiding domination by older, patriarchal, church-based groups. SNCC provoked confrontations with segregationists, local police, and the southern power structure. Members launched massive voter registration drives. SNCC had a profound effect on the radicalism of the 1960s. Other activists emulated SNCC members' bravery and egalitarian ethics. Like SNCC workers, many accepted jail terms, beatings, and tear gas as the price to be paid for dissent.

The Freedom Rides began in May 1961 when seven black and six white volunteers from various groups boarded two buses in Washington, D.C., and set out to test compliance with the 1960

Supreme Court decision in *Boynton v. Virginia* that desegregated waiting rooms and restaurants for interstate passengers. Volunteers on one bus were attacked in Rock Hill, South Carolina, and in Anniston, Alabama, they were beaten and their bus was burned. The second bus met a similar fate in Birmingham, Alabama. Volunteers on a third bus that left from Nashville, Tennessee, on May 17, 1961, were beaten, and some of the black volunteers were jailed for two months for attempting to use a white restroom. The press publicized the events widely, and some participants began to wonder about the wisdom of nonviolence.

Blacks focused on gaining their civil rights, while the New Left had a broader political and economic view. Made up mostly of college students, the New Left was distinguished from the Old Left, which was composed mostly of communists, socialists, and social democrats. Unlike the Old Left, which tried to achieve political change through unions, people in the New Left thought everyone could be a rebel if they could be led to a greater understanding of the political and economic plight of the poor. Rather than drawing their ideology from traditional leftist sources such as Karl Marx, Friedrich Engels, and Vladimir Lenin, the New Left drew its wisdom from a variety of places, including the Beatles.

In the fall of 1964, the Free Speech Movement (FSM) at the University of California at Berkeley brought together veterans of the Freedom Rides. When the university administration forbade all political activity not related to campus life, the students questioned the operation of the institution and launched a massive sit-in. The FSM became a model for other campus protests, until more violent disruptions began in the late 1960s.

The antiwar movement of the 1960s and early 1970s caught people up in an examination of many of America's favorite myths and reached conclusions far more subversive than those President Eisenhower made about the risks to democracy of a massive military buildup. Activist organizations helped to take these discussions out of the living rooms and classrooms and into the streets.

Despite prosperity and the passage of civil rights legislation in the mid-1960s, most blacks in northern inner cities lived in poverty. During the summer of 1964, Harlem exploded in a riot. The uprising was quelled by massive police violence. Many blacks, like Malcolm X, a member of the Nation of Islam, questioned the effectiveness of nonviolent resistance. He advocated black self-defense and a separate black nation. Although Malcolm X later changed his mind about separation, his earlier stance continued to have an influence on black radicals for the remainder of the decade. He was assassinated on February 21, 1965.

Between 1964 and 1967, 101 major riots and scores of minor disruptions took place in cities across the nation. Police made 28,932 arrests. On April 4, 1968, the Reverend Martin Luther King, Jr., was murdered. His death provoked nationwide riots. During this period of riots and surging black anger, SNCC purged its white staff members and abandoned nonviolence. The SNCC chairperson, Stokely Carmichael (now known as Kwame Ture), popularized the slogan "Black Power." The shift by SNCC away from a nonviolent philosophy was a reopening of a longstanding argument within the black community. One view strives toward assimilation within the overall American culture. The other advocates separateness. The tension between the two views continues into the 1990s.

From 1968 to 1971, women who had dropped out of other movements because of sexism brought skills learned in other protests with them. They organized large demonstrations for "free abortion on demand" and an end to job discrimination, pornography, and violence against women.

In the early 1970s, these movements gradually declined. On March 29, 1973, the North Vietnamese released sixty American prisoners of war, who left Vietnam with the last U.S. troops. Remaining Americans were evacuated from the top of the U.S. Embassy on April 30, 1975. More than 58,000 Americans had died in Vietnam. Legal segregation and the war in Vietnam were over. Yet despite the victories they had won, many radicals felt like failures. The conservative era of the 1980s increased some activists' feelings that the struggle had all been for nothing. Yet many movements that blossomed in the 1960s and 1970s were incorporated into mainstream America. The environmental movement, the women's movement, the consumer movement, the disability rights movement, the gay movement, and many others still labor on behalf of their causes.

Nor did the search for social justice die. President Jimmy Carter, in office from 1976 to 1980, championed human rights around the world and continued to do so after he left office. Noam Chomsky, MIT linguist and expert on international policy, asserted that many more people have been and continue to be involved in the sanctuary movement than in all the movements of the 1960s and 1970s. The need for the sanctuary movement did not end with cease-fires in Central America. In the April 18, 1997, issue of the *National Catholic Reporter*, sanctuary movement workers were asked once again to take a stand to prevent mass deportations of Salvadorans and Guatemalans.

The deportations had been deferred for six years as a consequence of a suit by the American Baptist Churches against U.S. Attorney General Richard Thornburgh. The American Baptist Churches (ABC) represented eighty religious and refugee assistance organizations. Settlement of the case stipulated that requests for asylum would be held up until the Immigration and Naturalization Service (INS) could deal with a backlog of cases.

By the time the INS was ready to deal with those deferred, six years had passed and, in the interim, new immigration restrictions had been enacted that dramatically reduced chances for approval. The old law permitted suspension of deportation for undocumented immigrants of good moral character who had lived in the United States continuously for seven years and who would experience extreme hardship if deported. The new law, which went into effect April 1, 1997, required ten years of continuous residence and "exceptional and extremely unusual hardship" for the family of the deported who are U.S. citizens or lawful permanent residents.

The flood of asylum seekers being returned threatened fragile Central American peace agreements, and the loss of money the refugees had sent regularly from the United States jeopardized unstable economies.

Although many problems in the 1990s were nationwide in their scope, activists were less likely to think they could solve them for the whole society. They focused on finding solutions on a local level. Teachers were delegated to take on more burdens as they were asked to civilize their students, teach them about birth control and sexually transmitted diseases, encourage them to abstain from drugs and alcohol, and manage a rising tide of violence.

As the amount of violence among adults in the nation dropped and violence among the young rose, local activists formed small groups to launch programs to divert youngsters into less destructive modes of behavior. Nevertheless, accidents, suicide, and murder remained principal causes of death among young males. A spate of murders in rural America by youngsters who brought guns to school shattered comforting notions that crime and violence were confined to inner-city neighborhoods.

Binge drinking by high school and college students became of increasing concern to parents and teachers. Binge drinkers consume large quantities rapidly to get drunk quickly and risk exceeding the body's ability to process alcohol, which can result in coma and death. Some students began practicing drinking in high school to get ready for college. When admonished by parents, they reminded their parents that they had done drugs in the 1960s.

Activism on behalf of children in the 1990s received a boost when Marian Wright Edelman, the founder of the Children's Defense Fund, enlisted the aid of First Lady Hillary Rodham Clinton. In connection with a book she wrote called *It Takes a Village and Other Lessons Children Teach Us*, the First Lady toured the country urging adults to take more responsibility for the well-being of children.

By the 1990s, the theatrical techniques of the 1960s and 1970s on behalf of social issues had lost much of their power to gain media attention. The success of activist campaigns increasingly depended on enlistment of a celebrity as spokesperson, such as actress Elizabeth Taylor for AIDS, actor and producer Robert Redford for the environment, and comedian Jerry Lewis for muscular dystrophy.

Reasons for a lessened interest in social causes in the 1990s were not clear. Perhaps because grassroots movements are labor intensive and the generation that followed the baby boomers was substantially smaller, there are fewer hands to go around to take on causes.

One of the most successful efforts by activists during the 1970s through the 1990s was not a grassroots movement. It was a no-smoking campaign waged by public health professionals. In the mid-1970s nonsmokers could not escape from the smoke generated by colleagues, friends, and family. By the mid-1990s, smokers were forced to go outdoors to smoke and the attorneys general of several states were suing the tobacco companies for recovery of state monies spent for smokers' health care costs.

One promising trend of the 1990s was the inclusion of "community service learning" as a requirement for high school graduation. High schools arranged for students to spend time working in community programs such as nursing homes, nursery schools, recreational programs, and town or municipal government. This trend may result in a new generation being inspired by grassroots activism.

Encyclopedia of
American
Activism
1960 to the Present

Abernathy, Reverend Ralph (1926–1990)

Following the arrest of Rosa Parks in 1955 for refusing to give up her bus seat to a white passenger on a Montgomery, Alabama, bus, the Reverend Ralph David Abernathy enlisted his close friend and colleague the Reverend Martin Luther King, Jr., to help organize a community effort to boycott the city's buses. Abernathy and King were among the founders of the Southern Christian Leadership Conference (SCLC), a major organizing force in the civil rights movement.

The grandson of a slave and the tenth son of a farmer, Abernathy grew up in a devoutly Christian home. His father was a leader in the black community. Perhaps because he lived within a respected black farm family and had little contact with whites, until he joined the Army during World War II, Abernathy had never left Alabama or personally suffered from the effects of Jim Crow laws (laws that permit segregation, named for an old minstrel song). After service overseas during the closing months of World War II, he pursued his two passions, the ministry and mathematics. Abernathy was ordained in the Baptist ministry in 1948 and received a bachelor of science degree in mathematics from Alabama College in Montgomery in 1950. In graduate school, he turned from mathematics to sociology because, as he said, "I realized my life was with people." Abernathy was awarded a master's degree in 1951 from Atlanta University in Atlanta, Georgia.

While studying in Atlanta, he met Martin Luther King, Jr., at the Ebenezer Baptist Church, where King's father was pastor. The two men resumed their friendship in Montgomery, Alabama, where they also became colleagues. In 1951 Abernathy was appointed pastor of the First Baptist Church. Three years later King moved to Montgomery to become pastor of the Dexter Avenue Baptist Church.

Following their success in the Montgomery bus boycott, in an ongoing struggle to end Jim Crow laws, King, Abernathy, and the SCLC brought the philosophy and practice of nonviolent resistance into cities and towns throughout the South and north to Chicago. Protests and

marches were not welcomed by many white residents. Abernathy and King often found themselves in situations in which "we really didn't know which were the worst, the police or the angry mob."

For striving to achieve equal civil rights for black Americans, Abernathy and King were often jailed. Each time the two ministers went to jail together, they spent the first twenty-four hours fasting, in Abernathy's words, "to purify our souls, in order that we would have no hatred in our hearts toward the jailer and a strong determination to tear down the system responsible." From Abernathy's perspective, violence is the weapon of the weak, and nonviolence is the weapon of the strong.

In time Abernathy and King realized that a full array of constitutional rights alone would not bring equality to blacks until the United States dealt realistically with the plight of the poor. With that in mind, they planned the Poor People's Campaign, a massive demonstration in Washington, D.C., during which poor people of all races would confront government leaders. The demonstration, scheduled for March 1968, was postponed to permit King to intervene in the sanitation workers' strike in Memphis, Tennessee. On his second trip to Memphis in connection with the strike, King was assassinated, on April 4, 1968. He died in Abernathy's arms.

Anticipating his own death, King had structured the leadership of SCLC to ensure that his philosophy of nonviolence would not be lost after he was gone. Abernathy was the logical successor. Before taking the reins, as he had so often with King when they were jailed, Abernathy fasted. After seven days of prayer, he felt prepared to take over his new responsibility. Abernathy's retreat was viewed by some observers as a lack of confidence in himself. When he emerged from his brief exile, he told reporters that the demonstration would go on as planned. Participation in the Poor People's Campaign vastly exceeded all expectations.

After an unsuccessful run for Congress, in the late 1970s Abernathy developed a model program to help people escape from welfare. When he could not gain either private or financial support or funding from Democrats in Congress, he turned to the Republicans. His well-publicized endorsement of Ronald Reagan for president, which gained him nothing, was a continuous source of embarrassment for him.

Abernathy died in 1990 after a lifetime spent in the pursuit of racial harmony.

See also King, Reverend Martin Luther, Jr.; Poor People's Campaign; Young, Andrew
References Ralph Abernathy. *And the Walls Came Tumbling Down: An Autobiography,* 1989; Andrew Young. *An Easy Burden: The Civil Rights Movement and the Transformation of America,* 1996.

Abzug, Bella (1920–1998)

Her family claimed that Bella Abzug was born yelling. As an outspoken advocate for women's rights, she played a prominent role when the women's movement revived in the 1960s after forty years of being dormant. Abzug said that she was born a feminist in the year that women gained the vote (1920) after more than a half-century of campaigning. Her father was a pacifist.

As a child, Abzug lived in an Orthodox Jewish household with her parents, Emanuel and Esther Savitsky, along with her maternal grandfather, Wolf Tanklefsky, his wife, and their bachelor son. Whenever Abzug was not in school, she went with her grandfather to the synagogue, where he went three times a day to pray. By the time she

was seven, Abzug could recite complicated Hebrew prayers with ease. Her grandfather would set her on a table to show off her competence to his friends, an encouragement seldom given to girls, especially for learning Hebrew.

Abzug's early exposure to the teachings of her faith, combined with the way her family lived, served as a strong guide to her as an adult. In her words, "To be a Jew is to care—not only about ourselves, but about others." Abzug's strong faith was tested when she was forbidden at the age of thirteen, following her father's death, to say kaddish—a mourner's prayer—traditionally said by the sons or brothers of the deceased man. Undaunted, Abzug went to the synagogue and said the kaddish. It was her first confrontation with Judaism's unequal treatment of women. About the experience, she said later, "I learned that I could speak out and no one would stop me."

While attending Columbia Law School, Abzug met and married Martin Abzug, a gentle, witty man who took great pride in his wife and typed her law school papers. During the 1950s, she concentrated on labor law and civil rights. Like her father, Abzug hated war; she helped found Women Strike for Peace. Her friends in the peace movement encouraged her to run for Congress. Supported by a veritable army of peace movement women, Abzug won an upset victory in the primary for Manhattan's nineteenth congressional district and went on to win the election. The media seemed to enjoy writing about Abzug, an outspoken radical whose trademark was her large floppy hats. During three terms in the House of Representatives, she gained a reputation for being vocal, controversial, persistent, and hardworking.

Abzug coined the phrase "A woman's place is in the House"—the House of Representatives. With Betty Friedan and others, Abzug founded the National Organization for Women (NOW) in 1966. Over the next three decades, she organized many other women's organizations. In 1990, Abzug founded the Women's Environmental and Development Organization (WEDO), an internationally based lobby group. In her role as president of WEDO, Abzug organized the World's Women's Congress for a Healthy Planet and a

This woman's place is in the House...
the House of Representatives!

Bella Abzug
for Congress.

Congressional campaign poster for Bella Abzug.

series of women's caucuses at international conferences that have had a major impact on United Nations' policies in connection with the environment, economic justice, reproductive rights, and human rights.

During five decades of activism, Abzug inspired young women not only to struggle on their own behalf but to labor on behalf of others and of the planet on which they live. She died on March 31, 1998.

See also Feminist Organizations; Friedan, Betty; Women's Movement
References Joyce Antler. *The Journey Home: Jewish Women and the American Century,* 1997; Marcia Cohen. *The Sisterhood: The Inside Story of the Women's Movement and the Leaders Who Made It Happen,* 1988; Doris Faber. *Bella Abzug,* 1976.

AIDS

The disease known as acquired immune deficiency syndrome (AIDS) is an incurable disease passed along by the transfer of bodily fluids, typically semen and blood. There is no evidence that other body fluids, such as saliva or tears, are transmitters. Transfer of the disease generally takes place during intercourse, particularly anal intercourse, during childbirth, or by sharing needles contaminated by blood during drug use.

The date of onset of the disease in the United States is not certain. Some researchers believe the first U.S. case may have been seen as early as 1960. Some scientists think it might have existed in isolated populations long before the 1960s. It may have killed off those infected without reaching the outside world.

In the spring of 1981, reports from both the East Coast and the West Coast informed physicians that otherwise healthy young men had developed unexpected illnesses. The illnesses were *pneumocystis carinii* pneumonia (PCP) and Kaposi's sarcoma (KS), a form of skin cancer formerly found among Central Africans and Central and Eastern Europeans. By late August 1981, 108 cases of KS and PCP had been reported in the United States. Over 90 percent were among men who were known to be homosexual. Both PCP and KS were found to be associated with patients who had, for some reason, a suppressed immune system. Kaposi's sarcoma was apt to be seen in people taking drugs to suppress their immune systems after a transplant.

Researchers found that the virus that caused AIDS—known as human immunodeficiency virus (HIV)—set in motion a chain of events that led to the host having opportunistic diseases (illnesses the body could not prevent because of a compromised immune system). When the AIDS virus enters the human bloodstream, it is attracted to one particular type of white blood cell, the lymphocytes, called T-helper cells. These white blood cells, like all white blood cells, are parts of the body's immune system, the body's defense against infection. The AIDS virus invades the T-helper cells and in time destroys them. Once the immune system is suppressed by destruction of the T-helper cells, the body becomes vulnerable to "opportunistic infections," infections normally handled easily by the immune system.

The isolation of the virus in 1978 enabled French and U.S. companies to develop blood tests to detect the presence of antibodies to the virus. Luc Montagnier of the Pasteur Institute in Paris and Robert Gallo of the National Cancer Institute are codiscoverers.

To predict who was at risk for the disease, researchers looked for risk factors in the gay lifestyle. The Centers for Disease Control developed a twenty-two-page questionnaire called Protocol no. 577, which they used with people who were HIV-positive and with selected control subjects. The data collected revealed that the oral and anal sexual practices of gay men added to their susceptibility to a host of infections.

The public, the press, governmental officials, and even some physicians and researchers viewed the disease as a problem for the gay community that posed no threat to the rest of society. Because of the lack of perceived threat and because of the stigma attached to homosexuality, research into origins of the disease and into treatments to counteract its lethal effects was slow in getting started.

The concept of AIDS as a homosexual's disease was jolted by the discovery of AIDS among drug users, Haitians, and hemophiliacs—and among blood transfusion recipients. The concept was further challenged by a small but growing number of cases among women and babies. Most of the women were exposed to the disease through sexual contact with a bisexual male or with an intravenous (IV) drug user. The numbers of victims remained higher among gay males than among other groups.

By early 1985, 60 percent of all cases of patients known to be positive for the presence of HIV in the United States had been reported in five cities (New York, San Francisco, Los Angeles, Miami, and Newark, New Jersey). The highest per capita concentration of AIDS cases was in a migrant worker's town, Belle Glades, in Palm Beach County, Florida. The high incidence of AIDS in Belle Glades prompted some observers to suspect the disease might be transmitted by insects. The Centers for Disease Control, after a brief study, disagreed.

Confirmation that the disease could be passed from women to men—not just from men to men or men to women—alarmed the general public. Dissemination of information about prevention and the reduction of risk picked up in 1986 and 1987. Yet the content of explicit information needed to inform the public about AIDS created a furor about the use of street names for sexual acts. Educators pointed out that information packaged in scientific and clinical words could not inform a public that did not know the meanings of the professional words. In 1987 school boards, parents, and health officials battled over sex education in schools.

Words like "condoms" and phrases like "safe sex" became familiar through repetition on the nightly television news. Possible breakthroughs in the origins and treatment of the disease were reported almost daily. Some reports suggested therapies or vaccines would be soon forthcoming, whereas others suggested years of trial and error faced researchers.

A theme of promiscuity, that is, that frequent exposures to infections with multiple partners made people vulnerable to AIDS, continued in the minds of the public and of researchers. The frequent exposure theory had to be rethought when a woman developed signs of viral exposure after one sexual encounter with her husband, who had acquired the HIV virus via a transfusion.

On the treatment scene, a drug called azidothymidine (AZT) began clinical trials in twelve hospitals in February 1986. The drug was given to AIDS patients who had been stricken with PCP within the previous four months. Some patients who displayed some less-frightening symptoms of full-blown AIDS were also included.

The trials were discontinued in September 1986 by an independent board sponsored by the National Institutes of Health when among the 145 patients receiving the drug there had been only one death, while among the 137 patients receiving a placebo there had been sixteen deaths. The trials were halted because it was felt that it was no longer ethical to give some of the participants placebos. AZT was found to be an effective treatment for AIDS, but it had serious side effects.

By the spring of 1987, experts in AIDS research were complaining of delays in drug testing due to technical, ethical, and financial problems; bureaucratic inertia; and lack of cooperation by major drug manufacturers. The government had planned to license Hoffman-LaRoche to manufacture a promising antiviral drug, dideoxycytidine (DDC), when the plan was challenged by two other drug companies. In spite of apparent industry competition, the president of the Hoffman-LaRoche Exploratory Research division, when asked why pharmaceutical companies gave a low priority to developing drugs for AIDS, said, "one million people isn't a market that's exciting."

The concentration of AIDS in urban areas placed a burden on health care facilities serving large patient population with AIDS. Health care staffs in institutions such as Bellevue Hospital in New York City faced patients on a daily basis who they knew were going to die despite their best efforts. Under those conditions, staffs burned out. Moreover, the fear of being infected remained ever present. Guidelines were established for health care workers to protect themselves against exposure to the blood or bodily fluids of infected patients, although the risk of chance infection from AIDS proved to be minimal.

Gay communities in large cities, particularly in Boston, New York, and San Francisco, lobbied for and organized treatment facilities for severely ill AIDS patients. With considerable success, they also lobbied for additional government funding for treatment and research. Desperate patients were willing to take any substance that offered a glimmer of hope. Activists badgered the Food and Drug Administration (FDA) into speeding up the slow process of new drug approval.

Also in the spring of 1987, the National Academy of Sciences, in a 390-page report, criticized the government's response to AIDS as woefully inadequate. The report called upon the government to allocate $2 billion a year by 1990 for educational campaigns, for the development of a vaccine, and for therapeutic drugs. The report predicted that at least a quarter, and perhaps more than one half, of those infected with the AIDS virus—a group estimated to number between 1 and 1.5 million people—could develop the disease within ten years.

The surgeon general estimated in the spring of 1987 that by 1991, 145,000 AIDS patients would need health and supportive services, at a total cost of $8 to $16 billion. Harvard historian of science Barbara Gutman Rosenkrantz remained unimpressed by projections of the havoc that could be expected from AIDS. By comparison, she pointed out, at the turn of the century, tuberculosis killed as many as 150,000 Americans annually.

Estimates of the number of people who would become infected were difficult to confirm, in part because the time between becoming infected with HIV and the onset of obvious symptoms of AIDS could be as long as ten years. As a consequence, there are many more people who have been infected with HIV than there are people with clear symptoms of AIDS.

By the mid-1990s, AIDS had become a pandemic, a worldwide epidemic. During 1994 alone, an estimated 4 million people worldwide became newly infected, an average of almost 11,000 people each day, more than the total number infected during the entire period from 1975 to 1985. The worldwide cumulative total of people with AIDS, as of January 1, 1995, was 8.5 million in sub-Saharan Africa; 700,000 in Latin America and the Caribbean; and more than 550,000 in North America, Europe, and Oceania.

During the 1990s, conflicts over prevention strategies continued in the United States. Many public health officials advocated needle-exchange programs, provision of clean needles to drug addicts to prevent them from taking drugs with needles used by infected addicts. Some drug rehabilitation experts and some of the public insisted that providing needles encouraged drug use. The issue of condoms in schools divided people into two camps. One group believed that sexual experimentation among teenagers was inevitable and safer when protected by condoms. The other group advocated abstinence and pointed out that the quality of condoms purchased by the school systems was often inadequate.

While the FDA's shortened approval time brought several new drugs into treatment use, it couldn't solve the problem of mutations (genetic changes). The changes were the result of a virus that survived the impact of the drug and passed on the traits that enabled it to survive to succeeding generations. Researchers raced to develop new drugs faster than the virus could mutate.

By 1998, some AIDS researchers felt hopeful enough to look forward to a time when AIDS would be a chronic disease that could be controlled rather than an acute disease that threatened life.

See also Glaser, Elizabeth
References Elinor Burkett. *The Gravest Show on Earth: America in the Age of AIDS,* 1995; Daniel Leone. *The Spread of AIDS,* 1997.

Albany Movement

In May 1961, the first large-scale civil rights uprising following the Montgomery bus boycott took place in Albany, Georgia. Located in the heart of the "Black Belt," Albany had once been a trading center to provide slaves for the plantations of southwest Georgia. Albany's black population comprised 40 percent of the town's 56,000 residents, yet despite their sizable numbers, they lived a segregated life from the cradle to the grave.

With a goal of loosening the hold segregation had on the minds of Albany's blacks, two staff members of the Student Nonviolent Coordinating Committee (SNCC), Charles Sherrod, age 22, and Cordell Reagan, age 18, moved into Albany to set up a voter registration drive. Initially, black ministers would not let the students hold meetings in their churches. They feared the churches would be burned and their homes would be stoned.

The president of the conservative Albany State College for Negroes resisted recruitment of students for fear the all-white state board of regents would cut off the school's funds. The dean of students at the college, Irene Asbury Wright, resigned in protest and opened her home to the activists. Wright was a force behind a coalition formed between the Youth Council of the Na-

tional Association for the Advancement of Colored People (NAACP), the Baptist Ministers' Alliance, and several SNCC groups. The coalition set out to test compliance with the Interstate Commerce Commission's (ICC) ruling that barred segregation in bus terminals. NAACP officials told the Youth Council members they could not participate. The youngsters resigned from NAACP and joined SNCC.

On the weekend before Thanksgiving in 1961, Albany's sheriff (the chief law enforcement officer), an ardent segregationist, arrested Albany State student Bertha Gobe when she entered the terminal's waiting room. After Gobe was arrested, student Bernice Johnson joined a campus protest. The sheriff arrested her. In jail, Johnson, who later became a singer known by the name of Bernice Johnson Reagan, sang protest songs. Several students were also suspended by the college. During the protest, the sheriff packed his jail and sent several protesters to jails in nearby counties. At one point, 15,000 people were in jail. More than 400 high school and college students were arrested when SNCC volunteers tried to integrate the railroad terminal.

The protests inspired a bus boycott in January 1962 when Ola Mae Quarterman, age 18, seated herself in the front of an Albany city bus. She told the white driver, "I paid my damn twenty cents and I can sit where I want." She was arrested.

When, after six months, the federal government had done nothing to respond to the intense protests, Martin Luther King, Jr., traveled to Albany and was arrested. Most blacks, including King, feared jail, not only because the living conditions were horrendous, but because blacks often disappeared after being jailed. Washington responded to King's arrest, and he was hastily released, but not much else changed. Activists kept the pressure up. SNCC's young people tested access to every public facility in the city.

When 16-year-old Shirley Gains attempted to enter a bowling alley, she was dragged down stone steps by police officers and kicked repeatedly. When Mrs. Maria King, who was five months pregnant and carrying a 3-year-old, brought food to the jailed protesters, she was knocked unconscious. Her baby was born dead a few months later. She later thanked SNCC workers for providing her children with an example of courage.

Without federal intervention to enforce federal laws, the sheriff's strategy of jailing protesters to avoid angry mobs was difficult to counteract. The protests continued throughout 1963 and 1964. When the city's library was desegregated, the seating was removed to prevent whites and blacks from sitting together. A judicial decree to integrate the schools was met with token compliance. To prevent mixing of the races, the city's swimming pool was sold to a private corporation.

Eventually, King and SNCC decided further protest would not be productive, and the city remained highly segregated. The Albany movement provided a model for the desegregation of Birmingham, Alabama, the most segregated city in the United States. Birmingham's reaction to protesters was to confront them with snarling dogs and high-powered fire hoses. The publicity that followed made Birmingham's sheriff, "Bull" Connor, the nationally recognized symbol of a segregationist sheriff.

See also Southern Christian Leadership Conference; Student Nonviolent Coordinating Committee
Reference Zita Allen. *Black Women Leaders of the Civil Rights Movement,* 1996.

Alcatraz, Occupation of

In November 1969, fourteen Indians, eleven men and three women, landed on Alcatraz Island, a federal prison facility in San Francisco Bay that had been abandoned in 1963. The Indians approached the resident caretakers and offered to buy the island for $24 in glass beads and cloth, the price Indians wre allegedly offered by the Dutch for Manhattan Island in 1626. Before departing, the protestors proclaimed that the island should be made into a Native American institute and museum.

Two weeks later approximately eighty Indians returned and declared, "We have come to stay." Signs that read "Keep Off U.S. Property" were repainted to read "Keep Off Indian Property." The American flag was replaced with a flag with a red

teepee under a broken peace pipe on a field of blue. Bay-area activists in boats kept the occupying force supplied with food and water.

On Thanksgiving, three hundred Indians celebrated together on the island. They cited an old Sioux treaty that gave Indians the right to occupy unused federal land. With an announcement that federal funds were needed to create a cultural complex, they gave the government two weeks to surrender Alcatraz.

Negotiations between the Indians and the government began and continued into 1970. *Newsweek* declared that Alcatraz had become a symbol of the red man's liberation.

See also Banks, Dennis; Means, Russell; National Indian Youth Council
Reference Terry Anderson. *The Movement and the Sixties: Protest in America from Greensboro to Wounded Knee,* 1995.

Alinsky, Saul (1909–1972)

A social activist, Saul David Alinsky described himself as a "professional radical." In the late 1930s, he began organizing poor communities in Chicago to take action on their own behalf. Alinsky understood the value of media attention in furthering the causes of the people he set out to help. He could always be counted on to provide a quip that deflated some politician or stirred up controversy. For example, in 1964 following a bloody race riot, he was invited to Rochester, New York, by the members of the white churches and the black community to help build a community organization. Alinsky enraged corporate executives of the Eastman Kodak Company, based in Rochester, by saying that "Kodak's only contribution to race relations was the invention of color film." Throughout his life as an activist, Alinsky created tactics and strategies designed to enable those people left out of the game of politics to participate. He inspired succeeding generations to carry on the struggle on behalf of social justice.

During the 1960s and 1970s, college student activists regularly consulted Alinsky about tactics and strategies for organizing. In 1972 college students planned to protest a speech by George Bush in defense of President Richard Nixon's Vietnam War policies. Alinsky advised the students against disrupting the speech with protests because they might be thrown out of school for their efforts. Instead, he suggested they dress as members of the racist group the Ku Klux Klan and cheer and wave whenever Bush said anything in defense of the conduct of the war. The students carried placards that read "The Ku Klux Klan Supports Bush," which they waved along with their cheering.

Alinsky's career as a community organizer began at the University of Chicago. While still an undergraduate, he discovered that the university's sociology faculty were pioneers in their field. Among them were zealots who pursued an understanding of problems in America's industrial cities. They argued that social disorganization, not ethnicity, was the source of disease, crime, and other undesirable characteristics of slum life. It was a common practice for the sociology faculty to send students into Chicago's neighborhoods to observe behavior, collect data, and write reports about a variety of behaviors common to urban life. Among the social organizations studied were dance halls, skid rows, and gangs.

In 1930, Alinsky accepted a graduate fellowship in criminology at the university. As his doctoral project, he chose to study, from the inside, the organized crime gang led by Al Capone. For three years, Alinsky dropped out of school to take a job with the Illinois State Division of Criminology. When he returned to the university, he went to work for Professor Clifford Shaw and the Institute for Juvenile Research. Shaw's philosophy assumed that after gaining the consensus of a neighborhood's residents to work on reform in their own community, larger social reforms, such as a reduction in crime and violence, would follow. Alinsky's experience in criminology made him less sure that improvement would automatically follow. In a 1968 interview with a *Chicago Daily News* reporter, Alinsky said, "All the experts agreed the major causes of crime were poor housing, discrimination, economic insecurity, unemployment, and disease. So what did we do for our

kids? Camping trips and something mysterious called 'character building.' We tackled everything but the issues."

Shaw sent Alinsky into an immigrant Chicago neighborhood called the "Back of the Yards," located behind the Union Stockyard (a holding area where animals were kept until shipped elsewhere or slaughtered for meat and other animal products). Shaw thought homogeneity was critical to organizing. Prior to Alinsky's assignment to the Back of the Yards, neighborhoods that had been organized had been ethnically and religiously homogeneous, which made organizing easier. The Back of the Yards was diverse. Earlier in the century, novelist Upton Sinclair had made the Back of the Yards famous in his graphic book *The Jungle*. Sinclair had portrayed the filthy conditions in Chicago's meatpacking houses and slaughterhouses and the tragic living conditions of those who worked in this industry. Three decades later when Alinsky arrived, not much had changed.

Alinsky's work in the Back of the Yards led him to form three firm principles critical to successful social action:

1. Forget charity. A community gets only what the residents are strong enough to get; therefore they must organize.
2. The residents of a community must be shown that they can have a way of life in which they make their own decisions. Once that is done, the organizer must get out of the way.
3. The organizer either has faith in the people, as did America's Founding Fathers James Madison and James Monroe, or the organizer lacks faith in the people, as did Founding Father Alexander Hamilton. Alinsky had faith.

In 1940, with moral support from the Roman Catholic auxiliary bishop of Chicago, Bernard Sheil, and financial support from Marshall Field III, the merchant-philanthropist, Alinsky established the Industrial Areas Foundation (IAF). IAF's purpose was to contract with communities that sought help in building a community organization. During the decade following World War II, Alinsky organized economically depressed and oppressed communities throughout the United States. His work drew little national attention, but he became a hero to those concerned with the well-being of the poor.

In one midwestern city, the police chief jailed Alinsky on a regular basis. The jail stints gave him time to think and to work on his book *Reveille for Radicals*, in which he described the radical as that person to whom the common good is the greatest social value. He explained that American democracy operates on the basis of pressure groups and power blocks. When the poor are not organized, they are excluded from the democratic process and left to make do with the crumbs from society's table.

Alinsky's wife, Helene, drowned in 1947 while trying to save a child. Her death had a profound effect on the activist. Two decades later, he said about the experience, "When you accept the fact of death, you begin to live. You don't care about your reputation."

During the 1950s, Alinsky organized Italian anticommunist labor unions under contract with the Bishop of Milan, who later became Pope Paul VI. In 1960, with support from the archbishop of Chicago, he made his first move into a black inner-city neighborhood, where he organized The Woodlawn Organization (TWO).

Alinsky's experience with TWO added two principles to his social action philosophy:

1. People are moved by self-interest, not by altruism.
2. Organizers should not bother with official machinery when they want something. Instead, they should go to the person who can give the organizer what the community wants and make that person hurt until he or she gives in.

Acting on the second principle, TWO solved housing grievances by picketing the suburban homes of slumlords. Another group, the Northwest Community Alliance (NCO), provoked an al-most instant improvement in garbage collection by gathering up uncollected garbage and depositing it in the driveway of a council man. In 1965 Alinsky told a group of ministers whom he had been hired to train, "The only way to upset the power structure in your communities is to goad them, confuse them, irritate them, and most of all make them live by their own rules."

Alinsky turned his attention in 1968 from the poor to the white middle class. His work was subsidized by the Midas International Foundation of Chicago. The president of the foundation explained that a lack of organization in middle-class, white neighborhoods on behalf of community goals could be just as harmful to the total society as a lack of organization in poor, black communities.

Alinsky's books have kept his influence alive. His 1989 book *Rules for Radicals* has become a Bible for community and labor organizers. In the 1990s, the issue of economic inequality loomed as large as ever. The gap between rich and poor widened, wages stagnated, layoffs were widespread, and unions lost ground. The percentage of unionized employees in the private sector had dropped from 16.8 percent in 1983 to 10.4 percent in 1996.

In 1994 the AFL-CIO organized "Union Summer," a program designed to attract college and community activists and to channel their quest for social justice into the moribund labor movement. Union Summer was modeled after "Freedom Summer," the 1964 effort by 1,000 college students to register blacks to vote in Mississippi. *Rules for Radicals* was a part of the Union Summer curriculum.

See also Union Movement Rebirth
References Saul Alinsky. *Reveille for Radicals,* 1947; and *Rules for Radicals,* 1989.

Alternative Religions Movement

Although most American religions and clergy supported the status quo of the 1960s, a religious and moral thread wove through the various movements that emerged. Christian and Jewish clergy had been at the forefront of the civil rights movement and participated at high levels in the antiwar movement. Counterculture hippies preached themes of love and peace.

In the minds of many activist clergy, a religious person was one who was committed to action based on conscience. Catholics discussed the idea that priests, in the manner of Jesus, should be advocates for the poor and the outcast. Priests such as Leonard Dubi of Chicago, James Groppi of Milwaukee, and the Berrigan brothers, Daniel and Philip, sought social justice.

Despite exposure to clergy who shared their ideas, many of the 1960s generation turned their backs on mainstream religion and adopted alternative religions. Mainstream magazines like *Time* and *Newsweek* expressed amazement that the generation regularly accused of copping out with drugs or sex or violence was embracing purity, selflessness, and love.

Jesus Freaks, also known as Street Christians, the God Squad, Children of God, or Straight People, established several hundred small communes nationwide and opened coffeehouses, such as the Way Word in Greenwich Village and the Catacombs in Seattle. In San Antonio, they turned a strip joint into a club where musicians played Christian rock. An audience of 8,000 attended the "Sweet Jesus Rock Concert" at Stanford University in California. Fans by the thousands saw *Godspell* and *Jesus Christ Superstar*. Religious activists established 24-hour hotlines, sold T-shirts and bumper stickers, and gave the Jesus power salute—arm raised, fist clenched, and index finger pointing to heaven. At revival meetings in Houston, 11,000 declared themselves for Jesus. In Chicago's Grant Park, an evangelist led a thousand converts in Jesus cheers.

By 1971, well-groomed evangelical Straight People were active on more than 450 campuses. The two largest organizations were Campus Crusade for Christ and Inter-Varsity Christian Fellowship. The Campus Crusade attracted 75,000 to the Cotton Bowl in Dallas for the "Fundamentalist Woodstock."

Near Boston, Rabbi Arthur Green organized Havurot Shalom, where young Jews joined fellowships that rejected traditional authorities and emphasized experimental worship, communal living, and political action. The Catholic Charismatics attracted Catholics to emotional meetings where shouting, rolling on the floor, and speaking in tongues were not unusual. One evangelical pastor said, "My concern is that the staid, traditional churches will reject these kids and miss the most genuine revival of our lifetime."

See also Neal, Sister Marie Augusta; Plowshares Movement; Sisters of the Immaculate Heart of Mary **References** Charles Glock and Robert Bellah, eds. *New Religious Consciousness*, 1976; James Sleeper and Alan Mintz, eds. *The New Jews*, 1971.

American Association of Retired People (AARP)

In 1947, when Dr. Ethel Percy Andrus, the first woman to become a high school principal in California, was forced to retire at age sixty-five, she founded the National Retired Teachers Association (NRTA). An idealist and an organizational wizard, Andrus at age seventy-six created AARP as a parallel organization to bring to nonteachers the benefits she had brought to retired teachers.

The cofounder of AARP was Leonard Davis, a young insurance agent who fashioned a method to provide group health insurance for NRTA members. With his own money, Davis financed the creation of AARP primarily to expand his own mail-order health insurance market.

Until he was forced to break his ties to AARP in 1980, Davis kept AARP almost entirely under his control. He operated it as a sales network to sell high-priced, often inadequate, insurance and many other Davis-created products. Following his departure, AARP struggled to rid itself of the shadow Davis had cast on the organization's other activities.

AARP has 150,000 volunteers around the country. Only a few Fortune 500 companies have a professional staff that large. None has a staff that dedicated. No other volunteer organization, including the Democratic and Republican Parties, can marshal so large a unified force. Volunteer jobs are not just handed out. Volunteers must submit a resume and go through several interviews before being "hired" to work for nothing except reimbursement of expenses.

AARP is a $500 million-a-year organization, by far the largest lobbying group in the country. AARP, with 32 million members, jockeys with the American Automobile Association as the largest member organization.

AARP's political profile has grown in part because of recognition that aging baby boomers, born between 1946 and 1964, pose serious public policy questions about how income and health security will be financed when baby boomers reach retirement age. Such policy questions need solutions before the first wave of baby boomers reach sixty five in 2011. AARP will be a major player in decisions made.

Before becoming acting director in 1989 and director in 1990, Horace Deets began with AARP as an educational volunteer almost twenty years earlier. A former Catholic priest, Deets has the air of a committed idealist, which impressed those with whom he came in contact.

Deets envisioned AARP as the nerve center of a national network of older Americans dedicated to solving the nation's social problems. Among areas in need of attention are the care and protection of the dependent aged; inspiration and drive to mount community improvement programs; service to deprived children as mentors, tutors, and caregivers; and revival of interest in the political process.

The largest of AARP's many service programs are Tax-Aide and 55-Alive. Tax-Aide volunteers provide tax assistance to an estimated 1.5 million low-income aged, many of whom are housebound. Upgraded driving skills and defensive driving techniques are taught by thousands of 55-Alive drivers. The Widowed Persons Services, another large program, is run by volunteers who are themselves widowed. A breast cancer initiative reminds older women of the importance of mammograms. A couple of thousand volunteers aid state nursing home ombudsmen. A grandparents' initiative focuses on the tangle of legal issues that face grandparents who are raising grandchildren.

See also Baby Boomers; Children's Defense Fund; Gray Panthers

Reference Charles Morris. *The AARP: America's Most Powerful Lobby and the Clash of Generations,* 1996.

American Friends Service Committee

The American Friends Service Committee (AFSC), a Quaker organization, was founded in 1917 during World War I to develop opportunities for conscientious objectors to assist civilian victims of the war. Its work is based on the Quaker belief in the worth of every person and faith in the power of love to overcome violence and injustice.

From the 1950s until the 1970s, while continuing its commitment to provide service to civilians in war-torn countries, AFSC was involved in the peace movement, the migrant farm workers' strike, the civil rights movement, and the antiwar movement. AFSC published *Speak Truth to Power, A Quaker Search for Alternatives to Violence: A Study of International Conflict* (Philadelphia, 1955).

In 1965, based on a long-term desire to end school desegregation, AFSC helped place 7,000 children in previously all-white schools. In 1966, AFSC provided aid to civilians in Vietnam in both the north and the south. In 1970, AFSC members counseled thousands of draft-age American citizens on their options. And in 1972, AFSC addressed immigration and unemployment issues on the U.S.-Mexican border. For the film *Witness to War,* a documentary about the war in El Salvador, AFSC won an Oscar and other awards.

See also Antiwar Movement

American Indian Movement
See Banks, Dennis; Bellecourt Brothers, Vernon and Clyde; Means, Russell; Wounded Knee

American Medical Students Association

During the early 1970s, federal funds became available for community groups to start up community health centers. Many were staffed by students in medicine, nursing, allied health, and optometry, who were supervised by medical, dental, and optometric school faculty or volunteers in private practice. Many medical student participants belonged to the American Medical Students Association (AMSA), founded in 1950.

AMSA's community involvement was still evident in the 1990s. For its Forty-eighth Annual Convention in March 1998, the theme was "Leading Medicine into the 21st Century." Students were offered a session on student-run community and public health projects. Another session covered how to work with the homeless, either as a student or as a career option.

At the convention, AMSA developed a minority medical assessment tool to help medical schools assess the adequacy of their environment for minorities. The controversial issue of "physician-assisted suicide" was also addressed in a mock trial.

On March 13, 1998, patients, medical students, and other health care providers-in-training mobilized on Capitol Hill to lobby Congress for health care for all Americans. Invited speakers included President Bill Clinton and Marian Wright Edelman, president of the Children's Defense Fund.

See also Children's Defense Fund; Community Mental Health Center Movement; Homelessness

Antiabortion Movement

Antiabortion advocates refer to themselves as "pro-life," whereas abortion advocates refer to themselves as "pro-choice." Most pro-life groups seemed to have been caught off guard by the *Roe v. Wade* decision in 1973 that legalized abortion under certain conditions. The immediate response was an organized deluge of protest letters to the Supreme Court. Around Easter of 1973, a similar organized flood of letters was aimed at Congress. At their spring meeting, the Catholic Bishops' Conference advised the National Catholic Conference to organize right-to-life groups in every state, call on dioceses to fund church and ecumenical antiabortion efforts, and help the National Right-to-Life Association in every way.

Efforts to enlist the help of government have been quite successful. Various "human life amendments" have been introduced in both houses of Congress; the most common bill seeks to protect the embryo from conception onward. In October 1973, Senator Jesse Helms (R-NC) succeeded in adding an amendment to the Foreign Aid Bill that forbade the use of U.S. funds for abortions or abortifacients (substances that induce abortions). In 1977, Senator Henry Hyde (R-IL) introduced bills that limited the use of public funds for abortions. Beginning in 1980, public funds were restricted to abortions only in cases of rape, incest, or a threat to the life of the mother. Presidents Jimmy Carter, Ronald Reagan, and George Bush all contributed to restrictions placed on abortions. Presidents Reagan and Bush between them appointed five Supreme Court justices who added further restrictions.

Researchers have identified several pathways that lead people to the pro-life/antiabortion movement. Physicians and attorneys who opposed abortion liberalization formed opposition organizations. Religious networks were a primary source of recruits. Feminists for Life was founded by women in the feminist movement. Sojourners, an evangelical group concerned with social issues such as poverty and racism, holds an antiabortion position.

Most pro-life participants say their reason for participation is altruistic, to defend the fetus, which is incapable of defending itself. They point to what researchers have learned via modern technology about how the human child develops in the womb; how active it is; and how aware—responding to sound and light. Pro-life advocates also point to various physicians and scientists who, though pro-choice, support the pro-life contention that life begins at conception, not at birth.

A description by Dr. Paul Rockwell illustrates the point. "While giving an anesthetic for a ruptured ectopic pregnancy . . . I was handed what I believed was the smallest living human ever seen. . . . This tiny human was perfectly developed, with long, tapering fingers, feet, and toes. . . . The baby was extremely alive and swam about in the sac approximately one time per second, with a

An antiabortion rally in Washington, D.C., January 23, 1980.

natural swimmer's stroke." In his book, *ProLife Answers to ProChoice Arguments*, Randy Alcorn disputes the pro-choice allegation that medical facts or illustrations presented by pro-life activists are fake. Whenever he is accused of doctoring photos, Alcorn suggests the accuser check medical textbooks or journals or even *Life* magazine.

Pro-choice advocates accuse pro-life supporters of wanting to "keep women in their place." Dallas Blanchard, chair of the Department of Sociology and Anthropology at the University of West Florida in Pensacola and a United Methodist minister, concluded that the motivation of pro-life activists was broader than just keeping women in their place. He proposed that the dominant motivation of the movement, particularly among the more activist organizations, such as Operation Rescue, was cultural fundamentalism. Blanchard described cultural fundamentalism as a protest against cultural change.

Such changes include the rising status of women, deviant lifestyles such as homosexuality, the absence of prayer and Bible readings in school, and sexual openness and freedom.

Failure to mobilize public opinion toward a ban on abortions provoked some groups to become more activist in the late 1970s and 1980s. Such groups included Joseph Scheidler's Pro-Life Action League, which sponsored picketing and disruption of abortion clinic activities. Scheidler wrote a book called *Closed: 99 Ways to Stop Abortion* (Rockford, IL: Tan Books, 1993), which, although it claimed not to support illegal activities, described many aggressive techniques. Among other things, Scheidler advocated picketing the homes of abortion workers, tracing patients through their license plate numbers for the purpose of accosting them at their homes, and jamming clinic telephone lines to prevent patients from scheduling appointments.

Dissatisfaction with picketing and forms of "mild violence" led to an increase in clinic bombings, which peaked in 1984 and remained relatively high until 1986. When bombings appeared to be counterproductive, Operation Rescue invaded and blockaded clinics for weeks at a time as an alternative. Other tactics included selective boycotts. Perhaps the most effective effort of the antiabortion movement was obstetrician and gynecologist Bernard Nathason's 1985 film *Silent Scream*, produced by the Cleveland-based American Life Films. Nathason had been a cofounder of the organization now known as the National Abortion Rights Action League. He claimed that his own participation in abortions had changed his mind. Producers said it was a sonogram of an actual abortion. Other physicians claimed the film was not a sonogram. The film was widely distributed to churches and to members of Congress, where it had an impact.

Pro-life organizations devoted to education and lobbying tend to be dominated by upper-middle-class professionals. Picketers tend to be working-class males and homemakers. Those engaged in bombings have been mainly self-employed working-class males who had the freedom to travel to other cities and to spend time in jail. The most successful counterstrategies of the pro-choice advocates have been suits against the picketing organizations and individual picketers under federal Racketeer-Influenced and Corrupt Organizations Act (RICO) statutes. RICO was enacted by Congress to attack organized crime and front organizations used by organized crime to take over legitimate businesses. Nevertheless, federal courts have upheld broader applications of the statute. On October 10, 1989, the Supreme Court upheld the use of RICO laws against 26 defendants at a Philadelphia abortion clinic, which alleged a conspiracy to shut down a legal business. Large fines and injunctions in several states significantly hampered the effectiveness of Operation Rescue. Fines were often designated to be paid to clinics that had been targeted.

While the Supreme Court ruled against suits against classes of persons brought under the so-called Ku Klux Klan act (which forbids acts against classes of persons, such as blacks), a Washington, D.C., federal judge levied a fine against Operation Rescue on the basis of district trespassing and public nuisance laws. Many physicians who perform abortions in clinics are harassed and threatened. Their families are also targeted for intimidation. Some physicians have been murdered.

See also *Roe v. Wade*
References Randy Alcorn. *ProLife Answers to ProChoice Arguments*, 1992; Dallas Blanchard. *The Anti-Abortion Movement and the Rise of the Religious Right: From Polite to Fiery Protest*, 1994.

Anti–Drunk Driving Movement

In 1970, the National Highway Traffic Safety Administration (NHTSA) set in motion the first major federal initiative against drunk driving. Called the Alcohol Safety Action Project (ASAP), the program was implemented in thirty-five communities around the nation. The program's goal was to achieve a significant reduction in drunk driving through a mix of law enforcement, rehabilitation, and public information.

Arrests in ASAP jurisdictions increased significantly and rehabilitation programs were pro-

vided to tens of thousands of offenders. But the program was facing an indifference in the courts, well entrenched for decades, that treated the there-but-for-the-Grace-of-God-go-I driver leniently and refused to treat catastrophic accidents as avoidable. When no significant reduction in drunk driving could be confirmed, the program was terminated. By that time, NHTSA had anti–drunk driving strategies in place that states had to adopt in order to qualify for federal highway funds.

The demise of ASAP did not spell the end of attacks on drunk driving. During the late 1970s and early 1980s a major grassroots anti–drunk driving movement organized and lobbied across the United States.

In 1979, Doris Aiken in Schenectady, New York, founded Remove Intoxicated Drivers (RID) after a local teenager was killed by a drunk driver. In 1980, Candy Lightner in Sacramento, California, founded Mothers Against Drunk Driving (MADD) after Cari, one of her twin daughters, was killed by a drunk driver with a prior history of driving while drunk. A short time later, friends of Cari and her twin organized Students Against Drunk Driving (SADD).

Another version of SADD was organized in 1981 by Robert Anastas, the director of health education for the Wayland, Massachusetts, public schools. John, a seventeen-year-old hockey player on Anastas's team, was killed while driving after drinking. Four days after John was buried, nineteen-year-old Buddy, a student who had formerly played for Anastas, was driving home from the beach with a friend when his car flipped over and both boys suffered severe head injuries. Buddy died; his friend regained consciousness to face a life with severe limitations. In his grief, Anastas felt as if his twenty years as a health educator and coach had been a waste because he had not been able to convince students that drinking and driving were lethal. Organizing SADD was his effort to engage students in helping each other.

The late 1970s and early 1980s were an opportune time for organizing an anti–drunk driving campaign. A public health drive against alcohol abuse had achieved significant success in defining alcohol abuse as a significant social and health problem.

Aiken and Lightner obtained NHTSA grants to engage in organization building. Newspapers and magazines reported on the efforts of RID and MADD to finally force an unresponsive criminal justice system to adequately punish and deter drunk drivers. In March 1983, NBC aired a documentary entitled "Mothers Against Drunk Driving: The Candy Lightner Story." The number of MADD chapters grew to almost 300. In December 1984, a made-for-TV movie based on Anastas's family life and the lives of John and Buddy aired. The movie won an Emmy award. In 1985, SADD branched out into junior high schools and colleges.

Institutionalization of the anti–drunk driving movement was promoted through state drunk-driving programs, federal recognition of drunk driving as a national problem, and the continued involvement of NHTSA in the issue. Nevertheless, in the late 1990s, drivers who killed someone while driving drunk were still less likely to go to jail than offenders who killed other ways.

By the 1990s, binge drinking had become a lifestyle in many colleges. The idea that they could be killed while driving drunk had still not penetrated the consciousness of many students. In the spring of 1998, law enforcement officers on both sides of the U.S.-Mexican border at Tijuana implemented a joint crackdown on students who traveled across the border to get drunk in Tijuana, where the drinks were much cheaper and the legal age for drinking is eighteen rather than twenty-one. Many students were so drunk they could barely stagger across the border, yet they had no qualms about climbing into their cars to drive home. The police had other plans for them.

See also Federal Student Right-to-Know Act of 1990
References Robert Anastas. *The Contract for Life*, 1986; James Jacobs. *Drunk Driving: An American Dilemma*, 1989.

Anti–Land Mine Movement

Land mines are a destructive legacy left behind after warring factions end combat. Land mines buried in fields during World War I are still, on occasion, accidentally blown up by farmers. The anti–land mine movement gained many supporters and much needed publicity in 1997 when the U.S.-based International Campaign to Ban Land Mines and its director, Jody Williams, were awarded the Nobel Peace Prize. The movement also sustained a significant boost when Britain's Diana, Princess of Wales, traveled to Bosnia in August 1997 to take part in a demonstration of the dangers involved in disabling and removing a land mine. She urged a worldwide ban.

According to the International Red Cross, more than 100 million mines have been planted in seventy countries. At least 26,000 people lose their limbs or their lives to mines each year, and only 13 percent of mine victims are military personnel. The other 87 percent of victims are civilians—many are children. Land mines cost very little—only $3 to $30 each—but removing them costs $150 to $1,500 each.

According to Red Cross surgeon George Kundent, working in Kenya, even if the practice of planting land mines was stopped, physicians would be kept busy repairing their deadly consequences for another thirty years.

See also Child Warriors

Antipsychiatry Movement

Antipsychiatry perspectives on mental illness became commonplace in the 1960s. The political left picked up the 1950s antipsychiatry books of two psychiatrists, Scottish-born Ronald David Laing and Hungarian-born Thomas Szasz.

Laing took the position that the irrationality of the mentally ill made sense when examined in the context of an irrational family. Szasz was a libertarian, one who believes in free will, freedom of action and thought, and minimum control by others. He claimed that mental illness did not exist. In 1959, he wrote, "Mental illness is a myth, whose function is to disguise and thus render palatable the bitter pill of moral conflicts in human relations."

Laing proved a disappointment to his followers on the left. He was more interested in various religions and mysticism than he was in politics. In the early 1970s, he complained that his work had been misinterpreted. He said, "I would never recommend madness to anyone." For example, Laing recognized that schizophrenics were people in desperate pain. Although Laing distanced himself from his early work, his enduring legacy was the idea that mental illness was liberation from the falsities of society.

Szasz never changed his mind, repeating his themes in 400 articles and twenty books over three decades. Szasz viewed mental illness as an issue of human liberty. Autonomy was his religion. Autonomy is freedom to make reasoned choices among alternative courses of action without assistance. Among the various symptoms of mental illness as categorized by the *Diagnostic and Statistical Manual (DSM) IV* (published by the American Psychiatric Association) are obsessions, impaired reality testing, delusions, hallucinations, inability to maintain minimal hygiene, and the inclination to hurt self or others. Such aberrations interfere with making reasoned choices. To insist that those labeled "mentally ill" must have autonomy, Szasz could not admit the existence of mental illness.

The antipsychiatry perspective was picked up by sociologists of the "labeling" school. Howard Becker, in his 1963 book *Outsiders*, wrote: "Social groups create deviance by making rules whose infraction constitutes deviance and by applying those rules to particular people and labeling them as outsiders . . . Deviant behavior is behavior that people so label."

Antipsychiatry was also given a boost by sociologist Erving Goffman. His 1961 book *Asylums* was based on fieldwork at St. Elizabeth's Hospital in Washington, D.C., a federal institution with 7,000 patients. *Asylums* became one of the most commonly assigned books in introductory sociology and social deviance courses. The mental hospital, for Goffman, was only one of several noxious "total institutions," including army barracks, concentration camps, boarding schools, ships, and monasteries. In Goffman's view, the institution provokes acting out. Goffman ignored

the introduction of phenothiazines, antipsychotic medications that had been available to psychiatrists seven years before his book was published. Yet he admitted, unlike many who quoted him, that if mental hospitals were done away with, an equivalent institution would have to be created in their place.

Sociology was not the only antipsychiatric academic arena. Historians of social welfare argued that the care of mental illness had regressed. The antipsychiatry movement was given a major boost by a study done by David Rosenhan, a professor of psychology at Stanford University, who had been influenced by the major proponents of the antipsychiatry movement. Rosenhan sent several pseudo-patients (three psychologists, a pediatrician, a psychiatrist, a painter, and a housewife) to twelve different hospitals in five states on the East and West Coasts. All but one of the cases were diagnosed as schizophrenic. The other was diagnosed as manic-depressive. The misdiagnosis of these pseudo-patients bore out Goffman's thesis that hospitals were agents of depersonalization and dehumanization. Rather than concluding that psychiatrists could be easily fooled, Rosenhan concluded that if psychiatrists could not distinguish between real patients and pseudo-patients, then insanity did not exist.

In the late 1960s, an offshoot of the Students for a Democratic Society (SDS) called itself Psychologists for a Democratic Society and published a journal called *Radical Therapist*. Radical therapists saw themselves as a part of a movement to build a revolutionary new world. They debated whether therapy was appropriate for oppressed people.

Some former patients responded with enthusiasm to the antipsychiatry model. Several mental patient liberation groups sprang up. In the United States, although many patients subscribed to the anticapitalist sentiments of their New Left therapists, most, shunned and stigmatized, saw themselves engaged in a civil rights struggle. Many recovered patients did not want to jeopardize the secret of their mental illness by speaking out.

In Europe the mixture of left-wing politics

and antipsychiatry became explosive. In Heidelberg, Germany, the Socialist Patients' Collective, formed in 1970, transformed itself into a political organization. It propounded doctrines such as "illness and capital are identical: the intensity and extent of illness multiply in proportion to the accumulation of dead capital." In her 1988 book *The Europeans*, Jan Kramer pointed out that most of the second generation of Baader-Meinhoff terrorists came out of this group. She wrote: "They followed a psychiatrist guru by the name of Wolfgang Huber—a kind of Leninist R. D. Laing, who convinced the people in his charge that the society was their real disease, and apparently inspired a lot of them to try to cure it."

In Italy, psychiatrist Franco Basaglia, with the backing of the Communist Party, secured passage in 1978 of Law 180, which banned any new admissions to state mental hospitals. Basaglia made clear that his intention was, at least, in part to have mentally ill patients in the streets serve as examples of the contradictions inherent in capitalism.

Except for young psychiatrists who were swayed by the antipsychiatric movement, the profession did not seem to notice the furor. As the antipsychiatry movement mounted, psychiatry had few defenders. Freudian psychiatrists had blamed parents for years for the illness of their children. These parents weren't anxious to help. Most important, American psychiatry had lost faith in large institutions. The great surge of asylum building in the nineteenth century had been in response to the vision of Dorothea Dix, who promised they would provide a quick cure. Until Dix, there was little to distinguish between jails and housing for the mentally ill. Some psychiatrists pointed out that drug therapy had limits. They were ignored. Between 1960 and 1980, loss of faith in institutions made possible the rapid dismantling of the system of care for the mentally ill, which left many living in the streets.

Several studies have concluded that 30 to 40 percent of America's homeless are mentally ill. Some advocates for the homeless refuse to believe that mental illness is a major factor keeping many in the streets. They insist that homelessness is simply an economic problem. They propose that a society that fails to provide jobs and homes has no right to prevent the homeless from living and panhandling in the streets, subways, parks, and transport terminals.

See also Community Mental Health Center Movement; Homelessness
References Howard Becker. *Outsiders,* 1963; Erving Goffman. *Asylums,* 1961; Rael Jean Isaac and Virginia Armat. *Madness in the Streets,* 1990.

Antiredlining

Housing discrimination practices directed toward residents of working-class and poor neighborhoods are called redlining. Common before the 1970s, redlining was supported by an interlocking network of behaviors. Banks refused to lend money for mortgages or home improvement loans, insurance companies turned down policies, real estate companies avoided handling such properties, and construction companies seldom worked in such neighborhoods. Redlining resulted in the deterioration of neighborhoods and white flight to the suburbs. Urban blight encouraged demolition and urban renewal, which eliminated housing for the working class and poor and created offices and housing for the affluent.

In 1971, Gail Cincotta and the West Side Coalition in Chicago set out to put a stop to redlining. Six hundred residents marched on the city council. When no change was forthcoming, 1,200 demonstrated at the U.S. Department of Housing and Urban Development (HUD). The coalition demanded an investigation. Within months, HUD issued seventy federal indictments for discrimination against real estate agents, building inspectors, and HUD officials.

The West Side Coalition sponsored a national housing conference in Chicago in 1971. It drew 2,000 neighborhood representatives from almost forty states. Chicago mayor Richard Daley and Democratic presidential contender George McGovern attended. The representatives formed a network, the National People's Action, directed by Gail Cincotta. The network proposed national legislation to inhibit redlining by requiring lenders to disclose the locations of their loans.

The success of the West Side Coalition encouraged resident Jeanine Stump and others to grapple with the local bank. Seventy percent of the bank's deposits came from the neighborhood, yet the neighborhood received only 15 percent of its loans. When neighborhood residents heard rumors that the bank planned to move to the suburbs, they staged a "bank-in." The residents tied up the bank's daily activities. Scores of children brought in pennies to cash. Parents opened new accounts with $1. Others bought $1 money orders. The bank agreed to stay and to invest $3 million in the neighborhood.

Neighborhood organizing emerged across the country. More than 1,000 residents in Southeast Baltimore formed the Southeast Baltimore Community Organization (SECO), representing more than ninety groups. SECO's ranks included hippies, small businesses, welfare mothers, union workers, churches, and even the Little League. Mothers with baby carriages blocked trucks from traveling on residential streets. A wheelchair march prevented the closing of the only nursing home in the district. A demonstration kept the library open. Protests at city hall resulted in a health cooperative, two public schools, the creation of a youth program, and an investigation of redlining leading to a compromise with the banks.

Reference Robert Fisher. *Let the People Decide: Neighborhood Organizing in America*, 1984.

Antiwar Movement

The 1960s were a decade of tumultuous change in the United States. Americans of many races joined hands with black Americans to struggle in the civil rights movement. The long overdue crusade for social and economic justice captured the imagination of young people. Another social trend that appeared during the same period, called the counterculture, attracted many young Americans with its vision of a world without violence, hatred, and prejudice. Participants were committed to a spirit of rebellion and dismissed the values of their parents and "anyone over thirty."

Still another set of attitudes and actions coalesced into the antiwar movement, which was motivated by opposition to the Vietnam War. Members of other movements joined with antiwar activists to work on behalf of shared concerns. For many activists, the war seemed to symbolize the struggle of the "have-nots" with the "haves." Along with their questions about the war, young Americans—mostly college students—questioned previously accepted facts of life in the United States such as racism, sexism, poverty, and corruption among the establishment.

Clergy and college students and faculty were among the earliest to stage antiwar protests. Anger among individuals at America's involvement in the war had gradually accelerated for a long time before it became organized into a mass movement of people who used demonstrations, parades, and sit-ins to force politicians to recognize that the war was unpopular. America's military involvement in Vietnam went on for more than twenty years. By the time U.S. troops withdrew from Vietnam in 1973, five American presidents had dealt with the complex issues of American entanglement in this Asian country.

The United States became embroiled in Vietnamese affairs as early as 1950, when French general Jean de Lattre de Tassigny spoke at the Pentagon to ask for American assistance. France wanted American help to prevent southern Vietnam from being lost to communist forces in the north. Preoccupied with the Korean War, the United States sent only equipment. In July 1954 an agreement was reached in Geneva between the French and the Vietminh, a communist military force. The agreement divided Vietnam, a strip of land shaped like a comma, into north and south at the 17th parallel. North Vietnam emerged from the division in a stronger military position than did South Vietnam.

From the beginning, there were prominent Americans who believed the United States should avoid any commitment to South Vietnam. General Matthew Ridgway, the well-respected American commander of United Nations forces in Korea, warned that the United States might encounter disaster if it tried to defend the fledgling Asian

Antiwar activists work diligently in the Peace Moratorium offices, 1969.

state. Ridgway not only feared intervention by China if the United States intervened, but also he believed any effort to keep ground forces supplied at such a great distance from the United States was unmanageable. Moreover, he knew from his experience in Korea that American troops were not trained for the kind of warfare they would encounter in Vietnam. Some opponents of the war felt that American efforts to save South Vietnam from communism would cause a loss of American lives on behalf of a dubious cause. Others felt that the extent of American commitment in other parts of the world made it impossible to devote enough attention to save South Vietnam.

Many critics, both inside and outside the government, believed that South Vietnam's leaders were not only incompetent, but they were too interested in benefiting from America's enormous resources to give sufficient attention to the war and too greedy to win the allegiance of their own people. Under the lax and corrupt leadership of the government in Saigon, the capital of South Vietnam, great quantities of American military

supplies and equipment disappeared into the black market.

After the French pulled out, American advisers took over the training of the South Vietnamese army. Up until 1960, the United States' participation remained limited. The nation supplied military equipment, financial aid, and about 700 advisers.

More realistic than the president he served, Kennedy's undersecretary of state, George Ball, advised the president that the Vietnam War might one day require as many as 300,000 troops. Kennedy did not believe Ball. He did not live long enough to see his undersecretary's prophecy come true. By the end of 1963, the number of advisers had increased to 17,000. In March 1965, a combat force of 3,500 U.S. Marines arrived in Vietnam. By 1968, more than 510,000 combat troops were present.

The longer the United States stayed in Vietnam, the more the escalating losses increased the desire of American leaders to justify past losses to the public. Although it was becoming increasingly imperative to rationalize the American presence in Vietnam, the chances for successfully forcing out the communists were dwindling. As the war dragged on and the numbers of troops sent to fight climbed, Vietnam became a presidential nightmare. Johnson confided to presidential press secretary Bill Moyers that he felt "like a hitchhiker caught in a hailstorm on a Texas highway. I can't run. I can't hide. And I can't make it stop."

Until early 1966, Congress had given presidents freedom to conduct the war as they saw fit, but congressional attitudes underwent a change. In February 1966, the nation watched on television while U.S. senators questioned Secretary of State Dean Rusk about the conduct of the war. Hearings in both the House and the Senate exposed America's Vietnam policy planners to many difficult questions. In 1966 it became apparent that the American public would no longer support the war in Vietnam without a clearer picture of America's reason for being there. Throughout 1966 and 1967, as casualty lists lengthened and military operations escalated, dissent became more strident.

The threat of the draft brought the impact of the war into most American homes. Many male college students attended or stayed in college or graduate school as a way to avoid being drafted. Fearful that they would be drafted if their grades slipped, many young men fled to Canada. A disproportionate number of black males, too poor to go to college, died in Vietnam.

On October 16, 1967, 120 antiwar demonstrators were arrested after a staged sit-in at the Oakland, California, draft induction center. A massive demonstration against the war took place in Washington, D.C., on October 21, 1967, when the spectrum of antiwar activists—writers, students, pacifists, clergy, and even some disillusioned Vietnam veterans—marched on the Pentagon. The march on the Pentagon was so large that troops of the 82nd Airborne Division were called in to protect the Capitol and were stationed at entrances to the Pentagon and the White House.

At a time when the government was calling up 30,000 men a month to serve in the armed forces, draft cards were being burned in open defiance.

By the final months of 1967, polls showed that a majority of Americans felt U.S. intervention in Vietnam was a mistake. For many blacks and for many young people, Vietnam became a symbol of America's lack of direction, an evil, immoral undertaking. In 1967, Martin Luther King, Jr., incurred the ire of many other civil rights leaders—who viewed Lyndon Johnson as an ally—when he attacked the Vietnam War as a senseless drain on America's scarce spiritual and economic resources. President Johnson, who shared with many of the disgruntled activists a dream of an America in which poverty and racism were reduced, had become a target of hate.

The Tet Offensive, an attack launched by the North Vietnamese on January 31, 1968, moved the sites of battle in Vietnam from the countryside to urban areas. One hundred South Vietnamese cities were attacked at the same time. American troops were shocked at the ferocity and distribution of the communist attacks. Two months before, troops had been assured that the end was in sight.

In the United States, nightly news broadcasts revealed the horror of desperate combat. Wounded soldiers were being taken out by helicopters. Dead bodies lay everywhere—on U.S. embassy grounds, on Saigon streets, and on the streets of South Vietnam's largest cities. False optimism and inadequate intelligence research had lulled the Americans and the South Vietnamese into a sense of security. The Tet Offensive increased already existing disagreements in America over what should be done in Vietnam.

Discouraged and sensing he might not win the 1968 presidential race, Johnson decided not to run for reelection. Richard Nixon won the 1968 election with a campaign promise to end the Vietnam War. Nixon sent Secretary of State Henry Kissinger to peace talks with North Vietnamese representatives that lasted five years. Nixon expanded the war into Cambodia. The North Vietnamese retaliated by strengthening their hold on Cambodia.

The escalation of the war into Cambodia sparked a disaster on the campus of Kent State University in Ohio. As students had on other campuses, Kent State students staged a protest at the reserve officers' training building. Ohio governor James Rhodes ordered the National Guard to the campus to impose order. A volley of shots fired into a crowd killed four youths. The Kent State deaths provoked protests across the nation. The campuses of more than 400 colleges and universities were shut down by strikes. Nearly 100,000 protesters marched on Washington.

Despite political chaos and widespread corruption in South Vietnam, Nixon felt obligated by his campaign promise to maintain a schedule of U.S. troop withdrawal without knowing whether the South Vietnamese had the will or the capacity to defend themselves. By the time the United States withdrew the last of its troops in 1973, 2.5 million Americans had served within the borders of South Vietnam. As no other issue had since the Civil War, the Vietnam War had divided the nation.

Even veterans who had served in Vietnam were divided in their opinions. An average soldier who served as an adviser in the Mekong Delta in 1959 would have encountered a black pajama–clad Vietcong guerrilla armed with an outdated weapon. A soldier or marine who served in the mountains in the north of South Vietnam in 1969 would have faced North Vietnamese regular troops armed with sophisticated weapons and protected by artillery and tanks.

Long after the war ended, the issue remained divisive and continued to be debated and to affect the lives of Americans. For example, an estimated one-third of America's homeless are Vietnam veterans.

See also Ho Chi Minh; Kent State; Southern Christian Leadership Conference
References Marshall Cavendish Corp. *The Vietnam War: People and Politics*, 1988; James Warren. *Portrait of a Tragedy: America and the Vietnam War*, 1990.

Asian-American Movement

The Asian-American movement, or the "movement" as it was popularly called, began in the late 1960s. Two social developments converged: public protests against the Vietnam War and the first wave of a significant number of Asian-American college students. Earlier in the history of Asian Americans in the United States, exclusionary immigration laws had barred male Asian laborers from bringing their wives and thereby prevented Asian immigrants from establishing families. The elimination of some discriminatory laws, in conjunction with a baby boom of Asian-American children following World War II, gave rise to the large numbers of Asian-American college students. The students came of age in the 1960s, a decade during which Martin Luther King, Jr., and John and Robert Kennedy were assassinated, riots erupted in inner cities, and the nation became increasingly involved in the Vietnam War.

Discrimination against Asians began early in U.S. history. The Naturalization Law of 1790 specified that naturalized citizenship was reserved for whites. This law remained in effect until 1952.

In the mid-nineteenth century (1840–1870), no formal immigration policy barred Asian immigration. Anyone willing to work was welcome. Chinese immigrants filled a severe shortage of laborers needed to work in mines and in construction of railroads. Chinese immigration became an issue only when the Chinese were perceived as competitors for other types of jobs. The competition was effectively eliminated by the Chinese Exclusion Act of 1882, which barred them from coming to America. Other Asian laborers were excluded by the "barred zone" clause included in both the 1917 Immigration Act and the 1924 Immigration Act. There was little Asian immigration until China became an American ally during World War II.

Fear of Asians escalated after World War II began and the United States went to war with Japan. Based on the assumption that Japanese immigrants might threaten the safety of the nation, thousands of Japanese immigrants on the West Coast and their American-born children were rounded up and interned in concentration camps.

Many had lived in the United States for decades. They lost everything they had worked so hard to gain. State laws had prevented these Asian immigrants from buying their own land, and federal law had prevented them from becoming citizens. Many had coped with the exclusions by purchasing land in the names of their American-born children. Their losses while interred included the loss of land in their children's names.

One family fought back. Kajiro and Kohide Oyama had bought 6 acres of farmland in San Diego, which they registered in the name of their 6-year-old son born in the United States. Officially, the couple served as the guardians of their son's property. In 1944, after the Oyamas had been taken to a camp, the state claimed the Oyamas' property, charging they had broken the law that prevented them from owning land.

After they were released from internment, the Oyamas took the case all the way to the U.S. Supreme Court. They insisted the land was a gift to their son, who was legally entitled to own it. The Supreme Court agreed with them. In 1948, the Court ruled that California's land law was "nothing more than outright racial discrimination." In 1956, a drive by the Japanese American Citizens League (JACL) succeeded in removing California's old land laws from the books.

Good relations between the United States and China did not last long after World War II. Shortly after the war ended, China was plunged into a civil war. Communists under the leadership of Mao Zedong won control and established a government. The nation became known as the People's Republic of China. The former leaders of China fled to the island of Taiwan to set up a rival government. The events in China split Chinese in America into two camps. Intellectuals cheered Mao's triumph, but other groups supported the campaign to overthrow the communists.

The involvement of the People's Republic of China in the Korean War, in which U.S. forces fought communist troops in Korea, set off anti-Chinese reactions in the United States. In 1955, an American official in Hong Kong warned that spies from the People's Republic of China were entering the United States using passports based on false birth certificates. Soon U.S. authorities began investigating thousands of Chinese Americans.

In the late 1950s, Congress passed a law that permitted communists to be rounded up and sent to concentration camps during a national emergency. Fear spread through America's Chinese communities. To help in its investigation, the government devised the "confession program." In exchange for protection from internment, Chinese residents who had entered the country illegally were encouraged to confess their guilt to the Immigration and Naturalization Service (INS) and give details of the status of friends and relatives. A single confession could involve dozens of people. The policy created deep divisions and distrust within the Chinese community.

In the early 1960s, as individuals or as Asian contingents, Asian Americans joined movements such as the antiwar movement. Their participation raised their consciousness about oppressive conditions in their own communities. When they were treated as "token" members, they became estranged from the antiwar movement.

Feelings about the treatment of Japanese immigrants during World War II may have provided the spark needed to bring diverse Asian ethnic groups together. The Asian-American Movement began as an inter-Asian coalition. It included a wide range of Asian groups, among them Chinese Americans, Filipino Americans, Korean Americans, Japanese Americans, and Pacific Islanders. In defining their identity as Asian Americans, participants acknowledged that as people of Asian heritage they suffered similar discrimination.

During the late 1960s, Asian Americans became activists on their own behalf. On the West Coast, community activists focused attention on conditions in San Francisco's Chinatown. Campus activists lobbied for inclusion of the Asian-American experience in college curricula. Campus demonstrations led to creation of community-based organizations to provide social services to the Asian ethnic communities. In the Midwest, activism began among college students who came together to gain support and participate in collective actions.

Contributions made by the Asian-American Movement are seldom recognized. In 1974, a landmark trial, *Lau v. Nichols,* involved non-English-speaking Chinese students, who won a suit against the San Francisco Board of Education for failing to provide educational opportunities for all students. The outcome of *Lau v. Nichols* mandated bilingual/bicultural education for all students.

Perhaps the movement lacked visibility because it never had a well-known, flamboyant leader. It also lacked an ideology or plan of action to attract followers, and its numbers remained small. Discriminatory immigration laws had limited the overall population of Asians in America; their numbers reached only 878,000 in 1960 and 1,369,000 in 1970. Given the small size of the overall population, the proportion of activists was large.

The Immigration Act of 1965 abolished quotas based on national origin, thereby removing restrictions on Asian immigration. Current policy gives preference to Asian immigrants with special skills or financial capital. Partly as a result, the number of Asian Americans climbed to 3.8 million in 1980 and to 7.3 million in 1990.

Even though the roots of many Asian Ameri-

cans go back for generations in the United States, they are perceived as foreigners by other Americans. Ironically, they are also perceived as a "model minority," one that, despite racial barriers, has successfully integrated into American society.

The Asian-American Movement focused separate and sporadic episodes of resistance to racial oppression into a collective action. The movement did not disappear as did many others but continues to bring Asian Americans together. Defined by the movement as Asian Americans, they organize into inter-Asian coalitions to raise their political status and improve their lives.

See also Lin, Maya; Women's Sex Workers Project
References Geraldine Gan. *Lives of Notable Asian Americans: Arts, Entertainment, Sports,* 1995; Harry Kitano and Roger Daniels. *Asian Americans: Emerging Minorities,* 1995; Ronald Takaki. *Strangers at the Gates Again: Asian Immigration after 1965,* 1995; William Wei. *The Asian American Movement,* 1993.

Baby Boomers

Seventy-five million babies were born between 1946 and 1964, the largest generation in American history. The "baby boom" was preceded and followed by much smaller generations. As babies, the baby boomers overtaxed maternity facilities, as children they caused a surge in school building, and as adults they crowded employment offices and mortgage markets. To the extent that boomers shared tastes in music, clothing, food, purchases, and opinions, they shaped the culture. The first wave became teenagers during the 1960s and participated in demonstrations, picket lines, and marches. They were approaching middle age when the nation elected conservative president Ronald Reagan.

In spite of many boomers' support of President Reagan and President George Bush, they retained many of the liberal views they had held on the picket lines of the 1960s. They still favored aid to minorities and abortion on demand. In fact, boomers often held contradictory opinions. They wanted less government but thought government should guarantee a job to everyone who wanted to work; believed government should do more for the poor, but not for those on welfare; wanted to protect the environment, but not at the cost of jobs; and conversely, wanted new jobs, but not at the cost of the environment.

In his 1988 book *Baby Boomers,* political scientist Paul Light cites an explanation for boomers' conflicting opinions formulated by sociologist James Davis, who said that boomers' opinions reflected "a conservative weather in a liberal climate." By this he meant that a conservative wave hit all generations at the same time, but the liberal boomers of the 1960s moved into the more conservative mode from a position far more liberal than that of their parents.

Boomer affiliation with political parties was weaker than that of their parents and grandparents. With fewer bodies to do the grassroots day-to-day work, the influence of political parties lessened in the 1980s and 1990s. More than prior generations, boomers were committed to self-reliance. They took self-development seriously. They were more apt to blame individuals, themselves included, than society for failure. Boomers tried to stay competitive physically and mentally. Boomers in the 1980s were much less willing to take on volunteer tasks in their communities. The Bush administration called for a return to volunteerism and the number of volunteers began to slowly increase.

Within the boomer generation, there was enormous diversity. Younger boomers were different from older ones. The worldview of those who served in Vietnam did not resemble that of those who marched on picket lines or avoided the draft by going to Canada. A difference in perspective between boomer men and women was wider than in earlier generations.

Women had gained the power to make a significant impact on elections. The influence of women was evident in 1992, when a record number of women were elected to office. During the 1996 presidential election, politicians and the media took "soccer moms" into account. Soccer moms spent much time chauffeuring their children to various kinds of after-school activities, including soccer, and felt strongly enough about issues affecting their children and their communities to find time to register and vote.

Soccer moms made up just one of many smaller diverse groups within the boomer generation. During the early 1980s, the media often mentioned the activities of yuppies (young urban professionals). To distinguish among the various subgroups of baby boomers, Light adopted terms coined by *American Demographics*, a journal that covers consumer trends for business leaders. Yuppies were defined as 25-to-39-year-old boomers who lived in metropolitan areas, worked in professional or managerial occupations, and earned at least $30,000 if they lived alone or $40,000 if they were married or living with a partner. The definition fit only 5 percent of boomers—perhaps the most visible segment.

At the other end of the scale, in 1985 four out of ten boomers lived on incomes of less than $10,000. They were sometimes called yuffies, or young urban failures. Those in the income bracket just above the yuffies were referred to by analysts and the media as the "new collars." To be a new collar required a boomer to have at least a year in college and an income above $10,000 but below $40,000. To emphasize the difference in worldview between yuppies and new collars, Paul Light used a joke in his 1988 book *Baby Boomers:* "You tell a new collar voter about $600 toilet seats at the Defense Department and he'll want to fire the people involved. You tell a Yuppie about one and he'll want to know what colors they come in."

Besides the yuppies, the yuffies, and the new collars, the media quipped about the grumpies (grim, ruthless, upwardly mobile professionals) and the dinks (dual income, no kids). Less amusing was the impact yuppies had on the housing of the poor when they engaged in a movement known as "gentrification." In many cities, after older family members died and younger ones moved to the suburbs, old houses that had once housed large middle-class and upper-income families deteriorated. Many were subdivided into rooms or small apartments and became low-rent housing for those who could not afford more. Yuppies, bored by their childhood in the suburbs, began buying the old houses and restoring them with "sweat equity," or their own labor. In time, whole neighborhoods were restored. Some yuppie owners went into business and restored homes for their less ambitious or less talented acquaintances. On the positive side, once-beautiful houses were restored to their former glory by their owners' sweat equity. On the negative side, the poor had to look elsewhere.

Yuppie restoration was only one factor that contributed to a shortage of affordable housing. Subsidized housing (subsidies for rent and support for new housing) virtually disappeared during the Reagan years. More than earlier generations, boomers were likely to leave home and set up their own households before they were married. The additional households put a further strain on a housing market already tested by the sheer numbers of boomers.

In the late 1990s, the boomers' children swamped existing schools, when, as their parents had earlier, they moved like a bulge through the local systems. The impact of the boomers and their children will continue well into the twenty-first century.

See also Hippies; Women's Movement
Reference Paul Light. *Baby Boomers: Those Born Between 1946 and 1964*, 1988.

Backlash against Feminism

Pulitzer Prize–winning investigative reporter Susan Faludi addressed the intense resistance during the 1980s against the advancements made by women in her book *Backlash*. Faludi proposed that the resistance came from the anxiety men felt at modest gains women had made toward equality. As it had in earlier periods of America's history, antifeminism stemmed from the struggle of major social institutions to ensure male supremacy.

Repressive measures against women during the decade were extensive. Public support for rape crisis centers, battered women's shelters, women's health facilities, and abortion centers for the poor dwindled. A conservative Supreme Court threatened repeal of *Roe v. Wade*, the 1973 decision that legalized abortion in America. Picketing and harassment of abortion clinic staff and their families began in the late 1970s. In 1993, David Gunn, a Pensacola, Florida, abortion clinic physician, was murdered and a Wichita, Kansas, physician was shot. Intermittent bombings of clinics kept workers in a state of constant anxiety.

In July 1964 Congress included sex in Title VII of the Civil Rights Act, which provided for the establishment of an Equal Employment Opportunity Commission (EEOC). At the outset, Title VII provided no real enforcement powers. Many women were not covered, and the EEOC showed little inclination to pursue gender-based grievances. In 1972, the agency was given authority to pursue its complaints in the courts, a process that may take years. Many women grow weary after years of postponed hearings and withdraw their complaints.

Some in the media claimed that women had won the fight for equality and that there was no longer a need to push for equal employment opportunities. Others claimed women were unhappy with their success—professional women suffered from burnout and anxieties about infertility, and single women yearned for an end to the man shortage. Health reporters asserted that high-powered women were being stricken with stress-induced disorders.

Women did not agree with the media that they had gained equality. Almost 70 percent reported in a *New York Times* poll that the movement for women's rights had just begun. The number one problem they faced was job discrimination. At the bottom of their list of priorities was a quest to find a husband, to switch to a less-pressured job, or to stay home. More than one-half of the black women and one-quarter of the white women told the pollsters that men were trying to take back the gains women had made in the preceding twenty years. Proof that women had achieved equality was hard to find. Two-thirds of all poor adults were women. Almost 75 percent of full-time working women were making less than $20,000. Women were twice as likely to live in substandard housing and to have neither health insurance nor pension benefits.

A 1990 poll of Fortune 1,000 chief executive officers found that 80 percent agreed that discrimination impeded women's progress. Less than 1 percent regarded remedies against sex discrimination as a goal their company should pursue.

In Faludi's opinion, the antifeminist backlash did not arise because women had achieved full equality but because it seemed increasingly possible that they might win it. The backlash was a preemptive strike and was eerily reminiscent of earlier reactions, such as that described by Rebecca West in 1913: "I myself have never been able to find out what feminism is. I only know that people call me a feminist whenever I express sentiments that differentiate me from a doormat."

See also Black Feminist Organizations; Feminist Organizations; Friedan, Betty; Steinem, Gloria; Women's Movement
References Susan Faludi. *Backlash: The Undeclared War against American Women*, 1991; Miriam Scheir. *Feminism in Our Times: The Essential Writing, World War II to the Present*, 1994.

Baez, Joan (b. 1941)

Singer-songwriter Joan Baez was an active participant in both the civil rights movement and the antiwar movement. She was born in Staten Island, New York, to Albert Baez and Joan Bridge Baez. Joan protested not only the Vietnam War but all wars, and she did more than just participate in the antiwar movement. When she learned that 60 percent of the nation's budget was being spent on the war, she declared she would pay only 40 percent of the income taxes she owed. She wrote a letter to the Internal Revenue Service (IRS) informing them of her decision and sent a copy of the letter to the news media. The content of her letter was printed all over the world. For ten years, Joan Baez persisted in her refusal to pay 60 percent of the tax she owed each year. The IRS put a lien on her house, her car, and her land. Agents sometimes showed up at her concerts and took cash from the registers. Eventually, the government collected everything owed, plus fines.

Joan's parents played a significant role in the development of her philosophy about war. Her parents became Quakers early in their marriage and raised their children to believe in nonviolence. Her father, Albert Baez, came to the United States from Puebla, Mexico, when he was 2 years old. His father, a Methodist minister, had been assigned to work with the Hispanic community in Brooklyn, New York. After Albert earned a Ph.D. from Stanford University in California, he took a job as a research physicist at Cornell University and moved his family to Ithaca, New York.

Folksinger Joan Baez.

From 1950 to 1951, the Baez family lived in Baghdad. The sight of animals being beaten, children searching for food in the garbage pails, and legless children dragging themselves through the streets affected Joan profoundly. When the family returned to the University of Redlands where her father was teaching, Joan entered junior high school. She told her biographer that because her name and her coloring were Hispanic, she was ignored by the non-Hispanic community. Because she spoke no Spanish, she felt isolated from the Hispanic community, many of whom were immigrants or illegal aliens.

Joan's loneliness prompted her to spend one summer learning how to play the ukulele and sing. Her singing enabled her to make new friends whenever her father moved to another university. When Albert Baez took a job teaching at the Massachusetts Institute of Technology in Cambridge, Massachusetts, Joan enrolled in the Boston University School of Drama.

The Baez family lived in Cambridge, close to Harvard Square. In the late 1950s and early 1960s, coffeehouses that featured folksingers, jazz musicians, and poets were plentiful in Cambridge. After Baez developed a passion for coffeehouses, she was invited to perform at the Mt. Auburn 47, a jazz club. Offers to sing in area coffeehouses followed.

In 1959, Baez sang at the Newport, Rhode Island, Jazz Festival. Her overwhelming success at the festival launched her career as a singer. To the astonishment of many of her contemporaries, she refused to make a Coca-Cola advertisement that would have brought her $50,000 because she didn't want to become a product—something to be sold for a price. Within a single year, she turned down several concerts that collectively would have earned her an income of $100,000. Baez told a *Newsweek* reporter in 1961, "I know I'm getting paid a hell of a lot. But really, I don't care about the money."

A search for social justice became a driving force in Baez's life. In 1962, she joined Martin Luther King, Jr., in the civil rights march on Birmingham. In 1963, she and singer Bob Dylan sang duets throughout the day on which King gave his famous "I Have a Dream" speech. She joined Dr. King again in a 1964 civil rights march from Selma to Montgomery.

At her many concerts, Baez always spoke out against the war in Vietnam. Just before John Kennedy was assassinated, she was invited to perform at a White House reception. Then Kennedy was assassinated, and the reception was held after his funeral to honor the new president, Lyndon Johnson. When Baez took the floor, she told the president to listen to the youth of the nation who wanted to stay out of the war in Vietnam.

Baez's husband, David Harris, whom she married in March 1968, was jailed on July 15, 1969, for refusing to be drafted. When she was six months pregnant with her son Gabriel, she performed at the music festival held at Woodstock, New York, an event that with the passage of time became a symbol of the coming together of the youth movements of the 1960s. During three days of rain, performers entertained the huge crowd who camped in muddy parking lots, sharing food and blankets.

After her husband was paroled on March 15, 1971, Baez concluded that it was impossible for her to adjust to living with another person. She and David divorced in 1973, and each moved to a separate, nearby home.

In late 1972, at the invitation of a Vietnamese group called the Committee for Solidarity with the American People, Baez and three other Americans visited North Vietnam. Veterans' groups severely criticized her visit, saying that she impeded rather than aided the peace process. In time, she apologized to the veterans for any suffering she might have caused them.

During the 1980s, Baez raised millions of dollars by giving concerts for suffering people around the world. She was one of four performers to play both Woodstock and Live Aid, a concert to raise money for Africa's people. On July 11, 1988, she appeared at a concert in London's Wembley Stadium to celebrate the seventieth birthday of South African activist Nelson Mandela.

During more than three decades of a music career, Baez has recorded more than thirty record albums, eight of which went gold. She has never stopped performing.

See also Rustin, Bayard; Seeger, Pete
Reference Joan Baez. *And a Voice to Sing With,* 1987.

Baldwin, James (1924–1987)

Writer James Arthur Baldwin was an eloquent spokesperson for the civil rights movement. He was born in Harlem, New York, to David and Berdis Emma (Jones) Baldwin, who raised him in the strict moral standards of the rural South.

Baldwin's father, a clergyman, came from New Orleans. Baldwin described him as a proud, bitter man, whose children were never glad to see him come home. In Baldwin's essay collection, *Notes of a Native Son,* Baldwin wrote that "we did not know that he was being eaten up by paranoia and the discovery that his cruelty to our bodies and our minds had been one of the symptoms of his illness was not then, enough to enable us to forgive him." In an interview twenty years later, Baldwin said, "Part of his problem

was he couldn't feed his kids, but I was a kid and I didn't know that."

A literary award Baldwin received in 1948 when he was twenty-four enabled him to go to Paris and develop his skills as a writer in an atmosphere less fraught with racial tensions. During ten years spent in Paris, Baldwin wrote his first three books. The first, *Go Tell It on the Mountain,* is a partially autobiographical novel about the religious conversion of a fourteen-year-old boy. The second, *Notes of a Native Son,* is a collection of essays published earlier about race relations. The third, *Giovanni's Room,* a novel, involves the persecution of homosexuals.

Critics were harsh. In reply to criticism of a 1962 book, *Another Country,* Baldwin said that Americans did not want to know how disastrously they were living. Baldwin's thesis was that whatever happens to black Americans also happens to everyone else in the society. He believed that the myth of white supremacy prevented whites from facing their own weaknesses. He told Kenneth Clark, "I'm not a nigger. I'm a man, but if you think I'm a nigger, it means you need it."

Baldwin's ability to put white readers into the minds of blacks in his books and in his later plays was eventually recognized as a creative gift. *Amen Corner,* a play Baldwin wrote in the early 1950s while still in Paris, was well received when it was produced in March 1964 at the Robertson Playhouse in Beverly Hills, California. A month later, on April 23, 1964, his play *Blues for Mister Charlie* opened on Broadway. The story was loosely based on the murder of Emmett Till, a Chicago teenager killed for violating a rule of segregation while on vacation with relatives in the South.

Critics accused Baldwin of mixing his role as an artist with his role as a civil rights advocate. One critic wrote, "Mr. Baldwin has mustered all his pamphleteering skill and written a raw, stinging denunciation of racial oppression. The play is as much a civil rights pageant as a drama—militantly propagandistic in intent, often crudely oversimplified, but unfailingly vivid, moving, and powerful."

Baldwin wrote most of *Blues for Mr. Charlie* while traveling on buses and trains to and from civil rights activities. He was on the National Advisory Board of the Congress of Racial Equality (CORE) and gave fifteen lectures to benefit CORE. Baldwin discussed civil rights issues with Attorney General Robert Kennedy and appeared often on radio and television to talk about the struggle for racial equality.

The death of Martin Luther King, Jr., profoundly affected Baldwin, and he felt forced to leave the United States. He bought a home in southern France and began to write *No Name in the Street* (1972), an autobiography recounting his activities during the civil rights movement. Reviewers described it as angrier than earlier books. A 1974 novel, *If Beale Street Could Talk,* bitterly attacked America's judicial system. *The Devil Finds Work,* published in 1976, was an extended essay on the roles blacks played in American movies. Baldwin's 1979 novel, *Just Above My Head,* received mixed reviews. His final book, *The Price of the Ticket,* a collection of his nonfiction from 1948 through 1985, received little attention.

In 1978 Baldwin was invited to teach at Bowling Green State University in Ohio. He returned in 1979 and 1981. He was asked in 1983 to become a visiting professor for Five College, Inc. in Massachusetts. The five colleges were the University of Massachusetts at Amherst, Hampshire College, Mount Holyoke College, Smith College, and Amherst College. A mild heart attack in 1983 curtailed his teaching career. After his death from cancer in France in 1987, his body was returned to the United States for a funeral at the Cathedral of St. John the Divine in New York City. Family, friends, reporters, writers, and politicians joined in mourning.

> **See also** Civil Rights Movement; Southern Christian Leadership Conference; Till, Emmett
> **References** James Campbell. *Talking at the Gate: A Life of James Baldwin,* 1991; James Tackach. *The Importance of James Baldwin,* 1997.

Banks, Dennis (b. 1937)

A charismatic leader and one of the founders of the American Indian Movement (AIM), Dennis Banks, a Chippewa, patrolled the streets of Min-

neapolis, Minnesota, in the late 1960s, to protect Indians from police brutality. He protested to both local governments and the federal government about the plight of Native Americans, who suffered from racism, poor health care, inadequate education, malnutrition, and high rates of alcoholism and suicide.

Banks demanded prosecution of the murderers of Indians. He also demanded respect for Indian customs and heritage. Most essential for the long-term well-being of Indians, he brought attention to the ongoing governmental disregard for the terms of treaties between the federal government and Indian tribes.

To call attention to Indian needs, in 1969, 200 Indians, including Banks and other AIM leaders, reclaimed Alcatraz Island in San Francisco Bay, the site of an abandoned federal penitentiary. When Richard Oakes, the Mohawk leader of the Alcatraz occupation, was later murdered, his death served as a catalyst for an Indian march on Washington called "The Trail of Broken Treaties." The march was staged in the fall of 1972, shortly before the presidential election.

The disrespect shown to tribal chiefs by officials after the marchers reached Washington inspired the occupation of the headquarters of the Bureau of Indian Affairs (BIA). The occupation ended with a shake-up of BIA's administration and promises from President Richard Nixon to appoint a special panel to investigate.

The next major AIM protest came in connection with the 1973 barroom stabbing of Wesley Bad Heart Bull in Buffalo Gap, South Dakota. The dead man's mother, Sarah Bad Heart Bull, was infuriated when the white man accused of killing her son was only charged with involuntary manslaughter. She asked AIM to intercede with state authorities. On February 6, 1973, two hundred Indians assembled at the courthouse in Custer. A few Indians, among them Banks, were allowed to confer with officials. When Sarah Bad Heart Bull tried to enter the courtroom, the police beat her and others. Indians set fire to a police car and the chamber of commerce. Because Banks was an AIM leader, he was charged with arson, burglary, and malicious damage.

Dennis Banks stands with 250 American Indians on Alcatraz Island during an "unthanksgiving" ceremony. Banks said the prison was a reminder of the large bureaucracies that have hurt the Native American.

Discouraged by their failure to obtain justice by peaceful means, the Indians took a more drastic stand. On February 28, 1973, armed with mostly shotguns and at least one AK-47 automatic rifle, Banks, in the company of Russell Means and other AIM leaders, occupied the hamlet of Wounded Knee in South Dakota. Recently returned Vietnam veterans built fortifications around the perimeter. Three hundred U.S. marshals and Federal Bureau of Investigation (FBI) agents, armed with M-16 automatic rifles and protected by armored personnel carriers, surrounded the area.

Wounded Knee is the site where Sioux leader Big Foot and about 350 (estimates vary widely) unarmed men, women, and children were massacred by the Seventh Cavalry on December 29, 1890. The 1973 occupying force hoped that the site's symbolism would prevent a repeat of the past. If it did not, they were willing to die.

The seventy-one-day occupation of Wounded Knee not only publicized the dire poverty of Indian reservation life but also offered urban Indians an opportunity to become familiar with traditional Indian customs practiced on the reservations. The action failed to achieve its stated goal of getting Congress to investigate corruption in the BIA or to honor the terms of the 1868 Treaty of Fort Laramie between the United States and the Lakota (Sioux) Nation.

During the occupation, the Indians and the FBI agents and federal marshals exchanged sporadic gunfire. When the action ended on May 9, 1973, two Indians had been killed and several wounded. Two FBI agents and one federal marshal had been wounded. In exchange for laying down their arms and surrendering, the Indians were promised a White House investigation of their grievances. The investigation did not lead to changes.

During a highly publicized eight-month trial in the federal district of St. Paul, Minnesota, Banks and Means—each charged with ten felonies—were prosecuted for their participation in Wounded Knee. The judge ended the trial by dismissing the charges against Banks and Means on grounds of prosecutorial misconduct.

Although Banks was not prosecuted for his participation in Wounded Knee, on July 26, 1975, a South Dakota jury found him guilty of riot and assault with a deadly weapon in the February 6, 1973, Custer courthouse incident. Facing fifteen years in jail, Banks did not appear for sentencing on August 5, 1975.

On November 14, 1975, Kenneth Moses Loud Hawk, Russ James Redner, and Banks's wife, Darlene "Kamook" Nichols, were arrested near the Oregon-Idaho border after Oregon state police searched their car and motor home and found firearms and 350 pounds of dynamite. Banks and another man fled on foot. The two fleeing men were arrested by FBI agents in northern California. Banks was freed when Governor Jerry Brown interceded to reduce his bail. Then South Dakota officials demanded Banks's extradition. He appealed to Governor Brown for refuge, and Brown refused to extradite him. Banks remained safe in California until Republican George Deukmejian became governor in 1983.

Banks next found sanctuary on the Onondaga Reservation near Syracuse, New York. Governor Mario Cuomo told federal authorities that since Banks's unlawful flight to avoid imprisonment was a federal offense, New York state police would not become involved. However, the eight reservations in New York are not under federal jurisdiction. Their treaty is with the state; therefore, federal officials could not arrest Banks.

While living on the reservation, Banks ran 6 miles each day, coached a cross-country running club for young Indians, organized food and clothing drives, and helped with reservation chores. In time, he tired of being confined to the reservation. In the fall of 1984, he turned himself in. He was sentenced to three years in the South Dakota penitentiary on October 8, 1984, and paroled on December 9, 1985. Meanwhile, the government pursued its relentless efforts to convict Banks for the 1975 weapons violation charge, the claim that the police had found weapons and dynamite sufficient to cause an explosion in the car and motor home. The case was dismissed four times for constitutional violations.

Despite the cost, after each dismissal, the government prosecutor reformulated the charge and charged the defendants again. It became the longest pretrial case in history, lasting from 1975 to 1988. To bring the thirteen-year ordeal to an end, Banks pleaded guilty to one charge in exchange for dismissal of charges against the other defendants. The judge gave him probation.

Attorney Kenneth Stern, who began working on the weapons violation case as a volunteer for the defense while still a law student, stayed through the thirteen years of frustration. Along the way, he pleaded the case before the U.S. Supreme Court. Stern traced the story in his book *Loud Hawk: The United States versus the American Indian Movement.*

In 1978, Banks became the director and coach of Sacred Run, an organization dedicated to spreading the message of the sacredness of living things and the delicate balance between nature and humankind. Except for his time in jail, he maintained his relationship with the group.

See also Bellecourt Brothers, Vernon and Clyde; Means, Russell; National Indian Youth Council; Wounded Knee

Reference Kenneth Stern. *Loud Hawk: The United States versus the American Indian Movement,* 1994.

Beat Generation

The Beat Generation of the 1950s is best remembered for its poetry and its lifestyle. Poet Allen Ginsberg is often considered the father of the Beat Generation. A practicing Buddhist, Ginsberg wove strong spiritual values into his poetry. His nonviolent protests at demonstrations and rallies raised the level of awareness of young people about America's involvement in war and about the destruction of the environment.

In his 1995 book *Beat Voices: An Anthology of Beat Poetry,* David Kherdian described the beats as trying to live like the mad, desperate nineteenth-century French poets Rimbaud and Baudelaire. They hung out with jazz musicians, hobos, and criminals and saw American history through the eyes of victims like anarchists, segregated blacks, and hunted homosexuals. One of the best-known poems by Allen Ginsberg begins:

"I saw the best minds of my generation destroyed by madness."

Jack Kerouac was another highly influential member of the beats. He helped coin the term "Beat Generation" and was an unofficial spokesman for the participants. When Kerouac's literary work was scorned, he withdrew and became alcoholic. He died at the age of forty-seven without suspecting that he would become one of the most widely read writers of his generation. His best-known works are *On the Road* (1957), *The Subterraneans* (1958), and *The Dharma Bums* (1958). The beats came together in and around Columbia University in New York. Ginsberg, with his friends, William Burroughs, Kerouac, Gregory Corso, Peter Orlovsky, and Neal Cassady, read the work of William Blake, Walt Whitman, and William Carlos Williams.

Strictly defined, the beats consisted of William Burroughs, Allen Ginsberg, Jack Kerouac, Neal Cassady, Herbert Hunke, Gregory Corso, and Peter Orlovsky. More broadly, the beats included innovative poets associated with San Francisco, Black Mountain College, and New York's Greenwich Village. The media pictured the male beats dressed in black shirts and pants, wearing goatees, and the women dressed in leotards. Although the images tended to be exaggerated, the beats' intention was to be as unlike the rest of the society as possible.

They gathered in coffeehouses around the country, particularly in North Beach in California and Greenwich Village in New York City, whose history of accepting bohemian groups stretches back to early in the twentieth century. Most beats had been raised on stories of political and economic victims, such as the shunned black singer Paul Robeson; the condemned anarchists Nicola Sacco and Bartolomeo Vanzetti; the falsely accused Scottsboro boys; and Ethel and Julius Rosenberg, who were executed for spying. Ginsberg wrote in 1959: "America is having a nervous break down. San Francisco is one of the many places where a few individuals, poets, have had the luck and courage and fate to glimpse something new through the crack in mass consciousness, they have been exposed to some insight into their own nature, the nature of God." Ginsberg's focus was on a few individuals rather than mass consciousness. In his view, newspapers and movies were the purveyors of stereotypes. Mass communication was the "enemy of divine insight."

Beats spoke on behalf of many causes that had persisted from earlier decades and were to become issues in the decades to come: ecology, black civil rights, Eastern thought, meditation, and poetry. Being a beat meant disdaining society, seeking free love, and revering speech as art. Beats believed in the power of poetry to shape a better world. They found the task so difficult that they did whatever they could to reach a plane where they were free, including self-destructive methods such as sniffing glue, taking heroin, drinking to excess, and engaging in indiscriminate sex. Their excesses carried some to addiction, some to the brink of insanity, and some to suicide.

In David Kherdian's view, the singer Bob Dylan serves as a symbol of the disappearance of the beats and the emergence of the hippies. Dylan, a folksinger, went to England and had an opportunity to see the rising popularity of the Beatles. Dylan experimented with the electric guitar and "changed his look from humble folk singer to a rock star." In the summer of 1965, at the Newport Folk Festival, Dylan went electric. In Kherdian's view, "This was no mere change of instrument; it caused a great scandal and suggested a much larger shift for a whole generation." Dylan no longer played for small groups in coffeehouses; instead, he aimed at the mass culture of rock.

Neal Cassady, who searched with Jack Kerouac for the soul of America, later drove the bus named "Further" that Ken Kesey's group of "Merry Pranksters" used in their own expedition. Their adventures were recounted in the classic book about hippies, *The Electric Kool-Aid Acid Test* by Tom Wolfe.

The original beats preferred to be outsiders and to find life and truth in other outsiders. They were most content out of the mainstream, and they preferred poetry and songs that proclaimed their isolation. Their influence dwindled when being alienated from society became trendy. The movement was over by about 1963, replaced by hippies, who were less interested in individuals and more interested in exerting influence on a mass scale. Hippies, dressed in colorful tie-dyed shirts, did not picture themselves as isolated from America but as the apostles of a new way of life. Many joined rock bands and dreamed of big record contracts.

See also Ginsberg, Allen; Hippies
Reference David Kherdian. *Beat Voices: An Anthology of Beat Poetry,* 1995.

de Beauvoir, Simone (1908–1986)

In 1949, Simone de Beauvoir, an internationally known existential philosopher, left-wing political activist, and writer of fiction and nonfiction, wrote a book about women called *The Second Sex,* in which she insisted that womanhood is a social construct and that the subordination of the female to the male does not reflect the dictates of nature. She also believed that civilization, culture, knowledge, art, and values were of men's making. De Beauvoir may have been pessimistic about women's past, but she had hope for their future. She believed that technology, contraception, and abortion would enable women to overcome their physical disadvantage of smaller size and lesser physical strength, and that socialism would enable them to overcome economic and social disadvantages.

De Beauvoir's book served as a beacon for an emerging European women's movement. Miriam Schneir, editor of *Feminism in Our Time: The Essential Writings, World War II to the Present,* wrote, "And in the United States, de Beauvoir was mentor to those who arrived at feminism via the sixties student movements for social change."

Among many others, eminent historian Mary Beard, a veteran activist, disagreed with de Beauvoir. She believes women played an essential part in making civilization and have been a force in history. Later feminists perceived women's so-called disadvantages as strengths.

See also Black Feminist Organizations; Feminist Organizations; Friedan, Betty; Steinem, Gloria; Women's Movement
Reference Simone de Beauvoir. *The Second Sex,* reprint, 1989.

Bellecourt Brothers, Vernon and Clyde

Among the founders of the American Indian Movement (AIM) were two young Minnesota Chippewas, the Bellecourt brothers, Vernon and Clyde. AIM was the most militant of various Indian protest groups that emerged in the late 1960s.

Vernon Bellecourt left the reservation at age 15. Angry at the Anglo (white) economic and political system that had kept him in poverty, he became an armed robber. For his crimes, Vernon was sentenced to forty years in a Minnesota prison. Because of his youth, he was released in a short time, with the proviso that he refrain from committing further crimes.

Still angry, Vernon committed another crime and was returned to prison, where he served three and one-half years before he was again paroled. Reluctant to go back to prison, he worked hard and became a successful businessman.

Clyde, serving a long sentence in prison, gave up in despair and stopped eating. His depression lifted when a fellow inmate, a young Ojibwa named Eddie Benton—a spiritual leader from a family of spiritual leaders—told him about his own Ojibwa heritage. The bond between the two men inspired them to start an Indian awareness program in the prison. Their goal was to keep young Indian men who had been released from jail from returning.

A few months after Clyde was paroled, he held a meeting in the poverty-stricken urban Indian community in Minneapolis. The residents suffered constantly from police harassment and brutality. That first meeting became the nucleus for the American Indian Movement (AIM). Drawn to AIM's goals, Vernon gave up his career and his life in a white suburb to join the group.

To document the community's complaints against the police, AIM formed a patrol that used tape recorders and cameras to record the methods police used to handle calls in the Indian community. The patrol obtained ample evidence to show prisoners were beaten and restrained by handcuffs so tight they cut the skin. With its evidence, AIM began filing suits against the police.

To protect Indians who were arrested from being harmed after they were jailed, AIM members routinely raced to the police station with an attorney and a bondsman to post bail.

A sacred dimension was added to AIM's mission when members traveled to South Dakota to visit with a twenty-five-year-old medicine man, Leonard Crow Dog. They asked Leonard Crow Dog and his father, also a medicine man, what it meant to be an Indian. They were told to be an Indian meant to be spiritual.

This emphasis on spirituality strengthened the ties between AIM members despite their diversity. In Vernon Bellecourt's words: "That circle around the drum brings us together. We can have two or three hundred people around that drum, all from different tribes, all singing the same song."

See also Banks, Dennis; Means, Russell; National Indian Youth Council
Reference Peter Nabokov, ed. *Native American Testimony: A Chronicle of Indian-White Relations from Prophecy to the Present, 1492–1992*, 1991.

Birmingham Baptist Church Bombing (September 15, 1963)

In the fall of 1963, black citizens in Birmingham had reason to feel encouraged by recent civil rights actions. The sight on national TV of Birmingham black children, who were marching with Martin Luther King, Jr., being knocked down by fire hoses and threatened by vicious dogs had hastened repeal of some of the city's segregation laws. Lunch counters had become open to blacks, and the federal court had ordered the Birmingham school administration to admit black children to white schools.

Hopes were shattered at 10:22 A.M. on September 15, when a bomb planted in an outer wall of the 16th Street Baptist Church went off, killing four young girls. Addie Mae Collins, age 14, and Denise McNair, age 11, were scheduled to sing in the choir during worship service. Carole Robertson and Cynthia Wesley, both age 14, were to serve as ushers. The four girls died in the ladies' lounge in the basement, a few feet from the site where the bomb had been placed eight hours earlier. In addition, more than twenty people were hospitalized by the blast. Addie Mae's sister was blinded in one eye.

The 16th Street bombing was not the first in the area. Bombs had wrecked ministers' homes, other churches, and a black-owned hotel.

Efforts by civil rights leaders to channel the anger of black youth into nonviolent channels in the wake of the destruction went unheeded. Gangs of white and black young men battled in the streets, and some businesses went up in flames. Federal Bureau of Investigation (FBI) investigators discovered the bombing had been planned by Ku Klux Klansmen in revenge for the new school desegregation order. Klansmen celebrated the event. Klan leader Connie Lynch said the bombers deserved medals. According to Lynch, the four children who died were not children. "Children are little people, little human beings, that means white people . . . if there's four less niggers tonight, then I say 'Good for whoever planted the bomb.'"

At a joint funeral for three of the girls, King told the mourners, "God has a way of wringing good out of evil." The good that emerged from the four deaths included a surge in federal civil rights legislation and an intensive voting rights campaign in Selma, Alabama.

Although an eyewitness claimed to have seen four white men plant the bomb, for fourteen years no one was charged. At last Alabama attorney general William Baxley reopened the case. He charged seventy-three-year-old Klansman Robert Chambliss with first-degree murder. A jury found him guilty, and he was sentenced to prison, where he later died.

See also Civil Rights Movement; Ku Klux Klan; Little Rock, Arkansas', Central High
Reference Sara Bullard. *Free at Last: A History of the Civil Rights Movement and Those Who Died in the Struggle*, 1993.

Black Feminist Organizations

Despite the impressive growth of the women's movement in numbers and a great deal of media attention, the movement attracted only a narrow segment of the society—mainly white, middle-class women. From the outset, black women were underrepresented in feminist organizations. In 1970, NOW elected a black woman, Aileen Hernandez, to be its president, but the organization was never able to attract a sizable black membership.

Although black women were in agreement with white women about issues of inequality based on gender, they were in disagreement about several other issues. For example, white women typically viewed paid employment as a road to independence and self-fulfillment. Many black women perceived it as an unpleasant part of life—most likely because they were restricted to poorly paid, menial jobs. White feminists lobbied for abortions free of restrictions. Some black women feared overuse of abortion might become a kind of population control that amounted to genocide.

Although black women were late in becoming involved in the women's movement, by 1970 they were engaged in college campus workshops, work-study groups, discussion groups, and in the founding of black women's magazines. In January 1973, fifteen women in the San Francisco Bay Area formed Black Women Organized for Action. Within a few years, the group had 300 members.

The National Black Feminist Organization (NBFO) was organized in August 1973 and put on a conference in November 1973 that drew 400 participants. Issues discussed at the conference included unwed mothers, reproductive freedom, rape, lesbians, domestic work, welfare, addiction, prisons, media treatment of blacks, and blacks in the arts.

The first paragraph of NBFO's statement of purpose suggested why many American black women didn't join the women's movement. In the opinion of the writers, the media had obscured the importance for Third World women, particularly black women, of the women's liberation movement. The media suggested that if black women joined "a white, middle-class women's movement," they would be selling out and dividing the black race. About this notion, novelist Alice

Walker once said, "Many black women are more loyal to black men than they are to themselves."

NBFO's document focused on black women's dual status: "black women have suffered cruelly in this society from living the phenomenon of being black and female in a country that is both racist and sexist. . . . Our above ground presence will lend enormous credibility to the current Women's Liberation Movement, which unfortunately is not seen as the serious political and economic revolutionary force that it is."

Lacking time and money, poor, economically oppressed women, both white and black, did not join feminist organizations in great numbers. From the outset, some feminists sought ways to include poor women, but most were too caught up in trying to solve their own immediate problems to spare the attention.

See also Feminist Organizations; Women's Movement
Reference Toni Cade, ed. *The Black Woman, An Anthology,* 1970.

Black Friday

Students involved in the various movements of the 1960s joined for different reasons, but most held a common view that segregation was morally wrong and un-Christian and that the status quo of the 1950s was intellectually bankrupt. The civil rights movement became a catalyst drawing activists together.

The early student activists had been educated in liberal universities and colleges, as had most of their parents. Their families' incomes were secure, and the children were raised in an essentially egalitarian home environment. A small percentage of parents were political leftists and raised "red diaper babies," but most were liberal and voted Democratic.

Paul Goodman's *Growing Up Absurd* became a best-seller on campuses. C. Wright Mills declared academic life of the era to be drab and became an oracle of the New Left. Students became concerned with issues related to the atomic bomb and revelations of radioactivity in the atmosphere and in food. They joined older peace ac-

tivists. In the spring of 1960, 1,000 Harvard students held a protest march for nuclear disarmament, and that same summer hundreds of students joined 15,000 older protesters in a rally at Madison Square Garden aimed at ending the arms race and creating a test ban treaty.

The flurry of activity on select campuses triggered concern in the government. In May 1960, the House Un-American Activities Committee held hearings in the Bay Area to investigate "communist activities." A thousand students from the University of California at Berkeley protested the hearings at San Francisco City Hall. Students were singing the phrase "the land of the free and the home of the brave" when the police arrived armed with nightsticks and fire hoses. One student recalled, "Here students were being dragged by their arms and legs down the stairs so their heads were bouncing off the stairs."

Students called the incident "Black Friday"; for many it was the day on which their commitment to activism began.

See also Free Speech Movement
References Terry Anderson. *The Movement and the Sixties: Protest in America from Greensboro to Wounded Knee,* 1995; Paul Goodman. *Growing Up Absurd,* 1960.

Black Muslims

Although Black Muslims did not participate in marches, sit-ins, acts of civil disobedience, or riots during the 1960s, their attitude toward whites made police officers and white communities uneasy. The Federal Bureau of Investigation (FBI) kept them under close surveillance.

One of many black nationalist groups that have come and gone over time, Black Muslims advocate black self-sufficiency and independence from white dominance. Black nationalism rejects the "alien" white culture and the symbols of that culture and supports pride in black culture. In the opinion of historian C. Eric Lincoln, some black nationalists revise history to establish that they are descended from glorious ancestors. Black nationalist movements establish a focus around which they build their resistance to the white culture, such as religion or politics. For the religious groups, creation of a separate state is of little interest. For political groups, it is a central focus.

The black nationalist group that came to be known as the Black Muslims organized around religion. It was known to the public by various names prior to 1956, when C. Eric Lincoln, author of *The Black Muslims in America,* coined the term. The group's various names included the Temple People, the Muhammadans, the Muslims, the Voodoo Cult, and the Nation of Islam. Members did not want to be associated with orthodox Muslims because they did not agree with the Muslim belief that submission to the god Allah eliminated racial differences. A fundamental tenet of the Black Muslims' teaching is that all blacks are Muslims by nature and that Christianity is a white religion. They deny the possibility that a black could truly accept Christianity or that a white could accept Islam, because whites by their nature are devils incapable of becoming Muslims.

In day-to-day living, Black Muslims are governed by a strict code of private and social morality. Belief in an afterlife does not dictate their morality. Rather, they believe that a moral life is appropriate to divine black men and women in their roles as the true rulers of the planet. In addition, some temple activities are morally binding. Among these is the requirement for male Muslims to "fish for the dead," that is, go into the streets in search of potential members. This practice has been particularly successful through prison programs put on by Black Muslims.

The Black Muslims emerged in the inner cities of Detroit and Chicago during the Great Depression of the 1930s. Sometime during the summer of 1930, a peddler appeared in Detroit. Some observers thought he might have been Arabic. He told his potential customers that the silks and other items he had for sale were like those used by black people in their homeland across the sea. The peddler's customers were so entranced by his stories that he began holding meetings in various homes. At the outset, he told them stories about his experiences in foreign lands. Later he gave them suggestions about improving their health.

Kindly and unassuming, he became known as the Prophet.

The Prophet used the Bible to demonstrate religious principles and to teach the blacks who came to listen about the religion practiced by blacks in Asia and Africa. He introduced them to the Quran, the sacred book of Islam, which contains the revelations made to Muhammad by Allah. The Prophet's teaching included bitter denunciations of whites and attacks on the Bible as interpreted by whites and imposed on slaves. As the numbers of his listeners grew, the meetings moved from people's homes to a rented hall, which the followers named the Temple of Islam. Thus began the Black Muslims.

The Prophet never told his followers much about his background. He called himself by various names. One early convert recalled him saying, "My name is W. D. Fard and I come from the Holy City of Mecca. More about myself I will not tell you yet, for the time has not come yet. I am your brother. You have not seen me in my royal robes."

Within three years, Fard had developed such an effective organization that he was able to withdraw almost entirely from active leadership. A minister of Islam was appointed to run the entire organization, aided by a staff of assistant ministers. Fard founded a University of Islam (a combined elementary and secondary school), a Muslim Girls Training Class to teach girls how to be proper wives and mothers, and a military organization called the Fruit of Islam. One of the earliest officers in the movement was Elijah Muhammad, born Elijah Poole. Muhammad became Fard's most trusted lieutenant, his minister of Islam.

In June 1934, shortly after he made Muhammad his minister of Islam, Fard disappeared as mysteriously as he had appeared. Some of Muhammad's critics hinted that Fard's disappearance following Muhammad's rise to power was no coincidence. In the years that followed, Muhammad perpetuated Fard's teaching and almost single-handedly raised him to the level of a deity.

After his disappearance, some of Fard's 8,000 followers began to drift away. Muhammad was forced out of the Detroit temple and set up a new headquarters in Temple Number 2 in Chicago. An effective leader, Muhammad opened schools and additional temples and purchased apartment houses, grocery stores, restaurants, and farms. Most important, he gave blacks a sense of dignity. Black Muslims could be a formidable political force but choose not to vote in the belief that America is already corrupt and doomed.

In time, a true Black Muslim came to be defined as an African American who was a follower of Elijah Muhammad, the "Spiritual Leader of the Lost-Found Nation in the West." The Black Muslim is distinguished from orthodox Muslims in their belief that the Honorable Elijah Muhammad is the messenger of Allah. He was directly commissioned by Allah, who came in person under the name of Fard to arouse the sleeping black nation and rid them of white domination.

Elijah Muhammad twice ran afoul of the law. In 1934, he was arrested for failing to transfer his child from the University of Islam to the public school and was given probation. In 1942, he was arrested, along with twelve other black leaders, and sent to prison for teaching blacks that their interest was in a Japanese victory in World War II and that they were racially akin to the Japanese. He was not released until 1946. During his years in prison, Muhammad was able to expand the movement.

No one person could carry Muhammad's immense load of responsibility alone. Muhammad had a close-knit circle of leaders, the most effective of whom was Malcolm X, who eventually broke with him, adopted beliefs more in keeping with orthodox Muslim principles, and repudiated the idea that whites were devils.

Muhammad died on February 25, 1975. Many of his followers refused to believe he was dead. Others drifted into four main camps that competed for leadership. The most effective splinter group was led by Louis Farrakhan and was based in Chicago. Like his mentor, Malcolm X, Farrakhan has extraordinary charisma, wit, and charm. He proclaims a fervent belief in the vision of Elijah Muhammad and criticized Malcolm X for his break with Muhammad. Some members of Malcolm X's family believed Farrakhan was involved in Malcolm's assassination. One of Malcolm's daughters was indicted for participation in a plot to kill Farrakhan.

During the 1990s, Farrakhan was frequently criticized for anti-Semitic remarks in his speeches. He received high praise—often grudging—among black leaders for the Million Man March on Washington in October 1995, which he conceived and helped organize. Black men from all walks of life joined together to celebrate being black and to make a commitment to be better parents and to help those hopelessly mired in the nation's inner cities. Controversy swirled around Farrakhan once again in March 1998, when it became known that he had hired Muhammed Abdul Aziz, one of three men convicted of assassinating Malcolm X, as captain in charge of Mosque No. 7, the Harlem temple that Malcolm X presided over before his murder.

See also Malcolm X; Million Man March
References C. Eric Lincoln. *The Black Muslims in America,* 3d ed., 1993. Elijah Muhammad. *Message to the Black Man in America,* 1965.

Black Panther Party

An ultramilitant urban black liberation organization, the Black Panther Party was founded in 1966 by Huey P. Newton and Bobby Seale in the slums of Oakland, California. The organization began as a self-defense force. Membership was limited to black youth committed to armed revolution as a strategy for social change in America. Dressed in black jackets, armed with guns and law books, the Panthers patrolled the streets to protect the residents from police harassment.

Panthers believed that blacks in America were "colonized" and oppressed by the white establishment. They called for an independent black community. Eldridge Cleaver, the Panthers' minister of information, appealed to all oppressed people and those who empathized with them to join in the Panthers' revolutionary struggle, in which the question of racial integration and segregation would become irrelevant.

Panther chapters organized in most major American cities between 1966 and 1969. Many

Members of the Black Panther Party stand on the steps of the Alameda County Courthouse in California, July 15, 1968. They are showing support for their leader, Huey Newton, who is on trial inside for the killing of an Oakland policeman.

chapters became involved with positive community self-help programs, such as children's lunch projects, and antidrug clinics. Yet despite worthwhile Panther activities, local police forces remained hostile to them. During the late 1960s and early 1970s, clashes between the police and the Panthers in inner cities became commonplace, and Panther leaders were routinely jailed. Although civil rights activists committed to nonviolence deplored the Panthers' philosophy of violence, they became alarmed and outspoken as the toll of Panthers killed by police mounted.

On July 3, 1969, three months after he had moved to Guinea, Stokely Carmichael, formerly head of the Student Nonviolent Coordinating Committee and former Black Panther prime minister, resigned. Apparently unhappy with the direction the Panthers seemed to be headed, he wrote an open letter to the organization, which read, "The history of Africans living in the United States has shown that any premature alliance with white radicals has led to complete subversion of the blacks by the whites, through their direct or indirect control of the black organization."

By 1971, the Panthers had split into two groups, a New York–based group headed by Eldridge Cleaver (living in Algeria to avoid a prison sentence) and an Oakland group headed by Huey Newton.

See also Carmichael, Stokely; Student Nonviolent Coordinating Committee
References Philip Foner, ed. *The Black Panthers Speak*, 1970; C. Eric Lincoln. *The Black Muslims in America*, 3d ed., 1994.

Black Power Movement

The meaning of the term "black power," first coined by militant black activist Stokely Carmichael, varied. Initially, for militants it meant revolution and violent resistance to segregation. For moderates, it meant possible destruction of gains they had made through nonviolent protest. Despite the differences, all those who used it included in its meaning a sense of pride in their blackness and a sense of solidarity.

Introduction of the idea of black power shifted the emphasis of the civil rights movement from nonviolence, Christian humility, and a goal of integration to taking pride in separateness and questioning the value of a goal of integration.

Use of the term "black power" gradually dwindled, but questions about the value of integration versus a need for separateness resumed in the 1990s in the wake of losses in gains made earlier.

See also Black Muslims; Black Panther Party; Carmichael, Stokely
Reference James Haskins. *Profiles in Black Power*, 1972.

Black Studies

A black student strike at San Francisco State College began with an incident in 1967, escalated in the fall of 1968, and ended in the spring of 1969 with the institution of a black studies program. Except on the campuses of black schools, academic programs that reflected the philosophy and culture of America's black people had been absent on American college campuses.

In 1967, tensions were running high at San Francisco State College. After a white editor of the campus newspaper allegedly mocked boxer Muhammad Ali, a dozen blacks attacked him in his office. The president of the college suspended the black students, along with two white students who had published a poem about masturbation. Black and white radicals responded with angry demonstrations.

The college of 18,000 students had only 700 black students, less than 4 percent in a city with a black population of 20 percent. The Black Student Union (BSU), made up of about 100 students, together with the local state representative, Willie Brown, demanded that the university establish a black studies department. The administration hired a few instructors, but by 1969 many students and community blacks believed that the university was stalling about doing any more.

Frustration brought about by a scarcity of black scholars was not confined to students. After years of exclusion of blacks at all levels of education, black scholars were in short supply. Salary bidding wars among institutions to hire black scholars during the 1970s created dissension among existing faculty, who resented the fact that new hires earned more than they did.

Negotiations between the BSU and the administration became testy. The BSU wanted the university to hire a dozen faculty members to form a core black studies program. The administration agreed to hire one full-time professor and a secretary. The BSU also demanded that admissions standards be lowered, even abolished, and that scholarships be increased or tuition lowered. The administration agreed to admit 400 black students who would not normally qualify. The BSU countered with the demand that all blacks be admitted without tuition. Tempers grew short.

Conflict grew within the BSU. The group began excluding radical whites, claiming that their meetings were for only "Third World," that is, minority American and non-Western foreign, students. Talk increased within the BSU about black nationalism and separatism. George Murray, a graduate student and Black Panther who had been hired to teach a black studies course, soured relations with the administration further with the suggestion that Third World students "should bring guns on campus to defend themselves against racist administrators." When the university president, Robert Smith, suspended Murray rather than fire him as he had been ordered to do by the board of trustees, the BSU declared a general strike in November. After a speech by Stokely Carmichael, black radicals roamed the campus, setting small fires, turning over file cabinets, and breaking windows. Smith called police to campus, and they attacked with batons swinging. Some faculty, irritated by the presence of the police on campus, joined the strike.

Like so many of the college administrators of the era, Smith was caught in the middle. His offer to resign was accepted, and he was replaced by Acting President S. I. Hayakawa, a semanticist and conservative professor with no administrative experience. Hayakawa denounced his liberal colleagues who supported the students. He had spoken out against radical students in connection with the Free Speech Movement at Berkeley in 1964, five years earlier. Most faculty viewed Hayakawa as a puppet of the conservative board of trustees and Governor Ronald Reagan.

Hayakawa proceeded to fan the flames of dissent. He announced that the campus would not be shut down by a strike and would be kept open by the police, that faculty supporting the students would be fired, and that students were not to give speeches with microphones. When he climbed on a students' truck and pulled out the wires to their amplifier, a shoving match followed. The same afternoon radicals began throwing stones to break windows, and police chased them all over campus.

The acting president suspended 5 students, which encouraged about 2,000 students to stage a rally. Local black politicians and community leaders came to campus to support the students. After Hayakawa tried to drown out the strikers by blasting the radio through loudspeakers, some radicals hurled stones at his office and the police waded into the crowd. One policeman was knocked unconscious, many students were beaten, and thirty were arrested.

Throughout December, the strike escalated. Attendance at classes dropped to 20 percent. Only about a third of scheduled classes met. The governor and the trustees tried to defuse the strike by closing a week early for the holiday break. However, the strike resumed in January. By the end of the month, repression and weariness began to take a toll. With help from the mayor and community leaders, striking students and faculty began meeting with Hayakawa and his administrators.

Under the settlement that was reached, the administration agreed to found a black studies department with eleven professors, waived admission requirements, and allowed numerous "Third World" students into the college. A black administration officer was given additional money for minority student financial aid. But the price was high. Charges were not dropped against 700 students, and 24 faculty members were fired. A few, like George Murray, served six months in jail. The strike had lasted 134 school days. Fortunately, no one had been killed. The strike had also inspired militancy among other campus minority students. Asian Americans, Chicanos (Mexican Americans), and Native Americans all demanded classes in their own ethnic histories and cultures. For his tough stance, Hayakawa was later elected to the U.S. Senate. For idealistic students, he inspired hatred for the major institutions of their country.

Demands for minority studies programs erupted during the spring of 1969 among minority students at 230 colleges across the country at such diverse campuses as Harvard, Memphis State, and Yakima Valley College in Washington State. At Rutgers University in New Jersey the black student organization took possession of the main classroom building and rechristened it Liberation Hall. Black students at the University of Texas took over the Lyndon B. Johnson Presidential Library and renamed it for Malcolm X. A coalition of blacks and other minority students at the University of California, San Diego, demanded a Third World College, to be named for the African revolutionary Patrice Lumumba and the Mexican revolutionary Emiliano Zapata. Similar demands at the University of Wisconsin and the University of California, Berkeley, resulted in riots and occupation of the campuses by the National Guard.

The rebellion that seemed to upset the public the most took place at Cornell University in Ithaca, New York, where the student population of about 14,000 included 250 African Americans. In December 1969 about 100 black students demanded a black studies program, for which the university approved funding in April 1970. Some white fraternity members who objected to the plans burned a cross at a black women's cooperative. The following day, which coincided with Parents' Weekend, an estimated 100 black students took over the student union building. When they left after negotiations had been completed, school officials and the public were shocked to see the students carrying rifles out of the building.

See also Free Speech Movement
Reference Terry Anderson. *The Movement and the Sixties: Protest in America from Greensboro to Wounded Knee*, 1995.

Bloody Sunday (March 7, 1965)

The day known as "Bloody Sunday" demonstrated graphically for white Americans why black Americans were adamant in their demands to have their civil rights respected and protected by local, state, and federal officials. The events leading up to that day revolved around Selma, Alabama, an industrial city in Dallas County, 40 miles west of the capital of Montgomery. Selma symbolized white resistance to the idea that blacks had civil rights.

Selma had a black majority, and Dallas County was almost 60 percent black, yet less than 1 percent of blacks were registered to vote. In the adjoining counties of Loundes and Wilcox not a single black voter was registered. In 1965, despite two years of rigorous efforts by the Student Nonviolent Coordinating Committee (SNCC), few voters had become registered. Blacks had not registered because they had been intimidated by local residents and by Sheriff Joe Clark and his police force. In January 1965, Martin Luther King, Jr., and Southern Christian Leadership Conference (SCLC) activists led a march to the courthouse, where blacks attempted to register.

Clark responded to the march by arresting King and keeping him in jail briefly. Over the next month, Clark arrested 3,000 demonstrators. White business owners supported the sheriff by firing 150 black employees. In the presence of the national press, Sheriff Clark kept his temper and restrained his officers from violence, thereby defeating SCLC's tactics of provocation.

However, restraint was absent in the small rural town of Marion, about 30 miles from Selma. On February 7, 1965, a few hundred blacks held an evening church rally and decided to march around the courthouse to protest the arrest of one of their friends. As the protesters began their march, a formidable police presence of local and state troopers attacked. They shot out all the lights and then began to beat the marchers. When one protester tried to go to the aid of a man whose head had been split open by a police baton, the sheriff shoved a gun in his mouth and threatened to kill him. The police did shoot a man named Jimmie Lee Jackson, who died several days later.

Local blacks wanted to march to Montgomery carrying Jackson's body. Under pressure from President Lyndon Johnson to call off demonstrations long enough to get legislation to help the poor passed, King vetoed the march and left for Atlanta.

Local activists ignored King's wishes and planned a march from Selma to Montgomery one week after Jackson's funeral. On Sunday, March 7, 1965, almost 600 singing and chanting activists left Brown's Chapel. They headed for Selma's Edmund Pettus Bridge, the route to Montgomery. A hundred of Sheriff Clark's deputies lined the bridge, and 100 state troopers, some on horseback, blocked the bridge on the far side. After the marchers stopped in front of the blue line of state troopers, an officer shouted that for public safety the crowd had two minutes to turn around and return to their chapel. After a brief pause, despite the presence of the media, the police charged the marchers from all sides, swinging nightsticks and throwing gas canisters.

One young woman marcher recalled, "I saw those horsemen coming toward me and they had those awful masks on; they rode right through the cloud of tear gas. Some of them had clubs, others had ropes, or whips, which they swung about them like they were driving cattle." Another marcher saw an officer swing a club and split open a woman's head as if it were a watermelon. The police chased the marchers all the way back to the chapel. According to a marcher, "They even came into the yard of the church, hittin' on folks. Ladies, men, babies, children—they didn't give a damn who they were." Sheriff Clark was heard to say, "Get those god-damned niggers."

Blacks called the day Bloody Sunday. The nation saw it that evening on television, and activists poured into Selma. Black sharecroppers, ministers, and students mingled with white professors, physicians, and 400 clergymen and nuns. The White House and Congress were besieged by phone calls and mail. Four thousand people traveled to Washington, D.C., to demonstrate for voting rights. Across the nation, 10,000 walked in marches of sympathy.

SCLC planned a second march from Selma to Montgomery, but a judge issued an injunction that upheld the governor's ban on the march. President Johnson privately demanded that the activists cool down. Johnson's envoy met with King in Selma, and he agreed to compromise. At the same time, he told his followers, "We have a right to walk the highway, and we have a right to walk to Montgomery if our feet will get us there." Whether deliberately or through oversight, King did not tell his followers about his agreement with Johnson. SNCC members and many other activists rushed to Selma to join SCLC.

On Tuesday, March 9, King led 3,000 marchers singing "Ain't Gonna Let Nobody Turn Me 'Round." Once again, state troopers blocked the route, but suddenly they moved off the road, clearing the way to Montgomery. King knelt down and prayed. Then he turned to the crowd and ordered them to return to Selma. Militants were outraged and labeled the incident "Tuesday turnaround." That Tuesday was a decisive point in King's relationship with militants. SNCC activists called SCLC "slick." They were tired of nonviolence when faced with people like Sheriff Clark.

But when three northern white ministers were violently attacked by local thugs with baseball bats, the differences between the two groups were set aside for a while. One minister, James Reeb of Boston, died from multiple head traumas. Thousands demonstrated across the nation, and Lyndon Johnson, on March 15, 1965, addressed a joint session of Congress to ask for the passage of a voting rights bill. Johnson informed Alabama governor George Wallace that citizens had the right to march on public highways, and, on March 21, more than 3,000 white and black activists began the journey from Selma to Montgomery, protected by the federalized Alabama National Guard.

Most of the marchers were young students, but they were joined by politicians, clergy, historians, and Jimmie Lee Jackson's grandfather. The trip took five days. Despite being incredibly disorganized, it was festive. The last night the marchers camped 3 miles outside of Montgomery, where they were joined by a flood of celebrities. The next day they were joined by thousands for the final walk to the capital. The crowd swelled to 30,000.

In August 1965, Johnson signed the Voting Rights Act into law. To enforce it, the law placed federal examiners in states with a history of discrimination. Poll taxes (which in 1964 had already been barred for federal elections by the Twenty-fourth Amendment to the Constitution) and literacy tests began to disappear altogether. Within two weeks, more than 60 percent of blacks in Selma were registered to vote. By the 1966 election, more than half of adult blacks in the South were registered, and they began electing black officials. Registration of eligible black voters was easily accomplished because activists had spent years locating them and trying unsuccessfully to get them registered. The events at Selma—particularly Bloody Sunday—transformed southern politics and also galvanized uninvolved students across the nation into action.

See also Abernathy, Reverend Ralph; King, Reverend Martin Luther, Jr.; Southern Christian Leadership Conference; Student Nonviolent Coordinating Committee; Young, Andrew
Reference Terry Anderson. *The Movement and the Sixties: Protest in America from Greensboro to Wounded Knee*, 1995.

Bond, Julian (b. 1940)

Born in Nashville, Tennessee, Bond grew up in Lincoln, Pennsylvania, where his father was president of Lincoln University, a black institution. He attended nearby George School, a Quaker preparatory school, where he was the only black student. Because of his gentle temperament, the Quaker philosophy had a profound impact on him. However, Bond's experience at the George School was not all positive. There he had his first exposure to white racist attitudes, when the headmaster asked him not to wear his school jacket on dates with white girls in Philadelphia.

The Bond family moved to Atlanta in 1957. Bond enrolled at Morehouse College, a black school, where he majored in English and took a philosophy course from Martin Luther King, Jr. Verse he wrote during the late 1950s and early 1960s was published in Langston Hughes's *New Negro Poetry U.S.A.*

While Bond was a student at Morehouse, he cofounded the Committee on Appeal for Human Rights (COHAR), a civil rights group. In Atlanta, COHAR began the desegregation of lunch counters. In April 1960, COHAR and other civil rights groups coalesced into the Student Nonviolent Coordinating Committee (SNCC). During his senior year, Bond left college to work full time for the *Inquirer*, an Atlanta-based, black, weekly newspaper. He also became the communications director of SNCC, a post he held for six years. Among other things, as communications director Bond supervised civil rights drives and voter registration campaigns.

In 1965, the Georgia state legislature reapportioned voting districts. As a result, a new district made up mainly of blacks was created in southwestern Atlanta. After Bond won the right to represent that district, the Georgia House of Representatives voted to exclude him. The excuse they used was that he had endorsed a SNCC statement that accused the United States of pursuing in Vietnam "an aggressive policy in violation of international law." The U.S. Supreme Court ruled the legislature's exclusion of Bond was unconstitutional in December 1966, and he was seated in January 1967.

In August 1968, Bond and fellow state representative Ben Brown led a rebel delegation, the Georgia Loyal National Democrats, to the national convention in Chicago. The insurgents charged that blacks were excluded from becoming delegates to the national convention because they were denied significant participation in the regular Georgia Democratic Party. To be permitted to participate in a convention, a delegation must first be approved by the political party's credentials committee. The insurgents won the right to cast half of the delegation's forty-two votes on measures to be voted on by the convention. The presence of the rebels helped defeat the unit rule, which until 1968 had forced delegation members to cast their vote with the majority as a unanimous vote. The unit rule had stifled dissent at earlier conventions.

Julian Bond, a member of the Georgia State Legislature, during a visit with college students, 1968.

Bond seconded the nomination of peace candidate Eugene McCarthy. He was asked to make some statements on the podium about the violence going on between students and police outside the convention center. Bond allowed his own name to be placed in nomination for vice president, but later withdrew because he was seven years too young to run for that office.

Later in 1968, Bond ran unopposed for his seat in the legislature. To supplement his minuscule income as a legislator, he gave speeches all over the country—200 in 1969. In an address before black elected officials in October 1969, Bond described the constituents of the "new politics" as "urban militants, campus rebels, small farmers who can't compete with big ones, tenant farmers who refuse to pay rents, welfare people, housewives who are tired of rising prices, and high school students who want to wear their hair longer than one inch." Bond was surprised to find that he enjoyed politics. He was also surprised to find that "politicians don't lie to each other." In-

stead, they try to convince others of the soundness of their position.

A fast reader, Bond reads a book or two a day, particularly in American history. In the 1990s, he taught history at the University of Virginia and had a home in Washington, D.C. In February 1998, Bond was chosen at the annual meeting for the National Association for the Advancement of Colored People (NAACP) to be chairman of the organization's board.

See also Southern Poverty Law Center
Reference James Finn. *Pacifism and Politics: Some Passionate Views on War and Nonviolence,* 1968.

Brown, H. Rap (b. 1943)

Dubbed a "hate preacher" by the media, H. Rap Brown defined black power as "guerrilla war waged against the honkies [whites]." Radicals, both black and white, considered Brown a victim of governmental "preventive detention," a policy of bogging down radical spokesmen in a mire of arrests and trials until they either amass long jail terms or are forced to leave the country.

Brown was born in Baton Rouge, Louisiana. His light skin, in contrast to the darker skin of his siblings, prompted his mother to give him preferential treatment and prevented him from becoming close to his older brother Ed, whom he admired. To protect himself from older boys, Brown began carrying a gun during childhood. He gained a reputation of always being ready to fight. Brown attended Southern High School, which was affiliated with Southern University, a black college. In the spring of 1960, Brown's high school class attended a meeting at the college in connection with civil rights demonstrations. The class was suspended for two days, a penalty that heightened the students' interest.

Brown's brother Ed, after being expelled from the college two years earlier for participation in a sit-in, had gone to Howard University in Washington, D.C., where he joined the Non-Violent Action Group (NAG). In 1962, Brown began to spend summers with Ed in Washington, where he attended NAG meetings with his brother. During his second summer with Ed, Brown also attended meetings held by the Student Nonviolent Coordinating Committee (SNCC) and began to do some organizing for the two groups.

In 1964, Brown participated in the Mississippi Summer Project organized by SNCC to bring northern—mostly white—students to the South to help register blacks to vote. Hundreds were arrested or beaten and two whites and one black were murdered. Most participants were profoundly affected by the experience.

Brown felt he could not return to Southern University when so much needed to be done for black people. He began to work with NAG in Washington and SNCC, headquartered in Atlanta. He became a powerful spokesman for the movement. Although not a Howard student, he was elected chairman of NAG.

In the summer of 1965, SNCC launched a voter registration drive in Selma, Alabama. After an attempt to march from Selma to Montgomery ended on "Bloody Sunday" with police clubbing marchers and spraying them with tear gas,

Brown became impatient with the politeness and patience required by nonviolent tactics.

By the spring of 1966, many SNCC members were leaning toward adoption of the Black Power slogan and militant self-defense tactics. In May 1967, Brown succeeded Stokely Carmichael as chairman of SNCC. Brown continued "hate preaching" and was considered an even greater menace than Carmichael had been.

After a speech in Cambridge, Maryland, in July 1967, during which Brown said, "Violence is as American as cherry pie," police and blacks clashed in a riot. Brown was hit in the head with shotgun pellets. After he received first aid, Brown returned to Washington. Officials issued a thirteen-state warrant for his arrest.

Attorney William Kunstler worked his way through a legal tangle among various states who wanted Brown and had him released after posting an enormous bail. Brown was followed constantly. He was arrested again in September for violating the National Firearms Act. He had asked a stewardess on a return flight from Baton Rouge to New York to hold a gun for him. For the next couple of years, Brown was in and out of custody. On March 2, 1970, the preliminary hearings on charges that he incited a riot and arson were held in Bel Air, Maryland, but Brown was absent.

On March 10, 1970, two miles from the courthouse, an explosion shattered the car of Ralph Featherstone, a leading militant in the area. That same morning, a bomb had ripped a hole in the courthouse in Cambridge, which was to have been the site of Brown's trial. An unidentified white woman was seen in the area. The police claimed Featherstone and his companion, William "Che" Payne, had been taking the bomb to the Bel Air courthouse when it accidentally exploded. Kunstler pointed out that the car had been headed away from the courthouse.

Brown disappeared and did not reappear, even after several charges against him were dropped.

See also Bloody Sunday; Student Nonviolent Coordinating Committee
Reference James Haskins. *Profiles in Black Power,* 1972.

Brown Power

The terms "Brown Power" and "Hispanic" are used to refer to people who speak Spanish regardless of whether they originated in Mexico, Cuba, Central or South America, or Spain. Most Spanish-speaking people in the United States originated in Mexico. Mexican Americans are sometimes called Chicanos.

Although there were few Jim Crow laws against Hispanics, there was ample segregation. Until the Brown Power movement and Cesar Chavez's farm workers began to demand their civil rights in the mid to late 1960s, Hispanics were routinely the victims of discriminatory customs. Ignoring compulsory school attendance laws, police in farm communities picked up Hispanic children and delivered them to growers for fieldwork. Local customs made it difficult for Hispanics to go to movies or use public facilities like swimming pools. They never served on juries. Police treated Hispanic prisoners harshly.

Between 1965 and 1968, Cesar Chavez's movement on behalf of farm workers (La Causa) received little attention in the American media. Despite this, Chavez pursued his larger goal: not just to unify farm workers but to ignite a Mexican-American civil rights movement. Other Hispanics moved in the same direction. In Denver, Colorado, Rodolfo "Corky" Gonzales and colleagues formed the first Mexican-American civil rights organization in the nation—the Crusade for Justice—to protest unfair treatment by the Denver city government. In Albuquerque, New Mexico, fifty Hispanics staged a walk-out of the Equal Employment Opportunity Commission, charging paternalism. The commission did not have a single Hispanic member.

The first militant behavior took place in 1967, when Reis "Tiger" Tijerina and six cars of armed followers descended on the Tierra Amarilla, New Mexico, courthouse. They claimed that Anglos (whites) had stolen millions of acres from Hispanics after 1848, when Mexico ceded the Southwest to the United States. In the spring of 1968, high school student walkouts, called blow-outs, took place in Los Angeles, Denver, and San Antonio. For many Mexican Americans, the blow-outs marked the beginning of their participation in a Mexican-American revolution. The blow-outs received little publicity in the national media, where attention focused on the Tet Offensive, a massive attack by the Vietcong in Vietnam, and the New Hampshire presidential primary. What did attract attention was a hunger strike by Cesar Chavez to publicize La Causa. When Chavez broke his fast after twenty-five days, he was joined by Robert Kennedy at mass.

In East Los Angeles, David Sanchez organized the Brown Berets, a paramilitary group designed to fight police brutality. In New Mexico, militants organized the Los Comancheros, to "go all the way in the struggle and by any means necessary."

Black Power also stimulated Brown Power. Because college officials were listening to black student power, brown students became militant, particularly in California, where there were more Hispanics enrolled than in any other state. At Berkeley, 100 Hispanics occupied the president's office during the spring of 1969, and another group invaded the chambers of the Los Angeles Board of Education, where they stayed for six days and nights. The most significant meeting in 1969 took place in Denver, where Corky Gonzales organized the Chicano Youth Liberation Conference. Gonzales gave the movement a homeland, Aztlan, the mythical land of the Aztecs.

Besides education, another issue that captured Hispanic attention was equal employment opportunities. Although Hispanics made up 10 percent of the California population, they held only 3 percent of federal jobs. In San Antonio, Hispanics made up 45 percent of the workforce, yet held only 30 percent of the jobs at Kelly Air Force Base and only 12 percent of the better jobs.

Much more than blacks, Hispanics were divided by class and generation. For years, many had worked hard to assimilate into middle-class Anglo society. For those who had achieved or aspired to middle-class status, the term "Chicano" was pejorative. To the militants, establishment Hispanics were traitors to their race, or "coconuts," brown outside and white inside.

The Brown Power revolutionaries wanted equality everywhere and possibly some rectification for past wrongs, but unlike Cesar Chavez, they did not have a plan. Plans began to take shape with the formation of the National Council of La Raza (NCLR) in 1968 with a goal of reducing poverty and discrimination and improving opportunities for Hispanic Americans. By 1998 NCLR had 200 formal affiliates in all regions of the nation and a network of more than 20,000 groups and individuals. The organization has been described as the preeminent Hispanic think tank and principal Latino advocacy group.

Despite some improvements in the daily life of Hispanic Americans, as a group they are the most undereducated ethnic group in the United States, and farm workers still suffer from discrimination. In 1998, labor, civil rights, religious, and environmental groups joined in a national campaign to improve the lives of 20,000 California strawberry workers in one of the largest union drives in the United States. In various suits, the multinational company Driscoll Strawberry Associates of Watsonville, California, was accused of widespread sexual discrimination for denying women work in the fields early in the season; failure to warn workers about the cancer-causing pesticide Captan; and violation of wage laws by failing to pay workers full overtime pay.

See also Brown Power in Classrooms; Chavez, Cesar **References** Terry Anderson. *The Movement and the Sixties: Protest in America from Greensboro to Wounded Knee*, 1995; Stan Steiner. *La Raza: The Mexican Americans*, 1970.

Brown Power in Classrooms

In their struggles to obtain civil rights and respectful treatment by America's Anglos (white people), activists from Spanish-speaking neighborhoods, known as barrios, waged few battles in the streets. Most of their energies were focused on schools.

Schools were the most visible, best known, and most vulnerable Anglo institutions in the barrios. They were arenas where the language, philosophy, and goals of Anglos were taught. They were the institutions that could most easily be attacked and the institutions where parents could demand that the language, philosophy, and goals of La Raza (Mexican-American civil rights) be taught.

The daily humiliation Spanish-speaking children suffered in classrooms can be seen in a story told by author Stan Steiner in his 1970 book *La Raza*. A shy boy of about ten whispered to his teacher in Spanish that he needed to go to the bathroom. She told him he had to speak in English. He repeated his urgent message in Spanish. Once again, she said he must speak English. Desperate, he said in Spanish, "If you don't let me go to the bathroom, I'll piss on your shoes." Years later, as an adult, the man looked back on the incident with shame and rage.

Various devices were used to prevent children from speaking Spanish. Some teachers made children feel ashamed of the language. Others made them pay a fine for every Spanish word they spoke. Some children were paddled for infractions. When East Los Angeles high school students left their classes in a walkout, one of their demands was the abolition of corporal punishment, which mostly involved paddling.

The idea of community control of schools and a better education for children united barrios. Almost by mutual consent, Mexican Americans and Anglos seemed in agreement that their battlefield over cultural values would be the classroom. Yet new textbooks, a curriculum based on the heritage and needs of La Raza, and a bicultural and bilingual teaching system would not change the economic power Anglos had over the barrios. Hence, "revolution in the schools" became a platform that satisfied Mexican-American activists and did not threaten Anglo leaders.

In the fall of 1969, Mexican-American students declared a national walkout in celebration of Mexican Independence Day on September 17. To avoid a replication of a riot they had experienced the previous year on September 17, school officials in Denver, Colorado, held a special assembly at the high school. Leaders of the walkout were permitted to present their views to the student body.

The classroom continued to be a battleground in subsequent decades. Bilingual education was adopted in many school systems with large Spanish-speaking student bodies, but it remained controversial. Many Anglos and some Mexican Americans became convinced that bilingual education failed to adequately educate students. In 1998 a statewide ballot referendum offered California voters an opportunity to support or eliminate bilingual education.

See also Brown Power; Chavez, Cesar
References LeRoy Ashby and Bruce Stave, eds. *The Discontented Society,* 1972; Stan Steiner. *La Raza: The Mexican Americans,* 1970.

Cambodia, Invasion of

In 1953, Cambodia became independent from France. The recognized leader of its government was Prince Norodom Sihanouk. The cornerstone of Sihanouk's plan for survival was noninvolvement with either side in the Vietnam War. The prince's opponents objected to the presence of Vietnamese communists in their country, and he was deposed by General Lon Nol in 1970.

Lon Nol's attempts to suppress the Vietnamese and a small group of communists known as the Khmer Rouge disrupted the country and encouraged the growth of the Khmer Rouge. Communists engaged in the Vietnamese War had sanctuaries in Cambodia in two main areas.

One area, known as the Parrot's Beak, was a sliver of land that pushed into South Vietnam within 33 miles of Saigon, the capital. The second area, known as the Fishhook, was a curving strip that jutted within 50 miles of Saigon. In April 1970, President Richard Nixon put into operation a plan to send South Vietnamese troops into the Parrot's Beak and a combined U.S.–South Vietnamese force into the Fishhook to eliminate the risks posed by the sanctuaries.

Nixon insisted that the operation was not an invasion of Cambodia. The British magazine the *Economist* supported the president's position in an editorial. "For years, North Vietnam has violated the neutrality of this country [Cambodia] with barely a chirp of protest from the rest of the world. . . . To condemn the United States for 'invading' neutral Cambodia is about as rational as to condemn Britain for 'invading' formerly neutral Holland in 1944."

The reaction from antiwar activists in the United States was hostile. Within minutes after the president's speech announcing the operation, some students took to the streets. The following day, demonstrations began all over the United States. Students went on strike on sixty campuses. Two hundred State Department employees marched. On the campus of Kent State in Ohio, National Guard troops fired into a crowd of approximately two hundred students throwing stones at them, wounding nine and killing four. Student strikes spread to four hundred campuses.

As the furor of the protest began to ebb, white state troopers in Mississippi fired on black students at Jackson State, wounding twelve and killing two women bystanders. The public became outraged at the students, and the protests diverted attention from the reason they were protesting.

See also Antiwar Movement; Kent State
Reference Terry Anderson. *The Movement and the Sixties*, 1995.

Carmichael, Stokely (b. 1941)

In 1966, while Stokely Carmichael, who later changed his name to Kwame Toure, was chairman of the Atlanta-based Student Nonviolent Coordinating Committee (SNCC), a civil rights organization, he coined, or at least popularized, the slogan "Black Power."

Carmichael was born in Port-of-Spain, Trinidad, British West Indies, on June 29, 1941. When he was 2 years old, his parents immigrated with two of his sisters to the United States, leaving Carmichael behind to live with his grandmother and two aunts in an impressive house his father had built. Until he was 11, he remained in Port-of-Spain, where he attended Tranquillity Boys School and received a British-style education.

Although Carmichael received an excellent education that later shaped his intellectual bent, as an adult the thought of it infuriated him. During a July 23, 1967, interview with a *London Observer*

Activist Stokely Carmichael popularized the phrase "Black Power" when he published Black Power: The Politics of Liberation in America *in 1967.*

reporter, he said, "At school we were made to memorize Kipling's 'White Man's Burden,' told we didn't exist until Sir Walter Raleigh discovered us, and we went to the movies and yelled for Tarzan to beat the hell out of Africa."

In Trinidad, the black majority filled positions in government, law enforcement, education, religion, and business. When Carmichael rejoined his family in New York, he found whites held the major positions in law enforcement and education and owned property and businesses. With regret and anger, Carmichael said of his father, "He believed genuinely in the American dream. And because he believed in it he was just squashed. Squashed! He worked himself to death in this country and he died the same way he started: poor and black."

Carmichael's family moved to Morris Park, a white neighborhood in the Bronx, and he became the only black member of the Morris Park Dukes,

a neighborhood gang. For a time, Carmichael drank, became aggressive, and committed petty theft. His behavior changed when he entered Bronx High School of Science.

About the time Carmichael graduated from high school in 1960, he learned about the sit-ins at lunch counters in the South and was inspired to join picket lines with members of the Congress of Racial Equality (CORE). Rejecting several offers of scholarships from white universities, he enrolled in predominantly black Howard University in Washington, D.C.

Carmichael joined the first Freedom Rides in 1947 aimed at integrating interstate travel in the South. For the first of many times to follow, he was jailed. After his graduation from Howard in 1964, Carmichael became an organizer with SNCC, which sent hundreds of young, middle-class, white and black volunteers from the North into the rural South to teach residents how to read, write, and register to vote. Carmichael worked primarily in Lowndes County, Mississippi, where the black majority had no power.

Under Carmichael's leadership, the number of registered voters in Lowndes County increased from seventy to 2,600, exceeding the number of white voters by 300. Carmichael bypassed the Lowndes County Democratic and Republican Parties and organized the all-black Lowndes County Freedom Organization, which adopted as its ballot symbol a leaping, snarling, black panther.

In the mid-1960s, more militant civil rights organizations, including SNCC, turned their backs on what they considered white paternalism and purged their rolls of white members. SNCC elected Carmichael as its chairman to succeed the more gentle John Lewis. On June 10, 1966, while leading the James Meredith Freedom March along Highway 50 in Mississippi, Carmichael used the term "Black Power" for the first time. He shouted the slogan to black sharecroppers who lined the route.

Carmichael envisioned Black Power as winning political power on voter participation in activities that generated economic power. In his 1967 book *Black Power,* written with Charles V.

Hamilton, he wrote: "Before a group can enter the open society, it must first close ranks."

During 1966 and 1967, Carmichael traveled and lectured on many American college campuses and in several foreign countries. Statements he made in his speeches abroad alienated him from many SNCC members, because they led the American public to associate SNCC with violence. They particularly objected to his words in a speech given in Havana, Cuba. Carmichael said, "We are preparing groups of urban guerrillas for our defense in the cities ... It is going to be a fight to the death."

In August 1967, SNCC severed its ties with Carmichael, who had become the prime minister of the Black Panther Party, a particularly militant black liberation group. The Panthers had adopted the black panther symbol Carmichael had used in Lowndes County.

Carmichael quickly lost his enthusiasm for the Panthers. In the spring of 1969, he moved to Guinea, West Africa, and on July 3, 1969, he made public his resignation from the organization. In an open letter to the Black Panther Party, Carmichael objected to the Panthers' "dogmatic party line favoring alliances with white radicals." He referred to himself as a Pan-Africanist and asserted that blacks needed to "wage an unrelenting armed struggle against the white Western empire for the liberation of our people."

Two days later, David Hilliard, national chief of staff of the Black Panthers, made a public response. He was quoted in a *Washington Post* article as saying, "We tried to bring him around. But he just did not come to understand that you can't fight racism with racism. The world is our neighborhood. All oppressed people are a part of it." In 1973, Carmichael and his South African wife became citizens of Uganda. On the Charlie Rose talk show in the spring of 1998 he said he had no intention of ever making his home again in the United States.

See also Black Panther Party; Freedom Riders; Sit-ins; Student Nonviolent Coordinating Committee
References Stokely Carmichael, with Charles Hamilton. *Black Power*, 1967; Philip Foner, ed. *The Black Panthers Speak*, 1970; C. Eric Lincoln. *The Black Muslims in America*, 1994.

Carson, Rachel (1907–1964)

Three books written by Rachel Carson made her one of America's best-known and most controversial environmentalists. Her painstaking work had an enormous impact on the environmental movement. Carson's writings brought into common use the word "ecology," the interrelationship between diverse species and the environment they share. The Greek root of ecology means "house," and Carson made the public aware of how fragile humanity's house is.

When she entered the Pennsylvania College for Women, Carson intended to be an English major and possibly a professional writer. A required course in biology changed her mind, however, and she switched to zoology. Between college and graduate school, she had a summer fellowship at the Woods Hole Marine Biological Laboratory (MBL) in Massachusetts. After she earned a master's degree in zoology at Johns Hopkins University, she taught there and at the University of Maryland and continued to work summers at MBL.

The sudden death of Carson's father in 1935 led her to assume support of her mother. When her sister died the following year, Carson and her mother took over the care of her two nieces. To increase her income, Carson applied for a job as a junior aquatic biologist at the Bureau of Fisheries. Her first job with the bureau was to write a series of radio broadcasts called "Romance under the Waters." The broadcasts were the beginning of a long writing career at the bureau. For many years, Carson wrote and edited bureau publications.

The chief of the biology division, Elmer Higgins, asked Carson to write a general piece about the ocean. He thought the finished product was too detailed for what he envisioned and suggested she send it to the *Atlantic Monthly*. The article, which appeared in the September 1937 issue of the magazine, brought her to the attention of Quincy Howe, an editor at Simon and Schuster. He encouraged her to write a book. For the next four years, Carson spent her limited free time writing *Under the Sea Wind*. Unfortunately, the book was published just one month before the Japanese attack on Pearl Harbor and, as a consequence, did not get the kind of attention it might otherwise have had.

The Bureau of Fisheries merged with the Biological Survey to become the Fish and Wildlife Service. After World War II, Carson was promoted to chief editor of all Fish and Wildlife Service publications.

In 1948, to make available to the public the enormous amount of new information generated by marine scientists during World War II, Carson began work on *The Sea around Us*. The book was published in July 1951. It was chosen as a Book of the Month Club selection and made the bestseller list, where it remained for eighty-six weeks. A quarter of a million copies were sold the first year. The book made Rachel Carson famous and won her the John Burroughs Medal and the National Book Award.

The money from *The Sea around Us* enabled Carson to build a cottage in Maine overlooking a bay, where she could do research on a new book, *Edge of the Sea*. At all times of the day and night she explored tide pools along the shore. The book's illustrator, Bob Hines, sometimes had to carry her out of the icy water after her legs became numb from staying in too long. *Edge of the Sea* was published in 1955 and became another best-seller. It emphasized the fragile interdependence of life along the ocean shore. Carson made her readers feel the wonder and mystery of the ancient forms of life.

The idea for Carson's last and most famous book came from a friend, Olga Owens Huckins. Huckins and her husband owned a private bird sanctuary in Duxbury, Massachusetts. The day after a plane spraying DDT for mosquito control flew over the sanctuary, the Huckinses found seven dead songbirds. All had died in agony. Outraged, Mrs. Huckins wrote a letter to the *Boston Herald* and sent a copy of the letter to Carson.

Her friend's letter spurred Carson into action. For several years, she had been concerned about the indiscriminate spraying of DDT and other pesticides. She later wrote: "The more I learned about the use of pesticides the more appalled I became . . . everything which meant most to me

as a naturalist [a direct observer of plants and animals] was being threatened."

In May 1958, she convinced Houghton Mifflin to sign a contract with her for a book about the impact of pesticides. Carson set out to explore what spraying was doing to the balance of nature; whether "good insects" were being destroyed along with "bad" ones; what the effects of pesticides were on birds, fish, and other wildlife; and what the long-term effects of pesticides might be on humans.

As she had always done, Carson gathered facts thoroughly before she began to write *Silent Spring*. Early in 1960, she had a cancerous breast tumor removed. The cancer spread, and she began radiation treatments. The illness delayed the book. Prior to publication, it appeared as a condensation in the June 16, 1962, issue of *The New Yorker*. Within a week a storm of controversy arose. Chemical companies and the U.S. Department of Agriculture launched major public relations campaigns attacking Carson as a nonscientific, emotional crank. The attacks continued and escalated after the book's publication in September 1962.

Silent Spring had supporters as well as detractors. In time it became evident that the attacks were based on misinterpretations. Carson never suggested that all pesticides be banned. She urged that decisions about pesticides be made by biologists able to assess the risks. As an alternative to chemical pesticides, Carson favored biological controls, the use of living organisms that are natural enemies of specific pests.

Gradually the tide of public opinion turned in favor of Carson's interpretation. By the end of 1962, more than forty bills had been introduced into state legislatures to regulate the use of pesticides. In November 1969, the U.S. government began to phase out the use of DDT over a two-year period.

Carson did not view control of pesticides as the only vital environmental problem to be solved. She was growing concerned about careless disposal of radioactive wastes. She felt that twentieth-century civilization had become too complicated to be dealt with by specialists working in isolation.

Carson was not only a gifted scientist but also a writer with a unique ability to share her passion. In an article for parents, Carson advised them to take their children and a flashlight to explore their nighttime backyards, with the goal of nurturing "a sense of wonder." During the last year of her life, Carson was the recipient of many awards, but she was often too ill to attend the ceremonies. She died in April 1964.

See also Environmental Movement; Leopold, Aldo
Reference Nancy Veglahn. *Women Scientists,* 1991.

Center for Constitutional Rights

By 1966, when the Center for Constitutional Rights (CCR) was operating out of a small office in Newark, New Jersey, the founding attorneys, Arthur Kinoy, William Kunstler, Morton Stavis, and Ben Smith, had spent years defending hundreds—perhaps thousands—of black people in the South. Kunstler had defended the Reverend Martin Luther King, Jr., and others in Albany, Georgia, and had represented the Freedom Riders in their successful efforts to desegregate interstate travel facilities in the South. Fifteen years after CCR filed a civil suit in Kentucky in 1966, the fees collected from the large settlement enabled CCR to move to New York.

Ben Smith, one of a few white lawyers in the South who was sympathetic to the civil rights movement, became a defendant when members of the Louisiana Un-American Activities Committee burst into his office and charged him and others with sedition (inciting rebellion against the authority of the state). However, the U.S. Supreme Court prevented prosecution of Smith and the other arrestees. The court's opinion used the phrase "chilling effect" to describe what might happen to the First Amendment if such prosecutions were allowed.

Attorneys Kinoy and Kunstler reinvented the practice of "removal"—a procedure seldom used since Reconstruction. When discrimination issues were involved, cases that otherwise would be heard in state courts could be "removed" to federal courts.

In 1964, the Mississippi Freedom Democratic Party (MFDP) asked the founders of CCR and dozens of other attorneys to help them unseat the all-white regular Mississippi Democratic delegation to Congress. More than 100 attorneys, mostly organized by Morton Stavis and members of the National Lawyers Guild, traveled to Mississippi and took hundreds of depositions from local residents and civil rights workers who had witnessed voting rights violations. Based on the depositions, the MFDP formally challenged the constitutionality of the elections. The MFDP succeeded in forcing the Mississippi delegation to "stand aside" while the other members took their oath of office. One-third of the members of Congress voted to unseat the Mississippi delegation. By the end of the year the Voting Rights Act of 1965 was passed by Congress.

A goal of CCR was to develop new legal approaches based on the idea that litigation could be more than just defensive; it could also become an affirmative means to preserve individual liberty and freedom. CCR attorneys, including Kunstler, and others defended the "Chicago Seven" against conspiracy prosecutions arising from the demonstrations staged at the 1968 Democratic National Convention in Chicago. The Chicago Seven were originally the Chicago Eight, but Bobby Seale refused to accept the CCR lawyers and the judge separated his case, leaving seven to stand trial together.

Beginning in 1969, when attorney Nancy Stearns joined CCR, the center became involved in the issue of women's reproductive rights. Stearns met a group of women, the Women's Health Collective, who were talking about the politics of health care. At the time, the only way for a woman to obtain an abortion was to have two psychiatrists declare she was likely to commit suicide if she did not have one. In many states she didn't even have that option.

Stearns and the Women's Health Collective decided to file a lawsuit, thus using the court as a political forum. They filed a complaint with 350 plaintiffs against the state of New York, the attorney general of the state of New York, and the district attorney for Manhattan. The lawsuit *Abramowitz v. Lefkowitz* (Louis Lefkowitz was attorney general) focused on a woman's right to control her own body.

From the outset, CCR became involved in cases with international implications. Two former attorneys, Beth Stephens and Michael Ratner, shared the 1995 "Trial Lawyers of the Year" award for work on cases concerning torture in Guatemala, Haiti, and East Timor. CCR's interest in international litigation began with the precedent-setting *Filartiga v. Pena-Irala* case. After seventeen-year-old Joelita Filartiga was tortured to death by a Paraguayan police official, family members located the killer in Brooklyn in 1979 and asked CCR to represent them in a civil damage suit against him. CCR used a 200-year-old law, the Alien Claims Act. The law permits noncitizens to sue in federal court for human rights violations, even those committed outside the United States, provided the accused is under the jurisdiction of a U.S. court.

The precedents set in the *Filartiga* case were upheld at the highest judicial levels. They have been used to obtain multimillion-dollar judgments against torturers from Paraguay, Guatemala, Haiti, Ethiopia, and East Timor.

Still based in New York City, CCR celebrated its thirtieth birthday in 1996.

See also Mississippi Freedom Democratic Party; Southern Poverty Law Center
Reference Arthur Kinoy. *Rights on Trial: The Odyssey of a People's Lawyer*, 1983.

Chaney, Goodman, and Schwerner, Murders of

James Chaney, Andrew Goodman, and Michael Schwerner were activists working to register voters in 1964 during the Mississippi Freedom Summer Project. Schwerner and Goodman were whites from New York. Schwerner was a graduate of Cornell and had been active in the Congress of Racial Equality (CORE), and Goodman was a student at Queens College. Chaney was a black Mississippian and a CORE activist.

Whites were working to register voters in Mississippi because, even after three years of intense effort by Student Nonviolent Coordinating Com-

mittee (SNCC) members, only about 5 percent of blacks eligible to vote in Mississippi had been registered. A coalition of civil rights organizations decided to invite 1,000 white northern students to Mississippi for the summer to help register black citizens. Their rationale was that northern public opinion and federal officials would not tolerate southerners assaulting white college students.

During the evening of June 21, 1964, Chaney, Goodman, and Schwerner disappeared. Because there had been four "mystery killings" of blacks in the state during the first half of 1964, coworkers became immediately fearful and called for a search. Mississippi governor Paul Johnson declared their absence a publicity hoax. Two days later authorities found the volunteers' burned-out car.

President Johnson ordered sailors from a nearby base to join the Federal Bureau of Investigation (FBI) in a massive search. Federal agents searched for six weeks before they found the bodies buried in an earthen dam. Goodman and Schwerner had been shot through the heart. Chaney had been beaten. A pathologist and medical examiner said that he had never seen a body with bones so severely shattered except in high-speed accidents or plane crashes.

In an interview, Schwerner's widow told the nation that the massive search was conducted only because her husband and Goodman were white. If only Chaney had been involved, nothing would have been done.

See also Freedom Riders; Mississippi Freedom Democratic Party; Student Nonviolent Coordinating Committee
Reference Terry Anderson. *The Movement and the Sixties: Protest in America from Greensboro to Wounded Knee*, 1995.

Charisma

A quality of leadership that captures the imagination, charisma inspires devotion, fascination, and sometimes fanaticism on the part of others. In the arenas of social and political issues, the 1960s and 1970s brought to the attention of the public many charismatic leaders, including Bella

Abzug, the Berrigan brothers, Fidel Castro, the Reverend Martin Luther King, Jr., Ronald Reagan, Mario Savio, and Gloria Steinem, to mention a few. Unfortunately, charismatic leaders often don't have the qualities needed to maintain change after it is brought about. If they are lucky, they will have followers with the capacity to carry out the mundane tasks required for daily living.

Revolutionary leader Fidel Castro, who took over the governance of Cuba, is an example of a leader who allowed the infrastructure (for example, roads and bridges) of Cuba to deteriorate. Castro did not have the administrative skills, nor did he delegate the tasks to people who did. Castro was kept in power by massive financial and technical support from the Soviet Union.

The socialist Norman Thomas once said, "Every dissenter who is worth his salt—better every dissenter who wants to be numbered among the salt of the earth—is primarily concerned about some positive value that he not only wants to assert for himself but to recommend to others." He went on to say, "Angry men, young and old—assertive, nonconformist, although not of Hitler's stripe—have no great value to themselves, much less to society if they are merely angry, merely objectors to the dominant institution and idea of their time." In other words, the dissenter, at whatever level, needs more than charm and a glib tongue. He or she needs a plan and the personal skills to carry out the plan or the ability to recognize the skills in others who can be responsible for the details of the plan.

See also Free Speech Movement; Independent Living Movement; Neal, Sister Marie Augusta
Reference Norman Thomas. *The Great Dissenter,* 1961.

Chavez, Cesar (1927–1993)

Cesar Estrada Chavez spent his entire adult life struggling to improve the working and living conditions of America's farmworkers. In general, to maintain maximum profits, growers held down the cost of labor. They could pay whatever they chose, require laborers to work twelve- or fourteen-hour days, and fire workers for no rea-

son. Nevertheless, farm workers did on occasion "strike" a farm, refusing to work. For their efforts, they were apt to be jailed, beaten, or terrorized. Cesar Chavez set out to change all that.

By the 1960s, migrant farmworkers included Mexicans, Mexican Americans, blacks, Asians, Asian Americans, and whites. By far the largest group was Mexicans and Mexican Americans. Regardless of their ethnic or racial background, migrant laborers were the most poorly paid, housed, and educated workers in America. They were not protected by the National Labor Relations Act (NLRA). The NLRA stipulated that all workers must be paid a minimum wage and could not be forced to work long hours every day. The act also forced employers to permit the formation of unions among the workers. However, the NLRA specifically excluded farmworkers.

In 1965, the best-paid farmworker earned only $1.50 an hour, and his or her family income amounted to less than one-half the poverty level. Few could afford three balanced meals a day. Proper clothing was scarce, particularly shoes. Housing was apt to be a converted chicken coop, an old car, or a cardboard shelter. Water for drinking or bathing might come from an irrigation ditch.

Most workers began work in the fields at 6:00 A.M. and worked ten or twelve hours. Although temperatures in the fields often reached over 100 degrees, growers provided scant water to drink, and toilet facilities were nonexistent. Out of perversity, farmers often made their workers use short-handled hoes, which meant they had to work in a stooped-over position for hours. Preventable accidents caused severe injuries. If a farmworker was injured, the employer was likely to force the family to move out of their flimsy quarters. Inadequate food, water, housing, and toilet facilities, together with dangerous working conditions, caused migrants to have the highest rates of disease and death among American workers.

Because migrant families moved constantly from one area where they had finished harvesting a crop to another area where their help was needed, their children's schooling was sporadic.

AFL-CIO president George Meany (left) presents a charter setting up a new United Farm Workers organizing committee to Cesar Chavez and an unidentified man. The two men were leaders of groups who successfully led strikes of California grape pickers.

Too often economic necessity forced children to drop out of school at age 8 or 9. Children who did attend school often felt humiliated because they were poorly dressed and had fallen behind the other children in their studies. Teachers frequently refused to let them speak languages other than English.

Cesar Chavez's grandfather, Cesario Chavez, was a farm laborer in Mexico and had worked on a railroad in the United States. After he saved enough money to bring his wife and fourteen children from Mexico to the United States in 1888, he settled in North Gila Valley in Arizona before Arizona became a state. In the valley, he claimed a 100-acre homestead and built a home. In 1925 Cesario's son, Librado, and his wife, Juana Estrada, bought a grocery store with an adjoining gas station and pool hall and continued to do farm work. On March 31, 1927, Cesario Estrada

Chavez was born and named after his grandfather and his mother.

Two years later, the United States fell into the Great Depression, a time when millions of Americans lost their jobs and their homes. People who would normally buy a farmer's crops had little or no money. Most of the farmers who lived in Gila Valley had been poor even before the Depression. Librado let destitute people buy food for the family from his store on credit. When they couldn't repay him, he went into debt and was forced to sell his business. The family moved into Librado's childhood adobe home.

Cesario's childhood home was a happy one, except for school. The teachers and the principal punished and humiliated children for speaking Spanish. One teacher took the liberty of changing his name to Cesar because it sounded less Mexican. For his future role as a leader, Cesar's most important education came from his family. His deeply religious Catholic mother taught her children Mexican proverbs, including the proverb "What you do to others, others will do to you." Stories she told her children often illustrated the virtue of nonviolence. When her children argued, Cesar's mother would say, "It takes two to fight, and one can't do it alone."

She believed it was her Christian duty to help the poor. The family frequently had someone who was poor share the family's meals. Farm families living in severe poverty often bartered, that is, traded eggs for flour or bread and watermelons for medical services. However, the one thing the families could not barter was the taxes that had to be paid on their land. By 1937, the Chavezes' bill for taxes totaled more than $4,000. The government took possession of the family farm, and it was sold at public auction. The horrified family watched trees they had nurtured being knocked down by a tractor. Then they packed the family car and headed for California, for life as migrant laborers. The first winter, the family lived in a tent in the yard of a kind woman. Over the next several years, the family traveled constantly. By the time he was 12, Cesar worked every day after school and ten hours on Saturday and Sunday. His parents left at five in the morning and didn't return for fourteen hours. They were often so tired they could do nothing except fall into bed. Not only were their wages meager, but farmers often cheated laborers out of the wages they earned. Being cheated robbed them of their dignity.

Cesar's father suffered an injury to his chest in 1942, and at age 16 Cesar dropped out of school to support his family. By then he had learned most farm jobs. He had cut broccoli in wet, muddy fields and had planted crops in soil so thorny it constantly punctured his fingers. He had spent days hunched over, thinning and weeding rows and rows of plants. He had pulled 15-pound sugar beets from soil so resistant he had split open his hands. Each day he set a goal for himself and did not leave the field until he had met it. One day he told his mother that she was never to do another day of work in a field. She did not. The years of work blurred for Cesar.

In 1944, to avoid being drafted into the army, Cesar joined the navy and spent the next two years as a deckhand on ships transporting troops. After his service, he returned to the migrant labor fields. While he was picking cotton in 1948, a caravan of cars drove by the field. The passengers waved flags and shouted, "Huelga! Huelga!" (strike, strike). Cesar left the field and joined the strikers. Although the walkout was initially effective, its effect was not lasting. Nevertheless, the experience changed Cesar. His father had once belonged to unions, and the thought of organizing the farm workers gnawed at Cesar's conscience.

In 1948, Cesar Chavez married Helen Fabela. In 1952, they were living in an overcrowded barrio (neighborhood) of San Jose, California, called Sal Si Puedes (get out if you can), where Chavez met Father Donald McDonnel. With the Catholic priest, Chavez talked about the plight of the farmworkers. Father McDonnel helped him to recognize the disparity between the workers' grinding poverty and the landowners' wealth. From the priest, he learned about such people as St. Francis of Assisi, who in the Middle Ages was born into a wealthy family and devoted his life to the poor. He also learned about Monads Karamchand Gandhi (1869–1948), who had used nonviolent methods to lead India to political independence from Great Britain in 1947.

The second major influence in Chavez's life was Fred Ross, who had been hired by Chicago sociologist Saul Alinsky. Ross was sent to Los Angeles to organize hundreds of poor Mexicans and Mexican Americans and help improve their lives. After six years, Ross had created a community service organization (CSO), an organization intended to unite people and give them political power. One of the CSO's main goals was to get people registered to vote in Sal Si Puedes. Day after day, the two men went door-to-door convincing residents to vote. By the 1952 general election, the CSO had registered 4,000 new voters.

Disaster struck on election day. When Mexican Americans who had been born in the United States of Mexican parents appeared at the polls on election day, officials questioned whether they were U.S. citizens. Some were asked to show that they could read. Few were literate. Almost all were frightened by the officials, so much so that many left without voting. The CSO leaders wrote a letter of protest about the harassment to the U.S. attorney general. But all except Chavez were afraid to sign it for fear of losing their jobs. Chavez's signature of the letter won him respect throughout the community. Many Mexicans in the community were qualified to become U.S. citizens. To build the community's power base, Chavez helped them with the paperwork and tutored them on tests.

When Chavez was laid off from the lumber mill where he worked, Saul Alinsky hired him and asked him to organize DeCoto (now Union City), California. Once Chavez overcame his natural shyness, his organizing skills improved steadily. One of his co-workers said he had a spiritual quality. Another described his spiritual quality as a kind of "humble innocence that is the bearer of the words of another world."

Chavez listened well. When he went to Oxnard in 1958, he planned to start up a CSO and register voters. However, the people of Oxnard were not interested in voting. Their immediate problem was competition for jobs from *braceros,* Mexican laborers who had permission from the U.S. government to work. Growers bussed them in to work for less money and under worse conditions than Mexican-American laborers. But U.S. law required that braceros be used only when there were not enough Americans to work the fields. For thirteen months, Chavez protested and filed complaints with local, state, and federal authorities. His most effective strategy was a march through Oxnard. The approximately 10,000 marchers were filmed by several television stations. The attention in 1959 forced growers to stop hiring braceros. Chavez had organized his first major victory on behalf of farmworkers.

The Oxnard victory convinced Chavez that it was time to build a union of farmworkers, despite prior failed attempts, during which workers had been threatened, beaten, and jailed. Only Chavez's wife, Helen, believed he would succeed. In 1962, with $1,200 in the bank, Chavez resigned from leadership of the CSO and returned to Delano,

where Helen's family lived. Delano was surrounded by 30,000 grape vineyards and eighty-six farmworkers' camps.

Using the same methods he had used to organize a CSO, he organized a union. He and his organizing crew of friends and relatives drew in members one by one. The Reverend Jim Drake, one of Chavez's organizers, said that the pains Chavez took "were a very real extension of his philosophy that human beings are subjects to be taken seriously." By the fall of 1962, enough farmworkers had joined the union to hold a convention. When the National Farm Workers Association (NFWA) came to order in Fresno on September 30, 1962, 200 people were present. The union motto adopted that day was "Viva la Causa!" which means "Long live the cause." The farm movement was often referred to as La Causa, meaning the fight for justice. However, ten months after the convention, all but ten members had dropped their membership. In 1963, recruitment began again. By August 1964, 1,000 farmworkers had joined.

In the summer of 1965, a small association of farmworkers walked off their jobs. Although Chavez was not ready to strike, he felt he had no choice but to help. On September 17, 1965, Mexico's independence day, the NFWA's membership voted to go on strike. In response, the growers hired strikebreakers, and some growers harassed the strikers.

The local police decided that the strikers could not shout at the strikebreakers in the field. NFWA believed the police were infringing on their right to free speech. To gain publicity, volunteers challenged the police on a day Chavez was scheduled to speak at the University of California at Berkeley. Students donated their lunch money to the strike effort. To help with the strike, Chavez recruited people other than farmworkers, particularly people who had participated in the civil rights movement and been trained in nonviolent protest tactics.

Once the strike was under way, NFWA began a boycott of grapes. Strikers followed truckloads of grapes to buyers and formed picket lines. To increase the chances of success, Chavez narrowed the scope of boycott to grapes produced by Schenley Industries, which owned about 3,350 acres of grapes near Delano. However, grapes were only one of Schenley's products. Chavez reasoned that a boycott of all Schenley's products would have the greatest impact on the company's profits. He chose thirteen major cities and sent volunteers to picket stores and encourage buyers to refrain from buying Schenley's products. In March 1966, a U.S. Senate subcommittee came to Delano to investigate. Democratic senator Robert Kennedy became an avid supporter.

Chavez organized a 250-mile march from Delano to Sacramento, California's state capital. Public support and press coverage increased at every stop along the way. In Stockton, where 5,000 people came out to show their support, Chavez received a phone call from Schenley headquarters saying they were ready to negotiate a labor agreement with NFWA. In the agreement, they recognized NFWA as the representative of their laborers, agreed to use the union hall for hiring, and gave field laborers a thirty-five-cent-an-hour wage increase. After twenty-five days on the road, the strikers arrived in Sacramento, where 10,000 people waited to greet them.

The strikers' work had just begun. A week later, NFWA began picketing at DiGiorgio, a large corporation that owned vineyards in Delano and other regions. In May, DiGiorgio obtained a court order that permitted only a few strikers to picket the fields at any one time, thus effectively crippling the strike. Chavez was discouraged but had faith that a nonviolent solution would be found. Three women asked if the court order prohibited the strikers from praying at DiGiorgio's field. The court had no objection. A chapel with a shrine to Our Lady of Guadalupe was built on the back of Chavez's station wagon, and farmworkers were invited to attend every morning. Hundreds came. For two months, after each daily mass, NFWA signed up new members.

To counter the effectiveness of NFWA, the DiGiorgio company permitted the Teamsters Union to recruit workers in its fields. The Teamsters had a reputation for engaging in illegal practices. Their behavior in Delano was no exception.

NFWA protested to the governor, who appointed an arbitrator. The arbitrator permitted NFWA to talk to the DiGiorgio workers and ordered a secret ballot.

The election was set up so that the workers could choose among the NFWA, the Teamsters, and AWOC (a small union associated with the national American Federation of Labor–Congress of Industrial Organizations [AFL-CIO]). If NFWA lost the election, the union would be finished. Chavez reasoned that if NFWA merged with AWOC, the chance of winning the election would be increased. The two unions merged in August 1966, becoming the UFW (the United Farm Workers). UFW won with 530 votes to 331 for the Teamsters. Congratulations and support came from Americans around the nation. In a telegram, Martin Luther King, Jr., wrote: "Our separate struggles are really one—a struggle for freedom, for dignity, and for humanity."

In the summer of 1967, the UFW struck the largest table grape grower, Giumarra. When Giumarra obtained a court injunction to keep the number of strikers around their fields to a minimum, the union organized a boycott. The company countered by placing the labels of other growers on their boxes. With any one of sixty separate labels, it became impossible to tell which boxes were Giumarra's. When the boycott stalled, the union proposed to strike all grape growers. Chavez was opposed. He didn't want to hurt the uninvolved growers. Reluctantly, he called for a nationwide boycott. The public rallied to the cause. A secondary boycott—a boycott of stores carrying California grapes—spread.

Although they were losing money, the growers refused to negotiate. Some of the frustrated workers wanted to resort to violence. Following an hour-long meeting during which Chavez insisted on the need to maintain a nonviolent philosophy, he announced he was going on a fast as a symbol of his commitment to nonviolence. At Forty Acres, a plot owned by the union, friends pitched tents to join Chavez in a nightly mass. Chavez's fast became more than his personal act of worship; it encouraged the workers to pull together. Public sympathy for La Causa grew. He ended his fast after twenty-five days, when Senator Robert Kennedy served him the communion bread.

By 1969, the growers claimed that they were willing to offer UFW a contract, but the terms were no improvement over existing conditions. The AFL-CIO, whose members belonged to AWOC when it merged with NFWA, and some workers wanted to accept the terms, feeling that recognition of the union as a bargaining unit was sufficient and terms could be strengthened later, but Chavez ignored the pressure. After four years of resistance, an inadequate contract was not enough. An estimated 17 million consumers had boycotted California grapes. In 1970, growers conceded. Catholic bishops experienced in labor relations negotiated twenty-six contracts, which were signed on July 29, 1970, providing substantial gains for the workers. The workers had sacrificed whatever worldly possessions they had. Chavez had sacrificed his health.

The UFW planned next to go after lettuce growers. To keep out the UFW, the lettuce growers raced to sign contracts with the Teamsters. For the next several years, UFW was locked in a struggle with the Teamsters, who used violence and threats. Chavez refused to permit his workers to respond in kind. President Richard Nixon's administration seemed to support the Teamsters and the growers. The assassination of King and Robert Kennedy robbed UFW of two of its strongest and most public allies. By 1973, UFW membership had significantly declined.

In 1974, Chavez met with Pope Paul VI in Rome. In 1975, California governor Jerry Brown helped sign the Agriculture Labor Relations Act, which required the growers to recognize an elected union. With renewed vigor, Chavez led one struggle after another to rid the fields of the Teamsters. Suddenly, in 1977, the Teamsters asked for a truce. The two unions signed a pact that allowed the Teamsters to organize farm cannery workers and truck drivers and left the field workers to the UFW.

When the peace pact expired in the early 1980s, the Teamsters began recruiting field workers once again. The Teamsters' membership grew, while UFW's rolls declined. There were several theories about why UFW membership declined, mostly revolving around Chavez's single-mindedness. A serious factor unrelated to Chavez was a mass influx of braceros, who were afraid to complain about working conditions.

In two decades, Chavez had brought about a miraculous change. Real wages of California farm workers had increased by 70 percent, and many had access to pension benefits, health care, and disability insurance. Despite the miracle, a 1980s study found that one-third of the nation's farm laborers still did not have access to toilet facilities in the fields, and one-half were not provided with drinking water while they worked. Nevertheless, the U.S. Occupational Safety and Health Administration refused to force growers to provide such necessities. Chavez and the UFW continued to fight for water and toilet facilities and added protests about the grave risk pesticides posed for workers.

On April 23, 1993, at the age of sixty-six, Chavez died in his sleep. On April 28, crowds gathered at Forty Acres to keep a vigil through the night. By morning, 35,000 people had come to Delano to pay their respects. Although celebrities and government officials were among the mourners, many more were farmworkers, many of whom had traveled long distances and brought their children.

Despite Chavez's sacrifices, migrant workers remain among the most unprotected and underpaid of America's workers. As many as 5 million migrant workers, predominantly black and Hispanic, wend their way north each year through the nation's farm fields. Many have not lost hope. Chavez's example lives in young leaders of small unions organized on the model provided by Chavez and the UFW. In 1994, Chavez's friends and family established the Cesar E. Chavez Foundation. Posthumously, President Bill Clinton awarded him the Presidential Medal of Honor, the highest honor a civilian can receive.

See also Brown Power; Brown Power in Classrooms; King, Reverend Martin Luther, Jr.

References Delores Gonzales. *Cesar Chavez: Leader for Migrant Farm Workers,* 1996; Jacques Levy, *Cesar Chavez: Autobiography of La Causa,* 1975.

Chicago Seven Trial

At the outset, the defendants tried for conspiracy and inciting a riot in connection with the 1968 Chicago Democratic convention numbered eight: Dave Dellinger, Tom Hayden, Rennie Davis, Abbie Hoffman, Jerry Rubin, Lee Weiner, John Froines, and Bobby Seale. Black Panther chief Bobby Seale's case was eventually separated from the white activists and the Chicago Eight became the Chicago Seven.

The seven were members of two groups that played a part in the protests that disrupted the convention. The National Mobilization Committee, "the Mobe," planned to demonstrate that politicians did not speak for them. They hoped to encourage discontented Democrats to seek new forms of protest and resistance. The Mobe had two leaders. Tom Hayden was the founder of the New Left organization Students for a Democratic Society (SDS). Rennie Davis was a former member of SDS's Economic Research and Action Project (ERAP), which recruited students to organize white and black inner-city residents to take control of their communities. The experience of dealing with unyielding bureaucracies radicalized ERAP organizers and taught them that confrontation was the only way to gain attention.

The second group was the nonviolent Youth International Party, "Yippies." They aimed at shaping youth culture into a revolutionary force through media events rather than through organizing. Jerry Rubin, a creative antiwar organizer from the University of California at Berkeley, was a key Yippie organizer. He was aided by Abbie Hoffman, a New York hippie, who had earlier staged an exorcism at the Pentagon, and by Paul Krassner, editor of the *Realist*, a countercultural journal.

The Mobes and the Yippies, different in style and purpose, joined in an uncomfortable alliance to orchestrate protests. Mobe concentrated on having a "counterconvention" with marches and rallies. Yippies staged a "Festival of Life" with rock music and nominated a pig for president.

Student march protesting the trial of the Chicago Seven.

The reaction of Mayor Richard Daley and the Chicago police to the presence of the protestors sparked riots. Scenes of police officers beating protestors were broadcast across the nation.

In early 1969, the Nixon administration ordered FBI agents to arrest the Chicago Eight, the presumed leaders of the protest, for conspiracy to cross state lines to incite a riot. They were brought to trial and the trial went on for months. It ended in February 1970.

Federal Judge Julius Hoffman demanded respect in his courtroom. Instead, he faced obscenities and defendants dressed in strange costumes. Defiant defendants and their attorneys engaged the judge in verbal warfare. Before his case was separated from the others, Bobby Seale contributed substantially to the courtroom uproar. Seale wanted his own lawyer, who was unavailable, and refused to accept the lawyers handling the other defendants. To put a stop to Seale's shouts and constant motion, the judge had him chained to his chair with his mouth taped. Despite the chains and tape, Seale continued to be disruptive until the judge elected to try him separately.

All seven were acquitted of conspiracy charges, but all except two were found guilty of inciting a riot. The judge added convictions for contempt of court for the defendants and their attorneys. A federal appeals court overturned all the convictions.

See also Daley, Richard; Hoffman, Abbie; Yippies
References Terry Anderson. *The Movement and the Sixties: Protest in America from Greensboro to Wounded Knee*, 1995; Stewart Burns. *Social Movements of the 1960s*, 1990.

Child Warriors

Founded in 1987 in Eureka Springs, Arkansas, the Center on War and the Child dedicated itself to arousing interest in the public about the use of children as soldiers. The goal of ending the use of child warriors is not solely humanitarian. The United States and the United Nations (UN) are frequently drawn into peacekeeping roles in conflicts around the world that are internal—ethnic

and religious wars. Children are used to keep internal wars going—often despite peace accords. Such wars are characterized by butchery. More than 80 percent of the victims are noncombatants, mostly women and children.

Although it is difficult to count this population, the UN in the late 1980s estimated that 200,000 children under the age of fifteen were bearing arms, most of them fighting in rebel groups. The M-16 assault weapon had made warfare easier to conduct using children as warriors—and as fodder. In the mid-1990s, the number of child soldiers, current or recently demobilized, was estimated to be about one quarter of a million around the world. The estimate was based on a series of case studies in twenty-six countries conducted by the Swedish division of Save the Children (Radda Barnen). The studies were part of a larger UN study led by children's rights advocate Graca Machel, former first lady of Mozambique, which found that in some countries, children constituted a significant percentage of the nation's combatants.

In El Salvador, the FMLN (Farabundo Martí National Liberation Front) enlisted both young boys and young girls. During the Khmer Rouge regime in Cambodia, children massacred civilians, including their own parents. Iranian ten-year-olds served as human minesweepers. In areas of the world where most of the battles took place in the 1980s and continued to take place in the 1990s—Africa, Southeast Asia, and the Middle East—nearly half of the populations were young.

Mike Wessels, a professor of psychology at Randolph-Macon College of Virginia and a former president of the Division of Peace Psychology of the American Psychological Association, has done extensive consultation on conflict resolution in war-ravaged countries. According to Wessels, children who are reluctant to take up arms can be coerced by a desire to please their elders. Because they crave approval and affection from adults, children can be taught quickly to hate. For some, the excitement of battle, if they survive, serves as a motivator. For some, the brutality of their training forces them to cooperate.

One Mozambican fourteen-year-old told researchers, "When it [the training] was over, they did a test. They put someone in front of me to kill. I killed."

Once the war comes to an end, participation in a peaceful community becomes difficult for the former soldiers. Some societies shun the child warriors, assuming they are potential assassins. In many indigenous cultures, healers use traditional rituals to reintegrate the child back into the community.

Advocates like the Center for War and the Child and APA's Division of Peace Psychology believe prevention of the use of child warriors is preferable to finding ways to repair them after participation in war. They have lobbied to raise to age eighteen the minimum age of military recruitment set at fifteen in Article 38 of the Convention on the Rights of the Children.

See also Children's Defense Fund; Killing Fields
Reference Rachel Brett and Margaret McCallin. *Children: The Invisible Soldiers,* 1996.

Children's Defense Fund

The founder of the Children's Defense Fund (CDF), Marian Wright Edelman, has spent most of her life defending the rights of children. Born in 1939, she grew up in a small town in South Carolina, where black people like her were forbidden to buy a soft drink or use the local parks. Edelman's father, a Baptist minister, created a playground and opened a canteen in his church for black children. From his example, Edelman learned that if you don't like the way the world is organized, you are obligated to change it.

In the United States, one in five children lives in poverty. A black child is twice as likely as a white child to die before his or her first birthday. Edelman explained during an October 22, 1989, interview with Harry Reasoner on the television program *60 Minutes* why children are so neglected. She said, "Everybody is for them in general … But when they get into the budget rooms, or behind closed doors—to really decide how they're going to carve up the money—children get lost in the process because they're not powerful."

Edelman attended law school from 1960 to 1963. During the Mississippi Freedom Summer Project in 1964, she spent a great deal of time securing releases from jail for northern college students who had come south to register voters. During that summer, she learned such survival skills as starting a car with the doors open in case the car had been fitted with a bomb. The first woman admitted to the Mississippi bar. Edelman broadened her focus from civil rights to a goal of improving the economic conditions of blacks because she felt that, without enough to eat, civil rights were meaningless.

As counsel to the Child Development Group of Mississippi, Edelman helped restore federal funding for Head Start. She took Democratic senator Robert Kennedy on a tour of Mississippi shanties, which lacked heat, electricity, and running water. Saddened and angered by the plight of children, Kennedy helped put elimination of the conditions of poverty high on his brother John F. Kennedy's list of priorities.

Edelman married Peter Edelman, legislative assistant to Robert Kennedy, and moved with him to Washington, D.C., where she began the Washington Research Project, a public interest research and advocacy organization. The memory of the misery in Mississippi haunted her. On the day after Martin Luther King, Jr., was killed, Edelman tried to divert a group of teenagers bent on violence by suggesting their actions could destroy their futures. One said to her, "Lady, I ain't got no future."

The youngster's words spurred Edelman to create the Children's Defense Fund. CDF's research projects have included an investigation of why so many school-aged children do not attend school, treatment of institutionalized children, the use of children in medical experiments, infant mortality, homelessness, prenatal care, nutrition, school dropouts, and increasing rates of teenage pregnancy. CDF's advocacy campaigns urged the poor to immunize their children. Edelman lobbied to reform the nation's foster care system and to create a system of support for children in single-parent households.

Edelman keeps CDF in the public eye through

her writing and frequent speeches. She regularly points out that the children of the world do not get fair treatment. Each day, at least 40,000 children in the world die of malnutrition or infection. Malnutrition makes children vulnerable to infection. Each day, the nations of the world spend $2.7 billion on weapons.

During the 1992 presidential campaign, CDF ran a series of provocative ads created, without charge, by ad agencies. One showed a squalling infant lying in a basket—evoking an air of abandonment. The print read: "Maybe America is really going to hell in a handbasket." Edelman became close friends with Hillary Clinton when Bill Clinton was governor of Arkansas. The two women worked on children's issues together. Since becoming First Lady, Hillary Clinton, like Edelman, has spent substantial time promoting the welfare of children.

When critics accuse Edelman of being impractical in an era of financial crisis, she typically responds, "People ought to be able to distinguish between throwing money at problems and investing in success."

See also Child Warriors; Homelessness
References Marian Wright Edelman. *Families in Peril: An Agenda for Social Change,* 1987; and *The Measure of Our Success: A Letter to My Children and Yours,* 1994.

Chisholm, Shirley (b. 1924)

Most newcomers to a profession remain more or less quiet until they get a sense about what they need to know. Shirley Chisholm, the first black woman elected to Congress, was an exception. She had been a maverick since childhood. Born in Brooklyn, New York, Chisholm was the first child of Charles and Ruby St. Hill, who had emigrated from Barbados in the early 1920s in search of a better life. Home ownership and a good education for their children were goals that eluded the family, despite hard work. By the time Chisholm was three, she had two younger sisters.

Chisholm's mother took her three daughters home to Barbados to live with her mother, while she and her husband tried to accrue some savings in New York. The St. Hill girls stayed in Barbados for six years. Chisholm's grandmother and the British schools she attended imposed a strict discipline on the independent and outspoken Chisholm. After a rocky period following her return to New York, Chisholm excelled and went to Brooklyn College, a free public college with high admission standards. She obtained a master's degree in early childhood education from Columbia University.

Chisholm's education in practical politics came after she joined a local Democratic club. Blacks who came to meetings customarily allowed the white club leaders to take charge. Chisholm asked embarrassing questions, such as "Why isn't trash collected more often in black neighborhoods?" From the experience, she learned that people in power don't like those who question authority. She wasn't intimidated.

In 1960, Chisholm joined a group of rebels in the Democratic club who attempted to throw out those in power. They failed in 1960 in getting a black man elected to the state assembly but succeeded in 1962. When their candidate decided two years later to run for a judgeship, the voters of the black Bedford-Stuyvesant district where Chisholm lived picked her to replace him. She served in the New York state legislature until 1968.

Chisholm moved on to national politics after the Supreme Court handed down a decision that required congressional districts to be roughly equal in proportion in numbers of voters. In response to the decision, the New York state legislature created the Twelfth Congressional District in Brooklyn, which included Bedford-Stuyvesant. A citizen's committee chose Chisholm as a candidate. With very little money, she won over two other Democrats in the primary election by going door-to-door to talk with voters.

In the general election, Chisholm had a more difficult time. Both the Republicans and New York's liberal party nominated James Farmer, a black civil rights leader, the founder of the Congress of Racial Equality (CORE). Surgery to remove a large tumor curtailed Chisholm's time to campaign. When James Farmer began asking potential voters where Chisholm was, she announced to her husband and her doctor, "The stitches aren't in my mouth. I'm going out." Chisholm rode around in a truck equipped with a loudspeaker. She campaigned with the slogan "Unbought and Unbossed." Farmer's campaign, which called for "a strong male image" and "a man's voice" in Washington, was self-defeating in a district where women outnumbered men more than two to one. Chisholm appealed to women voters to support her as a way of fighting discrimination against women. Women's organizations mounted a strong campaign on her behalf, and she won by a substantial margin.

Almost immediately upon arrival in Congress, Chisholm bucked the committee assignment system. She was assigned to the Agriculture Committee, an inappropriate slot for an urban specialist in childhood education. When Wilbur Mills, the powerful chairman of the Democratic selection committee, repeatedly refused to recognize Chisholm at a meeting of the Democratic caucus to approve assignments, she marched up to the speaker's platform and stood there until he allowed her to speak. Her tactic worked. The caucus removed Chisholm from the Agriculture Committee and assigned her to Veterans' Affairs. Although the assignment was not one of her choices, she said later, "There are a lot more veterans in my district than trees."

During Chisholm's second term in the House of Representatives, she became the first black woman to run for president. In the fall of 1971 in a closed-door meeting, black politicians and civil rights activists decided that if they put a black candidate up for president, a man would make a better candidate. Chisholm ignored their opinion, and on January 25, 1972, she formally announced her candidacy.

She told prospective voters she was neither the candidate of black America nor of women, although she was proud of both her race and her gender. Chisholm declared, "I am a candidate of the people." She entered eleven primaries in 1972 and waged a vigorous campaign in several states. Chisholm had enthusiastic support but little money. By the time of the Democratic National Convention in the summer of 1972, she had only a handful of delegates pledged to support her. Chisholm's dignity and a gracious speech of withdrawal charmed the delegates into giving her an enthusiastic round of applause.

In 1977, fellow Democrats assigned Chisholm to the powerful House Rules Committee. In February of that same year, she and her husband, Conrad Chisholm, were divorced. In November 1977, she married Arthur Hardwick, with whom she had served in the state legislature. Then Hardwick was severely injured in an automobile accident. Her husband's health and the increasingly conservative climate that accompanied the election of Ronald Reagan in 1980 led to Chisholm's decision to retire at the end of the 1982 session to teach college. The first black woman in Congress, she had served for fourteen years and run for president, a record of which she could be proud.

In 1985, she became the first president of the newly organized National Political Congress of Black Women.

See also Women's Movement; Year of the Woman
References Shirley Chisholm. *Unbought and Unbossed,* 1970; and *The Good Fight,* 1973; Isobel Morin. *Women of the U.S. Congress,* 1994.

Christian Identity Movement

Many of the social movement organizations active in the 1960s and 1970s actively recruited new members to help them work on behalf of social justice for America's disenfranchised. In contrast, Christian Identity churches recruit new members by preaching hate and by blaming segments of America's population, such as Jews, for whatever they perceive as wrong with the nation.

Protected by the rights to freedom of speech and religion, church leaders publish pamphlets and newsletters, share speakers, and hold conferences. Although the fiery rhetoric may provoke violence among individuals, building a case against church leaders that will hold up in court is difficult.

The Center for Democratic Renewal in Atlanta, Georgia, estimates that there may be as many as 30,000 followers who belong to over 100 Christian Identity churches. Local parishes have a variety of names, such as the Church of the Jesus Christ Christian, the Mountain Church, the Cosmotheist Church, and the New Christian Crusade Church.

The focus of the Christian Identity Movement is on justification of white supremacy and anti-Semitism. According to the movement's beliefs, Jesus was a northern European, and white Anglo-Saxon Christians are the true chosen people of the Bible. Jews are the children of Satan. In contrast to the northern European chosen people, southern and eastern Europeans and all people of color have no souls. They are the "mud people." Women are weak vessels. Each must serve the "one man God has given to rule over her." Homosexuals are perverted.

Members contend that a Zionist Occupation Government (ZOG) controls not only America's banks but also the federal government, the media, and most major institutions. ZOG must be overthrown before the Second Coming. Identity preachers hold "race mixing" and the lies of Jews to blame for whatever they perceive to be social problems. Heavily mortgaged farmers are a particular target for recruitment.

In 1985, Thom Robb, an Identity minister from Arkansas who in 1989 became a Ku Klux Klan Grand Wizard, wrote to his congregation: "The anti-Christ Jews want to kill you and your children in a gigantic genocidal bloodbath . . . They want to steal the souls and destroy the minds of your children with their hell-inspired teachings."

Although there is no central church, the religion provides a unity for different racist political groups and brings religious people in contact with the racist movement. In 1986, Robb said: "You can't stop a religious movement the way you can a political one because people believe they are being led by God."

Many Christian Identity churches are linked with paramilitary, white supremacist groups, such as the Aryan Nation, some Ku Klux Klan groups, and neo-Nazis. The church teachings include armed warfare techniques, curricula for teaching children at home, and tax information for those who object to taxes on the grounds that they go to ZOG.

See also Duke, David; Ku Klux Klan
References Elaine Landau. *The White Power Movement,* 1993; Susan Lang. *Extremist Groups in America,* 1990.

Civil Rights Movement

Many observers limit the civil rights movement to the period between the Supreme Court decision in the 1954 *Brown v. Board of Education of Topeka,* which declared segregated schools to be unconstitutional, and the Voting Rights Act of 1965, which permitted African Americans to participate freely in local and national elections. The general public tends to think of the civil rights movement as having continued throughout the 1960s and 1970s.

Some observers believe the civil rights movement began as early as January 31, 1865, when the Thirteenth Amendment prohibiting slavery everywhere in the United States became law. The hostile reactions of southern whites forced blacks to immediately begin a struggle to achieve equality. The possibility that blacks might be elected as government officials offended southern leaders. Beginning in Mississippi in 1890, they set out to pass laws that would make voting more and more difficult. To prevent blacks from voting, governments routinely applied restrictive requirements. The requirements included payment of a poll tax and demonstration of an ability to read and explain obscure sections of the constitution. Collectively, the laws were known as Jim Crow laws—named after a minstrel song.

In 1896, the U.S. Supreme Court strengthened local and state segregation laws through its decision in *Plessy v. Ferguson.* Homer Plessy, who was one-eighth black, was arrested for riding on a Louisiana train in a section reserved for "whites only." Plessy sued on grounds that a Louisiana statute requiring segregated streetcars violated his right to equal protection under the Fourteenth Amendment. Eight of the nine members of the Supreme Court ruled that the Fourteenth

Dr. Martin Luther King, the 1964 Nobel Peace Prize winner, and Ralph Bunche, the 1950 winner, march to Montgomery to support the right of African Americans to vote.

Amendment was not intended to enforce social, as distinguished from political, equality or a mixing of the two races on terms unsatisfactory to either. The decision held that "separate but equal" accommodation laws throughout the South were constitutional. The doctrine of separate but equal prevailed until the 1954 unanimous Supreme Court vote in the *Brown v. Board of Education of Topeka*, which ruled that separate educational facilities were inherently unequal.

Pursuit of the *Brown* ruling was only one of many actions taken by blacks to achieve equality during the years from 1954 to 1965. The organization of resources required to sustain the Montgomery city bus boycott, which brought the Reverends Martin Luther King, Jr., and Ralph Abernathy to national prominence, raised the hopes of many blacks in the South. The sit-ins and Freedom Rides of the early 1960s inspired a commitment among blacks who gave their time and their resources. They also focused national attention on the festering issue of race relations.

Following the Selma-to-Montgomery march, from March 21 through March 25, 1965, and the passage of the Voting Rights Act, attention shifted away from King's nonviolent theme of "we shall overcome." A new set of people with a more confrontational philosophy became more interested in "Black Power" than they were in civil rights.

During the years between the *Brown* decision in 1954 and the Voting Rights Act of 1965, more court decisions related to equal rights were handed down than during any other decade in America's history.

See also Abernathy, Reverend Ralph; Freedom Riders; King, Reverend Martin Luther, Jr.; Parks, Rosa; Sit-ins; Southern Christian Leadership Conference; Young, Andrew

References Sanford Wexler. *The Civil Rights Movement,* 1993; Andrew Young. *An Easy Burden: The Civil Rights Movement and the Transformation of America,* 1996.

Cleaver, Leroy Eldridge (1935–1998)

One of the most popular figures in the black power movement, Eldridge Cleaver appealed to a broad spectrum. He attracted blacks who had grown up in inner cities as he had; black prisoners, because he too had served time; radicals, because he was dedicated to overthrowing the power structure; and students and intellectuals, because he was a talented writer and a fine speaker.

Because he had to fight to survive on the streets of Los Angeles, Cleaver spent his time with youngsters who committed crimes and was sent to Juvenile Hall. The experience did not impress him. At twelve he went to reform school, where he learned the business of selling marijuana. Cleaver was sent to California's Soledad Prison in 1954, the same year that the Supreme Court in *Brown v. Board of Education of Topeka, Kansas* ruled that segregation was illegal. The lack of any visible change following *Brown* made Cleaver realize that he was a second-class citizen. He was in prison for breaking a law, but politicians who were ignoring the Supreme Court decision were not being jailed.

After a great deal of reading, Cleaver concluded that the only laws he would obey in the future were his own. When he was released from Soledad, he went on a rampage of crime, concentrating on rapes against white women. When Cleaver was apprehended, he was sentenced to two to fourteen years for assault with intent to kill and, at age twenty-two, sent to California's Folsom Prison. Ashamed, he turned to writing to find himself.

In 1958, he discovered the Black Muslims and became devoted to Malcolm X. When Malcolm X was assassinated, Cleaver felt all he had left was his writing. A civil rights lawyer, Beverly Axelrod, showed his manuscripts to Edward Keating, the founder of *Ramparts,* who in turn sent them to some white writers in the East. The eastern writers pressured prison authorities into paroling Cleaver, who was released in November 1966. As an editor of *Ramparts* in Los Angeles, Cleaver met other black artists and founded Black House, a gathering place for young people interested in an emerging black culture. He decided to revive Malcolm X's Organization of African-American Unity and planned a three-day memorial to honor Malcolm X, but he became disgusted when his efforts resulted in pomp rather than substance.

At the memorial, Cleaver met Black Panthers for the first time and was awestruck. He joined the Panthers and became their minister of information. After Cleaver spoke to a crowd of 65,000 at an antiwar rally, his parole officers told him that in future he had to have all his speeches preapproved. The parole authorities backed down when his attorney went to court charging a violation of free speech.

In February 1968, Cleaver's book *Soul on Ice* was published. The book made him famous. Two months later, on April 4, when Martin Luther King was assassinated, Cleaver and other Panthers went to local high schools to plead with angry students to refrain from violence. Yet the next day, in *Ramparts,* he wrote: "The violent phase of the black liberation struggle is here, and it will spread."

Within days, Cleaver was back in jail. Driving home after making preparations for a black community barbecue on April 7, Cleaver and other Panthers were surrounded by Oakland police. A shoot-out left seventeen-year-old Panther Bobby Hutton dead and Cleaver wounded. Cleaver's parole was revoked without a hearing. A judge who ordered Cleaver's release told authorities that the real reason they had revoked the parole was that his ideas were unpopular. Corrections authorities appealed the judge's decision and had it reversed. He was ordered to surrender on November 27.

In the meantime, the Black Panthers had

joined the mostly white Peace and Freedom Party, whose members opposed the Vietnam War. The new allies obtained the 100,000 signatures needed to register the combined groups as the California Peace and Freedom Party. At the party's convention in the summer of 1968, Cleaver was chosen as candidate for president of the United States.

Cleaver's speeches became symbols of opposition to Governor Ronald Reagan. Cleaver was followed everywhere by law enforcement officers. Cleaver and his attorney feared he would be picked up by corrections authorities before his scheduled trial in Oakland. Four days before he was scheduled to surrender to authorities, Cleaver said in a speech, "I cannot relate to spending the next four years in the penitentiary." After U.S. Supreme Court Justice Thurgood Marshall turned down a last-minute appeal for more time, Cleaver disappeared for several months. He turned up in Cuba and later as a guest of the government in Algeria. He continued to write and participate in international revolutionary struggles, but he had lost his power base in the United States.

See also Antiwar Movement; Black Panther Party; Stokely Carmichael
Reference Eldridge Cleaver. *Soul on Ice,* 1968; James Haskins. *Profiles in Black Power,* 1972.

COINTELPRO

The counterintelligence program known as COINTELPRO was conceived by the Federal Bureau of Investigation (FBI) in 1956 during a field conference. The goal was to crush the remnants of the American Communist Party. COINTELPRO-CPUSA (Communist Party USA) was the largest and longest of several COINTELPRO operations. It lasted until 1971.

Several events during 1956 had disillusioned and fragmented the American Communist Party. A speech by Soviet premier Nikita Khrushchev had chronicled atrocities committed by revolutionary leader Joseph Stalin. Authoritative accounts were being circulated about Soviet anti-Semitism. Communist authorities killed 100 protesters in Ponan, Poland, and wounded hundreds more, in June 1956. In October of that year, Soviet tanks rolled into Hungary.

Biographers differ in their interpretations of why John Edgar Hoover, the director of the FBI, felt a need for COINTELPRO. Some cynics believe he knew the party was no longer of much consequence but used it as a way to obtain ample funding for the bureau. Other observers say Hoover was continuing a pattern set when he was a young lawyer with the Justice Department during World War I. His job was to target pacifists, socialists, and communists, whose presence in the United States was deemed a threat. Supporters believe the communist threat in the United States was real and Hoover was just doing his job.

COINTELPRO was an aggressive campaign to destroy the party by circulating disruptive rumors and by employing "dirty tricks" to disrupt its functioning. William Sullivan, the assistant director in charge of COINTELPRO, later described the program as an application of wartime counterintelligence methods to domestic groups. Some informants disrupted meetings by bringing up Stalin's behavior. If a party official was found to be homosexual, the FBI arranged to have that person arrested to embarrass the party. One of the most effective techniques was to put "a snitch jacket" on someone by framing them as an FBI agent. Anonymous phone calls prevented the party from renting halls. The only restraint on an informant's ingenuity was the fear of being caught.

As a legal basis for COINTELPRO, Hoover relied on a dubious interpretation of the Communist Control Act of 1954. The law stated that the Communist Party was not entitled to any of the rights, privileges, and immunities afforded to legal bodies under the jurisdiction of the laws of the United States. Party membership was not a crime, but the party was considered an outlaw.

COINTELPRO's methods were more conspiratorial than those of the American Communist Party, which for the most part operated openly, without apology. COINTELPRO's apparent success in reducing the ranks of an organization in demise encouraged the FBI to expand its techniques to other targets. In March 1960, a new program, COMINFIL (Communist Infiltration) was added to COINTELPRO-CPUSA. Earlier operations had had the goal of discovering communist infiltration. The new operation's aim was to prevent communist infiltration of mass organizations. The expansion represented an intrusion of a police force into the American political process. COMINFIL gave Hoover a pretext for conducting surveillance on such groups as the National Association for the Advancement of Colored People (NAACP), despite no evidence of illegal activity. The FBI justified regular surveillance of the Black Muslims because of its need to determine whether the group should be cited on the attorney general's list of subversive organizations, whose members were barred from government employment.

The initial draft of Hoover's 1958 book, *Masters of Deceit*, was produced in the Research and Analysis Section of the FBI's Domestic Intelligence Division, under its chief, William Sullivan. Some time later, Sullivan said, "We used to joke at the bureau, 'Masters of Deceit,' written by the Master of Deceit who never even read it." In his book, Hoover claimed that the real danger to the United States was "the destruction of the American way of life" through the spread of "a communist mentality representing a systematic, purposive, and conscious attempt to destroy Western civilization."

President Lyndon Johnson aided and abetted Hoover's surveillance of the New Left. In March 1966, Johnson asked Hoover to "constantly keep abreast" of contacts between foreign officials and "Senators and Congressmen and any citizen of a prominent nature." Until 1968, the FBI's surveillance of the antiwar movement was supposed to provide the government with advance warning of demonstrations. After 1968, the FBI intruded as an active participant with a goal of disrupting and discrediting opposition to the war. Hoover justified COINTELPRO–NEW LEFT to his agents as a defense of the social order not limited to the enforcement of specific statutes. The definition of the new target was broad. The New Left was "a subversive force" dedicated to destroying traditional values, with "strong Marxist, existentialist, nihilist, and anarchist overtones." The vague definition made any antiwar group a target, including student groups demonstrating about virtually any issue.

When Hoover died on May 2, 1972, the FBI's aura of impregnability collapsed. In December 1973 and March 1974, documents exposing COINTELPRO were released to NBC reporter Carl Stern as a result of his Freedom of Information Act lawsuit. The Freedom of Information Act was strengthened in 1974 and in 1975, and the FBI was forced to reveal the entire record of the covert COINTELPRO operation. During hearings by the House, chaired by Representative Otis Pike, and the Senate, chaired by Senator Frank Church, the bureau was forced to make full disclosures about COINTELPRO and other activities. Although the House committee's report was suppressed, the Senate committee's report was released on April 28, 1976.

On April 10, 1978, three FBI officials were indicted for authorizing burglaries of houses belonging to relatives of Weather Underground members. However, charges against the acting director were dropped. The acting associate director and the assistant director were fined $5,000 and $3,000, respectively.

See also Antiwar Movement; Old Left and New Left
References David Caute. *The Great Fear: The Anti-Communist Purge under Truman and Eisenhower*, 1978; Richard Gid Powers. *Secrecy and Power: The Life of J. Edgar Hoover*, 1987.

Columbia University Campus Protest

Several months before the protest at Columbia University, a decision had been made at a Students for a Democratic Society (SDS) conference in Maryland to take physical control of a major American university. Columbia was chosen because it had a liberal reputation, it was located in New York, and it was an Ivy League school.

Columbia's relationship with the West Harlem community, which borders it on two sides, had been deteriorating for years. A decision to build a gymnasium in Harlem's Morningside Park had united the community in its animosity toward the university. To permit expansion of the private university—and presumably to lower the area crime rate—several hundred people had been evicted from buildings around the university. The disenchantment of the Columbia faculty with the leadership of the university president, Grayson Kirk, and his chosen successor, David Truman, made Columbia vulnerable. The faculty were unhappy because the administration had refused to consider the establishment of a Faculty Senate or to create constitutional procedures that would enable the faculty to exercise power over academic and disciplinary matters.

Two issues were originally planned for the protest at Columbia. One issue was amnesty for student leaders who were threatened with not being allowed to return to the university after the end of the academic year because of earlier protests. The second issue was prevention of construction of the gym. Because the week of April 22, 1968, would bring thousands of antiwar protesters to New York, a third issue was added—the university was to sever ties with the Institute for Defense Analysis (IDA). However, these issues were pretexts. In a broad sense, the most radical members of the SDS Steering Committee didn't care about Columbia. They wanted to show that a major American university could be taken over by a well-organized group. The purpose of the demonstration was the destruction of American institutions in the hope that out of the general chaos a more humane America would emerge.

Using these three issues, SDS leaders were able to attract a large following of Columbia's students. After the protest had been going on for some time, the violent intentions of some of the leadership became evident, and more moderate students began demanding a nonviolent approach to solutions.

On Tuesday, April 23, about 100 students led by Mark Rudd, chairman of SDS, marched to Morningside Park to protest the building of the gym. When the police were called after the students had torn down some fences around the construction site, Rudd led the students away, giving the impression that the protest was over for the day. Instead, Rudd led the demonstrators in an attack on Hamilton Hall. After the building

had been secured, Tom Hayden, former SDS national chairman, arrived at Hamilton Hall and directed white students to leave and yield control of the building to blacks. The strategy effectively prevented the university from attempting to seize Hamilton Hall because black radicals threatened to burn the university to the ground.

Later in the day, Low Library was occupied, and the administration attempted to sow dissension by offering the blacks in Hamilton Hall amnesty, twenty-five new scholarships for black students, and termination of gym construction. The offer was refused. Shortly after midnight on Thursday, David Truman informed an ad hoc committee created to negotiate that the police had been called. An hour later, plainclothes police officers used nightsticks to push their way through a crowd of professors who had formed a blockade at the Low Library entrance. Many teachers were hurt. A teaching assistant was hospitalized with a head injury. Outraged faculty joined SDS as allies.

By Saturday morning, faced with cancellation of $11 million in donations and hundreds of threatened resignations, the administration appeared to give in to SDS demands. Kirk agreed to resign in a year, sever ties with IDA, and refrain from punishing participants with anything more than a reprimand. The SDS Steering Committee agreed to refrain from liberating any more buildings. It also agreed that if alumni and trustee pressure became too great, a police bust of white-held buildings was acceptable. A bust would give the appearance that the committee had resisted. The university would notify the Steering Committee in sufficient time to warn students who did not want to be arrested to leave.

On Tuesday, at 1:30 A.M., 2,000 police officers, including 50 on horseback, swept across Columbia's campus, surrounded the occupied buildings, and cleared them. Although the police were without weapons, they were violent. Mounted officers rode into terrified crowds on Broadway. For two and one-half hours, faculty watched through windows as the police destroyed furniture, urinated on rugs, and dumped files while injured students waited to be removed.

The reaction was swift. The faculty moved to increase its power. The Faculty Committee on Instruction ordered classes closed for a week. The SDS had succeeded in polarizing and paralyzing a major university.

See also Free Speech Movement
Reference Walt Anderson, ed. *The Age of Protest,* 1969.

Communes and Collectives

Many groups of hippies formed communes and collectives, arrangements in which they all lived together or worked together or both. The media tended to focus on communal sharing of sexual partners, which reflected the hippie philosophy of "make love, not war," but the communes that lasted were equally intent on developing an alternative culture.

Communes and collectives shared common themes, in particular the idea of free service to others. A San Francisco pamphlet offered thirty free services. These included crash pads (places to sleep overnight), a foot clinic, and a drug hotline. Hippie attorneys offered free legal aid. Drug use was so much a part of the lifestyle that some groups sold drug paraphernalia in so-called head shops.

Many college communes created their own teaching arrangements in which students became their own teachers or teachers to others. The Free Speech Movement began at Berkeley. Other campus towns sprouted their own free speech universities.

The hippie group Trans-Love Energies Unlimited, a Detroit commune and collective, produced rock concerts, light shows, posters, and pamphlets, including an underground pamphlet called *Sun.* The group also functioned as a booking agency for rock groups. Rock festivals were perceived as "gatherings of the tribe."

Hippie entrepreneurs were selective about the types of businesses they chose to run. The business could not discriminate or pollute the environment. It had to supply meaningful employment or improve society. Some groups went into the construction business. Others bought radio

stations. Printing and selling buttons and posters were substantial sources of income. Among the most successful publishing ventures were the magazines *Rolling Stone* and *Mother Earth News.* Even though particular members might put more into the development of a product or service than other members, the final result was viewed as an accomplishment of the whole.

Communes and collectives boycotted corporations that purchased fruits and vegetables from farms that paid migrant workers pittance wages. Groups began food cooperatives, and members urged their customers to avoid white bread and preservatives. Many groups specialized in carrying or producing organically grown foods.

See also Free Speech Movement; Grateful Dead; Hippies
Reference Timothy Miller. *The Hippies and American Values,* 1991.

Community Mental Health Center Movement

During the 1960s, a widespread antipsychiatry movement concluded that mental illness was a myth and mental hospitals were oppressive. Lawyers, zealous in pursuit of the rights of mental health patients, helped get them discharged or prevented them from being admitted. Politicians, anxious to get rid of the financial burden of maintaining large institutions, latched onto the antipsychiatry fever and the chance to stand up for civil rights and launched the "deinstitutionalization movement."

Large mental hospitals were closed, or their populations, which previously numbered in the thousands, were reduced to as few as 200. In 1960, there were half a million beds available in public mental health institutions. By 1980, there were less than 100,000.

Besides the notion that mental illness did not exist, other factors contributed to the demise of large hospitals. During the Depression, hospitals were grossly underfunded and understaffed. World War II robbed them of their limited professional staffs, who were in high demand in the military services. Exposés drew public attention to conditions in mental hospitals. In 1945, Mike Gorman, just out of the army and a fledgling reporter for *The Daily Oklahoman*, embarked on a campaign to wave "the reek and the stench" of state mental hospitals under the public's nose. Other reports followed.

Another factor that opened the doors of mental hospitals to scrutiny was the presence of outside observers. During World War II, many conscientious objectors (COs) were assigned to alternative service as attendants in state mental hospitals. They communicated with each other and assembled massive affidavits about the wretched conditions in state mental hospitals and turned over the information to reporters and politicians. Some hospital attendants who agreed with the COs also spoke out. By then, many psychiatrists had concluded that large mental hospitals should be abolished.

The negative attitude of psychiatrists toward mental hospitals also had its origins in World War II. Battlefront psychiatrists had developed methods for quickly treating servicemen suffering from battle fatigue. Psychiatrists presumed they could apply lessons learned during war to all manner of peacetime problems. They yearned to exercise their new therapeutic powers in a broader arena. Fueling psychiatrists' urge to work in communities were the conclusions of large mental health studies, which claimed that less than 20 percent of the general population was free of psychiatric impairment.

British psychiatrist Maxwell Jones's book *The Therapeutic Community: A New Treatment Method in Psychiatry* (1953), about the Industrial Neurosis Unit he had set up at Belmont Hospital in London, inspired others to emulate him. Jones's method involved restructuring an individual's waking hours to form new attitudes and adopt new behaviors. Jones's emulators overlooked the fact that he screened out the seriously ill from his therapeutic community.

Faith in the idea of preventive community psychiatry received a tremendous boost from the work of Boston psychiatrist Erich Lindeman. In 1943, Lindeman studied bereavement reactions among the survivors of 429 people killed on November 28, 1942, in Boston's Coconut Grove nightclub fire. Lindeman established a community mental health program to implement his ideas about preventive intervention in crises.

In 1955, Congress passed legislation requiring the National Institute of Mental Health (NIMH) to appoint a commission to reevaluate the nation's approach to mental health. NIMH appointed the Joint Commission on Mental Illness and Mental Health. After six years of work, the Joint Commission issued a report, *Action for Mental Health*. The report identified major mental illness as the core problem. By that they meant that major mental illnesses were not only difficult to treat, but they also disrupt all aspects of daily living, which requires treatment providers to be responsible for seeing that their patients are fed, clothed, and housed. The commission was not opposed to state mental hospitals but believed that they had to be transformed and should house no more than 1,000 patients, although many on the commission felt that 1,000 was too many.

The commission called for the establishment of community mental health clinics, one for each 50,000 people. The clinics would serve as a main line of defense, reducing the need for people with a major mental illness to undergo prolonged or repeated hospitalization. The clinics would care for "incompletely recovered mental patients short of admission to a hospital or following discharge from the hospital." The report called for a range of aftercare services, such as halfway houses, social clubs, and sheltered workshops. The commission proposed that funds currently being spent on the mentally ill be tripled.

The commission emphatically rejected the idea of primary prevention, describing it as an "article of faith rather than an applicable scientific truth." Those in the vanguard of the community psychiatry movement were unhappy with the report. However, a problem that went unrecognized by psychiatrists who had great faith in their own ability to prevent mental illness was that no one really knew how. Community-oriented psychiatrists misunderstood the nature of mental illness just as profoundly as those who claimed it did not exist.

Few of those in NIMH leadership positions had ever worked with the type of patients who filled state hospitals. When NIMH sent a report to President John F. Kennedy in the spring of 1962, it ignored the Joint Commission's central proposal for a new system of small, treatment-intensive state hospitals. As a result, during a special message to Congress, Kennedy focused on the goal of primary prevention and reduction in state hospital populations. (Kennedy had a personal interest in mental health legislation. His sister Rosemary was both developmentally disabled and mentally ill.)

Subsequent congressional hearings dwelt on proposed mental health centers as organizations to care for severely and chronically ill patients, which would permit state hospitals to fade away. Members of Congress had no intention of tripling funds for care of the mentally ill. They hoped to save money. No one asked where all the people released from mental hospitals would live.

Although the NIMH report to the president had described eight essential services to be provided by community mental health centers (CMHCs), NIMH's final regulations virtually ignored chronic patients. CMHCs were required to provide only five services to qualify for federal funds. Services for chronic patients came under an optional second group of five services that would make the center "comprehensive."

From the outset, CMHCs were not equipped to serve chronic patients in the community. Patients released from state mental hospitals needed income support, vocational training, social opportunities, and housing. Yet the staffs at many CMHCs tried desperately to make them work. When a CMHC psychiatrist would try to get a patient in acute distress admitted to one of the few beds at mental hospitals, the hospital psychiatrist generally could not admit that person. The criteria for admission set by antipsychiatry legislators and attorneys made it virtually impossible.

At a mental health conference during the mid-1970s, a psychiatrist and an attorney had a shouting match. The psychiatrist said, "Where are you when the former patient needs a place to live? You're off protecting the civil rights of more patients so they too can live in the streets."

"Patients have a civil right not to be locked up," said the attorney.

"So they can die in the street with their civil rights on," said the psychiatrist. The attorney shrugged, and the psychiatrist left the meeting.

The schemes and legislation intended to do away with mental illness overlooked the needs of the almost half a million patients in 1963 who were residents in state hospitals. Only a fraction of the chronically mentally ill patients benefited from the new perspective. Many more wound up living in the streets.

Of the estimated 400,000 homeless people who live in shelters and in the streets, several studies have found that 30 to 40 percent suffer from a major mental illness—schizophrenia, manic depression, or clinical depression. In his book *Nowhere to Go*, psychiatrist Fuller Torey took issue with homeless advocate Mitch Snyder's suggestion that all the mentally ill need is love. Torrey wrote: "You can put them in a home and give them love, but they're still schizophrenics out of touch with reality. Until they are treated for the disease you can give them all the love and all the homes in the world and you still have a chaotic situation."

Seldom mentioned in discussions of community mental health centers is the formula by which they were funded. With the expectation that CMHCs would become a necessity in their communities, funding was set on an eight-year cycle. Each year the federal funding was reduced. After the eighth year, it disappeared. Local and state funding seldom made up for each year's lost funding. Most CMHCs could not survive; indeed, they had been set up to fail.

About the euphoria that fueled the community mental health center movement, psychiatrist Donald Light wrote in *Becoming Psychiatrists*: "Given the difficulty psychiatrists have in treating disturbed individuals, the assertion that it could also treat whole communities, carry out primary prevention, and eradicate mental illness was extraordinary." Light suggested psychiatry should have taken itself on as a patient.

If the Joint Commission's recommendations had been implemented, the public policy mistakes that left the mentally ill abandoned would not have been made. Even though a fully functioning community mental health program would not have cured mental illness, it would have provided a humane quality of life. It would also have increased the time a mentally ill person is in remission. Without staff to remind them, many patients stop taking antipsychotic medication.

See also Antipsychiatry Movement; Homelessness
References Rael Jean Isaac and Virginia Armat. *Madness in the Streets: How Psychiatry and the Law Abandoned the Mentally Ill,* 1990; Maxwell Jones. *The Therapeutic Community: A Treatment Method in Psychiatry,* 1953; Donald Light. *Becoming Psychiatrists,* 1980; E. Fuller Torey. *Nowhere to Go: The Tragic Odyssey of the Homeless Mentally Ill,* 1988.

Congress of Racial Equality
See Freedom Riders

Consciousness-Raising Movement
Consciousness refers to both awareness of one's own existence and the normal waking state. The 1960s and 1970s were a time of general change, during which the civil rights movement, the feminist movement, and the Vietnam War all contributed to a sense of unrest and alienation. The cohort of young people born between 1946 and 1964, known as the baby boomers, were skeptical about American society, particularly its politics, arts, fashion, and lifestyles. Many "dropped out"—they left school or avoided ordinary jobs.

Many young people escaped their disillusionment by taking drugs. Others used drugs in the hope that chemicals would provide a better understanding of the world in which they lived. Some turned to philosophies based on such religions as Hinduism, Buddhism, and Taoism. However, few young Americans actually converted, although they were attracted to meditation, an approach to thinking and contemplation. Hindus regard meditation as a way to get closer to God. Americans used meditation to cope with the fast pace and high pressure of everyday life. Some

found meditation helped them to get along better with others and gain inner peace.

As American interest in meditation and other facets of Eastern philosophy increased, gurus (teachers) from Asia, particularly India, came to America. Among them were genuine philosophers whose goal was to spread peace and harmony, as well as opportunists intent on making money. Some Americans began their own versions of Eastern philosophies. In time, many organizations, groups, and individuals offered many techniques—the majority involved meditation and self-realization.

Two of the reasons the consciousness movement became so popular in America were that it reflected a traditional belief in the goodness of human beings and embodied a basic concept written into the Declaration of Independence, the idea that people are entitled to the pursuit of happiness. In addition, ideas about raising consciousness were not new to America. During the 1830s and 1840s, a group of New England writers and scholars who called themselves "Transcendentalists" tried to introduce ideas from older, different cultures into American culture, which they perceived as strict and unimaginative. Among the Transcendentalists were Ralph Waldo Emerson, Nathaniel Hawthorne, and Henry David Thoreau. Thoreau's *Walden, or Life in the Woods*, which he wrote about living in the woods by Walden Pond near Concord, Massachusetts, became enormously popular among students during the late 1960s and 1970s. In Thoreau's view, to be alive—to transcend—meant to be awakened in one's thoughts, feelings, and body.

The American psychologist Abraham Maslow (1908–1970) also had a significant impact on student thinking in the 1960s. Maslow proposed "peak experience" as a goal of consciousness raising. A peak experience is a "happening" of intense joy, ecstasy, and excitement. Maslow coined the term "self-actualizing" to refer to people able to make the most of whatever abilities or talents they have and to enjoy the process. A peak experience can come from almost any life experience, particularly love, passion, accomplishment, or a religious experience.

During the early and mid-1960s, some psychologists experimented with drugs like LSD (lysergic acid diethylamide), both on themselves and on research subjects. The federal government eventually outlawed the use of LSD in psychological research. After the ban on LSD, psychologists found they could achieve many similar results, such as serenity and the ability to ignore external stimuli, using Eastern techniques. Yoga is one of the better known of the meditation techniques. During the 1960s, the Esalen Institute in California became famous as part of the consciousness movement. Founder Michael Murphy studied yoga in India. The Esalen staff believed they were bringing about a "new humanity," a less competitive and materialistic society devoted to uplifting the human spirit.

Martial arts gained popularity in the 1970s. A combination of meditative and fighting techniques, martial arts embrace the idea of a continuous or eternal inflow and outflow of "divine," universal energy thought to be everywhere in all living and nonliving things. The goal of a person practicing the martial arts is to blend the mind-body with the energy of the universe.

Zen, another meditative movement that enjoyed some popularity in the United States during the 1960s and 1970s, is a sect of Buddhism. Zen is a path to enlightenment. Zen, which originated in China but came to the United States by way of Japan, in subtle ways is one of the strongest influences on Japanese life. A Zen experience much sought after is a flash of enlightenment called *satori.*

Perhaps the most famous of the meditative movements was est (Erhard Seminars Training), founded by Jack Rosenberg, who changed his name to Werner Erhard when he left behind his old lifestyle to travel around the United States and sample a variety of consciousness-raising techniques. Erhard borrowed the Zen idea of satori. He called satori "getting it." He combined "getting it" with the notion that minds create a false sense of reality.

New recruits signed up for a rigorous, two-weekend Erhard course. The trainees were exercised to the point of physical and mental exhaus-

tion and forced to give up their "acts" (their false reality). They were instructed in techniques of self-hypnosis intended to alleviate the aches and pains of the severe training. By the end of 1976, more than 80,000 had signed up for the sixty-hour course, and by the late 1970s est training employed more than 5,000 teachers and workers.

One consciousness-raising movement of the era did not compromise Eastern concepts to fit in with Western ideas. The founder of the American Hare Krishna movement was A. C. Bhaktivedanta Swami Prabhupada, who was said to be one of an unbroken chain of spiritual masters that originated with Krishna, an incarnation of Vishnu, the second god of the Hindu trinity. Prabhupada was 70 years old when he arrived in Boston in 1965. He had less than $10 and a suitcase filled with books, including translations of the *Vedas,* ancient Hindu writings that are among the oldest in the world.

Translations of Vedic literature were popular in the United States during the 1960s and 1970s, particularly in universities. Sales of the translations of the *Vedas* brought in enough revenue to finance a large independent publishing operation. Publishing funds supported growth of the movement. In less than ten years, Prabhupada built a huge organization.

Singing and chanting, devotees of the International Society for Krishna Consciousness appeared in large cities around the United States, particularly in New York and San Francisco. For several years, they were a frequent sight in American airports and on America's streets selling flowers. Despite rebuffs from people in a hurry, they appeared serenely happy. They wore flowing, deep yellow robes. The men had shaved heads, except for a single lock that hung down the back of the head. Some wore dabs of white paint on their faces. As part of a daily ritual, every Hare Krishna follower was expected to frequently chant a mantra (everyone's was the same) to the accompaniment of music and dancing. The followers lived the austere life of monks in one of the Hare Krishna centers located in several large cities and on farms throughout the world.

Even greater than Prabhupada's accomplishments were those of Maharishi Mahesh Yogi, the founder of the Science of Creative Intelligence, better known as Transcendental Meditation (TM). Based on Hindu concepts, TM was not a religion, nor did it require devotion of one's life to its practice. All that was required was a short course of instruction and twenty minutes of meditation twice a day.

Maharishi came to the United States in 1959. Within months, he had established the Spiritual Regeneration Movement in Los Angeles. The movement grew slowly until 1969, when members of the Beatles were initiated into TM. Other celebrities, among them members of the Beach Boys, joined. By the early 1970s, it was estimated that as many as 800,000 people in the United States had taken instruction.

The interest of politicians and businesspeople kept the TM movement going. In the early 1970s, the federal government provided grants through the National Institute of Mental Health (NIMH) to study TM. During the early to mid-1970s, many high schools offered courses in TM, and later in the decade, some corporations encouraged their employees to learn it. In 1976, the United Nations allowed a TM center to be set up in the UN headquarters in New York City.

Religious opposition to TM grew, mainly from fundamentalist Christian groups but also from Catholics, Jews, and more liberal Protestant groups. In the court case *Alan B. Malneck et al. v. Maharishi Mahesh,* filed in New Jersey in March 1976, it was argued that the initiation ceremony and textbook used in the course were religious in nature and therefore violated the important American concept of separation of church and state. The court ruled against Maharishi Mahesh, thereby stopping all TM instruction in New Jersey public schools. Because the suit had been filed in federal court, the adverse decision had the effect of banning TM instruction in all states if the instruction was supported with public funds.

A fatal blow was struck at the movement in January 1977, when Maharishi announced the TM-Siddhi program. A Siddhi is a supernormal power, such as the ability to fly, to become invisible, or to move through walls. Maharishi invited 1,000 TM teachers from around the world to take the course at his headquarters in Switzerland. The result was ridicule from which the movement never fully recovered.

The consciousness revolution began with the young, mostly students, and spread to other age groups. Questioning old values, concentrating on self-improvement, and "doing your own thing" became important. As the rebels of the 1960s grew older and accepted the responsibilities of making a living and raising a family, many of them forgot their rebellion, but the impact of their questions remained. When TM became subject to ridicule, some people ignored public opinion and continued to practice meditation. Many turned to other forms of self-improvement, such as eating health foods, going on diets, and working out.

See also Alternative Religions Movement
Reference Aaron E. Klein and Cynthia L. Klein. *Mind Trips: The Story of Consciousness-Raising Movements,* 1979.

Consumer Movement

Although the boycotts of the early years of the civil rights movement are generally not included in discussions of the consumer movement, they had an economic impact and served as models for later actions. Most accounts of the consumer movement begin with Ralph Nader, who moved to Washington, D.C., in the early 1960s and became a self-appointed guardian of the American consumer.

Nader's 1965 book *Unsafe at Any Speed,* about General Motors' Corvair, stimulated a national debate about automobile safety features. For decades, American car manufacturers had balked at the inclusion of safety features because, in their view, safety features did not sell cars, and Americans would not pay for the costs. Nader forced them to change their minds.

Student interns, or "Nader's Raiders," conducted investigations and pressured politicians. Congress responded with the Truth in Lending and Fair Packaging and Labeling Acts. When

Nader called for more student participation, 700 applicants applied for a job that lasted ten weeks and paid between $500 and $1,000.

In the spring of 1970, feminists became involved in consumer issues. One hundred women working for *Ladies' Home Journal* conducted a sit-in at the office of the editor, John Mack Carter. They demanded an end to the "exploitative" advertisements in the magazine. They also wanted a free day care center and a special feature in a future issue on the women's liberation movement. Women working for *Time* and *Newsweek* filed a complaint with the Equal Employment Opportunity Commission charging discrimination. Of the writers at *Newsweek,* fifty were men and one was a woman. Bread and Roses feminists in Boston converged on radio station WBCN and demanded withdrawal of an add that read "If you're a chick, we need typists." The manager changed the ad.

The feminists were mixing two themes, liberation and empowerment, thereby expanding the movement to include those interested in community, consumerism, and conservation. Activists used sit-ins, picketing, and boycotts to put economic pressure on companies they felt paid low wages, practiced discrimination, or cheated the consumer. Among them were Gallo Wine, Polaroid, Levi's, Farah, AT&T, Coors, Coca-Cola, and Philip Morris.

Activists united behind consumerism. Job discrimination, pollution, war production, low wages, and a lack of opportunities for women and minorities, in their view, were symptoms of a sick business establishment. The consumer movement expanded as college and law school graduates of the 1970s were hired by businesses. They were interested in profit but were also concerned with corporate social responsibility and quality of life. Young attorneys organized groups such as the Center for Constitutional Rights. Nader set up Public Interest Research Groups on college campuses. Hundreds of law students filed suits in cooperation with new groups such as Common Cause, Environmental Action, and Friends of the Earth.

Activists passed out flyers recommending that those interested in stopping the Vietnam War withdraw their money from such financial institutions as Bank of America. Demonstrators at corporate headquarters mocked company slogans, for example, "At GE, Profits Are Their Most Important Product."

By 1972, fifty cities and half of the states had established consumer protection offices. To the surprise of automobile manufactures, safety features sold cars. By the 1990s, television stations routinely had reporters assigned to consumer affairs.

See also Alinsky, Saul; Nader, Ralph
References Terry Anderson. *The Movement and the Sixties: Protest in America from Greensboro to Wounded Knee,* 1995; David Farber. *The Sixties: From Memory to History,* 1994.

Cousteau, Jacques (1910–1997)

From the outset of his career, oceanographer, undersea explorer, filmmaker, and writer Jacques Cousteau shared findings from his research with the public out of his sheer love for the sea. Later, as he became increasingly aware of the interconnectedness of all organisms, including humans, with each other and with their habitats, he appealed to the public to take care of the earth's fragile environment. Jacques Cousteau amassed vast amounts of information on the biology, botany, and ecology of the world beneath the sea. He invented the Aqua-Lung (equipment that enables a diver to swim underwater). He wrote books that became best-sellers and produced documentaries that won awards. Over the course of his life, he became increasingly committed to ensuring that those generations inheriting the planet would not make the same mistakes under the sea that their predecessors had made on land.

Born in France, Cousteau spent most of his childhood on the move. His father, a lawyer, was employed by an American millionaire, who loved to travel and live in various parts of the world, often seaside resorts. The Cousteau family accompanied him. As a child, Cousteau suffered from chronic enteritis (inflammation of the intestines).

Doctors warned him to avoid strenuous physical activity. His father's boss, who was committed to fitness, encouraged Cousteau to swim. Swimming improved his health, and he developed a lifelong love of the sea.

A precocious child, at age 11 Cousteau built a 4-foot working model of a 200-ton marine crane. At 13, he built a 3-foot-long, battery-powered car. He was bored by school routines and acted out his dissatisfaction via pranks. After he broke seventeen windows by throwing stones, his parents put him in a school run with strict discipline, where he excelled.

After Cousteau graduated from the Ecole Navale, the French naval academy, he completed a round-the-world cruise on a training ship, served a tour of duty in Shanghai, and participated in a map-making survey along the Indochina coast. Shortly before he was due to graduate from naval aviation school, he broke both arms in an automobile accident. Again he turned to swimming to rehabilitate his badly injured arms.

Cousteau became interested in underwater diving while watching Chinese fishermen dive to catch fish barehanded. His interest turned to fascination when a friend gave him a pair of underwater goggles worn by pearl divers in the South Seas. The goggles introduced him to the enchanting world beneath the water. Calling on the inventiveness he had displayed as a child, Cousteau set out to develop an apparatus that would enable swimmers to travel underwater without being hampered by conventional deep-sea diving equipment. The result in 1946 was the manufacture of the Aqua-Lung. The same year, Cousteau founded the French navy's undersea research group. He also founded two organizations during the 1950s, which were devoted to undersea research. They operated ships, designed and built equipment, and investigated the human aspects of deep-sea exploration.

In the early 1950s, Cousteau converted a British minesweeper into an oceanographic research ship and named it *Calypso*, a name that became synonymous with his own for the next four decades. Sponsored by the National Geographic Society and the French Academy of Science, Cousteau conducted a four-year exploration of the world's seas. Using equipment specifically designed for the task, Cousteau anchored above the 24,500-foot-deep underwater valley called the Romanche Trench to take pictures of the ocean bottom 4.5 miles below.

With August Picard and French naval engineers, Cousteau worked on construction of the first bathyscaphe (apparatus for reaching great ocean depths without being cabled to a ship). Beginning in 1957, he directed the Conshelf Saturation Dive Program, experiments designed to enable people to live and work on the ocean bottom along the continental shelf. The continental shelf is submerged land that slopes gradually from the edge of a continent until it reaches the continental slope, where the rate of descent becomes much steeper.

Cousteau resigned from the French navy in 1958 to devote his attention to a far-flung set of enterprises collectively known as the Cousteau Group. The group was engaged in a wide variety of marine-related activities, including research, engineering, equipment manufacturing, production of film and television documentaries, and lobbying efforts to protect the ocean's ecology. The group's profit-making ventures supported research, education, and lobbying.

Cousteau enjoyed television enormously. For a September 10, 1972, *New York Times Magazine* article, he told a reporter, "Making films and writing books are good, but not thrilling. With television, you know that on one evening, 35 to 40 million people are going to see a dolphin." For a series called *The Undersea World of Jacques Cousteau*, in 1968 he began producing four documentary films a year for ABC. One highly praised special, "Beneath the Frozen World," shared with millions of viewers a view of exotic formations of ice sculpted beneath the sea in the Antarctic.

Cousteau continued to be active in his eighties. The more he learned, the more committed he became to protecting the whole planet, not just the sea. In his words, "The earth is a living body, an interlocking system of delicately balanced forces, endlessly changing in the sea and the cliff, the tree and the desert." His documentaries made it easier for the public to understand that destruction of a species or a habitat creates a chain of destructive changes. Increased understanding has made ideas like habitat protection and clean-up of the environment more acceptable. Many scientists, particularly oceanographers, can trace their interest in science back to watching Cousteau on television. Cousteau died in 1997.

See also Carson, Rachel
References Jacques Cousteau. *World without Sun,* 1965; Catherine Reef. *Jacques Cousteau: Champion of the Sea,* 1992.

Daley, Richard (1902–1976)

Mayor of Chicago and chairman of the Cook County Democratic Central Committee, Richard Daley was one of the most powerful politicians in the United States during the middle of the twentieth century. For more than two decades, he controlled a tightly organized political machine. Presidential nominees deferred to him because he could deliver Illinois votes during a Democratic National Convention.

A strong party supporter at age 12, Daley, at 21, became a precinct captain and secretary of Chicago's eleventh ward, in which he lived. He served in the state legislature from 1936 to 1946. In 1953, Daley gained control of his political machine by being elected the chairman of the Cook County Democratic Central Committee, a seat he was able to retain after he was elected mayor of Chicago in 1955 and 1959.

Daley gained national prominence when, during the 1960 Democratic National Convention, he delivered Illinois' vote to John F. Kennedy. Between Kennedy's nomination during the summer and the November election, Daley rallied his machine to get out the vote. According to television network polls, Kennedy led in Cook County by about 250,000 votes. He defeated his opponent, Richard Nixon, in Illinois by only 8,858. Daley's machine had made the difference between winning and losing.

Daley's stature on a national level enabled him to lure federal aid and new business into Chicago. City services improved dramatically, and he was reelected in 1963. Three months after his 1963 election, Daley claimed Chicago had no ghettos. Later that same month, minorities demonstrated in white neighborhoods against de facto segregation in the schools. When minority complaints escalated, Daley blamed communists and Republicans.

On April 4, 1968, the day of the assassination of Martin Luther King, Jr., rioting broke out on Chicago's West Side and lasted three days. On April 15, Daley blamed conspirators, ordered a shoot-to-kill policy for arsonists, and advocated maiming of looters. Four months after the riots, in a speech to the 1968 Democratic National Con-

vention, Daley welcomed the delegates and told them, "There's going to be law and order in Chicago." Protesters had come to Chicago in droves to picket the convention.

Trouble began almost immediately between the police and the demonstrators. Each night, the hostility escalated, until it culminated in a major riot in Grant Park. The media dubbed the riot the Battle of Michigan Avenue. Television cameras captured brutal confrontations between the police and the demonstrators. Daley told the press that only sixty people were injured. In reality, 300 people were injured. The Medical Commission for Human Rights reported that 1,000 people needed aid. While the demonstrations went on outside, at the convention Daley delivered 112 of Illinois' 118 votes to candidate Hubert Humphrey.

As some delegates became aware of the violence in the streets, they spoke up on the floor of the convention and criticized the "Gestapo tactics" of the police. Daley called the demonstrators a "lawless, violent group of terrorists." The sight of police wielding batons against college students tarnished Daley's national reputation. Nevertheless, a September 17, 1968, Gallup poll indicated that 56 percent of the American public supported the actions of the police. On December 1, 1968, a committee formed by the President's Commission on the Cause and Prevention of Violence, led by Daniel Walker, the president of the Chicago Crime Commission, issued a special report about the convention-related disorders. The report accused the Chicago police of precipitating the violence and labeled the disorder a "police riot." The committee pointed to Mayor Daley's shoot-to-kill policy during the April riots as the reason for the excessive use of force by police.

In the 1970s Daley suffered several political disappointments. Nevertheless, he won still another reelection in 1975, obtaining 78 percent of the vote. He died in December 1976.

See also Riots
References Milton Rakove. *Don't Make No Waves— Don't Back No Losers*, 1974; Mike Royko. *Boss: Richard J. Daley of Chicago*, 1971.

Deaf Student Protest

A 1988 protest at Gallaudet University in Washington, D.C., was a pivotal moment for the disability rights movement. Although protesters with a variety of disabilities had taken over the U.S. Health, Education, and Welfare headquarters in 1977, the event had not received much publicity and not been widely perceived, even by the disabled, as a civil rights issue. Yet only two months after the 1988 Gallaudet protest, the Americans with Disabilities Act was introduced and, for a law with so many potential enemies, passed swiftly.

In August 1987, Jerry Lee, the school's president, who was not deaf, announced his plans to leave in December. At a meeting in early February, six young Gallaudet alumni discussed the search committee's process of selecting presidential candidates. They were angry that for 124 years the world's premier university for the deaf had operated under the premise that the university itself could not be led by a deaf president. In the 1980s Gallaudet had experienced a quick turnover of presidents. However, the average tenure for a president was twenty years. The group realized they might not have another opportunity for several years. They decided to hold a rally. Financial support came from two local alumni entrepreneurs, John Yeh and David Birnbaum. Both men were bitter that the university had little interest in giving business contracts to local business owners. There were two reasons

that the Gallaudet "student" protest about the appointment of a new president began with alumni rather than students. First, the students had been taught to accept limits. Second, the student body included both those who were completely deaf and those with a profound hearing loss that was helped by hearing aids. Those with hearing aids were more sanguine about their future. The two groups functioned as factions.

Flyers Yeh had printed up carried the message: "In 1842, a Roman Catholic became president of the University of Notre Dame. In 1875, a woman became president of Wellesley College. In 1886, a Jew became president of Yeshiva University. And in 1926, a Black person became president of Howard University. AND in 1988, the Gallaudet University presidency belongs to a DEAF person." Thousand of buttons read "DEAF PRESIDENT NOW," which became the slogan for the protest.

At the rally on March 1, 1988, about a dozen speakers standing on the bed of a truck signed civil rights messages. The rally moved from site to site on campus, followed by about 1,500 students, alumni, and faculty chanting and waving the sign for applause—hands stretched above the head with fingers fluttering. On the day of the rally, Greg Hlibok took office as the new student body president. He became the national spokesperson for the students. Together with the outgoing president, Tim Rarus, and two students who had campaigned for a woman student, Jerry Covel and Bridgetta Bourne, Hlibok led the protest. All four students had deaf parents and had grown up feeling self-confident.

Coincidentally, a few minutes before the rally began, the names of the three finalists under consideration by the Search Committee were announced. They were I. King Jordan, the popular dean of the college of arts and sciences, who had been deaf since young adulthood; Harvey Corson, president of a Louisiana residential school, who had been deaf since birth; and Elisabeth Zinser, the administrator of the University of North Carolina at Greensboro, who was a hearing person.

On Sunday, March 6, approximately 500 students and alumni gathered at 8:30 P.M. at the

Hundreds of students demonstrate at Gallaudet University as part of a seven-day protest against the appointment of a hearing president in 1988.

main gate of the campus to await the announcement of the name of the new president by the board of trustees. The press had been notified two hours before. Hearing reporters had been told before the university's students that Elisabeth Zinser had been selected. When the group learned the news, they marched downtown to the Mayflower Hotel, where the trustees were said to be at a party to celebrate the choice. Hlibok, Rarus, and Jeff Rosen were invited upstairs to meet with the board. There, according to the protest spokespeople, Jane Bassett Spilman, chairwoman of the board of trustees, said: "Deaf people are not ready to function in a hearing world." Spilman later denied she had made the statement and claimed she had been misquoted by the sign language interpreter. This comment insulted the protesters further. She had been on the board of trustees for seven years and had never bothered to learn sign language.

The following morning, the students shut down the university. They hot-wired university cars and buses and at 5:30 A.M. began positioning them to close all campus entrances. Security guards cut a hole in a chain-link fence to enable the university's provost to enter the grounds. Classes were canceled. An assembly of students, faculty, and staff gave a list of demands to Spilman. They wanted Zinser's selection cancelled; appointment of a deaf president; the resignation of Spilman; and appointment of a majority of deaf trustees to the board. Spilman rejected the demands but agreed to address an assembly, which turned out to be a disaster for her. One thousand protesters screamed and held their left hands over their left ears—the sign for deafness—while raising their right fist in the air—the sign for power. They signed the sign for "sinner" as a close approximation of Zinser's name and said they wanted her out.

Before Spilman could speak to the crowd, Harvey Goodstein, a mathematics professor and a member of the delegation that had met with her, walked onstage and signed to the crowd that their demands had been rejected. He urged the crowd to leave. Most left to head toward the Capitol and the White House, snarling rush-hour traffic on the way. The departing students had pulled a fire alarm. Spilman told those who remained behind, "We aren't going to hear you if you scream so loudly that we can't have dialogue. It's very difficult to be heard over the noise of the fire alarm."

"What noise?" the students responded. One student said, "If you could sign, we could hear you."

Spilman insisted that the choice of Zinser was lawful, proper, and final. The students experienced her condescension as one more example of oppression by the hearing world.

Classes resumed on Tuesday. Only about 10 percent of the student body attended. National media attention brought support from students at other schools for the deaf, and local businesses made donations. Quickly the students set up a sophisticated operation. The protest leaders took up residence in the alumni house, where there was ample telecommunications equipment to enable them to contact reporters around the country and to raise funds.

The students prevented Zinser from setting foot on campus and, because Gallaudet is a federally chartered university, took their cause to Congress. (In 1988, 75 percent of the school's budget was allocated by Congress.) By Thursday, it became clear to Zinser, despite the board's reaffirmation of her appointment, that her best move was to resign. The students were not ready to back down. They still wanted a deaf president appointed and their other demands met.

On Sunday, one week after the protests began, seventeen members of Gallaudet's board selected Jordan as the school's first deaf president. The new chairperson of the board was deaf, and half of the trustees would be deaf. Spilman resigned.

A few days later, Hlibok wrote a letter to Zinser, who had returned to North Carolina. In it, he said, "You were, of course, an innocent victim and an unfortunate target of our collective anger." Zinser began wearing a necklace with a silver charm shaped in the sign for "I love you."

There was irony in the success Gallaudet had in equating disability with civil rights, because for most deaf people, deafness is not a disability but rather a culture—much the same as being Jewish, Irish, or Navajo. The American Sign Language (ASL) is as complex as other languages. It has its own syntax and grammar; it is not merely an offshoot of English. For those who are deaf at birth or become deaf before they learn to speak, ASL is an innate language. The deaf in every country develop their own version of the innate language. Sign languages have dialects. In the southern United States, blacks who are deaf and are isolated from whites who are deaf develop a separate sign dialect.

Researchers believe deaf children who learn ASL first have an easier time learning English later. For most of the twentieth century, hearing educators of the deaf tried to stamp out the use of sign language and have their students learn to speak and read lips. At residential schools where ASL was forbidden, students who had hearing parents learned to sign from students who had deaf parents. The denunciation of sign language did not change until after young linguist William Stokoe published a seminal paper in which he argued that ASL was a complex, three-dimensional language. In 1965, he published *A Dictionary of American Sign Language*, the first manual of sign language in print since 1918. Stokoe's interest began when he came to Gallaudet in the late 1950s to teach Chaucer and English literature. He became fascinated with the graceful sign language students used outside class and began to study the signing of children of deaf parents. The administration frowned on his work until after the publication of his paper.

The resurgence of interest in ASL sparked a deaf cultural renaissance, which began with the decision of the National Theater of the Deaf in 1972 to use ASL. There has been a blossoming of sign poetry, song, dance, storytelling, and oration.

See also Disability Rights Movement
Reference Joseph Shapiro. *No Pity,* 1994.

Dees, Morris
See Southern Poverty Law Center

Democratic National Convention of 1968
See Daley, Richard; Hoffman, Abbie; McCarthy, Eugene; Yippies

Demographics of Protest

Demographic factors had a major impact on the protests of the 1960s and 1970s. Their contribution was explained in a July 1971 *Harper's Magazine* article entitled "The Surprising Seventies" by Peter Drucker, a social scientist, economic analyst, and management consultant. Demographic data about populations include such factors as distribution by age, sex, income, incidence of disease, number of people in a geographic location, and vital statistics (births, marriages, and deaths). Drucker focused on the impact on America of the baby boom that followed World War II, beginning in 1946 and ending in 1964. Within a few years, mainly between 1948 and 1953, the number of babies born in the United States rose by almost 50 percent, the biggest increase ever recorded. The baby boom overturned an established principle of demography, the assumption that birthrates change slowly except in times of major catastrophes like war or famine. All developed countries except Great Britain experienced a similar boom.

The boom crested in 1953, and by 1964 the total number of births began to drop sharply and kept dropping for seven years, the sharpest fall in population history. In 1960, 4.3 million babies were born in the United States, but in 1967 only 3.5 million were born—a 20 percent decline. In 1960 the largest age group in the country was the 35- to 40-year-olds. In 1964, 17-year-olds became the largest single age group in the country. For the next seven years, until 1971, the 17-year-old age group became larger every year. Thus within four years, the largest population group shifted from age 35 to age 17—younger than it had been since the early nineteenth century. The

psychological impact on America's culture was enormous.

According to Drucker, 17 is a crucial age. It is the age when youngsters make career decisions and trade opinions with peers, rather than with family. Although such statements may sound sweeping, they are made about large populations. Minor variations within the population don't affect the overall impact. Young people get ready to move out of the family home to go to work or attend college. In urban and developed economies, the four years that separate 17 from 21 are, in Drucker's opinion, the true generation gap. Seventeen-year-olds are traditionally rebellious and in search of a new identity and new ideas.

In 1965, almost half of the 17-year-olds did not join the workforce. They stayed in school—outside of adult society and without adult responsibilities, where they could encourage each other to participate in the protests of the era. From 1977 to 1985, however, the number of 17-year-olds dropped sharply. By 1985, the dominant age group was 21- and 22-year-olds. The most conventional group in a population tends to be 21- to 35-year-olds. This age group is concerned with concrete problems, such as mortgages, job advancement, and doctors' bills.

In 1971, Drucker predicted conservatism would increase in the late 1970s and 1980s. His prediction came to pass, made obvious by the election of Ronald Reagan as president.

Baby boomers as a whole had more discretionary income available than the teenagers who had preceded them. Particularly jarring for some baby boomers was the shift from being a 17-year-old with discretionary money to being a homeowner whose income had to be devoted almost entirely to recurring expenses, such as food, shelter, and transportation. One factor that contributed to the baby boomers' shift from the liberalism of their teen years to a growing conservatism stemmed from the shock they created in the job market. Jobs had to be found for 40 percent more people than in the previous ten years. In a tight job market, they had to compete.

Although no one could have predicted the form it would take, in Drucker's opinion, because of demographics, the youth revolution of the 1960s and early 1970s would have taken place even in the absence of stimulus provided by the Vietnam War and the civil rights movement.

See also Baby Boomers
Reference LeRoy Ashby and Bruce Stave. *The Discontented Society: Interpretations of Twentieth-Century American Protest*, 1972.

Disability Rights Movement

Until the early 1970s, many of America's 25–50 million disabled people lived in institutions. In less than two decades, their numbers were reduced to about 2 million. Estimates of the number of disabled Americans in and out of institutions vary due to differences in the inclusion or exclusion of particular groups. People with such disabilities as heart conditions or dyslexia may be included or excluded.

People who are wheelchair bound are commonly assumed to be the largest disability group, but in reality they are not. About 500,000 adults and 150,000 school-age children use wheelchairs. Their numbers grow each year by about 10,000 due to head and neck injuries sustained in automobile accidents. However, an estimated 8 million Americans have learning disabilities. Approximately 6.5 million have arthritic restrictions in their arms and legs. About 5 million are developmentally disabled. Some 2 million suffer from mental illness. An estimated 3.5 million have central nervous system disorders, including muscular dystrophy, cerebral palsy, paraplegia, and quadriplegia. The counting is complicated by overlapping. Some people with central nervous system disorders are in wheelchairs. Some people may have more than one disability. Poor vision or blindness afflicts about 1.7 million. Approximately 346,000 Americans are deaf, and about 22 million suffer some hearing loss.

Two trends influenced the transfer of the disabled from institutions to community settings. The first trend was caused by social movements for civil rights and equality waged by African Americans, Hispanics, Native Americans, and women. Successes encouraged young activists to

Gregory Mansfield is assisted onto a wheelchair-accessible bus in 1982. Despite the passage of the Americans with Disabilities Act of 1990, disability movement advocates claim that not enough has been done to enable those with disabilities to participate fully in society.

lobby on behalf of other disadvantaged groups, including the disabled. The second trend stemmed from the perceptions of politicians around the country that they had to reduce the costs incurred in running large institutions.

With promises to provide support services in communities—many of which never materialized—the disabled were turned out of institutions. It became apparent almost immediately that the architects and planners of houses, buildings, and cities had never considered the needs of the disabled. The Rehabilitation Act of 1973 focused their attention. It required that all federal buildings be made handicapped-accessible. In 1977, the requirements were extended to all structures built with federal grant money.

The mandated changes turned out to have advantages for more than just the disabled. Universities with sagging enrollments tapped the population of disabled students. Ramps and curb cuts proved useful for parents pushing strollers, vendors delivering merchandise, couriers racing on bikes through cities, and skateboarders practicing stunts. Hydraulic lifts on buses that lower to accommodate wheelchairs encouraged installation of hydraulic mechanisms that lower the bus for elders with restricted motion. Washing machines with large dials to increase ease of use for the handicapped proved equally useful for elders with reduced vision.

The Paralyzed Veterans of America (PVA), founded after World War II, had a variety of goals, among them improved therapy and rehabilitation programs. Many PVA members wanted to continue involvement in sports competitions they had enjoyed prior to being injured. Sport participation contributes to rehabilitation: therefore PVA members became a driving force behind the first wheelchair basketball teams. Participation of young disabled athletes in sporting events, such as marathons and basketball games, had an enormous impact on the design of wheelchairs. Old wheelchairs weighed as much as 70 pounds and featured bulky frames, hard rubber tires, small fluttery front wheels, and uncomfortable sling seats. Constant modifications in design and materials not only made wheelchairs more comfortable but reduced their weight dramatically. In the 1990s, a wheelchair for playing basketball can weigh as little as 13 pounds.

Engineers and manufacturers rose to the challenge of providing equipment to the disabled living in the community. The needs of quadriplegics sparked innovative designs that enabled patients to move equipment by regulating their breathing or blinking their eyes. Computers that operate with voice commands made use possible for those who could not use a keyboard.

President George Bush signed into law the Americans with Disabilities Act (ADA) on July 26, 1990, the first comprehensive civil rights law for people with disabilities. In a speech during the event, President Bush said, "Let the shameful walls of exclusion finally come tumbling down."

A continuing inspiration to those who are disabled has been Stephen Hawking, a world-renowned physicist and cosmologist. At age 21, he was stricken with amyotrophic lateral scleroris (ALS), an incurable disease that would increasingly cripple him and was likely to end his life at an early age. Despite the obstacles, Hawking has made major contributions to science. In 1988, he published *A Brief History of Science,* a popular science book that became a bestseller.

See also Community Mental Health Center Movement; Deaf Student Protest; Independent Living Movement

References Fred Pelka. *The ABC-CLIO Companion to the Disability Rights Movement,* 1997; Joseph Shapiro. *No Pity,* 1994.

Disappeareds

Several factors drew the attention of American human rights activists to the cause of Latin America's *desaparecidos,* or disappeareds. Foreign policy played a role. President Jimmy Carter made human rights advocacy a cornerstone of his foreign policy. President Ronald Reagan, who succeeded Carter, so feared communists that he ignored human rights abuses by noncommunist countries in Latin America.

Reagan directed the Immigration and Naturalization Service (INS) to give political asylum only to refugees from communist countries. Reagan's policy gave rise to the sanctuary movement, which began when individuals and churches broke the law to give sanctuary to refugees from El Salvador and Guatemala. The need for secrecy makes estimates of the number of Americans involved in helping refugees from Latin America impossible, but some scholars believe many more people were involved in the sanctuary movement than were involved in the civil rights movement. Human rights organizations such as Amnesty International, Physicians for Human Rights, and Americas Watch called attention to the disappeared by asking Americans to write letters on behalf of those jailed and those who had disappeared. The organizations also hired forensic specialists to help document atrocities.

In Latin America, disappearance is a strategy used to terrorize a population. The technique has been used in many countries since the method began in Guatemala in 1966. Although kidnappings are occasionally done by antigovernment forces, Latin American *desaparecidos* are typically abducted by representatives in legal authority. Often the kidnapped are thought to have information or to hold an unfavorable opinion of the government. At the height of General Jorge Rafael Videla's repressive regime in Chile, between 1976 and 1978, some 15,000 people were made to vanish by civilian death squads or the army.

In the early 1980s, the Salvadoran army carried out a campaign against civilians suspected of supporting the opposition. Each month, approximately 800 Salvadorans were killed. By 1987, at least 42,000 had been killed or had disappeared.

Regardless of the country doing the abduction, the majority of disappeareds were arrested, tortured, and killed, then buried anonymously in mass graves. To end the uncertainty of not knowing whether their missing loved one was alive or dead, relatives repeatedly made the rounds of morgues to view bodies.

In 1984, the American Association for the Advancement of Science (AAAS) sent forensic anthropologist Dr. Clive Collins Snow and several American colleagues to Buenos Aires, Argentina, to look into the forensic challenge of identifying the bodies of 10,000 *desaparecidos.* Following a talk in Buenos Aires, Snow was approached by several Argentines, who asked his help in identifying remains that might be loved ones. Snow recruited a band of young Argentine volunteers, mostly college students, to apply his techniques to what was left of the bodies. The amateurs became skilled enough to positively identify many skeletons and prove the guilt of their killers. Evidence collected by the group provided the basis for Snow's testimony in court, which sent some culpable officers to prison.

In 1991, Snow made a series of trips to Guatemala on behalf of Americas Watch to investigate suspected atrocities. On one such trip, accompanied by Dr. Robert Kirschner, a medical examiner from Cook County, Snow examined three male bodies discovered in a shallow grave near a highland village called Quiche. The bodies bore the customary pattern inflicted by a quasi-

military organization called the Civil Patrol, which terrorized remote villages. Two of the skulls had been shot from behind with rifle bullets. The lumbar vertebrae (lower back) of the third man had been slashed by machetes at the time of his death.

In the countries to which Snow lent his skill, he devoted almost as much time to training apprentice forensic anthropologists as he did to his own investigations. Snow explained why independent observers were needed in repressive Latin America countries. "If you're a medical examiner at a morgue in, say Cordoba, Argentina, and a bunch of cops with guns bring in a shot-up corpse they say died of a heart attack, you may not feel like arguing when they insist that you sign a death certificate saying the person died of natural causes."

In Argentina, under a military dictatorship, an estimated 12,000 people were picked up and never seen again, and at least 210 children were either kidnapped or born in captivity. In 1977, a year after the military regime in Argentina came into power, an Argentinian group called the Grandmothers of the Plaza of May began a weekly vigil in the plaza across from the military government's offices. They demanded return of their missing children and grandchildren.

The grandmothers had become a skilled fact-finding organization. By the time the military regime gave up power in 1983, it was apparent that most of the adult disappeareds had been killed, but the fate of the disappeareds' children remained unknown. Some children had been given to military couples. Others had been given or sold to collaborators. The grandmothers' goal was to find their grandchildren and return them to their families. To do so, they had to be able to prove a relationship to the children that courts would accept. They appealed to the AAAS for help and were referred to Mary-Claire King, a geneticist at the University of California, Berkeley. Because a grandmother might be the only member of the family left, King developed a test that required only one maternal relative.

See also Physicians for Human Rights, Sanctuary Movement

References Christopher Joyce and Eric Stover. *Witness from the Grave: The Story Bones Tell,* 1991; Jacobo Timerman. *Prisoner without a Name, Cell without a Number,* 1991.

Duke, David (b. 1950)

In the 1970s, many Ku Klux Klan leaders set out to clean up their racist public image. Among them was Klan Grand Wizard David Duke, founder of the Knights of the Ku Klux Klan and the National Association for the Advancement of White People (NAAWP). As the leader, Duke shed his white robes for a business suit, and his soft-spoken white supremacist views on talk shows attracted thousands of sympathizers. Among other things, he suggested that minorities could be relocated to specific geographical areas.

Raised in a family with an absent father and an alcoholic mother, Duke developed his racist views early. While preparing a high school term paper on the down side of integration, Duke visited the offices of the segregationist group known as the White Citizens' Council. There he found father figures who introduced him to the Klan and Nazi doctrines. In high school, Duke openly revealed his preoccupation with white power. One of his high school social studies teachers recalled that in twenty-eight years of teaching, Duke was the only student that she had ever feared. At Louisiana State University, Duke's obsession with Nazism and Aryan (Northern European) superiority intensified. He tried to convert fellow students to his fascist philosophy.

Eventually realizing that his extremist views were not attracting followers, Duke stopped talking about his fanatical devotion to Nazism and transformed himself. Although considered physically attractive, he underwent cosmetic surgery, apparently to enhance his Aryan appearance. In 1989, Duke won the 81st District seat in the Louisiana state legislature. To broaden his appeal, he claimed he had found God and thrown off the racial hatred that had once dominated his life. Duke asked voters to forget his past and concentrate on his message of lower taxes and less government. He softened his racist arguments into less abrasive language. Duke talked about the "welfare underclass" that must be eliminated by getting rid of "shirkers and the lazy." In answer to questions about his Nazi past, he said, "I was an angry young man. I wanted to make the world a better place." He compared his youthful radicalism to Jesse Jackson's.

Duke's publishing history is bizarre. Under a pseudonym, he wrote a sex manual, *Finderskeepers,* in which he enumerated the advantages of loving a married man and advised "women's libbers" on how to use their careers to find men. Under another pseudonym (Mohammed X), Duke wrote *African Atto,* a street-fighting manual for blacks. It is filled with deliberate misspellings and strange advice, such as the avoidance of fatty, weakening white milk. He claimed it was a satire.

Despite the Republican Party's disavowal of him when he announced his intention to run, Duke became the Republican nominee for governor in 1991. He lost the general election, having been defeated by a record turnout of black voters and fears of white voters that he would tarnish the image of the state. Duke also lost a bid for the U.S. Senate. However, in doing so he collected 60 percent of the white vote.

Thom Robb, who in 1989 assumed the position of Grand Wizard in the Klan to which Duke once belonged, announced plans to operate a high-tech training facility for white supremacists who wanted to follow Duke into American politics.

See also Ku Klux Klan
References Elaine Landau. *The White Power Movement: America's Racist Hate Groups,* 1993; Susan Lang. *Extremist Groups in America,* 1990.

Dylan, Bob (b. 1941)

Social protest singer, composer, and poet Bob Dylan was said to be a spokesman for the generation coming of age during the 1960s. His songs scorned war, racial intolerance, and poverty. His themes are exemplified by his best-selling "Blowin' in the Wind."

Born in Minnesota, Robert Zimmerman, the son of an appliance dealer, changed his name to Bob Dylan in honor of the poet Dylan Thomas. At age ten, he taught himself to play the guitar. By age fifteen, he had also taught himself to play the piano, autoharp, and harmonica and had written a ballad dedicated to the French film star Brigitte Bardot. Between the time he was ten and seventeen, Dylan ran away from home seven times, finally leaving for good at age nineteen. In an autobiographical poem, he claimed that he created his own Depression. "I rode freight trains for kicks / An' got beat up for laughs / Cut grass for quarters / And sang for dimes."

Dylan's music draws inspiration from many directions, the folk music of Woody Guthrie; the blues of black musicians Leadbelly and Big Bill Broonzy; the country western music of Jimmy Rodgers, Hank Williams, and Hank Snow; the harmonica techniques of Sonny Terry; and the silent films of Charlie Chaplin. During a visit to his idol, Woody Guthrie, in February 1961, the singer convinced Dylan that he should not try to write in a Guthrie style, he should write what he felt. In the summer of 1961, Dylan furnished harmonica accompaniment for a friend who was cutting a record for Columbia Records. Columbia's director of talent acquisition, impressed by Dylan, signed him up for a recording contract. His albums became best-sellers. Many of Dylan's songs have been sung by other singers, including Pete Seeger and Joan Baez, and many have been published in song books.

Uncompromising in his beliefs, Dylan canceled an appearance on the *Ed Sullivan Show* in the spring of 1963 because the network refused to allow him to present his satire of the John Birch Society, an ultra-right organization. Although he sympathized with civil rights causes and contributed financially to them, Dylan refused to join organizations. In an interview with Nat Hentoff for the October 24, 1963, issue of the *New Yorker,* Dylan said, "I do a lot of things no Movement would allow. . . . I just can't make it with any organization." Singer Joan Baez, a friend who often performed with Dylan in the 1960s, remarked, "Bobby Dylan says what a lot of people my age feel, but cannot say." George Harrison of the Beatles said, "I like his whole attitude … the way he doesn't give a damn."

Preferring isolation, Dylan often retreated to the Catskill Mountains. His popularity escalated in 1965 when he combined folk songs with the electronic beat of rock and roll to create "folk rock." Dylan did not just write angry songs, he also wrote love songs. His music was still popular in the 1990s.

See also Baez, Joan; Grateful Dead; Rock and Roll; Seeger, Pete

Reference Clinton Heylin. *Bob Dylan,* 1996.

Earth Day (April 22)

Conceived in 1970 by Wisconsin Democratic senator Gaylord Nelson, the first Earth Day was a nationwide afternoon teach-in about the environment. Organized by Denis Allen Hayes, a Harvard Law School student who had earlier hitchhiked around the world, it took place at approximately 1,500 colleges and 10,000 other schools on April 22, 1970. Thousands of students heeded the call to organize events on their campuses. Coordination of the first Earth Day was done by nine staff members, most of them students in their twenties, working out of a small Washington office on a budget of $125,000. They secured the participation of an estimated 20 million people throughout the United States. The first celebration used many techniques borrowed from student movements of the 1960s. To protest litter, demonstrators in West Virginia dumped five tons of roadside trash on the steps of a courthouse. To protest auto emission pollution, students in San Jose, California, buried a car.

The event became annual and grew each year. Increased awareness of the environment generated additional participation. Spurred by Earth Day's annual reminders and prodding from other environmental groups, agencies and protective measures came into being, among them the Environmental Protection Agency, the Clean Air Act, and the Clean Water Act. By 1990, on the twentieth birthday of Earth Day, 76 percent of Americans considered themselves to be environmentalists, that is, people who are concerned about and are anxious to improve the world's environment.

Protesters in 1970 focused on local and regional problems, such as the Cuyahoga River, which sometimes caught fire from pollutants as it made its way through Cleveland, Ohio. The first year's optimism was based on a belief that existing knowledge would solve most environmental problems. Environmentalists hoped their campaigns would bring about a reversal of the spiraling global loss of plant and animal species.

By Earth Day 1990, optimism had been tempered by understanding that solutions to some problems might not come fast enough to avoid disaster. Increased knowledge had also broadened the focus of Earth Day 1990 to encompass global

issues. Narrow issues, such as species whose survival was threatened by a dam, a development that would eliminate a wetland, and California smog that killed trees, were recognized as part of larger environmental risks that endangered the entire planet. California smog, for example, comes from local emission of industrial gases, which rise into the atmosphere to join similar gases produced worldwide by people burning fossil fuels.

Production of some gases, particularly carbon dioxide, can lead to global warming by preventing heat from the sun from escaping back into space. Global warming is predicted by many scientists to dry up lakes and streams and raise the level of the sea, which will flood many heavily populated seacoast areas. The increase in temperature caused by global warming could be too swift for flora and fauna to adapt.

The 1970 Earth Day did not pay much attention to the issue of population growth. By 1990, it had become a major issue. The ingenuity of technological inventions and economic progress will, in the opinion of many experts, ultimately be defeated by a rising world population, which has gone from 1.4 billion in 1875 to a projected 6.2 billion in the year 2000.

By Earth Day 1990, the event had become a vast, elaborate affair, involving the expenditure of millions of dollars and months of preparation. The 1990 demonstrations included 100 million participants. The Harvard law student Denis Hayes, who had organized the 1970 event, had, by

THE WHOLE
EARTH IS WATCHING

Earth Day poster.

1990, become a San Francisco lawyer. He chaired the twentieth birthday celebration from headquarters in Palo Alto, California, with a staff of 120 and a board of 115 directors made up of celebrities, prominent politicians, religious leaders, labor officials, and business executives. The board served as an umbrella group lending technical assistance to local and international groups. The headquarters staff plotted strategy as if they were orchestrating a political campaign. Posters and ads carried the slogan "Who Says You Can't Change the World?" As part of a drive to raise $3 million, Earth Day 1990 licensed its logo.

The marketing of Earth Day 1990 and the inclusion of American businesspeople evoked some sharp criticism. The staff responded by pointing to some remarkable changes in corporate America. Many corporations had dropped the argument that pollution control meant a loss of jobs. Moreover, the public's changed attitude toward the environment had corporations scrambling to demonstrate how "green" they were, in order to gain a competitive edge. Even so, many environmentalists were skeptical about whether some corporations had become green.

The original 1970 half-day of activities had grown by Earth Day's twentieth anniversary into a weekend of participation in 3,600 communities in the United States and in 140 other countries. Among many other issues, the worldwide protest aimed attention at pollution in Eastern Europe, destruction of the Latin American rain forest, and the deterioration of the ozone layer. Events took many forms around the world, including parades; proclamations; protests; teach-ins; trash-ins; ecofairs; a bicycle procession in Bengal, India; and a team of climbers who cleaned up debris on Mount Everest.

The Earth Day staff set out to counter the criticism that it had become too cozy with corporate America and the working-class perception that the environmental movement was limited to upper-class bird-watchers. A group from Earth Day 1990 toured the nation to urge minority members to become involved because four out of five toxic waste dumps in the United States are located in or near minority communities.

See also Environmental Movement; Hippies; Kent State; Urban Forestry

References Terry Anderson. *The Movement and the Sixties: Protest in America from Greensboro to Wounded Knee,* 1995; Paul Erhlich. *The Population Bomb,* 1975; and *The Population Explosion,* 1990.

Edelman, Marian Wright
See Children's Defense Fund

Environmental Medicine
Interest in environmental medicine, also known as alternative medicine, grew out of a number of separate trends. During the 1960s, students and young practitioners in a variety of health care professions discovered the wretched health status of the rural and urban poor and set out to find remedies. Volunteers set up local health care centers. Federal grants often enabled the local health care centers to stay open after private sources of funding dried up. In addition, natural food stores became common in urban areas.

The poor who used the local health care centers included such ethnic groups as Hispanics, Native Americans, and Asians. Ethnic groups often have traditional therapies in which group members have strong faith. Alternative medical practitioners put a strong emphasis on the mind-body connection and believe that the patient's frame of mind, that is, belief in the treatment, influences the effectiveness of treatment. Grudgingly, Western-trained doctors have learned that therapies delivered by acupuncturists, chiropractors, and naturopathic practitioners often work when traditional medicine fails.

Environmental practitioners tend to believe that the health of people living in developed countries suffers severely from the myriad of chemicals they encounter in daily life, which compromise immune system functioning. An immune system struggling to neutralize chemicals becomes too depleted to fight off infection. Therefore, the alternative practitioner attempts to restore the immune system to its natural balance, often through natural medicines rather than synthetic ones. Some patients with chronic fatigue syndrome and Gulf War syndrome, unable to find relief through traditional medicine, have turned to alternative medical practitioners.

Europeans use more natural medicines than Americans. Pharmacies in Europe sell not only prescription drugs but herbal and homeopathic remedies. Homeopathy is based on the theory that some diseases can be cured by giving very small doses of substances that in a healthy person would cause the symptoms from which the ill person suffers.

A German compilation of research called the Commission E Monographs provides a standard reference to physicians about herbal medicine. A problem for physicians prior to translation of the Commission E Monographs was that herbal remedies were not standardized, which made it difficult to arrive at proper dosages and to monitor their effectiveness. The American Botanical Council (ABC) had the monographs translated and made them available for purchase in the United States in June 1996.

Alternative medicine, long left on the fringe, had by the mid-1990s achieved some respect. In 1992 the Office of Alternative Medicine was formed at the National Institutes of Health. After several years of criticism, a highly respected scientist, Wayne Jones, the director of Medical Research Fellowship at Walter Reed Army Institute of Research, was appointed director in July 1995. In February 1995 two landmark events signaled increased acceptance. The first issue of the *Journal of Alternative and Complementary Medicine* was published, and the Seattle–King County Council voted to establish a natural medicine public health clinic using public funds. Eleven of the thirteen members of the council had used alternative medicine, and their acceptance reflected statewide acceptance—a poll found that 44 percent of Washington residents had used alternative medicine.

The mission of the clinic under a two-year pilot program was to show that integrated care—a combination of traditional and alternative medicine—was effective. An additional goal was to demonstrate a high demand for alternative medicine among the poor. Ideally, the budget permitting, the clinic was expected to include naturopathic physicians (N.D.'s), traditional medical physicians (M.D.'s), nurses, acupuncturists, chiropractors, social workers, and massage therapists.

By the 1990s, alternative medicine, with roots in the care of the poor, appeared to have been assimilated into the domain of the well-educated upper middle class. Perceiving a potential for savings, some insurance companies began paying for alternative therapies.

See also American Medical Students Association
References William Collinge. *The American Holistic Health Association Complete Guide to Alternative Medicine,* 1996; Isadore Rosenfeld. *Doctor, What's My Alternative? An Establishment Doctor Looks at Complementary Medicine,* 1996.

Environmental Movement

Many conservationists, preservationists, environmentalists, and ecologists of the 1990s can trace their roots back to being student activists in the 1960s and 1970s. Their separate activities are often lumped together as environmental. All work toward essentially the same goals of protecting part of the natural or manmade world from outside threat.

Conservationists are often dedicated to protecting oceans, waterways, and open spaces to ensure the survival of species in a particular area. Poverty increases the threat to many of the world's most precious environmental areas, such as the rain forests. Poor farmers slash and burn the forests in order to plant crops in the soil beneath the forest. Because the soil is fragile and easily exhausted, it cannot sustain more than a few plantings before the farmer must move on and slash and burn more forest.

Further loss of trees and erosion of soil are caused by logging companies that build roads into the forests. To prevent the destruction of such areas, conservationists often create "preserves." The Ordway Preserve, created from gifts of land to the University of Florida, gives scientists an opportunity to learn about the volatile environment of the Florida sandhills.

Preservationists are typically concerned with preserving links to the past, such as old neighborhoods and buildings. One preservation project involved the purchase by New York State over a twenty-year period of a 250-acre site near Rochester to be the first Native American Historic Site.

Ecologists focus on ecosystems, the interrelationships among diverse species and their environments. They believe a diverse environment is more flexible than a homogeneous one, and an environment that contains wild crops and domestic ones protects the future of domestic ones. When the latter fall victim to disease or insect infestation, wild plants can contribute genes not found in domestic plants toward the creation of a more resistant hybrid.

Environmentalists are concerned with the quality of life and with issues of human health and welfare. For example, a Boston-based public interest group, the Conservation Law Foundation (CLF), sued local and federal agencies to clean up Boston Harbor, which in the 1980s was the most polluted harbor in the country.

One reason these distinct arenas of knowledge

seem to be linked together is that activists during the 1960s and 1970s moved into battles beyond the original one that captured their attention. Activists from other movements joined in marches and demonstrations, planned strategies, and shared ideas and techniques. Although the majority of student activists over time matured, married, had children, and became more conservative in their politics, many retained their concern for the environment.

Hippies and the counterculture in general did a great deal to promote interest in the environment. Although various factions of the counterculture movement disagreed about issues, most of those who believed in the hippie philosophy considered themselves environmentalists. For example, many hippies were involved in establishing "people's parks." A Seattle hippie wrote: "A park is for living things, squirrels, children, growing things, turned-on things, people, love, food, lush green colors, laughter, kites, music, God, the smell of life." Many hippies formed a coalition consisting of the Hog Farm, Wartoke Unlimited, Ecology Action Council, the Sierra Club, and several underground newspapers to establish Earth People's Park. The goal was to have "the people" send one dollar to purchase a permanent living space for the present generation and generations to come, to be purchased and built in New Mexico or Colorado.

But hippies were not alone in their interest in the environment. Throughout the decade of the 1960s, many citizens became concerned about pollution. In her book *Silent Spring,* Rachel Carson warned about the impact of pesticides. In *The Population Bomb,* Paul Ehrlich linked population growth with ecological disaster. Barry Commoner wrote in his book *Closing Circle* that if environmental degradation continued on its present course, "it will destroy the capability of the environment to support a reasonably civilized society."

Smog alerts in Los Angeles kept the environment in the news. In 1969, an oil-rig line ruptured off the coast of Santa Barbara, California, and gushed for two weeks, fouling 200 miles of coastline. One hundred thousand citizens signed a petition to end drilling off Santa Barbara. In 1970, Chevron oil wells off the Louisiana coast burned out of control, creating the largest spill in history. And Cleveland's Cuyahoga River was so filled with oil and chemical pollution that it actually caught on fire. Dumped chlorides and sulfates rendered Lake Erie virtually dead.

The radical wave of the feminist movement also contributed to the development of the environmental movement. Feminists mixed themes such as liberation and empowerment and set an example for other groups interested in community, consumerism, and conservation. During the spring of 1970, all kinds of demonstrations became regular fare on nightly news broadcasts, and the first Earth Day on April 22, 1970, received great publicity.

The Kennedy and Johnson administrations had encouraged various community action programs. The Nixon administration shifted much of the funding elsewhere, but the idea of community action did not disappear. Local activists adopted the slogan "Think Globally, Act Locally." Neighborhood activists recognized that issues decided outside their neighborhoods had an impact within their community. One such issue was highway construction. White suburbanites welcomed city planners' efforts to link growing suburbs with downtowns by building freeways. The plans often required wiping out older neighborhoods.

In Baltimore, the city council planned a six-lane highway through the southeast part of the city. The road would have displaced 100,000 residents, many of whose families had lived in the area for generations. Activists organized the Southeast Council Against the Road (SCAR). The group succeeded in stopping the road by getting part of the neighborhood included on the National Register of Historic Places.

In Philadelphia, the city and state highway departments, with support from the Chamber of Commerce, planned an eight-lane expressway that would have displaced 5,000 residents from their old neighborhood and cut off the black population from the newer downtown. Organizers established a citizen's council and blocked construction of Philadelphia's "Mason-Dixon line."

In 1970, local neighborhood revolts sprang up across the nation. In Chicago, much of the pollution was created by Commonwealth Edison, the local utility, which burned soft coal. Columnist Mike Royko asked longtime activist Saul Alinsky to organize citizens to stop the increasing pollution. Alinsky suggested Royko write a column about the issue. Letters poured in. A meeting Alinsky scheduled brought together an audience of scientists, hippies, workers, students, and housewives. The group decided on a strategy of protesting at the company's rate request hearing. Guards barred most of them from the hearing. Undaunted, they formed the Citizen's Action Program (CAP), chaired by activist Father Leonard Dubi and Paul Booth, one of the founders of Students for a Democratic Society (SDS). The group took several actions. Among them were demands that both sulfur emissions and rates be reduced. Flyers were passed out suggesting that consumers delay paying their bills. The most colorful strategy involved gaining "proxy power." CAP members bought stock in the company, which gave them the right to attend the annual meeting of the board of directors. At the meeting, Father Dubi led a group of senior citizens, some singing the "Star Spangled Banner." Writer Studs Terkel led 800 in a chant, "Let Us Breathe!" CAP won all its demands and expanded its efforts. Its next target was the pollution generated and the level of taxes paid by the local U.S. Steel plant.

Many students were moved to join the environmental movement by the writings of Aldo Leopold, particularly by his *Sand County Almanac*. Leopold, a dedicated ecologist, has been called the father of wildlife management and, before his death in 1948, was the world's most outstanding spokesman for conservation.

Berkeley students formed an activist group called Ecology Action, and membership took off on campuses across the country. The rising participation of students in environmental actions, often referred to as "Green Power," led one University of California at Berkeley student to say, "We haven't forgotten Vietnam or the problems of blacks." She added, "Vietnam is a big environmental problem in itself."

Polls taken during the spring of 1970 revealed that Americans were more concerned about the environment than about any other issue. Participation in the first Earth Day supported those findings. During the month before and after Earth Day, Congress passed clean air and clean water acts and mandated environmental impact statements. States did the same. During the week in which Earth Day occurred, 20 million people participated in varied activities.

See also Alinsky, Saul; Earth Day; Greenpeace; Leopold, Aldo; Rainforest and Chico Mendes; Urban Forestry
References Saul Alinsky. *Rules for Radicals,* 1989; Rachel Carson. *Silent Spring,* 1962; Barry Commoner. *Closing Circle: Nature, Man, and Technology;* 1971; Paul Ehrlich. *The Population Bomb,* 1968, 1975; Susan Flader and J. Baird Callicott, eds. *The River of the Mother of God and Other Essays by Aldo Leopold,* 1991; Aldo Leopold. *Sand Country Almanac: Sketches Here and There,* 1987.

Evers, Medgar (1925–1963)

Appointed the first National Association for the Advancement of Colored People (NAACP) field secretary for Mississippi, Medgar Evers spent much of 1955 investigating race-related murders in the state. His record was compiled in a nationally distributed pamphlet entitled *M for Mississippi and Murder.*

Despite the fact that Medgar Evers had lost a friend to a lynch mob, had been prevented from voting by a gang of armed white men, and had been denied admission to a Mississippi law school because he was black, he loved the state. When he returned home from serving overseas during World War II, Evers was determined to steer Mississippi toward racial harmony.

Being the NAACP's highest official in the state made Evers a natural target for attack. It also meant that he was responsible for tasks fraught with danger and anxiety. He counseled James Meredith, while the young student suffered from the white resistance that followed his enrollment at the University of Mississippi. For Mose Wright, an elderly man who risked death to testify against the white men who murdered Emmett

Till, Evers set up a safe escape route. Till, a black teenager from Chicago, had made a flip remark to a white woman and whistled at her and had been murdered for his audacity.

In the spring of 1963, Evers led a drive against Jackson City government to attain integration and fair employment practices for blacks. The mayor, Allen Thompson, replied to a list of black demands in a televised speech. He told black listeners they lived in a beautiful city and made a comfortable living. He warned them against listening to rumors. The television station granted Evers equal time. He told his listeners that a black man in the Congo could hold a job as a locomotive engineer, while a black man in Jackson could not drive a garbage truck. City officials remained unmoved.

On May 28, 1963, an integrated group of students sat in at a whites-only lunch counter. A group of whites sprayed paint on the seated students and poured salt and pepper on their heads. When photographs of the incidents appeared in the national media, the mayor felt compelled to negotiate. As the momentum of civil rights actions increased in Jackson, the number of arrested protesters became so large that the police had to use the state fairgrounds to detain them. The level of violence in retaliation also increased.

In response to increased violence in the South, President John F. Kennedy addressed the nation in a speech on the evening of June 12, 1963: "A great change is at hand and our . . . [responsibility] is to make that revolution, that change, peaceful and constructive for all." Following the president's speech, Evers and other NAACP officials held a strategy session. By the time Evers finally pulled into his driveway, it was about midnight.

His wife and his children had waited up for him. They heard a car door slam—followed by gunfire. As they had been taught to do by their father, the children dropped to the floor. Evers's wife, Myrlie, rushed to open the door and flipped on a light. On the other side of the door, she found her husband, who, despite mortal wounds, had dragged himself there from the spot where he had been shot. Neighbors lifted Evers onto a mattress and drove him to the hospital. He died within an hour.

On the night following Evers's death, Myrlie Evers spoke to a group of about 500 and urged them to remain calm and to carry on her husband's work. On June 15, three days after Evers's death, a group of black youths broke off from a crowd of 5,000 who had come to pay their respects and began to march in defiance of a court order. When police officers drew their weapons, a Justice Department official, John Doar, who had come to attend Evers's funeral, walked between the youths and the police. The young people responded to Doar's request that they turn back, and violence was avoided. The day after Evers was buried in Arlington National Cemetery, Mayor Thompson appointed the city's first black police officer.

On a high-powered rifle equipped with a telescope that had been left at the scene, Federal Bureau of Investigation (FBI) agents found fingerprints belonging to Byron De La Beckwith, a charter member of Jackson's White Citizens' Council, a racist group dedicated to a doctrine of white superiority. After two trials that resulted in hung juries, Beckwith went free for almost three decades. In 1990, prosecutors found new evidence and brought him to trial a third time. On February 5, 1994, Evers's killer was sentenced to life imprisonment.

See also Sit-ins; Till, Emmett
Reference Sara Bullard. *Free at Last: A History of the Civil Right Movement and Those Who Died in the Struggle,* 1997.

Farmer, James
See Freedom Riders

Federal Student Right-to-Know Act of 1990

Campus crime spurred the passage of the Federal Student Right-to-Know Act of 1990. The law requires colleges that receive federal aid to make crime data available to students and university employees and to the U.S. Department of Education. Until the Right-to-Know Act was passed, only slightly more than 300 of the nation's 2,100 four-year colleges and universities reported crime data individually to the Federal Bureau of Investigation's (FBI's) voluntary Uniform Crime Reports system. Many schools did not report crimes for fear such information would damage their reputations and hurt their fund-raising efforts.

Campus administrations, some very reluctantly, were forced to deal with crime issues in the 1980s and 1990s because of pressure from women students and faculty to address date rape, gang rape, and sexual harassment. Added incentives were several widely publicized crimes and an increase in lawsuits claiming negligent campus security.

Campus crimes occur at about half the rate for the nation. Nevertheless; campuses are not the tranquil settings presented in college and university brochures. Sexual assaults by students on students are the crimes college administrators most often ignore or hush up. Experts believe that gang rape is more common on college campuses than in the society as a whole, is seldom reported, and is almost never prosecuted. According to national surveys, all crime is underreported. Rape is far more underreported than other crimes, particularly if the rape is perpetrated by an acquaintance and especially if the rapist is a campus acquaintance. Eight campus rape-prevention centers in the University of California system revealed that they saw about 240 rape victims annually who had failed to report the assaults to police.

There are two broad categories of campus crime: crime against students by outsiders and student-on-student crime. Urban campuses have

long been faced with the problem of outsider crime. Outsider thieves are tempted by the large quantity of stereos, computers, and bicycles. Outsider sex offenders are drawn by the congregation of young women. Serial killer Ted Bundy was attracted to college campuses by the presence of a large pool of potential female victims.

At least 80 percent of campus crime is committed by students. Fraternities are responsible for a great deal of on-campus crime, often in connection with rituals such as hazing or as expressions of fraternal solidarity achieved through verbal or physical attacks on women. A 1989 University of Illinois at Urbana-Champaign self-study found that fraternity men, who represented one-quarter of the male student population, perpetrated 63 percent of student sexual assaults, ranging from verbal abuse (which typically refers to sex) to acquaintance rape to gang rape.

A 1990 survey of 2,000 randomly selected students conducted by the Towson State University's Center for the Study and Prevention of Campus Violence revealed that one-third of the students surveyed had been the victims of crime. Alcohol and drugs played a part in many of the crimes. The more the students had used alcohol and drugs, the more likely they were to have been the victims of crimes or to have committed crimes.

About two-thirds of the total number of crimes against college students took place on campus. The crimes ranged from theft (most common) to vandalism, fights and physical assaults, rape by an acquaintance, and sexual assault and rape by a stranger (least common). Although men and women were about equally likely to be victims, only 29 percent of those who committed crimes were women.

In the late 1960s and early 1970s, most colleges dropped rigid codes of conduct that had governed college life. Relaxed standards about liquor on campus were adopted. In the 1980s and 1990s, binge drinking became an epidemic on campuses. Fraternities often held keg parties on weekends that began on Thursday and ended on Monday.

Being high can be lethal. The body can process alcohol, which is a toxin, at a fixed rate that depends on size, health, and amount of food taken in. When the rate is exceeded, death is likely to occur. A Massachusetts Institute of Technology (MIT) freshman died in 1997 from drinking at a fraternity party. Two weeks later, another MIT fraternity was suspended when beer kegs were delivered and underage students accepted their delivery.

In addition to getting rid of rules about liquor in the 1970s and 1980s, colleges created coed dorms. In the mid to late 1980s and 1990s, women students living in coed dorms reported being subjected to sexual harassment. They urged colleges to take a more active role in student life. Often, administration efforts were inadequate. In 1986, Jeanne Ann Clery was raped and murdered in her Lehigh University dorm. Students had propped open the dorm's locked doors. Clery's parents sued the school for $25 million on grounds of negligence.

Jeanne Ann Clery was killed by a Lehigh student who had been in trouble with the law earlier. In addition to suing the university, her parents mounted a campaign to develop federal legislation that would require all colleges to disclose crime statistics for the previous three years, policies on student drug and alcohol abuse, and data on the admission of convicted felons. By February 1991, the Clerys' efforts had led to the passage of the Federal Student Right-to-Know Act of 1990 and had prompted twelve states to require universities to report campus crime, either

to law enforcement agencies or to the public. The Clerys also began an organization called Security on Campus, which sent out 200,000 Security Questionnaires to prospective students and their parents.

In the fall of 1990, women adopted new tactics to protect themselves and each other against sexual assaults. On the bathroom walls of the Brown University library, women wrote lists of names of male students who they said had raped them. When the lists were removed, they reappeared with names added, and lists appeared in several other bathrooms on campus. Since the compilers of the list remained anonymous, the university could not take action against them.

At Hampshire College in Amherst, Massachusetts, women who were dissatisfied with the university's response to their complaints gathered 700 signatures on a petition and presented it to parents and administrators on the morning of Parents Weekend. As a consequence, Hampshire officials ordered additional campus lighting and had doors with locks installed for dormitory showers.

Although the lists on bathroom walls became catalysts for change and the installation of protective devices offered some protection against future crime, lawsuits seemed to be the most effective leverage for change in universities. Several successful suits resulted in large judgments being levied against colleges. However, most college administrative policy changes dealt with sexual assaults by strangers. Many experts believe that major changes have to come in approaches to acquaintance rapes and gang rapes conducted by fraternity brothers and athletic team members.

References Walter DeKeseredy and Martin Schwartz. *Woman Abuse on Campus: Results from the Canadian National Survey,* 1997; Martin Schwartz and Walter DeKeseredy. *Sexual Assault on the College Campus,* 1997.

Feminist Organizations

Following President John F. Kennedy's election in 1960, he looked for a national organization that represented all women and with which his "New Frontier" spirit of reform could work. He found none. A dedicated band of women connected to Eleanor Roosevelt, the wife of the late President Franklin Delano Roosevelt, had disbanded during the years of President Dwight D. Eisenhower's presidency.

In 1961, Esther Peterson, Kennedy's director of the Women's Bureau and a longtime friend of Eleanor Roosevelt, proposed that the president set up a President's Commission on the Status of Women. The goal of the commission was to explore women's opinions on laws and practices that affected them. Kennedy asked the frail Eleanor Roosevelt to chair the commission, which was formed in 1962. Despite her poor health and her personal dislike of Kennedy, she agreed.

The U.S. Civil Service had a stated policy of equal opportunity for both sexes, but women routinely went unpromoted, the reason being that officials in need of a candidate had the option of stating a sex preference. To no effect, beginning in 1941, Eleanor Roosevelt had often questioned the contradiction between policy and practice. In 1962, her influence brought about a change. While presiding over a meeting of the Commission on the Status of Women, Roosevelt was informed that Attorney General Robert Kennedy had ruled that the president had the power to order civil service officers to consider women for jobs on an equal basis with men. By the time the influential Commission on the Status of Women disbanded in 1963, it was succeeded by state commissions all over the country.

In 1966, Betty Friedan, author of *The Feminine Mystique,* was in Washington, D.C., as a representative of her state commission at a conference. For months before Friedan's arrival, women's rights advocates working in the nation's capital had been telling her that the prohibition against sex discrimination in Title VII of the Civil Rights Act of 1964 was in jeopardy. The advocates urged women to form a women's equivalent to the National Association for the Advancement of Colored People (NAACP) to lobby on behalf of women. Friedan agreed to try.

One evening during the conference, she invited about fifteen women to her hotel room to

Activist leaders Karen de Crow and Eleanor Smeal pose in front of a National Organization for Women (NOW) poster in 1976.

discuss formation of a group. The majority of the women rejected the idea. They felt that working within existing groups would be more effective. The following morning, a few conference delegates who had participated the night before in the debate in Friedan's room attempted to introduce a resolution. The resolution urged the Equal Employment Opportunity Commission (EEOC) to enforce its mandate to end sex discrimination in employment. The conference officials told the women that as a body they had no authority to take any action, not even to pass a resolution.

Nothing further was needed to convince the women that a women's organization was critical to bring about change. The National Organization for Women (NOW) was founded, with Kathryn Clarenbach, the head of the Wisconsin Commission on the Status of Women, named temporary coordinator. On October 29, 1966, the first NOW organizing conference was held in Washington, D.C., and Betty Friedan was elected president. In its first year, NOW went from an initial 300 members to 1,200. At its 1967 convention, NOW endorsed reproductive rights.

Through the late 1960s and early 1970s, countless new women's groups emerged around the country. Most organized on a local basis and lasted only a year or two. On the national scene, NOW continued as the predominant organization. By 1970, its membership had grown to 3,000. By 1971, more than 100 journals and newspapers devoted to women's issues were being published. In July 1972, the preview issue of *Ms.* magazine appeared, the first nationally distributed commercial feminist publication.

Less visible than the organizations with official names—but possibly more influential in numbers of women influenced—were countless small groups of women who met weekly in college dorms, city apartments, and suburban homes. These so-called consciousness-raising groups arose spontaneously out of the needs of women. Participants discussed sexism as it affected them in personal terms. By giving voice to their discontent, these women became committed to the movement. Many joined larger groups.

Feminist organizations were jolted by three key factors in the 1980s and 1990s. When the Equal Rights Amendment, passed by the House of Representatives in 1971 and by the Senate in 1972, failed on June 30, 1982, to gain the necessary 38 states needed for ratification, some discouraged women dropped out of the struggle. Others were galvanized into renewed action.

Modest gains in employment and education generated a backlash in the 1980s and 1990s. Women were blamed for a variety of ills in society, particularly those that could be traced to the absence of women in the home due to employment. The backlash reinforced women's awareness of their unequal status.

In October 1991, during hearings for Senate confirmation of Clarence Thomas for nomination to the Supreme Court, law professor Anita Hill testified that she had been sexually harassed by Thomas when she worked for him. The sena-

tors' scornful treatment of Hill enraged American women. As a consequence, a record number ran for office and a record number won.

See also Backlash against Feminism; de Beauvoir, Simone; Black Feminist Organizations; Friedan, Betty; Steinem, Gloria; Women's Movement

References Betty Friedan. *The Feminine Mystique,* 1963; Miriam Schneir. *Feminism in Our Time: The Essential Writings, World War II to the Present,* 1994.

Fish-ins
See National Indian Youth Council

Fonda, Jane (b. 1937)

Actress, activist, and fitness entrepreneur Jane Fonda decided to become a radical in 1970. She attacked being a radical with the same fervor she had previously learned acting roles. Her new career began in early 1970, when self-styled 1960s revolutionaries David Horowitz and Peter Collier, new editors of the radical magazine *Ramparts,* received a telephone call from Fonda's press agent, Steve Jaffee. He called about a story Collier had written on the Native American takeover of Alcatraz. Fonda wanted to be taken to Alcatraz to meet the leaders.

Fonda found radical influences everywhere. At a Beverly Hills party in 1970, Fonda was introduced to Fred Gardner, a part-time screenwriter who was an outspoken Marxist and an antiwar activist. Gardner had set out to radicalize the army by appealing directly to disgruntled enlisted men. To do so, he had opened a string of GI coffeehouses outside military bases across the country. Servicemen could hear antiwar sentiments with free coffee and rock music. Fonda fell under Gardner's spell.

Gardner told her that Mark Lane, a radical lawyer who popularized the assassination conspiracy theory about President John F. Kennedy's death, was planning a major Indian rights protest in Seattle. On March 8, 1970, with Lane, Fonda entered the world of militant protest. She joined 150 Indians on a march on Fort Lawson to reclaim their property. Lane and ninety-six demonstrators were arrested. Fonda was not, but because she was shoved around during the melee, she charged the military police with brutality. Collier, Gardner, and Jaffee arranged a whirlwind tour of reservations, bases, campuses, and coffeehouses for Fonda.

With Lane and Indian activist La Nada Means, Fonda appeared on television on the highly rated *Dick Cavett Show*. Once seated, she raised her hand in the clenched fist salute of the Black Panthers. The appearance was a disaster. Shrill and arrogant, Fonda's comments were filled with factual errors. Indian activists pleaded with her not to help them anymore.

Fonda turned to the Black Panthers. The actress was drawn to Huey Newton, the Panthers' founder and "minister of defense." The Panthers remained a local Bay Area group until a bloody incident gained them national attention. As Newton was leaving a party celebrating the end of his probation for a knifing incident, he was stopped by an Oakland officer, John Frey. Following a brief struggle, a backup officer and Newton were wounded and Frey lay dead from five gunshot wounds. The Newton trial became a celebrated legal case. Defense attorneys claimed the backup officer had accidentally shot his partner. Newton was convicted of manslaughter, but the conviction was overturned on a technicality. Of Newton, Fonda said, "He's the only man I've ever met who approaches sainthood." She agreed with the Panthers' premise that black capitalism would solve nothing. Instead, it would create a black elite who would exploit black people.

A wave of protest swept across American campuses after the U.S. invasion of Cambodia. Following the May 4, 1970, deaths of four students who were fired upon at Kent State by the National Guard, Fonda resumed traveling around the country. At the University of New Mexico, she led a march on the president's office and demanded that the school shut down to protest the shootings at Kent State. After a speech at the University of Maryland, a man asked if she was "in it for the publicity." When Fonda failed to respond, he said, "Well, you must be getting something out of this." She snapped, "You think this is fun? Standing in the heat talking to a bunch of lethargic students?"

Fonda didn't mention that her fee—about $2,000—was among the highest paid to speakers. She used the money to support her anticapitalist causes.

By the time Fonda finished filming *Klute* in October 1970, she freely admitted she was out to "change the American system through socialism." When a coalition of antiwar groups planned to hold a hearing in Detroit during which Vietnam veterans would describe atrocities they claimed they had witnessed, Fonda volunteered her services. The event was called the "Winter Soldier Investigation," an allusion to Tom Paine's "sunshine patriots" and those truly committed to a cause.

Fonda saw only what she hoped to see in her adopted causes. In November 1970, she cited Fidel Castro's Cuba as an example of a utopian society. In March 1971, Fonda flew to France, where she met privately with North Vietnam's negotiator at the Paris Peace Talks, Madame Binh. Fonda emerged from the meeting to tell the French press that the U.S. government, the Pentagon, and the Central Intelligence Agency (CIA) were responsible for the My Lai massacre, an occasion when soldiers under the command of First Lieutenant William Calley, Jr., herded together hundreds of Vietnamese—old men, women, and children—and slaughtered them.

While in France to make a film in 1972, Fonda met with the North Vietnamese–sponsored International Assembly for Peace and Independence in Indochina. In clandestine meetings, she met with Vietcong and North Vietnamese operatives to plan a trip. Fonda returned home filled with indignation. At the Embassy Theater in Los Angeles, she showed slides provided to her by the communists she had met in Paris. After the showing, activist Tom Hayden, who had met Fonda previously, climbed on the stage and reintroduced himself.

On July 8, 1972, Fonda arrived in North Vietnam with greetings from "revolutionary comrades in America." For the next two weeks, Fonda toured bombed-out hospitals, schools, and factories. A photograph of her on a mobile North Vietnamese antiaircraft gun normally trained on

American planes was taken. The photo came back to haunt her for years after the trip. Twenty-five years after Fonda's trip to North Vietnam, veterans still felt enmity toward her. Some still carried stickers on their car bumpers that read "Vets Are Not Fonda Jane." Not satisfied just to have her picture taken, Fonda volunteered to do ten propaganda broadcasts over Radio Hanoi. The broadcasts were intended to demoralize American combat troops. Calls to charge Fonda with treason when she returned to the United States went unanswered. The Justice Department did not want to make a martyr out of Fonda.

In November 1972, Fonda and Hayden decided to have a baby. The decision was followed by a ninety-day speaking tour to raise money for presidential candidate George McGovern, during which her divorce from her husband. film director Roger Vadim, was processed. The marriage lasted seventeen years, during which Fonda spent an estimated $10 million supporting Hayden's political career.

During the 1970s, Fonda made thirteen movies and appeared in Henrik Ibsen's *A Doll's House* on television, a play with a feminist theme. Her movie *Coming Home* was about a Vietnam veteran confined to a wheelchair, and her movie *The China Syndrome* had an anti–nuclear power theme.

In the spring of 1982, *Jane Fonda's Workout Book* was published by Simon and Schuster and became an instant best-seller. A video version of her book did equally as well. By the end of 1982, the Fonda fitness empire was earning $20 million annually.

Fonda and Hayden divorced, and in 1991, Fonda married the founder of Turner Broadcasting, Ted Turner, a billionaire and consummate capitalist.

See also Black Panther Party; GI Antiwar Protests; Hayden, Tom
Reference Christopher Anderson. *Citizen Jane: The Turbulent Life of Jane Fonda*, 1990.

Free Speech Movement

Civil rights activist Mario Savio spent the summer of 1964 working in the civil rights movement in Mississippi. When he returned to the University of California at Berkeley in the fall, he found that university officials had established new rules that restricted the university's students from participating in political activities. Savio reacted by organizing campus protests and becoming an articulate spokesperson for the protesters.

In his 1993 book *The Free Speech Movement: Coming of Age in the 1960s,* author David Lance Goines described some of the social elements that contributed to student unrest. On September 30, 1964, eight University of California at Berkeley students were suspended indefinitely by Chancellor E. W. Strong because they had violated university rules about the form, place, and manner of speech allowed students while on campus.

The suspensions sparked a period of student unrest at Berkeley that ended in the largest mass arrest in California history on December 3, 1964. At issue was the restoration of First Amendment rights on campus. A major contributor to the escalation of the disagreement was the president of the university. Clark Kerr, a professor of industrial relations, had become president in 1958. Kerr perceived the university as a "series of processes producing a series of results—a mechanism held together by administrative rules and powered by money." In Goines's perception, Kerr viewed the university as a handmaiden of industry, a perspective common to the leaders of many American universities. Such institutions do not encourage dissent.

In Kerr's 1963 book, *The Uses of the University,* he wrote, "The university and segments of industry are becoming more and more alike. As the university becomes tied into the world of work, the professor—at least in the natural and some of the social sciences—takes on the characteristics of an entrepreneur. . . . The two worlds are merging." Caught up in his own view of the world, Kerr failed to notice the campus unrest around him. The university's post–World War II enrollment tripled from 7,748 in 1944 to 21,909 in 1946 and produced a housing crisis both on and off campus. Between 1959 and 1964, the size of the population grew by another 7,000, as the first wave of baby boomers (those born between 1946 and 1964) arrived at college.

The new students found themselves adrift on a 1,232-acre campus where no one cared what happened to them. Lecture classes often had enrollments of as many as 800 students. Some large lecture classes were broken down into smaller study groups led by underpaid, overworked, graduate teaching assistants, who often didn't know much more than their students did about the subject. Young professors, who would be expected to engage their students in their chosen fields, labored under the pressure of "publish or perish." In order to pursue research that would result in publication, professors could not spend adequate time on teaching preparation. In that respect, conditions at Berkeley were not that different from those at many other large universities around the country. For many students, on-campus protests not only gave them a sense of camaraderie but provided the only intellectually stimulating events in their lives.

Factors outside the university also contributed to unrest on American college campuses. The 1963–1964 academic year brought an escalation in the participation of students in the civil rights movement. Student participation was given added impetus by the assassination of Medgar Evers, the Mississippi field secretary of the National Association for the Advancement of Colored People (NAACP).

Civil rights activists on the Berkeley campus such as Mario Savio believed that change is best accomplished by direct action and confrontation. Savio was the son of devout Italian-American Catholics. He had been educated at the Christian Brothers Manhattan College before transferring to Queens College. During the summer of 1963, Savio had worked for a Catholic relief organization in rural Mexico. In the fall of 1963, his parents moved to Los Angeles, and he enrolled at Berkeley as a junior. During the summer of 1964, Savio taught freedom school to black children in McComb, Mississippi. By the fall of 1964, he was angry about what he had seen.

In part, Savio's power came from his physical presence—he was 6'1" and 195 pounds. More

came from his articulateness. He could express the anger, frustration, and anxiety of his generation. On September 30, 1964, Savio brought 300 or more students to see Chancellor E. W. Strong at the Dean of Students' office in Sproul Hall. Several students had been directed to make an appointment with the chancellor for violating the university's policy on the use of campus facilities for political activity. Each person in the large group with Savio acknowledged violating the policy and wanted to make an appointment.

The chancellor ordered the five students who had been cited to enter the dean's office to meet with two deans. Savio told the chancellor that he, the chancellor, had misunderstood the students' request. They wanted him to talk to each and every student present, if he wanted to talk to any of them. The chancellor told them to leave the building. Savio replied that (1) the students' equal protection under the laws was at stake; (2) the group would leave only if the chancellor guaranteed that the same disciplinary action would be given to each student; and (3) without such assurances, he would urge the students to stay where they were. At a few minutes past 4:00 P.M., Savio announced to the group that they would spend the night in Sproul Hall. Without any preplanning, the student invasion of Sproul Hall had become a sit-in. At 11:30 P.M., the dean of the graduate division announced that eight students had been suspended. The sit-in ended about 3:00 A.M.

The next day, October 1, members of the Congress of Racial Equality (CORE) set out to violate the university's regulations against distribution of information and collection of donations for nonuniversity causes on campus. As a consequence of the CORE action, Jack Weinberg, who had graduated from the university with great distinction in mathematics the year before, was singled out as a nonstudent to be arrested. The university police lieutenant told Weinberg that if he was not a student, he was trespassing, and if he was, then he was violating university policy. Weinberg refused to give his name and was arrested.

The cry went up, "Take us all." While the lieutenant went to get help, Weinberg gave a rousing speech to a rapidly growing, enthusiastic crowd.

In characteristic civil rights activist fashion, Weinberg refused to cooperate in being arrested. His limp body was carried off by four officers, each lifting one limb. The police brought a car to shorten the distance they would have to carry Weinberg. Someone yelled "sit down." The crowd of 200–300 sat down, surrounding the car. The car became a platform for making speeches.

When the chancellor refused students' demands, Savio escalated the confrontation. He told the crowd, "I recommend that 500 of you stay here around this auto and others of you join me in taking our request to the dean." In short order, there were 500 students blockading the deans' offices and more than 1,000 surrounding the car. The deans and secretaries crawled out windows to escape. A faculty committee offered to make contact with Vice Chancellor Alex Sheriff. The professors were ineffective at getting the word back to the students once they had made contact, and the sit-in went on after it could have ended. When a large group of police officers tried to close the doors of Sproul Hall, the students occupied the building, with half of the students outside and half of them inside. Neither side reckoned on the enormous resources of the other side and the incredible damage that could be inflicted. No one thought the disruption could continue. But it did.

Finally, Savio and other student representatives in negotiations with the chancellor agreed on the following: illegal forms of demonstrations would be stopped; a committee to conduct hearings on all aspects of political behavior on campus would be set up; the arrested man would be booked and released on his own recognizance and the university would not press charges; the suspended students would be dealt with by the Student Conduct Committee rather than the administration; and an area where students traditionally conducted political activities would be turned over to the city or to the Associated Students of the University of California (ASUC). Although not all students were happy with the terms, they agreed, and the crowd dispersed. The students perceived the end of the sit-in as a cooling-off period. Kerr seemed to think the danger was past. According to Goines, university officials hinted to the district attorney that they would not object to Weinberg being prosecuted, but no charges were ever pressed.

The Free Speech Movement (FSM) coalesced in the days that followed. The chairman of the university's Board of Regents treated the events as if they were student highjinks and law and order had been reestablished thanks to Kerr and his staff. Participatory democracy, which requires consensus, takes an enormous amount of time. The first meeting of FSM to form the organization took a week. Within hours of the end of the sit-in, a clearinghouse for information and communication was set up to run around the clock. By October 4, 1964, the Northern California chapter of the American Civil Liberties Union had become interested in the student Free Speech Movement. Support had also come from the Executive Committee of the Association of California State College Professors.

On October 5, the FSM held its first official rally on Sproul Hall's steps. About 1,000 students showed up to hear Savio tell them that the battle was not over but that the students had won the biggest battle by making the administration admit that there was a problem and that student representatives were agents with whom the university had to negotiate. On that same day, Chancellor Strong announced appointments to the Study Committee on Campus Political Activity (CCPA). The formation of the committee, stacked with students and faculty in disagreement with the students' complaints, began another escalation of bad feelings and accusations. Kerr was unavailable to meet with FSM representatives.

On December 2, following a huge noon rally in Sproul Plaza, about 1,500 people packed all four floors of Sproul Hall. At 3:00 A.M. the following morning, an announcement was made that students were to leave or face disciplinary action. At 3:45 A.M., the governor announced that he had instructed the California Highway Patrol and the Alameda County Sheriff's Department to arrest the demonstrators. The arrest of 800 students by almost as many police officers took twelve hours. Area jails overflowed, and a loosely guarded group was lodged in the National Guard Armory in San Leandro. By 4:45 P.M. on December 3, all that was left in Sproul Hall was a lot of tired police officers and trash. Students were released in time to attend a noon rally on December 4. Pickets encouraged faculty and students to boycott classes to protest the arrests. Picketers from the University of California at Davis demonstrated at the governor's office.

Graduate teaching assistants, poorly paid and shabbily treated, lacked representation. They bore the brunt of day-to-day teaching and identified with the undergraduates. They ensured that the strike, which lasted until December 8, was a success. The faculty were enraged at the administration for having had police on campus, a violation of a long tradition that barred civil authorities from campuses.

Departmental chairmen announced that all university classes between 9 A.M. and noon on December 7 would be cancelled to hear an address by Kerr in the Greek Theater. At 11:00 A.M., to an estimated audience of 16,000 students, faculty, and staff, Kerr said he would accept a proposal concerning free speech on campus—which said, in effect, that the administration would think about it—amnesty for pending disciplinary action against specific student leaders, and no university action against students arrested during the sit-in.

Kerr was laughed at and booed. Savio, who had been denied an opportunity to speak, walked up to the microphone carrying a rolled-up piece of paper in his hand. Opinions differ about whether he planned to make a speech or to simply announce a rally at Sproul Plaza. Two police officers grabbed him and dragged him off the stage to a small room—one tugging on his tie. Two students who went to his aid were knocked down and immobilized. The crowd was electrified. The professors onstage were shocked. The students began to chant, "We want Mario." Cooler heads prevailed, and Savio was released and allowed to announce the rally. Professors who had opposed the demonstrations had been converted by the sight of seeing Savio dragged off the stage.

On December 8 a set of resolutions hammered out by 200 professors was presented to the entire faculty in the Academic Senate. The resolutions passed. Joseph Tussman, chairman of the philosophy department, announced the meaning of the Academic Senate's position. He said, "Anything that is illegal in the community at large is still illegal on campus. The question is: Should the University impose more restrictions on its students in the area of political activity than exist in the community at large? The Senate said: No." To prevent the faculty of other campuses in the University of California system from undermining the gains won by the students at Berkeley, the faculty formed a speakers' bureau whose members gave presentations at the other campuses.

In early March 1965, after much discussion and delay, the wheels of justice began to move for the 800 or more students who had been arrested in Sproul Hall. On March 10, 1965, after months of wrangling, the defendants were offered three choices. One hundred and one chose "nolo," not to make a defense but not to admit guilt. Five hundred chose "stipulation," to agree to a bargain. One hundred and fifty-five chose a collective trial before a jury. One defendant, a schoolteacher from San Francisco, insisted on a trial by jury. He was released when a hung jury could not make a decision.

The majority of the students were given probation, a fine, and a suspended sentence. Following the trial, the judge asked the defendants to write out an explanation. Fines ranged from $25 to $400. Rather than pay fines they could not afford, some defendants chose to serve ten to thirty days. The leaders were given actual sentences ranging from thirty to 120 days. The average age of the students was 21. They were drawn from sixty different disciplines. Dean of Students Arleigh Williams described the participants as "only mildly deviant from University norms."

See also Civil Rights Movement; Columbia University Campus Protest

References David Lance Goines. *The Free Speech Movement: Coming of Age in the 1960s,* 1993; Clark Kerr. *The Uses of the University,* 1982; Leonard Levy. *Freedom of the Press from Zenger to Jefferson,* 1966.

Freedom Riders

Of the many types of segregation, segregated transportation was among the most humiliating and difficult to avoid. It became a major target of the civil rights movement, which began to build momentum in 1954 and peaked in 1965. But long before 1954, public transportation had been a source of racial friction.

In 1890, Homer Plessy, who was seven-eighths white, sat in the white car of a train. After being arrested for violating Louisiana law, Plessy challenged the state law on the grounds that his constitutional rights had been violated. He lost in state court, and the U.S. Supreme Court ruled against him in 1896. The Court's decision stated that the states could offer separate but equal services under the constitution. The *Plessy v. Ferguson* decision served as a signal to the southern politicians that they could pass laws that segregated the races.

In areas of the South where blacks and whites traveled in the same cars, the black sections were always smaller. Blacks were required to give up their seats to whites who were standing. Sometimes entire cars were designated white or black. The black cars were always shabbier and less well maintained. In 1900, blacks in Montgomery, Alabama, boycotted the city's streetcars until the city changed its ordinance to state that no one would be forced to give up a seat unless another was available. The ordinance was not enforced, and segregation in city transportation became entrenched. When bus transportation supplanted travel by trolley or train, the rules of segregation were continued.

Almost fifty years after the *Plessy v. Ferguson* decision, black veterans, who had served in large numbers during World War II, came home to find the discrimination they had experienced before they left. They were vocal about their disenchantment. President Harry Truman agreed and appointed the President's Commission on Civil Rights. He spoke at the annual convention of the National Association for the Advancement of Colored People (NAACP), the first president ever to do so. He said, "We must make the federal government a friendly, vigilant defender of the rights and equalities of all Americans. And again I mean *all* Americans."

The members of the Supreme Court in 1946 held quite different attitudes than those who had voted in favor of segregation in 1896. Although they were not prepared to attack state laws, they were prepared to intervene when the laws of more than one state were involved. Interstate travel was one such area.

Black passengers on trains and buses headed south could sit anywhere in a vehicle while it was north of the Mason-Dixon line, the boundary between Pennsylvania and Maryland. (Surveyed by Charles Mason and Jeremiah Dixon in the 1760s, the line is regarded as a dividing line between the North and the South.) But when a bus or train reached the line, black passengers traveling from the North had to transfer to the back of the bus or, in the case of a train, to another car. Irene Morgan, a black woman holding an interstate ticket, challenged the practice in Virginia. She was arrested for not moving to the back of the bus. On June 3, 1946, in *Morgan v. Commonwealth of Virginia*, the U.S. Supreme Court ruled that segregation on interstate buses was unconstitutional. In a later decision, the Washington, D.C., Court of Appeals extended the Morgan decision to trains.

To test whether the Interstate Commerce Commission's rules to abolish racial discrimination against interstate passengers on buses were being enforced in the South, the Congress of Racial Equality (CORE), a small civil rights organization, undertook a risky venture. CORE had been founded in 1942 by the young race-relations secretary of the Fellowship of Reconciliation (FOR), James Farmer. FOR was a pacifist organization whose philosophy did not permit direct confrontation.

Farmer founded CORE to be an organization that would attempt to change racial discrimination practices by employing the same kind of nonviolent confrontation used by Mahatma Gandhi in India. CORE's workers were mostly black or white University of Chicago students. Following the *Morgan* decision, the leaders of CORE and the Racial-Industrial Committee of FOR voted to sponsor a "Journey of Reconciliation" through the upper South to determine if bus and train companies were enforcing the *Morgan* decision. The participants deliberately chose the upper southern states to avoid the physical risks inherent in the Deep South.

Despite Irene Morgan's example, women were excluded from the journey. Sixteen men, both black and white, participated. One of the black travelers, Bayard Rustin, kept a diary of the journey. There were several unpleasant incidents and arrests but only a few court convictions. Five Journey of Reconciliation participants who had been arrested in Chapel Hill, North Carolina, had expected to plead not guilty and escape prison. Two days before they were to go on trial, they learned that a local black attorney had lost their interstate bus tickets, the proof they needed. Because fear had made local black officials unwilling to help, NAACP attorneys decided they did not have enough evidence to mount a successful Supreme Court challenge. Roy Wilkins, the head of the NAACP, had to tell those in jail they would have to plead guilty and spend time on the chain gang.

The judge told Bayard Rustin he was a "poor misled nigra from the North" and gave him thirty days. To Rustin's white friend, Igal Roodenko, the judge said, "It's about time you white Jews from New York learned that you can't come down here bringing your nigras with you to upset the customs of the South." His sentence was ninety days. Rustin took notes about his experiences and those of others on the chain gang in Roxboro, North Carolina, and smuggled them out. His account of the inhumane conditions on chain gangs was serialized in the *New York Post*. Two years later, North Carolina's chain gangs were abolished.

Following the Journey of Reconciliation in 1947, Farmer worked as an organizer for the American Federation of Labor's Upholsterers' International, as student secretary of the League for Industrial Democracy, and at District Council 37 in New York City. In 1959, he joined the national staff of the NAACP. While Farmer's attention was turned elsewhere, his wife and a few friends had kept CORE functioning. In 1961, he was persuaded to leave NAACP and devote his full attention to CORE.

Although CORE was the smallest and the least well funded of established civil rights organizations, it was still in a position to mount a public action quickly. It had engaged in desegregation campaigns in the early 1940s and had been encouraged by the results of the Journey of Reconciliation in 1947. At the first CORE staff meeting under Farmer as the new national director, a suggestion was made to test the December 1960 Supreme Court decision in *Boynton v. Virginia*. The Court had held that segregated waiting rooms and restaurants to serve interstate passengers were unconstitutional. The CORE staff knew that attempts to test the law would be met with violent resistance. The publicity would also thrust CORE into the national spotlight. Farmer did not believe President John F. Kennedy would enforce the *Boynton v. Virginia* decision for fear of losing the support of southern Democrats.

The planned trip was to be called a Freedom Ride rather than a second Journey of Reconciliation. Thirteen people, men and women, black and white, ranging in age from 21 to 60, volunteered. James Peck had been on the Journey of Reconciliation fourteen years earlier. Farmer planned to go, but his participation was cut short when his father became gravely ill. The youngest participant was a black member of the Student Nonviolent Coordinating Committee (SNCC), John Lewis. The oldest participants were white, 60-year-old Walter Bergman and his wife Florence. Bergman was a Wayne State University professor and a teachers' union activist. Simeon Booker of *Jet Magazine* also joined the group. The journalist told Attorney General Robert Kennedy that he expected trouble, but Kennedy took no notice.

On May 4, 1961, after three days of nonviolent training, the group split in two; one group left on Greyhound and the other on Trailways. The CORE groups sat in the buses in various racial combinations, some whites in back, some blacks in front, and at least one interracial pair together. Nothing happened at stops in Fredericksburg, Richmond, Petersburg, or Farmville, Virginia. The peaceful trip turned ugly in Rock Hill, South Carolina, where three months earlier ten students had been arrested for sitting in at McCrory's lunch counter. Each had been sentenced to a $100 fine or thirty days' hard labor. Nine students had chosen hard labor. The Rock Hill jail-in held so much meaning for Lewis that he was the first Freedom Rider off the Greyhound bus to enter the Rock Hill terminal. Lewis and the man behind him, Albert Bigelow, were severely beaten by white youths in the terminal. To the disgust of the Rock Hill police captain, Lewis and Bigelow refused to press charges against the culprits. When the Trailways bus arrived two hours later, the station was closed.

A large white mob met the Greyhound bus in Anniston, Alabama. Men beat the bus with baseball bats and bricks and slashed the tires. The Anniston police were curiously missing until the bus eased through the mob in an attempt to leave. Then police appeared to direct the bus out of town. A parade of fifty cars followed. When the tires deflated from the slashes, the driver pulled the bus off the road and fled. The hoodlums smashed windows, ripped open the luggage compartment, and pried open the door. When a firebomb was tossed inside and the mob blocked the exits, one of two Alabama state police investigators who had joined the group threatened the mob with a gun. As the frightened passengers exited, the crowd beat them with clubs. Ultimately, a contingent of Alabama state troopers arrived and dispersed the crowd with warning shots in the air.

A Federal Bureau of Information (FBI) informant who had infiltrated the Ku Klux Klan told the bureau that when the Greyhound bus arrived in the city of Birmingham, police planned to give the Klan fifteen minutes of time to attack before they appeared. Reporters were waiting along with the mob. When news came that the Trailways bus would arrive first at the Trailways terminal four blocks away, the mob and the press rushed there. A Birmingham *Post-Herald* reporter took pictures of the mob beating two of the Freedom Riders. He managed to remove the film from his camera before he, too, was beaten and clubbed.

Simeon Booker, the reporter from *Jet*, escaped and made his way to the home of the Reverend Fred Shuttlesworth, who began organizing a res-

cue effort. Before the rescue crew could leave, black-owned taxis began to arrive carrying the wounded. After James Peck was refused admittance at the Carraway Methodist Hospital, doctors at Hillman Hospital closed his six wounds with fifty-three stitches. Peck astonished reporters and photographers by promising to be on the bus headed for Montgomery the following day. Shuttlesworth received a call from the Freedom Riders who had been on the burned Greyhound bus. They had been taken to Anniston Hospital and followed by the mob. Frightened hospital personnel had refused to treat them. Heavily armed volunteers drove the 60 miles to Anniston to rescue the stranded group and deliver them without incident to Birmingham hospitals.

The violence in Anniston and Birmingham made national and international headline news. To the chagrin of the new president of the Birmingham Chamber of Commerce, who was attending an international conference in Tokyo, the Japanese promptly lost interest in doing business in Birmingham.

The Freedom Riders decided they had had enough. They planned to fly from Birmingham to New Orleans, but they were pursued by a group of hoodlums who reached the airport before them. Bomb threats grounded all scheduled flights. Robert Kennedy's aide, John Seigenthaler, arranged to have airport personnel refrain from answering calls until the eighteen boarded the next plane to New Orleans and were off the ground.

Their departure did not end the Freedom Rides. Students in Nashville took over the bus trip in Birmingham that the CORE group had abandoned. The Freedom Rides continued, as did mobs, beatings, and arrests and the resulting publicity. New volunteers kept replacing those who were jailed—so many that the Freedom Riders were able to replicate a tactic used by Mahatma Gandhi—the overcrowding of jails.

Beatings and psychological intimidation went on inside the jails and prisons. The Freedom Riders irritated their jailers by singing freedom songs they had sung on the buses. Jailers became even more irritated when prisoners taught the

Freedom Riders work songs, protest songs, and gospel songs. John Lewis was jailed on forty occasions and beaten so often he later suffered a speech impediment. Four months after the beatings he received in Anniston, Wayne State Professor Walter Bergman suffered a cardiac arrest and was confined to a wheelchair for the rest of his life.

The Freedom Rides lasted for three months. They finally ended when Attorney General Robert Kennedy convinced the Interstate Commerce Commission (ICC) to issue an order he could enforce. In September 1961, the ICC ordered that all "For Colored Only" and "For White Only" signs be taken down from buses and terminal facilities used by interstate passengers. The signs were to be replaced by signs that said that segregation by race, color, creed, or national origin was unconstitutional and was punishable by fines or imprisonment or both. Farmer called off the Freedom Rides but warned that on November 1, 1961, he would send out interracial teams to crisscross the South to test enforcement of the order. If it was not obeyed, the Freedom Rides would resume immediately.

The Freedom Rides and the student sit-ins opened up a new era of confrontation for the civil rights movement. Southerners resisted, and demonstrations became more violent. The Freedom Rides occupied the stage only briefly during the long civil rights struggle, but nevertheless, they had a profound impact. Mary King, a white SNCC worker involved with a 1964 voter-registration drive in Tougaloo, Mississippi, wrote in her 1987 book *Freedom Song*, "Local black communities had been stunned by the daring of the Freedom Rides of 1961 into the mob-packed segregated bus stations of Anniston, Birmingham, and Montgomery, and finally into Jackson. For years afterward, the local people in southern hamlets called any and all civil rights workers by the stock name Freedom Riders." The Freedom Rides inspired students to think of the movement as a solemn vocation.

See also Civil Rights Movement, Sit-ins; Southern Christian Leadership Conference; Student Nonviolent Coordinating Committee; Young, Andrew

References James Farmer. *Lay Bare the Heart: An Autobiography of the Civil Rights Movement*, 1988; James Haskins. *Freedom Rides: Journey for Justice*, 1995; Mary King. *Freedom Song: A Personal Story of the 1960s Civil Rights Movement*, 1987.

Friedan, Betty (b. 1921)

The publisher of Betty Friedan's 1963 best-selling book *The Feminine Mystique* claimed that she was the "mother of the current feminist movement." Although she was by no means the only such "mother," Friedan did give a name to a growing discontent among American woman.

Born to Harry and Miriam Goldstein in Peoria, Illinois, Friedan was the oldest of their three children. She attributed her sensitivity to discrimination to her experience growing up Jewish in the Midwest. Friedan graduated summa cum laude from Smith College in 1942 and accepted a fellowship at the University of California at Berkeley. Afraid it would upset her boyfriend, Friedan turned down a renewal of the fellowship. The boyfriend lost interest in her. In 1947, after a series of dead-end jobs, she married Carl Friedan, a producer of summer stock theater, and they had three children. Friedan later described the time she spent in suburban living and raising children as "schizophrenic years of trying to be the kind of woman I wasn't."

The genesis of her book was an intensive questionnaire Friedan designed and sent out to her Smith College classmates. Friedan found restlessness and misery among educated women who stayed home. Questionnaires sent out by other colleges to their own alumnae corroborated her findings. *The Feminine Mystique* analyzed the post–World War II lives of middle-class women. Many had held responsible jobs during the war. At war's end, they were sent home to make way for returning servicemen. During the "back to the home" movement that followed, young couples moved to the suburbs and had large families. So large were their families that their offspring became known as the baby boomers, the largest population of babies in America's recorded history. The boom lasted from 1946 through 1964. Friedan accused advertisers, educators, sociologists, and psychologists of conning American women into believing they could find fulfillment only by having children. In Friedan's opinion, the feminine mystique left women without a sense of identity.

The book's popularity made Friedan a sought-after speaker on lecture circuits. As she met women around the country and asked them about their jobs and their lives, she became convinced that women, who made up more than half the population, were the world's only discriminated-against majority.

In 1966, along with other women, Friedan founded the National Organization for Women (NOW) and became its first president. At the outset, NOW focused mainly on job discrimination and on changing women's image of themselves. As the ideas of the movement spread, younger, more militant women scorned NOW as hopelessly middle class. Despite the criticism, NOW remained the largest feminist group in the country.

Friedan and her husband divorced in 1969. After Friedan stepped down from the presidency of NOW in 1970, she headed a loosely knit coalition of women's groups with the goal of having a strike on August 26, 1970, the fiftieth anniversary of the states' ratification of the Nineteenth Amendment guaranteeing women the vote. Two weeks before the strike, the U.S. House of Representatives hurriedly passed an amendment to the Constitution prohibiting discrimination on the basis of sex. The amendment had been introduced every year since 1923 but had never before come up for a vote. On the day of the strike, women in forty cities across the nation took part.

Although smaller than antiwar and civil rights demonstrations, the turnout of women was the greatest since the days of the suffragists. The largest demonstration took place in New York, where estimates of participation ranged from 10,000 to 25,000.

In 1981, Friedan published *The Second Stage*, in which she asserted that women had succumbed to the feminist mystique, which denied the core of a woman's personhood that is fulfilled through love, nurturing, and home. She suggested that women should take a fresh look at how they arranged their work lives with such possibilities as flextime, part-time work, job-sharing, and split shifts. Many feminists were offended by the book.

In 1988, she told a *Life* reporter that she was appalled at signs of a neofeminist mystique—extremely short skirts and extremely high heels. She wondered how a woman could conduct serious business in that kind of attire. She feared economic bad times could bring a return to a philosophy of a-woman's-place-is-in-the-home.

Less controversial was Friedan's 1994 book, *Fountain of Age*. In her 1997 book *Beyond Gender: The New Politics of Work and Family,* she called for a new paradigm of social policy that transcended "identity politics," the simple political issues of women, blacks, gays, and the disabled.

See also Baby Boomers; Black Feminist Organizations; Feminist Organizations; Women's Movement

Reference Betty Friedan. *The Feminine Mystique,* 1963; *The Second Stage,* 1981; *Fountain of Age,* 1994; *Beyond Gender,* 1997.

Gandhi, Mohandas (1869–1948)

Born in India to a middle-class family and trained in England as a lawyer, Mohandas Gandhi changed the status of Indians in South Africa and the status of India in the world. His strategy of nonviolence served as a model for the leaders of many social justice movements in the 1960s.

Gandhi's social activism began when he was traveling on a train in South Africa. Although he had paid for a first-class ticket, he was ordered to move to the baggage car because people with brown skin were not allowed to ride in first-class cars. When he refused, a police constable threw him off the train. For the next twenty years, Gandhi worked in South Africa to overcome discriminatory laws that relegated Indians and blacks to second-class citizenship. Gandhi called his technique of mass opposition *satyagraha,* a combination of *satya* (truth) and *agraha* (firmness). He defined it as truth-force or love-force, which inflicts suffering on oneself rather than one's enemy. Gandhi's first satyagraha campaign was against the Black Act enacted on July 1, 1907, in Transvaal, a self-governing area in the Union of South Africa. The act discriminated against all people of color—native Africans, Indians, and other Asians.

Gandhi was arrested in December for failing to register under the new law. After Gandhi and many of his followers had spent a few weeks in jail, Transvaal official General Jan Christian Smuts promised Gandhi that if Indians registered voluntarily, he would repeal the act. Indians registered, but Smuts failed to repeal the act. Gandhi announced that Indians would burn their cards in a huge bonfire. Gandhi was jailed twice more during this campaign. While in jail, he read and was impressed by American writer and philosopher Henry David Thoreau's "Civil Disobedience." (Thoreau also exerted an influence on many American antiwar activists during the 1960s.)

After the Cape Colony Supreme Court declared that only Christian marriages were valid, which meant that Indian wives had no status or rights, women persuaded miners to strike. The

protest spread. General Smuts met again with Gandhi and agreed to improve the status of Indians in South Africa. An agreement called the Indian Relief Bill was worked out, and Gandhi felt free to return to India. He spent the next thirty years in a struggle to free India from British rule.

India was wracked by social divisions in religion, caste (social class), and geographic region. Gandhi was able to mediate among the conflicting interests, all of whom were opposed to British rule. Despite the divisiveness of religion in India, Gandhi was convinced that all religions were based on holy principles worthy of respect and emulation. His lifestyle, comparable with that of ancient Hindu religious leaders, earned him the respect of all Indians—even those who disagreed with his goals.

In developing his ideas, Gandhi was influenced by the Hindu principle of working for what is right without fear. He was also inspired by Jesus Christ's Sermon on the Mount: "Blessed are the meek, for they shall inherit the earth. Blessed are the poor, for theirs is the Kingdom of God." He followed Christ's advice to "love thy neighbor." Gandhi believed in self-reform by reducing personal desires and self-indulgence. He wore only a coarse white cloth. When out of prison, he lived in a collective retreat. The retreat was located in a primitive village populated mostly by untouchables, a poverty-stricken class despised by the rest of Indian society.

Mohandas Gandhi walking with his supporters.

In appearance, Gandhi resembled an undernourished bird. Despite large ears, an enormous nose, wrinkled skin, a bald head, and a toothless smile, he had an aura of such childlike charm that his enemies, both Indian and British, tried to avoid personal encounters with him for fear he would win them over. Gandhi thought people could be taught to behave more justly. He believed oppressors would in time feel humiliated as they recognized their cruelty.

During World War I, British officials implied that India would be given self-rule and asked Gandhi to encourage Indian men to join the British army. Although he was a committed pacifist, Gandhi agreed. He felt citizenship carried obligations. Thousands volunteered. When the war was over, Britain reneged on its promise and in 1919 imposed the repressive Rowlatt Act on India. The act called for severe penalties for anyone disloyal or resistant to the government. Civil rights were curtailed, and secret trials and trials without the right of appeal were permitted.

In response to the act's passage, Gandhi called for a national day of *hartal* (mourning) to be held on March 30 in New Delhi and a week later throughout the rest of India. He asked that people close their businesses to fast and pray for freedom. Not all Indians adhered to Gandhi's nonviolent principles. In some cities, there were riots. He canceled the strike and asked supporters to fast with him in atonement for the violence.

To protest the Rowlatt Act, on April 10, 1919, about 5,000 Indians gathered at Amritsar, the holy city of the Sikh religion. Such meetings were banned. Once the crowd was inside the high walls, British general Reginald Dyer ordered soldiers, mostly native troops, to fire at the unarmed people. Ten minutes of gunfire left 379 people dead and 1,200 wounded. The massacre wiped out any lingering faith Gandhi had in the British. He became committed to a nonviolent course to free India. Twenty-eight years later, on August 15, 1947, India was declared officially independent from Great Britain. Colonial India was partitioned into Hindu India and Muslim Pakistan. Jawaharlal Nehru, a follower of Gandhi's, became the first prime minister of India. Gandhi was so saddened by the division that he did not attend the independence ceremonies.

As an estimated 15 million people displaced by the division moved during the weeks following partition, violence broke out. In response to the violence, seventy-eight-year-old Gandhi went on a fast. After six days, calm returned, and he ended his fast.

Five months later, Gandhi was dead, assassinated on January 30, 1948, by a fanatical Hindu. Nehru urged people around the world not to deify Gandhi—to see him instead as a human being striving to achieve greatness. Gandhi would have agreed. He often said he was "not a saint trying to be a politician, but a politician trying to be a saint."

See also King, Reverend Martin Luther, Jr.; Mandela, Nelson; Nonviolence; Rustin, Bayard

References Mohandas Gandhi. *Autobiography: The Story of My Experiments with the Truth*, 1963; Victoria Sherrow. *Mohandas Gandhi: The Power of the Spirit*, 1994.

Gangster Rap

The lyrics of the songs sung by young inner-city black males during the 1980s and 1990s known as gangster rap served to spread a message of dissatisfaction with life. Such young black males faced the same bleak future their fathers and grandfathers had faced. A major difference was that the angry message of the 1960s was delivered by theatrical protests and demonstrations, which had attracted media coverage. By the 1990s, the novelty had worn off.

Until 1984, the music identified with black Americans was mainly blues, jazz, gospel, and soul. In 1984 Russell Simmons and Rick Rubin created Def Jam Recordings, a company that featured music called rap (conversation or discussion). Until Def Jam came along, rap music had been thought of as East Coast street music. The new company became an almost instant success. If fans of rap had been restricted to young black males, the message of the songs would not have been heard outside the boundaries of inner-city neighborhoods. A large part of the audience turned out to be young, white, suburban males who were attracted by the music's themes of being a street gangster and of being larger than life. A lyric from one of Simmons's rap songs reflects these themes: "I've got a big, long, Caddy not like a Seville / and written on the side, it says dressed to kill."

The lyrics of East Coast rap songs focused on material acquisitions, but West Coast rap themes were substantially different. They reflected significant differences in inner-city street life between the East and West Coasts. On the East Coast, New York rappers dreamed about leaving the low-rent housing projects where they lived in the Bronx and moving to a high-rent district in Manhattan. On the West Coast, California rappers proclaimed their allegiance to the neighborhoods they lived in, such as East Los Angeles, Long Beach, and Compton.

A Compton group called NWA (Niggaz with Attitude) achieved almost instant commercial success. One NWA performer, Andre Young, also known as Dr. Dre, was in large part responsible for the music that came to be known as "'gangsta' rap."

Other groups quickly followed. The lyrics of the West Coast rappers were often violent and provoked harsh criticism from police officers and women. In just two weeks, an NWA album called *EFIL4ZAGGIN* (NIGGAZ4LIFE spelled backwards), containing a typical song "To Kill a Hooker," reached the top of the album charts. Dr. Dre told a reporter, "People are hungry for N.W.A. Nobody can do it as good as us. We're underground reporters. We're just telling the truth."

One California man, Suge (pronounced like sugar) Knight, loved the violent rap and perceived its potential for commercial success. In 1992, he persuaded Dr. Dre to join him in starting up a new recording company called Death Row. A slight problem delayed the start-up, however. Dr. Dre was under contract to Ruthless Records, owned by Eazy E, another member of NWA. According to documents filed in the Ninth Court of Appeals in San Francisco, Suge Knight and a couple of other men threatened Eazy E with baseball bats and pipes. Dr. Dre was released from his contract. Death Row's first record, *The Chronic*, sold 2 million records. ("Chronic" is slang for marijuana.) Between 1992 and 1996, Death Row sold 15 million records and grossed $100 million.

From the outset, critics accused Death Row of glamorizing violence, corrupting children's minds, and reinforcing an ugly image of black, urban life. The performers were often as violent as their lyrics. At least one was tried for murder, another for sexually assaulting a fan, and a third for violating probation for assault charges.

On May 18, 1995, former secretary of education William Bennett launched an anti–gangster rap campaign led by the conservative group "Empower America." An ad describing the campaign featured Bennett and the chairperson of the National Political Congress of Black Women. The ad attacked Time Warner for promoting music that celebrated the rape, torture, and murder of women. At the time, Time Warner controlled 22 percent of the music market. Time Warner's chairperson, Gerald Levin, asked executives to devise standards for labeling explicit music. Levin's action was a reversal of his attitude in

1992, when he defended a song called "Cop Killer," performed by Ice-T.

To many in the music industry, attacks by groups like Empower America are fueled by ignorance. One performer said, "This is our voice. If it wasn't for rap, you would never know that these horrors are going on in the community."

See also Rock and Roll
References "Cop Killer: The Sequel." *Rolling Stone,* 1995; "Rhyme or Reason?" *Time,* 1997.

Gay Liberation

Although homosexual organizations such as the Mattachine Society and the Daughters of Bilitis and student homophile groups existed before June 28, 1969, many view the events of that day as the beginning of gay liberation. At the time, police often raided gay bars and harassed patrons. They raided the Stonewall Inn in Greenwich Vil-

lage because they said the club was selling liquor without a license.

For the first time in memory, gay men fought back. Thirteen people were arrested, and four police officers were injured. The next night, the police swept the area. They were met by 400 young men and women. Many hurled bottles and coins. The Stonewall Inn had boarded-up windows covered with graffiti that read "Legalize gay bars." Members of the crowd shouted, "I'm a faggot and I'm proud of it."

Gays had never been accepted in mainstream American society. They were ridiculed, and mental health professionals labeled homosexuality an illness that should be treated with drugs, hypnotism, or electroshock therapy. When thugs drove into gay neighborhoods to beat up gays, cops ignored them. Even in the civil rights movement, they were outcasts. Black Panther Eldridge Cleaver proclaimed that homosexuality was evil.

Protesters march on Washington in support of gay and lesbian rights, October 15, 1979.

Most gays hid their sexual orientation. "Coming out of the closet" carried too many penalties, yet Stonewall galvanized many into doing just that. Activists met and announced in the underground newspaper *Rat*: "We are creating new social forms and relations, that is relations based upon brotherhood, cooperation, human love, and uninhibited sexuality."

One of the most outspoken of about fifty groups that quickly formed after Stonewall was the Gay Liberation Front. The groups began picketing companies that discriminated against them and publishing underground newspapers. By New Year's Eve, New York had fifty gay bars, San Francisco had seventy, and the Gay Liberation Front held the first gay street dances in New York, Chicago, and Berkeley. On the first anniversary of the Stonewall Inn incident, 10,000 gays marched down Sixth Avenue in New York.

In the succeeding decades, gays became a potent political force. They were elected to office, and politicians had to take them into account. Congressman Barney Frank of Massachusetts came out of the closet while in office and was reelected. But like other minorities, as individuals they continued to suffer from prejudice.

The AIDS epidemic, which came to the medical community's attention in the spring of 1981, first struck gay men. Cities with large gay populations like New York and San Francisco were hit hard. Gay organizations began a vigorous campaign to change gay sexual practices that contributed to the spread of the sexually transmitted disease, and the campaigns achieved considerable success. Gay organizations then took on the task of lobbying for treatment and research funds. Again they had considerable success. Knowledge about the basic biology of the disease accumulated rapidly. Although many new treatments came into use, the chances of a quick cure became dimmer as research continued. At the same time they lobbied, gay organizations focused on the state of care for the dying as well as on developments abroad: although AIDS was being held in check somewhat in the United States, it raged out of control in Third World countries.

See also AIDS
Reference Jonathan Katz. *Gay American History*, 1985.

Gentrification
See Baby Boomers

GI Antiwar Protests
Early in 1969, eight soldiers based at Fort Jackson, South Carolina, circulated a petition asking their commander, Brigadier General James Hollingsworth, for permission to hold an open meeting "to freely discuss legal and moral questions related to the war in Vietnam and the civil rights of American citizens within and outside the armed forces." Three hundred soldiers signed the petition. The general refused permission.

In March, 100 gathered outside their barracks and began discussing the war. Officers came, observed, and left. They later returned and restricted seven soldiers to the base and put four in the stockade. Within a few days, the army charged eight soldiers with breach of peace, inciting a riot, and disrespect to an officer. Prominent lawyers offered free counsel. College students from around the country and activist actress Jane Fonda traveled to the base to demonstrate outside. Soldiers from other bases collected signatures and sent petitions to the general. Hollingsworth did not back down.

Although the court-martial of the Fort Jackson eight was closed to the press, it received national attention. Under public scrutiny, the army dropped most of the charges and rid itself of the soldiers by giving most of them dishonorable discharges. After the trial, ten Fort Jackson soldiers sued Hollingsworth and the army for harassment and intimidation. Eventually the army won the case in federal court. In the meantime, eighty soldiers on the base signed a statement in which they accused the army of trampling on their lives in the most unpopular war in history and following a policy that would continue the tragedy for years to come.

Similar sentiments began to be voiced by

troops in Vietnam that same spring of 1969. News of antiwar feelings among GIs surfaced in connection with "Hamburger Hill." Two battalions of the 101st Airborne Division were ordered to attack Hill 937. North Vietnamese soldiers, who were deeply entrenched in bunkers, repulsed the attack, inflicting heavy casualties on the Americans. After a thirty-six-hour artillery attack, soldiers were ordered once more to attack the hill. Again they were repulsed, with heavy casualties.

After ten days, the colonel in command ordered reinforcements and another attack. It took four battalions to drive the North Vietnamese off the hill. After controlling the hill for a few days, the colonel ordered the troops to withdraw. He commented to the press, "the only significance of Hill 937 was the North Vietnamese were on it." The casualties had been so great that the troops referred to it as Hamburger Hill. A few days after the American troops left, the North Vietnamese reoccupied the hill.

A GI underground newspaper advised soldiers, "Don't desert. Go to Vietnam and kill your commanding officer." Soldiers advertised a $10,000 bounty to anyone who "fragged" (killed) the colonel who ordered the attack. The army shipped the officer back to the United States after numerous attempts on his life. A few months later, after five days of a battle similar to Hamburger Hill, the strength of Company A of the 196th Light Infantry Brigade had been cut in half—sixty soldiers were dead. When the lieutenant in charge of the men radioed his commander that Company A refused to move out, the commander flew in a sergeant who was able to cajole the exhausted men back into battle.

Company A was the first unit to refuse to obey orders, but not the last. In 1970 troop disobedience became so common that the army gave it a name, "combat refusal." In previous wars, combat refusal was viewed as treason, punishable by death. Vietnam changed that policy.

See also Antiwar Movement

Reference Melvin Small and William Hoover, eds. *Give Peace a Chance: Exploring the Vietnam Antiwar Movement*, 1992.

Ginsberg, Allen (1926–1997)

One of the most influential leaders of the Beat Generation, Allen Ginsberg was born to a couple who held leftist political philosophies. His father, Louis, was a socialist, and his mother, Naomi, was a communist. His mother was also schizophrenic. She first displayed symptoms in 1919, the year she married Louis.

Irwin Allen, the family's second child, usually called Allen, was born in 1926. When Allen was three, his mother checked herself into a sanatorium. In the years that followed, she had intermittent stays in sanatoriums. During the periods when she was home, her paranoid delusions dominated family life. Allen became increasingly torn by his identification with his mother's paranoia and his father's complaints.

Allen's mother often took him and his brother Eugene to communist meetings and spun fairy tales about princes who helped the working classes. His father, who taught English at the Paterson, New Jersey, Central High School, strove to maintain stability for his two sons. On weekends, he took his sons to family get-togethers, where Allen experienced generosity from relatives that carried over into his adult life. In his spare time, Louis wrote poetry, which was often published in small magazines.

Allen was often frightened by images in his mind that appeared later in his poetry. He began writing his thoughts in a journal at age 11. In 1943, he received a small scholarship that enabled him to switch from Montclair State College in New Jersey to Columbia. At Columbia, he met Jack Kerouac, a former student, Lucien Carr, William Burroughs, and Neal Cassady. Together they formed the nucleus of the Beat Generation.

Over time, Ginsberg became known as the poet laureate of the Beat Generation. The most significant influences on his poetry came from eight months in a psychiatric hospital in 1949 and the poets William Blake, Walt Whitman, Ezra Pound, and William Carlos Williams. Many supporters and detractors believe his poem "Howl!", written in 1955–1956, served as a blueprint for the sexual revolution in the decades following the 1950s. Candor was a Ginsberg hallmark. He advo-

Poet Allen Ginsberg.

cated freedom of expression, and long before the gay liberation movement, he was open about his own homosexuality. "Howl!" not only served as a symbol of open sexuality, it also became a landmark case in an ongoing struggle with censorship. U.S. Customs agents seized a booklet of "Howl! and Other Poems" and charged Ginsberg with obscenity. After a long trial, Judge Clayton Horn ruled that the poem did not lack "redeeming social importance."

Three years after his mother's death, Ginsberg wrote "Kaddish for Naomi Goldberg (1894–1956)," an elegy that many consider his finest poem. "Kaddish" enhanced his reputation and established him as a major voice. Over the years he continued to write. Later major works included "TV Baby" in 1960; "Wichita Vortex Sutra" in 1966; "Wales Visitation" in 1967; "Don't Grow Old" in 1976; and "White Shroud" in 1983. Ginsberg received several awards, and in 1985 Harper and Row published his *Collected Poems,* an anthology of his work in one volume. The book signaled his acceptance as a poet in mainstream American literature.

Ginsberg's celebrity status enabled him to travel widely during the 1960s and 1970s and to participate in a succession of social movements: the sexual revolution and drug culture of the 1960s, the antiwar and anti-CIA demonstrations of the 1970s, and the anti-Shah and anti-Reagan protests of the 1980s.

In 1986 Ginsberg became a full-time faculty member at Brooklyn College, where he remained until his death. He nurtured young poets and gave active support to the Poetry Project at St. Martin's Church. Although Ginsberg was famous worldwide, his work remained rooted in lower Manhattan, where he lived most of his adult life. A few months before his death, he participated in a rally to support squatters occupying an apartment building on East 13th Street.

A negative critique of the impact Ginsberg had on American society came from Norman Podhoretz, who was the editor-in-chief of *Commentary* for 35 years before become an editor-at-large. He wrote in an August 1997 article entitled "My War with Allen Ginsberg," which appeared in *Commentary,* "It always struck me as odd that so many of the dissidents in Czechoslovakia, all of whom were passionate anti-Communists, should have made heroes out of Ginsberg and other icons of the counterculture, all of whom were equally passionate anti-anti-communists."

See also Beat Generation
References Allen Ginsberg. *Collected Poems, 1947–1980,* 1984; Wilborn Hampton. "Allen Ginsberg, Master Poet of Beat Generation, Dies at 70," 1997; Barry Miles. *Ginsberg: A Biography,* 1989; Norman Podhoretz. "My War with Allen Ginsberg," 1997.

Glaser, Elizabeth (1947–1994)

On July 14, 1992, AIDS activist Elizabeth Glaser spoke at the Democratic National Convention about the ordeal that had propelled her into action on behalf of AIDS victims. (AIDS, or acquired immune deficiency syndrome, destroys the immune system, leaving its victims vulnerable to infections.) She said, "I started out as just a mom—fighting for the life of her child . . . I learned how unfair America can be. Not just for people who have HIV [human immunodeficiency virus], but for many, many people—gay people, people of color, children."

Glaser told the delegates that she had been raised to believe that other people's problems were her problems, but most people did not want to hear about AIDS. "Two HIV commission reports," she said, "with recommendations about what to do to solve this crisis are sitting on shelves, gathering dust." Glaser reminded the delegates that a young boy named Ryan White, a hemophiliac who contracted AIDS, had been banned from his school. His parents had then moved to another community, where the school welcomed him. Worldwide, he served as a symbol of courage to young people.

Glaser told the delegates about her daughter Ariel, who died of AIDS at age 7. "In her last year, when she couldn't walk or talk, her wisdom shone through. She taught me to love when all I wanted to do was hate. She taught me to help others, when all I wanted to do was help myself. She taught me to be brave, when all I felt was fear."

A former early childhood teacher and happy wife and mother, Glaser was married to television actor Paul Michael Glaser. She contracted AIDS during Ariel's birth, when she was given blood contaminated with HIV to replace blood lost in a hemorrhage. The virus was passed on to Ariel in breast milk. When Ariel was 4, she began to exhibit symptoms that confounded physicians until she was finally tested for HIV. Elizabeth and Jake, Ariel's younger brother, also had HIV. Elizabeth's husband did not.

In her book *In the Absence of Angels*, Glaser talked about years of being cut off from friends, of trying to find preschools that would accept her children, of dealing with Ariel's constant physical pain. On August 12, 1988, Ariel died. Glaser then felt she had to find a way to save Jake from the same fate. Late in President Ronald Reagan's second term in office, she obtained a meeting with the president and his wife. Apparently moved by her story, Reagan promised to spearhead a push to increase attention to AIDS in children and to give serious attention to a report on AIDS, which he had ordered. He did neither.

By June of 1990, in the United States, 2,380 children had full-blown AIDS and at least 20,000 children had contracted HIV but had not yet exhibited symptoms. Worldwide, there were more than 700,000 infected children. The World Health Organization (WHO) predicted that by the year 2000, 10 million or more children would have been infected, and most would be dead.

Glaser understood that the period of time between when Congress approved funding for research and the time when researchers received funds could be eighteen months to two years or longer. To save Jake's life, she had to do something other than lobby the government. With two friends, Susan De Laurentis and Susan Zeegan, she established the Pediatric AIDS Foundation. Glaser approached an elderly, wealthy aunt of her husband's for help in raising money to start the foundation. The aunt pledged $500,000. Glaser's approach to fund-raising was unusual. She would say, "Could you please give the Pediatric AIDS Foundation everything you are ever going to give? We need the research going immediately. Three years from now is too late. I need as much money as you can spare and then if you never want to see me again, tell me and that will be fine."

Glaser and her two friends didn't want the foundation to duplicate research already being done by government researchers. They wanted to work in tandem on basic unanswered questions. Why did only a third of all mothers with AIDS pass it on to their children? What therapies might be most effective for the opportunistic infections to which children were vulnerable? The three women were stunned to find there was no basic government research being done.

Among the researchers Glaser met was physician Jim Oleske of Newark Children's Hospital. He saw his first patient with AIDS in 1976, five years before June 1981, when the Centers for Disease Control published a report about five men with the strange symptoms that came to be known as AIDS. Oleske was never able to get government funding. It was difficult to make people believe that the disease affected children. The first funding Oleske received was from prisoners at a nearby prison, who gave him $1,000. He had taken care of one of the inmate's children.

Glaser and her friends set out to pressure the Food and Drug Administration to speed up drug research for children. The AIDS drug azidothymidine (AZT) was available to adults two years before it was available for children. Their pressure succeeded in whittling the time down to a year, which they felt was still too long.

She and her friends succeeded in having a benefit in Washington, D.C., sponsored by Democratic senator Howard Metzenbaum of Ohio and Republican senator Orrin Hatch of Utah, two men who seldom agreed on anything. The benefit raised $1 million.

To protect Jake from the ostracism children with HIV often suffered—in spite of all her lobbying—Glaser was able to keep her and Jake's health status a secret. When her family's privacy was threatened by the tabloid the *National Enquirer*, she and her husband gave the story to the *Los Angeles Times*. Her fears that her son would be shunned did not materialize.

Elizabeth Glaser died of AIDS in 1994. At the time, her son was still free of AIDS symptoms.

See also AIDS
Reference Elizabeth Glaser. *In the Absence of Angels*, 1991.

Goodman, Andrew
See Chaney, Goodman, and Schwerner, Murders of

Grateful Dead
The band known as the Grateful Dead began in San Francisco in the 1960s, during a transition period between the beats and the hippies. The band members aspired to the bohemian, unconventional, nonconformist philosophy of the beats. They became a symbol of their generation to millions of fans. Members of the Grateful Dead were also fascinated by jazz and Zen, a form of Buddhism that seeks to achieve an illumination of the mind and spirit. They believed in existentialism, a doctrine that asserts individuals are free and responsible for their own acts. Beats did not admire the Grateful Dead members in return.

Particularly, they did not like electronic music, nor they did welcome changes brought by hippies. The hippies in time became bored with the beats and their seemingly endless discussions of French existentialist philosophers.

The members of the Grateful Dead were all born in northern California and proud to be a part of San Francisco's tradition of long-haired, bearded poets and eccentrics. Jerry Garcia, who was generally thought of as having been the Grateful Dead's leader, played banjo and guitar, sang in a gravelly voice, and had an extensive knowledge of folk, bluegrass, and gospel. His father, who was a clarinetist and a band leader, died when Garcia was young. Garcia was 15 when Jack Kerouac's book about the beats, *On the Road*, came out. The pursuit of pleasure and mysticism outlined in this book became a blueprint for his life.

Band member Ron McKernan, better known as "Pigpen," had an encyclopedic knowledge about blues music. His father was one of the first white rhythm and blues disc jockeys on a black station in Oakland. Pigpen played keyboards, was an alcoholic by age 13, and was dead by age 27—the band's first casualty.

Band member Bobby Weir had a band in high school called the Uncalled Four. He spent his last year of high school skipping classes and teaching himself to play the guitar. Bobby met Jerry on New Year's Eve in 1963. While wandering the streets with a friend, too young to be admitted to clubs, he heard the sound of banjo picking coming from the rear of Dana Morgan's music store. Garcia, unaware that it was New Year's Eve, was waiting for his guitar students to put in an appearance. The boys persuaded Garcia to let them come in and join him. After a couple of hours of playing on the store's guitars, Garcia and the boys decided to form a jug band, a group that uses unconventional or improvised instruments, such as jugs, washboards, and kazoos (toy instruments).

For about six months, Mother McCree's Uptown Jug Champions played the local folk circuit. A variety of people dropped in and out of the band. Dana Morgan, the owner of the music store, whose son played bass, offered to pay for electric instruments for the group, and they changed their name to the Warlocks. Band member Phil Lesh, a horn player, played trumpet for the Berkeley High School jazz band and was an engineer for "The Midnight Special," a folk music program on Berkeley's station KPFA. Jerry was a regular guest on the program, and the two became friends. Phil shared Garcia's enthusiasm for the beats. When Dana Morgan became too busy to play the Warlocks' gigs, Phil learned to play the bass in a week. Jerry found the band's drummer, Bill Kreutzmann, through the music store. He had played in a few rock and roll bands. Until 1965, rock and roll was considered crass and commercial in the area.

The Warlocks had a better chance of becoming a cohesive group than other local bands for whom music was an activity they did in their spare time. They played together in noisy, rowdy pizza pubs, unlike the hushed reverence of coffeehouses where other bands played. Folk music did not fare well in a demanding setting like a pizza pub. Pigpen encouraged the band to focus on traditional blues and on rhythm and blues.

The band's first gig as the Grateful Dead was in December 1965. Musically, the band members were not an ideal fit. They learned to play to each other's weaknesses. The result was the unique sound characteristic of the Grateful Dead.

Ken Kesey set up most of the band's early gigs, most of which were "Acid Tests," which meant that everyone present partied furiously and was on lysergic acid diethylamide (LSD), a psychedelic drug that produces hallucinations. Many observers have wondered how two ragtag groups like the Rolling Stones and the Grateful Dead, who used drugs and subscribed to a bohemian perspective, managed to hold together as bands. Despite their chaotic behavior and drug use, the Grateful Dead thought of themselves as professionals. No matter what else happened, the band showed up on time and played the whole gig. Pigpen, who didn't take acid, and Rock Scully, the band's manager, kept the band anchored during Acid Tests. Scully would say, "It not just another Acid Test; it's a gig. We're selling tickets, you guys! Must remember: these people paid *money* to hear you."

After 1968, none of the band members wanted to live any longer in the Haight-Ashbury area, the neighborhood where hippies had settled around the intersection of Haight and Ashbury streets. After three years of communal living, they gradually drifted to Marin County and into separate homes. According to Scully, "For the oldest juveniles in the state of California, it was a bit like leaving home."

With a goal of breaking a cycle of gang violence in the Bay Area, in 1969 Rock Scully suggested the Grateful Dead and the Rolling Stones give a free concert at Golden Gate Park. To reduce the size of the crowds, the Park Department required the bands to refrain from announcing the concert until twenty-four hours before it was due to take place. Mick Jagger of the Rolling Stones blurted out their plans, and the Park Department revoked the permit.

The Altamont Speedway was selected as an alternative site, a disastrous choice. By the time the bands arrived, fights were breaking out. The Grateful Dead left without playing. The Rolling Stones had hired members of the Hell's Angels to handle security, a task for which they had no aptitude. Fans were killed: one was stabbed; one drowned in an irrigation canal; and two were run over in their sleeping bags. Woodstock, a rock and folk festival held in Woodstock, New York, also in 1969, remembered by many who participated as a highlight of their young lives, was a celebration of peace and love. Altamont was a celebration of violence, guns, and drugs.

In his book *Living with the Dead* (1996), written with David Dalton, Rock Scully proposed that Woodstock and Altamont were the end products of the same disease. "The bloating of mass bohemia in the late sixties. The Haight [Haight-Ashbury community] worked because it was a small, closely knit community where everyone knew each other and shared a common vision. Then came the attempt to re-create the vibe on a larger and larger scale. At that point, Mercury, the patron of the merchants and thieves, took over and started setting up bleachers on Highway 61."

The band's failure to play at Altamont was a rare occurrence for the Grateful Dead. They played a couple of hundred concerts a year. One reason they played so many was that the band allowed fans to bring tape recorders to concerts. The circulation of fan-recorded tapes of their concerts reduced sales of their records. As a consequence, they had to play more concerts than other bands that made more income from records.

In 1972, the band undertook a tour of Europe with the same casualness they did everything else. It meant traveling in twin buses for two months with seven musicians and a singer, five managers, five office staff, ten equipment handlers (to handle 15,000 pounds of sound equipment), four drivers, and an assortment of seventeen friends, wives, elderly ladies, and babies. To pay for the expense of the trip, the band had to record every concert. When the entourage of forty-nine returned from the tour, the band found sacks containing thousands of letters from fans. The fans had responded to a message Garcia put inside one of the Grateful Dead's albums. Garcia's message read: "DEAD FREAKS UNITE. Who are you? Where are you? How are you? Send us your name and address and we'll keep you informed."

The letters—reputed to be as many as 25,000—inspired in the Grateful Dead visions of having their own recording company and a list of fans to whom they would sell their records. The major flaw with their reasoning was that the day-to-day business of running a record company involved the kinds of tasks they had spent their lives avoiding. In addition, they knew nothing about operating a record company. Undaunted, the band's company, Grateful Dead Records—along with Round Records for band members' solo projects—came into being on April 19, 1973. It lasted until 1976.

On September 9, 1974, the band began its second European tour. As it had during the 1972 European tour, drug use seemed to dominate the band members' lives. Fire marshals all over Europe were made anxious by the band's equipment, a complex arrangement of wires, cables, and generators. In Munich, Germany, the band provided great quantities of beer backstage for the firefighters present during the concert. Beer

drinking on duty in Germany was not frowned on. The firefighters were rendered harmless by acid-laced beer.

Garcia was a perpetual fire hazard, given his beard and his penchant for smoking cigarettes and joints (marijuana cigarettes). During the concert, Garcia was smoking a huge, loosely rolled joint laced with hashish (another drug made from the hemp plant, like marijuana). The joint was coming apart, spilling chunks of tobacco and drugs onto the stage. On the amplifier rested another joint and two cigarettes. Smoke curled up into the klieg lights, and ashes drifted off the amplifier. One firefighter still able to function perceived Garcia and his amplifier as a conflagration about to happen. He threw a bucket of water over Garcia and another over his amplifier. The house went black. The audience began lighting matches and cigarette lighters, creating another fire hazard. The shut-off circuits of the band's transformers protected their equipment. However, the surge of electricity blacked out a large section of Munich.

Starting in late 1974, the band took a year off. For most of the members, the layoff brought with it the shock of adjusting to no income while supporting an expensive lifestyle and a huge, ongoing drug bill. For a friend who was in trouble with the Federal Bureau of Investigation (FBI) over drugs, Scully secured false identity papers. The friend was an informant, and Scully spent eight months in jail.

When the Grateful Dead band was not scheduled to play, Garcia played clubs with his Jerry Garcia Band. He lived a constant round of playing gigs and taking drugs. To get away from fans, in 1982 Garcia and Scully moved into a house with two apartments. Garcia lived on the first floor and Scully on the second. Garcia's apartment—all black—resembled a tomb. He no longer wanted to be Garcia and began to withdraw. He stopped showering and changing his clothes and became belligerent if someone suggested he should.

By 1983, Garcia's life had been reduced to being secluded in his apartment with music, drugs, junk food, ice cream, and cigarettes. His and Scully's daily life revolved around getting sufficient drugs to get through the day. Garcia had an uncanny ability to convince himself that their drug addictions were temporary. When one of the band members threatened to fire Garcia, he reminded him that the band could not get along without him. Alarmed at Garcia's deteriorating physical condition, Scully called a physician. The band blamed Scully for Garcia's condition and gave him six months off with pay.

At the end of six months, Scully realized he didn't want to return. After devoting twenty years to the Grateful Dead, Scully's life with the band was over. After detoxification, Scully tried drugs one more time. He awoke to find himself on a hill with his car straddling cable car tracks. Drugs lost their attraction.

Garcia was never able to overcome his drug habit. He suffered a fatal heart attack at a drug rehabilitation center in Marin County in April 1996. The estate he left behind was no less chaotic than the life he had led.

Garcia's widow, Deborah Koons Garcia, who was his third wife, refused to permit his second wife, Carolyn "Mountain Girl" Adams Garcia, to join the shipboard memorial service to scatter Garcia's ashes. Despite inheriting an estate worth hundreds of millions of dollars, Koons Garcia, who had been married to Garcia only twenty-six months, refused to honor a divorce settlement Garcia had made with his second wife, with whom he had lived on and off for twenty-six years and by whom he had fathered two children. Adams Garcia took her former husband's widow to court. During the trial, Koons Garcia insisted that the agreement to pay Adams Garcia $5 million and the marriage between Garcia and his second wife were not valid. The judge ruled that a marriage that required a divorce was a valid one. Koons Garcia was ordered to honor the agreement.

In clubs around the country, the fans who had responded to Garcia's plea to hear from his fans continued to cherish Garcia and the Grateful Dead after Garcia's death. They called themselves Dead Heads. A Dead Head testified at the trial filed by his second wife against his widow that the band did not have a designated leader and

subscribed to a beat/hippie democratic ethos of joint decisionmaking.

In an afterword to his book, Scully wrote: "However much he would have protested, Jerry was the heart and soul and magic of the Grateful Dead and in the end that was too much of a burden for him to bear." About Garcia's drug use, Scully wrote: "I think for Jerry drugs were a way of reconciling his contradictions. He was a nest of paradoxes: outgoing recluse; gullible hipster; ironic Utopian; self-effacing star. . . . He was an oddity in the narcissistic world of rock 'n' roll: a true beatnik who cared nothing for his image, a bashful lead singer, an introvert with such debilitating stage fright he was unable to eat anything before going on stage."

See also Beat Generation; Rock and Roll
Reference Rock Scully with David Dalton. *Living with the Dead: Twenty Years on the Bus with Garcia and the Grateful Dead*, 1996.

Gray Panthers

In 1970, the United Presbyterian Church told Maggie Kuhn that she had to retire from her executive position following her up-coming sixty-fifth birthday, although male executives had been allowed to continue to work following theirs. The church permitted her to stay on until the end of the calendar year. Emotionally, Kuhn was unprepared for the edict. After months of being dazed and hurt, she became outraged. She realized that the problem was not hers alone. An activist most of her adult life, Kuhn did what activists do—she called other activists.

Five professional women, all associated with nonprofit social and religious groups, met with Kuhn for lunch. Eleanor French had been the director of the student division of the World Young Women's Christian Association (YWCA) in Geneva. Helen Smith worked for the United Church of Christ. Polly Cuthbertson was the director of the American Friends Service Committee College Program. Anne Bennett was a religious educator who had worked on the Women's Strike for Peace. Helen Baker was a former editor of *The Churchwoman* and a reporter with the

United Nations. All faced retirement. All wanted to continue their involvement in social action bearing on important policy issues of the day— war and peace, the presidential elections, poverty, and civil liberties. Seasoned bureaucrats, they called a meeting to which a hundred people came.

The meeting participants agreed to form a social action group. The first order of business was unanimous agreement that the group was opposed to the Vietnam War. Over the next several months, the group educated themselves and worked out priorities. Some members wanted to work on specific problems of the aged, such as a national health plan, pension rights, age discrimination in the workplace, and participation in organizations that governed their lives. Others wanted to work on larger public issues, such as the Vietnam War, availability of affordable housing, health care, and the 1972 presidential elections. Ultimately, the group decided to work both on behalf of the old and for the common good.

The initial name the group gave itself was the Consultation of Older Persons. Opposition to the Vietnam War put group members in contact with the young who were opposing the war. When two of the founding members, Eleanor French and Helen Smith, died within weeks of each other in early 1971, a young student from Haverford College said, "You old people are as transient as the students—here one year, gone the next."

Maggie Kuhn and Hobart Jackson, a social worker and director of the Stephen Smith Geriatric Center, a nursing home for poor blacks in Southwest Philadelphia, sought to have input into a White House conference on Aging scheduled for the fall of 1971. Jackson opted to organize a Black House Conference on Aging and Kuhn assisted him. Two weeks before the scheduled White House conference, nine hundred people, mostly elderly blacks, assembled at the New York Avenue Presbyterian Church in Washington, D.C., for a two-day Black House conference. Lacking money for hotel rooms, many slept overnight in the church.

Arthur Flemming, whom President Nixon had appointed to head the White House conference, asked for a meeting with the organizers of the Black House conference. Before the meeting, seventy-five of the conference participants, mostly elderly women, marched from the church to the White House gates with a list of demands for reducing disparities between blacks and whites in health care, housing, and income. At the locked gates, group members asked the guards to deliver their message to the president. A team of police on horses approached and ordered the group to move away. Fannie Jefferson, the march leader, refused. Whistles sounded and the horses charged. Kuhn was knocked down. Jefferson was handcuffed, whisked away, and charged with disorderly conduct.

The charges against Jefferson were dropped at the request of officials connected with the White House conference. Flemming arranged for more minority representation and added the Black House conference issues to the White House conference agenda. Kuhn obtained press credentials to attend the White House conference for herself and two of Consultation's young members. The three wrote press releases every day criticizing the proceedings of the conference and distributed them among the reporters present. Reporters sought them out for interviews. President Nixon closed the conference with a speech in which he proposed an allocation of $100 million to a new nutrition program for the elderly. The conference brought unprecedented attention to the problems of the old.

At Hobart Jackson's suggestion, the Consultation of Older Persons changed its name to the Gray Panthers and opened up an office in a former janitors' broom closet of the Tabernacle Church in West Philadelphia.

In 1972, Ralph Nader launched an organization called the Retired Professional Action Group with the goal of using retired people as volunteers or employees on social action projects. He asked Maggie Kuhn to move to Washington, D.C., to lead the new organization. Because the health of her mentally ill brother was deteriorating, she reluctantly declined. Nader moved the operation to the basement of Kuhn's house. Having outgrown the janitors' closet at the Tabernacle Church, the Gray Panthers moved into an assembly room and hired two full-time staff members. By 1974, the Gray Panthers had chapters in most major U.S. cities and many smaller ones.

The Gray Panthers set out to change attitudes of gerontologists. Most assumed that intellectual and emotional deterioration was an inevitable consequence of advancing age. Kuhn was convinced that gerontologists had a vested interest in maintaining an illusion that age was incapacitating. During the 1970s, she engaged in a running debate with the American Gerontological Society that peaked in a debate with the society's president at the 1978 annual meeting in San Francisco.

The Gray Panthers focused attention on America's health care system. Passage of Medicare in 1966 helped ease some financial burdens of health care for the elderly, but it did nothing to help the aged to live with chronic diseases and disabilities, find home health care services, arrange transportation to and from medical services, or obtain financial help when Medicare and personal funds were not enough to pay for services.

To capture the attention of the American Medical Association (AMA) during the group's 1974 annual meeting at the Palmer House in Chicago, Panthers, dressed as doctors and nurses, tried to revive a comatose AMA on the front steps of the hotel. A Panther dressed in a hospital gown labeled "Sick AMA" lay on a stretcher in the lobby while a team tried to resuscitate him. Vital signs returned only after the team removed wads of paper money from his chest.

At the twentieth anniversary of the founding of the Gray Panthers, representatives attended from many groups the Panthers had founded: the Older Women's League, the Black Caucus for the Aged, the National Shared Housing Resource Center, and the National Coalition for Nursing Home Reform.

Maggie Kuhn died in 1991. The Gray Panthers carried on.

See also American Association of Retired People; Black Panther Party
Reference Maggie Kuhn with Christina Long and Laura Quinn. *No Stone Unturned: The Life and Times of Maggie Kuhn,* 1991.

Great Peace March (March 1–November 15, 1986)

The Great Peace March, also known as GPM or Peace City, came together to form a small community of people organized around the idea of nuclear disarmament. GPM began with more than 1,000 people pledged to march across the United States to alert the world's governments that the nuclear arms race could destroy the global human and animal populations.

The idea for the march came from David Mixner, a 39-year-old partner in a Los Angeles public relations firm. He was galvanized by his 6-year-old niece, who said she was afraid she would not grow up because of the bomb. In April 1985, he announced the organization of People Reaching Out for Peace (PRO-Peace). Mixner's charisma inspired a staff of 150 men and women to join him. Most were quite young, and most were white. PRO-Peace's biggest obstacle became Mixner's behavior—he operated as if he were accountable to no one.

When big bills began to flow in and big donations did not materialize, the march looked doomed before it could get started. Mixner suggested the faint of heart should go home, but people who had given up homes, jobs, and a way of life to join were not about to give up before they started. Despite the difficulties, the march began on March 1, 1986, in Los Angeles. The marchers were convinced that nuclear disarmament was essential for human survival and contended that money spent on weapons became unavailable for life's necessities. The cost of a nuclear submarine could build 450,000 homes.

The first of many astonishing rescues happened in Claremont, California. When the march couldn't get insurance to protect organizers and owners of sites where they stayed from any liability in case of accident, church organizations found overnight homes for some and space on church grounds for others. Gagni Trotter, whose husband was a theology professor, organized the Claremont arrangement. She later said, "The march was one of the most exciting things that happened to Claremont. It was a unifying thing that brought all kinds of people together."

Early in the march, the group camped on a Bureau of Land Management (BLM) site in the Mojave Desert. The BLM supervisor, Alden Siever, compiled a sixteen-page document about the march and sent it along with a handwritten letter to every BLM office with which he thought the march might come in contact. In the letter, he said the marchers had treated the land with "tender, loving care and flagging was put around little creosote bushes to keep them from getting crushed." Siever's help was immeasurable.

The marchers ranged from toddlers to octogenarians. They came from a wide range of socioeconomic backgrounds. Two participants wrote a book about the eight-and-a-half-month march. The authors were Frank Folsom, age 80, writer, scholar, and longtime activist, and Connie Fledderjohann, age 57, teacher and psychotherapist. They were aided in their research by fellow marcher Gerda Lawrence, age 65, a clinical social worker, who conducted extensive interviews with other marchers. Their book, *The Great Peace March,* traced the impact the march had on the marchers and on the communities through which they passed.

Communities reluctant to have the march pass through became impressed by the marchers' commitment and friendliness. The marchers left communities neater than they found them. In Cedar City, Utah, Mayor Robert Linford planned to present the key to his town to Peace City during a rally at the local park. While marcher Diane Clark, the march's "litter lady," was at City Hall to make arrangements about litter pickup, she was asked about how the presentation should take place. The ceremony became a ritual repeated across the country. Clark became Peace City's ceremonial mayor. On each occasion, she exchanged keys with local officials, and the group planted a peace tree.

Almost everywhere the marchers stopped, they met people who had been encouraged by the march's example to do something about working for peace. A reporter from the Iowa City *Press Citizen* quit her job and joined the march. A chance meeting with marchers in Colorado made Pennsylvania dentist Edward Bronall want to help. His staff and several colleagues cleaned marchers' teeth when they passed through Philadelphia.

For many marchers, the walk fostered a newfound positive attitude toward Americans, a "belief in the people of this country in their wonderful goodness." After PRO-Peace failed to provide financial support, those left had little except their few personal possessions and tents. The march turned them into a community. There was always a crisis, but the marchers pulled together. The consensus form of government kept most feeling included, and the physical acts of walking and camping bonded them together.

At the outset, few marchers had experience with large-scale food preparation to feed 300–1,000 people three times a day. They learned well enough to cook for guests. Whenever the marchers neared a state line, they made a cake in the shape of the state the march was leaving. The cake was shared with the highway patrol and police officers who had helped the group and the people from the peace organizations from the new state who had come to meet them.

The logistics of keeping the march organized, fed, and housed were only one aspect of keeping the march on course. Others involved scouting sites, getting permits, alerting police, planning routes, and attending to cleanup and restoration of the sites used. About thirty-eight separate people or committees were needed to get everything accomplished.

As the marchers approached Washington, D.C., the ranks of marchers swelled with people who bused or flew in to join. By the time they reached the capital, they numbered 1,800. In silence, the marchers walked down 16th Street toward the White House, accompanied only by a lone bagpipe and the beat of Buddhist drums. President Ronald Reagan did not acknowledge their presence. The 3,701-mile walk from Los Angeles by way of New York ended on November 15, 1986. Separation was almost as difficult as coming together and staying together had been. The wide variety of skills learned by the marchers during their trek across the United States enabled many to continue their efforts on behalf of peace. They fanned out across America as local peace organizers or as members of many other peace organizations, such as SANE/FREEZE, Physicians for Social Responsibility, and Women's International League for Peace. A group of marchers settled near Boulder, Colorado, to organize actions against the Rocky Flats plant, manufacturer of nuclear triggers.

"Collective Vision," one of several musical groups that sprang up on the march, went on a nationwide tour in 1987, spreading peace through music.

See also Peace Movement; Plowshares Movement
Reference Franklin Folsom and Connie Fledderjohann. *The Great Peace March: An American Odyssey*, 1988.

Great Society

The term "Great Society" was coined by President Lyndon Johnson to refer to his plans to reduce the level of poverty in the United States and to make the country a better place to live for everyone. Many of the programs had been conceived as part of the Kennedy administration's "New Frontier" programs but had little success in getting through Congress. Johnson exploited the public's guilt and grief to push through Kennedy's stalled New Frontier. Less than a week after the assassination, Johnson spoke to a special session of both houses of Congress. He endorsed pending civil rights legislation, the stalled tax bill, the delayed federal education bill, and a measure to stimulate youth employment. He announced that he intended to promote Kennedy's campaign against poverty, which at the time was little more than an idea.

In his 1996 book *The Best Intentions: The Triumphs and Failures of the Great Society under Kennedy, Johnson, and Nixon*, historian Irwin Unger points out that Johnson was not a standard liberal or a conventional conservative. He mingled with liberals and tycoons with equal comfort. He revered Franklin Delano Roosevelt and his own father, who had fought for the common man during his two terms as a Texas legislator. Regardless of ideology, Johnson was softhearted. Aide Larry O'Brien recalled that he became almost emotionally involved in the subject of poverty. Texas lawyer Harry McPherson said that Johnson was "as self-centered a man as ever was," but he had a rare capacity "to empathize."

Johnson never shared the class resentments and the antibusiness bias of populists and of Roosevelt's supporters. To defend the poor did not mean finding villains or creating enemies. He cherished consensus. Ideally, he converted opponents, he did not defeat them.

Johnson had not been included in White House discussions about poverty. He learned about them the day after the assassination. He told aides to make poverty his highest priority and to create a plan. He was unhappy with their first plan, which he thought was a puny demonstration program. He wanted a big and bold program that would have impact. In his State of the Union address on January 8, 1964, he said, "This administration today, here and now, declares unconditional war on poverty in America." The struggle would not be easy, he said, but "we shall not rest until that war is won." In his March 1964 speech to Congress accompanying the Economic Opportunity Act (the War on Poverty law), Johnson said, "today, for the first time in our history it is possible to conquer poverty."

Two theories exist about how the war on poverty came into existence. The bottom-up theory claims that the Reverend Martin Luther King, Jr., moved the nation with his "I Have a Dream" speech at the 1963 Washington march for "jobs and freedom" and shifted the attention of the civil rights movement from voter registration to issues of poverty. The top-down theory claims that poverty was not confined to blacks and that work was already in progress before the Washington march. Michael Harrington's book *The Other America* in 1962 had a significant impact. Middle-class Americans could better enjoy their prosperity if its benefits were not confined to the rich.

There was more than one reason that Americans accepted attempts to eliminate poverty. First, in the global struggle with communism, it was difficult to maintain a claim of superiority in the presence of a large group of poor. Second, America had a long history of distinguishing the "deserving poor" from the "undeserving poor."

Widows, orphans, and victims of acts of God deserved compassion and help, whereas those engaged in self-destructive behavior did not. For a time in the early 1960s, class blame abated.

In 1965, Johnson submitted eighty-seven bills of social legislation to the new Democratic-majority Congress. Within nine months, eighty-four of the bills had been signed into law. Those bills included the clean air and water acts, creation of the National Endowments for the Arts and Humanities, the Equal Employment Opportunity Act, and the development of the Head Start program for preschoolers.

The period of benevolence toward all the poor did not last long. By the 1980s, programs aimed at the poor, the aged, and inner-city children were deemed an unnecessary burden. Compassion had deteriorated to the extent that by the 1990s, the middle class and affluent complained when the homeless begged for money on city streets.

Because it failed to eradicate poverty and welfare programs, the Great Society is often proclaimed a failure. The programs designed to make life healthier and more comfortable for the middle class are seldom mentioned. In the foreword to his book, Unger lists a few of the advantages available to all Americans that came into being because of Great Society legislation. He made the list during a drive from New York to Austin, Texas. Once-common junkyards and commercial road signs had disappeared from the edges of highways. Clean, well-equipped rest stops were available every 100 miles or so. National Public Radio offered a fare of classical music, in-depth news, and sophisticated discussions and interviews. Seatbelts and collapsible steering columns made the trip safer. At Assateague Island in Virginia, a national seashore preserve established by Lyndon Johnson in 1965, nature walks provided glimpses of wild ponies.

See also Harrington, Michael
References Michael Harrington. *The Other America*, 1982; Michael Katz. *The Undeserving Poor: From the War on Poverty to the War on Welfare*, 1989; Irwin Unger. *The Best of Intentions: The Triumph and Failure of the Great Society under Kennedy, Johnson, and Nixon*, 1996.

Greenpeace

The predecessor of Greenpeace, an organization called "Don't Make a Wave," came into being to protest the testing of nuclear bombs on the tiny island of Amchitka. Near the tip of the Aleutians off the coast of Alaska, Amchitka was a haven for wildlife and located in one of the planet's most earthquake-prone zones. In 1964, it was the site of a massive earthquake that cut a 500-mile path of destruction and generated a series of tsunamis (tidal waves) from Oregon to Japan. In the eighteen months after the initial quake, there were 10,000 aftershocks. On October 2, 1969, Amchitka was rocked by the force of a one-megaton nuclear bomb exploded 4,000 feet below the island's surface. On the day of the explosion, an estimated 10,000 protestors blocked the major U.S.-Canadian crossing to protest. Their banners read "Don't Make a Wave. It's your fault if our fault goes."

One of the most active people in the American antinuclear movement was Jim Bohlen, who had been a deep-sea diver and a radar operator during World War II. Following the war, he had worked on American space-age weapons. Bohlen became alarmed at the threat of nuclear war raised by the 1962 Cuban Missile Crisis. When his stepson became eligible for the draft in 1966, Bohlen moved his family to Vancouver, Canada. There he and his wife, Marie, became involved in the peace movement and in helping American draft resisters.

During a 1967 antiwar march, Bohlen met Irving and Dorothy Stone, a Quaker couple who introduced the Bohlens to the Quaker philosophy of "bearing witness." To bear witness means to be present at the scene of an activity to which the witness objects in order to register his or her opposition. The Bohlens were frustrated that the peace movement was not getting the attention it deserved. Marie said, "The Quakers in 1958 tried to sail a ship near the Bikini Atoll in the South Pacific protesting the atmospheric testing of H-bombs. The name of the ship was the *Golden Rule*. They were arrested in Hawaii before they got to the site, and they made all kinds of national news. . . . Why don't we get a ship and take it up there?"

Don't Make a Wave was renamed Greenpeace to express concern for the planet and opposition to nuclear arms. The members found an aging halibut seiner, the *Phyllis Cormack,* which had numerous mechanical problems. On September 17, 1971, a little more than two weeks before the date set for the bomb test, the *Phyllis Cormack*—dubbed *Greenpeace* for the trip—and a crew of twelve set sail. The timing created grave risks. The autumn equinox is the season for hurricanes and riptides. When the test date was delayed, the ship had to return to Vancouver.

Interest generated by the aborted trip enabled Greenpeace to raise enough money for a faster ship, a converted minesweeper. A crew of twenty-eight set out when a test date was set for November 4. Beaten back by a storm, the new ship was 700 miles from the test site when the bomb was finally detonated on March 6. The detonation provoked a flood of protests and demonstrations. In response, the Atomic Energy Commission (AEC) announced an end to tests in the Aleutians.

American businessman and yachtsman David McTaggart became angry when the French government announced in 1972 its intention to cordon off thousands of square miles of international waters around the atoll of Mururoa, which lies mid-ocean in the South Pacific. He answered an ad placed by a Vancouver group on behalf of the New Zealand Campaign for Nuclear Disarmament, looking for someone who would sail a boat to Mururoa to protest the testing. McTaggart was not an activist, but he was furious at the French for defying the international maritime law that gave a nation the right to claim only a 19-kilometer (12-mile) territorial zone around its land. McTaggart reasoned that the way to challenge the French arrogance was to sail just outside its territorial limit.

Against severe odds, on June 1, 1972, McTaggart's 12-meter (38-foot) ketch, the *Vega,* carrying a banner attached to its sail that read "Greenpeace III," sailed into the forbidden zone. *Vega* took up a position 32 kilometers (20 miles) from the test site in the anticipated path of the fallout.

The three-man crew hoped that their presence would stop the test. Instead, French warships attempted to intimidate the crew of the small boat into leaving. Two warships began a game of squeezing the small yacht between them. The harassment went on for eight days. The exhausted crew were unaware that their persistence was generating headlines around the world, notoriety that caused the French to postpone the test.

A huge warship collided with the *Vega* and towed the boat in for repairs. While the crew ate lunch in the company of the admiral in charge of the testing, photographers surreptitiously took pictures. The photographs released to the press suggested that the crew was on good terms with the French and the mishap was the crew's own fault.

McTaggart met Jack Cunningham, an expert on maritime law, who agreed to handle a suit against the French government. To document his case, McTaggart spent a long, wet winter in Vancouver writing his case and wrote letters to supporters and politicians. A small local publisher gave him a $1,500 advance to publish his manuscript in a book called *Outrage.* The cost of repairing the *Vega* left behind in New Zealand was $1,300.

In April 1973, the French government's announcement of its intention to detonate a hydrogen bomb generated sufficient funds to make the *Vega* seaworthy for the trip back to the test zone. Testing began on July 21. Initially, the *Vega* was joined by vessels from New England and Australia. By August 14, the *Vega,* crewed by McTaggart, Ann-Marie Horne, Mary Lornie, and Nigel Ingram, was alone.

On August 15, a dinghy filled with men boarded the *Vega* and beat the crew severely. Horne photographed the beatings and was able to smuggle the film of the beatings past the unsuspecting guards by concealing it in her vagina. The French version was that the *Vega* crew had tried to throw the unarmed men into the sea. During the melee, McTaggart had sustained a severe injury to his eye.

Because the Canadian government refused to take McTaggart's claim against the French government to the International Court of Justice, which was eager to receive it, McTaggart had to sue in a French court. He won damages for having his boat rammed, but he had to appear in a second court on the more serious charge of piracy connected to the beating.

The court accepted the French government's position that boarding the *Vega* had been an "exceptional case" and that the issue of international waters and the conduct of the military were matters of state security that could not be questioned by the French court. The prosecutor made a surprising comment. "It should not be denied that McTaggart may have helped the French government to choose underground tests in place of atmospheric tests. It is possible that McTaggart's attitude, reinforced by the reactions of certain countries and certain groups caused the government of France to think again."

Until 1975, the major preoccupation of Greenpeace was nuclear testing, but the focus broadened to include the plight of the great whales, which were being driven to extinction by the whaling industry. The International Whaling Commission (IWC) had become essentially a whalers' club. The number of whales being killed each year continued to climb.

Photographs of the high-speed, inflatable French dinghies that had pursued the *Vega* suggested a new strategy. Dinghies could be lowered from a Greenpeace boat to position themselves between the whales and the whalers. The new owner of the *Vega,* a retired law professor, put himself and his boat at the service of Greenpeace. The *Phyllis Cormack* joined the *Vega.* On April 27, 1975, the two boats set sail from Vancouver, seen off by an estimated 23,000 well-wishers. Photographs taken of a harpoon exploding in the back of a defenseless whale were shown around the world.

By early summer 1976, Greenpeace had raised enough money to finance a second mission against the whalers aboard a retired Canadian minesweeper. At the dock, a Cree medicine man told the crew: "You are the Warriors of the Rainbow." The second trip directly saved 100 whales and by keeping whalers from their normal grounds, indirectly saved another 1,300. The battle to save the whales was still going on in the 1990s.

In the mid-1970s, Greenpeace took up the cause of the Newfoundland harp seal pups, who were clubbed to death each year by commercial sealing fleets. By 1977, the seal campaign had become an international cause.

A new vessel became identified with Greenpeace in 1977. With a grant from the World Wildlife Fund, the organization purchased a 418-ton trawler that had been a research vessel for the British Ministry of Agriculture, Fisheries, and Food. Teams of volunteers overhauled the vessel and it was christened the *Rainbow Warrior.*

While on a mission to oppose Icelandic whaling, the *Rainbow Warrior* took on a new mission: to intercept a British ship on its way to dump 2,000 tons of radioactive waste in international waters. Toxic waste became a new cause. On May 17, 1985, the *Rainbow Warrior* arrived at Rongelap Atoll in the Marshall Islands, which had been dusted by fallout from five U.S. nuclear tests between 1946 and 1958. Despite assurances from the American government that the island was safe, the inhabitants wanted to move. The *Rainbow Warrior* relocated 300 residents and 100 tons of supplies and materials to the island of Mejato 195 kilometers (120 miles) away.

At 11:38 P.M. on July 10, 1985, the first of two bombs blew up the *Rainbow Warrior.* Photographer Fernando Pereira was killed, and the destruction to the ship was massive. The crime was traced to two French agents, who pleaded guilty to manslaughter and willful damage. Although a lengthy trial was avoided, France was exposed to ridicule and humiliation.

The death of Pereira and the loss of the *Rainbow Warrior* underlined the seriousness of the ship's missions. In the late 1970s, groups calling themselves Greenpeace sprang up all over the United States and Canada. The bombing of the *Rainbow Warrior* spread the group's sense of urgency around the world.

In 1990, increasing concern over global warming inspired Greenpeace to publish many reports, participate in intense lobbying, and undertake a myriad of actions around the world. By the late 1990s, Greenpeace had spread itself so thin that it was forced to retrench. Many staff members were laid off and the focus of the organization was narrowed to a handful of its missions. By that time, other activist organizations had taken on the many causes Greenpeace had championed.

See also Environmental Movement
Reference Michael Brown and John May. *The Greenpeace Story,* 1991.

Guevara, Ernesto "Che" (1928–1967)

For students on the political left during the 1960s and 1970s, Che Guevara was a folk hero. Widely perceived as the leading intellectual in the Cuban government of Premier Fidel Castro, Guevara, a native of Argentina and a physician, participated in several leftist movements in Latin America. He played a major role in Castro's January 1959 overthrow of Cuban dictator Fulgencio Batista.

An avid reader in childhood of history and sociology, Guevara joined a youth group at age 14 to take part in street fights against supporters of Juan Perón, who was the most powerful behind-the-scenes figure through shifting alliances in the Argentine government. In a coup, Perón became dictator in 1943.

Guevara's grandmother's cancer prompted him to become a physician. Guevara met Fidel Castro in Mexico, where he joined his revolutionary 26th of July movement. He acted as a physician as needed, served as chief of personnel for Castro's expeditionary forces, and helped train guerrilla forces.

In 1960, one year after the Cuban revolution, Castro named Guevara head of the National Institute of Agrarian Reform and president of the National Bank of Cuba. He also took over the task of training Cuba's civilian militia, for which he wrote a training manual.

Because the United States had subsidized Cuban sugar production under Batista, Guevara accused Americans of "economic enslavement" aimed at hampering Cuba's industrial development. In reply to protests about expropriation of American property, he said, "The only way to carry out agrarian reform is to take the land first and worry about compensation later."

Ernesto "Che" Guevara listens as delegates to the Inter-American Economic and Social Conference choose President John F. Kennedy's program for economic and social development, the Alliance for Progress.

Although Guevara courted the Soviet Union, he vowed that the Cuban people would resist to their last drop of blood any attempt to make Cuba a Soviet satellite. During a trip to Moscow to build trade relations, he asserted that Cuba stood prepared to fulfill its goal as a model for armed revolution in Latin America. During the Cuban Missile Crisis from October 16, 1962, to October 28, 1962, when U.S. President John F. Kennedy learned of signs of a buildup of Soviet nuclear weapons in Cuba, Guevara is alleged to have said that in the event of aggression by the United States, Cuba was prepared to fire nuclear missiles at American cities. In August 1963, Guevara went on a special mission to the Soviet Union to obtain a firm commitment from the Soviet government for increased armaments and technical specialists to deal with "the threats of aggressor imperialistic elements."

Guevara was reportedly captured on October 8, 1967, and killed on October 9, 1967, in Bolivia during a clash between guerrillas and Bolivian troops. In 1995, a retired Bolivian army chief revealed the likely whereabouts of Guevara's body. Teams of French, Argentine, and Cuban archaeologists with aid from Bolivia began a search. They succeeded in June 1997. Guevara's handless skeleton was found buried with his three sergeants. Three more skeletons were found nearby. All were genetically identified.

On October 9, 1997, Bolivia embarked on its first "Che Guevara Week" to honor the anniversary of Guevara's death. The anniversary was heavily promoted by Bolivia's tourist board.

See also Kennedy, John Fitzgerald; Kennedy, Robert
References Jorge Castañeda. *Compañero: The Life and Death of Che Guevara*, 1997; *Economist*. "Riding the Che-Chic Route," 1997; Douglas Kellner. *Ernesto "Che" Guevara*, 1989.

Guthrie, Arlo (b. 1947)

During the late 1960s and early 1970s, Arlo Guthrie became the spokesperson for many young Americans who were alienated from the society they lived in. Arlo was the son of the late folksinger Woody Guthrie, who had been a spokesperson for migrant workers and those displaced by the harsh environmental conditions of the Dust Bowl during the 1930s. Woody wrote more than 1,000 songs, among them "This Land Is Your Land."

The Guthrie household of Arlo's childhood was filled with music. Legendary folksingers like Pete Seeger and the Weavers were frequent guests. During the 1950s, however, Woody became more and more incapacitated by Huntington's chorea, a hereditary disease that results in deterioration of the nervous system. To protect the rights to Woody's songs and literary works, his manager Harold Leventhal, Pete Seeger, and others set up the Guthrie Children's Trust Fund, which enabled

Arlo's mother to send him to private schools.

A major inspiration to Arlo as a musician was singer-composer Bob Dylan, who idolized his father. Arlo became a musician because he felt he could do nothing else as well.

In November 1965, Guthrie went to Stockbridge, Massachusetts, to visit Alice and Ray Brock, who had been on the faculty of his school when Arlo was a student in Stockbridge. The Brocks had become surrogate parents of an informal commune of young people who lived in an abandoned church. Alice Brock ran a nearby restaurant. After eating a typical Thanksgiving dinner at the restaurant, Arlo and his friends decided to do their hosts a favor by taking the garbage to the town dump. When they found the dump was closed, they threw the garbage in a nearby gully and were arrested for littering. After he was released, Arlo wrote a satirical, antiestablishment song called "Alice's Restaurant," which became a top seller and gave a major boost to his career. He later starred in a motion picture with the same name. The movie received mixed reviews from critics but was widely regarded as a significant commentary on the era.

Arlo's career as a musician escalated after he wrote "Alice's Restaurant." Managed by his father's former manager, Harold Leventhal, he developed as a concert and recording artist. Over the course of his career, Arlo chose a path of "diminished stardom," preferring to spend as much time as possible with his family on a farm in Massachusetts. His compositions included the whimsical "Motorcycle Song," the comic "Moses," the children's song "Me and My Goose," and the antiestablishment "Ring-Around the Rosy," about a group of young people arrested for frolicking in Philadelphia's Rittenhouse Square.

See also Youth Rebellion Movies

Haight-Ashbury

Until the late 1950s, San Francisco State College had its campus in close proximity to two traditionally low-rent districts: the Fillmore, largely populated by blacks; and the Haight-Ashbury, populated by a mix of white and Asian-ethnic groups. When San Francisco State moved its campus to 19th Street near the ocean, there were few facilities for student housing. The students stayed in Haight-Ashbury, where the rents were cheap.

The name Haight-Ashbury was derived from the busy intersection of Haight and Ashbury streets. Until 1965, "Hashbury," as the neighborhood was often called, was a quiet community of run-down Victorian houses, empty storefronts, and marginal businesses. It was home to white- and blue-collar workers, beatniks who had fled from the more repressive North Beach, black families inching their way up the economic ladder, and Asians migrating from crowded Chinatown. For five years beginning in 1965, Haight Street became center stage for hippie counterculture.

Haight Street begins at the eastern edge of Golden Gate Park and runs for twenty blocks through the Ashbury district, down through the Fillmore district, and on to Market Street. Three blocks north of Haight Street, another green strip called the Panhandle runs parallel to the Haight district for a mile. Nearby Golden Gate Park, one of the finest parks in the United States, offers sunny, green meadows, formal gardens, statues, and museums.

The combination of cheap rents, miles of parks, and a tolerant neighborhood attitude toward students drew the young in increasing numbers to the district. The vast majority of those attracted to Hashbury openly declared opinions counter to the prevailing culture. In particular, they opposed the Vietnam War. Also drawn to the neighborhood were artists, musicians, advocates of unrestricted sex, and practitioners of new religions. Many believed that drugs enhanced creativity, sexual sensation, and religious experiences.

Theatrics to be seen on the streets of Hashbury made the neighborhood an attraction for

tour buses. At the outset, the young people welcomed the tourists with good-natured enthusiasm. Eventually, they equipped themselves with mirrors so the tourists would see themselves.

The Diggers were an integral part of the Hashbury neighborhood. The Diggers traced their roots back to a seventeenth-century communal farming community in England, who lived on waste lands between scattered villages. The Diggers wanted their land to be free to all who needed to use it. To be a Digger in Haight-Ashbury, one had only to proclaim oneself a Digger. The Diggers regularly fed large numbers of people under the tall eucalyptus trees in the Panhandle. Often those who were fed became Diggers and joined in the daily effort to find food to serve the hungry.

Haight-Ashbury contributed to the development of several rock bands that later became well known, including the Grateful Dead. The uncle of a San Francisco State psychology major owned a house at 1090 Page Street in the district. The big old house, once the home of a wealthy man, had a ballroom in the basement that made an excellent rehearsal room for several beginning bands. The use of psychedelic lights with bands was developed in Hashbury. Bill Ham, who managed rooming houses in which itinerant musicians lived, was a painter who adapted an army surplus light apparatus and used it to project watercolor pigments through oil solutions, thereby creating wall-sized landscapes. By manipulating the liquids in concert with the rhythms of his tenants' bands, Ham created the first psychedelic rock and roll show.

One of the best-known events created by the Hashbury residents was the "Human Be-In." A press release announced: "A union of love and activism previously separated by categorical dogma and label mongering will finally occur ecstatically when Berkeley political activists and hip community and San Francisco's spiritual generation and contingents from the emerging revolutionary generation all over California meet for a Gathering of the Tribes for a Human Be-In at the Polo Fields in Golden Gate Park on Saturday January 14, 1967 from 1 to 5 P.M." Thousands came.

On October 6, 1967, the Diggers and hundreds of Haight-Ashbury "flower folk" celebrated "the Death of Hippie" with a parade and a ceremony that concluded with a burial of the storefront sign from the Psychedelic Shop. After the prime movers of the neighborhood left, a general exodus followed. The Haight-Ashbury counterculture had become a victim of its own success. An unwillingness to impose order sometimes resulted in anarchy and violence. The promise of free food, a place to stay, drugs, sex, and friendship had attracted a stream of young people. In time, their numbers overwhelmed the Diggers' ability to manage food, shelter, health care, and sanitation.

See also Grateful Dead; Hippies
Reference Gene Anthony. *The Summer of Love: Haight-Ashbury at Its Highest,* 1980.

Hamer, Fannie Lou (1917–1977)

Civil rights activist Fannie Lou Hamer convinced her neighbors to stand up for their rights despite the risks. Hamer was the twentieth child of Mississippi sharecroppers Jim and Lou Ella Townsend. Sharecropping in the South was set up by whites to make it impossible for tenant sharecroppers to escape poverty. Under the system, sharecroppers worked a segment of land owned by a white plantation owner and paid half of the family's income to the owner when the crop was sold. Not only did the sharecropper's family sup-

ply all the labor, but also the cost of seed, fertilizer, and other supplies came out of the family's half. Supplies were bought on credit at a store belonging to the landowner, whose prices were so high that they kept the family in debt. As long as they remained in debt, they could not leave.

One year Hamer's father did well enough to rent some land of his own and buy a few animals. One night a white man put poison in the animals' trough, and they died. The family was forced to return to the plantation.

In 1944, Fannie Lou married Perry "Pap" Hamer, a tractor driver and sharecropper who worked on a plantation in Ruleville owned by W. D. Marlowe. For the next eighteen years, Fannie Lou worked in the fields during the day, cleaned the Marlowes' house at night, and served as the plantation's timekeeper, keeping track of hours worked, bales of cotton picked, and pay due each worker.

On Sunday August 26, 1962, Hamer's dreams that one day she and her neighbors would have racial justice seemed a little closer to reality. Her minister announced that a mass meeting would be held in the church that evening, cosponsored by the Southern Christian Leadership Conference (SCLC) and the Student Nonviolent Coordinating Committee (SNCC). At the meeting, Hamer discovered that blacks had the right to register and vote.

Eighteen volunteers, including Hamer, agreed to travel by bus to Indianola, where the circuit clerk who registered voters had his office. Mississippi required potential black voters to pass a literacy test that involved explaining an obscure section of the state's constitution. Not surprisingly, all eighteen blacks were disqualified. When Hamer returned from Indianola, she learned that the plantation owner insisted that she refrain from registering to vote or leave the plantation. She left.

That winter, Hamer returned to Ruleville as a field secretary for SNCC and began organizing a local poverty program. By day, she went into the fields to tell workers about their right to vote. At night she talked to them in the churches. She quickly became one of SNCC's most effective fund-raisers.

On January 10, 1963, on her third try, Hamer became one of Sunflower County's first registered black voters. When election came in the fall, she wasn't allowed to vote because she could not afford to pay Mississippi's poll tax. A year later the Twenty-fourth Amendment to the Constitution outlawing poll taxes in connection with elections to any federal post was ratified.

SNCC had two goals for Mississippi—keeping the nation's attention focused on the state and helping blacks develop their own political leaders and groups. With those goals in mind, 1,000 young white volunteers were invited to spend the summer in Mississippi. They had two tasks: (1) to set up Freedom Schools to educate blacks as voters and train them for leadership; and (2) to register voters for the Mississippi Freedom Democratic Party (MFDP), which would challenge the authority of the state's white-dominated Democratic Party. Most volunteers suffered the same kind of harassment SNCC workers regularly faced: being taunted, followed, threatened, and run off the road. Three were murdered during the summer.

By the time MFDP's first state convention was held in August 1964, 60,000 voters had been registered. Sixty-four blacks and four whites were chosen to represent MFDP at the national convention in Atlanta. President Lyndon Johnson was furious because he feared the presence of MFDP would disrupt party unity and encourage Democrats to vote for his opponent in the general election.

During the hearing of the convention's Credentials Committee on August 22, 1964, most of MFDP's presentation was not shown on television because President Johnson had called a press conference for the same time. However, some of Hamer's speech was carried. She said, "If the Freedom Democratic Party is not seated, I question America. Is this America, the land of the free and the home of the brave where we have to live with our telephone off the hook because our lives be threatened daily, because we want to live like . . . decent human beings in America?" In support of MFDP, telegrams poured in to delegates.

The committee settled on a compromise that required all members of the regular party to sign a loyalty oath, gave MFDP two at-large seats, and required an integrated delegation by 1968. The MFDP delegation felt betrayed.

As part of the Mississippi Freedom Summer Project, Hamer ran against white congressman James Whitten. Only Whitten's name was listed on the Democratic ballot. SNCC ran a counter-election with both names. Whitten won one election. Hamer won the other. The U.S. Congressional House Committee on Elections spent nine months investigating. The full house voted against MFDP, but the investigation eventually led to Mississippi elections being declared illegal by the federal courts.

Between the 1964 Democratic National Convention and the 1968 convention, Hamer worked tirelessly to build MFDP. Some whites joined, and MFDP changed its name to the Mississippi Loyalist Democratic Party (MLDP). At the 1968 convention, once again there was a battle. MLDP refused an offer of a compromise. The segregationists were unseated, and Hamer received a standing ovation when she took her seat.

Hamer understood that poverty as much as discrimination in voting kept black people in Mississippi in place in the social order. According to Andrew Young, "if you talked too much economics in the fifties and sixties, you were called a communist. So we clearly avoided economic issues." Hamer did not avoid economics. She was poor and her neighbors lived with hunger. She worked on both a national and a local level.

In 1968, on a local level, she created the Pig Bank with the help of the National Council of Negro Women. The bank bought 35 female pigs and 5 male pigs. The bank loaned pregnant females to local families, who would keep the piglets and return the female to the bank. In 1969, also on a local level, she bought the first 40 acres of Freedom Farm to form a cooperative. Hamer's organizing efforts helped establish regular payrolls for black women in Sunflower County, Mississippi, where she lived. She also helped organize Head Start and the Fannie Lou Hamer Day Care Center. The latter served the children of women at a small garment factory Hamer helped establish in Doddville.

On a national level, she attended President Richard Nixon's White House Conference on Food, Nutrition, and Health. She participated on July 10, 1971, in the founding meeting of the National Women's Political Caucus. More than once during the 1970s, Hamer was hospitalized for nervous exhaustion. She hosted visitors from developing nations after a meeting in July 1975 of the International Year of the Woman. In March 1976, she died of heart failure brought on by breast cancer, diabetes, and hypertension. Hamer had never let her physical ailments interfere with her organizing.

In January 1997, President Bill Clinton proclaimed February National African American History Month. One of several people named as inspirations of courage, wisdom, and vision was Fannie Lou Hamer.

See also Chaney, Goodman, and Schwerner, Murders of; Mississippi Freedom Democratic Party
Reference Kay Mills. *The Little Light of Mine: The Life of Fannie Lou Hamer,* 1993; David Rubel. *Fannie Lou Hamer: From Sharecropping to Politics,* 1990.

Harbury, Jennifer

In 1985, Connecticut-born, Harvard-educated attorney Jennifer Harbury felt impelled to go to Guatemala when a man covered with acid burns received in a Guatemalan torture chamber was denied asylum in the United States. The U.S. Immigration and Naturalization Service (INS) claimed he had no reasonable fear of persecution and should be deported. Harbury traveled to Guatemala to collect firsthand evidence of atrocities to enable her to help Guatemalan refugees threatened with deportation. The crimes the attorney witnessed were committed by the military government, which for decades, despite a record of brutality and routine slaughter of civil rights leaders, had received strong support from the American government.

Centuries after the Spanish conquistadors robbed the Mayas of their civilization, their Spanish-speaking descendants lived in wealth on great plantations, while Mayas worked like serfs on those same plantations. Mayas, who make up 80 percent of the Guatemalan people, were allowed no lands, no money, no representation, and no rights. For seeking their own lands or asking for wages sufficient to feed their families, Mayas were routinely killed. Every Mayan generation that tried to break out of bondage had been crushed. Yet each time they rose again, all the while clinging to their Mayan language and customs.

In 1990, on another trip to Guatemala, Harbury met Efrain Bamaca Velasquez, a Mayan resistance leader known as Commander Everardo. In spite of their differences in age, nationality, and education, the two fell in love and married.

Everardo knew he would eventually be killed. He accepted the risk rather than stand by and permit his people to continue to be terrorized and subjugated. During combat in March 1992, Everardo vanished, and Harbury began a desperate search for him. Her search, if unsuccessful, threatened to embarrass both the U.S. and Guatemalan governments, which had lied to her. Obtaining orders to exhume bodies in unmarked graves mired her in governmental red tape. Being present at the exhumation was not only emotionally harrowing; it also carried the risk of being killed by a sniper. Each failure to find Everardo's body made follow-up on the next lead that much more difficult. In a crusade to force officials to tell the truth, Harbury staged three hunger strikes—two in Guatemala City and one in front of the White House. During the hunger strike in front of the White House, she came close to dying.

The worldwide publicity generated by Harbury's hunger strikes and an investigation by Mike Wallace of the television program *60 Minutes* forced official disclosures in the United States. Congress initiated an investigation of charges against the U.S. State Department and the Central Intelligence Agency (CIA). Representative Robert Torricelli, who championed Harbury's cause, was the person who told her that Everardo had been killed on the orders of Colonel Julio Roberto Alpirez, a CIA informant.

From papers turned over to her by the CIA, the Defense Department, the Guatemalan Embassy, and an investigation conducted for the president,

Harbury learned the details of her husband's death. She finally obtained the documents in part because of the public outrage and in part because she took the agencies to court. In the documents Harbury obtained was a picture of Alpirez bending over Everardo's torture table, the same month that the CIA had paid him $44,000.

In the waning years of the 1990s, Harbury was working with the United Nations Human Rights Commission and other human rights organizations to expose the brutal acts committed by the Guatemalan military. She filed civil rights suits against members of the CIA, the U.S. State Department, and the National Security Council.

In 1995, the Guatemalan government and leftist guerrilla forces (the Guatemalan National Revolutionary Units) signed the Accord on the Identity and Rights of Indigenous Peoples. Some of the changes in the lives of Mayas brought about by the accord became evident in 1998 when twenty-one Maya priests were sworn in by the vice-president as members of a new government-sponsored Council of Elders. New Maya political and cultural organizations began forming rapidly. A Maya renaissance was emerging as Mayas spoke for themselves about themselves.

Reference Jennifer Harbury. *Searching for Everardo: A Story of Love, War, and the CIA in Guatemala,* 1997.

Harrington, Michael (1928–1989)

Political activist and writer Michael Harrington was a socialist, meaning that he was in favor of a system of government in which the workers both hold political power and control the means of producing and distributing the products of their labor. Unlike many American socialists, Harrington willingly worked with liberals, especially Democrats. He hoped to bring about incremental changes in the United States that would create a welfare state, in which citizens would have adequate food, housing, and medical care, to offset the dehumanizing effects of capitalism. Harrington's first book, *The Other America,* helped lead to government funding of the War on Poverty during the Johnson administration. His book inspired many young medical workers to travel throughout the South documenting the swollen bellies of starving children.

In his youth, Harrington's studies began not with poverty, but with the law and then English literature, until a job with the St. Louis welfare department changed Harrington's life. In 1948, he left Yale and pursuit of a law degree to enter the University of Chicago with the intention of becoming a poet. After receiving a master's degree in English in 1949, he went home to St. Louis to take a job and save money in order to move to Greenwich Village. The job he found was with the welfare department, whose largest share of clients was sharecroppers who had migrated from Arkansas.

In Harrington's second autobiography, *The Long Distance Runner,* he wrote: "I went into a decayed, beautiful house near the Mississippi River, which stank of stopped-up toilets, dead rats, and human misery." He devoted his life to "putting an end to that house and all it symbolized."

In 1954, Harrington joined the Young Socialist League, which, although Marxist in its philosophy, was passionately anti-Stalinist and staunchly supportive of civil liberties. That same year, he joined in the civil rights struggle being waged by the National Association for the Advancement of Colored People (NAACP). For the next ten years, Harrington worked with a broad alliance of civil rights activists, labor union representatives, and pacifists. In the 1960s, he noted that various factions had emerged in the coalition. In his view, the movement for social justice had moved from protest to politics. Unlike the visions or slogans that inspire and unite protesters, practical politics involves making choices among politicians and pieces of legislation that don't suit everyone equally well. The escalation of the war in Vietnam by President Lyndon Johnson brought into sharp focus the differences among the allies. Peace activists and civil rights workers, for example, often alienated each other.

One of the most poignant events in Harrington's life came in 1962 during a battle between the Old Left and the New Left. An Old Left group, the League for Industrial Democracy (LID), an affiliate of the Democratic Socialist Party, became embroiled in a dispute with a student affiliate of LID, the Students for a Democratic Society (SDS). As "one of only three people over thirty who could be trusted," Harrington participated in SDS's development of the Port Huron Statement, a manifesto. During the drafting of the statement, Harrington lost his status as someone the students trusted.

Because the students had grown up during the Cold War anticommunist fervor of the 1950s and 1960s and had been alienated by it, they refused to accept Harrington's anticommunist stance. Harrington had to leave before the draft was finished. He had no way of knowing that the students had incorporated most of his concerns in the final draft. In fact, he was told his contributions were ignored. As a consequence, Harrington condemned the SDS, which led to the tie between LID and SDS being broken.

In *The Long Distance Runner,* he expressed his regret at the part he played. Harrington described his behavior as "insensitive to the students' struggle to forge a new identity." He had dealt with them as if they were seasoned factional fighters, perversely dedicated to principles he abhorred. He wrote: "I was one more horrifying example of the untrustworthiness of people over thirty."

The success of *The Other America* led to Harrington's participation in Lyndon Johnson's antipoverty task force. Revenues from the book and from many speaking engagements brought Harrington more money than he had ever had in his life before, a difficult moral position for a socialist. Unnerved, he spent four years in therapy. A prolific writer, Harrington's discomfort with his affluence did not prevent him from writing.

Among his many books, two on political theory, *Socialism* (1972) and *The Twilight of Capitalism* (1976), received high praise. He wrote two more books on poverty. *The Vast Majority: A Journey to the World's Poor* (1977) was nominated for the National Book Award.

Having mastered his emotional problems with affluence, he set out in 1973 to mend the splits within the socialist movement. During the 1970s and 1980s Harrington demonstrated in the

United States against apartheid in South Africa and protested America's intervention in the governments of Central America.

After he resigned as chairman of the Socialist Party of America, Harrington organized the Democratic Socialist Organizing Committee (DSOC), whose goal was to forge a coalition of trade unionists, environmentalists, feminists, and racial and ethnic minorities. In 1981, DSOC merged with the New Americans Movement to become the Democratic Socialists of America (DSA). With Barbara Ehrenreich, he became cochair of DSA.

At a 1988 fund-raiser to celebrate Harrington's life and raise money for the Next America Foundation, which he founded to do research on poverty, he summed up his political position: "I want to be on the left of what's possible."

See also Port Huron Statement; Weathermen
References Michael Harrington. *The Other America,* 1962; *The Twilight of Capitalism,* 1976; *A Vast Majority: A Journey to the World's Poor,* 1977; and *The Long Distance Runner: An Autobiography,* 1988.

Hayden, Tom (b. 1940)

Political activist Tom Hayden spent most of the 1960s and half of the 1970s working in a variety of movements. He has been described as the New Left's most ubiquitous worker. He was a member of the Student Nonviolent Coordinating Committee (SNCC), a cofounder of the Students for a Democratic Society, a community organizer in Newark's inner city, and a peace movement leader who was responsible for bringing prisoners of war (POWs) back home from North Vietnam.

Hayden was one of eight defendants indicted for the protest that took place during the 1968 Democratic National Convention in Chicago. The eight included a cross-section of various movements: Hayden and Rennie Davis were from the New Left, Abbie Hoffman and Jerry Rubin were part of the hippie counterculture, Dave Dellinger represented the antiwar movement, Bobby Seale was a Black Panther. The other two were Lee Weiner and John Froines.

When Bobby Seale's attorney was hospital-

Tom Hayden in the Santa Monica headquarters of the Indochina Peace Campaign, March 1973.

ized, he refused to accept any other counsel. The judge refused to delay the trial or to honor Seale's right to an attorney of his choice. Because of Seale's repeated protests, the judge had him chained to his chair and gagged. Even gagged, Seale managed to protest. To get rid of Seale, the judge declared a mistrial that applied only to him. Because of Seale's early participation and then removal, leaving the trial of the other seven to continue, the trial is referred to as either the Chicago Eight or the Chicago Seven.

The trial ended in February 1970 with the conviction of Hayden and four others. He was sentenced to five years in prison for inciting people to riot and for contempt of court. The riot convictions were overturned in November 1972 on the grounds that the judge had been guilty of improper rulings and conduct. A separate appeals court voided most of the contempt citations against Hayden and declined to pass sentence on the others. With his legal problems behind him, Hayden went to live in a commune in Berkeley,

traveled around the country speaking at peace rallies and demonstrations, and contributed articles to magazines like *Ramparts* and *Rolling Stone.*

Hayden proposed teaching a course on the Vietnamese to the dean of the Immaculate Heart College. The Sisters of the Immaculate Heart was an order of 500 nuns who engaged in quiet protest with the cardinal about flexible hours of prayer, modification of their habit, and the right to provide graduate studies for their sisters. In 1970, the order became a lay community with its own vows. The dean accepted Hayden's course proposal with enthusiasm. In September 1971, he taught similar courses at Pitzer College and at the University of California at Los Angeles extension service.

In July 1971, the Pentagon Papers were published in the *New York Times.* The documents provided a history of U.S. policies from 1945 through the summer of 1968 and included classified memos. The documents had been stolen and photocopied by Daniel Ellsberg and Anthony Russo. Ellsberg had been an adviser to the Pentagon on counterinsurgency, or military and political action to counter revolts against the government in power. Russo had interviewed Vietcong prisoners and done studies on the chemical spraying of rice crops.

Hayden read the thousands of pages of formal prose, which confirmed much of what the antiwar movement had been saying for years. A month after publication, a Harris poll revealed that a majority of Americans felt the war was "immoral" and 60 percent were in favor of withdrawal. Hayden set out to reduce the papers to a readable pamphlet for the public. Eventually, 100,000 copies were circulated free across the country.

He met the actress and antiwar activist Jane Fonda in 1971, and they married in January 1973. They participated in antiwar rallies and protests together. Their divorce seventeen years later was less than amicable.

Hayden ran for the state assembly from his home district in 1982. He had concluded that his protests and policy proposals would always be considered utopian as long as he worked outside the system. He won his seat and was reelected in subsequent elections. He served from 1982 to 1992, when he won a seat in the state senate. In 1997, he ran for mayor of Los Angeles and published a book he compiled and edited called *Irish Hunger: Personal Reflections on the Legacy of the Famine*. He continued to serve in the state senate.

See also Columbia University Campus Protest; Fonda, Jane; Pentagon Papers; Port Huron Statement; Yippies
Reference Tom Hayden. *Trial*, 1970; *Reunion: A Memoir*, 1988; and ed., *Irish Hunger: Personal Reflections on the Legacy of the Famine*, 1997.

Hearst, Patricia (b. 1954)

The Symbionese Liberation Army (SLA), whose members perceived themselves as part of the Black Power movement, were at the extreme edge of the long-standing controversy within the black community about whether nonviolence or violence was more effective in the struggle against discrimination. Although the rhetoric of many Black Power advocates might be violent, only occasionally was violent action taken. The SLA was different. Members not only preached violence, they acted violently. They accomplished little, but generated much negative publicity.

In 1973 at the age of nineteen, Patricia Campbell Hearst, granddaughter of the newspaper tycoon William Randolph Hearst, was kidnapped by the SLA. The police had earlier discovered a "hit" list that contained Hearst's name when members of the SLA were captured for the 1973 murder of Marcus Foster, the first black superintendent of schools in Oakland, but they never warned her of the danger.

Like many victims of terrorists, Patty Hearst fell under the influence of her abductors and became sympathetic to their cause. For fifty-seven days following her kidnapping, Hearst was brutalized, raped, abused, and kept bound and gagged in a closet. The SLA used classic "thought-reform" (brainwashing) techniques: debilitation, dependency, and dread. As her reeducation progressed, Hearst's captors became friendlier. To survive, she became a model prisoner, subservient, obedient, grateful, and eager to learn. The SLA had Hearst in its custody for a year and a half.

Therapists call the change in Hearst's state of mind "posttraumatic stress disorder with dissociative features." Posttraumatic stress results from a serious threat to one's life, the lives of one's children, or close friends or relatives; sudden destruction of one's home or community; or the sight of another person being seriously injured or killed. Dissociation refers to an interruption in the integration of one's identity, memory, or consciousness.

During her captivity, Hearst participated in several robberies with SLA members, including the robbery of a branch of the Hibernia Bank in the Sunset District of San Francisco. For her participation, following her capture in 1975, she was sentenced to seven years in prison. After fourteen months in prison, Hearst was freed on bail pending her appeal. After the U.S. Supreme Court refused to hear her appeal, she was returned to prison. Following her reincarceration, California Congressman Leo Ryan rallied forty-eight of his congressional colleagues to sign a petition on her behalf.

In the wake of Ryan's assassination in Guyana by a member of the California-based People's Temple cult, followed by the murder-suicide of 900 men, women, and children of the cult, public understanding of brainwashing swung in Hearst's favor. On February 1, 1979, President Jimmy Carter commuted Hearst's sentence to time already served, twenty-two and a half months. In 1979, Hearst married her former bodyguard, Bernard Shaw. She published an account of her experience with the SLA in 1982, *Every Secret Thing*, and co-wrote a murder mystery with Cordelia Frances Biddle called *Murder at San Simeon* (1996). Hearst appeared in the movies *Serial Mom* in 1995 and *Bio-Dome* in 1997.

See also Symbionese Liberation Army
References Shana Alexander. *Anyone's Daughter*, 1979; Patricia Hearst. *Every Secret Thing*, 1982.

Highlander Folk School
See Horton, Myles

Hill, Anita (b. 1956)
University of Oklahoma law professor Anita Hill brought the topic of sexual harassment worldwide attention during the October 1991 U.S. Senate confirmation hearings of Supreme Court nominee Clarence Thomas. Sexual harassment can take many forms, including lewd conversations; displays of lewd pictures; sex-related items left in a woman's desk or locker; remarks about her body; unwanted touching, particularly of her breasts and buttocks; and requests for sexual favors, sometimes coupled with promises of promotion or threat of demotion or firing. Although sexual harassment happens to men, it is seldom reported, perhaps because men are even less likely than women to reveal they have been victimized.

Although sexual harassment was a common experience for many women, it did not have a name until 1974, when Carmita Wood, a 44-year-old Ithaca, New York, mother of four quit her job because of unwanted sexual advances by her boss. She filed for unemployment benefits on the grounds that her boss's behavior forced her to resign. Several feminist activists at Cornell University took an interest in her case and organized a speak-out, labeling the problem sexual harassment. Wood's claim was rejected by the Unemployment Commission, but the issue did not disappear. Appellate courts ruled that sexual harassment in the workplace violated Title VII of the 1964 Civil Rights Act.

In 1986, the Supreme Court heard its first sexual harassment case. Michelle Vinson, the plaintiff, was represented by feminist attorney Catharine MacKinnon, the author of *Sexual Harassment of Working Women* (1979). The Court unanimously agreed with MacKinnon's argument that sexual harassment by an employer violated Title VII. The Court further stated that a hostile or abusive work environment can constitute sexual harassment, even in the absence of a job-related threat or reward.

The confirmation hearing of Clarence Thomas, a black nominee chosen to fill the seat vacated by Thurgood Marshall, was broadcast on television and polarized men and women around the world. Despite his strongly conservative record, Thomas had considerable support among blacks, even as they acknowledged that his actions during his leadership of the Equal Employment Opportunity Commission had been negative toward redressing racial inequality.

As the final Senate vote to confirm Thomas's appointment neared, the matter was referred to the Judiciary Committee for reconsideration. Under questioning by a Senate staffer, Hill, herself African American, had charged Thomas with sexual harassment. Reluctantly, Hill testified before the Senate Judiciary Committee. Women watching the proceedings on television around the world relived unhappy experiences of their own. From their questions, it was obvious that the committee did not want to believe Hill. Most watching women did not like Hill's treatment by the committee. Polls found that women's support of Thomas's confirmation dropped sharply as the hearings progressed.

The Senate's confirmation of Thomas came back to haunt members. In the next election, 150 women ran for the House of Representatives, and eleven women ran for the Senate, more than had ever run before. California elected two women senators. Many women who ran for office at all levels of government and the women who supported them by volunteering and giving money said they had made their decision as a consequence of having watched the Thomas hearings.

Anita Hill, the politically conservative law professor, dignified, religious, and reticent, had galvanized the feminist movement. In time, Hill tired of being a symbol of sexual harassment to many and a pawn or a perjurer to others. No longer an anonymous private individual, she elected to tell her story in *Speaking Truth to Power*. Asked frequently why she didn't complain of sexual harassment against Clarence Thomas, Hill wrote: "I do not believe that in the early 1980s I lived or worked in a society, either in Washington or in Tulsa, that would have supported my right to raise a claim of harassment against the head of the EEOC."

See also Women's Movement
References Margaret DiCanio. *The Encyclopedia of Violence: Origins, Attitudes, Consequences,* 1993; Anita Hill. *Speaking Truth to Power,* 1997; Miriam Schneir. *Feminism in Our Times: The Essential Writings, World War II to the Present,* 1994.

Hines, Bishop John Eldridge (b. 1910)

Despite the fact that he had held several important posts within the church, when Bishop Hines attended the sixty-first general convention of the Episcopal Church held in St. Louis, Missouri, in October 1964, he was comparatively unknown. Nevertheless, he emerged from the conference as the spiritual leader of 3.6 million Episcopalians, having been elected the twenty-second presiding bishop of the Episcopal Church in the United States. With his election to high church office, Bishop Hines brought change. At a news conference before the inauguration, the bishop told reporters that he supported President Lyndon Johnson's Great Society program, except for his proposal to extend federal aid to parochial schools.

One of the bishop's first official acts was to chair an executive council meeting that rescinded a ruling that curbed civil rights activities of Episcopal priests. In doing so, the executive council reaffirmed its support for the National Council of Churches' community and voter registration work in Mississippi. In his inaugural sermon, the bishop said, "The church is caught up today in the throes of a worldwide convulsion, the basic ferment of which is the thrust for freedom and dignity and hope on the part of the little people of the world. The church is an agent of God's reconciling love that cannot survive this revolution as an observer."

At the first national interreligious conference on peace, held in Washington, D.C., in March 1966, Bishop Hines served as cochair. Two hundred delegates from the Roman Catholic, Reformed Jewish, Unitarian, Greek Orthodox, and Methodist faiths unanimously called on President Johnson to seek a cease-fire in Vietnam. A majority asked the president to consider an end to bombing raids in North and South Vietnam. That same year, the bishop participated in two other interfaith conferences whose agendas condemned escalation of American involvement in Vietnam.

At the sixty-second general convention, held in Seattle in the fall of 1967, with Bishop Hines presiding, noteworthy reforms were passed. Laymen were granted permission to administer the chalice; a simplified liturgy of the Lord's Supper was approved for trial use; women were permitted to attend future conventions; heresy trials were made more difficult to institute; and the functions of the presiding bishop were more formally defined. Also approved was a program that called on the church to spend at least $3 million for the next three years to help nonwhites achieve more economic and political power.

Fifty-four when he was elected, Bishop Hines was expected to serve until age sixty-eight. When a reporter said, "Bishop, when your term is over, what do you hope to be remembered for?" the Bishop replied, "For having survived." Bishop Hines did much more than survive. He committed his church's resources and permitted his clergy to work on behalf of the disenfranchised.

At a General Motors shareholder meeting in May 1971, Hines used his church's shares to instigate a movement to divest American institutions' interests in South Africa with a goal of ending apartheid. His divestment movement spread to other churches and was credited in 1990 by South African Archbishop Desmond Tutu as having been a key factor in the collapse of apartheid.

Hines seemed to attract controversy. Despite severe criticism, he held fast to his belief that the church had to give itself away even at the risk of disappearing. The bishop was blamed for a decline in the population of the church and a loss of faith in the national church structure. He voluntarily resigned in 1974, but his philosophy prevailed. The church's involvement in social outreach ministries continued to increase.

See also Abernathy, Reverend Ralph; Young, Andrew
References Kesselus, Reverend Ken. "Former Presiding Bishop John E. Hines Dies after Leaving a Legacy of Social Action," 1997.

Hippies

The poets, writers, and musicians of the 1950s had a strong influence on the so-called counterculture, which gained prominence in the mid-1960s. Collectively, those who participated in the counterculture were referred to as "hippies." Although this movement lasted only four or five years, it made a strong impression on the American mainstream.

The beats of the 1950s advocated dropping out of society. They promoted new forms of art and literature, smoked marijuana, and listened to jazz, at that time still considered an unorthodox form of music. Swing, one part of the spectrum of jazz, had a wide appeal for the young who liked to dance, but other forms of jazz had only limited audiences. The beats popularized the word "hip." They tended to direct most of their attention toward their inner selves and isolated themselves from the larger world. Hippies, in contrast, directed their attention outward to the larger society, which they hoped to change. Hippies thought of themselves as "the people of ground zero," who would build a new society on the ruins of America's involvement in global power struggles, in rampant urbanization, and in creation of an environmental catastrophe. Their intent was to bring about a fundamental change in the way Americans thought and to forge a new ethic.

The popular American media ignored the hippie philosophy and focused on their offbeat clothing, use of drugs, and occasional nudity. A few perceptive reporters noted that hippies lived by a moral code. One *Time* reporter wrote: "It could be argued that in their independence of material possessions and their emphasis on peacefulness and honesty, hippies lead considerably more virtuous lives than the majority of their fellow citizens."

Timothy Miller, an assistant professor of religious studies at the University of Kansas, wrote about the ethics of the hippie culture in *The Hippies and American Values* (1991). In Miller's view, the predecessors of the hippies included not only the beats but also the bohemians of the 1920s and 1930s, and black Americans. Like blacks, hippies were outsiders. While blacks had no choice about their outsider status, hippies chose to become outsiders by rebelling against their culture. In a 1957 essay about beats that applied equally well to hippies, novelist Norman Mailer wrote: "It's no accident that the source of Hip is the Negro for he has been living on the margin between totalitarianism and democracy for two centuries."

Although some hippies were simply escapists, many were active opponents of the majority culture. Some were separatists. A "Declaration of Cultural Evolution," written jointly by Timothy Leary, Allen Ginsberg, Paul Krassner, and Abbie Hoffman, described the majority culture as deaf to reason and claimed that human beings ought to be absolved from allegiance to the present cultural arrangement.

Most hippies were young. They distrusted anyone much beyond adolescence. Age thirty was their upper limit. In their protest of middle-class values, hippies used obscenities to provide shock value. They asked their critics which was more obscene—sexual intercourse, an act of love, or killing, an act of hate? Hippies declared middle-class revulsion toward the body's normal dirt as

President Richard Nixon talks with hippies at an antiwar demonstration at the Lincoln Memorial in Washington, D.C., May 9, 1970.

absurd, given middle-class acceptance of pollution and slums.

By 1967, the youth culture in opposition had become widespread. The opposition never came from a single direction. One analyst proposed that there were three sources of opposition—the New Left, the militant poor, and the underground. The New Left was made up of radical political activists, many of whom were students involved with Students for a Democratic Society (SDS) and the Student Nonviolent Coordinating Committee (SNCC). The militant poor included ethnic activists, blacks, Chicanos, and Native Americans. The undergrounds comprised anyone who rejected rigid political ideologies, including beats, hippies, and commune dwellers.

In general, hippies tended to avoid politics, except when their businesses or communities were threatened, and as a result they were suspicious of the New Left. *Rolling Stone* columnist Ralph Gleason pointed out that the New Left shared political enemies with hippies. Nevertheless, he said, "They [hippies and the New Left] all have the old approach. You can't make an omelet without breaking eggs. True, man true. But you better figure out how to make a revolution without killing people or it won't work. We've had all that." His point was that if either group resorted to violence to bring about change they would be recreating the world against which they rebelled. Leftist philosopher Herbert Marcuse called the hippies "the only viable social revolution." Some analysts believe their attack on American society made a substantial contribution toward change.

In the main, hippies grew up in comfortable, privileged surroundings, but this didn't stop them from glorifying the nobility of poverty. They championed the rights of racial minorities while accepting the tradition of a male-defined society. At least in the beginning, they were disinclined to permit women equal rights and privileges.

The counterculture proclaimed the value of physical and mental pleasure, maintaining that pleasure is not immoral. Country Joe McDonald claimed: "Probably the most revolutionary thing in the U.S. today is hedonism. By that I don't mean wishing your life away, but doing something you enjoy. That really puts them uptight." To hippies, sex was good, healthy, and fun. Most proclaimers, like McDonald, were male. As the counterculture gained momentum, many women lost faith in the counterculture's notions about sex. Moderate women advocated withdrawing from relationships in which men were dominant. Some women became actively hostile toward men.

Hippies distinguished between "dope," that is, "good drugs" that gave pleasure, and other drugs that might be good or bad. One hip author claimed that the government was correct in its fear of drugs because they made people feel too good. One *Rolling Stone* reporter equated hippie drug use with the early Judeo-Christian and the Native American use of drugs in connection with religious experiences. Many believed drugs enhanced human beings' connection to nature, rural and urban. They also believed that drugs promoted a sense of intimacy among people and could be a way to bridge cultural chasms. On the other hand, according to Timothy Miller, "the counterculture regarded most drugs as harmful. . . . They destroyed the good that dope [good drugs] had done."

Hippies considered music a key ingredient in the generational rebellion. Until 1966, when the Beatles gained worldwide recognition, folk music served as the music of cultural rebellion. The revival of folk music during the 1950s and 1960s prepared the way for rock and roll. The protest music of Pete Seeger and others was filled with distrust of the cultural establishment. Bob Dylan incorporated rock into folk music, and "hip" bands, such as the Grateful Dead, gained prominence. Rock and roll became an integral part of the counterculture. Not only did the lyrics of rock

spread a communal message, but its driving 4/4 beat inspired listeners to dance. The liberating force of rock encouraged crowds to sing, holler, scream, and feel good.

Rock music and dope were almost inevitably linked. Ringo Starr of the Beatles once said that dope "made a lot of difference to the type of music and words." At least in the minds of some musicians, dope inspired new musical styles and inspired new subject matter for lyrics.

Capitalism posed a moral dilemma for rock musicians. Capitalists made much more money from the work of musicians than did the musicians themselves. In time, many of the best musicians became capitalists. Even hippies who bootlegged music by recording concerts and selling their records on the black market used the money they made to pay bills. Hence, they also became capitalists in an underground economy.

Festivals and concerts were perceived by the countercultural faithful as the hip equivalent of pilgrimages, crusades, and revivals. So important did the halls where concerts were held become that the names of the ballrooms took on a sacred aura. However, the ultimate experience came from great outdoor festivals. The chance to share a cultural identity was just as important as the music in drawing the huge crowds.

Two giant festivals in 1969 represented high and low points in the counterculture movement. The August Woodstock Festival in New York is mythologized as the pinnacle of joy and peace. A *Rolling Stone* magazine reporter described the Woodstock Festival as a new culture arising from the ashes of adult American life. In terms of arrangements, however, Woodstock was a disaster. Supplies of food, medicine, and sanitary facilities were inadequate for the size of the crowd. Rain turned the Woodstock meadow into a quagmire. A *Liberation News Service* release claimed the shortcomings of the preparations helped the crowd to coalesce. "When natural disaster strikes, people pull together in a rare way that they all remember with amazement years later."

The Altamont Festival in California had a different outcome. The Rolling Stones hired members of the Hell's Angels motorcycle gang to serve as security guards. Several people were beaten, one person was stabbed and died, and three more were killed in accidents. Critics blamed the crowd of 400,000 for failing to subdue the less than fifty people who were violent. Anniversaries of Woodstock are regularly remembered. Altamont is left unmentioned.

Many legacies of the counterculture live on. Rock and its many variations remain a major musical influence. Hipsters' preoccupation with their bodies lives on in the large number of people who eat health foods once identified with hippies, such as yogurt, carob, and organic fruits and vegetables. Many hippie communes where organics were first grown still exist. Hippies' interests in mysticism and spiritual growth live on in the New Age Movement, where the focus has shifted from the group to the individual. The environmental movement owes much to the counterculture. Hippies were deeply involved in the first Earth Day on April 22, 1970, and Earth Day is now celebrated around the world.

See also Beat Generation; Communes and Collectives; Environmental Movement; Grateful Dead; Yippies **Reference** Timothy Miller. *The Hippies and American Values,* 1991.

Ho Chi Minh (1890–1969)

The leader of the North Vietnamese during most of the Vietnam War, Ho Chi Minh was born in 1890 in Central Vietnam. He changed the name he was given at birth—Nguyen Sinh Cung—several times before finally settling on Ho Chi Minh, which means "he who enlightens."

Raised during a period when Vietnam was ruled by France, Ho received a French education. After he left school, he spent several years at sea visiting many countries, including the United States, where he was favorably impressed by the American way of life. In London, Ho became interested in politics, and in France he joined the French Communist Party. He became convinced that the Soviets might one day liberate Vietnam from colonial rule.

In 1930 Ho organized the communists in Vietnam. In 1940 when France fell to Nazi invaders, a pro-German government was set up in southern France. Japan took the opportunity to seize air bases and port facilities in French Indochina (Laos, Cambodia, and Vietnam). In early 1941, disguised as a journalist, Ho returned to Vietnam, where he recruited an army to defeat the Japanese and the French in Vietnam who were collaborating with the Axis powers. Although he did not live to see his native land unified, Ho struggled toward that end for thirty-five years.

Early in the endeavor, he sought help for his guerrilla troops from the U.S. Office of Strategic Services (OSS), the predecessor of the Central Intelligence Agency (CIA). Because Ho wanted not only to defeat Japan but also to be rid of the French, the OSS was reluctant to help him. Nevertheless, an OSS advisory team parachuted into his jungle camp in northern Vietnam in early 1945.

Two weeks after World War II ended on August 15, 1945, the Vietnamese emperor Bao Dai abdicated. Four days later, Ho declared the independence of Vietnam from colonial rule. However, when British forces were assigned to the port city of Saigon, later the capital of South Vietnam, the commander returned power to the French. Ho's guerrilla forces, the Vietcong, maintained control of Hanoi and other important centers in northern Vietnam. In March 1946, France recognized the regime in the north in exchange for permission to send troops into several cities. The French promised to quickly grant Vietnam independence within the French Union. By December France and the Vietminh, the Vietnamese army, were at war.

Preoccupied following World War II with the threat of communism in Europe, the United States took little notice of communism in Indochina and the emergence of war in Vietnam. American inattention came to an end on June 25, 1950, when North Korean forces surged into South Korea and four days later captured Seoul, South Korea's capital. Six months earlier Communist leader Mao Zedong had conquered all of mainland China. The Soviet Union and China both recognized as legitimate the regime of Communist leader Ho Chi Minh and the Democratic Republic of Vietnam (North Vietnam). This cluster of Communist governments led President Harry Truman to expand the U.S. policy of "containment" of communism in Europe to include Asia.

At the same time northern Vietnam had been turned into a battlefield, the French tried to keep prosperous southern Vietnam under their influence, even after all of Vietnam was granted independence on March 8, 1949. Ho Chi Minh set out to win over all the Vietnamese to communism. The French commander in chief, General Jean de Lattre de Tassigny, spoke at the Pentagon in September 1950 to warn the American military that the loss of northern Vietnam would open the rest of Southeast Asia to communism. Still preoccupied with Korea, the United States sent only equipment and supplies.

By late 1952, six years after the war with the communists had begun, 90,000 French troops had been wounded, were missing, or were dead. The war's most furious and decisive battle began in Dien Bien Phu in November 1953 and lasted until May 7, 1954, when the communist forces raised their flag over the French command bunker. The following day, delegates assembled in Geneva to begin peace talks.

The peace agreement reached on July 21, 1954, became a source of frequent disagreements. The General Accord called for a cease-fire and a truce. Pending a nationwide election to be held during the summer of 1956, the country was divided into two states at the 17th parallel. All Vietminh communist forces were expected to withdraw to the north of the 17th parallel, and all French and State of Vietnam troops to the south. Refugees from both sides were allowed to cross the border to find new homes.

The accord left the new state of North Vietnam in a stronger position than its counterpart in the South. The Vietminh leaders agreed to the truce only because they expected the election called for in the truce would unify the country under their control. Although Ho had always claimed that he was a Vietnamese nationalist first and a communist second, he organized the North along communist lines.

In the South, no trained politicians were ready to take over from the puppet emperor, Bao Dai.

He asked the Catholic politician Ngo Dinh Diem to form a government. With help and enormous financial aid from the United States, Diem succeeded in taking control of the political chaos in the South. He abolished groups that disagreed with his religious or political beliefs. He made himself president of the Republic of Vietnam in October 1955 and made no preparation for the agreed-upon election in the summer of 1956. The repressive conditions in South Vietnam encouraged the development of a communist-led insurrection. Ho Chi Minh's guerrilla army, the Vietcong, expanded its forces into the South. Diem's regime was overthrown by his own army on November 1, 1963, and he and his brother were killed. Over the next fifteen months, the Republic of Vietnam had nine governments. In June 1965, Air Vice Marshal Nguyen Cao Ky took over. The rapid changes of government stopped, but the military regime in power was no less repressive than Diem's.

Until 1960, the United States supported the government in the South with military equipment, financial aid, and the help of 700 advisers who took over the training of the South Vietnamese army from the French. By the end of 1963, the number of advisers had grown to 17,000, and a growing number of American helicopters and pilots had joined them.

An election in 1967 rigged to defeat the communists increased tension. Ho Chi Minh's government, the National Liberation Front (NLF), endorsed troops based in the jungles and hillsides of the South. These troops battled to neutralize the South with the goal of enabling the North Vietnamese Regular Army to take over. Infiltration of equipment and military experts from the North spurred the growth of the NLF from about 30,000 in 1963 to about 150,000 in 1965. The NLF troops were commonly referred to as the Vietcong (Vietnamese communists) or VC, although not all were communists.

The growth of the Vietcong threatened the survival of the South Vietnamese government in Saigon, and this risk escalated American involvement. In February 1965, President Lyndon Johnson ordered that North Vietnam be bombed. The bombing encouraged rather than discouraged the government in Hanoi. Four weeks after the bombing, Johnson sent the first U.S. combat troops to Vietnam. On March 7, 1965, 3,500 U.S. Marines landed. By July, the number of combat troops had reached 75,000. It continued to climb, and by early 1968, the numbers had reached 510,000. As the numbers of U.S. troops in Vietnam increased, opposition to the war grew at home.

There was no front line in Vietnam from which an army could advance or withdraw. The jungle favored the small guerrilla units of the Vietcong. For the communists, the number of troops they lost to the war appeared to be insignificant compared to their ultimate goal.

On January 31, 1968, the Tet Offensive began as the North Vietnamese Regular Army and the Vietcong moved the war from the countryside to the urban areas of South Vietnam. Although the offensive was repulsed by American and South Vietnamese forces, Lyndon Johnson concluded that it was time for the United States to pull out of the war.

Johnson's popularity as a president had waned as opposition to the war had grown. On March 31, 1968, he announced his decision not to run for reelection. He sent veteran diplomat W. Averell Harriman to open negotiations with the communists. Peace talks began on May 10, 1968, in Paris and quickly reached an impasse. When President Richard Nixon took office in 1969, he sent Secretary of State Henry Kissinger to the talks, which lasted five years. The last American troops left Vietnam on March 29, 1973. By war's end, more than 2 million American men and women had served in Vietnam.

Ho Chi Minh died at the age of 79 in September 1969. He had earlier turned over the day-to-day management of North Vietnam to a collective of leaders.

See also Antiwar Movement
References Marshall Cavendish. *The Vietnam War: People and Politics,* vol. 11, 1988; Edward F. Dolan. *America after Vietnam,* 1989.

Hoffman, Abbie (1936–1989)

Born in Worcester, Massachusetts, in 1936, Abbie Hoffman, a former pharmaceuticals salesman with a staid family life, became in the 1960s an antiwar activist and a self-proclaimed revolutionary. He was the founder of the Youth International Party (the Yippies) and delighted in creating pranks with a political message. Celebrated in the media, Hoffman became a leading spokesperson for many young people during the 1960s. They made him a best-selling author. *Revolution for the Hell of It* (1968), which jokingly suggested overthrowing the government, was a favorite.

Hoffman's father, John, was a pharmacist who worked in his brother's drugstore until it closed after World War II. John Hoffman then founded the Worcester Medical Supply Company, which sold supplies to doctors.

Hoffman's quarrels with authorities began early in life. Following a fight with his English teacher, Hoffman was expelled from Worcester Classical High School and had to attend a private school. He obtained a bachelor's degree from Brandeis University, where he came under the influence of the radical social views of philosopher Herbert Marcuse and the humanistic psychology of Abraham Maslow. A year spent at the University of California to get a master's degree in psychology introduced Hoffman to activist politics.

He returned to Worcester in 1963 to work as a pharmaceutical salesman for three years. During those same years, he devoted most of his energies to community organizing. In 1966, Hoffman moved to New York City and founded Liberty House, a store that sold crafts made by poor people's cooperatives in Mississippi. He left Liberty House in 1967 to devote his time to opposing the Vietnam War. Hoffman attracted a following among New York's East Village hippies, who were mostly made up of rebellious, middle-class youth. In his autobiography, *Soon to Be a Major Motion Picture* (1980), Hoffman made a distinction between the free-form lifestyle of the hippies and himself. He wrote: "A semistructure freak among the love children, I was determined to bring the hippie movement into a broader protest."

To achieve his broader perspective, Hoffman staged a variety of "happenings." During his first prank in April 1967, Hoffman and a group of friends threw dollar bills from the visitors' gallery onto the floor of the Stock Exchange. The result was chaos. In October 1967, during a massive antiwar demonstration in Washington, D.C., Hoffman staged an event to surround the Pentagon. The goal was to make the building rise using mental power. His antics reflected Hoffman's perception of the influence the communication industry, particularly television, had on modern American life. He wanted to create a "guerrilla theater" in the streets to wage a war of symbols that would be broadcast on the evening news.

The decisive battle for Hoffman and the Yippies came at the 1968 Democratic National Convention in Chicago. A series of staged demonstrations was met with such a massive police reaction that it was later characterized by a government investigation as a "police riot." Television viewers watched in horror as confrontations between the police and the young demonstrators were intercut with views of the convention.

Chicago made Hoffman well known and a target for police attention. He was arrested eight times in the next eight months. One arrest provided a spectacular stage for Hoffman's guerrilla theater. In March 1969, a grand jury indicted Hoffman and seven others on charges of conspiracy and crossing state lines to incite a riot. During the twenty-week trial, Hoffman and his fellow defendants refused to follow proper courtroom decorum, provoking authorities into reactions that made them seem like villains.

The jury acquitted the group of conspiracy but found five of them, including Hoffman, guilty of crossing state lines to incite a riot. The trial confirmed Hoffman as a celebrity. He found himself in demand as a speaker, writer, and television talk show guest. The stress of visiting campuses to speak in the United States and abroad during the years 1970 and 1971 exhausted Hoffman emotionally, and he began to withdraw from activism. He returned in 1972 to campaign for the presidential election of Democratic senator George McGovern.

Hoffman's career as a radical came to an end on August 1973, when he was arrested for participating in the sale of 3 pounds of cocaine to undercover agents. After spending six months in jail, Hoffman was released on bail. If convicted, he faced a mandatory life sentence without possibility of parole for fifteen years. He jumped bail and went underground in February 1974. During six years underground, Hoffman, using the alias "Barry Freed," worked in upstate New York as a community organizer and an ecological activist. On September 3, 1980, he surfaced on ABC television as a guest of Barbara Walters. He had a new book to promote.

After he surrendered to authorities, Hoffman was given a three-year sentence and served a year before becoming eligible for parole. Hoffman's flamboyant life ended April 12, 1989. He apparently committed suicide.

See also Black Panther Party; Daley, Richard; Hippies; McCarthy, Eugene; McGovern, George; Yippies
References Terry Anderson. *The Movement and the Sixties: Protest in America from Greensboro to Wounded Knee*, 1995; Abbie Hoffman. *Revolution for the Hell of It*, 1968; *Steal This Book*; and *Soon to Be a Major Motion Picture*, 1980.

Homelessness

Estimates of the number of homeless people in the United States vary from a low of 300,000 to a high of 3 million. The ranks of the homeless include those who have lost their homes because of social factors: mentally ill people; substance abusers; victims of family violence; handicapped people who are unemployable; and children and teenagers who are runaways or have been thrown out of their homes. The homeless also include those who have lost their housing because of economic factors: a rise in rent; the loss of a job; a calamity like an apartment fire; or a divorce that leaves a parent without child support and unable to pay for both food and shelter. An estimated 60 percent of the homeless are lone adult males in their thirties or forties, about a third of whom are veterans, both from the Vietnam era and from the 1970s and 1980s.

In the late 1950s new drugs made it possible

to control the psychoses of many mentally ill people. The idea gained credence that the mentally ill could live outside mental hospitals. Politicians anxious to reduce expenditures seized on the opportunity to cut the budgets of large mental institutions. They promised to fund mental health centers and support services to aid the newly released, but these promises were not kept.

Populations of mental hospitals were cut to a tenth of their former size. Many former mental patients found themselves with no place to live. With no home and no way of obtaining medication, many became psychotic once again. Despite the return of their psychoses, they were no longer eligible to reenter the hospital. New legislation permitted admissions only for those who posed a danger to themselves or to someone else, a difficult criterion to meet, since most mentally ill people are not violent.

The mentally ill made up a large portion of the newly homeless. A shortage of low-rent housing and a steep rise in the cost of housing accounted for the large percentage. In the 1970s and 1980s, several factors severely reduced the amount of housing stock available to the poor and near-poor. President Ronald Reagan's administration virtually eliminated federally supported low-cost housing programs for working-class and poor families. At the same time low-cost housing was disappearing, the poor and near-poor were thrust into competition for housing with the middle class and affluent. Middle- and upper-income individuals and families set up homes separate from parents and former spouses. Divorces, delayed marriages, and adult unmarried baby boomers moved away from their parents' homes. The number of separate households grew faster than in earlier decades.

Bidding for scarce shelter drove up the cost for the poor and increased the percentage of income paid for housing among all economic classes. It became the norm for 40 or 50 percent of total income to be spent on housing. Further shrinkage in the amount of available low-rent housing was caused by a process called gentrification. Young, upwardly mobile professionals, bored with the suburbs, purchased low-rent, multiple family housing to restore as single-family homes. Low-income families and the elderly were forced out into the streets. Poor people who lose their housing for whatever reason are unlikely to have the extraordinary amount of money needed to move into a new apartment. Before moving in, a new tenant may need as much as $500 to $1,000 to pay a deposit and two months' rent.

People who have no home have few options. Some double up with family or friends, an arrangement that tends to be short-term, because overcrowding frays tempers. Some commit crimes in order to go to jail. Many walk the streets during the daytime and sleep under bridges, in abandoned buildings, or huddled in doorways or cardboard boxes.

Having no home complicates ordinary acts of daily living such as cooking a meal, taking a bath, going to the bathroom, attending school, being safe from the weather, and, most important, being safe from intrusions from other people. Shelters and welfare hotels may get the homeless out of the weather and provide toilets, but most of the other aspects of daily living remain difficult and sometimes impossible. Violence in shelters makes many homeless people prefer living in the streets. Children living in welfare hotels are at risk of being preyed upon or instructed in violence.

Ambivalence among the public about the homeless continues to grow, because much homelessness is a direct result of economic dislocation. Homelessness raises doubts about the ability of the American economic system to create prosperity and provokes fear of joining their ranks. A loss of manufacturing jobs and a shift to a lower-paid service economy in the United States have left many people underemployed or unemployed. For many of them the specter of homelessness looms.

See also Community Mental Health Center Movement

References John Belcher and Frederick DiBlasio. *Helping the Homeless: Where Do We Go from Here?* 1990; Jonathan Kozol. *Rachel and Her Children,* 1988; Doug Marx. *The Homeless,* 1990.

Horton, Myles (b. 1905)

In 1932, Myles Horton founded the Highlander Folk School in Monteagle, Tennessee, an adult education center devoted to helping people solve problems and conflicts—whether social, economic, or political—by bringing to bear their own knowledge. From the outset, Horton and his folk school were controversial. During labor uprisings beginning in the 1930s, he worked with labor union organizers who were engaged in trying to obtain decent working conditions. During the 1950s and 1960s, Highlander provided an oasis of reason for civil rights workers. At Highlander, Rosa Parks was inspired to take her stand and refuse to move to the back of the Montgomery bus. Civil rights leader Martin Luther King, Jr., folksinger Pete Seeger, and First Lady Eleanor Roosevelt, who was committed to civil rights for blacks, all spent time learning at the Highlander.

Born in Savannah, Tennessee, and raised in the Appalachian Mountains, Horton graduated from Cumberland University. He believed that no one has the power to dictate what people think. It took him years to understand the forces that prevented people from acting in their own best interest. Horton concluded that revolutionary change could not come from the top down. Based on that conclusion, he decided to work with working-class people, many of whom were exploited because of their race and socioeconomic class. He felt it was not worth his time to work with poor people who had given up hope. People without hope don't look for a path out of their misery.

To gain knowledge that would be useful to mountain people and with no intention of becoming a minister, Horton attended the Union Theological School in New York. At the University of Chicago, he learned about group problem solving and conflict from the famed sociologist Robert Park. In Park's classes, Horton realized that learning that came from group effort was superior to learning from individual efforts.

In his autobiography, *The Long Haul (1990)*, Horton described how the group method works. He wrote:

George Bernard Shaw once said that you only begin to solve a problem when you have two people who passionately believe in something state opposite views.

In a workshop, conflict gets the whole group involved. You don't even try to referee between two people. At this point the group takes over the discussion, since the problem being debated is everyone's problem. And when this happens, everyone discovers that the issue is not as simple as the two people have stated it, and a lot of the complications surface and get aired.

Horton believed that a school should be organized only enough to get the students and teachers together. In time, he realized that he had to understand the nonverbal language of mountain people by seeing how they related to one another, how they took care of their children, and how their experience affected them.

In Horton's view, the Highlander's best work has been in connection with social movements. In 1932, he anticipated the growth of unions in the South. By the time the Congress of Industrial Organizations (CIO) began moving into the South in 1935, Highlander already had a network of connections to new union people. Horton predicted in the 1950s that schools in the South would be desegregated. In 1954 he recruited people for an integrated workshop on integrated schools. In South Carolina, he developed methods to reach black millworkers, who were paid substantially lower wages than white workers.

Highlander severed its connections with the CIO in 1949 when the union disassociated itself from left-wing unions. In 1955, in connection with Eleanor Roosevelt's search for people to do support work for the United Nations, the Highlander was contacted. From involvement with a UN workshop, a new direction emerged for the Highlander. Staff began working with blacks who lived on the Sea Islands of South Carolina. From these efforts emerged a literacy program and citizenship schools, which prepared participants to register to vote. The citizenship schools in time played a critical part in furthering the goals of the civil rights movement. Highlander's approach has always been to start programs and turn them over to other organizations. The citizenship schools were taken over by the Southern Christian Leadership Conference (SCLC).

In 1959, the attorney general of Tennessee accused Highlander of being subversive. In 1961, the state revoked the school's charter and confiscated the school. The buildings were destroyed in a fire two months after the staff left. Horton applied for a new charter and threatened to sue the state of Tennessee if it was not forthcoming. With a new name, the Highlander Research and Education Center, the school operated out of a large house in a black community in Knoxville for ten years before moving back into the country. The years in Knoxville were filled with harassment from governments, the Ku Klux Klan, socialists, and communists.

By the 1990s, Highlander alumni were scattered all over the world engaged in helping poor people work on their own behalf. The kind of influence Myles Horton and Highlander had on individuals is evident in an article entitled "Myles' Legacy," which appeared in the Winter 1991 issue of *Social Policy.* The author, Lucy Massi Phenix, is a documentary filmmaker and educator who produced and directed a film called *You Got to Move* about the history and impact of Highlander. She likened the influence of Horton to a garden without boundaries.

See also Civil Rights Movement; Parks, Rosa; Young, Andrew

References Frank Adams. *Unearthing Seeds of Fire: The Idea of the Highlander,* 1975; Myles Horton. *The Long Haul: An Autobiography,* 1990.

In Re Gault (1967)

On May 16, 1967, the U.S. Supreme Court decision known as *In re Gault* gave children some legal rights. For most of recorded history, children were chattels of their parents—usually their fathers. Not until the nineteenth century did society perceive a need to protect children from abuse, neglect, and exploitation in the workplace. For centuries, children who did nothing more than steal food to stay alive were jailed with hardened criminals. Despite a widely held belief that childhood was an evil state, nineteenth-century reformers labored to move children out of adult prisons. At the turn of the century, Jane Addams, founder of Hull House in Chicago, proposed the creation of a separate juvenile court for children. The first was set up in 1899, and by 1920 every state in the United States had some form of juvenile court.

From the outset, the juvenile court system was seriously flawed. Based on the idea that the court should be free to rehabilitate rather than punish the child, the judge was given total control over the child's life. This effectively deprived an accused child of any of those rights an accused adult possessed—facing one's accuser, trial by jury, and so on. The juvenile court judge operating in the "benevolent" juvenile court had powers unavailable to judges in the "adversarial" adult court. No safeguards protected the child. The state did not have to prove a crime had been committed. Because the scope of the juvenile court was so broad, it became a dumping ground for children other institutions could not handle. The combination of a court without constraints and overcrowding did extraordinary damage to children's lives.

Change came in the system with the *Gault* decision. The case began in 1964, when 15-year-old Francis Gault was placed on probation for being in the company of a boy who stole a wallet. While Gault was still on probation, a neighbor claimed that he had made an obscene phone call to her. Without notifying Gault's parents, the police picked the boy up. Only after Gault's older brother went looking for him did the family discover that he was in a local detention center. A deputy at the

center told the family that a hearing was scheduled the next day.

Two hearings were held. The woman who complained appeared at neither. Even though the judge had never seen or spoken with the complainant, he sentenced Gault to the state industrial school "for the period of his minority, unless sooner discharged by due process of law." The same offense for an adult would have drawn a fine or a month or two in prison. The judge concluded that Gault was a "habitual delinquent," because, in addition to being in the company of the boy who stole the wallet and being accused of making the phone call, two years earlier a boy had accused Gault of taking his baseball glove, a claim for which there was no evidence.

The Gault family instituted habeas corpus proceedings. Writs of habeas corpus require that a prisoner be produced for a hearing to determine the legality of his detention. The case worked its way up through the appeals system to the U.S. Supreme Court. The Court agreed with the Gaults. The Court's decision criticized the "lack of substantive standards" in the juvenile courts. The Court set down the rights of a child in any case that might deprive him or her of liberty.

The rights specified by the Court are as follows:

1. The child and his or her family must have written notification of charges brought and proceedings to be undertaken.

2. The child has a right to counsel and the right to have the court provide counsel.
3. Written records must be kept in order to be available in the case of an appeal to the court's decision.
4. The child has a right to remain silent. (Children may be awed by adults and say whatever the adult wants them to say.)
5. The child has a right to confront his or her accusers, and to cross-examine them, usually through an attorney.
6. Anyone making a charge against the child must appear in court to state the charge in the child's presence.

Following the *Gault* case, Congress passed several laws strengthening children's rights. Legal representation was expanded beyond delinquency cases to include status offenses—that is, illegal behaviors that would not be crimes if committed by adults, such as running away. Children also have a right to an attorney when they are victims of abuse or neglect or pawns in a custody battle. Children do not have as many legal rights as adults.

Although children gained many legal rights, by the 1990s the juvenile system was still not meeting the needs of children. The pendulum had swung from locking children up on flimsy grounds without regard to due process to seldom locking them up. An exception was murder. Prosecutors were beginning to ask that juveniles charged with murder be tried as adults. Presumably to rehabilitate youngsters, most were sentenced to probation and assigned a counselor. However, the counselors were untrained or poorly trained and given huge caseloads that were impossible to manage effectively. Drug dealers hired juveniles as lookouts for pushers and called them "minute men," because, if they were caught, they spent "only about a minute locked up."

On the premise that many juveniles mature and leave behind their juvenile misbehaviors, juvenile police and court records are routinely sealed when the juvenile becomes a legal adult. During the 1980s and 1990s, as violent crimes were being committed with frequency by chil-

dren at younger and younger ages, the police and the public began to clamor for the elimination of sealed records. Victims of crimes by juveniles demanded more appropriate punishments. To relieve prosecutors of the requirements of requesting permission to try juveniles as adults, several states lowered the age. In the early 1990s nearly half of all arrests in the United States for motor vehicle theft and for arson were of people under age 18. Nearly one-third of all arrests for larceny (theft) were of juveniles.

In any given year, about 4 percent of all children in the United States make an appearance in juvenile court. One-third of all male juveniles living in inner-city neighborhoods are likely to make an appearance in juvenile court at least once during their juvenile years. The greater likelihood of a minority youngster being arrested in contrast with a white juvenile remained a source of ongoing conflict between minority communities and the police. Between 1985 and 1995, the number of delinquency cases handled by juvenile courts rose 81 percent. Within the same time frame, juvenile cases involving blacks and other nonwhite youth rose 78 and 94 percent, respectively, while white youth cases increased by 26 percent.

References Hoyt Gimlin, ed. *Youth Problems: Editorial Research Reports,* 1982; Robert Horowitz and Howard Davidson, eds. *Legal Rights of Children,* 1984; Carl Lardiero. "Of Disproportionate Minority Confinement," 1997.

Independent Living Movement

The movement of the disabled toward independent living appears to have begun with a student named Edward "Ed" Roberts and the University of California at Berkeley. After a 1953 polio epidemic swept through the family of Verne and Zona Roberts and their four sons, everyone except 14-year-old Ed recovered. After twenty months of hospitalization, Roberts moved back home in an iron lung that enabled him to breathe. Prior to his paralysis, Roberts had been indifferent to school. He recognized that only his mind remained undamaged. For a time, he attended school by telephone. When he physically returned to school, he found his classmates were fascinated rather than repelled by him.

Despite Roberts's good grades, his high school principal refused to award him a diploma because he had not completed driver's education and gym requirements. His mother, a former labor organizer, created an uproar that took her all the way through the system to the school board. Roberts received his diploma. He spent two productive years at San Mateo Community College. Roberts planned to attend the University of California at Los Angeles, one of only four in the country set up to serve disabled students. Roberts's San Mateo adviser talked him into applying at University of California at Berkeley because it had a more rigorous program in political science, his major interest.

One Berkeley dean told him, "We've tried cripples before and it didn't work." Nothing was accessible at Berkeley. Roberts had to get an attendant to carry him. The biggest problem was the weight of his iron lung, for which dormitory floors were not structurally adequate. The dean of Student Health Services suggested Roberts be housed on the third floor of the university's Cowell Hospital. Soon, as the university began to admit other physically disabled students, Roberts had company on the third floor. He and his mates became caught up in the several political movements fermenting on the Berkeley campus. They called themselves "The Rolling Quads."

By 1967, Roberts was working on a doctoral degree. Not all students with disabilities were doing as well. A California Department of Rehabilitation counselor threatened to cut off support for those students not progressing at a fast enough rate. Roberts led a rebellion, and the counselor was reassigned.

In the fall of 1968, eight members of the Rolling Quads appeared before the Berkeley City Council to ask for curb cuts. The students' wheelchairs could not navigate the 5-inch-high curbs. The council allocated $50,000 a year to make the changes. The Rolling Quads talked frequently about their dreams of getting jobs and becoming independent of the whims of the state bureaucracies. They wanted to shed the role of student by day and patient at night. They wanted to stop being segregated in a disability commune.

The counselor at San Mateo Community College who had helped Roberts had developed an antidropout program at San Mateo. She enlisted other students to help at-risk students solve problems such as finding transportation or getting a job. A federal education official asked her to come to Washington and replicate her program on a national level. She, in turn, invited Roberts to come to Washington, D.C., and help her write provisions for disabled people.

In the fall of 1970, the Rolling Quads were awarded $83,000 in grant money to begin the Physically Disabled Student Program (PDSP) at Berkeley. They hired disabled counselors to find apartments for people in wheelchairs. They also developed a roster of attendants willing to do whatever was necessary to enable disabled students to live a student life, and they steered students through the bureaucratic obstacles related to paying the attendants. Wheelchairs turned out to be a stumbling block to living an active life. They broke down frequently. PDSP set up a 24-hour-a-day repair shop staffed by self-taught experts who set about developing their own wheelchair designs. They also learned to modify cars and vans for use by disabled students.

The activities of PDSP redefined the medical definition of independence from being able to move one's arms and legs to the ability to control the quality of one's life. When PDSP began operation, various disability groups operated separately from one another. In time, PDSP began getting requests from blind students to find them readers. They also received requests for help from nonstudents. Rarely did they turn anyone away.

In the spring of 1972, the Center for Independent Living (CIL) in Berkeley, California, opened on a shoestring budget. Roberts took over as CIL's director, and the center hired a new grant writer, who raised an extraordinary $1 million.

In 1975, California's new governor, Jerry Brown, appointed Roberts as the director of the state's Department of Rehabilitation. Fifteen years earlier that same agency had predicted that Roberts would never be able to hold a job. Until Roberts took over, the philosophy of the agency revolved around the staff's ability to place people in jobs. As a consequence, the staff had worked only with those easiest to place—the least disabled.

Berkeley was not the only place where civil rights and student protesters were developing a new definition of disability. In the spring of 1970, a year after she had graduated from college, Judy Heuman was denied a license to teach in New York City's public schools. Left a quadriplegic at the age of eighteen months, Heuman had to use a wheelchair. The principal of the local elementary school decided her wheelchair was a fire hazard and, instead of permitting her to attend school, sent a teacher into her home twice a week for an hour. The respect Heuman's German-Jewish immigrant mother had for education turned her into a fierce advocate on behalf of her daughter to see that she had a proper education.

Heuman absorbed her mother's lessons in advocacy, and at Long Island University in Brooklyn, she fought a series of battles with the administration. She organized other disabled students and forced the university to put ramps on its buildings. With a goal of helping elementary school–age children, Heuman majored in speech therapy. She was turned down for a teaching certificate because the testing physician did not believe she could go to the bathroom on her own or help children get out of a school building in the event of an emergency. Heuman sued the Board of Education for discrimination. When it became clear that the board would lose the suit, the members settled out of court. Although Heuman had obtained her teaching certificate, only the principal of the elementary school she had attended as a child was willing to hire her.

The publicity Heuman received in connection with the suit prompted hundreds of disabled people to write to her. At the age of 22, in 1970, Heuman founded The Disabled in Action, a disability rights group. The group engaged in protest and did not offer services. In 1975, Roberts asked Heuman to take over as director of CIL. From 1975 to 1982, she combined political activism with services to promote independent living.

The rise of a parents' movement following World War II was perhaps the most important factor in changing the public's attitude toward disabilities. The United Cerebral Palsy Association, in 1948, and the Muscular Dystrophy Association, in 1950, were organized by parents. The common concern parents had was to obtain an education for their children. As a direct result of parents' actions, in 1970, Congress established a federal bureau for the handicapped.

The most significant sources of change came about as an accident. The Rehabilitation Act of 1973 was a spending bill that authorized $1.55 billion in federal aid to the disabled to be spent over two years. Unnoticed at the end of the bill were four provisions—the most important, Section 504, made it illegal for any federal agency or any institution or company receiving federal funds to discriminate solely because of a person's handicap. After passage, aides could not remember who had suggested adding civil rights protection, which had been copied out of the Civil Rights Act of 1964. The Department of Health, Education, and Welfare (HEW) estimated the provision would cost the government a billion dollars.

During his bid for the presidency, Jimmy Carter had promised to complete regulations left unfinished by his predecessor. Carter's new HEW secretary, Joseph Califano, alarmed by the public reaction if he included coverage for alcoholics, drug addicts, and homosexuals, stalled about issuing regulations. To force the hand of HEW, Judy Heuman and a group of protesters occupied the sixth floor of the San Francisco HEW regional office for twenty-five days. HEW officials thought that by refusing to allow food into the building, cutting off telephones, and barring attendants, they could force the group into giving up. Some of the more severely handicapped risked their lives to stay.

HEW officials underestimated the commitment of the protesters and the public support they had. When an HEW official disclosed that Califano was considering changes that amounted to "separate but equal," Heuman told him they were not acceptable. Integration was key. On April 28, 1977, four years after the law had been passed, Califano signed the regulations. At the same time, he signed the regulations for the Education for All Handicapped Children Act passed in 1975. The San Francisco sit-in marked a turning point in the disability rights movement. It helped disabled people recognize their ability to protest, and it unified disability groups.

Despite its promise, the disability rights movement faltered in the 1980s. Opponents greatly exaggerated the potential costs of changes. The courts were not supportive, and the Reagan administration was hostile toward regulations that would affect business and government agencies. Despite these setbacks, the proliferation of centers promoting independent living spread the new philosophy to disabled people, their families, and the professionals who served them. The centers insisted that no one knew the needs of disabled people better than they did.

Disabled children who began school in 1977, after their rights were assured, began graduating in the late 1980s and launched a new era of activism. One area of student activism and social change can be seen in sports and physical education. The *Journal of Physical Education, Recreation, and Dance* in its March 1998 issue posed the question "Should students with disabilities be allowed to try out for and compete on school athletic teams or should schools be responsible for providing extracurricular athletic options for students with disabilities." The question stimulated a lively debate on the Internet. One respondent, Gil Fried, an assistant professor of sports and fitness at the University of Houston, reminded his colleagues that the Americans with Disabilities Act (1991) mandated inclusion. If a student with disabilities tries out and fails to make the team, then he or she may be motivated to try again the next year, but if the school blocks the student's participation, his or her motivation to test athletic skills in the future will be lost.

In March 1994, Ed Roberts, 42 years after becoming a quadriplegic, died from a heart attack. Some of the nation's first curb cuts were made in Berkeley, California. Curb cuts in cities across America serve as a monument to him. The Independent Living Center he established in Berkeley has 300 replicas across America. Roberts married

and fathered a son who was seventeen when he died. He established an Oakland, California–based disability think tank in the 1990s and began to spread his independent living philosophy around the world. When a healer in Russia promised to cure him, Roberts, the president of the World Institute on Disability, said, "Just don't make me walk. I'll lose my job."

See also Deaf Student Protest; Disability Rights Movement
Reference *Journal of Physical Education, Recreation, and Dance.* "Should Students with Disabilities Be Allowed to Try Out for and Compete on School Athletic Teams or Should Schools Be Responsible for Providing Extracurricular Athletic Options for Those Students with Disabilities," 1998; Joseph Shapiro. *No Pity,* 1994.

Infant Formula Action Committee

In the 1970s, the Swiss-based multinational Nestle Company targeted Third World mothers as a lucrative market for its powdered baby formula. This kind of formula serves babies well, provided it is prepared according to guidelines and under sanitary conditions. The bottles and nipples must be sterilized, the water used to turn the dry formula into a liquid must be relatively pure, and the proportion of formula to water must be accurate. In the Third World of the 1970s, even when the procedure was properly explained, pure water was rare, and sanitary conditions were hard to achieve. The greatest risk to infants came from mothers' efforts to stretch the expensive formula by adding extra water, thereby inadvertently reducing intake of food. As a consequence, Third World babies died of disease and malnutrition.

Outraged missionaries and health professionals contacted the Nestle Company with their complaints about the practice of selling dried baby formula in the Third World. The company responded that it had broken no laws. It was indifferent to the complaints.

As activists and nutritionists in the industrialized world spread the word, a boycott was launched by the Infant Formula Action Committee (INFACT) in the United States. Almost 100 organizations in sixty-five countries organized a transnational boycott of Nestle products. The boycott became a public relations nightmare for Nestle, which preferred to be thought of in terms of cozy cups of hot chocolate. The campaign forced the company to abandon Third World sales of its dried infant formula. The boycott also prompted the World Health Organization (WHO) to pass a code of conduct governing the marketing and sale of infant formula.

See also Nongovernmental Organizations
Reference Robert S. Walters and David H. Blake. *The Politics of Global Economic Relations*, 4th ed., 1992.

Jackson, Jesse (b. 1941)

Clergyman, civil rights leader, and presidential candidate, Jesse Jackson became prominent in the 1960s as a member of Martin Luther King, Jr.'s, staff and as president of Operation PUSH (People United to Save Humanity).

Jackson was born in Greenville, South Carolina, to Helen Burns, a domestic worker who later became a cosmetologist. Jackson's father, Noah Louis Robinson, a cotton grader, lived next door and was married to someone else. When Jackson was 2 years old, his mother married Charles Henry Jackson, a former athlete who became a postal worker and a janitor. When Jackson was 16, his stepfather adopted him. As an adult, Jackson attributed his drive to succeed as an attempt to "outdistance" those who tried to shame him because his parents were not married.

As a boy, Jackson worked at various jobs and represented his Baptist church at Sunday school conventions. An athlete like his stepfather, Jackson was a quarterback on a state championship team. He won a football scholarship to the University of Illinois but transferred to North Carolina Agricultural and Technical State College, an all-black school, after he learned that blacks at Illinois were expected to be linemen, not quarterbacks.

In 1963, Jackson became active in campus civil rights organizing. He arranged for sit-ins and picket lines to integrate lunch counters and other business establishments in Greensboro, North Carolina, gaining statewide attention for his labors. After college, Jackson attended Chicago Technological Seminary on a scholarship. A semester short of graduation, he left to work full-time for King at the Southern Christian Leadership Conference (SCLC) in Atlanta, Georgia.

In 1966, King sent Jackson to Chicago to lead the city's Operation Breadbasket, an effort to secure more jobs for blacks and improve services in black communities. Jackson achieved a triumph after a sixteen-week drive to make the A&P supermarket chain hire black workers. The chain signed an agreement to hire 268 more blacks and to stock brands produced by black manufacturers. In 1967, Jackson became leader of the national organization of Operation Breadbasket.

Although Jackson was mentioned as a possible successor to King as head of SCLC after King was assassinated on April 4, 1968, the Reverend Ralph Abernathy was chosen. Amid rumors that he was not happy with Abernathy's leadership, Jackson remained with SCLC for another three and a half years. In December 1971, Jackson founded Operation PUSH and built it into a thriving national campaign. A tireless traveler and a riveting speaker, he led audiences around the country in chants of "I am somebody. I may be poor, but I am somebody. I may be on welfare, but I am somebody. Nobody can save us, for us, but us." In 1976, Jackson founded PUSH-Excel (PUSH for Excellence), a crusade in inner-city schools to curb the growth of vandalism, drug abuse, teen pregnancy, truancy, and high dropout rates.

With help from President Jimmy Carter and Secretary of State Cyrus Vance, in the summer of 1979 Jackson secured a visa to visit South Africa, where he led black audiences in chants and hymns that stressed black pride and advocated civil disobedience. Not long after his trip to Africa, Jackson plunged into Middle Eastern politics when he toured Israel, the West Bank, Lebanon, Syria, and Egypt to promote acceptance of the Palestine Liberation Organization (PLO). Jackson was criticized by the Israelis for his pro-Arab bias and by the Arabs for his recommendation of a freeze on the Palestinian armed struggle and recognition of Israel.

On November 3, 1983, Jackson announced his

Jesse Jackson.

candidacy for president. He entered the race because Democratic leaders had been "too silent and too passive" in opposing President Ronald Reagan's economic, social, and foreign policies. Jackson promised to represent the poor and the dispossessed. He pledged to forge a "rainbow coalition" of those who are "rejected ... despised" and "left naked before the Lord in the wintertime." Although some key black leaders endorsed Jackson's candidacy, many opposed it, fearing that he would split Democratic support for former vice president Walter Mondale. Although his campaign was often disorganized, many journalists found Jackson the most interesting figure in a field of bland candidates.

Jackson's stature on the international scene rose when he appealed to Syrian president Hafez al-Assad for the release of U.S. Navy pilot Lieutenant Robert O. Goodman, Jr., whose plane had been shot down over central Lebanon by Syrian gunners. Jackson succeeded where U.S. diplomacy had failed.

The glow of approval disappeared when a black *Washington Post* reporter, Milton Coleman, revealed that in a private conversation, Jackson had referred to Jews by the derogatory term "Hymies" and to New York as "Hymietown." At a New Hampshire synagogue two days before the New Hampshire primary election, Jackson apologized. He declared, "It was not in the spirit of meanness, but an off-color remark having no bearing on religion or politics." He received 5.3 percent of the New Hampshire vote.

Jackson's credibility with America's Jewish community took another blow a few months later. In a March 11, 1984, speech, Louis Farrakhan, Jackson supporter and head of the Black Muslim group known as the Nation of Islam, made a remark interpreted by many to be a threat against the *Washington Post* reporter who had written the story about Jackson's remarks. To worsen the impact, in the same speech, Farrakhan described Adolf Hitler as a "great man," albeit "a wicked one." Jackson's biographer, Marshall Frady, described the difficulty he had in making a break with Farrakhan. Jackson felt that in repudiating the Black Muslim leader, he might be turning his back on millions of black people for whom Farrakhan was a leader.

Jackson regained credibility on "super Tuesday," the election day when five primaries and several state caucuses are held. The results left three contenders in the Democratic race. In New York State's primary, Mondale received 44.8 percent of the vote, Gary Hart received 27.3, and Jackson a respectable 25.5.

After it became evident that Mondale would be the Democratic presidential nominee, Jackson embarked on a six-day tour of Latin America. In Panama, he conferred with representatives of El Salvador's leftist guerrillas and conveyed their peace proposal to the president of El Salvador, José Duarte. He also met with Daniel Ortega, leader of Nicaragua's Sandinista government, and with Cuban president Fidel Castro. From Castro, he secured the release of twenty-two U.S. citizens imprisoned on drug charges or border violations, plus twenty-six Cuban political prisoners.

While Jackson was in Latin America, Farrakhan created new misery for him by reportedly calling Judaism a "gutter religion" and charging the United States with being engaged in a criminal conspiracy by supporting Israel. After several days of avoiding comment, Jackson finally said that Farrakhan's comments were reprehensible and morally indefensible.

When the long primary was over, Jackson had 384 delegates pledged to him, more than he had expected but not enough to force Democratic National Convention delegates to accept his controversial platform proposals. To the relief of many Democrats, Jackson neither bolted the party nor launched a third-party crusade. Instead, at the 1984 Democratic National Convention in San Francisco, Jackson made a passionate speech. He said, "If in my low moments, in word, deed, or attitude, through some error of temper, taste, or tone, I have caused anyone discomfort, created pain, or revived someone's fears, that was not my truest self.... When I see a missing door, that's the slummy side. Train some youth to become a carpenter, that's the sunny side. When I see the vulgar words and hieroglyphics of destitution on the walls, that's the slummy side. Train some youth to be a painter and artist, that's the sunny side ... I am not a perfect servant. I am a public servant doing my best against the odds. As I develop and serve, be patient. God is not finished with me yet." Some commentators declared that Jackson's speech may have been the most eloquent oration at a presidential nominating convention since William Jennings Bryan's in 1896. As Jackson spoke, the television audience kept increasing, until it reached 33 million viewers.

Following the convention, Jackson went on the road to campaign for the Democratic ticket, traveling more miles than either the presidential candidate, Walter Mondale, or the vice presidential candidate, Geraldine Ferraro. The huge black voter turnout Jackson had generated for his own candidacy in the primaries continued into the general election. Ten million blacks voted, more than in any other presidential election. This huge turnout had a significant impact on local elections. During his campaign, Jackson had said, "My running will stimulate thousands to run, and millions to register. If you can get your share of legislators, mayors, sheriffs, schoolboard members, tax assessors, and dogcatchers, you can live with whoever is in the White House."

In 1985, Jackson had a ceremonial meeting with Soviet leader Mikhail Gorbachev at which Jackson abruptly said, "There is great anxiety among the American people about the plight of Soviet Jews." Gorbachev insisted there was no problem. Jackson kept pushing him.

Jackson never paused after the 1984 convention. He traveled around the country preaching his political gospel—decrying the "economic violence" and "the merger maniacs and corporate barracudas," particularly the "American multinational firing free labor at home to hire repressed labor abroad." Months before the 1988 presidential campaign began, polls indicated that Jackson was a leading candidate.

Jackson brought into his campaigning a minister's belief that words can lift people out of their everyday selves into a larger reality. In Rome, New York, Jackson told 300 white machinists—who had been on strike for two years—that they were engaged in an important struggle. "It's against what's happening in the world economy, what corporations are doing to a lot more people like you. So when you fight here, you fight not just for yourselves, you're fighting for working folks all across this country."

At Jackson's Rainbow Coalition conferences, large delegations of farmers, destitute oil workers, and labor leaders began to appear. Jackson's rallies brought together huge numbers of citizens who had long felt estranged from the interests of those presiding over the country. He was the only civil rights leader trying to forge a link between blacks and white working people. By 1988, Jackson's campaign organization had become more cosmopolitan and professional. To his 1984 battery of issues he had added a comprehensive offensive against the blight of drugs. New York governor Mario Cuomo said that Jackson's 1988 campaign had "the single most identifiable and attractive message."

Some media criticized Jackson by comparing his ability to mesmerize the public with that of former President Ronald Reagan's, calling him long on grievances and short on alternatives.

After the New York primary, when the race was down to Massachusetts governor Michael Dukakis and Jesse Jackson, pressure was put on Jackson to step down in favor of Dukakis. He refused. When the Democratic primaries were over, Jackson finished second with 7 million votes; of those, 2 million had come from white voters. He went into the convention with 1,200 delegates, almost a third of the total.

Dukakis apparently couldn't stand being around Jackson. Bert Lance, a member of Jackson's campaign staff, met a few times with the Dukakis staff. He later said, "It was obvious that they had no real understanding of Jesse at all. They kept wanting to know how to handle him." As had Mondale's staff in 1984, Dukakis's staff didn't want to deal with Jackson. After the convention was over and the campaign for the general election began, the Dukakis staff worked to isolate Jackson from the campaign. With him gone, they lost the seventeen-point lead they had going into the campaign. When they lost the election, Jackson became a convenient scapegoat. They blamed the loss on his huge presence at the convention.

Andrew Young, who was not always a fan of Jackson's, said later, "Jesse paid a very high price for those campaigns, but I think he may well have saved the country with them, at that critical time during Reagan. He restored a mass focus on black concerns, on poverty and other conditions holding a real danger of social eruption if left ignored . . . his voter registration efforts brought a liberalization of the makeup of Congress—it was how we got forty blacks in the House . . . how we got Clinton elected." Political writer David Halberstam predicted that although Jackson would never become president as he wanted to be, he had a larger role to play. "He has become America's black media man on the world media stage."

After the 1988 election, Jackson's concerns became global. During a 1989 jaunt overseas, he said, "All our yards are much closer to each other now, which expands the compass of the golden rule about loving your neighbor as yourself." Jackson told his biographer, "When the curtain finally falls on me, all I want history to say is, 'He was part of the conscience of his age.' I'll rest then."

See also Sit-ins, Southern Christian Leadership Conference; Young, Andrew
Reference Frady Marshall. *Jesse: The Life and Philosophy of Jesse Jackson,* 1996.

Johnson, Lyndon
See Great Society

Jones, (Everett) LeRoi (b. 1934)
Poet, playwright, and black separatist leader, LeRoi Jones, later known as Amiri Baraka, gained recognition in the late 1950s. On the fringes of the beatnik literary movement, he became known to the public as the raging, often ironic author of one-act plays, among them *Dutchman,* which won the Obie, an award given by the *Village Voice.*

After several semiprofessional works were staged, Jones made his professional off-Broadway debut with *Dutchman.* The name alludes to a legendary ship without a port. The thirty-five-minute drama is about a confrontation between Lula, a white woman, who is attractive, unconventional, and immoral, and Clay, a black man who is a well-dressed intellectual. Mockingly, Lula flirts with Clay. Then she taunts him for trying to act white. Angry, Clay tells her, "If I'm a middle-class fake white man—let me be. The only thing that would cure my neurosis would be your murder." Pretending self-defense, Lula stabs him to death. In his plays, Jones tried to shock white Americans into becoming aware of the love-hate racial relations in the United States. In time, he concluded white audiences were hopeless and wrote only for black audiences.

Jones founded Spirit House, a community-service center in Newark, New Jersey, to serve inner-city blacks, disseminate Afro-Islamic culture, and build black political power in Newark. He told an interviewer in 1964, "Any artist has a lot of energy that won't respond to anything else. The reason I'm not a violent man—that's what I'm trying to say in *Dutchman*—is that art is the most beautiful resolution of energies that in another context might be violent to myself or anyone else."

While teaching a course at San Francisco State College in 1967, Jones consulted with Ron Karenga, the founder of a black politico-cultural group called US. Jones wanted to learn how to organize black people around bread-and-butter issues. After he returned to Newark, in January 1968, he founded the Black Community Development and Defense Organization (BCD). BCD was composed of approximately 100 men—including a military-style corps called the Simbas—and fifty women dedicated to creating a new value system for the black community. Members wore traditional African dress, spoke Swahili—in addition to English—and stressed such traits as courtesy, promptness, propriety, and willingness to share. Members were Muslim. Jones became minister of the faith and adopted the Arabic name Amiri Baraka.

Politically BCD fit into a larger organization called Committee for a United Newark, whose goal was to gain power for the black and Puerto Rican communities of Newark. Jones had no desire to enter into combat with whites. "Our thing now," he said, "is love—love ourselves. Let the whites work out their own salvation." In the 1990s Jones's play *Dutchman* continued to be produced in theaters in the United States and abroad. A 1984 book, *Eulogies,* included memories of Dizzy Gillespie and James Baldwin.

See also Baldwin, James
Reference Imamu Amiri Baraka. *Eulogies,* 1984; LeRoi Jones. *Autobiography of LeRoi Jones/Amiri Baraka,* 1984.

Joplin, Janis (1943–1970)

Producing sounds previously associated only with black singers, screaming and wailing the blues, Janis Joplin, a white singer, converted millions of predominantly white rock enthusiasts to her brand of "blue-eyed soul." Born in Port Arthur, Texas, Joplin never fit in. She described her hometown as a place where the chief amusements were going to drive-in movies, visiting the corner coke stands, and burning crosses on the lawns of blacks.

In a 1969 interview for the *New York Times*

Janis Joplin.

Magazine, Joplin said, "Port Arthur people thought I was a beatnik, and they didn't like beatniks, though they'd never seen one . . . I read, I painted, I thought, I didn't hate niggers. There was nobody like me in Port Arthur." At 17, Joplin ran away from home. She returned a couple of times and tried to fit in, but it never worked out. Eventually, she made San Francisco her base. Interested in blues music, for years she collected the records of Huddie "Leadbelly" Ledbetter and Bessie Smith. One night at a party, Joplin did an imitation of the folksinger Odetta. She recalled, "I had never sung before and out came this huge voice." She began singing in a small bar in Austin, Texas, and in folk clubs and bars in North Beach and Venice, California. In 1965, Joplin retreated back to Port Arthur, burnt out by too little food, too many drugs, and a broken romance.

She stayed a year, but an emerging hippie community and its new rock music lured her to San Francisco. In June 1966, Joplin made her debut with the band called Big Brother and the Holding Company at a hippie hangout, the Avalon ballroom. Entranced by the rhythm and power of the music, she danced while she sang, something she had never done before. Because she couldn't hear herself, she sang louder and louder. Word spread about the singer, and she and the band became regular performers. In June 1967, Joplin gained national attention with her performance at the Monterey International Pop Festival. As a result of the fame, she and the band began playing the rock circuit: the Electric Factory in Philadelphia, the Psychedelic Supermarket in Boston, the Kinetic Playground in Chicago, and the Whiskey-A-Go-Go in Los Angeles.

Shortly after a triumph at the Newport Folk Festival, Joplin and Big Brother and the Holding Company brought out an album entitled *Cheap Thrills*. Before its release date, advance sales amounted to a million copies. One critic claimed Joplin "possesses the kind of genuine womanness—uncleansed and intensely real—that Billie Holiday had and that many white vocalists have tried and failed to emulate."

Although Joplin was considered "the queen of the hippies," she identified herself as a beatnik. She explained that whereas hippies are optimistic, "beatniks believe things aren't going to get better and say the hell with it, stay stoned and have a good time." On stage she drank Southern Comfort. Joplin acknowledged that her music kept away her "super horrible downs." Joplin died on October 4, 1970, of a heroin overdose. After her doctor had told her she would die if she continued to take drugs, she had been off drugs for some time. Her death inspired speculations about whether she had committed suicide. The coroner and her biographer, Myra Friedman, both believe her death was accidental.

See also Beat Generation; Hippies; Rock and Roll
Reference Myra Friedman. *Buried Alive: The Biography of Janis Joplin,* 1973.

Journey of Reconciliation
See Freedom Riders

Kennedy, John Fitzgerald
(1917–1963)

The first Roman Catholic and the youngest man ever elected to be president, John F. Kennedy was also elected by an extraordinarily narrow margin. He was the second of nine children born to Joseph Kennedy and Rose Fitzgerald Kennedy. Both of his grandfathers were Irish immigrants who settled in Boston, where they succeeded and became involved in politics. Joseph Kennedy taught his children to be fiercely competitive. Their mother, a deeply religious woman, taught them a sense of religious obligation. To permit his children to participate in a life of public service, Joseph Kennedy set up trust funds, which gave his children $1 million each when they reached maturity.

While playing football at Harvard, Kennedy received a back injury that plagued him throughout his life. Some writers charge that there was no injury, but that the story was made up to cover the fact that he suffered from Addison's disease. His back problems were aggravated when, during World War II, his patrol boat was torpedoed. Despite his injury, Lieutenant John F. Kennedy saved the lives of several of his crewmen. In the summer of 1944, his older brother Joseph, a flier, died in action over the English Channel. Joseph's death changed the direction of John's life. Joseph's father wanted his oldest son to be president, and Joseph had shared his political ambition. John became the substitute to fulfill his father's ambition.

On July 13, 1960, Kennedy became the Democratic Party's nominee for president. Although Kennedy's religion was not an issue on which either candidate dwelled, a University of Michigan poll in April 1961 revealed that he had lost 1.5 million votes because he was Catholic. Because Kennedy was physically attractive and so young compared to most presidents, he was appealing to the first wave of baby boomers (those born between 1946 and 1964) to reach their teens. His inaugural command, "Ask not what your country can do for you. Ask what you can do for your country," inspired them. His support of the idea to form a Peace Corps and send young Americans to serve in poor countries around the world was met with enthusiasm.

The Cold War was a major issue during Kennedy's administration. The Cold War began following World War II, when the increasing power of the Soviet Union made many Americans and their Western allies uneasy—an unease made more severe by the realization that the then Soviet premier, Joseph Stalin, was as ruthless as Adolf Hitler. Soviet leaders predicted that the whole world would one day embrace communism, a system in which all property is owned by the community or the state. The term "Cold War" expressed the idea that, although physical conflict had not broken out, a war was going on between two conflicting ideologies, capitalism versus communism.

The United States and the Soviet Union each built an arsenal of nuclear warheads, and each believed the other was prepared to use them. While in office, Republican president Dwight D. Eisenhower continually fought ill-founded accusations, not only by Democrats but by Pentagon officials and some Republicans, that there was a missile gap in the Soviet Union's favor. Satellite photos eventually proved him right. But by the time Kennedy took office, that belief was too well rooted to be easily dispelled.

The Soviets had a tight hold on Eastern Europe, particularly East Germany. In Southeast Asia, a fragile government set up by the French in Vietnam was threatened by a communist-led guerrilla force. During Kennedy's administration, the number of military advisers rose from 700 to

President John Kennedy signs the nuclear test ban treaty at the White House on October 7, 1963, as members of Congress look on.

17,000. On the island of Cuba, 90 miles off the Florida coast, avowed Marxist Fidel Castro had taken power in 1959. Most embarrassing, in 1957 the Soviets had launched the world's first spacecraft, the Sputnik. During the presidential campaign, the State Department briefed Kennedy on plans to overthrow Fidel Castro. The plans called for American military experts to train a small force of Cuban exiles and were based, in part, on the idea that thousands of Cubans would spontaneously revolt against Castro. But in implementing the plan, the Kennedy administration provided no air support, no reinforcements, and far less naval support than originally envisioned. Furthermore, during the campaign, Kennedy indicated he wished to intervene militarily in Cuba, thus signaling to Castro an invasion might be coming.

The invasion by 1,500 Cubans at the Bay of Pigs was a disaster. Kennedy took responsibility for the fiasco but remained unrepentant. He had underestimated the toughness of Cuba and other developing countries and overestimated the ability of the United States to impose its will on other nations, particularly without a more thorough grasp of what their needs and perceptions were. Nor did he seem to realize it was better to overprepare for a military situation than it was to underprepare.

Cuba was the site of another threat to his administration. On the morning of October 16, 1962, National Security Adviser McGeorge Bundy showed the president photographs that revealed the installation by Soviet technicians of silos to hold nuclear missiles in Cuba. Kennedy feared the Soviets might be trying to bluff the United States into taking the first steps toward war. Yet he could not ignore silos that might within days contain weapons pointed at the United States.

The president was aware that the Soviets were unhappy about North Atlantic Treaty Organization (NATO) missile silos near them in Turkey, weapons that were obsolete. The Defense Department planned to place Polaris missiles aboard submarines, thus eliminating need for the Turkish silos. But Kennedy could not directly order that missiles controlled by NATO be removed.

He chose to create a naval blockade to prevent a stream of ships already underway from bringing weapons to Cuba. Secretly, via his brother Robert Kennedy, the president sent Soviet premier Nikita Khrushchev a message hinting at his support for removal of the Turkish missiles—a militarily pointless concession. For the next several days, the United States and the Soviet Union hovered on the brink of war. Eventually, the Soviet ships turned back, and Khrushchev agreed to dismantle the weapons sites if Kennedy would promise not to invade the island. By Kennedy's order, no one in his administration was to crow about making the Soviets back down—the balance was too delicate.

The Cuban Missile Crisis enhanced Kennedy's reputation internationally, but in a way it contributed to the intergenerational conflict that was building in the United States. The fears of the Soviet Union among those who had lived through World War II were increased by the Cuban confrontation. Baby boomers coming of age, particularly those who became part of the hippie counterculture, which promoted love and peace, felt their parents' generation was caught up in useless paranoia. When the president was assassinated in November 1963, for many the futility of hate was confirmed. The awareness of the good that young Americans could do for others inspired by Kennedy lingered long after his death.

See also Kennedy, Robert; Peace Corps
References Doris Goodwin. *The Fitzgeralds and the Kennedys: An American Saga*, 1987; Barbara Harrison and Daniel Terris. *A Twilight Struggle: The Life of John Fitzgerald Kennedy*, 1992.

Kennedy, Robert (1925–1968)

The seventh child and third son of Joseph Kennedy and Rose Fitzgerald Kennedy, Robert Kennedy was raised in a wealthy, competitive, political family. He managed his brother John F. Kennedy's political campaigns and became attorney general of the United States during his brother's presidential administration.

In 1953, Robert's father steered him to a job as a staff attorney for Senator Joseph McCarthy, a powerful Republican senator from Wisconsin and a noted anticommunist—as was Joseph Kennedy. After a period, Robert left McCarthy's staff because of a difference with another staffer but eventually returned. McCarthy chaired the Senate's Permanent Subcommittee on Investigations. Like many Americans, McCarthy feared that communists sympathetic to the way of life in the Soviet Union had infiltrated all walks of life in the United States, particularly the government and the entertainment industry.

People were brought before the committee because at some time they had or were suspected of having belonged to the American Communist Party. Witnesses were asked to name others. Many of those who appeared and those who were named were subsequently "blacklisted"; that is, employers agreed among themselves not to hire them. However, McCarthy began to lose favor with his Senate colleagues, and in 1954 they censured him. After elections, a new chairman took over the committee, and Robert Kennedy became its chief counsel. In later years, he was criticized for having worked for McCarthy. Kennedy explained that he liked McCarthy personally and that McCarthy was a friend of his father.

Kennedy shifted the committee's preoccupation with communism to a focus on organized crime and the activities of the "mob" (the American Mafia). Reports that the Teamsters Union was involved with the mob enraged him. Union leaders had grown rich by betraying their membership. Mobsters threatened union members who objected to the corruption.

Joseph Kennedy tried to divert his son to another cause, fearing that exposures of union corruption might erode union support of the Democratic Party and hurt the political futures of the Kennedys. Kennedy ignored his father's fears and convinced the committee chairman, John McClellan, to form the Senate Select Committee on Improper Activities in the Labor or Management Field, which became known as the "Rackets Committee." Once the Rackets Committee came into being, thousands of letters poured in each week reporting corruption. Most letters were anonymous because union members feared reprisals. An investigation Kennedy led against the Teamsters Union leader, Jimmy Hoffa, led to Hoffa's expulsion from the union. Robert Kennedy worked with his brother John, who was a senator at the time, to pass a bill to force unions to hold elections using a secret ballot and to regularly produce financial statements.

In 1960, Kennedy left his job to manage his brother John's campaign for the presidency. His superb organization was a key factor in his brother's winning the Democratic nomination. During the campaign, despite his commitment to his brother's candidacy, Kennedy risked losing voters in the South when Martin Luther King, Jr., was arrested by calling the judge and demanding King's release.

Robert Kennedy refused to take the job as attorney general in the cabinet until his father told him that his brother needed someone he could trust completely. At 35, he became the youngest attorney general in history. Under his leadership, the staid Justice Department became a lively, activist organization.

Kennedy's informality irritated J. Edgar

Robert Kennedy speaks to a crowd outside the Justice Department on June 14, 1963.

Hoover, chief of the Federal Bureau of Investigation. Hoover deplored the fact that the attorney general walked around the building in his shirt-sleeves. An imperious man, Hoover filed a complaint that Kennedy had brought his dog to work with him, an offense punishable by a thirty-day jail sentence and a $50 fine. Hoover had held the directorship of the FBI since 1924. His behavior suggested that he believed his powers exceeded those of the president. When Kennedy held a party in his office to celebrate Hoover's thirty-eighth year as director, Hoover refused to come. Kennedy held the party anyway, and his children ate the cake.

With John Kennedy in the White House, civil rights leaders began to look to Washington for help in enforcing laws that protected the freedom of blacks. As chief law enforcement officer in the nation, Robert Kennedy had an obligation to strike down laws that discriminated. For more than three centuries, frustration had been building among blacks, and whites had opposed rights for blacks. Kennedy was caught in the middle. No matter what he did, blacks complained that he had not done enough, and southern whites complained that he had done too much.

Unlike many of his countrymen, Kennedy perceived the connection between race and poverty as well as the connection between poverty and crime. He set in motion a series of programs he hoped would address juvenile needs before youngsters got in trouble. Volunteers in Service to America (VISTA) was organized in the Justice Department to fight poverty.

When the United States and Cuba were brought to the brink of war because of the presence of missile silos in Cuba, Kennedy advised against a military attack. He couldn't condone the possibility that thousands of Cubans might be killed. Kennedy advocated a selective naval blockade that would prevent Soviet ships from landing missiles and warheads at Cuban ports. At the end of thirteen frightening days, Soviet premier Nikita Khrushchev ordered his ships to return home, and the potential war was avoided.

Kennedy's relationship with Lyndon Johnson, which had not been friendly since the 1960 Democratic National Convention, deteriorated when Johnson became president after John Kennedy was assassinated. Robert Kennedy eventually resigned and ran for the Senate in New York. His years as a senator expanded his concerns about poverty. He visited Chile, Argentina, and Brazil, where he was drawn to the communities of shacks on the outskirts of cities. On such a visit, Kennedy, who remained firmly anticommunist all his life, said to a friend, Richard Goodwin, "Wouldn't you be a Communist, if you had to live here? I would."

He opposed South Africa's system of apartheid, which segregated whites and blacks and left blacks powerless and poverty-stricken. The South African government took five months before it would agree to issue Kennedy a visa for a visit. At the University of Capetown, Kennedy delivered a speech. He said, "Each time a man stands up for an ideal, or acts to improve the lot of others, or strikes out against injustice, he sends forth a tiny ripple of hope, and crossing each other from a million different centers of energy and daring, those ripples build a current which can sweep down the mightiest walls of oppression and resistance."

On March 16, 1968, Kennedy announced his candidacy for president. On April 4, 1968, Martin Luther King, Jr., was assassinated in Memphis. After King's death, the poor looked to Kennedy for help. During a speech to medical students at the Indiana University Medical Center, he said, "It's the poor who carry the major burden of the struggle in Vietnam. You sit here as white medical students, while blacks carry the burden of fighting in Vietnam."

Kennedy's pleas for compassion generated a large volume of hate mail. In Los Angeles, sometime during the first hour of June 5, 1968, he made a victory speech to his campaign staff after winning the California Democratic primary. To avoid the crush of the crowd, Kennedy left the Ambassador Hotel ballroom via the kitchen. A gunman propped his elbow on a counter and fired an eight-shot revolver at Kennedy's head. His press secretary announced at 2:00 A.M. on June 6 that Kennedy was dead. His younger brother, Ted Kennedy, described him as "a good and decent man, who saw wrong and tried to right it, saw suffering and tried to heal it, saw war and tried to stop it." Kennedy had enormous empathy for the poor and disenfranchised. When he died, many young activists became disillusioned. Within months, they had lost their two best allies, Robert Kennedy and Martin Luther King.

See also Kennedy, John Fitzgerald; King, Reverend Martin Luther, Jr.; Mandela, Nelson
References Lester David and Irene David. *Bobby Kennedy: The Making of a Folk Hero*, 1986; Barbara Harrison and Daniel Terris. *A Ripple of Hope: The Life of Robert F. Kennedy*, 1997.

Kent State (May 4, 1970)

In the spring of 1970 student protest focused on the environment, and the public shared their concern. The first Earth Day, on April 22, was extraordinarily successful. Eight days later, President Nixon announced that South Vietnamese and American troops were crossing the border from Vietnam into Cambodia. The invasion reignited the antiwar movement, which had been winding down. Minutes after the president's address, people took to the streets in Philadelphia and New York. The next day, student demonstrations began on campuses from Maryland to California.

After the president was quoted as having referred to students as "bums blowing up the campuses," even more students participated. Two hundred State Department employees resigned in protest. Hundreds of government employees marched with banners that declared "Federal Bums against the War." Strikes spread to sixty campuses. Most rallies were peaceful, but violence broke out at the University of Maryland, Ohio State, and Stanford.

A protest erupted on the usually placid campus of Kent State University on May 4, and the Ohio National Guard was ordered in. At one point guardsmen fired into a crowd of about 200 students, wounding nine and killing four. In the week after Kent State, strikes and protests closed down about 500 campuses, fifty for the remainder of the session. Police and students clashed at two dozen institutions. Students attacked and damaged ROTC buildings at thirty universities.

Bombings, arson, blocked traffic, and smashed windows became commonplace in and around campuses. The California branches of the Bank of America had two dozen fires caused by bombings. As the national eruption began to simmer down, at Jackson State University in Mississippi, white state troopers opened fire on black students. They shot 300 bullets into a dormitory, wounding twelve and killing two women who were watching through a window.

When the exhausted students stopped protesting, they found the public was enraged at them for demonstrating against American foreign policy. A Kent State student reported that his mother said to him, "It would have been a good thing if all the students had been shot." Her son responded, "Hey Mom! That's me you're talking about." Unmoved, she said, "It would have been better for the country if you had all been mowed down." A commission appointed by President Nixon and headed by William Scranton concluded that the guardsmen did not need to shoot. But a grand jury, rather than indict National Guard troops who fired into an unarmed crowd, indicted two dozen faculty and students, claiming the soldiers had fired in self-defense.

See also Antiwar Movement
Reference Terry Anderson. *The Movement and the Sixties: Protest in America from Greensboro to Wounded Knee*, 1995.

Killing Fields

In Phnom Penh, the capital of Cambodia, there is a museum whose purpose is to record the genocidal crimes of the nation's former ruler, Pol Pot. Cambodia is in Southeast Asia, bounded on the north by Thailand and Laos, on the east and southeast by Vietnam, and on the southwest by the Gulf of Siam.

The Museum of Genocidal Crimes of Pol Pot is a former high school that was taken over by Pol Pot's forces, the Khmer Rouge, and surrounded with barbed wire to turn it into a prison. At the prison, the Khmer Rouge carried out interrogations of an estimated 20,000 Cambodians. Often those being interrogated died from being tortured.

In the interests of efficiency, the Khmer Rouge carried out Pol Pot's policy of genocide by gathering people to be killed in an area in which they could be buried. The mass murder sites became known as "killing fields." Many of those killed were as young as 13. Many of the Khmer Rouge doing the killing were almost as young.

During the 1960s, Cambodia was ruled by Prince Norodom Sihanouk and was an attractive location for those touring Southeast Asia. In 1970, pro-American Cambodian generals began an anti-Sihanouk campaign, and Cambodia was drawn into the Vietnam War. Once the social fabric of the nation was destroyed, Pol Pot took over and began an era of atrocities.

In the spring of 1975, shortly after Cambodia's president fled the country, the withdrawal of U.S. military forces enabled Pol Pot to put into effect his vision of purifying Cambodia. He set out to eliminate religion and turn Cambodia into a rural, peasant country. Within days of the U.S. withdrawal, Pol Pot's troops forced hundreds of thousands to leave the cities and march to the countryside, where they lived in labor camps and worked in fields. Many did not survive the almost four years of being beaten and starved that followed. The rationale for keeping the population starving may have been to keep them too weak to revolt. In the camps, malnutrition contributed to the loss of teeth and feet. People's legs had unhealed infections from working in fields fertilized by human waste. Malaria often resulted in death.

Having an education made a Cambodian a target for murder. An estimated 90 percent of the nation's writers, actors, musicians, dancers, and teachers died in the killing fields. Some scholars believe that in the beginning of Pol Pot's regime, there were some reasonable people under his command, but they were eliminated, victims of his increasing paranoia. Everything, both inanimate objects and people, was sacrificed to his dream. Vehicles, even brand-new ones, were melted down to be turned into farm implements. Rubber tires were made into sandals for the Khmer Rouge. The rest of the population walked barefoot.

In late 1978, Vietnamese communists invaded Cambodia—which the Khmer Rouge had renamed Democratic Kampuchea. Over a twenty-year period, Cambodia had four names: the Kingdom of Cambodia, Khmer Republic, Democratic Kampuchea, and the People's Republic of Kampuchea. By early 1979, the Vietnamese invaders had driven Pol Pot's forces as far as the Thai-Cambodian border. Their presence enabled millions of starving Cambodians to escape from the labor camps.

Those who escaped too often found they were the sole surviving members of their families. Even those who had not been sent to the labor camps and remained alive suffered from nightmares and anxiety attacks from watching their parents, siblings, children, and neighbors starve to death or be shot. In one killing field near Siem Reap, the invading Vietnamese punished the Khmer Rouge by making them dig up the bodies they had buried. A monument built in memory of the millions killed by Pol Pot is located in Cheung Ek, a village near Phnom Penh. Within the narrow, two-story building with peaked roofs, glass shelves hold the skulls of some 9,000 people who were buried in the surrounding killing fields.

When the Vietnamese invaded in December 1978, they installed a procommunist government led by Prime Minister Hun Sen. Although the Cambodians enjoyed a respite under the government of Hun Sen, the indignities of occupation and their past history with invaders made them distrustful of the Vietnamese. Moreover, few districts ever became entirely secure against incursions by the Khmer Rouge.

The Vietnamese troops pulled out in September 1979, leaving the Cambodians to govern and protect themselves with their own inexperienced army. Outside observers hoped the psychological threat of a return of the Khmer Rouge would encourage the Cambodians to defend themselves. To cope with the threat from the Khmer Rouge, the government—the most benevolent one in modern history—armed the civilian militia, made up mostly of peasants, with weapons and minimal training. At the same time, the government began a program of forcible conscription into the regular army. Students exempted from the military had their identification cards torn up and were drafted.

The Khmer Rouge stepped up their attacks, introducing heavy artillery. Their most potent weapons against the population were land mines and terror. Village leaders in rural districts near Phnom Penh were attacked. Phnom Penh was decimated in 1979.

In an obvious effort to repair their image with the rest of the world, in July 1997 the Khmer Rouge brought Pol Pot to trial. They permitted one foreign reporter with a video camera to cover the trial. A frail, elderly Pol Pot was led by assistants to a seat, where he sat impassively while he was denounced.

Because of the scope of the atrocities committed under Pol Pot's directions, foreign commentators on the trial of the former leader felt that it should have been held in an international tribunal. Instead, it was held outdoors, in a building that resembled an open shed. To most observers, the participants seemed like amateur actors reading their lines with sham anger. The jury found Pol Pot guilty, and he was sentenced to life imprisonment. No one believed that Pol Pot would spend his last days in the kind of prison to which he had condemned so many of his fellow Cambodians.

A movie called *The Killing Fields* told the story of *New York Times* correspondent Sidney Schanberg and his Cambodian assistant Dith Pran, after they stayed behind when the United States withdrew its forces. Pran was forced to join his fellow Cambodians in the march to countryside labor camps. He and Schanberg were eventually reunited, and Pran now works for the *New York Times* as a photographer.

See also Antiwar Movement; Ho Chi Minh; Physicians for Human Rights
Reference Christopher Hudson. *Killing Fields*, 1984.

King, Reverend Martin Luther, Jr. (1929–1968)

When civil rights leader Martin Luther King, Jr., was awarded the Nobel Peace Prize in 1964, he was the youngest man and only the third black person ever to receive the award. Often called an Uncle Tom by other blacks for his efforts to draw whites into the struggle, King preached a doctrine of nonviolence. Steeped in the philosophy of Mohandas Gandhi, who helped win independence for India through passive resistance, King perceived the push for equal civil rights for blacks and other minorities as a moral crusade. For his participation in marches and protests, King was frequently threatened, often assaulted, and jailed on numerous occasions.

Although King's father and maternal grandfather were both ministers, originally he had no intention of following in their footsteps. He was embarrassed by the emotional displays characteristic of black religious services. King changed his mind in 1944 after he enrolled in Morehouse College in Atlanta. Exposure to the college president, Benjamin Mays, and to his philosophy professor, George Kelsey, convinced him that the ministry could be intellectually satisfying. King graduated from Crozier Theological Seminary in Pennsylvania and, in 1953, went on to obtain a doctorate from Boston University (BU). In Boston, he met Coretta Scott, a singer from Marion, Alabama, who was in the city to study voice and whom he married on June 18, 1953.

While at BU, King preached summers at his father's church, the Ebenezer Baptist Church in Atlanta. In September 1954, he became the pastor of the 400-member Dexter Avenue Baptist Church in Montgomery, Alabama, where he organized his parishioners into social and political action committees to get them involved in solving their community's problems.

King's life changed forever on December 1, 1955. On that day, Rosa Parks refused to give up her seat on a Montgomery bus to a white passenger. Her arrest inspired a citywide boycott of the city's bus system. Coordination of the boycott was handled by the Montgomery Improvement Association, which early in its formation elected King as its president. King's most formidable task in Montgomery was to stir his members and the community to take action while keeping that action within moral boundaries. During the year-long protest, King became the brunt of many

The Reverend Martin Luther King, the Reverend Fred Shuttlesworth, and the Reverend Ralph Abernathy (left to right) report at a news conference in Birmingham, Alabama, that demonstrations are being suspended and a settlement is near, May 1963.

threats. After his home was bombed on January 30, 1956, he begged angry crowds to forget their bitterness and embrace forgiveness.

In November 1956, the U.S. Supreme Court upheld a decision made earlier in the year by a district court that declared Alabama laws requiring segregation on buses to be unconstitutional. On December 21, 1956, a year and twenty days after Rosa Parks refused to give up her seat, the first integrated Montgomery buses set out on their routes.

In January 1957, black leaders from ten southern states met at the Ebenezer Baptist Church, where they formed the Southern Christian Leadership Conference (SCLC). A month later, they elected King as the organization's president. As SCLC's leader, in an ongoing struggle to end Jim Crow laws (named after an old minstrel song), King, his friend and confidant the Reverend

Ralph Abernathy, and SCLC spread the philosophy and practice of nonviolent resistance into cities and towns throughout the South and north to Chicago. Abernathy and King often found themselves in situations in which they didn't know which to fear most, the police or the angry white mob.

During 1957, King traveled 780,000 miles and made 208 speeches. While on a book tour following the publication of his first book, *Stride toward Freedom* (1958), a black woman stabbed him. He viewed her attack as just another example of the "climate of hate and bitterness in the nation." In early 1959, King traveled to India to visit the land of Gandhi, fulfilling a lifelong dream.

Sensing that he could do more to accelerate black protest, King moved to Atlanta in 1960 to become co-pastor of his father's church. In 1962, he met with John F. Kennedy to prod the president into taking a more decisive stance about minority civil rights. A year-long protest in Albany, Georgia, that ended in failure taught King and his followers lessons that served them well in a 1963 massive protest in Birmingham, Alabama. The aim of the protest was to obtain fair-hiring practices in the city. While locked up in April 1963 for defying a court order that barred demonstrations, King wrote a letter in reply to Birmingham religious leaders—Catholic, Protestant, and Jewish—who had criticized him for his "unwise and untimely actions." King's "Letter from Birmingham Jail" became a classic statement of the goals of the civil rights movement. Added to King's eloquent words was the impact of photographs, television coverage, and eyewitness accounts of the use of dogs and fire hoses on protesters, including children. Whites and blacks negotiated a settlement.

The example of Birmingham was repeated on a smaller scale in 800 other cities and towns throughout the United States. Formerly indifferent whites began to understand the grievances of blacks. On August 28, 1963, 250,000 people, 60,000 of whom were white, took part in the March on Washington on behalf of a civil rights bill pending in Congress. Several black leaders made speeches at the Lincoln Memorial. King's speech near the end of the day was the highlight of the event and subsequently became his most often-quoted remembrance. Referred to as the "I Have a Dream" speech, King's words touched on the Bible, the Constitution, and the National Anthem as he assured the crowd that equality and freedom would one day exist throughout the United States.

The following summer, Congress passed a civil rights bill that in King's view went far, but not far enough, to solve the problems of minority groups. During that summer of 1964, riots broke out in Harlem and several other urban centers. For many observers, the riots symbolized the tragic alternative to King's course of nonviolent demonstrations. In his acceptance speech for the Nobel Peace Prize, King said the prize was for those white and black people of goodwill who pursued "the crucial political and moral question of our time—the need of man to overcome op-

pression and violence without resorting to violence and oppression."

Early in 1965, King led a massive voter registration drive in Alabama. After leading a march to the Dallas County Courthouse on February 1 to protest that blacks were being prevented from registering to vote, he was arrested and jailed briefly. A few days later, he conferred with President Lyndon Johnson, Vice President Hubert Humphrey, and Attorney General Nicholas Katzenbach about voter registration for blacks. A march King tried to lead from Selma to Montgomery, Alabama, ended in failure when the marchers were turned back 1 mile from where they started. Nevertheless, a five-day march from Selma to Montgomery, during which King and the Reverend Abernathy led 3,200 demonstrators, ended in victory at the state capital on March 21, 1965.

Abernathy and King were jailed often. Each time, they spent the first twenty-four hours fasting to purify their souls, avoid hatred, and strengthen their determination to end segregation and discrimination.

King realized that a guarantee of their constitutional rights would not bring blacks equality until their economic rights were assured. Those living in poverty do not have the time or energy to participate in a democracy. With that in mind, SCLC planned the Poor People's Campaign, a massive demonstration in Washington, D.C. The march would bring poor people of all races to confront government leaders. Originally scheduled for March 1968, the march was postponed to permit King to energize a stalled Sanitation Workers' strike in Memphis, Tennessee. On his second trip to Memphis to help the strikers, King was assassinated on April 4, 1968. He died in Ralph Abernathy's arms.

Recognizing that the chances of his being killed were high, King had structured SCLC to ensure that nonviolence would not be discarded after he was gone. Abernathy was appointed his successor. After seven days of prayer and fasting, Abernathy took over his new responsibility. He told reporters that the Poor People's Campaign would go on as planned. Participation far exceeded all expectations.

A January 3, 1964, *Time* article described King as having "an indescribable capacity for empathy that is the touchstone of leadership." Seventeen of his sermons were published by Harper in 1963 in a book called *Strength to Love*.

See also Abernathy, Reverend Ralph; Civil Rights Movement; Poor People's Campaign; Young, Andrew
References Ralph Abernathy. *And the Walls Came Tumbling Down: An Autobiography,* 1989; Lerone Bennett. *What Manner of Man,* 1964; Martin Luther King. *Stride toward Freedom,* 1958.

Ku Klux Klan

Although the secret society commonly known as the Ku Klux Klan, KKK, or simply the Klan is concentrated in the South, it has groups throughout the United States. Most groups are small. Among hate groups in the United States with total memberships of at least 200,000, the Klan is the oldest. Founded in the South following the Civil War to defend the southern way of life against northern efforts to change it, the Klan became committed to keeping blacks from gaining rights that would ensure equality. Terrorism and murder achieved that end. The Klan was outlawed by Congress in 1871.

Reorganized in Atlanta, Georgia, in 1915, as the Invisible Empire, Knights of the Ku Klux Klan, the Klan continued with lynching as its preferred method for controlling blacks. During its brutal history, the Klan broadened its targets for hate to other people of color and Jews. The goal of the Klan's paramilitary hierarchy is to perpetuate the white race—but not all whites. Although Catholics in the United States are predominantly white, the Klan includes them among those they choose to hate. The characteristic dress for Klansmen on a nighttime raid to do violence is white robes with hoods, or sheets when robes are not available. Setting fire to people's houses or leaving a burning cross in front of their homes serves as a symbol of hatred and a warning of more violence to follow.

Those who join the Klan swear to "uphold the principles of White Supremacy and the purity of White Womanhood." White supremacist groups like the Klan characterize the women's movement as the "Jew-dyke conspiracy against the white race." The Klan tolerates women only in their proper place, under the domination of men. Although a few klans had auxiliaries, women could not join klans before the 1970s. David Duke, Grand Wizard of the Knights of the KKK from 1975 to 1980, opened the ranks of the KKK to women in an aggressive recruitment drive. Darlene Carver, the wife of the Grand Dragon of the Georgia KKK, became Grand Secretary when her husband was barred by court order from representing the Klan. One of Carver's first acts as Grand Secretary was to put a recorded message on the Klan hotline asking women to take up the cause of teenagers and drugs. But Carver's suggestion that women act independently was unlikely to be taken seriously.

The woman's job is to indoctrinate the family. If she steps out of line, fear for the safety of her children can be used against her to make her mend her ways. The husband of a woman who is under suspicion of not being submissive is told to "take care of the problem." Domestic violence is an acceptable method for ensuring conformity. A husband's womanizing is taken for granted. If a wife has an affair, she will be banished. A white woman who "race-mixes" with a man of color, especially if she has a child, deserves death.

Doug Seymour, a police officer who infiltrated the California KKK and headed up the Klan Bureau of Investigation from 1979 to 1981, likened the KKK's structure to another male bastion—organized crime. Each den of seven to fourteen members is expected to produce money for the Grand Dragon's coffers. If more affluent members do not produce funds, the poorer members may be forced into burglary or drug trafficking.

During the 1990s, the Klan perfected a technique for expressing its hatred in a lawful way. It applied for parade permits in communities likely to withhold permission. Once the parade permit was denied, the Klan asked the American Civil Liberties Union to defend its First Amendment right to assemble. Each suit before a federal judge asked the court to rule the denial unconstitutional and demanded legal fees. Thirty Klan members and Aryan youth groups marched in

Palm Beach, Florida, on July 28, 1990, before about 1,000 spectators, journalists, and police officers. The Palm Beach Police Department, reinforced by police from four neighboring cities and from the county sheriff's office, spent thousands of dollars to provide security at the march. One monitoring group reported that during the summer of 1990, there was a Klan marching somewhere every weekend.

See also Christian Identity Movement
Reference Susan Lang. *Extremist Groups in America,* 1990.

Leary, Timothy (1920–1996)

During the 1960s and 1970s, young rebels admired psychologist Timothy Leary as a kind of folk hero for daring to promote consciousness-altering drugs. As a doctoral student at the University of California at Berkeley, Leary became disenchanted with traditional psychotherapy. He recommended psychedelic drugs (which generate hallucinations, distortions of perceptions, and occasionally psychoses) as tools for the treatment of schizophrenia and alcoholism and as vehicles for visionary experiences. At Harvard, where he was a lecturer and researcher in clinical psychology, he was respected for pioneer studies in "games" theory of behavior, although he was deemed a little too adventurous. Leary was dismissed in 1963 because of personal experiments with consciousness-altering drugs.

In a 1966 lecture, Leary compared LSD (lysergic acid diethylamide) to a microscope, asserting that it is to psychology what the microscope is to biology. Following his conversion to Hinduism in 1966, he founded the League for Spiritual Discovery, which was dedicated to the ancient sacred sequence of "turning on, tuning in, and dropping out."

Leary's reputation as a "corrupter of youth" made law enforcement agencies anxious to jail him. In December 1965, accompanied by his teenage daughter, Leary drove south across the bridge connecting Laredo, Texas, with Mexico. He was turned back by Mexican border officials. On reaching the American side, Leary and his daughter were searched. A half-ounce of marijuana was found on his daughter. Tried on failure to pay tax on the marijuana, he was sentenced to thirty years in jail. The U.S. Supreme Court overturned the conviction on the grounds that the marijuana law required self-incrimination and therefore was unconstitutional.

After the reversal, Leary was again tried in Laredo. This time the charge was smuggling. Again, he was convicted and sentenced to ten years in jail. During prolonged litigation in connection with the conviction, Leary moved to California, where he was picked up and charged with possession of a half-ounce of marijuana and sen-

tenced to ten years in jail. Facing twenty years in jail, after six months, Leary escaped and fled to Algeria. In 1973, he was captured and returned to the California penal system, where he remained until Governor Edmund Brown ordered his release in 1976.

During the last twenty years of his life, Leary lectured on college campuses; did some stand-up comedy; pursued an interest in cybernetics (control and communication within and between machines, animals, and organizations); became involved in virtual reality; designed some computer games; and founded a software company.

See also Hippies
References Timothy Leary. *The Politics of Ecstasy,* 1968; and *Flashbacks: An Autobiography,* 1983.

Leopold, Aldo (1886–1948)

In the decade after his death, the father of the national forest wilderness system and of wildlife management, Aldo Leopold, became a guide to young environmentalists who took up the cause. He is best known for his last book, *A Sand County Almanac and Sketches Here and There* (1949). Written during the last ten years of Leopold's life and published after his death, *A Sand County Almanac* became the conservationist's bible and a natural history classic. Initially, the book's audience consisted of conservation professionals and dedicated amateurs. *A Sand County Almanac* eventually surpassed even Rachel Carson's *Silent*

Spring in number of readers. The credibility of the book rested on a lifetime of achievement and a large body of writing that preceded it.

During nineteen years with the U.S. Forest Service, from 1909 to 1928, Leopold's innovative approaches to the new profession of forestry, particularly to recreation planning, game management, and soil erosion control, provided models for others to follow. From 1933 until his death in 1948, Leopold held the nation's first chair of game management, created for him at the University of Wisconsin.

Leopold's stature as a scientist attracted professionals, but it was his philosophy that drew budding environmentalists into the movement—a philosophy of wilderness preservation, ecology, natural aesthetics, and ethics. From the 1920s to the 1940s, Leopold advocated a system of wilderness preserves. Perhaps because he had once been in charge of recreation for the southwestern district of the national forests, Leopold viewed recreation as an important component of preserves. A practical man, he suggested that a distinctive area of each state, unsuited to industrial development, be set aside as a preserve—sufficient for a two-week pack trip. As a possible site, he favored the headwaters of the Gila River, which flows from southwest New Mexico to southern Arizona.

In 1922, Leopold drew up a plan for the Gila Forest that became the basis for its designation in 1924 as a wilderness. The Gila Forest set the pattern for the nationwide system that followed. Leopold expanded his view of wilderness as a recreation site. In a 1920s essay, influenced by his neighbor and American historian Frederick Jackson Turner, he proposed that the remnants of America's frontier be preserved for future generations.

Leopold's work during the 1930s was influenced by two trips, one to Germany, the other to Mexico. The German trip depressed him. He returned to America determined to avoid that country's overly artificial management of land and wildlife. The trip to Mexico, however, had a positive and profound effect. He wrote: "It was here that I first clearly realized that land is an organism and that all my life I had seen only sick land, whereas here was a biota [animal and plant life of a region as a whole] still in perfect aboriginal health."

Based on the German and Mexican contrasts, Leopold began to devise a set of principles supporting wilderness preservation based on ecology (the relationship between plants and animals and their environment). His earlier argument that each state should have a wilderness that provided affordable recreation for its citizens was discarded. He now proposed that each biome (major ecological region, such as a desert or a seacoast) should have a wilderness preserve to serve as a standard against which ecologists could measure the disruption created by various ways in which other land was used.

Aesthetics (sense of beauty) were also important to Leopold. In 1936, he told a student audience, "Our tools are scientific whereas our output is weighed in esthetic satisfaction rather than in economic pounds or dollars." In a paper he presented in June 1941, Leopold said, "Land then, is not merely soil; it's a fountain of energy flowing through a circuit of soils, plants, and animals. Food chains and the living channels which conduct energy upward; death and decay return it to the soil."

At the beginning of his career, Leopold's perspective on land ethics was essentially utilitarian. As his knowledge and philosophy of the relationship between people and nature changed, his views evolved. Later in life, he perceived an ethical obligation to preserve the health of the system by encouraging the maximum diversity and complexity and by minimizing the violence done in connection with human activities.

See also Carson, Rachel; Environmental Movement; Hippies
Reference Susan Flader and J. Baird Callicott. *The River of the Mother of God and Other Essays by Aldo Leopold*, 1991.

Liberation Theology

Liberation theology is an interpretation of Christian faith based on the experiences of the poor. It is an effort to understand the Bible and key

Christian doctrines from the perspective of the poor. At the same time, it attempts to enable the poor to interpret their faith in a new way. Liberation theology, which developed primarily in Latin America, focuses on the life of Jesus and his message. Because poverty is a product of the way a society is organized, liberation theology involves a critique of economic institutions that enable some Latin Americans to live in luxury while many fellow citizens do not have even safe drinking water.

Liberation theologians critiqued ideologies that justified such inequality. They also questioned how the church organized its pastoral work on behalf of the poor. Such questions brought liberation theologians into conflict with church authorities. The theologians also posed a threat to repressive governments, and some were murdered.

Until Vatican II, 1962–1965, Roman Catholicism in Latin America was rooted in unchangeability. After Vatican II, Latin American Catholics took a critical look at their church and their society. In the 1960s, church people felt they had a right to respond to questions about the social order. Hopes rose because revolutionary social change appeared to be under way, but change came in the form of military dictatorships and with them even greater restrictions of freedom.

Latin American liberation theology is not an isolated phenomenon. Parallel theologies—Asian, African, black, and feminist—have arisen. Each has criticized the interpretation of Christian symbols they were taught, and each has reinterpreted the past. Interchange among the new theologians became formalized in Detroit in 1975 and 1980 at conferences on theology in the Americas. Beginning in 1976, additional dialogue took place at several conferences sponsored by the Ecumenical Association of Third World Theologians.

Finding common ground among the different perspectives often proved difficult. Latin Americans, who focused on economic oppression, seemed to blacks to be insensitive to racism. In turn, Latin Americans felt blacks failed to sufficiently understand systems of oppression. Feminists believed both to be mired in Western male interpretations.

Historical circumstances make Latin American Catholicism significantly different from that found in Asia and Africa. Catholicism arrived in Latin America in the sixteenth century with conquest by the Spanish and Portuguese, and it still exercises a cultural quasi-monopoly in Latin America. But Catholics are the minority in Asia and in Africa, even though their numbers have grown in recent years. Catholicism was introduced into Asia and Africa in the nineteenth century in a wide diversity of ways and has existed in political cultures as different as apartheid in South Africa and socialism in Tanzania.

During the 1960s, the author of *Liberation Theology* (1987), Phillip Berryman, served as a Catholic priest in a barrio of Panama City. While in Central America, he traveled to South America to meet and talk with liberation theologians. After Berryman resigned from the priesthood in 1973, he continued to travel to Latin America as a representative of the Quaker American Friends Service Committee. In Berryman's view, perspectives on liberation theology differ among Latin Americans and their North American and European counterparts. Americans and Europeans ask questions about violence and Marxism. Latin American liberation theologians ask questions that compare the kingdom of God with efforts to achieve dignity in the world.

When the native people of the New World were conquered by Spain and Portugal, they had imposed on them an aggressive form of Catholicism that reflected the church's reaction to the Protestant Reformation. Some of the early missionaries that came to bring Catholicism protested to little avail the cruelties of the conquerors. The social order imposed on Latin America embodied the model of order that had existed in Europe since the fall of the Roman Empire. Civil authorities backed the church, and the church supported the civil order. The form arrived in Latin America about the time it was beginning to unravel in Europe.

The Latin American church became tied to conservative parties. Liberal parties that emerged viewed the Catholic Church as backward. Locked into an uneasy position, the church became an ineffectual force—so ineffectual it was unable to produce sufficient local clerics and was forced to depend on a flow from Europe. Between 1808 and 1824, Latin American countries broke with Spain and Portugal. The independence movements were largely the work of local elites. The poor served in the armies fighting for independence, but they gained few benefits for their efforts.

During the first half of the twentieth century, Latin American Catholicism gained strength. Catholic action movements developed among workers and students. In 1955, Catholic bishops from all over the continent traveled to Rio de Janeiro to meet. Although their principal concerns were Protestantism, communism, and secularism, they also discussed social problems.

Despite the rise in activity, in the 1980s, approximately 80 percent of Latin American clergy were foreign-born. The number of liberation theologians is relatively small. Those who have published significant works on the subject comprise an even smaller group. Almost all are male, and most are Catholics—although a few Protestants have played important roles in the movement.

Liberation theology has had a significant impact in the United States. According to Berryman, during the latter decades of the twentieth century, at almost any public action staged in protest of U.S. policy in Central America, one-half or more of the participants were linked to church organizations. American church activists were horrified by the murder of Archbishop Oscar Romero in El Salvador in March 1980. The murderers were graduates of the School of the Americas (SOA), often called the School of the Assassins. The SOA, located in and funded by the United States, has given training to 59,000 Latin Americans since 1946. When the U.S. government began to target Central American refugees for deportation, more than 300 American religious congregations declared their churches to be sanctuaries.

Although by the late 1980s most dictatorships had given way to civilian governments, most were incapable of producing basic social and economic change. Nevertheless, many Latin Americans were convinced that their struggles were a second independence movement taking up unfinished business.

See also Neal, Sister Marie Augusta; Sanctuary Movement; Sisters of the Immaculate Heart of Mary
Reference Phillip Berryman. *Liberation Theology: Essential Facts about the Revolutionary Movement in Latin America and Beyond,* 1987; Gail Lumet Buckley, "Left, Right, and Center," May 9, 1998.

Lin, Maya (b. 1959)

At the age of 21, Maya Ying Lin won the competition to design the Vietnam Veterans Memorial in Washington, D.C. Lin was born in Athens, Ohio, where her parents, immigrants from China in the 1940s, were academics at Ohio State University, her father a dean of fine arts and her mother a professor of literature. Although Lin does not identify strongly with her Chinese heritage, she recognizes that the simplicity of her work and its sense of introspection is "distinctly Asian." During a talk at the Metropolitan Museum of Art in 1990, she told her audience, "Architects call me a sculptor and sculptors call me an architect."

In college, she excelled in math and took courses in existentialism, a philosophy that emphasizes the uniqueness and isolation of an individual in an indifferent world. She became preoccupied with the concept of death, and while an architecture major at Yale, she often visited cemeteries to photograph headstones. During her senior year, she enrolled in a course in funerary architecture. The class involved designing monuments, including the gateway to a cemetery and a memorial for World War III. The professor urged all the students in the class to enter a contest for the proposed Vietnam Veterans Memorial.

Lin traveled to Washington, D.C., to see the proposed site on the Mall between the Lincoln Memorial and the Capitol. While she was taking photographs, the basic idea for the design that eventually won her the competition came to her. Her concept was to open the earth and evoke an apolitical serenity. The design consisted of two long black granite walls that meet to form a slight V shape. On the granite walls were engraved the

Maya Lin's winning design for the Vietnam Memorial. The design was a student project at Yale University's School of Architecture.

names of the 58,156 servicepeople killed or missing in Vietnam, in chronological order of their deaths.

Lin's design served as a statement that war is not solely about victory or loss but about individual lives. The chronological order signifies that each listing represents a moment in history; Lin avoided alphabetical order because people do not die in such neat, orderly ways. She chose black granite as "more peaceful and gentle than white." Its polished surface indicates an unseeable space behind and beyond the walls, where the dead lie, and acts like a mirror, making mourners see themselves among the living. The V shape of the walls stretches into space, pointing to the Washington Monument on the left and the Lincoln Memorial on the right, bringing the Vietnam Memorial into the context of America's history.

Lin's entry in the competition won from a field of 1,420 entries because, in the opinion of the judges, it was superbly harmonious. The an-

nouncement on May 6, 1981, was met with protest by some veterans and their families. Some called it a degrading ditch and a wall of shame. Others insisted they could not accept having a wall "built by a gook." Former Secretary of the Interior James Watt tried to deny the Vietnam Memorial project a permit.

Support arose in early 1982 for an alternative to Lin's design. Sculptor and former antiwar demonstrator Frederick Hart had designed *The Three Servicemen Statue,* which had placed third in the competition. Protesters petitioned to have the bronze statue of three soldiers brandishing an American flag erected in the center of Lin's two-walled monument. Lin compared the idea to "drawing mustaches on other people's portraits."

A compromise was reached in February 1982. Hart's statue was erected near the entrance to the memorial site, about 120 feet away from Lin's wall. Lin received $20,000 in prize money from the Veteran's Memorial Fund, but the same fund paid ten times that amount to Hart for his commission. The dedication program featured Hart's sculpture on the cover, and Lin's name was not mentioned during the ceremony. Her name appears only on a separate stone placed a few feet behind the memorial.

During the controversy, a group of prominent critics pronounced Lin's the best design. It became the most visited monument in Washington. Every day Park Service crews collect flowers, photos, and dog tags left by veterans' friends and relatives at the base of the wall. Letters to Lin from veterans tell her how much her memorial helped them.

By the time the memorial was dedicated, Lin was enrolled in Harvard's Graduate School of Design. Attention from the press distracted her, and she took time off from school to disappear and become a virtual recluse for a time. She later told reporters that she was "terrified that at 21 I might have already outdone myself." She returned to school in the fall of 1983.

In February 1988, Lin was asked by the Southern Poverty Law Center's executive director, Morris Dees, to design a monument to the people who had given their lives in the civil rights struggle.

And in 1992 her commissioned monument, called *The Women's Table,* was installed in Yale's main quadrangle to commemorate the centennial of the first year Yale admitted women to its graduate school. Lin continues to do large-scale public works. She also pursues her other love, which is sculpture.

See also Antiwar Movement; Asian-American Movement
Reference Geraldine Gan. *Lives of Notable Asian Americans: Arts, Entertainment, Sports,* 1995.

Lipkis, Andy
See Urban Forestry

Little Rock, Arkansas', Central High

The Supreme Court's 1954 decision in *Brown v. Board of Education of Topeka* did not set a deadline to desegregate schools. A year after the decision was handed down, in May 1955, the Court issued guidelines that instructed local school boards to implement desegregation plans "with all deliberate speed."

Five days after the Supreme Court handed down its 1954 decision, the Little Rock, Arkansas, school board announced its intention to comply with federal constitutional requirements. On the surface Little Rock was ready for integration. The city's newspaper, *The Arkansas Gazette,* was one of the South's oldest and most respected newspapers. The student body of the University of Arkansas Graduate Center was about 50 percent black. Libraries, parks, and buses were already integrated. No one expected Little Rock to become a battleground over school integration. Nevertheless, the roots of segregation ran deep in the city.

During the interim between the Supreme Court's 1954 decision and the ambiguous guidelines it set in 1955, Virgil Blossom, the Little Rock superintendent of schools, drafted a plan for implementing desegregation on a gradual basis. He planned to begin integration when two new high schools opened in the fall of 1956. A few days after the Supreme Court's "with all deliberate speed" directive, the school board revised Blos-

som's plan. Its plan would integrate only one high school, include only a few black students, and be delayed until the fall of 1957.

Despite the arbitrary revision of the superintendent's plan, Little Rock school administrators expected no problems when nine black students entered Little Rock's Central High on September 3, 1957. The night before the students' first day, Arkansas' governor, Orval Faubus, announced on statewide television that it "would not be possible to restore or to maintain order" if forcible integration were carried out the next day. He ordered the National Guard to surround Central High.

The school board asked the nine students to postpone their first day while they obtained a ruling from Federal District Judge Ronald N. Davies, who was in Arkansas on a temporary assignment from North Dakota. Davies ordered that the desegregation plan be put into effect. When the black students arrived on September 4, the National Guard blocked their entrance, thus directly challenging the federal government. President Dwight D. Eisenhower, who had not supported the *Brown* decision, was reluctant to intervene, but he could not ignore Faubus's defiance of a federal court. He met with Faubus and told him the National Guard could remain, but they were there to protect the black students.

On September 20, Judge Davies ordered the governor to stop interfering with school desegregation at Central High and remove the troops. That evening, Faubus once again went on statewide television to tell the public he was going to comply with the order, but he asked the black students to stay away from school until he could work out a peaceful plan. Then he left town for a governor's conference in Georgia.

A thousand angry segregationists from across the South surrounded Central High on the morning of September 21. White students chanted, "Two, four, six, eight, we ain't gonna integrate." Unnoticed by the mob, Daisy Bates, the president of the Arkansas branch of the National Association for the Advancement of Colored People (NAACP), accompanied by the "Little Rock Nine," entered the school through a side entrance. When someone noticed that the students had entered,

A federal escort protects these African-American girls as they make their way to Little Rock's Central High School in the fall of 1957.

there were shouts of "The niggers are in our school." The crowd began to chant, "Come on out! Come on out!"

Groups of white students emerged from the school and were greeted by shouts of approval from the crowd. Fearful of violence, Little Rock's mayor ordered the nine students to be withdrawn. Daisy Bates told the press that the black students would not attempt to enter Central High again unless the president provided them with protection. That evening President Eisenhower denounced the actions at Central High as disgraceful. He declared that the Supreme Court's orders "cannot be flouted with impunity by an individual mob or extremists." He ordered those who were obstructing federal law to cease and desist and for the mob to disperse.

The determined segregationists ignored the president. An even larger mob assembled outside the high school on the morning of September 22. Little Rock's mayor, whose police force was vastly outnumbered, called the U.S. Justice Department and asked for federal help. On September 24, 1957, President Eisenhower ordered 1,000 troops of the 101st Airborne Division to Little Rock and federalized 10,000 members of the Arkansas National Guard. By 5:00 A.M., paratroopers carrying fixed bayonets had surrounded the school. Federal troops picked up the Little Rock Nine from the home of Daisy Bates and escorted them to school.

The idea that soldiers with obvious southern accents were there to protect them seemed incredible to the students, but the soldiers did so for two months. After the 101st was withdrawn, the federalized Arkansas guardsmen continued to patrol Central High for the rest of the school year. Despite the presence of the military in the high school, the Little Rock Nine suffered from constant harassment throughout the year. Their parents received frequent phone calls during which the callers threatened to shoot their children with acid-filled pistols.

After being called a "nigger bitch," Minniejean Brown called a white girl "white trash" and was expelled. She moved to New York, where she entered a private school and graduated the following year with a high standing in her class. At graduation ceremonies in 1958, no one clapped when the name of Ernest Green, the first black boy to graduate from Central High, was announced.

At the request of the Little Rock school board, Arkansas Federal District Judge Harry Lemley suspended the integration plan for two and one-half years. The NAACP filed an appeal with the Supreme Court. A special session of the Court on August 28, 1958, took up the case *Cooper v. Aaron* (Cooper was a Little Rock school board member; Aaron was a black student). In response to the contention by the school board's attorney that desegregation should be postponed until a national policy was established, Chief Justice Earl Warren asked how the law would be clarified if all school boards took the same position.

On September 27, 1958, Governor Faubus closed all public schools in Little Rock and helped a hard-line segregationist group set up the Little Rock Private School Corporation, which tried to lease the public schools. The public schools stayed closed for the entire school year. Some white students went to private schools,

some attended schools outside the city, and some stayed home. Most black students went to segregated schools outside Little Rock.

Two days after Faubus closed Little Rock's public schools, on September 29, 1958, the Supreme Court handed down a unanimous decision that declared that the *Brown* case could not be nullified directly or indirectly through evasive schemes for segregation. On June 18, 1959, a three-judge federal panel unanimously declared the governor's scheme to lease public schools to private corporations as unconstitutional. Two months later, one of the black students who had braved the mob two years earlier, Elizabeth Eckford, enrolled at Central High without incident. The police kept the mob that gathered to see her in check.

The press coverage of the events at Central High focused national attention on enforcement of the *Brown* decision. It also added fuel to the fire of the growing civil rights movement.

See also Civil Rights Movement
References Daisy L. Bates. *The Long Shadow of Little Rock: A Memoir,* 1962; Sanford Wexler, *The Civil Rights Movement: An Eyewitness History,* 1993.

Mainstreaming

The enrollment in conventional classrooms of children handicapped by physical or psychological problems that interfere with learning is known as mainstreaming. The theory driving the mainstreaming movement is that even the most handicapped child can benefit intellectually and socially by attending class with normal and gifted children. The theory presumes that non-handicapped children also benefit by learning tolerance and appreciation of children who are different from them.

The movement began when a series of reports aired on television about cruel living conditions in public mental hospitals. Advocates and parents lobbied Congress to pass the landmark Education for All Handicapped Children Act (1975). Amended in 1983 and 1986, the act mandated that all public schools guarantee handicapped children free and appropriate public school education.

The law provides federal funds to state and local districts for three major purposes: to make schools accessible for handicapped students and faculty; to provide schools with support staff to work with students, parents, and teachers; and development of individual education plans designed to provide instruction tailored to each handicapped student's needs.

Even though mainstreaming has benefited both handicapped and nonhandicapped children, it has not been universally welcomed. Some teachers complain that the normal teaching routines are disrupted by the presence of aides who serve as interpreters for individual children or help with their physical needs. Other teachers are overwhelmed by their students' problems because their districts have no or an insufficient number of trained aides. Occasionally teachers are given a disproportionate number of handicapped students.

Complaints also come from some parents of handicapped children, who feel the gains made by being in a conventional classroom do not offset the loss of individual attention available in small special education classrooms. Some parents of nonhandicapped children are dismayed

by the substantial portion of the school budget that must sometimes be spent on behalf of handicapped children. Some profoundly handicapped children must be sent to expensive residential schools, which are often out of state.

Objections to creating barrier-free schools echo those to making barrier-free public accommodations. Critics claim they benefit only a few. In practice, barrier-free accommodations benefit many nonhandicapped people, such as mothers with strollers, vendors, and the elderly.

See also Deaf Student Protest; Disability Rights Movement
Reference Judy Wood. *Mainstreaming: A Practical Approach for Teachers*, 1989.

Malcolm X (1925–1965)

In 1919, the year that the father of black activist Malcolm X, Earl Little, married his mother, Louise Norton, there were many lynchings across the United States. Despite the risk of holding radical views, Earl Little did not accept the attitude of whites that kept blacks despised and at the bottom of the economic ladder. Little was inspired by the work of Marcus Garvey, the founder of the Universal Negro Improvement Association (UNIA). Garvey believed that blacks were too dependent on handouts from whites. He advocated that they create their own businesses, jobs, and schools. Garvey also advocated that American blacks move to Africa, their spiritual home.

When Little moved his family to Omaha, Nebraska, he carried with him Garvey's ideas and became head of the Omaha chapter of the UNIA. Although the 1926 Omaha city directory listed Little as a laborer, the members of his church considered him a man of ideas, their minister. He was an excellent speaker, who not only preached about the message of Christian salvation but also about the politics of race.

Life was not easy for the Little family. Ku Klux Klansmen forced them to move several times. Malcolm, born on May 19, 1925, was the fourth child of Earl and Louise. He was just four when the family moved into a farmhouse on the outskirts of Lansing, Michigan. Two weeks later, during the night, the farmhouse was set on fire. The local fire department did nothing to put out the fire. When the family moved to a house in East Lansing, white neighbors stoned them.

Malcolm often accompanied his father to UNIA meetings and heard his father speak about the issues facing blacks in the United States and their need to unite. On September 28, 1931, when Malcolm was 6, he was awakened by his mother's screams. The police had come to the house to tell Louise that her husband was dead, run over by a trolley. The conductor of the trolley claimed that he had not seen Little and that he must have somehow fallen beneath the wheels. Earl's eight children were left fatherless.

Malcolm's mother, in time, became mentally ill. In January 1939, she was declared legally insane and committed to an institution. The children were scattered to foster homes. Malcolm lived in a variety of boardinghouses and institutions. At the age of 15, after a teacher—despite his excellent grades—told Malcolm that his ambition to become a lawyer was unrealistic for "a nigger," he lost interest in school.

Malcolm went to live with a half-sister, Ella, in Boston. To Ella's dismay, he made friends in a local pool hall and began leading a reckless life. In 1946, Malcolm was sentenced to eight to ten years in prison for theft. While in prison, he learned from his family about the Black Muslim movement, whose official name was the Lost-Found Nation of Islam. Malcolm began to study

Malcolm X.

the teachings of Elijah Muhammad, the leader of the Black Muslims. After he was released from prison in 1952, Malcolm traveled to Chicago to meet Elijah Muhammad. He was accepted into the movement and renamed Malcolm X to signify throwing off a name given by slave owners. The adoption of X symbolized that Malcolm's African name had been lost. In January 1958, Malcolm married fellow Muslim Betty X.

Malcolm had a genius for organizing. He was first sent to the Black Muslim mosque in Detroit as an assistant minister. In 1953, he was assigned to organize a mosque in Philadelphia, and in 1954 he took over leadership of a mosque in New York City's Harlem. During his lifetime, Malcolm learned to talk to people at all socioeconomic levels. He could recruit young people because he spoke the language of the streets.

The Black Muslims' goal of racial separation ran counter to the goal of integration held by most other national black organizations. Malcolm criticized the philosophy of nonviolence championed by Martin Luther King, Jr. Malcolm advocated self-defense for blacks confronted by violent whites. He urged black people to give up the Christian religion and the lifestyles of Western society. In black communities, the Muslims established restaurants, grocery stores, and other businesses in which the prices were reasonable. Business ownership instilled pride and kept money in black communities.

In April 1957 in Harlem, a black man named Johnson Hinton complained loudly when he saw two police officers beat a black man. After Hinton turned to leave, an officer grabbed him from the rear and assaulted him. As Hinton tried to defend himself, other officers joined in beating him. Dazed and bleeding, he was taken to the police station. Upon hearing the news, Malcolm organized members of his Harlem storefront mosque, Temple Seven, to march to the police station, where they demanded to see Hinton. At the sight of the almost unconscious man, they demanded that he be taken to the hospital. News of the confrontation convinced the community that the Nation of Islam was a force worthy of respect.

Like his father, Malcolm was a gifted speaker. By early 1959, he had become the chief spokesperson for the Nation of Islam and its most effective minister. Membership in the Black Muslims rose in part due to acute disappointment that the landmark 1954 Supreme Court decision in the case of *Brown v. Board of Education of Topeka*, which had outlawed school segregation, had not had a significant impact.

Malcolm, as a representative of Elijah Muhammad, traveled the world. Muslims in Africa and the Middle East became interested in American blacks who were fighting for their rights in the United States. Outside observers began to suspect that for various reasons some people within the Black Muslim movement wanted Malcolm thrown out. He inadvertently gave them ammunition. On November 22, 1963, President John F. Kennedy was assassinated. The black community was relieved that the accused assassin was white rather than black and grief-stricken because Kennedy had been popular among black Americans. The ministers of the Nation of Islam were ordered not to comment on the assassination.

On December 1, 1993, Malcolm, substituting for Elijah Muhammad as a speaker, was asked questions about the assassination. He said that Kennedy had permitted the assassination of the South Vietnamese president Ngo Dinh Diem and his brother, and the president "never foresaw that the chickens would come home to roost so soon."

Malcolm claimed later that he meant that the Kennedy administration had tolerated an atmosphere of violence and that violence had claimed the life of the president. The press and the public interpreted his remarks to mean that he took pleasure in Kennedy's death. Elijah Muhammad suspended him and ordered him not to speak on behalf of the movement for ninety days. Malcolm accepted the punishment, but he felt hurt and betrayed.

In the months that followed, Malcolm heard rumors about his "betrayal" of Elijah Muhammad. At the time, he had begun his autobiography with Alex Haley and had assigned any potential royalties from the book to the Nation of Islam. However, death threats forced Malcolm to accept that the Nation of Islam was finished with him. On March 8, 1964, he announced his split with the organization. Four days later, Malcolm told the press he had formed the Muslim Mosque, a religious group.

Malcolm journeyed to Boston to talk with his half-sister Ella. While he was there, he told her he wanted to make a pilgrimage to Mecca. The pilgrimage would serve as a symbol of his faith and of his break with the Nation of Islam. Before he left, he referred to the Nation of Islam as a separatist organization. On April 13, 1964, Malcolm set off on his journey. On May 21, 1964, he returned a changed man with a new name, el-Hajj Malik el-Shabazz. In *The Autobiography of Malcolm X,* Malcolm wrote about his pilgrimage, a journey only a small percentage of Muslims are privileged to make. "There were tens of thousands of pilgrims from all over the world. They were of all colors, from blue-eyed blondes to black-skinned Africans. But we were all participating in the same ritual displaying a spirit of unity and brotherhood that my experience in America had led me to believe never could exist between the white and non-white."

Malcolm hoped to created a worldwide bond

among black people. In a letter to the black newspaper the *Amsterdam News,* he claimed that pan-Africanism would accomplish for people of African descent what Zionism had done for Jews around the world. Blacks from the United States, Ghana, Nigeria, Mali, South Africa, Brazil, and all the other countries where they lived would share a common bond that would be a source of identity and strength. On June 8, 1964, Malcolm announced formation of the Organization of Afro-American Unity, a secular group.

Malcolm's separation from the Nation of Islam alienated him from some within that organization and from militant groups, who did not like his willingness to work with all groups. At the same time, his new attitude attracted support from the black middle class. In an open letter to Elijah Muhammad, Malcolm suggested the two men work together toward a common goal. Muhammad made a statement that he would be willing to forgive Malcolm, but no reconciliation took place. *Muhammad Speaks,* a newspaper that Malcolm had established within the Nation of Islam, began to print articles denouncing him. Death threats arrived often. Anonymous callers on radio talk shows said he would be "bumped off" and he was "as good as dead."

By the middle of October 1964, Malcolm had traveled to meet with eleven heads of state. At an airport press conference when he returned to the United States on November 24, 1964, Malcolm told the press that he had gathered support for an appeal to the United Nations about the violations of human rights of African Americans.

In February 1965, Malcolm, his four children, and his wife Betty, who was pregnant with twins, were awakened by the sound of glass breaking. His living room was on fire. Fireman found broken bottles in the scorched room and a bottle of gasoline in a rear bedroom where Malcolm's three older daughters slept. C. Eric Lincoln, the author of *The Black Muslims in America,* invited Malcolm to talk with students at Brown University. Malcolm said, "Professor Lincoln, I may be dead by Tuesday." Once Lincoln realized Malcolm was serious, he asked why he did not go to the police. "They already know," said Malcolm.

Understanding that any minute might be his last, Malcolm vowed to go on. Still building his Organization of Afro-American Unity, he gave a speech on October 15, 1964, to 600 people at the Audubon Ballroom in Harlem. He was scheduled to speak again on February 21. At 3:05 P.M., as Malcolm began to speak, a man wearing a three-quarter-length black leather coat jumped to his feet and yelled at the man next to him, "Get your hand out of my pocket." Trying to calm the two men down, Malcolm stepped from behind the podium. The man who had jumped up pulled something from inside his coat. A series of rapid shots and a booming noise followed. The crowd scattered, and Malcolm's wife, Betty, pulled her children to her and tried to cover their bodies with her own. While police and security guards pursued the gunman, a small gathering of people surrounded Malcolm's body. When Betty reached her husband, she found a Japanese woman, who had brought her son to hear Malcolm speak, holding his head. Malcolm was dead.

At the murder scene, police arrested a man named Talmadge Hayer. A few days later they arrested Norman 3X Butler and Thomas 15X Johnson, both identified as members of the Nation of Islam. The detectives working the case did not believe that they had acted on their own. Someone had arranged Malcolm's murder. The three men were convicted on March 11, 1966, and sentenced to life imprisonment. There were various theories about the murder. Some thought that the Nation of Islam was worried that Malcolm's new organization would threaten the organization's existence. Others said the Central Intelligence Agency viewed Malcolm's visits to international leaders as a threat to America's social order.

Thousands who had denounced Malcolm in life identified with him in death. His admirers crossed racial and socioeconomic class lines. He was memorialized with t-shirts, plaques, and busts. A vast literature by interpreters arose. In the opinion of C. Eric Lincoln, the impact of Malcolm X's death shook the Nation of Islam. It raised questions about the judgment of Elijah Muhammad, and Malcolm's charisma and his organizing genius were sorely missed. Irritation among Nation of Islam leaders at the continuing presence of a cult of Malcolm X was evident in a May 1971 article in *Muhammad Speaks*. The article included a line that read, "In worshipping Malcolm, you are hated before God and before his Angels."

A 1991 Spike Lee movie called *Malcolm X* brought a whole new generation of admirers. Youngsters born years after Malcolm's death wore buttons and t-shirts proclaiming his influence.

When Malcolm met his wife Betty, she was studying to be a nurse. Following his death, she strove to raise her six children out of the limelight. She became certified at the Brooklyn State Hospital School of Nursing and went on to obtain bachelor's and master's degrees in public health education and administration. In 1975, she earned a doctorate in education administration from the University of Massachusetts at Amherst.

On June 23, 1997, Shabazz died from burns over 80 percent of her body, the result of a fire allegedly set by her 12-year-old grandson, Malcolm. He was thought to be angry that he had been sent to live with her. The boy was the son of Qubilah, Betty and Malcolm's daughter, who in January 1995 was indicted for what authorities called a macabre plot to kill Louis Farrakhan, the leader of the Nation of Islam. Farrakhan took over one of the fragments of the Nation of Islam left after Elijah Muhammad died and built the splinter group into a strong organization. Some members of the Shabazz family had long believed that Farrakhan was involved in Malcolm's death.

At the time of her death, Betty was the head of the Office of Institutional Advancement at Medgar Evers College in Brooklyn, a respected educator, a champion for human rights, and a supporter of education for young people who otherwise might not be able to obtain higher education. Her funeral on June 27, 1997, was attended by a wide range of black leaders and politicians, including the mayor of New York and many of the young people she had helped.

See also Black Muslims
References Alex Haley. *The Autobiography of Malcolm X*, 1965; C. Eric Lincoln. *The Black Muslims in America*, 1994.

Mandela, Nelson (b. 1918)

South African political activist and attorney Nelson Mandela was the son of a tribal chief. His tribal name was Rolihlahla, which means "one who brings trouble on himself." The trouble Mandela brought on himself forever changed the racial politics of his country. Rather than become a tribal chief like his father and his uncle, who became a substitute father after Mandela's father died, Mandela left home and studied law. He hoped to free black people from the tyranny of South Africa's all-white government.

In 1941, at the age of 23, Mandela took a job in Johannesburg as a guard outside compounds that housed black people who worked in the area's gold mines. The living conditions in the compounds appalled him. Any miner who quit faced being sent to jail. Living conditions for those employed outside the mines were not much better. Whereas whites lived in comfortable secure housing, blacks lived in "townships," sprawling slums near the city. Blacks slept four or more to a room, and their homes had no plumbing or electricity. Disease and crime were sources of constant fear.

In Johannesburg, Mandela met Walter Sisulu, who in 1939 had labored to convince black South Africans to avoid enlisting in the army. He reasoned that blacks had no stake in fighting to end tyranny in another land when they were treated just as badly by their own racist government.

With great difficulty, in 1952, Mandela opened a law practice in Johannesburg with Oliver Tambo. Theirs was the first black law practice in South Africa. The attorneys' clients were daily reminders of the misery brought on black South Africans by the government's policy of separation of the races.

Afrikaners (Dutch for African) are South Africans descended from the Dutch, German, and French who established the first colony in 1652 in Africa. More than any other South Africans, Afrikaners, who were among the poorest whites in the nation, consistently considered any gains in education or skills among blacks to be a threat to their economic well-being. They called for a doctrine of racial separation.

A group called the African National Congress (ANC) had organized in 1912 when a conference of black leaders met to oppose the policy of racial separation sponsored by Afrikaners. The leaders came from widely different backgrounds, represented all parts of South Africa, and spoke different dialects and languages. The ANC resolved to use nonviolent means to improve the lives of black South Africans. However, by the mid-1940s, younger members of the ANC like Nelson Mandela had become tired of waiting for whites to be influenced by the reasonableness of blacks' demands. In 1944, the Youth League, to which Mandela belonged, forced ANC to work toward becoming a mass movement.

In 1948 the Afrikaners' party, the National Party, took over the reins of government, winning with a slim margin. The National Party put into effect more than 100 laws aimed at keeping blacks and whites separate, a political philosophy called *apartheid*. Blacks were required to carry identification papers called "passbooks" everywhere, all the time. An average of 200,000 black South Africans were arrested and penalized each year for passbook violations. By the mid-1950s the National Party had become all-powerful. Blacks had lost their homes and land they had owned for generations, were restricted in their movements, and could do little to improve their economic conditions.

In 1951, Mandela became president of the Youth League. In 1952, the ANC organized South Africa's first nationwide protest against apartheid. Mandela recruited 8,577 volunteers to defy the laws and use white-only entrances, ignore curfews, and enter forbidden areas. Over the next six months, thousands were jailed in a successful demonstration of orderly, passive resistance. In response, the government cracked down. Rioting, thought to be government-provoked, broke out. Hundreds were killed and thousands were wounded. The number of oppressive laws increased.

In 1956, with other groups, ANC brought together 2,884 delegates to a Congress of the People, where they drew up a Freedom Charter. Six months later, everyone associated with the Freedom Charter, including Mandela, was taken into custody. On December 10, 1956, 156 defendants were brought to trial for treason. The trial, which lasted four and a half years, attracted international attention. Representatives from judicial organizations in Europe came to witness and record the events. Highly skilled lawyers took on the defense. The state's case was badly organized and the witnesses often unconvincing. Mandela's 441 pages of testimony eloquently explained ANC policy. From the outset of his career, it had never been Mandela's intention to exclude whites who supported the cause of black equality. Mandela's composure and good humor won him worldwide respect. In 1961, all the defendants were acquitted.

A major goal of the Afrikaner government was to prevent blacks from becoming South African citizens. To ensure segregation, they set aside 13 percent of South Africa's territory as rural reserves for eight tribal "homelands" in which they intended to force millions of blacks to live. Blacks would be allowed to work in the 87 percent of land reserved for whites, but they would be considered immigrants.

Forced migration to the homelands called into question ANC's continued policy of nonviolence. Out of frustration with ANC's perceived inaction, the Pan African Congress (PAC) was born. Led by Robert Sobukwe, PAC did not accept white participation. On March 21, 1960, in a move aimed at abolishing the pass laws, PAC asked blacks to turn in their passbooks and allow themselves to be arrested. The move was intended to fill the jails and deprive white South Africans of black labor. In most areas, arrests were made without incident. In Sharpeville, 50 miles south of Johannesburg, frightened police killed sixty-nine people and wounded 180. Most were shot in the back trying to flee. The Sharpeville massacre became international news—a brutal image of apartheid.

The ANC created an armed wing, Umkhonto we Sizwe (Spear of the Nation), to use violent methods against the government. Mandela became its commander in chief. Nonviolence as a tactic for change disappeared, and the ANC leadership was forced to go underground. Mandela eluded the police for eighteen months. Betrayed by an informer, he was captured on August 5, 1962, tried, and sentenced to five years in prison. Then he was tried a second time, charged with recruiting and training for sabotage and violent revolution, and was given life imprisonment.

Prison did not change Mandela. He exercised, studied, helped tribal chiefs solve problems, and represented prisoners' grievances. Constant pressure to release Mandela came from within and outside South Africa. By the mid-1970s, international criticism of apartheid began to affect South Africa's business and financial affairs. In response, some of the more visible examples of apartheid disappeared, but nothing fundamental changed.

In January 1976, the government announced that some high school subjects would have to be taught in Afrikaans, the language of the Afrikaners. Black South Africans wanted to continue to be taught in English. Outside Johannesburg, in Soweto (South West Townships), the largest black urban community in South Africa, 20,000 high school students spontaneously gathered to protest the new policy. The students were on a collision course with the police. When the violence was over, an estimated 700 to 1,000 people were dead. Soweto made it clear that apartheid was no longer acceptable to the majority of South Africans. Cosmetic changes that followed did nothing to soothe the unrest. In 1980, South African Prime Minister P. W. Botha told white South Africans they must "adapt or die."

A campaign to free Mandela got under way in 1980 and attracted worldwide support. In 1985, Botha offered Mandela his freedom if he would formally reject violence and agree to live in the Transkei, the place where he had been born, which was now a homeland. He refused. Then in August 1988 Mandela was hospitalized for tuberculosis. Government officials feared he might die in prison and spark violence they would not be able to control. In October 1989, F. W. de Klerk was elected president. Although he did not believe in integration, he accepted the inevitability of a multiracial state. On February 11, 1990, after twenty-seven years in jail, Nelson Mandela was released. He was 71 years old.

Soon after he was released, Mandela renounced violence, and de Klerk repealed or canceled many of the apartheid laws. Mandela and the government pledged to work together to end the violence. Many black youth who had grown up with violence continued to believe that violence rather than discussion would bring about change. Mandela patiently explained ANC's position. Nevertheless, tens of thousands of people died in political violence. In November 1993, Mandela and de Klerk agreed to set up the country's first free election. A new government would rule for five years, during which a new constitution would be written.

On April 29, 1994, Nelson Mandela was elected president of South Africa. Strangers, black and white, danced in the streets in celebration. President de Klerk said, "Mr. Mandela has walked a long road and now stands at the top of a hill. A traveler would sit down and enjoy the view. But a man of destiny knows that beyond this hill lies another. The journey is never complete. As he contemplates the next hill, I hold out my hand to Mr. Mandela in friendship and cooperation." Mandela and de Klerk were awarded UNESCO's peace prize and the Nobel Peace Prize in recognition of their efforts to end segregation in South Africa.

See also Baez, Joan; Gandhi, Mohandas; Jackson, Jesse; Kennedy, Robert; Terrorism
References Barry Denenberg. *Nelson Mandela: No Easy Walk to Freedom*, 1991; Jack L. Roberts. *Nelson Mandela: Determined to Be Free*, 1995.

Mao Zedong (1893–1976)

At the Tiananmen Gate (gate of Heavenly Peace) in the wall that surrounds Beijing, the capital of China, revolutionary Mao Zedong rose to power. China's last emperor declared the end of the empire in 1912 at the Tiananmen Gate. Mao declared the founding of the People's Republic of China (PRC) on October 1, 1949.

The gate had once opened on a grove of large silk trees. By 1949, the grove had become a 98-acre paved square, which held 100,000 people who came to listen to the man who had brought a new communist China into being. Mao arrived at the festivities in an American-made Sherman tank, symbolic of the might he had used to overcome all resistance and the power he would use to rule China.

Mao liked to portray himself as a peasant, but the Maos were a rich peasant family. His father Mao Shunsheng, although illiterate, was shrewd and ambitious. The family became prominent in the village of Shaoshan in southern China. Early in his life, Mao rebelled against his father and his teachers and learned that rebellion brought him concessions. About the same time Mao noticed injustices on a larger social scale. When crop failures brought famine to southern China, his father was unwilling to share his stocks with his starving neighbors. Unrest generated by famine hinted that change was about to disrupt the smooth sameness of village life.

By the late nineteenth century, warlords, local rulers or bandit leaders with some sort of military following, ruled many areas in China. The Chinese imperial dynasty had grown weak. European countries and the United States had taken control of sections of China. The impact of outsiders was to generate a growing sense of nationalism among the Chinese and a desire to control their own fate. In Shanghai, a city where foreigners were concentrated, a sign at the entry to the foreign residents' quarters warned, "Dogs and Chinese Not Allowed," a sentiment that further fueled Chinese nationalism. In 1899, the Society of the Righteous Harmonious Fists (better known as the Boxers) organized an uprising. Although short-lived and unsuccessful, the Boxer Rebellion fueled growing Chinese nationalism.

Mao overcame many obstacles and educated himself. He obtained a job as an assistant librarian at the library of the Beijing University. When he discovered the theories of Karl Marx, he was intrigued by the idea that the world was moving toward a classless, collective communism. Mao became convinced that the Chinese must embrace socialism, a system in which those who produced goods and services also had the means to distribute them and had political power. At a secret meeting in July 1921, confident that China must become a communist state, he became one of the founders of the Chinese Communist Party (CCP).

Sun Yatsen, a physician, emerged as one of the principal opponents of the Manchu dynasty. A nationalist movement gained force under his leadership. In 1912 Sun Yatsen and a Manchu general named Yuan Shikai signed a truce that forced Pu Yi, the emperor, to step down from the throne. The Republic of China was proclaimed with Yuan Shikai as president.

In 1915, the Japanese government tried to make a deal with the emperor that would have given Japan control over China's economy. When word of the possible arrangement leaked out, the Chinese people were outraged. All over the country, army garrisons rose up in revolt. When Yuan Shikai died in 1916, the Republic of China collapsed and the country was left without effective government. Army generals set themselves up as warlords of provinces. Sun Yatsen's followers, the Kuomintang (KMT) or Nationalist party, joined the fray.

Marxist theory, which held that revolutions began with industrial workers in cities, did not fit the realities of China, a primarily agricultural country. Mao argued that revolution should begin among rural peasants, the backbone of China. Other CCP leaders overruled him.

The Kuomintang, much larger and better organized than the CCP, shared goals with the CCP, but was not committed to a socialist revolution. The Nationalist party included many landowners and aristocrats, but CCP needed their help. Mao stayed involved with the Nationalist Party, writing articles, organizing labor unions and protests, and doing the work of the CCP and the Nationalists.

When Mao went home to visit his brothers in Shaoshan village, he noticed signs that the peasants were starting a revolution on their own. They had organized fighting bands and seized land from rich owners, then divided the land among themselves.

In the meantime, the Nationalist army under the leadership of Chiang Kaishek was building its strength. The Nationalists promised to drive out foreigners and their puppet warlords. Chiang's army swept north, kindling revolt as it marched. The Nationalists had no intention of handing over China to the CCP. In the spring of 1927, the Nationalists declared war on their former allies. The communists fought for their survival and for "the soul of China."

Mao ignored the command of CCP leaders to engage the Nationalists at Changsha and like the outlaw heroes he had admired as a child, he holed up on a shrouded peak called Well Mountain in the Chingkang Mountains, where he gathered lawless bands under his command. He laid down strict rules for his soldiers. No one was allowed to steal from peasants. Loot taken from the rich was turned over to Mao's staff. Everyone was educated in socialist principles. Transgressors were killed.

Maoism—Mao's brand of socialism and revolution—took shape on Well Mountain. Mao insisted that China must follow a course dictated by its history and conditions, not a blueprint laid down by Russian Marxists. Mao joined forces with communist general Zhu De, a crucial move for China's future. Zhu was a brilliant military commander, and Mao was an inspired thinker and long-range planner.

Mao was constantly at odds with the strategy of the CCP. At a point when the Red Army, outnumbered six to one by the Nationalist forces, was losing badly and the CCP central committee was in disarray, Mao stepped into the breach and convinced the army to abandon its traditional fixed line of march and to adopt guerrilla tactics—such as sudden changes of direction and frequent backtracking. He also split up the army to confuse the Nationalists.

Because routes north were blocked by Nationalists, Mao ordered his troops to travel through the steaming rain forest of Yunnan, on the Vietnamese border, to begin what came to be known as the Long March. A year later, after a journey of 6,000 miles, he reached a new stronghold with 20,000, one-fifth of the force with which he had begun. The march made Mao a legend and brought millions of Chinese into contact with the Red Army and Mao's revolutionary goals. Maoists regarded it as a sacred pilgrimage and those who survived it as national heroes. As Red Army sol-

diers brought areas under Communist control, they cut taxes, took land from the rich and gave it to the poor, worked with the peasants in the fields, and introduced programs for literacy and medical care. Everyone was induced to wear peasant clothing—a loose-fitting blue jacket and trousers.

In 1937, Mao and Chiang Kaishek signed an agreement to stop fighting each other and attack the invading Japanese. Chiang broke the agreement in 1940 when he attacked one of the communist armies. Many Chinese who had no love for the communists were outraged. When the United States entered the war with the Japanese, U.S. supplies were funneled to China. Chiang Kaishek insisted that the Americans deal with him alone, which quenched Mao's positive feelings toward America.

A few months after the end of World War II, fighting resumed between the communists and the Nationalists in 1946. Mao launched an all-out offensive, taking city after city. By September 1949, the long struggle was over and all of China was under communist rule. Chiang and the Nationalists fled to Taiwan, an island off China's coast. When, on October 1, Mao climbed onto the Gate of Heavenly Peace to proclaim the birth of the People's Republic of China (PRC), he became the leader of the most populous nation in the world.

Reference Rebecca Stefoff. *Mao Zedong: Founder of the People's Republic of China,* 1996.

March on the Pentagon

On October 21, 1967, Stop the Draft Week climaxed with a march on the Pentagon that drew middle-class liberals, student radicals, hippies, civil rights workers, black power advocates, Vietnam veterans, and federal workers.

The radicals present proclaimed they were ready to fight. The counterculture hippies joked that they planned to exorcise demons from the military control center by chanting "om" and levitating the Pentagon building. A few dozen radicals attacked. The military responded by beating them and placed them under arrest. A few hundred people sat down in the Pentagon parking lot. Diggers (hippies who took responsibility for feeding people) brought the sitters-in food and marijuana.

The mood was festive. The participants laughed, hugged, and chanted to the military police, "We love you," and "We'd love to turn you on." They used guerrilla theater, pretending to be soldiers acting out death in war. Some smoked dope into the evening, sipped wine, and built campfires. Some sang "Silent Night." Despite those who sat in the lotus position and hummed "om," the Pentagon refused to levitate.

As midnight neared, the military police were replaced by paratroopers of the 82d Division. The paratroopers massed in the center of the sit-in and prepared to attack. U.S. marshals formed at the rear of the crowd. The combined forces beat the nonresisting participants over their heads. Although most activists deemed the march on the Pentagon a success, for many it was the end of passivity. A number of disciples of Gandhi's nonviolence vowed to become guerrillas.

House Democratic Leader Carl Albert asserted that the march on the Pentagon was organized by international communism. House Republican Leader Gerald Ford proclaimed that the administration had a secret report that confirmed that Stop the Draft Week was "cranked up" in Hanoi.

See also Antiwar Movement; Hippies; Nonviolence
Reference Terry Anderson. *Movement and the Sixties: Protest in America from Greensboro to Wounded Knee*, 1995.

March on Washington for Jobs and Freedom (August 28, 1963)

The March on Washington for Jobs and Freedom proposed by Southern Christian Leadership Conference (SCLC) member James Bevel did not meet with immediate enthusiasm. Bevel, who had helped organize the Mississippi Delta in 1960 and 1961 by bringing singing groups to friendly black churches, wanted to put 8,000 young people on the road from Birmingham, Alabama, to Washington, D.C. The logistics of moving, feeding, and taking care of thousands of people during a 1,200-mile trek proved unrealistic for SCLC. Nevertheless, the idea ultimately inspired a march that took place on August 28, 1963.

The National Association for the Advancement of Colored People (NAACP) and the Urban League were initially opposed to the march, as was the Kennedy administration. In favor of the march was A. Philip Randolph, who during World War II had used the threat of a march to persuade President Franklin D. Roosevelt to sign an executive order forbidding discrimination in war industries. In 1950 Randolph had cofounded, with Arnold Aronson and Roy Wilkins, the Leadership Conference, which was made up of religious, labor, and civil rights organizations. His opinion carried considerable weight—enough to change the opinions of the NAACP and the Urban League.

The Kennedy administration, fearful that an all-black march would threaten passage of civil rights legislation, urged white union leaders to join the effort. The march became a joint undertaking of unions, religious leaders, and the "Big Six" civil rights organizations: SCLC, Student Nonviolent Coordinating Committee (SNCC), NAACP, Urban League, Council of Negro Women, and Congress of Racial Equality (CORE).

The grassroots march Bevel had envisioned, made up of people dressed in denim who had sacrificed and gone to jail for the movement, instead included mostly middle-class blacks and liberal whites dressed in Sunday suits, the majority of whom had been reluctant in their support of earlier struggles. According to Andrew Young, in his book *An Easy Burden* (1996), Bevel complained, "You all turned my march into a picnic," and refused to attend.

Despite Bevel's disgruntlement, the 1963 march brought an estimated 250,000 people to Washington. Trainloads and busloads of people poured into the capital on a steamy hot day to sing and listen to speeches at the foot of the Lincoln Memorial. Behind the scenes, jockeying went on about the order of the speakers. The leaders of NAACP and the Urban League lobbied for early slots when the cameras would be present. Martin Luther King, Jr., whose organization,

SCLC, had originated the idea, was scheduled last. Fortunately, the cameras stayed to the end.

The words King delivered highlighted the reasons for the march and came to be known as his "Bad Check" speech, or as his "I Have a Dream" speech. He said, "We came here to dramatize a shameful condition. In a sense, we've come to our nation's capital to cash a check. When the architects of our republic wrote the magnificent words of the Constitution and the Declaration of Independence, they were signing a promissory note to which every American was to fall heir. The note was a promise that all men, yes black men as well as white men, would be guaranteed the unalienable right to life, liberty, and the pursuit of happiness. It is obvious that America has defaulted on this promissory note insofar as her citizens of color are concerned. Instead of honoring the sacred obligation, America has given the Negro people a bad check: a check which has come back marked insufficient funds."

See also Civil Rights Movement; King, Reverend Martin Luther, Jr.; Young, Andrew
Reference Andrew Young. *An Easy Burden: The Civil Rights Movement and the Transformation of America,* 1996.

Marcuse, Herbert (1898–1979)

A benign philosopher, already in his seventies during the 1960s, Marcuse wrote indignant critiques of the status quo, both East and West. Some scholars credit Marcuse as being a significant influence during the era on young radicals of the left. Other scholars believe that Marcuse's influence, as well as the influence of many other intellectuals of the period, has been overemphasized. Young people did not have to read Marcuse to discover the presence of injustice. They could simply look around, tune into the music of the age, and read underground newspapers.

Regardless of whether Marcuse actually had a significant influence, he was attacked by defenders of both capitalism and communism as a pernicious influence on youth. Marcuse's writing is difficult to read. Nevertheless, in the 1960s his ideas seemed to become widely disseminated.

The best known of Marcuse's books are *Eros and Civilization* (1955) and *One-Dimensional Man* (1964). The former synthesized Marx and Freud and is said to have made a major contribution to the hippie movement.

The heir of a prominent, upper-class Jewish family in Berlin, Marcuse was educated at the University of Berlin and received a Ph.D. from the University of Freiburg. As a university student, Marcuse belonged to the Social Democratic Party. He left the party after the murder of two Communist Party leaders that had allegedly been ordered by the Social Democratic government. With Theodor Adorno and Max Horkheimer in the 1920s, Marcuse founded the Frankfurt Institute of Social Research. Throughout his life he remained preoccupied with politics.

Three factors shaped Marcuse's worldview. One was the development of the discipline of sociology. A second was the failure of democracy in Germany under the Weimar Republic, which permitted the Nazi party to come to power. A third was the work of Wilhelm Reich, a young Viennese psychiatrist, which gave Marcuse a perspective on the sadism rampant in everyday German life.

Marcuse believed that in an advanced technological civilization like the United States, it was irrational to keep people engaged in "exhausting, stupefying, inhuman slavery." The wasteful misuse of technology under both capitalism and communism, in his view, actually made work more inhumane in such countries than it was in societies without the advantages of technology. Yet the leisure available in technological societies did not inspire workers to explore options, but soothed them into stupefaction. Marcuse wrote: "They have dozens of newspapers and magazines that espouse the same ideals. They have innumerable gadgets that keep them occupied and divert their attention from the real issue—which is awareness that they could both work less and determine their own needs and satisfactions." Marcuse felt that workers tended to get caught up in the status quo, and he believed that students and minority groups would be better at challenging the prevailing order.

The Frankfurt School of Social Research was a

target of the Nazis and was closed once Hitler took power. Marcuse fled to Geneva, Switzerland, in 1933, where he stayed a year before moving on to a post at Columbia University in New York. During World War II, Marcuse became a European intelligence analyst with the U.S. Office of Strategic Services. After the war, he held the job of chief of staff of the Central European section in the Office of Intelligence Research. Fluent in Russian, he was an expert on Soviet affairs.

In 1954, Marcuse joined the faculty at Brandeis University, where he taught for eleven years. When he reached mandatory retirement age at Brandeis, Marcuse moved on to the University of California at San Diego. Conservative, wealthy citizens of San Diego demanded that Marcuse's contract not be renewed. In July 1968, a death threat sent him into hiding for a month.

Marcuse didn't take himself seriously. He once said, "If somebody really believes that my opinions can seriously endanger society, then he and society must be very badly off indeed."

See also Beat Generation; Hippies; Hoffman, Abbie
References Herbert Marcuse. *Eros and Civilization,* 1955; and *One-Dimensional Man: Studies in Ideology of Advanced Industrial Society,* 1964.

Marxism

A political and social system of beliefs developed by Karl Marx and Friedrich Engels called Marxism serves as a blueprint for revolution aimed at bringing the industrial working class to power with the aim of eliminating social classes. Marxism proposes that the economic forces associated with the production of goods and services determine the form taken by a society's social classes, religions, and patterns of thinking. Marx theorized that humankind has evolved through several successive types of society.

The type of society called feudalism was replaced by the economic system called capitalism. Capitalism encourages open competition in a free marketplace, private (individual or corporate) ownership of the means (wealth or property) necessary to create goods and services, and the accumulation and reinvestment of wealth. Marx-

ism predicts that a proletarian (working-class) revolution will erode capitalism and replace it with a communistic, classless society that will no longer need a state, and the apparatus of government will wither away. Communism is defined as a social system in which the means of production and subsistence (food, clothing, and shelter) are owned in common by the people and the organization of labor is designed to benefit everyone.

Different interpretations of Marxism have arisen. Disagreements center mostly on whether the proletarian revolution will be democratic or violent. Whenever communist political parties have taken control of a nation, Marxism has been declared the state's official philosophy. In each communistic country, the official interpretation of Marxism has been controlled by the government in order to justify its policies.

Marx and Engels worked out their theory over an extended period in the nineteenth century. Following the publication of their inflammatory *Communist Manifesto* in January 1848, the two men devoted the next five years to revolutionary political agitation. From 1852 until the mid-1860s, Marx elaborated on his economic theory of capitalism. In 1864, he once again became involved in practical political activism. After 1875, extension of Marxism was carried on by Engels.

Marxism has been referred to as dialectic materialism. Dialectic alludes to a process of change in which a state of affairs ("thesis") generates opposing forces ("antithesis") that destroy the original situation, which leads the way to a new one ("synthesis"). The synthesis then becomes the thesis and generates an antithesis that results in another synthesis. Materialism indicates the material world rather than the world of ideas common to most philosophies.

Marx was convinced that the laws of history that had destined the development of capitalism would break down when confronted by proletarian revolutions. The synthesis that the revolutions would bring about would create an ideal world in which the separation between the ruling class and the workers would disappear. The process of the dialectic, given the absence of opposing forces, would also disappear.

Like any other broad theory of society, Marxism has been the target of many critics. The theory is replete with inconsistencies and ambiguities. It has been interpreted in a wide variety of ways by both its supporters and its detractors. Marx failed to predict the rise of a salaried middle class of professional, technical, and white collar workers.

In most countries, Marxism has aroused violent antagonism from the political, social, and religious sectors. As the Marxist revolutionary threat subsided, social scientists in Europe and America have recognized it as a major contribution to understanding social change and social problems. Marxism goaded scholars to examine the interrelatedness of political, social, economic, and cultural forces in society. In the latter part of the nineteenth century, Marxism was adopted by a majority of the rising labor and socialist movements in Europe, with the exception of Great Britain. It became the official philosophy of social democratic parties. During the same period, the political emphasis of Marxism shifted from revolutionary to peaceful democratic change.

During the first two decades of the twentieth century, two opposing interpretations of Marxism appeared within the social democratic parties. On the right or moderate side, theorists wanted to revise Marx to replace his idea of revolution with a democratic program of evolutionary socialism. On the left, a radical view, particularly among the Russian Marxists, advocated violent revolution.

Russian Marxist theorist Vladimir Lenin's vision of a party was a disciplined organization of professional revolutionaries who would overthrow the government and seize power in the name of the working class. He argued that the Social Democratic party should establish a "democratic dictatorship of the proletariat and peasantry" pending the economic development that would make the transition to socialism feasible. Leon Trotsky predicted that a revolution against the propertied class would initiate a permanent state of revolution in which the workers could seize power in the major cities. This would in turn set up a permanent state of revolution internationally as the Russian example triggered forces of proletarian revolution in the West. Trotsky's views were used to support the rationale for the 1917 Bolshevik ("majority") revolution and help explain the emphasis placed on world revolution by the Bolsheviks.

Marxists' reactions to the 1917 Russian revolution both inside and outside Russia were deeply divided. A struggle for power in Soviet Russia, just preceding and following Lenin's death in 1924, profoundly changed the meaning of Marxist theory for the communist movement. Joseph Stalin, the general secretary of the Communist Party, coined the expression "Marxist-Leninism." In dogmatic terms, he laid down the theoretical justifications followed by the Soviet regime until the 1990s: the necessity of violent revolution by the Communist party, of Communist Party dictatorship during the "building of socialism," of iron discipline within the party, and of the "theory of socialism in one country," which held that Russia could overcome its backwardness and achieve socialism without the aid of international revolution.

Once Stalin had overcome his rivals and taken control of Russia, he put his principles into practice. He collectivized the peasantry. Privately owned farms and business were taken over by the state and economic planning became centralized. Stalin rationalized the abandonment of egalitarianism with the argument "to each according to his needs." Management personnel needed more economic resources than the peasants. Stalin's programs of collectivization caused millions to die of starvation.

The idea that the state would wither away was rejected on the basis that governments played a positive role in the promotion of economic and cultural development, as well as the defense of the country against "capitalist encirclement." Soviet interpretations of Marxism were reinterpreted in countries brought under Soviet control during and after World War II. Those Eastern European countries dominated by the Soviet government, together known as the Eastern Bloc, enabled the Soviet Union to become a superpower in world politics.

The Soviet Union's goal of spreading communism around the world fueled U.S. fears that the Soviet Union would take over more countries. In the absence of outright warfare between the two superpowers, a series of diplomatic controversies developed to the point of open hostility. Once the Soviet Union could produce an atomic bomb, hostility carried the threat of mutual annihilation. The tension between the two countries became known as the Cold War.

In the 1950s and 1960s, a philosophy of Marxist existentialism (the isolation of individual experience in a hostile or indifferent universe) revived interest in the early writings of Marx as a theory of individuals isolated from society. This movement was reinforced by the "Frankfurt School" philosophers who applied the dialectical method to the psychological oppressiveness of modern society. An advocate of the Frankfurt School, Herbert Marcuse, influenced some American New Left student groups.

See also Ho Chi Minh; Mao Zedong; Marcuse, Herbert; Old Left and New Left
Reference David McLellan. Marx: *His Life and Thought*, 1974.

McCarthy, Eugene (b. 1916)

Antiwar presidential candidate Eugene McCarthy, who ran as a students' choice in 1968, was born in the village of Watkins, Minnesota. The gentle nature of McCarthy's mother, who attended mass every morning, made a deep impression on her children. His father, a feisty, rugged individual with a short temper, also had an impact, by teaching his son to stand for what he believed. McCarthy attended St. John's Preparatory School, run by Benedictine monks. There he was exposed to the thinking of the Reverend Virgil Michel, a formidable figure in the American Catholic Church.

Michel tried to help Americans understand that a renewal in the prayer life of the church had already started in Europe. As he delved into the issue, the priest saw a connection between a renovation of the church's prayer life and a renovation of church philosophy. He was strongly influenced by 1897 papal encyclicals that dealt with the rights of working men to organize. (A papal encyclical is a letter from the pope to the bishops of the church or to the hierarchy of a particular country.) Michel's explanations were published in a book entitled *On the Reconstruction of the Social Order*, which McCarthy read as a student. Michel laid out the course of liturgical and social reform that would make its way into the plans of the Second Vatican Council.

The views of the world-renowned priest, who died in 1938, strongly influenced McCarthy's political views later when he served as a senator and ran as a presidential candidate. McCarthy spent nine months studying for the priesthood. Although he left the monastery, he never forgot the Benedictine principles about moral and social values.

McCarthy spent the years of World War II working as a civilian analyst in Washington, D.C. In 1946, he took a job teaching economics and sociology at the College of St. Thomas in St. Paul, Minnesota. In St. Paul, he became involved in politics. Hubert Humphrey, then mayor of Minneapolis, advised him to take over St. Paul's weak Democratic organization. In 1948, McCarthy was elected to Congress from Minnesota's fourth congressional district. His campaign speeches were a paradoxical mixture of humility, arrogance, idealism, and pragmatism. As a member of the House Agriculture Committee, McCarthy launched a long campaign to improve the working and living conditions of Mexican-American migrant farmworkers. In 1959, he became a senator. In the Senate, McCarthy became chairman of the newly created Senate Special Committee on Employment Problems. Although he was not successful in gaining passage of the committee's proposals, many were later incorporated into President John F. Kennedy's legislative agenda.

In a speech delivered November 9, 1967, McCarthy questioned whether the U.S. commitment in Vietnam was morally defensible. He believed President Lyndon Johnson corrupted people and eroded the institutions of government. On November 30, he announced he planned to enter some presidential primaries. McCarthy took little

Senator Eugene McCarthy.

interest in organizing his McCarthy-for-President staff. Most members were young and inexperienced—few had worked in a national campaign. The effectiveness of his campaign was attributable to calamities in Vietnam.

McCarthy's student crusade, one of the most significant features of the 1968 presidential race, destroyed conventional wisdom that a campaign could be put together only by professional planners. It brought together a large group of alienated young people who wanted to revitalize the political process. With unpaid volunteers, McCarthy's staff mounted a door-to-door campaign in New Hampshire that reached most of the state's 90,000 registered Democrats and 100,000 independents. McCarthy thought he had a chance to win because Robert Kennedy and Hubert Humphrey might cancel each other out, leaving a clear field for him. When Robert Kennedy was assassinated, McCarthy appeared to lose faith in his chances.

Although Lyndon Johnson decided not to run

again, he managed the convention by telephone. His forces rammed through a plank that supported Johnson's Vietnam policy. At 8:00 P.M. on the night the nominations were made, as the process began, a clash broke out in the streets outside between the police and antiwar demonstrators. Television cameras shifted back and forth between the nominations and the police beating demonstrators. Later in the evening, as Humphrey was introducing his vice presidential candidate to the convention, McCarthy, accompanied by his Secret Service escort, walked to Grant Park, where the demonstrators were camped. He gave a speech reminiscent of St. Paul. He said, "I have not departed from my commitment to you, nor have you departed from your commitment to me . . . So we go on in this same spirit."

At 5:00 A.M. the following morning, the National Guard invaded McCarthy's hotel campaign headquarters. They claimed something had been thrown from the windows. They beat workers and herded them into elevators to the main lobby. When McCarthy arrived on the scene and asked who was in charge, no one could tell him. "Just as I thought," said McCarthy. "Nobody's in charge."

McCarthy did achieve something at the convention. He won an end to the "unit rule," which required everyone in a delegation to vote with the majority. It was the issue that had first led to McCarthy's involvement in politics twenty years earlier. The change in the unit rule drastically changed the party and played a critical role in the candidacy of George McGovern, who in 1972, like McCarthy, ran a campaign largely supported by students.

In 1971 Congressman John Blatnik of Minnesota mourned the confrontation in 1968 between Eugene McCarthy and Hubert Humphrey. He said, "They both knocked each other out of the ring in 1968 and the loss was for the whole liberal philosophy." Looking back from the vantage point of 1996, shortly before the Democratic convention, McCarthy did not take responsibility for any losses. He told *New York Times* reporter Francis X. Clines that he might have made more of 1968 if Robert Kennedy had not entered the race and diffused the antiwar vote.

The consequence of the selection processes for convention delegates that he helped bring about didn't please him. In his view, they shortcut the public's involvement in politics. Retired and living in rural Virginia, McCarthy writes an occasional poem or essay and gives ten or twelve speeches a year on campuses, to students who have little interest in him. "But," he said, "there's always about ten faculty people who invited me to talk about the old days." In his eighties and an avid reader of political news, McCarthy seemed to have lost most of his disdain for politics.

See also Bond, Julian; McGovern, George; Yippies
References Francis X. Cline. "The Sting of Tear Gas and Regret," 1996; Albert Eisele. *Almost to the Presidency: A Biography of Two American Politicians,* 1973; Eugene McCarthy. *The Year of the People,* 1969; Virgil Michel. *Christian Social Reconstruction: Some Fundamentals of the Quadragesimo Año,* 1937.

McGovern, George (b. 1922)

A former history professor, McGovern served in the U.S. House of Representatives from 1957 to 1961. During four years in the House, McGovern urged the United States to use its abundant food resources to feed the hungry people of the world. He proposed the establishment of an executive office for that purpose. In 1961, McGovern left the House to direct President John F. Kennedy's Food-for-Peace program. And in November 1962, McGovern became the first Democratic senator to be elected from South Dakota in fifty years. He told a reporter in January 1963 that his overriding interest since the end of World War II was attainment of world peace.

Despite having been a U.S. Air Force bomber pilot and winner of the Distinguished Flying Cross and Air Force Medal with three Oak Leaf Clusters during World War II, McGovern was a severe critic of the Vietnam War. In his first speech as a U.S. senator, McGovern criticized what he called America's fixation with Fidel Castro, the premier of Cuba. He declared that instead of making anticommunism an end in itself, the United States should "point the way toward a better life." In August 1963, he proposed a $4 billion

cut in the nation's defense budget, which he described as having a vast "overkill" capacity.

In late 1965, McGovern visited South Vietnam, where he talked with military and civilian officials and toured refugee camps. On his return in January 1966, he declared that U.S. policy toward Vietnam was flawed. It was based on the assumption that the issue dividing Vietnam was military rather than political.

McGovern was instrumental in bringing about a major change in the Democratic Party. For many activists, the campaign for the 1972 presidential campaign began the day after the Chicago convention in 1968. "New Democrats," many of whom had participated in the 1968 campaigns of Eugene McCarthy and Robert Kennedy, lobbied for changes in delegate selection for the 1972 convention. They wanted youth, minorities, and women to be represented. New Democrats demanded formation of a commission. Party regulars agreed, and George McGovern was appointed chairman of the commission. It heard 500 witnesses, most of whom were women, minorities, and local party organizers.

The conversion of the Democratic Party became evident in 1970, when activists worked for New Democratic candidates, many of whom won primaries. Two months after the elections, in January 1971, McGovern announced his candidacy for the Democratic nomination for president. He pledged to "call America home to those principles that gave us birth." McGovern gave more speeches at universities than any other candidate. He drew crowds whose numbers were enlarged by passage of the Twenty-sixth Amendment, which had lowered the voting age from twenty-one to eighteen.

In March 1972, the North Vietnamese launched a major assault. Within weeks, they threatened the South Vietnamese regime in Saigon. President Richard Nixon responded by ordering a massive escalation in the air war. By the spring of 1972, the peace movement had become part of the Democratic establishment, and both spoke out against escalation of the war.

After a bitter fight with forces supporting Hubert Humphrey, McGovern won the 1972

Democratic nomination. Union leaders, urban political bosses, "white ethnics" (European Americans), and moderate blacks resented the new party. American Federation of Labor–Congress of Industrial Organizations (AFL-CIO) boss George Meany labeled the delegates "hippies, women liberationists, gays, kooks, and draft dodgers." Despite a break-in at the Democratic National Headquarters at the Watergate Hotel that was traced to the White House, the outcome of the election was never in doubt. Opinion polls revealed that voters supported Nixon over McGovern two to one.

McGovern was the most liberal candidate ever nominated by a major party. His supporters at the convention shocked mainstream America. His positions on issues reflected those of the various movements of the 1960s, positions held by only a minority of Americans. McGovern continued to serve in the Senate until 1980. He is the president of the Middle East Policy Council, an educational organization founded in 1981 to promote better understanding of the issues in the Middle East. He frequently serves as a visiting professor at various universities and is a contributing editor to IntellectualCapital.com, an Internet site where issues are discussed.

In connection with the 1996 publication of his book about his daughter's struggle with alcoholism, McGovern used the opportunity to lecture about the impact of alcohol on families.

See also McCarthy, Eugene
References George McGovern. *War against Want: America's Food for Peace Program,* 1964; *Grassroots: The Autobiography of George McGovern,* 1977; and *Terry: My Daughter's Life and Death Struggle with Alcoholism,* 1996.

McLuhan, Herbert Marshall (1911–1980)

Activism depends upon the dissemination of ideas to potential supporters. By the 1960s, door-to-door campaigns to rally supporters had become obsolete. Communications specialist and writer Marshall McLuhan called attention to radical changes in the twentieth century that could be traced to electronic communications. He became famous in the 1960s for his assertion that "the medium is the message." An explorer of ideas, McLuhan straddled the disciplines of literature, art, education, philosophy, physiology, and sociology. He provoked responses in his readers, rather than explaining or offering proof of his assertions.

A Canadian, McLuhan began teaching at the University of Wisconsin in 1936, where he met young Americans he found impossible to understand. In order to make contact with his students, McLuhan studied their popular culture. He understood how to influence students. About a year after he began teaching at Wisconsin, McLuhan converted to Catholicism and subsequently taught at several Catholic institutions. In 1951, a year before he became a full professor at St. Michael's College, the Roman Catholic unit of the University of Toronto, he published *The Mechanical Bride: Folklore of the Industrial Man.* In it, he attacked the pressures exerted on people by the mechanical agencies of newspapers, radio, movies, and advertising.

McLuhan's reputation as a communications specialist led to his appointment in 1959–1960 as director of a media project for the U.S. Office of Education and the National Association of Educational Broadcasters. His book, *Gutenberg Galaxy: The Making of Typographic Man* (1962), won the prestigious Governor-General's Award for critical prose and brought him worldwide attention.

In *Gutenberg Galaxy*, McLuhan proposed that the nature of television, computers, and other electronic media reshaped civilization more than the contents they conveyed. In his opinion, the fifteenth-century invention of movable type had a profound effect on the culture of Western Europe. When print succeeded oral communication, the eye rather than the ear became the primary sense organ. Linear development—items that follow one another in succession—led to linear developments in music, mathematics, and science. In McLuhan's opinion, the linear revolution produced self-centeredness in humans.

With the advent of electronic circuitry in the electronic age, humans were restored to their tribal ways, and the world became "a global village." Electronic media, in particular television, heightened sensory awareness, brought an immediacy in communication, reduced separation of thought from action, and diminished isolation.

Even McLuhan's critics recognized the importance of his controversial book *Understanding Media* (1964). He described how and why radio, telephones, television, movies, computers, and all other forms of electronic communication restructured civilization. His critics ridiculed him for suggesting books are obsolescent. They pointed out that McLuhan's acclaim rested on his books. One severe critic described *Understanding Media* as "impure nonsense, nonsense adulterated by sense." Most critics agreed that McLuhan pushed his insights too far by trying to include every facet of contemporary society.

Acknowledging that his own "stuff" was so difficult he sometimes had trouble understanding it, McLuhan wrote *The Medium Is the Massage: An Inventory of Effects* with Quentin Fiore (1967). It contained more than 100 examples of how the media transformed modern life. The title was intended to draw attention to the fact that the medium is not neutral. It rubs off on people, massages them, and bumps them around.

McLuhan's thinking has proven prophetic in many areas. Music television (MTV) and music videos do not present linear ideas. They cross-cut flashes of ideas. Political campaigns are designed as much around how the medium will affect the message to be delivered as they are about the content. The concept of the world as a "global village" has also been widely accepted. News— events the media finds interesting or important—is rapidly distributed around the world by global journalism networks, such as Cable Network News (CNN). Communication satellites make it possible to locate and track people on highways and ships at sea. The intrusion of cameras has made privacy as elusive as it once was for people who lived in small villages.

References Marshall McLuhan. *Gutenberg Galaxy: The Making of Typographic Man,* 1962; *Understanding Media: The Extensions of Man,* 1964; *Mechanical Bride: Folklore of the Industrial Man,* 1967; and *The Medium Is the Massage: An Inventory of Effects,* 1967.

Means, Russell (b. 1939)

Russell Means was born on the Pine Ridge Reservation in South Dakota. During World War II, his father moved the family to California to work in a navy yard near San Francisco. The family made frequent trips back to the reservation. Means was relatively happy in school until he transferred from a racially mixed high school to one that was almost all white. Ostracized by fellow students, Means became resentful and began experimenting with drugs. After high school, he worked at a variety of jobs and attended five colleges but never graduated.

In the late 1960s, Means took a job directing the government-funded Cleveland American Indian Center. There he met Dennis Banks, a cofounder of the American Indian Movement (AIM). Means founded a Cleveland chapter of AIM. He brought national attention to AIM in 1970, when he and a handful of Indians seized control of the *Mayflower II* in Plymouth, Massachusetts, on Thanksgiving Day. During the next two years, Means was active. He staged a prayer vigil at the top of Mount Rushmore, attempted to take over the Bureau of Indian Affairs (BIA) control information office, and sued the Cleveland Indians baseball team for $9 million, charging the team's mascot demeaned Indians.

After Means resigned his job in Cleveland in 1972, he returned to the reservation in South Dakota, where he planned the "Trail of the Broken Treaties," a series of cross-country caravans scheduled to converge on Washington, D.C., during election week in November 1972. The purpose of the demonstration was to call public attention to the chain of treaties with the Indians that the federal government had broken.

The group planned to present a list of twenty demands. Means was assured by the BIA that the group would be given adequate housing on its arrival in the capital on November 2. The quarters for the Indian leaders who had traveled across the country turned out to be shabby, cramped, and insect-ridden. A minor official sent to meet the delegation was patronizing. Infuriated, Means led a protest against the BIA. The group took over the building.

Attorney William Kunstler, Russell Means, and Dennis Banks (left to right) meet at Wounded Knee, South Dakota, in 1973 to negotiate with Justice Department authorities.

In February 1973, Means and about 300 members of AIM occupied the small village of Wounded Knee, South Dakota, the site where, in 1890, the U.S. Seventh Cavalry massacred Big Foot and 350 members of his tribe, mostly women and children. Under federal siege, the AIM members controlled the hamlet for seventy-one days. Means, an Oglala Sioux, contended that the Indian's occupation of the village was a "liberation," justified by the federal government's breach of the 1868 Treaty of Fort Laramie and the breach of 300 subsequent treaties.

After several weeks of fruitless talks, Means negotiated a stand-down to allow him to be escorted to the White House. Asked to have the group at Wounded Knee lay down their arms, Means refused and stalked out of the meeting. He told the media that the last treaty the government made with the Indians had lasted only seventy-two hours. Trailed by FBI agents, Means crisscrossed the country to raise funds to support his cause. When he announced his intention to return to Wounded Knee in defiance of a court order, he was jailed. On May 8, 1973, 120 Indians surrendered. The government agreed to open an investigation.

Means was indicted on ten felony charges for taking part in Wounded Knee. The trial lasted from February 12, 1974, until September 16, 1974. Six defense attorneys kept government witnesses on the stand for days. The defense obtained evidence of illegal wiretapping, perjured testimony, and government misconduct. The judge dismissed the charges and severely criticized the prosecution.

See also Banks, Dennis; Bellecourt Brothers, Vernon and Clyde; National Indian Youth Council; Wounded Knee
Reference Russell Means. *Road to Wounded Knee,* 1974.

Militias

At an increasing rate during the 1990s, bands of armed right-wing militants, many of them calling themselves "militias," cropped up across the

United States. The term "militia" probably stems from their focus on the Second Amendment of the Constitution, which states: "A well-regulated militia being necessary to the security of the free state, the right of the people to keep and bear arms shall not be infringed." Although the militias had no centralized organization, they were loosely linked through sharing publications and speakers. A 1994 survey by the Anti-Defamation League (ADL) found evidence in thirteen states of militia activity.

Militia goals are stated in warlike terms. They are aimed at the creation of massive resistance to the federal government and its law enforcement agencies. To many militant militia members, the government is the enemy, which constantly increased its control and planned war over its citizens.

Gun control legislation is a particular target for militia ire. They believe gun control is a secret government strategy to disarm the American people and abolish the right to bear arms. Militias rail against the Brady Law—named for Jim Brady, the former press secretary of President Reagan, who was shot in the head during an assassination attempt against the president. The Brady Law requires a five-day waiting period during which a background check is run against the purchaser. The militia also resents the 1994 federal crime bill that banned the sale of nineteen different types of assault weapons and limited gun clips to a maximum of ten bullets.

As evidence of a government conspiracy, they point to two events. The first took place in Waco, Texas. The Bureau of Alcohol, Tobacco, and Firearms (ATF) attempted to enter the Branch Davidian compound to seize illegal weapons and arrest those responsible for stockpiling them. The residents of the compound resisted the raid, killing four ATF agents. A standoff between the agents and the compound residents went on for weeks. A second attempt to enter ended in a fire that killed eighty residents, including several children. ATF was severely criticized for the raid, and a congressional hearing was held to determine whether the agency could have handled the incident differently.

The second event the militias cite took place in Idaho. In 1992, Randy Weaver, a white supremacist, failed to appear in federal court on a weapons charge. Weaver hid out in a remote cabin in northern Idaho with his wife, his children, and Kevin Harris, an associate. When the U.S. Marshals Service learned of Weaver's whereabouts, they surrounded the cabin. During the eleven-day siege that followed, William Degan, a deputy marshal, and Weaver's wife and son were killed. Ultimately, Weaver and Harris surrendered. At the subsequent trial, Harris was acquitted of all charges. Weaver was acquitted of all but two lesser charges. He served fifteen months in prison.

Militia spokesmen routinely offer threats. Randy Trochman, a white supremacist leader of the Militia of Montana (M.O.M.), claimed: "If and when the government decides to confiscate weapons, people will band together to stop them." Robert Pummer of the Florida State Militia was a drug dealer in Michigan in the early 1970s and served time for second-degree murder. He alleged Russian and other foreign troops operate on American soil. He claimed his group was capable of "defending ourselves against chemical and biological weapons."

Although the militias are most concerned with controlling gun ownership, they hope to force the government to give up any involvement in education, abortion, and the environment. Most observers hope the militias will use rights granted under the Constitution to pursue their conspiracy theories—rights such as freedom of expression, the courts, and the right to petition the government, yet they wonder what the militias might do with their weapons stockpiles.

Evidence that at least one militia did not intend to use lawful means came during the arrest of the Blue Ridge Hunt Club in Virginia. The group's leader, James Roy Mullins, and three others were arrested for illegal possession of weapons. During the course of the investigation, stockpiles of weapons were found in the homes of the men and in storage facilities. A computer disk in Mullins's home included a draft of the group's newsletter, which contained plans for terrorist raids.

Many militia leaders were once active, or may still be active, in such hate groups as the Aryan Nation, the Neo-Nazis, and the Ku Klux Klan.

See also Ku Klux Klan; Southern Poverty Law Center; Terrorism
Reference Anti-Defamation League. *Armed and Dangerous: Militia Takes Aim at the Federal Government: A Fact Finding Report,* 1994.

Million Man March (October 16, 1995)

On October 16, 1995, hundreds of thousands of black men gathered together in a rally on the Mall in Washington, D.C. The day's theme was atonement and reconciliation. The message that many of the speakers delivered was for black men to unify and take responsibility for themselves and their families. One speaker, Damu Smith of Greenpeace, addressed violence in inner cities, an issue that troubles many middle-class blacks and whites. He told the crowd: "[We] must lay down our Uzis and Tech 9's [firearms] and not kill each other any more."

From the outset, the idea of the march was controversial. It originated with the Black Muslim leader, the Reverend Louis Farrakhan, who over the years had often alienated other black leaders by making racist remarks in his speeches about whites and about Jews. However, the march would not have succeeded if it had been left to Farrakhan alone. It went forth because thousands of people representing black social, civil rights, and civic organizations made it possible for hundreds of thousands of men and boys to travel to the nation's capital.

Because of inadequate video and audio systems, it was impossible for many in the crowd to hear and see everything coming from the speakers' platform. Instead, they interacted with each other. One of the editors of the *Million Man March/Day of Absence: A Commemorative Anthology,* Haki Madhubuti, wrote: "The men and boys communed, touched, shared, laughed, cried, introduced themselves to strangers, formed new relationships, testified to sons, grandsons, confessed, rejoiced, wrote notes and letters to their wives, girlfriends, and mates."

Most of the speakers stressed the theme of responsibility. Only Minister Farrakhan sounded an aggressive note. Like the others, he called for leadership building among African Americans, but he also criticized Lincoln, the founding fathers, and President Bill Clinton. During Farrakhan's speech, the crowd was quieter than at any other time during the day.

Madhubuti felt the minister's two-and-one-half-hour speech should have been shortened to no more than an hour—before he finished, the crowd began to disperse to catch their buses home. Nevertheless, he felt that the minister had stirred men to take local action; to maintain their families; to join churches, mosques, and temples; to register to vote; to become politically and culturally active; to support an African-American Development Fund; and to respect themselves and women.

The crowd was deeply stirred by a foreign visitor, Boubacar Joseph Ndiaye, the chief curator of Goree Island, Senegal. He hailed the crowd as the gifted descendants of 15 million slaves kidnapped from Africa. "You have broken the chains," he told those assembled.

Two years after the Million Man March, black women held a Million Woman March on November 1, 1997, in Philadelphia. A theme of the day was that black women have taken care of everyone else since their arrival in the United States. The time had come for them to take care of themselves. The keynote speaker for the afternoon was Winnie Madikizela-Mandela, the controversial ex-wife of South African President Nelson Mandela. She told the estimated 500,000 marchers, "We have a shared responsibility to save the world from those who attempt to destroy it." The organizers planned a Million Woman March for the year 2000, which would focus on the black family. Also in the planning stage were international Million Woman Marches.

See also Black Muslims
Reference Haki Madhubuti and Maulana Karenga, eds. *Million Man March/Day of Absence: A Commemorative Anthology,* 1996; Eric Westervelt. "Sisterly Love," 1997.

Milton Eisenhower Foundation

In 1990, on the tenth anniversary of its founding, the Milton Eisenhower Foundation reviewed its work in a publication entitled *Youth Investment and Community Reconstruction.* Inspiration for the foundation came from two sources: the 1968 National Advisory Commission on Civil Disorders (the Kerner Commission) and the 1969 National Commission on the Causes and Prevention of Violence (the Eisenhower Violence Commission). The Kerner Commission, whose findings were published under the title *Report* by Bantam in 1968, proposed that the United States was headed toward two separate societies, one black and one white. The Eisenhower Violence Commission, whose 1969 findings were published in sixteen paperback volumes as *Violence in America* by Chelsea House in 1983, concluded that safety in America required progress in reconstructing urban life.

The agenda of the Milton Eisenhower Foundation was to empower youth, to revitalize communities, and to stimulate grassroots action; that is, to encourage those adversely affected by social conditions and social policies to act on their own behalf in order to bring about change. The foundation discovered that preschool programs like Head Start are among the most cost-effective programs for combating inner-city decline and drug use. The foundation was not alone in that assessment. The Committee for Economic Development, made up of major corporate executives, reported in 1985 that every $1.00 spent on early prevention and intervention saved $4.75 in later costs of remedial education, welfare, and crime.

The foundation identified or evaluated a variety of successful programs for disadvantaged youth of junior and senior high school age. Among the most successful on a national level was the Job Corps, which provided intensive and supportive job training. Also successful on a national level was the JobStart program for school dropouts ages 17 to 21. Successes among local programs included Program Redirection, offered in several locations, which targeted disadvantaged teenage mothers, 17 and younger, who lacked a high school diploma. The goal was to move them into employment and reduce dependency on welfare. Also successful at the local level were the Argus Community in the South Bronx and the public housing crime prevention program at the Fairview House in Charlotte, North Carolina.

Like preschool programs, successful programs for young people offered multiple solutions to multiple problems. Most programs were tailored to provide social support and discipline, introducing a daily structure often not a part of the lives of at-risk youth. Some participants had to be taught to be on time, to dress appropriately, and to be courteous. Many successful programs developed an "extended family" of people who cared about the youngsters on an individual basis. The programs served as sanctuaries, an escape from the streets and the risk of being a victim or a perpetrator of crime.

The multiple approach of the successful programs yielded increased self-esteem, continued attendance at school, postponement of parenthood, improved skill in management of daily life, enhanced employability, and reduced use of drugs and involvement in crime. Some successful local programs were replicated in other communities.

The Washington, D.C., community organization called "Around the Corner to the World" employed at-risk youth in housing rehabilitation. Participants supported each other in extended family group sessions and served as role models to younger children. The Boston Massachusetts community organization called the Dorchester Youth Collaborative encouraged at-risk youth to design their own Prevention Clubs. Among the Prevention Clubs' accomplishments were a break-dancing video aimed at prevention of crack use.

In its tenth anniversary annual report in 1990, the Milton Eisenhower Foundation was critical of the assumptions that guide conventional crime-prevention tactics proposed for poor communities. Many call for a level of energy, time, resources, and stability more common to working-class and middle-class neighborhoods. For crime prevention in poor neighborhoods to work, there must be active police support. Block watches and foot patrols of citizens and police can make mothers feel safe enough to take their children to nutrition programs and preschool centers. Increased safety can encourage corporations and local governments to provide training and jobs in the community.

Reference Leon Friedman, ed. *Violence in America*, vols. 1–16, 1983.

Mississippi Freedom Democratic Party

During the Mississippi Freedom Summer Project of 1964, young civil rights volunteers traveled throughout the state to talk to black sharecroppers. During an entire summer, 1,000 workers were able to register less than 1,600 black voters with the Mississippi Democratic Party. Over the summer, segregationists beat eighty workers, shot thirty, and killed four. Southern police officers had arrested 1,000 workers and local citizens on flimsy charges. One coordinator, Hunter Morey, was arrested three times in the same city in less than four hours. Black homes, churches, and businesses were burned and bombed.

Anticipating their failure, the activists had prepared another plan. Under the rules of the national Democratic Party, they could form an alternative party. Volunteers enrolled 60,000 blacks in the Mississippi Freedom Democratic Party (MFDP). The new voters elected forty-four "freedom delegates" to attend the 1964 Democratic National Convention in Atlantic City.

Black delegates testified before the party Credentials Committee, which had the power to determine whether delegates could participate in the convention. They told the committee that they had not been allowed to participate in state elections and that MFDP represented the only freely elected party in Mississippi. On national television, delegates told of violence and intimidation in Mississippi. Nevertheless, the credentials committee refused to seat the MFDP.

Southern white delegations told Lyndon Johnson that they would walk out of the convention if MFDP members were seated, which might help

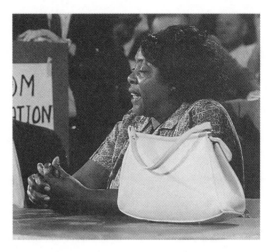

Fannie Lou Hamer testifies before the Credentials Committee at the 1964 Democratic National Convention.

Republican senator Barry Goldwater of Arizona to win the election. In addition, in 1964 Johnson had signed into legislation the Civil Rights Act and programs that created food stamps and an Office of Economic Opportunity. He need southern support to pass even more social legislation he had planned for 1965.

To appease angry liberals in the party, Johnson chose Minnesota senator Hubert Humphrey as his vice presidential candidate and offered a compromise regarding MFDP. The compromise permitted two MFDP delegates to be seated at the convention and stipulated that, in the future, only delegations from states that enfranchised all their citizens would be permitted.

Some blacks and some organizations, such as the National Association for the Advancement of Colored People (NAACP), felt the compromise was the best they could get and represented a massive leap beyond what they had had in the past. Other activists, especially younger ones in the Student Nonviolent Coordinating Committee (SNCC) and the Congress of Racial Equality (CORE), were disillusioned. Some had spent four dangerous years, and all they had received for their efforts were two seats and a promise for the next convention four years hence.

The convention convinced many SNCC activists that racism was a national problem rather than a southern one. One activist, Cleveland Seller, recalled that "afterward, things could never be the same. Never again would we be lulled into believing our task was exposing injustices so the 'good people' of America could eliminate them. We left Atlantic City with the knowledge that . . . our struggle was not for civil rights but for liberation."

See also Abernathy, Reverend Ralph; Bloody Sunday; Freedom Riders; King, Reverend Martin Luther, Jr.; Southern Christian Leadership Conference; Student Nonviolent Coordinating Committee

Reference Terry Anderson. *The Movement and the Sixties: Protest in America from Greensboro to Wounded Knee,* 1995.

Nader, Ralph (b. 1934)

In 1966, attorney Ralph Nader launched the modern version of the consumer movement. In the preface to his 1965 book, *Unsafe at Any Speed,* he wrote: "The automobile has brought death, injury, and the most inestimable sorrow and deprivation to millions of people." Nader accused American automobile manufacturers of routinely marketing vehicles they knew to be unsafe.

A graduate of Princeton University and Harvard Law School, Nader practiced law in Hartford, Connecticut. While working on an automobile accident case, he became appalled at the number of deaths on the highways. A self-taught expert, Nader became an unpaid adviser to a Senate subcommittee preparing to hold hearings on safety. He believed car design, rather than human error, was responsible for most injuries and deaths.

Initially, car manufacturers ignored the opinion of an obscure writer on a subject in which most of the public had little interest. A wide audience was not expected to be attracted to a book with the words "safe" or "unsafe" in the title, especially one written by an unknown lawyer. Although the book was not a best-seller, in just a few months it sold more than 20,000 copies. During that time, Nader testified before the Senate subcommittee on automobile safety. He described the facts covered in his book.

Alarmed by Nader's book sales and testimony, General Motors (GM) hired detectives to investigate his private life. In three states and the District of Columbia, the investigators scrutinized Nader's family, politics, travel, and sexual preference. He was followed, received anonymous late-night calls, and was approached by women with sexual propositions.

When the Senate subcommittee learned about the surveillance, they summoned John Roche, the president of General Motors, to testify. Roche admitted under oath that GM had paid for the investigation. According to Roche, the company wanted to know whether Nader was connected to several suits against GM pending in the courts. The suits all involved the popular Corvair. The first chapter of Nader's book portrayed the lethal

handling qualities of the Corvair. His evidence ranged from detailed engineering data to clinical descriptions of severed limbs lying on the highway at the scene of the accident. The Corvair's design caused it to go out of control.

Roche publicly apologized to Nader and confirmed the lawyer's unimpeachable character. The attorney sued GM for invasion of privacy and won a settlement of $425,000. In addition, the publicity spurred sales of Nader's book. Public reaction to the book pressured Congress into speedily passing an auto safety bill. On September 9, 1966, President Lyndon Johnson signed the National Traffic and Motor Vehicle Safety Act. After a 93 percent drop in sales, the Corvair was taken off the market.

Devoted to public service, Nader broadened his scope from cars to other consumer concerns, such as food, drugs, dyes, pension reform, and ethical government. In 1969, he founded the Center for the Study of Responsive Law, a think tank staffed by lawyers, engineers, and scientists. Young people—mostly students—known as "Nader's Raiders" worked under the center's permanent staff, carrying out investigations.

The center seeded dozens of other Washington-based Nader organizations. Not all remained directly connected with Nader, but all maintained close ties. Many other advocacy groups were inspired by his ideas and example. Most of Nader's groups were supported by foundation grants and by fees from his numerous speaking engagements.

Consumer activist Ralph Nader speaks before a House-Senate Economic Subcommittee, January 14, 1974.

One exception was Public Citizen, a membership organization begun in 1971 that is made up of several specialized groups. The goal of Public Citizen is to encourage its supporters to organize or join local groups dealing with a specific abuse or ongoing issue. Public Citizen keeps its supporters informed about legislation pending in Congress.

During the 1970s, Nader spoke to overflow audiences at college campuses all over the United States. Never held in high esteem by many businesspeople and some politicians, Nader has been called the most effective antagonist of American business. In the 1990s, Nader was still widely acknowledged and respected as a powerful and effective advocate for ordinary citizens. By that time, consumer advocates warning about shoddy goods and practices had become regular features on television.

See also Consumer Movement
Reference Ralph Nader. *Unsafe at Any Speed*, 1972.

National Association for the Advancement of Colored People

The National Association for the Advancement of Colored People (NAACP) was founded following a riot on August 14, 1908, in Springfield, Illinois, during which a white mob attacked blacks. The state militia was called to restore order. During the riot, two elderly blacks were deliberately killed, four whites were killed by stray bullets,

and fifty blacks were seriously injured. Springfield resembled a city devastated by war; nevertheless, most whites condoned the mob's action.

One man who did not approve of the mob's behavior was the wealthy Kentucky writer, William English Walling. His Jewish wife had suffered similar discrimination in Russia from anti-Semites. Walling wrote an article for the *Independent*, a publication that had long defended human rights, expressing his shock at Springfield's shamelessness. He described boycotts intended to drive blacks out of the city as terrorist tactics that could ultimately undermine a democratic way of life.

In response to the article, Mary White Ovington, a wealthy social worker and granddaughter of a white abolitionist, contacted Walling. Ovington had dedicated herself to solving blacks' problems. In January 1909, Ovington and Henry Moskowitz, another social worker, met with Walling in his New York apartment, where they conceived a national biracial organization of fair-minded whites and intelligent blacks to address wrongs endured by blacks. Three white people founded the NAACP.

In the years that followed, the NAACP crusaded against lynchings, laws that prevented blacks from voting, discrimination in transportation and housing, and segregation in the armed forces. From the outset, NAACP used the courts to secure black equality in the voting booth, the classroom, and public places.

Among those not supportive of NAACP's goal to be an aggressive watchdog of African-American liberties was Booker T. Washington. An ex-slave who had founded Tuskegee Institute, Washington believed that blacks had to earn the right to be citizens.

Six months after the NAACP was founded, Fisk University sociologist George Haynes proposed a new organization to help blacks with employment and social problems. The new group was called The Committee on Urban Conditions Among Negroes; it focused on blacks who migrated from the rural South to large cities. In time, the committee merged with three other organizations to become the Urban League.

In July 1910, William E. B. DuBois joined NAACP as the director of publications and research. He established NAACP's magazine *The Crisis*. By the end of the first year, the magazine had 10,000 subscribers. By the end of its tenth year, it had 100,000. In 1919, the NAACP published *Thirty Years of Lynchings*. During those thirty years, 3,224 blacks had been lynched.

From time to time, the NAACP was pressured to expand its focus on legal issues in order to deal with social and economic problems of American blacks. The presence of the Urban League allowed the organization to ignore the pressure and concentrate their resources in the courts.

The profound impact of the Great Depression forced the NAACP to confront economic issues. At a conference held in Amenia, New York, a proposal emerged to have the NAACP work toward bringing white and black workers together into one labor movement. DuBois found the idea of an integrated labor union unrealistic. To succeed, it meant that white labor unionists would have to accept the argument that race did not exist. A better route, in DuBois's opinion, was for blacks to recognize the reality of segregation and cooperate with one another to create their own schools, jobs, and support systems.

A debate between the two positions—working to eliminate segregation versus building a life within the black community—went on in the pages of *The Crisis* for months. Unaware that the NAACP's board had begun to discuss his idea for addressing economic problems within the black community, DuBois resigned in June 1934. The board abandoned the idea a year later.

For the next twenty-five years, the NAACP pursued the rights of blacks in the courts, at the White House, and in Congress. In 1954, the organization won a historic decision in *Brown v. Board of Education of Topeka, Kansas*, in which the Supreme Court found that segregation in schools was unconstitutional.

The result of the *Brown* decision was not instant desegregation. It soon became apparent that the NAACP would have to argue a case against every bus company and restaurant in the South. Many blacks were no longer willing to wait. Raising many of the arguments DuBois had made in 1934, other civil rights advocates accused the NAACP of being overly concerned with the opinions of whites. They took direct action to secure their rights via sit-ins, protests, and marches.

In March 1960, Roy Wilkins, the NAACP's executive director, ordered NAACP branches around the country to support sit-ins. His staff picketed two New York stores carrying signs that declared that the companies' southern stores discriminated against blacks. The NAACP's annual convention in 1960 marked a turning point in the organization's attitude toward direct action. An estimated 80 percent of the young people arrested in the South during the 1960s were NAACP members or supporters. During the Montgomery bus boycott, the NAACP filed suit. On the day Montgomery officials were about to declare illegal the private taxis blacks were using to commute to work, the Supreme Court handed down a decision that separate seating on buses was illegal.

As many civil rights gains made in the 1960s and 1970s began to be whittled away during the 1980s and 1990s, NAACP attorneys geared up to once again do battle in the courts. At the same time, the organization recognized the overwhelming problems of poor blacks by adopting an economic development plan. The debate between integration and black self-development showed no signs of abating as the 1990s drew to a close.

See also Black Muslims; Freedom Riders; Parks, Rosa
Reference Jacqueline Harris. *History and Achievement of the NAACP,* 1992.

National Indian Youth Council

Founded in 1961, the National Indian Youth Council (NIYC) became a leader in the struggle for Indian civil rights. NIYC was the first formally organized pressure group to adopt a new confrontational approach to Indian–non-Indian relations. NIYC had emerged on college campuses where, in the 1950s, campus Indian clubs formed regional associations.

The 1950s generation of college-educated Indians who were being groomed for tribal leadership positions and had strong ties to their cultural heritage were also knowledgeable about the ethics and social mores of the white world. Herbert Blatchford, a New Mexico Navajo and one of the founding members of NIYC, said: "Very few of us crossed the gap between the two cultures. Those who found it difficult to indulge in the new culture developed into a hybrid group, belonging to neither culture . . . But we were a group. There was group thinking. I think that surprised us the most. We had a group world view."

By 1972 NIYC had fifty chapters and 15,000 young members. Chapters had been formed in junior and senior high schools, in boarding schools run by the Bureau of Indian Affairs (BIA), on reservations, in communities, and in prisons. On behalf of Indian youth, NIYC drew up a bill of rights. It filed the first discrimination complaint against BIA in the bureau's 126-year history and filed petitions to deny network and cable stations license renewals on the grounds of neglect of their obligations to Indian people. NIYC members participated in marches and protests around the country. A journal of opinion called either *Aborigine* or *American Aborigine* was published from 1961 to 1965. In 1963 the first issue of a newsletter called *Americans before Columbus* (ABC) was published and, with occasional interruptions, was still being produced in the spring of 1996.

The new militancy of Native Americans could be traced to their experiences during World War II. By war's end, 30,000 Indians had served in the armed forces. Two had won Congressional Medals of Honor, and seventy-one had been awarded Air Medals. More than 40,000 Indians left the reservations to take jobs in war-related industries. Twenty thousand worked on the Pacific coast and lived in a massive enclave in Los Angeles. About those who left the reservation to participate in the war effort, the commissioner of Indian Affairs, John Collier, wrote in 1942: "It may be that they see in the victory of the democracies a guarantee that they too shall be permitted to live their own lives." Their perception was wrong.

Congress and President Dwight D. Eisenhower supported legislation that would assimilate the Indian people into mainstream American society and end federal responsibility for all Indian affairs. Referred to as the "Termination and Relocation" policy, the legislation comprised ten bills that were placed before Congress in 1954. The six that were passed had disastrous effects when applied to the Menominees in Wisconsin and the Klamaths in Oregon. The result was the loss of Indian livelihoods and their reservation land base and a massive assault on their traditional organizations, which galvanized Indians across the United States. The termination doctrine unified Native Americans in an unprecedented way. Tribal leaders began to scrupulously examine policies directed toward Indians for evidence of attempts to renege on treaty obligations. The civil rights movement heightened Indian awareness that poverty and discrimination affected both races. Whereas blacks suffered from cultural expulsion, Native Americans received intense pressure to assimilate.

Sioux Vine Deloria, Jr., said: "Black power, as a communication phenomenon, was a godsend to other groups. It clarified the intellectual concepts which had kept Indians and Mexicans confused and allowed the concept of self-determination to become valid . . . Red Power means we want power over our own lives. We do not want to threaten anyone. . . . We simply want the power, the political and economic power, to run our own lives in our own way." NIYC members demanded the right of Indians to determine their own policies and to control their lands and resources according to their own needs. They asserted that Indian sovereignty rested on the inviolability of treaty rights and obligations guaranteed by the federal government.

Following the passage in 1953 of Public Law 280, which granted certain states jurisdiction over Indian lands within their boundaries, violations of tribal sovereignty increased dramatically, particularly in the Pacific Northwest. The State of Washington repeatedly repealed the Indians' right to fish for salmon. NIYC decided to participate with the Northwest Indians in the first tribal direct action in modern history.

When Christopher Columbus landed in the Bahamas, North America was home to an estimated 2 to 10 million people, divided into 300 distinct cultures, with 200 different languages. They lived on land abundant in bear, deer, elk, berries, and roots. Salmon accounted for 80–90 percent of the Indian diet. By 1853 the federal government had assumed control over the region known as the Oregon Territory and split it into two territories. Governor Isaac Stevens, appointed to administer the Washington Territory, set out immediately to eliminate Indian title to the land and to win congressional approval to make Puget Sound a terminal for the transcontinental railroad. The governor pressured the tribes until they relinquished more than 64 million acres of land, leaving them with 6 million.

All the treaties the governor signed with the tribes contained restrictive provisions in connection with fishing rights. For example, in the Treaty of Medicine Creek signed on December 26, 1854, Governor Stevens inserted a clause saying that "the right of taking fish at all the usual and accustomed grounds and stations is further secured to said Indians in common with all citizens of the Territory." In explaining the treaty provision, Stevens remarked, "It was also thought necessary to allow them [the Indians] to fish at all accustomed places, since this would not in any manner interfere with the rights of citizens, and was necessary for the Indians to obtain subsistence." Although their rights were guaranteed, within a few decades the Indians lost access to many of their accustomed fishing sites. As processing technology improved, commercial canning operations proliferated in Washington along with non-Indian fishers who supplied the canneries. The Indians and the salmon were the losers.

Non-Indian, open-sea gillnetters and purse seiners rapidly depleted the salmon runs. Washington State officials accused Indians of overfishing and began to arrest them in the early 1960s. The crisis came to a head in 1963, when the Washington State Supreme Court ruled in *State v. McCoy* that Washington possessed the authority to regulate Indian fishing for conservation purposes. This ruling defied an earlier federal court injunction that held that the state could regulate Indian fishing only after exhausting all other methods of conservation, including restructuring non-Indian fishing and sport fishing and prohibiting pollution of salmon habitat. *State v. McCoy* gave Washington game and fish authorities the ammunition to eliminate all Indian fishing rights within the state.

A call for action originated on the Makah tribal reservation. The Makah Tribal Council requested help from college-educated NIYC members. Bruce Wilkie, a Makah, along with Mel Thom and Hank Adams, sent messages to fifty tribes to attend an organizational meeting. More than forty sent representatives. NIYC formed the Washington State Project as an umbrella group, from which a group called Survival of the American Indians Association (SAIA) emerged.

To publicize the theft of their treaty rights, the Washington tribes conducted "fish-ins." The first fish-in took place on January 1, 1964, at Frank's Landing on the Nisqually reservation. Twelve Indians were arrested for fishing. The U.S. Justice Department refused to intervene. With a $50 retainer, SAIA employed Frank Tanner, an NAACP lawyer. Fish-ins and arrests spread to other reservations. Widespread media attention encouraged celebrities to come to the state to lend support, which spawned more publicity. A march to the State Capitol in Olympia brought out 1,000 Indian and non-Indian supporters, including the actor Marlon Brando. In response to the march, the governor promised that the tribes would be protected as long as he remained in office. He was not reelected, and the battle continued.

For the next ten years, confrontations—sometimes violent—occurred frequently between the Indians exercising their treaty rights and the State of Washington exerting its authority. On February 12, 1974, Federal District Court Justice George H. Boldt rendered his decision in *The United States v. Washington*. The judge had spent three years in research. He based his decision on one sentence common to all the Northwest treaties: "the right of taking fish . . . is further secured to said Indians in common with all citizens of the Territory." Boldt interpreted "in common with" to mean "to share equally." Therefore, he declared nontreaty fishermen had the opportunity to take up to 50 percent of the harvestable fish, and treaty-right fishermen (Indians) had the right to take the same percentage. The judge became the target of white hate groups. Boldt said publicly, "It came as a shock to me to discover that the vast majority of Washington residents, at least those who fish, don't give a damn about Indian rights." When Boldt's decision was appealed to the U.S. Supreme Court, it was upheld in 1979.

Unlike many other groups that arose during the social upheaval of the 1960s, NIYC did not fade away during the 1970s or with the termination of the Vietnam War. Mel Thom said, "The movement grew in the Indian way. We decided we needed a movement. Not an organization, but a movement. Organizations rearrange history. Movements make history. That's what we decided to do. That's what we did."

See also Banks, Dennis; Bellecourt Brothers, Vernon and Clyde; Means, Russell; Wounded Knee

References Vine Deloria, Jr. *Custer Died for Your Sins: An Indian Manifesto,* 1969; Francis Paul Prucha. *The Great Father: The United States Government and the American Indians,* 1984; Stan Steiner. *The New Indians,* 1968.

Natural Childbirth and Birthing Centers

Members of the counterculture generation of the 1960s, particularly feminists, were determined to take control of their bodies away from the medical profession. They advocated a return to childbirth done without instruments and drugs. However, the idea of natural childbirth wasn't new in the 1960s. British obstetrician Grantly Dick-Read published his book *Childbirth without Fear* in 1944. He believed that education, exercise, and breathing techniques could eliminate pain. American women accepted Dick-Read's ideas, but the medical establishment did not. Stories circulated that women who experienced pain felt like failures and suffered from postpartum depression.

Dick-Read's method was replaced by the Lamaze method, named for Fernard Lamaze, a French physician. Lamaze grounded his concept in the theories of Ivan Pavlov's conditioned response, which linked physical responses to outside stimuli. Lamaze proposed that women could avoid pain by concentrating on controlled breathing or by staring at a focal point. Lamaze did not object to delivery taking place in a hospital or to the use of drugs, views that provoked criticism among some women. Lamaze advocates gained acceptance of the presence of fathers in the delivery room.

The Bradley husband-coached method emphasized natural childbirth without medication. Raised on a farm, Robert Bradley saw animals give birth peacefully. He sought to duplicate the natural birthing behavior of mammals: quiet, physical comfort, relaxation, controlled breathing, and closed eyes. He favored a squatting position as best during delivery.

Obstetrician Frederick Leboyer's concept of a "gentle birth" was at odds with his words in his book *Birth without Violence.* He described it as a "monstrous, unremitting pressure crushing the baby." Leboyer proposed that the baby be delivered in a darkened, quiet room and immersed in warm water. His method provoked strong reactions, both positive and negative. Proponents viewed it as a gentle alternative to the impersonal, hurried atmosphere of many hospitals. Professionals pointed out that the cool air of the delivery room stimulated the newborn to breathe.

Discussions of the various methods encouraged increasing numbers of women in the 1960s and 1970s to demand natural childbirth. Beginning in 1975, hospitals faced with the loss of deliveries to out-of-hospital alternatives set up birthing centers. Some hospitals set up a special room; others merely permitted women to forgo routine hospital procedures and deliver in the labor room rather than the delivery room. Many urban area hospitals set up home-birth services, operated by nurse-midwives or family physicians. Some designed their service around a birth center where a prospective mother came for prenatal care and actual delivery. As concepts of managed care emerged in the 1990s, the cost savings of natural childbirth and birthing centers ensured continued acceptance.

See also Women's Movement
References Robert Bradley. *Husband-Coached Childbirth,* 1996; Margaret DiCanio. *The Encyclopedia of Marriage, Divorce, and the Family,* 1989; Grantly Dick-Read. *The Original Approach to Natural Childbirth,* 4th ed., 1972; Frederick Leboyer. *Birth without Violence,* 1975.

Neal, Sister Marie Augusta (b. 1929)

During the 1960s, Sister Marie Augusta Neal, a member of the Sisters of Notre Dame order, became one of the best known among a group of Catholic scholars and nuns who called for changes in the Roman Catholic Church and in the role women played in the church. Following the Second Vatican Council, a 1962–1965 conclave that undertook to bring the church into the modern world, Neal emerged as one of the most influential figures in the movement to make the church deal with contemporary issues. In her writings and her speeches, Neal, who taught at Emmanuel, a women's college in Boston, became a revolutionary voice that questioned centuries-old practices in the church. On November 23, 1997, Neal was honored by the college for a lifetime of achievement and for her influence upon scores of students and other Catholic activists, many of whom credited her with shaping their lives.

Sister Grace Pizzimenti, a former student of Neal's who became a fellow teacher, said of her: "If it weren't for her and some of the others working with her, nuns might still be living in the Middle Ages. When many were accepting the status quo, she was very independent-minded." And Sister Helen Prejean, an anti–death-penalty activist whose book formed the basis for the movie *Dead Man Walking,* cited Neal as an inspiration for her work with death-row inmates.

A sociologist steeped in the church's writings on social justice, Neal challenged nuns to leave their cloistered lives and deal with the social and economic maladies of the world they lived in. A landmark survey she conducted in 1965 provoked religious orders to rethink and overhaul their religious missions. In a 1965 essay, Neal wrote: "Some religious did not learn . . . that we,

modern Christians, and not the devil were responsible for the genocide of Jews, the exploitation of Negroes, and the noneducation of the poor in the most forsaken places—responsible, because our Gospel called for more concern than we gave. We cannot be contemporary Christians fully cloistered."

Neal's scholarly criticism of capitalism and what she viewed as its unfair distribution of wealth branded her a Marxist in the eyes of some priests and other nuns. A friend of Neal's for thirty years, Kip Tiernan, who founded Rosie's Place, the nation's first shelter for homeless women, said of Neal: "Some people were interested in giving the poor what was left over. She would have none of that. She was talking about global redistribution of wealth . . . she wasn't a revolutionary. She was and is an angry daughter of Christ."

About her work, Neal told a *Boston Globe* reporter: "I was never afraid of what I wrote or said because it was based on careful research and church documents. It wasn't anything outrageous."

See also Abzug, Bella; Friedan, Betty; Plowshares Movement; Women's Movement
Reference Diego Ribadeneira. "Compassion in Action: Nun Honored for a Lifetime of Work," 1997.

Neo-Nazis

One of the many hate groups in the United States, neo-Nazis often form groups or alliances with radical far-right organizations. The American far right finds acceptable a society that has only a single language (English), a single race (white), a single religion (Christian), and a single sexual orientation (heterosexuality). Members of the extreme far right hate those who are not carbon copies of themselves. Neo-Nazis and militant white supremacists espouse violence to impose their way of life. They are contemptuous of the "liberal left," Americans who believe government has a role to play in solving major social problems, such as providing welfare benefits for poor mothers to care for their children and development of crime prevention programs rather than construction of more prisons.

According to Raphael Ezekiel of Harvard School of Public Health, the goal of the movement is power and domination. Its philosophy and language of violence draw those attracted to violence and willing to use it. There are no central neo-Nazi or white supremacist organizations. Far-right groups spread like a web across the nation, linking members of various groups and networking through a variety of means of communication—the latest being the Internet.

Most neo-Nazis claim a love for Adolf Hitler, the leader of Germany's National Socialist (Nazi) Party during the 1930s and 1940s. Hitler set Germany on a path of conquest, which, in 1939, resulted in the outbreak of World War II. Early in his life, Hitler developed a hatred of Jews. He became obsessed with a fantasy that Jews around the world plotted to destroy the Aryan (Indo-European) race. He believed that Aryans were born to rule because they were superior. Hitler called on Germans to become nationalistic, that is, singlemindedly devoted to their nation.

Hitler's Nazi party believed in fascism, a form of government led by a dictator. To set up his will, he created two brutal forces, a private army called the Schutzstaffel (SS) and a state police known as the Gestapo.

Neo-Nazis do not trace their roots to the few small Nazi groups in the United States during the 1930s and 1940s. Their roots lie in other white supremacist groups, particularly the Knights of the Ku Klux Klan. The Klan emerged following the Civil War with a goal of keeping blacks from exercising their civil rights. Because Klan methods of keeping blacks "in their place" were extremely violent, the group was outlawed in 1870.

Klans were revived in various guises to proclaim allegiance to white Anglo-Saxon Protestant (WASP) supremacy. To their hatred of blacks, they added Jews, Catholics, immigrants, and women, once women obtained the right to vote. The Klan reached a high point when they were supported by a large number of fundamentalist Protestant groups—they believed in literal interpretation of the Bible and in rigid adherence to fundamental principles. Such fundamentalists had become convinced that American values were decaying and that Armageddon—the biblical final battle between good and evil—was fast approaching.

A widely held belief—not just among fundamentalists—was that Jews conspired to take over the world and control it. The alleged Jewish plot was believed to have been revealed in a manuscript called *The Protocols of the Elders of Zion*. The myth is centuries old, but the manuscript was based on an essay written in the 1880s by the Russian secret police, who claimed that a Jewish council planned to destroy Christianity and control the world. The manuscript was widely distributed in Europe and the United States in the 1920 and 1930s and became a classic example of anti-Semitism.

The American Nazi Party (ANP), founded by George Lincoln Rockwell in 1959, produced numerous racist and anti-Semitic materials. The ANP had no more than 2,000 members when Rockwell was shot to death by one of his own party. His successor changed the party's name to the National Socialist White People's Party. An anti-Semitic essay on the Internet's World Wide Web in the early 1990s hailed Rockwell as a Nordic hero.

The approximately 300 white supremacist or Hitler-like groups that formed in the years following the 1970s were mostly local and never achieved much publicity. Although no two groups were exactly alike, all openly or covertly hated Jews, people of color, and homosexuals. According to the Center for Democratic Renewal, the number of Klan groups was declining while Hitler-inspired groups were growing in numbers and influence. Many groups honor their roots in the Klan by including "KKK" or "Knights" in their name, such as the Flaming Sword Knights of the KKK organization.

During the 1970s, self-proclaimed Christian Identity minister Richard Butler formed the Aryan Nations, the military arm of his Church of Jesus Christ Christian. Since 1979, each year, the Aryan Nations has held a world congress that brings together neo-Nazi and Klan leaders from North America and Europe.

Skinheads began as working-class youth in

Britain who banded together as street toughs, shaving their heads and provoking fights at soccer games. The neo-Nazi skinhead movement began in the United States during the 1980s. By 1995, there were an estimated 3,500 to 4,000 members in America and about 70,000 worldwide.

The Internet, faxes, and broadcasts make it easy to distribute neo-Nazi ideas and far-right propaganda worldwide at a fast pace. The Anti-Defamation League (ADL) calls the neo-Nazi skinheads "bigotry's shock troops." In Germany, skinheads mobilized against Turks; in Hungary, against Slovakia, the Czech Republic, and the Gypsies; in Britain, against the Asians; in France, against the Africans; and in the United States, against racial minorities and immigrants. In all countries, homosexuals and Jews are targets, and in many countries, the down-and-out are included.

See also Christian Identity Movement; Ku Klux Klan
Reference Kathlyn Gay. *Neo-Nazis: A Growing Threat*, 1997.

New Left
See Old Left and New Left

Nongovernmental Organizations
Frustrated by the failure of political organizations to bring about reform, activists in the 1970s and 1980s began to form coalitions that crossed borders, so-called transnational social movements. The coalitions became known as nongovernmental organizations (NGOs). When an NGO's activities crossed more than two or more national boundaries and the activists formed a central office with one or more staff members, often referred to as a secretariat, they became known as an international nongovernmental organization (INGO). In 1972, there were an estimated 2,100 INGOs. By 1982, there were in excess of 4,200, and by 1993, more than 4,800 were registered with the Union of International Organizations in Geneva, Switzerland.

Since the 1970s, it had become clear to many activists that certain social problems, such as human rights, the fate of refugees, and the destruction of the environment, were not confined within national borders. Because of the ever-widening distribution of personal computers, modems, and fax machines, citizen-activists, particularly students, around the world were able to share their concerns. It became virtually impossible for governments to prevent the flow of information by imposing restrictions or jamming broadcasts. Equally important to the increased transmission of information was a sharp increase in the number of private citizens committed to solving transnational social and political problems.

Unfortunately, even transnational movements committed to peace and justice, if they are dominated by activists from Western countries, address problems in the Third World based on Western assumptions that have little relevance to local conditions. This bias is often coupled with an unwillingness to listen to approaches favored by local activists.

NGOs have been formed to address a wide range of issues: the environment; social justice; the plight of refugees; and protection of economic, cultural, and environmental resources, among others. Women's NGOs have been quite effective. In September 1995, women from around the world, many representing NGOs, met as participants in the World Conference on Women in Beijing, China. Two of the participants were American feminists Bella Abzug and Betty Friedan. One of the issues addressed was violence against women—a worldwide problem.

The seeds of an NGO often begin as a program within one country that spreads across borders. For example, Dr. Muhammed Yunus began a bank for the rural poor in Bangladesh in 1983. By 1995, 1,042 branches served half of the nation's villages. The bank loaned over $500 million a year to about 2 million clients, 94 percent of whom were women. The model demonstrated that small local collectives could approve, guarantee, and monitor loans, and women wage earners could improve the nutrition and level of schooling in their families.

Pressure from NGOs and examples such as banks for the poor have forced international lending institutions, such as the World Bank and the International Monetary Fund (IMF), to reconsider their lending criteria. Often in the past, international loans have been for destructive activities, such as building roads to rainforests and building dams that displace tribal peoples. Such money is better spent on local initiatives that are self-sustaining.

See also American Friends Service Committee; Infant Formula Action Committee
References Ana Amado. "Women's Rights—No Buts About It," 1995; Amy Otchet. "Muhammed Yunus: On Tour with Grameen Bank," 1995.

Nonviolence

Nonviolence, the doctrine of rejecting violence in favor of peaceful means, particularly in connection with political issues, came into prominence in the United States during the civil rights movement. The theory of nonviolence is closely linked to that of pacifism, the belief that disputes between nations should be settled peacefully. Many people who favor nonviolence are also pacifists. Among these was Bayard Rustin, who helped found two major civil rights organizations, the Congress of Racial Equality (CORE) and the Southern Christian Leadership Conference (SCLC).

The ideas of peace and nonviolence can be found early in human history, but the oldest evidence of pacifism is found among the first Christians who lived within the Roman Empire. Scholars do not know whether Jesus condemned war. They do know that he preached a message of reconciliation. Religious sects and individuals have differed in their interpretation of pacifism. Some refused to become soldiers and instead became conscientious objectors, serving as ambulance drivers or in community service. Others refused to perform alternative service, or to do anything, even pay taxes, that would support war. The degree of tolerance with which the larger society has accepted pacifists has varied.

The Reverend Martin Luther King, Jr., based his campaign for black civil rights on a commitment to nonviolence. King modeled his tactics on those of India's Mohandas Gandhi, who helped his nation escape from its status as a British colony and become an independent nation. Gandhi was able to weld together India's conflicting interests, including illiterates and intellectuals, unionists and industrialists, poor peasants and wealthy landlords, conservatives and radicals, and Hindus and Muslims. They shared a common opposition to British rule. Despite his commitment to changing the political situation in India, Gandhi did not set out to reform India's economic system. Any follower of satyagraha, Gandhi's technique of nonviolence to achieve political reform, was expected to aim at individual reform. In an ideal society, the wealthy would serve as trustees of the surplus wealth they possessed. In any case, Gandhi felt it was better to reduce one's individual wants to a minimum, a way of life Gandhi himself followed.

King wanted whites and blacks to live in harmony. He never wavered from his commitment to nonviolence. In time, however, King deviated from Gandhi's lack of concern about economics. He concluded that poverty contributed to violence. King's commitment to nonviolence often created opposition within the black community because many people felt this method was too slow.

During a speech given in Harlem by Bayard Rustin in August 1964, a young man in the audience suggested that nonviolence was out of date. Rustin gave him three reasons why violence was not a practical solution in the United States: Blacks would have to be near the border of a friendly country willing to sell them arms, would need high mountains and jungles into which they could retreat, and would need to have the majority of Americans on their side.

Rustin, as a close adviser to King, may have been the one to convince him that poverty fostered violence. In a 1964 *Commentary* article, he expressed the belief that the major obstacle to black freedom was not simply racism. The problems came from a technological revolution that had altered the fundamental structure of the labor force and thereby destroyed unskilled and semiskilled jobs. When the protests and marches diminished in the United States, the memories of nonviolent tactics remained. Freedoms gained in Eastern Europe owed a great deal to nonviolent strategies. Until his death in 1987, Bayard Rustin helped to carry the idea of nonviolence around the world.

See also Freedom Riders; Mandela, Nelson; Rustin, Bayard

References Jervis Anderson. *Bayard Rustin: Troubles I've Seen: A Biography,* 1997; Peter Brock. *A Brief History of Pacifism: From Jesus to Tolstoy,* 1992.

Old Left and New Left

The Old Left in the United States, socialists and communists who were active during the 1930s, became disillusioned with the behavior of the Soviet Union in Eastern Europe following World War II. In 1956, Socialist Party leaders Earl Browder and Norman Thomas held a meeting to discuss a revival of the left. The meeting did not produce any definitive ideas, but it raised the question of what a new left should look like. For the next couple of years, the idea was discussed in the British journal *New Left*.

In September 1960, tired of the intellectual apathy of the 1950s and sensing a restlessness among the young, sociologist C. Wright Mills suggested the left needed a new organization and that older intellectuals would have to look to the young. Mills was apparently unaware that on the campuses of several select colleges, such as the University of Michigan, young intellectuals were engaged in what he had suggested, the formation

of new organizations. At Michigan, Robert "Al" Haber launched Students for a Democratic Society (SDS), which played a significant role in the antiwar movement over the next few years.

In the mid-1960s, even though the number of antiwar protesters was small, the idea that dissi-

Protesters outside the White House carry pleas for clemency for the Rosenbergs, February 15, 1953.

dents would question foreign policy alarmed the government. Federal Bureau of Investigation (FBI) director J. Edgar Hoover declared that Communist Party members and other subversives were the ones supporting and participating in demonstrations. Most historians agree that no one ever was in control of the antiwar movement, and certainly not the communists.

In 1965 the liberal and radical antiwar protesters split. The liberals, including such organizations as the American Friends Service Committee, Catholic Worker, and SANE (National Committee for a Sane Nuclear Policy), worried about the morality of the war and opposed escalation, but they feared that openly criticizing the president could jeopardize passage of important civil rights and Great Society legislation. Radicals, including such organizations as the Student Nonviolent Coordinating Committee (SNCC), the Northern Student Movement, and SDS, wanted out of Vietnam immediately. SDS member Richard Flacks said the United States had to make a choice between maintaining military superiority and channeling its resources to meet the needs of its people.

Disillusionment among the New Left began to set in after the 1968 Democratic National Convention and the death of Senator Robert Kennedy. When the nation elected conservative president Richard Nixon, members of the New Left felt they had failed. Such organizations as SDS and SNCC began to disintegrate. Many dropped out to join hippie communes and find themselves.

The New Left failed to recognize that it had made a difference and that its arguments had filtered into the minds of the general public. Older Americans had begun to wonder about the wisdom of America's foreign policy. By 1968, as the New Left began to fall apart, a second wave of students were participating in protests. Investigative journalist Mike Wallace, a student at Columbia in 1968, participated in the occupation of a building. Six months earlier he would have been horrified at the idea.

By 1968 the elements of SDS's Port Huron Statement had been co-opted by most liberals. The New Left's male chauvinism drove female participants toward a radical feminism, which had a profound effect on the women's movement. The New Left had not died. It had been transformed.

See also Antiwar Movement; Harrington, Michael; McCarthy, Eugene; Port Huron Statement; Radical Feminists

References Julian Foster and Durward Long, eds. *Protest! Student Activism in America,* 1970; Maurice Isserman. *If I Had a Hammer . . . The Death of the Old Left and the Birth of the New Left,* 1987.

Parks, Rosa (b. 1913)

Rosa Parks, a Montgomery, Alabama, seamstress, instigated one of the most important events in the civil rights movement. Parks, who was tired, refused to move when a bus driver ordered her to give up her seat to a white passenger in December 1955.

Bus seating arrangements almost everywhere in the South were a product of many so-called Jim Crow laws (named after an old minstrel song) that discriminated against blacks. In Montgomery, the first ten rows of seats of every city bus were reserved for white people. Blacks were not allowed to use those ten rows, even if it meant standing. When the whites-only section filled, bus drivers frequently forced blacks seated in the rows following the tenth row to give up their seats to white passengers. Even if only one white passenger needed a seat, a driver would make both sides of the aisle move to preserve the segregation of the row.

On December 1, 1955, the driver on Parks's bus, J. F. Blake, noticed that a white man was standing. Although the man had made no objection, the driver stopped the bus and ordered the row behind the white section to move. Parks was seated on the aisle. No one moved initially. The driver yelled at the four blacks. The man beside Parks stood, and she let him pass, then moved into the window seat. The two women on the opposite side of the aisle moved, but Parks stayed put. When the bus driver threatened to call the police, Parks said, "Go ahead."

Many of the stories about Rosa Parks imply that this was a spur-of-the-moment action by a tired woman. They overlook the sequence of events that led Parks to her historic action. During her childhood, Parks's mother, an elementary school teacher, and her grandparents, former slaves, had always taught her not to regard herself as inferior to whites. Parks's grandfather, Sylvester Edwards, was the son of a white plantation owner and a black house slave. After both of Edwards's parents died, the new overseer beat Edwards severely and often, leaving him with a permanent limp. Edwards raised his children and grandchildren to refuse to accept bad treatment from whites. Parks's father, Ray Parks, was a

member of the National Association for the Advancement of Colored People (NAACP) and discussed civil rights issues with her.

In 1943, Parks attended a meeting of the Montgomery NAACP chapter and found that she was the only female attending. Parks was elected secretary and thrived on the responsibility. She helped the chapter president, E. D. Nixon, make written records of cases of racial discrimination. Through Nixon, she met many of the leaders actively working to secure civil rights for blacks. Parks became an adviser to the NAACP's Youth Council and recruited young people to become recipients of United Negro College Fund scholarships.

The day when Parks refused to give up her seat was not the first conflict between Parks and the bus company. After she had been told that she had not passed the voter registration test for a second time, she was thrown off a city bus because she refused to comply with the custom that forced blacks to get off the bus once they had paid their fare in the front and reenter through the rear door. Some bus drivers would drive off before the passenger could reach the back door.

On that December day in 1955, civil rights organizations were poised to test whether the Supreme Court's May 17, 1954, ruling in *Brown v. Board of Education of Topeka,* which declared that separate schools for blacks were unconstitutional, could be assumed to cover other public services. A likely test case was segregated seating on buses. However, Parks didn't get on the bus

Rosa Parks.

A question was posed. "Should the boycott end?"

"No! No!" shouted the people.

Initially, MIA did not ask for an end to segregated seating. It simply wanted more courteous treatment. MIA spent an estimated $4,000 per week to transport 30,000 to 40,000 people to work in car pools. The Montgomery bus company lost an estimated $3,000 a day in revenues and faced bankruptcy less than a week after the start of the strike. The downtown merchants took in $2 million less than they had the previous year.

In response, the police commissioner orchestrated a campaign of police harassment against blacks. MIA vehicles were charged with carrying a mutilated license, staying too long or too short a time at a stop sign, carrying too many passengers, and having misaligned headlights. King was arrested for speeding. Montgomery insurance companies refused to issue insurance policies to MIA vehicles transporting blacks to work. Out-of-work bus drivers harassed and threatened blacks. Teenagers rode through black neighborhoods throwing balloons filled with urine. King received nightly death threats against him, his wife, and his baby daughter. A bomb was set off on the porch of his home. Parks also received constant threats. Her husband suffered an emotional breakdown from the harassment.

On February 1, 1956, NAACP attorneys, with MIA's approval, filed suit in federal court seeking to overturn segregation on public transportation in Montgomery. On February 21, 1956, a grand jury indicted 115 of the boycott's leaders under a 1921 Alabama statute that prohibited boycotts. The editor of the Montgomery *Advertiser* declared the indictments and the arrests as "the dumbest act ever done in Montgomery." They brought national media attention to the city. King was the only one to go on trial. He was found guilty and fined $500, plus $500 court costs or 386 days in jail at hard labor. The conviction made him a revered martyr.

The trial to end segregated public transportation began May 11, 1956. On June 4, 1956, the three-judge federal panel voted two to one that

intending to test the law. In her autobiography, she said, "If I let myself think too deeply about what might happen to me, I might have gotten off the bus. But I chose to remain."

Word of Parks's arrest spread through Montgomery's black community. Two articulate young ministers, Ralph Abernathy and Martin Luther King, Jr., were invited to join a group of influential black ministers to discuss what to do next. The group formed the Montgomery Improvement Association (MIA) and elected the well-educated King as its president. The MIA circulated thirty-five thousand copies of a petition urging blacks to boycott the city buses on Monday, December 5, 1955. With her attorney, Parks appeared in the city court of Montgomery on the day of the boycott. She was convicted and fined $10, plus $4 court costs.

The courthouse steps were filled with 500 or more supporters, the first public evidence of the impact Parks's arrest had made on Montgomery's black community. A meeting that same night, at the Holt Street Baptist Church, included 1,000 seated people and a crowd that surrounded the church for several blocks.

Montgomery's segregated seating ordinances were unconstitutional. On November 13, 1956, the U.S. Supreme Court upheld the lower court's ruling. The bombings, threats, and harassment continued, but on December 21, 1956, the first integrated Montgomery city buses rolled out, a little more than a year after Rosa Parks's small act of rebellion.

In 1988, Parks retired after working twenty-three years for Democratic senator John Conyers of Michigan. Much of her time and energy has been devoted to supporting an organization she founded with a friend, Elaine Steel, the Rosa and Raymond Parks Institute for Self-Development. The organization helps youngsters age eleven to seventeen pursue an education and create a promising future.

Her two autobiographical books, *Rosa Parks, My Story,* and *Quiet Strength,* reflect on her eventful life. Japan bestowed an honorary doctorate on her, and Sweden awarded her the Rosa Parks Peace Prize.

See also Civil Rights Movement; Horton, Myles; Southern Christian Leadership Conference
References Mary Hull. *Rosa Parks,* 1994; Hans Massaquoi. "Rosa Parks: Still a Rebel with a Cause at 83," 1996; Rosa Parks. *Rosa Parks, My Story,* 1990; and *Quiet Strength: The Faith, the Hope, and the Heart of a Woman Who Changed a Nation,* 1994.

Peace Corps

The idea of a Peace Corps (American volunteers sent to provide needed services in foreign, mostly Third World, countries) may have helped Senator John F. Kennedy (D-MA) to win his slim margin of victory in the 1960 presidential election. The concept was not new when Kennedy proposed it during a presidential campaign speech at the Cow Palace in San Francisco, and it provoked an immediate response. Thirty thousand Americans wrote letters in support of the idea. Thousands volunteered to join.

The origins of the Peace Corps can be traced to Franciscan friars, who in the sixteenth century worked with Native Americans to teach them skills, particularly medical skills, and to make converts to Christianity. In their quest, Christian missionaries from Europe traveled not only to the New World but also to Africa, South America, Asia, and the South Pacific. A second Peace Corps model developed in the early 1800s, when Thomas Fowell Buxton, a founder of London's Christian Missionary Society, preached that the slave trade could be eliminated by developing agriculture and commerce in Africa. He persuaded the British government to sponsor an expedition to West Africa. Later missionaries followed Buxton's advice and established hospitals; studied the languages of the natives; and supported trade, education, and industry throughout Africa. By the early 1960s, more than 400 different Protestant and Catholic organizations had a total of 33,000 missionaries around the world.

A third model for the Peace Corps was a U.S. government reconstruction and rehabilitation program in the Philippines that developed after the United States gained control of the islands following the Spanish-American War. When the war ended, many young soldiers remained in the Philippines to teach English in small barrio schools. The program was such a success that by 1926 the Philippines had more high school graduates than more developed countries such as Spain and Sweden.

A model closer to home, the Civilian Conservation Corps (CCC), was established in 1933 by President Franklin D. Roosevelt to supply employment to 2 million young men unable to find work because of the Great Depression. CCC workers planted trees and built roads, buildings, picnic grounds, and dams. A second group established by Roosevelt in 1935, the National Youth Administration (NYA), hired an estimated 5 million unemployed young people and students to clear swamps, build schools and hospitals, and teach illiterate adults to read.

A more immediate model was provided by Thomas Dooley, a U.S. Navy physician who served in Vietnam. After eight years of fierce fighting, Vietnam gained its independence from France in 1954 and was partitioned into communist-run North and pro-West South. In 1954, Dooley established large refugee camps in Haiphong, North Vietnam, to house, feed, and provide medical care

Peace Corps volunteers and villagers building a well for drinking water in Bichar, India, 1967.

to thousands of refugees waiting for U.S. ships to transport them out of the communist North to Saigon, the capital of South Vietnam. Appalled by the conditions of disease and poverty, Dooley vowed to return to Southeast Asia when his tour of duty was over.

With three of his former navy medical corps members and sponsored by the International Rescue Committee (IRC), in 1956 Dooley established a small hospital in Laos, a country in which 2 million people were served by one doctor. Dooley's efforts to raise funds and supplies made him a folk hero in the United States. Besides treating patients, the team trained nurses and midwives and gave courses in public health and nutrition to the villagers. Dooley said that he and his coworkers practiced "eloquence in deeds, not in words." When he died in 1961 from cancer, Dooley's organization, Medical International Cooperation (MEDICO), employed ninety-four physicians and sent medical teams worldwide.

Two American politicians were directly involved in stimulating interest in the idea of an American Peace Corps. One was Democratic congressman Henry Reuss of Wisconsin, who felt that American foreign aid was not reaching the people who needed it. In 1960, Reuss convinced the House of Representatives to approve a study that became a blueprint for the Peace Corps. The other politician was Minnesota Democratic senator Hubert Humphrey. In 1961, he submitted a bill that bypassed a study and asked for the establishment of a "peace corps" modeled after the International Voluntary Services (IVS), a private organization formed in 1953 to reach remote, impoverished towns and villages and to improve the "ugly American" image held by foreign countries.

Americans were made aware of foreign perception of Americans as uncivilized boors by a 1958 novel by Eugene Burdick and William Lederer called *The Ugly American*. The novel depicted American diplomats living in foreign countries in luxury in sharp contrast to the stark poverty of the native populations.

On March 1, 1961, President Kennedy issued

Executive Order 10924, establishing the Peace Corps as an agency within the Department of State. To secure funding, he sent a message to Congress explaining his executive order and asking it to recommend permanent adoption of the proposal. The Peace Corps Act was signed into law on September 22, 1961.

A few days after he signed the executive order, Kennedy appointed Sargent Shriver, a lawyer, journalist, and businessman who had long been interested in student projects, to head the agency. Key positions were filled by volunteers and a few officials loaned by other agencies. Shriver and his colleagues felt constrained to get it right the first time because many potential critics were poised to charge the youthful administration with naiveté. Not the least of their concerns were questions about whether privileged young men and women would stick to their assigned tasks despite frustration, dysentery, and boredom. Many critics thought not.

A Washington correspondent of the *Times of India* summed up the skeptics' viewpoint. He wrote:

> When you have ascertained a felt local need, you would need to find an American who can exactly help in meeting it. This implies not only the wherewithal (or what you inelegantly call the "know how"), but also a psychological affinity with a strange new people who may be illiterate and yet not lack wisdom, who may live in hovels and yet dwell in spiritual splendor, who may be poor in worldly wealth and yet enjoy a wealth of intangibles and a capacity to be happy. Would an American young man be in tune with this world he has never experienced before? I doubt it . . .
>
> One also wonders whether American young men and tender young girls reared in air-conditioned houses at a constant temperature, knowing little about the severities of nature (except when they pop in and out of cars or buses) will be able to suffer the Indian summer smilingly and, if they go into an Indian village, whether they will be able to

sleep on unsprung beds under the canopy of the bejeweled sky or indoors in mud huts, without writing home about it.

More than 50,000 Americans applied for the Peace Corps during the first three months of 1960. Although the Peace Corps began during the Vietnam War, service in the corps did not exempt a young man from being liable for military service upon his return after two years. No upper age limit was imposed. The oldest volunteer in service in 1960 was 76 years old. A tour of duty was limited to two years.

The new agency was divided into three sections: the headquarters staff, who recruited and trained volunteers and organized their projects; the Peace Corps representatives in particular countries or regions; and the Peace Corps volunteers who went into the areas' towns and villages and did the fieldwork. Shriver devised strategies for keeping the organization functioning effectively. With him as its leader, no formal policy was published. Every directive was marked "interim" to signify that it was in effect only as long as it worked.

Shriver's planned flexibility became evident when the government of the Dominican Republic was overthrown in a coup in 1963. Because the Peace Corps representative in the Dominican Republic decided the volunteers were in no danger, they were not removed. Shriver kept the Peace Corps from becoming bureaucratic by limiting the size of the headquarters staff. In contrast with other foreign-aid programs, which had one staff member for every four people abroad, the Peace Corps had one for every ten. He also limited staff tenure to five years.

From the outset, the Peace Corps made a distinction between its services and those of governmental agencies. Its separation from governmental functions convinced politically uncommitted nations to invite American Peace Corps volunteers into their homes, their classrooms, and schoolyards to teach future generations of national leaders. Peace Corps volunteers were deemed trustworthy. Peace Corps volunteers trained at host country universities and with private organizations, which proved to be vital to the

Peace Corps' success. Volunteers thereby gained access to expert knowledge and experience and, occasionally, monetary support.

Aside from cost, the major concern of Congress in 1961 was that young, unworldly Americans working in foreign countries would fall prey to communist influence. A related concern was that socialists, radicals, and beatniks would flock to join the Peace Corps. The law establishing the Peace Corps contained an amendment that required all volunteers to receive training in the "philosophy, tactics, and menace of Communism." During the first year, the FBI checked volunteers' backgrounds. Later, the Civil Service Commission took responsibility. By the end of 1961, 500 volunteers were on duty in 9 countries. By the end of 1962, 2,800 were at work in 31 countries. After President Kennedy's assassination, one volunteer wrote: "I am proud to have been a part of an already-established living memorial to Kennedy: the Peace Corps." Under President Lyndon Johnson, the Corps continued to grow, to 10,000 in 1964 and more than 15,000 in 1966.

Unlike officials in other governmental agencies in the early 1960s, Shriver and his colleagues went out of their way to recruit blacks for policy positions in the agency. By 1993, 24 percent of the agency's positions were filled by blacks, in contrast to 5.5 percent in other agencies.

One of the most difficult problems the Peace Corps discovered after a couple of years in operation was provision of adequate language training. Finding a Spanish-speaking hydrologist or a French-speaking bus mechanic was not always easy. Planners wrestled regularly with the question of whether to find skilled people and then teach them the native language needed or to find people with the language fluency and teach them the necessary skills.

After 1966, U.S. involvement in the Vietnam War brought the Peace Corps under attack by college students. President Johnson was charged with hypocrisy. Antiwar activists advised potential volunteers not to join the Corps. One volunteer, Bruce Murray, stationed in Chile, who had sent a letter protesting U.S. policy to a Chilean newspaper, was expelled from the Corps and lost his draft deferment. When Murray sued, the judge found in his favor on grounds that his right to free speech had been violated, and restrictions on volunteer antiwar activities were eliminated.

Antiwar restrictions were reinstated under Joseph Blatchford, who was appointed to direct the corps in May 1969 by President Richard Nixon. Under Blatchford, the agency hired more foreign staff to administer overseas projects. He also recruited more skilled workers. The average age rose from 23 to 27, and the number of generalists dropped from 47 percent in 1969 to 34 percent in 1972. Nixon also placed the Corps under a new bureaucratic unit called ACTION, an agency that combined all the government's domestic and overseas voluntary organizations. The Corps lacked real leadership during the 1970s. Seven different directors came and went. In 1981, the Corps found a steady direction under Miller Ruppe and regained its independent status separate from ACTION.

Political instability in host countries became an increasing problem in the 1980s. Another concern was that the Corps was not working in the poorest, least developed countries. Agency leaders decided to concentrate on the world's "absolute poor." High priority was given to volunteers in the fields of health care, nutrition, agriculture, and hydrology. The agency also focused on having volunteers work with women because, in developing countries, women handle much of the farm labor, trade, and commerce, along with their domestic duties.

In September 1986, to cap off a year of anniversary activities, 7,000 former volunteers met in Washington, D.C. A year-long examination developed proposals for the Corps' future. The Peace Corps was encouraged to reach out to larger countries, such as China, Pakistan, and Brazil. Congress was asked to fund the Corps for more than one year at a time. The Corps was asked to make the length of service for highly skilled volunteers variable and expand the Corps' evaluation and monitoring system.

By the end of the 1980s, the future of the Peace Corps looked promising. It was firmly established within the federal government and well accepted by both the American public and the Third

World. In the 1990s, an average of 6,500 volunteers served each year, and more than 100,000 volunteers had served in the Corps' three decades of existence.

See also Kennedy, John Fitzgerald
References Thomas A. Dooley. *Deliver Us from Evil,* 1956; Gerard Rice. *The Bold Experiment,* 1985; Madeline Weitsman. *The Peace Corps,* 1989.

Peace Curriculum

In May 1981, 1,000 people gathered at a conference pulled together by a Harvard University minister. Workshops at the conference spawned the development of organizations for concerned businesspeople, clergy, high school students, and media. It strengthened already existing groups of high school teachers, lawyers, and social workers. One major concern was nuclear proliferation. Forty-eight teachers who attended a workshop on nuclear education formed Educators for Social Responsibility (ESR).

In 1982, America's best-selling high school history book allocated one paragraph to a discussion of nuclear weapons. Bobbi Snow, a Brookline, Massachusetts, high school teacher, developed a curriculum she called "Facing History and Ourselves: Decision Making in a Nuclear Age." After *Parents Magazine* ran an article about Snow's work, letters poured in from other states asking how to form a local chapter of ESR.

An ESR brochure encouraged the Malcolm Shabazz High School (named after Malcolm X) in Madison, Wisconsin, to declare their school a Nuclear Free Zone. Their action sparked international attention. Eight students traveled to Washington, D.C., in 1982, to present a petition from their school to the White House, where they were shunted from department to department until they ended up in the mailroom. Ultimately, they presented their petition to the cultural attaché at the Soviet embassy. Within months, the city of Madison became a Nuclear Free Zone.

The 1.7-million-member National Education Association (NEA), in 1983, together with the Union of Concerned Scientists, drew up a draft of a nuclear curriculum called "Choices." They tested it in thirty-seven states. Albert Shanker, president of NEA's rival union, the American Federation of Teachers (AFTA), attacked the NEA's nuclear curriculum, and President Ronald Reagan echoed his words. Many people around the country agreed with Shanker and Reagan. They did not want nuclear issues discussed in their schools.

Brookline, where Bobbi Snow began her work, is adjacent to Boston, an area receptive to discussions of nuclear issues. Massachusetts Institute of Technology (MIT) faculty and students gathered 3,000 signatures for a petition supporting a freeze on nuclear arms, a no-first-use pledge, and a negotiated, comprehensive, nuclear test ban treaty. Among those who signed the petition were eleven scientists who had worked on the Manhattan Project that developed the atomic bomb.

More than 100 Greater Boston peace groups contributed to a national effort. The *Boston Globe* won a Pulitzer Prize for reporting on nuclear issues. Objecting to the dissent were members of the same Boston-area elite institutions that had spawned it. Solving the intellectual puzzles involved in creating a theoretical bomb may have been stimulating, but the destructive power of a real bomb changed the minds of many scientists, while scientists in the same institutions clung to the notion that science is removed from politics. Even though interest in nuclear curricula was replaced by other concerns, interest could be expected to be revived with nuclear testing taking place in India and Pakistan in 1998.

See also Great Peace March; Peace Movement; Plowshares Movement
Reference Paul Roget Loeb. *Hope in Hard Times: America's Peace Movement and the Reagan Era,* 1987.

Peace Movement

In November 1980, when President Ronald Reagan was elected president for the first time, the nuclear disarmament movement was almost invisible. A small core of dissident groups, such as the Fellowship of Reconciliation, the War Resistors League, and the American Friends Service Committee, raised the issue whenever they could. A larger, more diffuse group participated in an occasional march or rally. Organizations like the Palmetto Alliance challenged the use of atomic power, but nuclear weapons were largely ignored.

By 1987, in small towns across the nation, preachers, physicians, teachers, lawyers, and business leaders were bringing the issue to the attention of their institutions. California joined eight other states in passing a nuclear freeze referendum. Joan Kroc, the heir to the McDonald's fortune, ran full-page peace ads in ninety-two cities. The peace movement was made up of a great variety of individuals and organizations intent upon stopping the growing threat of a nuclear war. Few individuals became celebrities by reason of their involvement in the peace movement. Thousands of activists created local grassroots organizations and mounted local actions of protest. Many organizations began with the concern of one person who took on the Herculean task of convincing his or her neighbors.

Author Paul Loeb began his 1987 book *Hope in Hard Times* with the chronicle of the gradual involvement of Erica Bouza, wife of the Minneapolis police chief. Bouza began by attending vigils and distributing leaflets and moved on later to actions that she knew would lead to her arrest. Twice she was arrested at the Honeywell Project, a site where cluster bombs and missiles were manufactured. Her involvement included no leap of conviction; rather it was an accumulation of incidents.

Awareness of the threat of nuclear power began early in some communities. In Florence, South Carolina, a B-47 lost an atomic bomb due to a broken lock on its bay doors in 1958. The bomb fell 15,000 feet and landed just outside Florence. Fortunately for the citizens of Florence, the bomb failed to explode. Three years later, 130 miles away from Goldsboro, North Carolina, two more bombs fell. Five safety devices on one bomb failed before a sixth one held, thereby avoiding a nuclear blast. The explosion of the trigger device on one of the bombs dug a hole 100 feet across and 35 miles deep, sheared off trees, and collapsed adjacent homes.

Despite the two incidents, it came as a surprise to many people when, in 1982, 200 people signed peace pledges and joined in a march. Among the marchers was Southern Baptist minister Bill Cusak. His initial fears about nuclear power began after the atomic bomb was dropped on Hiroshima. They returned full force when his granddaughter was 2 years old and he heard a group of scientists predict an atomic war by the year 2000. Cusak met with a biologist at Francis Marion College, who was convinced that life would not survive an atomic war. The two men began meeting once a week with a rural Baptist minister, a Methodist minister, and a drama teacher. The group began speaking before various local organizations.

The group, which called itself the Pee Dee Nuclear Freeze Campaign, also bought a copy of a film called *The Last Epidemic* and lent it to churches, schools, and Rotary Clubs. The film, produced by Physicians for Social Responsibility, combines footage from the Hiroshima bomb blast with the testimony of scientists, statesmen, and an admiral about the consequences of a nuclear war.

In South Carolina, peace activists were recruited one at a time and joined communities of activists. South Carolinians had a great deal to protest. Charleston's naval complex included a major submarine facility and served as home to the Atlantic fleet. The Savannah River Plant (SRP), which produced plutonium, had come into being in 1950. The state's largest employer, the plant employed 10,000 workers in research labs, reprocessing plants, a 27-million-gallon radioactive waste dump, and five production reactors. One hundred and thirty miles from Florence, the *Augusta Chronicle*, the South's oldest newspaper, characterized acts of civil disobedience at the SRP as acts done by "shiftless failures as human beings."

Many people who protested the nuclear arms race did so because of religious beliefs. Many had read the 1982 book *Waging Peace,* published by radical evangelicals who put out *Sojourner Magazine.* A Florence counselor whose parents had been threatened twenty years earlier for talking to black activists was drawn into the struggle when Bill Cusak invited her to see a film about nuclear war. She and a young nurse formed a local chapter of Peace Links, a women's disarmament organization, founded by the wife of Democratic Arkansas senator Dale Bumpers.

Nuclear activists in Columbia, South Carolina, wore T-shirts that carried a picture of 84-year-old Modjeska Simkins. A college graduate and a lifelong activist, Simkins spoke in the style of a backwoods preacher. She could electrify a meeting within minutes. She sometimes drove 300 miles to give a speech about the Savannah River Plant, particularly if the speech would be delivered to young people.

For many people around the country, protesting nuclear arms meant taking a stance against their local economy, which depended on weapons production or research. Many feared being branded as radicals and shunned by their neighbors.

Several peace groups developed a document with the title "Call to Halt the Nuclear Arms Race." The document proposed a freeze on the testing, production, and deployment of all nuclear warheads, missiles, and deployment systems. In Massachusetts, the Deerfield Peace Center and the Northampton American Friends Service Committee worked for a year to get signatures to put a nonbinding public policy freeze referendum on the state ballot. The referendum won 59 percent of the vote. In 1980 a Los Angeles couple, Jo and Nick Seidita, decided to replicate the Massachusetts experience. Within nine months, they had involved eighty-four local groups. The effort became Californians for a Bilateral Nuclear Weapons Freeze. Harold Williams, who had founded a national organization of businessmen opposed to the Vietnam War and in 1978 had been a delegate to a United Nations special disarmament session, raised $250,000 for the California campaign. To put the petition on the ballot, the campaign had five months to get 500,000 signatures on a petition. They qualified with 750,000.

Attention turned to reaching the state's 25 million residents. Williams tapped his circle of wealthy contacts in an effort to blanket the state. Ads endorsing a November 1982 referendum, viewed by many as a potential watershed, ran in nearly every major paper. Actors, writers, and designers donated their services. Equipment was loaned. Producer Norman Lear provided funds more than once. To the surprise of many, the referendum passed.

The efforts in California created tension between individuals who held different philosophies of how to build support. Jo and Nick Seidita believed that those recruited to the movement by high-priced ads would not sustain their interest as long as those recruited one at a time. They felt the money would have been better spent building a network at the grassroots level. Williams believed that passing a statewide referendum that would reach all the voters was more important.

The peace movement suffered from other tensions. Freeze workers dissociated themselves from the vigils and civil disobedience of Catholic Workers. Working-class and middle-class organizers resented high-paid professionals who lived fast-paced lifestyles. A built-in problem of the peace movement, like many other movements, was that it brought a clash between working-class members and more affluent ones. Dissenters to the direction of the movement were attacked as naive outsiders. For example, Lord Zuckerman, the former scientific adviser to the British Ministry of Defense and a moderate critic of the arms race, called Jonathan Schell, who had been writing about issues of mass annihilation for fifteen years, a know-nothing newcomer.

In the long run, the village politics approach, which created human-scaled efforts, grew into a nationwide network of local activists opposed to nuclear war and the production of nuclear weapons and nuclear waste. Scale was a critical element in the peace movement. A hundred activists making a statement in Florence, South Carolina, would have an impact. A hundred activists in New York City might be hardly noticed.

Peace movement participants varied in their approaches to delivering their message. Some used drama; some cited statistics; some cited God's commandments; some were doggedly secular; and some, particularly younger religious participants, embodied countercultural views. At best the different styles complemented each other; at worst they pitted participants against each other.

Peace activist Jim Lawson, a Methodist minister, and the Reverend Ralph Abernathy opened a Fellowship of Reconciliation office in Nashville, Tennessee. Two months before black college students in Greensboro, North Carolina, held their now-famous lunch counter sit-ins, Lawson organized sit-ins in Nashville. When eighty of a group of 500 participants were arrested, the trustees of Vanderbilt University, where Lawson was a student, voted to expel him. The dean of divinity and fourteen divinity professors resigned in protest.

In Los Angeles, Lawson criticized peace activists for their failure to deal with difficult issues, such as how to convert an arms budget into a budget that addressed health care, education, housing, and the nation's infrastructure (roads, bridges, etc.). By avoiding such alternative visions, Lawson felt activists had helped to elect Ronald Reagan.

Weapons producers throughout the United States attempted to suppress peace activists' dissent. In Amarillo, Texas, the United Way, which is heavily dependent on the goodwill of local businesses, cut off funds to the Catholic Family Service when the bishop suggested workers at a local plant that assembled nuclear warheads should consider the moral implications of their work. Such opposition often brought activists closer together. A nonmilitary General Electric plant in Charleston, South Carolina, refused to permit the South Carolina freeze group to put an insert about a fund-raising race in a paper regularly handed to workers. The workers and activists were inspired to create a plan to convert the plant whenever General Electric decided to shut it down.

See also Great Peace March; Peace Curriculum
References Paul Rogat Loeb. *Hope in Hard Times: America's Peace Movement and the Reagan Era*, 1987; Jim Wallace, ed. *Waging Peace: A Handbook for the Struggle to Abolish Nuclear Weapons*, 1982.

Pentagon Papers

In the summer of 1971, some accusations against government officials by antiwar protesters were revealed to be true. The *New York Times* and the *Washington Post* published the Pentagon Papers, documents that laid out the history of U.S. policies in connection with Vietnam through the summer of 1968.

In 1967, Secretary of Defense Robert McNamara had gathered a team of forty researchers to examine how the United States had become embroiled in war. Two of the researchers, Daniel Ellsberg and Anthony Russo, stole the history from the Rand Corporation, copied the documents, and turned them over to the newspapers. Ellsberg was a former counterinsurgency adviser. Russo had interviewed Vietcong prisoners and done studies of chemical spraying on food crops. When the newspapers began publishing the papers, the U.S. Justice Department issued a restraining order, citing national interest. The *Times* took the case to the Supreme Court, where its attorneys argued that the government had failed to prove its case. On June 3, 1971, in a six-to-three vote, the Court agreed.

The documents revealed covert military operations and bombing missions in Laos at the same time such actions were being denied. President John F. Kennedy had approved a plot in 1963 to topple the government in South Vietnam. A reason often cited for the presence of the United States in Vietnam was the "domino effect," the belief that if Vietnam fell to communists, other countries in Southeast Asia would fall one after another—like dominoes. In 1964, according to the Pentagon Papers, the Central Intelligence Agency (CIA) reported it believed the theory to be false. Intelligence experts in Vietnam told President Lyndon Johnson that the revolt against the government in Saigon was indigenous and was not being directed by the communist government in North Vietnam. The papers also indicated that the various regimes in Saigon were not free and democratic but were controlled by Washington.

Support for the war among the American public and the Congress plummeted. President Richard Nixon was in an impossible bind. He had promised "peace with honor" to Americans and South Vietnamese. The Americans wanted their troops to come home. The South Vietnamese needed them to stay.

Although 200,000 troops were still in Vietnam, the antiwar movement petered out after 1971. In the spring of 1972, when Nixon ordered mining of North Vietnam's Haiphong harbor and intensified bombing, there were only a few massive demonstrations, mostly at a few campuses—Ohio State and the Universities of New Mexico, Minnesota, and Wisconsin. Some activists were hopeful because troops were coming home and casualties were declining. Others had grown cynical and felt powerless. Many were weary.

See also Antiwar Movement; Hayden, Tom
References Terry Anderson. *The Movement and the Sixties: Protest in America from Greensboro to Wounded Knee,* 1995; Tom Hayden. *Reunion: A Memoir,* 1988.

Physicians for Human Rights

Violence by governments toward their citizens is a worldwide problem. A common method used by repressive governments to keep their populations from rebelling is to crush protests and to prevent communication with the outside world. Those who complain or make contact with the outside world are severely punished.

In 1981, Boston physician Jonathan Fine was on a trip to Chile sponsored by the American Association for the Advancement of Science (AAAS). Fluent in Spanish, he had been asked by a friend to accompany a group of physicians to investigate the disappearance of three Chilean physicians, who were feared kidnapped, tortured, and possibly murdered by the Chilean police. Fine heard many stories about people whose only crime was a desire to restore normalcy and decency to their nation, a desire for which they paid a high price. One discussion with a 23-year-old preschool teacher in the office of a Chilean human rights group changed Fine's life. The young woman trembled as she told Fine that she had been at a peaceful protest rally when she was taken into custody by plainclothes police. The woman had been stripped and hooded, and her hands were tied. She was beaten repeatedly and not allowed to use a bathroom. After three days,

the men took her home. They warned her that if she continued her protests they would rape and kill her mother. Then they changed their minds about letting her free and took her back to prison, where they raped her.

After Fine and his group returned to the United States, he testified before Congress about what he had discovered in Chile. Fine urged congressional leaders to write letters of protest to Chilean foreign ministers on behalf of the three physicians. Five weeks after the letters were sent, the physicians were released. Fine was shocked to discover the difference one person could make. During the next two years, he became restless knowing that the people in Chile were suffering. Ultimately, he decided finding a replacement for himself as an internist delivering primary health care in a community health center would be easier than finding someone else to do the human rights work that needed desperately to be done.

Fine left the practice of medicine in 1983 and founded the American Committee for Human Rights (ACHR), an organization of professionals that sent delegations to countries around the world to investigate human rights violations. After three years, it was clear that ACHR needed to narrow its focus. In the fall of 1986, letters were sent to physicians throughout the United States who were known to be interested in human rights. ACHR was reorganized as Physicians for Human Rights (PHR), a group of physicians who specialized in documenting and trying to alleviate human rights violations involving medical issues.

For a May 26, 1989, article, Fine told an *American Medical News* reporter, "It is always critical for us to get some kind of dialogue going with the government of the country we are visiting . . . After all, the only way to do something like check on political prisoners is to get the government's permission. So it's in everybody's interest to communicate. And it's important for us to have an effective way to voice to a government any concerns we might have stemming from our findings."

PHR members talked frequently with the U.S. State Department and always contacted the U.S. embassy in the countries they visited. During the 1980s, PHR dealt mostly with countries that were politically to the right, because the U.S. government usually had closer ties with these countries than with leftist or Marxist governments.

By American standards, the crimes for which citizens are jailed in repressive countries are often difficult to comprehend. A 25-year-old dentist, Kim Chin-Yop, an Australian who headed up the dental clinic of the Comprehensive Maternal-Child Centre in Pusan, South Korea, was convicted of violating National Security Law and sentenced to eighteen months in prison. His crime was that he had helped 22-year-old Im Su-Kyong enter North Korea to attend the Thirteenth World Festival of Youth and Students. The young woman faced a five-year prison sentence.

Those who enter prison in some countries often don't come out. A PHR team gained unprecedented access to detention facilities in Haiti during the summer of 1990. They found horrendous living conditions. In all the prisons visited, food was either not provided or provided irregularly and in insufficient amounts. Prisoners had to rely on their families to bring food. Those who had no family had to beg from those who did. Common health problems included tuberculosis and infections of wounds sustained during beatings. In addition, physicians were hesitant to treat and document the injuries of those beaten by the Haitian military for fear of reprisals by Haiti's repressive government. To deter physicians from attending sick and injured prisoners, in November 1989, two private physicians were falsely accused of prescribing inappropriate and life-threatening medication to two political prisoners in the National Penitentiary.

In the mid-1990s, PHR members were involved in tracking atrocities committed during the civil war in Rwanda, in east-central Africa. They were documenting the presence of mass graves where bodies were buried after mass executions. PHR receives high praise from other human rights groups, such as Amnesty International, the Helsinki Watch, the Lawyers' Committee for Human Rights, and the J. R. MacArthur Foundation, a substantial contributor to PHR.

See also Disappeareds
References Ryan Van Berkmoes. "To Make a

Difference: Physicians for Human Rights Monitor Effects of Human Rights Abuse Worldwide," 1989.

Pill, The

Three scientists have been called "the fathers of the Pill," an oral contraceptive taken by women. Science writer Bernard Asbell, author of *The Pill: A Biography of the Drug That Changed the World,* contends that the Pill has no father, but does have two mothers, Margaret Sanger and Katharine McCormick. In 1914, Sanger coined the term "birth control" in her newspaper *The Woman Rebel,* and in 1916 she and her sister Ethel set up the first birth control clinic. Sanger went to jail to protest laws that prohibited the distribution of contraceptive information.

McCormick, heiress to the McCormick Reaper fortune, wrote to Sanger in 1950. She wanted to know two things: what organization or individual in the birth control movement was in greatest need of financial support and what the present prospects were for further contraceptive research. At Sanger's suggestion, McCormick wrote a check for $40,000 to Gregory Pincus, the world's foremost authority on the ovum. Pincus committed himself to the quest for a new form of contraception.

Pincus searched through the scientific literature to learn what was already known. He came across work by Russell Marker at Penn State, who in 1939 had changed a substance from sarsaparilla roots into the female hormone progesterone. Independent work on hormones was also being carried on by Carl Djerassi in Mexico and by Frank Colton in Chicago. Each created an oral progesterone pill as a cure for menstrual problems, without any notion that the pill could serve as a contraceptive.

In 1954, Pincus and gynecologist John Rock, who had been studying the potential of progesterone pills as an aid to fertility, decided to field-test Colton's pill. The Pill changed the lives of millions of women, who in other eras might have begun having babies in their teens and continued until middle age. The Pill also played a significant role in the sexual revolution of the 1960s because, even though the Pill has a small failure rate, the risk of pregnancy stopped being the overwhelming concern it had once been for young women. No longer was abstinence the only widely available option for women who wanted to avoid getting pregnant. Better-educated, more affluent women were more likely to know about other options such as condoms and diaphragms.

The Pill also made it easier for women to have careers, as it enabled them to postpone having children until after they had established themselves in the world of work. In the decades that followed the introduction of the Pill, research studies debated the health risks of taking the Pill. Long-lasting forms of the Pill that could be implanted under the skin or injected were introduced. They, too, sparked research controversy.

See also Antiabortion Movement; *Roe v. Wade;* Sexual Revolution
Reference Bernard Asbell. *The Pill: A Biography of the Drug That Changed the World,* 1995.

Plowshares Movement

In 1976, the Vatican issued a declaration that called the arms race "a machine gone mad." Many people in the world thought the endless production of weapons was a necessary "deterrent" to prevent a nuclear war. Others avoided thinking about the issue at all. However, some Americans noticed that in the United States, along with the production of so-called defensive weapons, there also existed a system capable of launching a first nuclear strike. Other nations interpreted the existence of the first-strike system capacity as a warning that the United States intended to use nuclear weapons.

A few Americans were unwilling to allow nuclear weapons production and the threat of a first strike to go unchallenged. At dawn on September 8, 1980, a group calling themselves the Plowshares Eight entered a General Electric plant in King of Prussia, Pennsylvania, that manufactures nose cones for nuclear warheads. The intruders poured blood on documents, and in a symbolic reenactment of the biblical prophecies (Isaiah 2:4 and Micah 4:3) about beating swords into plowshares,

they beat on two nose cones with hammers. Isaiah 2:4 says: "They shall beat their swords into plowshares and their spears into pruning hooks; nations shall not lift up sword against nation, neither shall they learn war anymore." All of the eight had spent time in jail because of their opposition to the Vietnam War. They knew that their actions on that night could result in their spending years in a federal penitentiary.

From the first incident at King of Prussia in 1980 to the last on February 6, 1989, on thirty-three occasions Plowshares activists symbolically and concretely disarmed components of America's first-strike nuclear weapons systems. Two other groups, thwarted by high security, were unable to reach the nuclear components. During almost eight and a half years, more than 100 individuals had taken part in these protests, and similar disarmament actions had occurred in Australia, Germany, Holland, and Sweden. Twenty-nine trials had been held—mostly jury trials—and all had ended in convictions. Members of a group that called itself the Epiphany Five had been tried an unprecedented five times. Three trials resulted in hung juries or mistrials.

Although it is difficult to trace a direct connection between the Plowshares Movement and the ongoing nuclear arms race, they focused attention on the manufacture of nuclear arms as an economic as well as a political issue. They, along with other peace activists, kept the threat of nuclear power before the public. They may have paved the way for the American public's reaction to the accident at the nuclear power plant on Three Mile Island in Pennsylvania in the fall of 1979. Nuclear power as a cheap form of energy lost its attractiveness.

Unfortunately, nuclear arms have not lost their appeal for some world leaders. Nuclear testing by India and Pakistan in 1998 reminded people around the world of the threat nuclear weapons pose to the planet.

See also Great Peace March; Peace Movement
Reference Fred Wilcox. *Uncommon Martyrs: The Berrigans, the Catholic Left, and the Plowshares Movement,* 1991.

Poor People's Campaign (May 12–June 19, 1968)

Martin Luther King, Jr., and his colleagues in the Southern Christian Leadership Conference (SCLC) hoped to call attention to barriers that kept residents of urban inner-city neighborhoods in poverty. One approach they used was called the "Poor People's Campaign" (PPC). Using techniques of nonviolence, they planned to confront America with the demoralizing reality of poverty. To do so, they intended to train and mobilize people in a social movement that would rise above racial divisions.

The plight of the inner-city poor did not suddenly arise in the 1960s. Over decades, displaced and dislocated workers had moved from rural areas to cities in search of jobs. By 1962, already overtaxed low-rent neighborhoods in urban areas had severely deteriorated. The crowded neighborhoods were plagued by high crime, poor health, and a lack of such services as garbage collection, street cleaning and repair, parks and recreation facilities, and adequate nighttime lighting. Activists in the 1960s referred to African-American slums as ghettos, places inhabited by people the rest of society had declared superfluous. Urban ghetto residents were hemmed in by economic, political, and psychological barriers. Although racial discrimination was not written into northern laws, residents were nearly as trapped as they had been under southern Jim Crow laws.

Planning for the PPC began only a few months before it went into operation. It was originally planned to be a massive, long-range campaign of civil disobedience, which means nonviolent opposition to a government policy or law by refusing to comply with it on the grounds of conscience. The SCLC leadership intended to bring 1,500 well-trained demonstrators to Washington, D.C., from fifteen regions of the country. While there, the demonstrators would live in temporary housing constructed by SCLC. They would petition government agencies and the Congress for what amounted to an "economic bill of rights." A second wave of 15,000 to 20,000 demonstrators from selected regions around the country was planned to coordinate local demonstrations with

those in Washington. The core group in Washington was expected to recruit and organize as many as 50,000 local high school and college students to rally behind the cause. Planners expected to stay a long time—perhaps a year or more—in Washington and be met with substantial repression for their efforts. Not everyone in SCLC was in favor of the idea.

Media coverage of plans for the campaign caused great consternation among officials in Washington. SCLC's attack on poverty called into question long-entrenched patterns of life in the United States.

Taking time out from his efforts to recruit support and funding for PPC, King traveled to Memphis to help the sanitation workers, whose grievances had been brought to a head in the wake of the deaths of two workers. Barred by segregation customs from taking refuge from a driving rain in the cab of their truck or in nearby neighborhood stores, the two men had huddled in the back of their truck and had accidentally been crushed by the machinery. The deaths prodded sanitation workers to engage in demonstrations. On April 4, 1968, during his second trip to Memphis to aid the workers, King was assassinated. On April 19, 1968, King's successor, the Reverend Ralph Abernathy, announced that the Poor People's March on Washington would take place.

District of Columbia officials provided the organizing committee with a temporary site in West Potomac Park, between the Lincoln and Washington monuments. A local architect designed plywood structures to be built on the site. The first people arrived in Washington on May 12, 1968. The site, known as "Resurrection City," quickly became a crowded urban ghetto taxed by the presence of too many people. The numbers climbed to 7,000 in June. The press and governmental officials were unsympathetic to the demonstrators and the needs of the poor.

On June 5, 1968, two months after Martin Luther King's assassination, Robert Kennedy, presidential candidate and brother of slain president John Kennedy, was also assassinated. His death shocked many of the PPC organizers and plunged them again into grief that may have curbed some of their work.

PPC culminated in a Solidarity Day Rally for Jobs, Peace, and Freedom on the afternoon of June 19, 1968, in front of the Lincoln Memorial. Fifty thousand people gathered. Resurrection City's permit expired on June 23 and was extended to June 25. On June 25, the National Guard and police surrounded the camp. By then, only a few people remained. That same day, Ralph Abernathy and about 300 people staged a demonstration at the Capitol, and Abernathy was arrested. By nightfall, the muddy ground was the only trace left of PPC and its efforts to deal with the seemingly intractable problem of poverty.

See also Abernathy, Reverend Ralph; King, Reverend Martin Luther, Jr.; Southern Christian Leadership Conference; Young, Andrew

Reference Andrew Young. *An Easy Burden: The Civil Rights Movement and the Transformation of America,* 1996.

Port Huron Statement

During the fall of 1959, Robert "Al" Haber was active in the Political Issues Club at the University of Michigan. He revived a defunct student political organization, renamed it Students for a Democratic Society (SDS), and began recruiting members, among them Tom Hayden, a reporter for and editor of the campus newspaper, the *Michigan Daily*. From the outset, SDS members were not only interested in a wide range of issues but also were willing to participate in actions such as sit-ins.

In May 1960, SDS held a conference at the university on "Human Rights in the North." Attendees included veterans of southern sit-ins, older leftists, and representatives from the Congress of Racial Equality (CORE), the National Association for the Advancement of Colored People (NAACP), and the Student Nonviolent Coordinating Committee (SNCC). The conference was such a success that the United Auto Workers (UAW) donated $10,000 to support SDS. At a conference in June, twenty-nine SDS members elected Haber president.

For the next two years, Haber visited cam-

puses to recruit activists and speak out on civil rights and individual liberties. Hayden went south to work with SNCC. He was beaten by whites in McComb, Mississippi, and jailed in Albany, Georgia.

To articulate SDS's social values and political positions, SDS set up a conference in June 1962 at Port Huron, a UAW camp. Among the fifty-nine who attended, forty-three were SDS members. The rest were older leftists and representatives of other student groups. Hayden had written a manifesto, or a declaration of principles. For five days, the group discussed the almost fifty-page draft, arguing in small groups about its topics: American politics, economics, racism, foreign policy, the nuclear issue, the role of students, communism, and the themes and values of SDS.

The document that resulted reflected the group's recognition of its middle-class status. The first lines said: "We are people of this generation, bred in at least modest comfort, housed now in universities, looking uncomfortably to the world we inherit." The young intellectuals were uneasy about inconsistencies between ideals and realities in the United States. Known as the Port Huron Statement, the agreement forged in the meetings was a radical document for the times. It condemned the loneliness, isolation, and powerlessness of ordinary people in the United States. In the statement, the advocates condemned the continuation of the Cold War, a U.S. policy that brought the world to the brink of nuclear war, and support of dictators in the name of democracy. It called for replacement of the arms race with a disarmament race.

The Port Huron Statement was also a traditional reform document. It demanded social programs to fight poverty, establish national health care, help farm families, construct decent prisons, and build more schools with smaller classrooms. The Port Huron Statement represented a break with the Old Left. Issues that had dominated the left since the 1930s—communism versus capitalism, labor versus management—were discussed but were less important to the young college students. The document declared that capitalism was not inherently immoral or undemocratic. Unlike organizations of the Old Left, SDS expected to recruit members from universities rather than labor unions. It wanted to build a student movement that would challenge apathy, increase individual participation, and transform society.

The statement was the first to issue from a new generation of white students, and it outlined a new ideology. How important the statement was to the events of the 1960s is impossible to judge. It was important to SDS organizers because it fused members into a network joined in a common destiny.

See also Old Left and New Left; Weathermen
Reference Terry Anderson. *The Movement and the Sixties: Protest in America from Greensboro to Wounded Knee,* 1995.

Elvis Presley, "The King of Rock and Roll."

Presley, Elvis (1935–1977)

Singer, guitarist, and actor, Elvis Presley was a catalyst for rock and roll, which was a symbol of protest for a generation of young people in the late 1950s and early 1960s. Seemingly unaware that he was crossing racial lines, Presley introduced music to white audiences that was customarily sung only by blacks.

Elvis Presley was born in Tupelo, Mississippi, to Gladys and Vernon Presley. His twin brother, Jesse Garon, died at birth, leaving him an only child whose mother doted on him. Often lonely, Elvis looked forward to church on Sundays so that he could sing. With a guitar his parents bought for his eleventh birthday, he taught himself to play as an accompaniment when he sang along with musicians he heard on the radio. When Elvis was 13, his family moved from Tupelo to Memphis, Tennessee, where he hung around in a neighborhood called "Shake Rag" and listened to African-American musicians play and sing rhythm and blues (R&B). The strong rhythms and the simple lyrics about the pain and suffering of the black experience appealed to Elvis.

Painfully shy in high school, he had no friends until his music class had a talent show. After he played a rhythm and blues song called "Long Black Train," the students were so impressed, they

stopped treating Elvis as an outsider. For his mother's birthday in 1954, he made a record of two songs to give her as a gift. One of the studio technicians made a copy of the record and played it for her boss, Sam Phillips, who operated Sun Records. He recognized the teenager's talent. For Sun Records, Elvis made his first commercial record in 1954, with "That's All Right, Mama" on one side and "Blue Moon of Kentucky" on the other. After the record was played by a local radio station, the phone rang constantly. A few listeners insisted that Elvis must have been black because he sang "race music," rhythm and blues. By playing his own version of music inspired by African Americans, Elvis helped to break color barriers that prevented black musicians from being heard by white audiences.

When Presley sang onstage, he tossed his head, shivered his shoulders, and shook his hips. Some spectators found his energetic, rhythmic motions offensive. Others, particularly teenagers, found his performance a delight. Fans outnumbered critics. Presley found the reactions to his physical involvement with his music a puzzle. He said in an interview, "The first time I appeared on stage, it scared me to death. I didn't know what the yelling was about. I didn't realize my body was moving."

Elvis's first national hit was "Heartbreak Hotel" in 1956. He had a series of hits and began making movies. He had made four when he was drafted into the army on March 24, 1958, where he spent two years. His career resumed when his term of service was over on March 1, 1960. Most of the 1960s was spent making movies, more memorable for the music than the plots. By the late 1960s, Elvis's career appeared to be over. Then he married Priscilla Ann Beaulieu on May 1, 1967, which seemed to rejuvenate him. A December 3, 1968, television special catapulted him back to stardom. He began a series of Las Vegas appearances, and more hits followed, but all was not well. Elvis's energy and good humor began to fail him. Finally fed up with his neglect of her, Priscilla divorced him in 1972. Rumors about drug addiction circulated.

Elvis died on August 16, 1977. Two days after he was found dead at Graceland, his mansion in Memphis, his wake was held in the foyer of his home. Thousands of mourners stood patiently in line for hours to pay their respects.

In the years following his death, fans from around the world visited Graceland, where they paid their respects and bought souvenirs. Elvis's gold Cadillac, with his first gold records embedded in the walls, became a permanent exhibit at the Country Music Hall of Fame in Nashville, Tennessee. Many performers built careers around being Elvis impersonators. A stream of books and articles tried to explain the enormous impact Elvis had made on music, on his fans, and on the culture of teenagers.

Irwin Stambler's *Encyclopedia of Pop, Rock, and Soul* described the loss of Elvis Presley. "His death in August 1977 shocked and saddened fans the world over who equated him with their own fantasies, a massive transference. Here was a man who loved his mother and father, served his country willingly, and embodied the young and restless spirit for all age groups. He was an American original who dispensed his gifts freely to all kinds of people, both in performing and in a personal way."

See also Rock and Roll
Reference Irwin Stambler. *The Encyclopedia of Pop, Rock, and Soul,* 1989.

Pro-Life Movement
See Antiabortion Movement

Radical Feminists

Like the women's movement in the nineteenth century, the women's movement in the 1960s split into two wings. A more conservative, middle-aged wing arose from the frustration of women like Betty Friedan who had married and had children in the 1940s and 1950s. A younger, more radical, activist wing arose from women who went south with groups like the Student Nonviolent Coordinating Committee (SNCC). The more radical groups are often referred to as women's liberationists or, in a derogatory sense, "women's libbers." The radicals included such women as Florence Howe, who founded the Feminist Press, and Susan Brownmiller, who wrote *Against Our Will*, an analysis of rape as a feminist issue. Still another was Rita Schwerner, who, during the Mississippi Freedom Summer Project, had accompanied her husband to work on voter registration in Mississippi, where he was murdered.

One of the most active women was Robin Morgan, a poet and former child actress. In 1967, she described herself as a "refugee" from the "serious, ceaseless, degrading, and pervasive" sexism of the male-dominated left. Morgan was a founding member of the influential women's group New York Radical Feminists. She criticized the reform agenda of the National Organization for Women (NOW) and similar organizations. She once said, "I have visions of women bleeding to death in the gutters while Betty Friedan has tea in the White House." In 1970, she took over the New Left magazine *Rat* and published it for two years as a feminist periodical. Her 1970 collection, *Sisterhood Is Powerful: An Anthology of Writings from the Women's Liberation Movement,* was characterized as the radical feminist Bible. She became a contributing editor to *Ms.* Magazine after it was founded in 1972 and took over as editor when it was reorganized in 1990 to eliminate advertising.

Another active radical was Meredith Tax. Following a women's liberation conference (the first national gathering of radical feminists) at Emerson College in 1969, Tax and some Boston colleagues founded a socialist-feminist collective called Bread and Roses. The name came from a 1912 mill strike in Lawrence, Massachusetts,

when women millworkers sang, "Hearts starve as well as bodies. Give us bread but give us roses." The goal of Bread and Roses was to build "a radical mass autonomous women's liberation movement to attack the many roots of women's oppression." A 1970 collection, *Notes from a Second Year,* included a four-part essay by Tax called "Woman and Her Mind." This essay became a major founding document of the women's liberation movement and sold 150,000 copies by mail. In her essay, Tax explained that although a revolutionary movement could be built out of personal need, there could be no individual solutions to women's oppression.

Although Bread and Roses eventually disbanded and its members moved on to other feminist pursuits, another group emerged from it and became the Boston Women's Health Book Collective. The group compiled the popular self-help manual *Our Bodies, Ourselves* and contributed to the emergence of a women's health movement.

The health collective remains in existence and has published other books and has a large library of material on women's health. Members spend time collecting new health information and disseminating it to women.

When Andrea Dworkin wrote *Pornography: Men Possessing Women* (1981), she became profoundly committed to the issue. While teaching a joint course on pornography with Catharine MacKinnon at the University of Minnesota in

1983, she and MacKinnon were asked by a group of Minneapolis residents to assist their efforts to limit the traffic in pornography in the city. The two feminists drafted an antipornography ordinance based on the argument that pornography is harmful to women. Most prior ordinances had been based on pornography as an offense against a community's moral standards. The Minneapolis City Council twice passed the ordinance and twice the mayor vetoed it. Similar legislation was stricken down in Indianapolis by the U.S. Court of Appeals as an infringement on the First Amendment right to free speech. The court, however, did accept the concept that pornography harms women. Feminists were divided in their willingness to pursue pornography suppression. Susan Brownmiller and Robin Morgan supported the Dworkin-MacKinnon initiative. Betty Friedan, Kate Millett, and Erica Jong feared it would be a threat to free speech.

See also Abzug, Bella; Black Feminist Organizations; Feminist Organizations; Friedan, Betty; Shelters for Battered Women; Steinem, Gloria; Women's Movement; Women's Sex Workers Project
References Joyce Antler. *The Journey Home: Jewish Women and the American Century*, 1997; Robin Morgan. *Sisterhood Is Powerful: An Anthology of Writings from the Women's Liberation Movement*, 1970; and *Going Too Far: The Personal Chronicles of a Feminist*, 1977.

Rainforest and Chico Mendes

Although rainforests cover only 6–7 percent of the Earth's landmass, they house 40–50 percent of all living species, making them the most biologically rich environments in the world. The destruction of the world's rainforests became news in America's press during the 1980s through the efforts of individual environmentalists and activist environmental groups.

A key figure was ethnobotanist Mark Plotkin, the director of Plant Conservation at the World Wildlife Fund, who publicized the argument that most of the world's effective medicines have come from plants. Yanomano Indians on the Suriname-Brazil border helped Plotkin in his search.

An organization that made the rainforests personal for many Americans was Earthwatch, a large nonprofit that sends volunteers to join research teams. The volunteers pay Earthwatch a fee for the privilege of working for two weeks with an eminent scientist. The fees help Earthwatch to fund the science projects. Many volunteers return year after year. In between their stints in the field, they set up programs at zoos, libraries, museums, and schools. They also mobilize corporate and foundation support to fund science training.

A heroic Brazilian rubber tapper, Francisco "Chico" Mendes, captured the attention of many Americans. The forty-two-year-old Mendes was already a legend when he was murdered on December 22, 1988, in the backyard of his home in the Brazilian village of Xapuri, near the border of Bolivia. Thousands—among them politicians, filmmakers, actors, journalists, scientists, and environmentalists—attended Mendes's funeral.

The son of a rainforest rubber tapper, by the age of seven Mendes had already learned to search for food in the forest and to tap rubber trees for the milky substance called latex, which can be turned into rubber. Mendes's simple life changed when the military took over Brazil's government and a dissident officer, Euclides Tavora, fled to the forest and became a neighbor. Tavora taught the teenager to read and write and to listen to the British Broadcasting Corporation's World Service. From the news broadcasts, Mendes learned the art of organizing workers to lobby for better working conditions.

In 1974 the Brazilian government built a road through the rainforest from Rio Branco to Xapuri. Ranchers, developers, and loggers moved into the area and drove the peasants from their homes. To make way for agriculture and cattle raising, many newcomers cut down large sections of the rainforest.

Cutting down a rainforest sets in motion a vicious cycle. Land beneath the trees remains rich only in the presence of trees, vegetation, and animals, which nourish the thin soil. After the trees are cleared, the soil loses its nutrients. Raising one or two crops in a cleared area renders the soil barren. The loss of trees and the biologically diverse animals and plants that live in the rainforest eliminates several self-sustaining sources of income. Not only does the forest yield latex and medicinal plants, it also provides fruits and nuts that feed the local population and are sold on world markets.

To halt the forest clearing, the Roman Catholic Church brought in union organizers to train rubber tappers. Mendes volunteered to become the leader of the effort. By the late 1980s, Mendes's Union of Rural Workers had 30,000 members. For fifteen years, Mendes was a tough, effective force in the fight to save the rainforest in the west Brazilian state of Acre from destruction. Mendes and his colleagues often sat in the path of bulldozers about to clear the forest. In spite of his work, by the time of his death, ranchers and loggers had destroyed one-tenth of the forest. Without Mendes and his fellow workers, much more of the 59,000-square-mile rainforest would have disappeared.

Three months after Mendes's death, 200 rubber tappers and Indians came together at a meeting Mendes had planned to form the Alliance of the People of the Forest. They issued a declaration: "The people of the forest wish to see their region preserved. This alliance embraces all efforts to protect and preserve this immense but fragile life-system, the source of our wealth and the basis of our cultures."

See also Environmental Movement
Reference Susan DeStefano. *Chico Mendes: Fight for the Forest*, 1992.

Reich, Charles (b. 1928)

Champion of the youth culture of the 1960s and early 1970s, Charles Reich wrote a best-selling book, *The Greening of America,* in which he predicted the future. Reich contended that the young would bring about a peaceful revolution that would replace the corporate state with a national community of individuals who lived in harmony. For Reich, the rock music, long hair, casual clothes, and other emblems of the young that angered and confused many adults were simply manifestations of a consciousness that valued community, the nonrational, and the sacred more than rationality and materialism.

After eight years as a corporate lawyer, Reich began teaching property and constitutional law in 1960 at Yale. About 1964, he began making friends with Yale undergraduates and spent hours discussing literature, philosophy, and political theory. He also audited English literature courses. In 1966, Reich obtained permission to teach a special undergraduate course called "The Individual in America," which became one of Yale's most popular courses. His interaction with undergraduates shifted the pessimistic framework of the book that would become *The Greening of America*, which he had been working on since 1960.

During a visit to the University of California at Berkeley in 1967, Reich saw "a revolution—a generation in revolt, a reversal of the corporate state underway." The visit generated the concept of levels of consciousness that became central to the book. Reich maintained that American consciousness had gone through three stages since the ratification of the Constitution. Consciousness I focused on an idealistic view of self pitted against threatening wilderness and isolation. The early American needed strength of character as well as body.

A fervor of destructive individualism was replaced by goals beyond self when Consciousness II emerged in the workshops of a growing industrial society, where robber barons and monopolies also grew. A hierarchy of authority became structured to protect society from the greed of a few individuals. Consciousness III evolved when the rigid government of Consciousness II, designed to protect citizens' rights, became all-encompassing. Consciousness III proclaimed the liberation of the individual and his or her right to create a personal life.

In Reich's view, Consciousness III became a revolutionary force to free Americans from the corporate state that sold them needless commodities, polluted the rivers, denuded the forests, and dangled the myth of the "American Dream." The force was made up primarily of those under age 25 who were willing to drop out of their parents' civilization to create alternative forms of community.

Critics did not like the book. Although many admired Reich's analysis of the corporate state, they found his perception of the youth culture flawed. One of the kinder critics, Robert Marin of the *New York Times Book Review,* found the book moving and intelligent but contended that Reich viewed the young from the outside. "Seen from the inside, the young are something else again, so much more lonely, more desperate. . . . The first wave of exhilaration is over and the young have moved on to something lonelier and far more real, a kind of mythic struggle in a darkness more profound than any Reich recognizes or has chosen to enter."

Twenty-five years later, in 1995, Reich's book *Opposing the System* was published. In it, he claimed that efforts at reform, including the counterculture and mainstream liberalism, had failed because of reliance on a false map of reality—one shared with conservatives. The time had come to oppose the system as a whole and reassert the sovereign power of citizens to create a society respectful of nature and human needs.

See also Carson, Rachel; Hippies
References Charles Reich. *The Greening of America,* 1970; and *Opposing the System,* 1995.

Resurrection City
See Poor People's Campaign

Riots

Ever since the Boston Tea Party, group violence in the form of mobs or riots has been a recurring theme in America's political and social history. Ethnic or religious groups have pitted themselves against other groups perceived as different or threatening. Youths, particularly university students, tend to play a significant role in political demonstrations. American university students were active in protests, disturbances, marches, sit-ins, and riots that took place during the 1960s and early 1970s.

Sociologists refer to mobs and riots as "acting crowds." Crowd members develop an unambiguous image of "we" versus "they." In the absence of facts, rumors define the situation and encourage the crowd to take action. After the fact, depending on the political perspective of the speaker, an acting crowd may be called a riot or a protest. In an effort to be neutral, speakers often call the incident a civil disturbance or civil disorder.

Since World War I, the largest and most destructive riots in the United States have involved race as a major issue: Chicago, 1919; Detroit, 1943; Rochester and Harlem, 1964; Watts in Los Angeles, 1965; Detroit and Newark, 1967; and Watts, 1992. Between January and September 1967, 164 civil disturbances took place in the United States in which residents of black urban neighborhoods attacked white-owned businesses and harassed law enforcement officials. The police and the National Guard, who described civil disturbances in Detroit and Newark as riots, were largely responsible for the toll of 68 deaths and 1,049 injuries over the course of all the riots. Citing a list of grievances, participants later interviewed perceived their behavior as a protest.

In an effort to understand the so-called race riots of the 1960s, the National Advisory Commission on Civil Disorders, better known as the Kerner Commission, undertook a vast study. Published by Bantam in 1968 under the title *Report,* the commission's analysis described events in twenty-three cities, ten of which had suffered serious disturbances in 1967. There was no "typical" disorder. Riots were not set off by a single precipitating incident. The rioters were not all "hoodlums" or the least educated. Although most were high school dropouts, the rioters tended to be more knowledgeable than the average. They were young men proud to be black and hostile toward whites and middle-class blacks. In most disorders, some individual blacks tried to prevent the action taken. In almost all disorders, militant blacks and civic authorities discussed the underlying grievances and negotiated to end the disruption.

The commission could find no pattern to the disorders; nevertheless, from the large body of data collected, the commission felt that it had identified a "chain." The chain's links were composed of "discrimination, prejudice, conditions of disadvantage, intense and pervasive grievances, and a series of tension-heightening incidents culminating in the eruption of disorder at the hands of youthful, politically aware activists." Often the final incident that set off a disturbance was trivial, but it was the last in a series. In Newark during 1967, the chain consisted of the arrest of fifteen blacks for picketing a grocery store, failure to prevent the use of 150 acres in their neighborhood for a medical-dental center, failure to get a black appointed as secretary of the Board of Education, and resentment at the participation of Newark police officers in an East Orange racial incident. The final incident on July 12 involved the injury of a black cab driver in a traffic accident.

The commission attributed the disorders to both long- and short-run factors. The long-range factors were three: pervasive discrimination and segregation, black migration into and white exodus out of urban centers, and development of black ghettos. The short-range, or "immediate," factors were lack of fulfillment of high expectations inspired both by the civil rights movement and by judicial and legislative victories and "legitimation of violence" by white officials, who had openly defied the law by resisting desegregation. A sense of powerlessness, together with advocacy of violence by some black militants, contributed to a feeling among inner-city residents that the system could only be changed through violence.

A riot in August 1965 in a Los Angeles neighborhood known as Watts fit the characteristics described by the commission. Watts was isolated from the rest of Los Angeles by poverty, a lack of adequate transportation, and the racial homogeneity of its population. Watts residents believed that the city administration and the police were racist. The police believed that Watts's black community was volatile. On August 11, 1965, a crowd of Watts residents gathered to witness an arrest. Bystanders speculated whether the arrest was lawful. The police failed to remove the prisoner promptly from the scene. Rumors spread that a police officer had kicked a pregnant woman. Looting and destruction of property began and targeted sources of grievances. The

property of black residents and black businesses was avoided.

Watts's rioters did not fit cherished stereotypes. Only 11 percent of those arrested had a criminal record; 58 percent were older than 25; 75 percent had lived in Los Angeles for more than five years; and as a group they had a median level of education comparable to the general population of Los Angeles, although they tended to be poorer. An analysis by members of the National Commission on the Causes and Prevention of Violence, better known as the Eisenhower Violence Commission, was submitted to the commission in December 1969. An edited version of the report was published by Chelsea House as *Violence in America*, vols. 1–16. The commission reported that over the five-year period from mid-1963 to mid-1968, protests or counterprotests and inner-city riots involved more than 2 million persons. Civil rights demonstrations brought together 1.1 million people, anti-Vietnam-war demonstrations 680,000, and inner-city riots 200,000.

Most casualties during this period, including 191 deaths, took place during the inner-city riots. Another estimated 23 deaths mostly involved white actions taken against blacks and civil rights workers. Although group violence in the 1960s was at a higher level than in the decades immediately preceding, it did not match the numbers of casualties per 100,000 population reached during earlier periods of American history.

Official interpretations during the 1960s perceived civil disturbances as irrational violence in which many were led by a few. Had officials interpreted the behavior as political protests, authorities would have had to acknowledge some rationality to the incidents and raised the possibility of a need for change.

More than a quarter of a century after the 1965 Watts riot, conditions of isolation and extreme poverty in Watts in 1992 replicated long-term factors responsible for the 1965 riot. Poverty was worse. Major companies like Bethlehem Steel, Goodyear, Firestone, and others had closed down local operations. In 1991 alone, almost 25,000 jobs were lost. South Central Los Angeles had become multiracial, and it suffered from the presence of violent gangs who were making vast sums of money from drugs.

Unlike many earlier riots, the trigger that set off the civil disorder on Wednesday, April 29, 1992, was known to the rest of the nation. The story began at about midnight on March 3, 1991. A drunk, unemployed, black construction worker named Rodney King led police officers on a high-speed chase. When the police caught up with King, his two companions got out of the car promptly when the police ordered them to do so. King refused. Officers dragged King from the car and beat him repeatedly with batons. To subsequent queries, they claimed they thought he was on PCP, a hallucinogenic drug known to make users behave violently. (He was not on PCP.) A man sitting on his balcony overlooking the highway videotaped the beating and turned the tape over to a local television station, whose broadcast of the tape was picked up by other stations and aired across the nation.

Four officers were arrested for the King beating and brought to trial. The four were acquitted of assault, and the jury could not agree about a charge of excessive force against one of the four. The verdict shocked almost everyone who had seen the tape and, in particular, residents of South Central Los Angeles. Within a few hours after the verdict was handed down, violence broke out. The Los Angeles Police Department (LAPD) seemed surprised by the violent response.

In civil disorders, police face a dilemma. If they act quickly, they may later be accused of escalating the violence. If they respond too slowly, they may later be accused of abdicating control and letting the violence get out of hand. LAPD may have chosen not to be accused of overreacting. Hours passed before the police entered many areas of 46-square-mile South Central Los Angeles, where stores were being looted and motorists were being dragged from their cars and beaten.

As late as 11 P.M. Wednesday night, at a time when at least two dozen fires were blazing out of control, Police Chief Daryl Gates, a target of much hostility among Watts residents, resisted black Mayor Tom Bradley's call for National Guard assistance. The first contingent of military police did not arrive until Thursday afternoon. The Los Angeles fire department had to let many fires burn unattended because there were not enough police officers to guard firefighters against snipers. The violence spread well outside the South Central area, to Hollywood, the San Fernando Valley, and Long Beach.

Many Watts residents refrained from participation, locking themselves and their children inside, not knowing whether they would be burned out of their homes or jobs. Many ordinary citizens, in the absence of the police, rescued victims of the violence. A white truck driver named Reginald Denny, on his way to deliver sand to a cement plant, was pulled from his truck and beaten. Barely conscious, he dragged himself back into his eighteen-wheel truck, but his eyes were too swollen for him to drive. At the risk of their lives, two black men and two black women, all strangers, helped him inch his massive truck away from the scene. They took him to a hospital, where he underwent four hours of brain surgery.

Unlike in the riots of 1967, many black stores were not spared—despite signs in the window declaring that they were owned by blacks. Korean-owned stores were a particular target, a reflection of tense relations between the area's blacks and Koreans.

When the forty-eight hours of violence were over, fifty-eight people were dead, 2,383 had been injured, and $735 million in property damage had been sustained. Many middle-class African Americans, who no longer lived in the inner cities, were stunned by the 1992 civil disorder in Watts. The violence may have been as much about class as it was about race. But, as in many other riots, most of the damage was done to the residents' own neighborhood rather than to more affluent areas surrounding Watts.

One factor distinguished the Watts riot of 1992 from earlier riots. The short-range injustice that precipitated the riot was clearly understood by many who lived outside the neighborhood. That understanding was symbolically acknowledged when a large number of people poured into the neighborhood to help with the cleanup, once the violence had subsided.

America's sporadic group violence was partially explained by the 1969 National Commission on the Causes and Prevention of Violence, which wrote in its report: "America has always been a nation of rapid social change. We have proclaimed ourselves a modern promised land, and have brought millions of restless immigrants to our shores to partake in its fulfillment. Persistent demands by these groups . . . and resistance to those demands by other groups, have accounted for most of the offensive and defensive group violence that marks our history. . . . And for all our rhetoric to the contrary, we have never been a fully law-abiding nation. . . . Lack of respect for the law and at least tacit support for violence in one's own interest have helped to make the United States, in the past as at present, somewhat more tumultuous than we would like it to be."

> **See also** Antiwar Movement, Civil Rights Movement; Milton Eisenhower Foundation; Sit-ins
> **Reference** Leon Friedman, ed. *Violence in America: Final Report of the National Commission on the Causes and Prevention of Violence*, vols. 1–16, 1983.

Rock and Roll

Over time, a genre that had begun simply as a form of musical expression evolved into a symbol of the counterculture's indulgence in drugs and sex. The parents of the young in the late 1950s and 1960s didn't like the hard-driving rhythms of the music and the loud volume at which it was played. They liked even less the lifestyle of many rock and roll musicians. For young activists, rock and roll evolved into a symbol of protest against their parents' bland acceptance of a culture that supported segregation, war, destruction of the environment, and second-class citizenship for women and minorities. Only a minority of rock and roll fans were activists. For the majority, rock and roll served as a ready symbol of adolescent rebellion. In its various mutations, it continues to play this role.

The term "rock and roll" is thought to have first been used in 1951 by Cleveland disc jockey Allen Freed. Freed claimed that he invented the term, but it appeared as early as 1938 in a song recorded by Ella Fitzgerald, which had a line that mentioned rock and roll. Some observers believe Freed took the phrase from the song "My Baby Rocks Me with a Steady Roll." In blues music, to rock, roll, or rock and roll referred to sexual intercourse.

One of the earliest recordings of rock was made in 1934, when two folklorists, John Lomax and his son Alan, made a bulky portable recording in a tiny, rural black church. A rough-voiced leader shouted one-line phrases in a kind of singsong. Dancers stamped out a steady rocking beat and responded rapidly to the leader's phrases. The rhythmic singing, hard-driving beat, stream-of-consciousness words, and blues melody resembled rock and roll as it emerged twenty years later. A "rocking and reeling" style evolved in maverick black churches (Sanctified and Holiness churches), which emphasized an ancient form called ring shouts. Guitars, drums, and horns—less expensive than pianos and organs—were welcomed in these churches.

Rock and roll blended much of the music that had preceded it. Jazz evolved among southern blacks in the late nineteenth century. It was characterized by improvisation, heavily accented rhythms, dissonance, and unusual tonal effects on the instruments, such as the trumpet, trombone, clarinet, and saxophone. Black church music influenced the blues, which is usually distinguished by a slow tempo, minor harmonies, and melancholy lyrics. Country and western is derived from the folk music of the southeastern and southwestern United States and typically includes stringed instruments. Rockabilly blends rock and roll with country and western music.

Rock and roll grew out of social and musical interactions between blacks and whites in the South and Southwest. Rural black blues influenced the folk songs sung by white performers. The rise of the recording industry during the 1920s made it possible for musicians to hear the traditions of other musicians. Jazz had mass appeal from the 1930s through the 1950s. The big band swing music of the 1920s to 1940s was a form of jazz, characterized by a strong, flexible understructure and improvisations—both solo and ensemble—on basic tunes and chords. Black popular music of northern inner cities influenced jazz, and to appeal to rural blacks, Lionel Hampton, a vibraharpist, developed a down-home style with a heavy beat. Rocking boogies became popular during the 1940s and 1950s. Rhythm and blues blended elements of blues and swing as it was played by the big bands.

Some characteristics of African music brought to the United States by slaves survive in current American music. African music was participatory. In a call-and-response arrangement, a song leader was often pitted against an answering chorus. Rhythms were often complex with a driving beat. Common was the use of falsetto, defined as a higher range having an unnatural or effeminate sound. Compared with European music, the vocal quality was hoarse. Music in Africa was always flexible, ready to incorporate influences from neighboring villages and foreign cultures.

Sam Phillips set up Memphis Recording services for black artists who wanted to make a record but had nowhere to do so. In 1952, he began his own label, which he called Sun. There are many records alleged to have been the first rock and roll record. Among them was one called "Rocket 88," cut at the Memphis Recording Service. The boogie-woogie (a jazz style of repeated rhythms and melodic patterns in the bass, usually on a piano) was carried by a fuzzed-out, overamplified guitar. The amplifier is said to have fallen off the car of the bandleader/pianist, Ike Turner. According to the story, Sam Phillips stuffed paper into the broken speaker to permit the recording session to be done on schedule. By 1952 western swing musician Bill Haley and his group, the Comets, were recording rock and roll records such as "Rock the Joint." They predated the records made by Elvis Presley a few years later for Sun Records, which are often cited as the first rock and roll albums.

Many of the 1950s rock and roll recordings contained disguised sexual themes. Raucous singing and suggestive lyrics were not new to black audiences. What was new was the appeal they began to have for white adolescents. By 1956 Elvis Presley, Chuck Berry, Fats Domino, and Lit-

tle Richard had crossed over to the popular music charts, and the era of rock and roll was under way. It was not long before popular music (ballads, novelty songs, and big band music) began to be overshadowed by the popularity of rhythm and blues, soul (music that expresses the emotional character of black culture), and rock and roll. As their popularity increased, the audience for popular bands and for jazz decreased.

The music and the performers influenced the culture, and the culture influenced the musicians in turn. Frequently unkempt, the mostly male stars wore jeans, long hair, beards, and odd combinations of clothing—statements of disdain for the establishment. Within the limits of their anatomy and pocketbooks, their adolescent fans shared the stars' preference in dress and appearance.

Rock and roll lyrics, often difficult to understand because of the loud volume, carried forbidden themes, such as sex and drugs, and messages about social protests, such as civil rights and women's liberation. Rock and roll maintained its hold over its adolescent fans and their parents during succeeding decades by spawning variations such as folk rock, heavy metal, speed metal, punk rock, reggae, and rap/hip-hop.

See also Gangster Rap; Grateful Dead; Joplin, Janis; Presley, Elvis
Reference Anthony DeCurtis and James Henke, eds. *The Rolling Stone Illustrated History of Rock and Roll,* 1992.

Roe v. Wade (January 22, 1973)

On January 22, 1973, the U.S. Supreme Court ruled in *Roe v. Wade* that a woman was free to have an abortion during the first three months of her pregnancy. During the second three months, state law could regulate where and by whom the procedure could be performed, and in the last three months the state could prohibit abortion. The *Roe v. Wade* decision sparked a national controversy that in the 1990s showed no signs of abating.

Until 1821, there were no laws in the United States prohibiting abortion. Abortions and abortifacients, herbs thought to be effective for bringing on a spontaneous abortion (a miscarriage), were freely advertised. Physicians mounted a campaign to outlaw abortion. Feminists in favor of legalized abortion hold the medical profession responsible for outlawing it. In 1847, the American Medical Association (AMA) was formed with the goal of improving the professional standing of physicians. Professions typically raise their status by setting standards of practice, regulating admission to the profession, and establishing a legal right to perform certain services. One of AMA's first goals was to make it illegal for nonphysicians, especially midwives, to perform abortions.

Reflecting the culture of the time, the campaign against abortion turned into a moral campaign aimed at encouraging chastity among women. Victorian morality viewed out-of-wedlock pregnancy as punishment for sin. Abortion enabled the culprit to escape public censure. Anthony Comstock, secretary of the New York Society for Suppression of Vice and post office inspector for the city of New York, led a campaign against vice and sin. His particular targets were pornography, sexual license, and abortion. Congress passed the Comstock Law in 1873, which forbade the use of the U.S. mail to transport obscene art and literature, and "any drug, medicine, or article for abortion or contraceptive use." By 1900 abortion had become illegal in every state in America.

Abortions did not stop because they were illegal. Poor women performed self-induced abortions with various instruments, from knitting needles to coke bottles, or sought help from untrained people under unsanitary conditions. Many died as a result. Many middle-class and wealthy women convinced their family doctors to break the law. Some wealthy women traveled to countries where abortion was legal.

From the 1950s to the 1970s, the number of middle-class occupations rose dramatically. New occupations came into being, and women slowly entered occupations formerly barred to them. World War II had given many women an opportunity to work outside the home. The GI Bill for veterans enabled more men to go to college, and overall prosperity increased, which enabled many more women to go to college. Women who worked were more apt to delay marriage or to obtain a divorce. Thus the use of birth control and abortion to limit pregnancies increased rapidly. In addition, the introduction of the Pill gave women new control over reproduction. When contraception failed, it was logical for women to turn to abortion.

In 1967, Colorado became the first state to modify its antiabortion laws. The new law permitted women to have "therapeutic abortions" when a pregnancy had been caused by rape or incest or when the mother's physical or emotional health was in jeopardy. By 1969, nine other states had passed similar statutes. By the 1970s, state laws varied widely. Many forbade abortion except to save the woman's life. New York, at the opposite extreme, allowed abortion on demand. Many women traveled from other states to obtain an abortion in New York. In most states that regulated abortions, many obstetricians and gynecologists quietly provided abortions on demand.

Support for abortion during the 1960s in the medical profession was spurred by two events extensively covered in the media. Thalidomide, a drug widely prescribed in Europe but barred from use in the United States by the Federal Drug Administration (FDA), resulted in the birth of 8,000 deformed babies. In 1962, an Arizona woman, Sherri Finkbine, was two months pregnant when she learned that she had taken thalidomide. The drug company, Richardson-Merrill, had been administering the drug to patients in clinical trials for nineteen months before submitting an application for approval to the FDA. Finkbine sought an abortion. When news about Finkbine's pregnancy appeared in the media, approval of her abortion was withdrawn by her physician and hospital. Ultimately, she had an abortion in Sweden. Publicity about Finkbine's case brought national attention to Arizona's law, which permitted abortion only to save the life of the mother.

The second medical issue involved an epidemic in the United States of rubella (German measles). Rubella during pregnancy often results in birth defects. Many American physicians performed abortions on their pregnant patients who had contracted rubella. Uncomfortable with being on the wrong side of the law, physicians began pressuring state legislatures to change the abortion statutes.

Other changing social conditions contributed to support for legal abortions. During the decades immediately following World War II, technologies such as mosquito control and vaccines reduced early deaths. The result was a worldwide population explosion, which sparked an awareness among the middle and upper classes of a global need for family planning services. In addition, other improvements in medical care lengthened life, which reduced the proportion of a woman's life spent in having and raising children. Careers and the companionship of their husbands assumed a greater importance in the lives of many women. For some, children were perceived as handicaps to their careers and their relationships with their husbands.

As middle-class and affluent women became more career-oriented, many working-class and rural women resisted the changes. They perceived work as a mere economic necessity rather than a career, placed a high value on their role as mothers, and looked on their husbands as providers. The increased availability of contraception and abortion, from their perspective, allowed men to avoid their responsibilities toward women. An increase in no-fault divorce laws in the 1970s and 1980s posed an added threat.

On March 3, 1970, a complaint on behalf of Jane Roe was filed in the U.S. District Court in Dallas. Attorneys Linda Coffee and Sarah Weddington had mapped out a strategy to have the Texas abortion statutes declared unconstitutional. A month and a half later, on behalf of Mary Doe, attorney Margie Hames asked the federal district court in Atlanta to declare the Georgia abortion statute unconstitutional. The attorneys of the two women, whose names were fictitious to protect their privacy, were notified that the U.S. Supreme Court had joined the two cases together because of their similar legal issues and that the cases would be heard as one. A classmate of Margie Hames, who had studied the personalities of the justices, told her to concentrate on the Fourteenth Amendment, which stresses the right to due process. The advice was crucial. When the Supreme Court announced its decision in favor of Mary Doe and Jane Roe, Justice Potter Stewart wrote: "The 'liberty' protected by the due process clause of the Fourteenth Amendment covers more than those freedoms explicitly named in the Bill of Rights."

The opposed views of the proper role for women—a career versus homemaking—undergird the philosophy of pro- and anti-abortion organizations and individuals. Those in favor of abortion rights refer to themselves as "pro-choice," and those opposing abortion refer to themselves as "pro-life." The two sides have become increasingly polarized over the decades. Pro-choice groups have varied in the degree of change they sought. Some wanted complete freedom of choice by women, which means a repeal of all restrictions. Others simply wanted the laws reformed to permit more women to obtain abortions.

Few organizations that support abortion are organized around that single issue. Most have a number of goals they support, only one of which is abortion, and many were organized before the *Roe v. Wade* Supreme Court decision. There are only three well-known abortion advocacy groups that are organized around that single issue. These pro-choice groups are the National Abortion Rights Action League (NARAL), whose core is made up of professionals engaged in delivering abortion services and which has a membership of 500,000; the National Abortion Federation (NAF), a federation of individuals and groups performing abortion; and the Religious Coalition for Reproductive Choice (formerly Religious Coalition for Abortion Rights), founded in 1973 in response to efforts to overturn *Roe v. Wade*.

See also Antiabortion Movement; Sexual Revolution
References Norma McCorvey. *I Am Roe: My Life,* Roe v. Wade, *and Freedom of Choice,* 1994; Leslie Reagan. *When Abortion Was a Crime,* 1997.

Rustin, Bayard (1910–1987)

Civil and human rights activist, organizer, and writer Bayard Rustin was a pacifist. His grandmother, who was a member of the Society of Friends, inspired his Quaker faith. In 1936, looking for a strong political organization opposed to war, Rustin joined the Young Communist League. While living in New York as a league organizer, he went to the City College of New York and sang in nightclubs. By 1941, Rustin left the league and joined the Fellowship of Reconciliation (FOR), a nondenominational religious organization devoted to solutions of world problems through nonviolent means. He served FOR for twelve years, first as a field secretary and later as race relations secretary. In 1942, he helped organize the Congress of Racial Equality (CORE), a secular wing of FOR.

Rustin went to California in 1942 to help protect the property of Japanese Americans who had been rounded up and imprisoned in camps. Sent to jail as a conscientious objector in 1943, he spent almost two and a half years in Ashland Correctional Institute and Lewisburg Penitentiary. Upon his release from prison, Rustin became the chairman of the Free India Committee and was frequently arrested for sitting in at the British Embassy in Washington, D.C. At the invitation of the Indian Congress Party, he spent six months of 1948 in India studying Gandhi's movement to free his country.

Much of Rustin's life was spent protesting war. In 1953, he left FOR to become executive secretary of the War Resisters League, a pacifist group. Five years later, he went to England to help the Campaign for Nuclear Disarmament mobilize the 1959 first annual 50-mile march from London's Trafalgar Square to Aldermaston, the site of England's nuclear facilities. Rustin was the only American speaker at Trafalgar Square. His speech, which linked the struggle against weapons of mass destruction with the struggle of American blacks for basic civil rights, was regarded by many as the most powerful speech of that Good Friday afternoon.

Rustin relished traveling. After a stint in West Africa in 1960 to protest the first French nuclear test explosion, Rustin traveled to Europe to orga-

Bayard Rustin.

nize the San Francisco–to–Moscow Peace Walk. A friend called him a "leading member of the radical jet set." Rustin's labors on behalf of civil rights went on simultaneously with his peace efforts. The War Resisters League loaned him to the Reverend Martin Luther King, Jr., in 1955, when King invited him to Montgomery, Alabama, to organize the bus boycott after Rosa Parks refused to give up her bus seat to a white man.

In Rustin's opinion, the victory won in Montgomery would have no lasting significance unless it was repeated throughout the South. To translate what had been learned into a broad strategy for protest, the movement needed an organization. That organization became the Southern Christian Leadership Conference (SCLC). In collaboration with Ella Baker and Stanley Levison, Rustin drafted a blueprint for a mass movement. A conference of sixty ministers from across the South made King the SCLC's first leader. On February 14, 1957, the day King became the SCLC's leader, he telegraphed President Dwight D. Eisenhower and urged him to visit the South to address racial segregation and discrimination. The telegram promised that if Eisenhower took no action, SCLC would lead a Pilgrimage of Prayer to Washington. There was no reply.

Rustin was the chief organizer of the pilgrimage. It massed at the Lincoln Memorial on the afternoon of May 17, 1957, the third anniversary of the Supreme Court's decision in *Brown v. Board of Education of Topeka,* which ordered that schools be desegregated. Rustin was also the chief organizer of another mass demonstration, the Youth March of Integrated Schools in October 1958, which was repeated in 1959. The pilgrimage and the youth marches were part of the gathering momentum of the civil rights movement.

As deputy to A. Philip Randolph, the director of the March on Washington for Jobs and Freedom held on August 28, 1963, Rustin was the chief organizer. To address racial imbalance in New York's public schools, he organized a school boycott on February 3, 1964, in which 44.8 percent of the schoolchildren participated—the largest civil rights demonstration up to that date. During the summer of 1964, Rustin walked the streets of Harlem trying to influence people to quell the riots. In late 1964, he became the director of the newly formed A. Philip Randolph Institute. There, he devoted himself to the development of radical programs to address social and economic ills.

On December 6, 1966, Rustin testified before a Senate subcommittee on "A Freedom Budget for All Americans," a ten-year plan. The plan was worked out by the A. Philip Randolph Institute in cooperation with several civil rights leaders and economists. The plan outlined a way in which the federal government could put all employable people to work rebuilding inner cities, constructing hospitals and schools, and improving air and water pollution. It would provide decent incomes for the unemployable. According to the plan, the goals could be met without an increase in taxes and with an increase in the nation's wealth.

Rustin had a gift for handling difficult audiences. He was addressing a hostile audience in Newark in January 1967 when, by accident or sabotage, the lights went out. After a brief pause, Rustin said, "This is the first time I've spoken in the dark. But as long as I'm here, there will be light." He completed his speech without interruptions. Oxford-educated British pacifist Michael Randle said of Rustin, "I had never met anyone who could order his thoughts so effectively: telling you in the heat of debate that there were x number of factors to consider and then laying them out—one—two—three—without pausing for reflection."

In the spring of 1981, Rustin visited Poland to address members of the Solidarity movement on techniques of nonviolent resistance. He asked union leader Lech Walesa, "How far can I go in criticizing the communist regime?" "You can't possibly say anything worse than I've already said," Walesa replied.

As vice chairman of the International Rescue Committee (IRC), Rustin undertook several missions to Southeast Asia to help alleviate the plight of refugees from Indochina. Rustin, the actress Liv Ullmann, Nobel Peace Prize–winner Elie Wiesel, and singer Joan Baez organized a March for Survival in February 1980 to aid Cambodian refugees. Blocked by a detachment of Cambodian troops at the border, the group used bullhorns— Baez sang songs, Rustin sang spirituals, and Wiesel recited Kaddish, the Jewish prayer for the dead. Leo Cherne, chairman of the IRC, said of Rustin, "Bayard had a remarkable gift for injecting reason, for reconciling a group of people at each other's throats. When he worked within a group, he was not interested in satisfying his own sense of importance."

At a memorial service for Rustin on October 1, 1987, more than 1,000 of his friends gathered at the Community Church in Manhattan. Lane Kirkland, president of the American Federation of Labor–Congress of Industrial Organizations (AFL-CIO), said: "He traveled the world on behalf of the helpless, the homeless, the poor, the exploited. He understood and he taught that human freedom was a seamless fabric that all of us have to repair whenever and wherever it is torn."

See also Freedom Riders; King, Reverend Martin Luther, Jr.; Nonviolence; Southern Christian Leadership Conference

Reference Jervis Anderson. *Bayard Rustin: Troubles I've Seen: A Biography,* 1997.

Sanctuary Movement

In 1982, retired rancher Jim Corbett, a Quaker, and John Fife, a Presbyterian minister, founded the Sanctuary Movement in Tucson, Arizona. The purpose of the movement was to offer refuge to Latin Americans fleeing political oppression. In time, fourteen of Tucson's congregations joined. As the movement spread, it was embraced by churches and synagogues in several states; two cities, Cambridge, Massachusetts, and Berkeley, California; several university groups; and for a brief time the state of New Mexico. From the beginning, the participants in the Sanctuary Movement made no secret of their intent. They conducted open meetings and gave interviews to the media.

The need for sanctuary was a direct consequence of the U.S. policy of refusing asylum to most Central American refugees. During the period from June 1983 to September 1986, 750,000 Salvadoran refugees fled to the United States, but only 528, or 2.6 percent, were granted political asylum.

In the minds of the Sanctuary Movement leaders, by giving asylum to refugees fleeing from political oppression, they were upholding the spirit of the 1980 U.S. refugee policy, which had been restructured by Congress to emphasize humanitarian considerations. Most sanctuary leaders were clergy or lay members of churches whose doctrines include an obligation to help those in need. They insisted that they helped oppressed people to escape from tyranny. The refugees' oppressors, in some cases governments, in other cases rebel forces, were often sponsored and aided by the U.S. government.

The U.S. government insisted that participants in the sanctuary movement were breaking the law. Government spokespeople claimed that those seeking asylum were not refugees. Instead, they were "economic migrants" simply trying to improve their standard of living. Designation of refugees as economic migrants is one of a number of devices governments employ to turn away immigrants they would prefer not to keep.

Critics of the U.S. policy charged that the United States accepted those fleeing from communist governments and rejected those fleeing

from governments with which the United States had friendly relations. Records seem to support their charge. Among the 125,000 refugees admitted in fiscal year 1990, more than 90 percent were refugees from communist countries. The minuscule quotas allotted to Africa and Latin America were granted mainly to exiles from leftist regimes in Ethiopia and Cuba. From 1981 through 1988, 103,355 immigrants from communist Cuba were admitted as permanent residents under the Refugee Act. During the same period, 2,823 from Nicaragua and 940 from El Salvador were admitted.

In 1980, when a small Marxist insurgency rebelled against a corrupt military government allied with wealthy coffee growers, civil war erupted in El Salvador. During the 1980s, the Reagan administration channeled more than $1 billion to aid the Salvadoran government. More than 60,000 civilians were killed in El Salvador between 1980 and 1989 by either government soldiers or rebels.

An estimated 435 U.S. churches and synagogues participated in helping illegal aliens from Central America to reach the United States, where they provided them with shelter and assisted them in obtaining legal status. Some of the sanctuary workers went to prison. In 1984 Stacey Merkt, a volunteer at a shelter for Central American refugees in San Benito, Texas, was convicted of violation of immigration laws and sentenced to 179 days in jail. Amnesty International adopted her as a prisoner of conscience when she began serving her sentence, which meant that the organization began a campaign to win her freedom. She had served only about half of her sentence when she was released to serve the remainder under house arrest.

The ancient principle of sanctuary in churches and synagogues has little support in modern law. Nevertheless, U.S. government agents recognized that the public would be outraged if they broke into churches to drag refugees away. Instead, the U.S. Immigration and Naturalization Service (INS) sent undercover agents and informers to meetings to gather evidence. One informant, who, until he was caught, had made a living smuggling aliens into Florida, made a deal with the government to pose as a sanctuary movement volunteer.

Using evidence gathered by informants, the government brought eleven Arizona sanctuary workers to trial in October 1985 on sixty-seven felony counts. Each count carried a possible five-year prison sentence. The workers' hope was to persuade the jury that international law, the Refugee Act of 1980, and the desperate plight of those trying to escape from Central America permitted them to help the refugees.

Even though a defendant's motive may be introduced in felony trials, the U.S. District Court Judge Earl Carroll ruled that the defendants could not base their case on religious beliefs and referred to their trial as a "simple smuggling case." In what defense attorneys assumed was a move to lessen the chances that jurors would hear any comment about the movement's motives, the prosecution did not use about 100 hours of taped movement meetings. Given the absence of a defense, the jurors felt they had no choice but to convict eight of the eleven.

The 9th U.S. Circuit Court of Appeals upheld the convictions of the eight workers in a 3-to-0 decision. In the court's opinion, they were not entitled to present evidence of their belief that immigrants are entitled to legal refugee status. The court said such a defense would have "essentially put the Reagan administration's foreign policy on trial."

In a July 1988 trial, a Lutheran minister and a journalist/poet were charged with smuggling two pregnant Salvadoran women across the Rio Grande two years earlier. U.S. District Court Judge John Conway permitted inclusion of evidence about conditions in El Salvador and about a proclamation by Governor Tony Anaya that designated New Mexico as a sanctuary state. The defendants were acquitted.

Following the 1986 convictions of the eight workers, three Arizona churches joined with the national organizations of the Presbyterian Church and the Lutheran Church to file suit against the government. They charged that the undercover investigation violated the First Amendment right to freedom of religion. Judge Roger Strand of the U.S. District Court in San Francisco ruled in December 1990 that the government does not have "unfettered discretion to infiltrate religious gatherings for criminal investigations." According to the judge, the government must have solid grounds for sending agents into religious gatherings.

The American Baptist Churches filed a class action suit against Attorney General Dick Thornburgh. It, too, was decided in U.S. District Court in San Francisco in December 1990. The suit charged that the INS routinely denied political asylum based on foreign policy decisions. In a landmark settlement, the INS agreed to stop the deportation of Salvadoran and Guatemalan refugees. The settlement required the readjudication of 150,000 denials and affected 500,000 Salvadoran and Guatemalan refugees in the United States.

Hostility among Americans toward immigrants, legal or illegal, appeared to increase in the early years of the 1990s. The hostility seemed to be a reaction to an enormous influx of immigrants in the 1980s. Yet the drawbacks of immigration are more than overcome by its advantages. A vast body of research shows that there is little direct competition for jobs between new immigrants and native-born Americans. According to Robert Suro, author of *Strangers among Us: How Latino Immigration Is Transforming America* (1998), an analysis of tax data by the Urban Institute in Washington, D.C., and an exhaustive study by the National Research Council, also in Washington, found that immigration brings identifiable economic benefits. It allows native-born workers to do more specialized work and stimulates new forms of consumption. Yet the perception of competition posed by legal immigrants, illegal aliens, and refugees regularly closes doors to those in desperate need of asylum.

See also Disappeareds
References Carole Kismaric, ed. *Forced Out: The Agony of the Refugee in Our Time*, n.d. (ca. 1989); Robert Suro. *Strangers among Us: How Latino Immigration Is Transforming America*, 1998.

Savio, Mario
See Free Speech Movement

Schwerner, Michael
See Chaney, Goodman, and Schwerner, Murders of

Seeger, Pete (b. 1919)
College students discovered Pete Seeger and other folksingers in the early 1960s, when the guitar became a favorite instrument for both professional and amateur musicians. Sometimes referred to as the "Thomas Jefferson of folk music," Seeger, for more than half a century, played a significant role in the widespread interest in folk music in the United States.

He was raised in a musical family. His father, a musicologist, conductor, and author, taught at the University of California, Los Angeles. His mother was a violinist and teacher. As a child, Seeger accompanied his father on field trips searching for folk music. He considered himself a professional singer who sang amateur music, which the composers usually played by ear, rather than a folksinger.

Hitching rides and hopping freight trains, Seeger began touring in the late 1930s. At his concerts in the United States and later around the world, he presented a cross-section of American life in song. For old favorites, audiences joined in.

While touring the United States, Seeger collected such music as sea chanties; "sod buster" (soil-breaking) ballads; and labor, anti-Fascist, and soldiering songs. Seeger believes five trends account for the surge of interest in folk music in the 1960s:

1. Following World War II, Americans searched for their roots.
2. During those same years, do-it-yourself activities boomed. Millions of guitar pickers were a part of the trend.
3. Folklorists' collections emerged from libraries to provide a rich lore of the nation's various music traditions.
4. Americans had gained enough sophistication to be able to sing old hillbilly songs without being worried they would be mistaken for old hillbillies.
5. Young people found that folk music permitted them to make social comments about America.

During World War II, Seeger spent three and a half years in Special Services entertaining troops in the United States and the South Pacific. After his discharge, he and others founded People's Songs, which comprised a union of songwriters, a research center, and a clearinghouse. Seeger expected the labor union movement to spur a major revival of folk music in the United States. Seeger helped bring about the folk music revival in 1948, when he and three other singers, Lee Hays, Ronnie Gilbert, and Fred Hellerman, formed the singing group the Weavers. Seeger sang with them until 1957, when he left because of other commitments. The Weavers appeared on national radio and television programs, sang in nightclubs and theaters throughout the United States, and turned such folk songs as "On Top of Old Smoky" and "So Long, It's Been Good to Know You" into perennial favorites.

In 1955, Seeger was called before the House Un-American Activities Committee (HUAC), which was investigating alleged subversive influences in the entertainment industry. He refused to answer questions regarding his political beliefs

Folksinger Pete Seeger.

and associations. Rather than plead the Fifth Amendment, which permits an individual to escape self-incrimination, Seeger chose to cite the First Amendment, which guarantees freedom of speech and association.

After his appearance before HUAC, Seeger and the Weavers were banned from some television networks. He was indicted on ten counts of contempt of Congress and went on trial in March 1961 before the U.S. District Court in New York City. A jury found Seeger guilty on all counts. Upon being sentenced to one year in prison, Seeger declared: "I have never in my life supported or done anything subversive to my country. I am proud that I have never refused to sing for any organization because I disagreed with its beliefs." The U.S. Court of Appeals reversed Seeger's conviction in May 1962 by a unanimous decision. The reversal was based on the indictment's failure to define with sufficient clarity the authority of the subcommittee to hold the hearings. Like the appeals courts, many entertainers

who lost their livelihoods after being called before HUAC wondered what right the committee had to question them.

Although Seeger's indictment was dismissed, some networks continued to ban him. When ABC banned Seeger and the Weavers from appearing in its weekly folk music program, *Hootenanny*, several singers, including Joan Baez, declined invitations. Indifferent to money, Seeger often turned down concert engagements to tour black colleges or give benefit programs. Seeger never stopped performing in concerts and benefits. His collection of American music continued to grow. In 1993, he published his musical autobiography.

See also Baez, Joan; Guthrie, Arlo; Hippies; Horton, Myles
References Ray Lawless. *Folksingers and Folksongs in America,* 1960; Pete Seeger. *Where Have All the Flowers Gone: A Musical Autobiography,* 1993.

Sexual Revolution

The public blamed hippies and their counterculture for an apparent widespread attitude change in the 1960s toward sex outside marriage. However, the change had been under way long before hippies made their presence known. The beats of the 1950s and the bohemians of the 1920s and 1930s disregarded conventional behavior. Because many were in the arts, they had a greater influence than their numbers would have warranted. In addition, biologist Alfred Kinsey's studies of sexual practices—*Sexual Behavior in the Human Male* (1948), *Sexual Behavior in the Human Female* (1953)—revealed a wider range of behaviors than was generally admitted. Kinsey's dry, science-oriented prose did not prevent the books from becoming best-sellers.

As the idea that sex before marriage was not uncommon spread, the practice became more common in a cyclical, self-fulfilling prophecy. Added to the already changing mores, the counterculture promoted its sense that sex was something to be enjoyed with multiple partners. The young carried their message into the multiple movements of the 1960s in which they participated. Although the counterculture and the participants in the various movements constituted only a small fraction of America's overall population, the idea of sexual freedom spread rapidly. By the 1990s, peer pressure in the United States to be sexual had filtered down to middle school students, ages 10 to 13.

Medical evidence began to accumulate in the 1980s about the risks of early sexual intercourse and multiple partners. The risks were not limited to unwanted pregnancies. They included the lethal possibilities of AIDS and other sexually transmitted diseases (STDs) that, untreated, also lead to death. Despite an acute need for information, in several countries, including the United States, research into sexual behavior was delayed or canceled due to political pressures. In Great Britain, after a government-funded survey of sexual attitudes and behaviors was vetoed by Prime Minister Margaret Thatcher in 1989, it was funded by the Wellcome Trust. Nearly 19,000 randomly chosen men and women between ages 16 and 59 in Great Britain took part, between May 1990 and November 1991, in the largest and most detailed study of sexual behavior ever undertaken. The findings were published in numerous journal articles and two books.

The survey revealed that 19 percent of teenage girls and 28 percent of teenage boys had had sexual intercourse before the age of 16. Boys typically had first partners their own age, whereas girls tended to have older first partners. This made the girls more likely to introduce STDs into their adolescent cohort. The groups having the larger number of partners tended to be upper class; to have had sex at an early age; and, regardless of age or previous marriages, to be single. Twenty percent of those between 25 and 34 had had ten or more sexual partners. Those with the largest number of partners, heterosexual or homosexual, were more likely to have been to an STD clinic.

By 1996, although the 1991 survey was still useful, the need for updated information on the spread of STDs, particularly AIDS, made a new study imperative. In 1996, the British launched a pilot project to determine the best approach to a nationwide survey.

See also AIDS; Hippies; Pill, The
References A. M. Johnson et al. *Sexual Attitudes and Lifestyles*, 1992; Alfred Kinsey. *Sexual Behavior in the Human Male*, 1948, and *Sexual Behavior in the Human Female*, 1953; K. Wellings et al. *Sexual Behavior in Britain*, 1994.

Shelters for Battered Women

Although incidents of women being beaten had existed in epidemic proportions for centuries, they had hardly caused a ripple in agencies of law enforcement, the judiciary, medicine, social agencies, or the psychiatric community. Change came in the United States, Great Britain, and Europe with the battered women's movement in the late 1960s and early 1970s. Estimates of the number of women beaten each year vary substantially depending upon how incidents are defined and counted. But regardless of whether an estimate of 2.8 million on the low end or 4 million on the high end is accepted, the numbers are great.

Groups of women met in feminist consciousness-raising groups where the issue of battering was raised. Awareness of the threat to battered women and their children prompted women to staff hotlines, offer their homes as refuges, and open up shelters. Battered women's groups were innovative in finding ways in which to get their hotline numbers to those in need. One clever approach was to put the telephone number on coupons for tampons.

Creating shelters for women and children was a major step in helping victims of domestic violence. Typically groups created nonhierarchical structures to avoid the superior-to-subordinate relationships of most work settings. Many shelters operated as collectives. Frequently, as soon as a shelter opened, it would fill up. When shelters overflowed, staff or volunteers contacted other shelters to find room. Links between shelters made it possible to transfer a woman from an area that was not safe to a distant shelter.

It quickly became clear that the best counselors for battered women were women who had escaped from being battered themselves. The risk with professional counselors was that they used a one-on-one technique that fostered the notion that the woman who was battered was sick, rather than suggesting that the fault lay in the customs of the society in which she lived. Professionals also tended to set up programs to deal with a limited number of women and to avoid the needs of other battered women in the community. By failing to devote attention and resources to working with the police, courts, hospitals, and other groups, such a program became just another social service that failed to mobilize community effort on behalf of battered women. For example, peer support is important for battered women. Sharing stories in a shelter with others dislodges the common idea in a battered woman's mind that somehow the battering was her fault.

Shelters are not new. Refuges have existed for hundreds of years. Most were associated with religious or charitable organizations and tended to be safety valves rather than agents of change. They bound up a woman's wounds and counseled her on how to adjust to her situation. One Amsterdam, Holland, woman reported her experience with a "relational counselor." When the woman told the counselor that her husband had tried to strangle her, the therapist said, "But ma'am, do you ever think how terrible it is for your husband that you're afraid of him?"

Some refuges in convents and hospitals solved a woman's problem by keeping her confined within the organization's boundaries. Women unwilling to accept relational therapy or confinement sometimes found the streets or brothels their only alternatives. As a consequence, feminists setting up shelters resisted replicating existing institutions that had held women in such disregard.

Prior to the advent of battered women's programs run by feminists, social agencies that helped a woman and her children relocate were also apt to give the abuser her new address on the grounds that a father had a right to know where his children were. They also failed to understand how trapped she was. The secretary-general of the Association of Shelters in France—welcome centers for women—told a reporter in 1975: "It's somewhat the same as dogs who attack only those who are afraid of them. There's a mutual exasperation. Some husbands defend themselves

against this exasperation by slamming the door and going out for a drink. Others by beating their wives. There are also, it's necessary to say, some women who adore being beaten."

Turf wars with other organizations posed a problem for battered women's project staffs and volunteers. After they put in long hours, weeks, or months to obtain funding, traditional agencies, institutions, and professionals would use bureaucratic methods to attempt to put their people in positions of control. Staffs and volunteers learned how to fend off encroachment.

The National Coalition against Domestic Violence, which was formed in 1979, raised national awareness about battering. By the 1990s, efforts of program staffs during the 1970s and 1980s to raise awareness had improved community understanding of the dilemmas faced by battered women. With greater understanding had come better working relationships with local police, courts, hospitals, and social agencies.

By the 1990s, battered women's program staffs and volunteers had learned a great deal about how to deal with individual women trapped by domestic violence. They no longer pressured women to leave, recognizing that pressure robbed her of an opportunity to make a decision on her own—perhaps for the first time in her life. They also understood that leaving was the most dangerous move she could make, since statistically that was the time she was most likely to be killed. Therefore, they told her the options and left the decision to her.

As the twenty-first century drew near, the police and the courts of some cities began to give domestic violence the kind of attention they gave homicides. The results were dramatic in lowering the number of deaths among women due to domestic violence. Nevertheless, on a national scale, the epidemic of domestic violence continued unabated, and the need for shelters continued to grow.

While many men may be emotionally abused by women, few are physically battered. Of those who are, few are likely to report the assault to the police. When they do, the police are likely to be skeptical.

See also Women's Movement
References Massachusetts Coalition of Battered Women's Service Groups. *Shelter and Beyond,* 1993; Betsy Warrior. *Battered Women's Directory,* 1982.

Sisters of the Immaculate Heart of Mary

In August 1967, the Sisters of the Order of the Immaculate Heart of Mary (IHM) took steps that dramatically changed their relationship with the Catholic Church. To what degree their actions affected other orders of nuns is difficult to assess, but they were an omen of sweeping change on the horizon.

Until the 1960s, Catholic nuns were highly regimented and were confined to a limited number of work roles. They served in great numbers on the front-line workforce in parochial schools and Catholic hospitals. The change the IHM requested came about not only in their own order but in many American orders over the next ten to fifteen years. Ultimately, in America, there were fewer nuns, fewer parochial schools, and fewer Catholic hospital nurses who were nuns.

The sisters elected 43 of their 560 members to meet at their retreat in Montecito, California, to address Pope Paul's *Motu Propio,* an urgent appeal for those in Catholic religious life to examine and renew their way of life by engaging in wide-ranging experiments. The delegates spent six weeks creating a fifty-eight-page document. The document outlined some of the values the nuns felt needed greater emphasis and some of the ways they intended to implement them. In the outline, the delegates said, "We believe, that our direct and immediate participation in the temporal order calls for a new style of communal existence, one which will not rigidly separate us by customs, cloister, or clothing from those we serve." In accordance with the general values they outlined, the sisters adopted proposals:

1. Sisters who are teaching without having completed their teaching credential would be replaced and enrolled in universities until they completed their education.

2. Classrooms would be limited to thirty-five students.

3. Any sister who served as a principal would be relieved of all other teaching responsibilities.

4. Sisters would be allowed to drop masculine religious names and reassume their family names.

5. Sisters could attend daily mass at their personal convenience and "pray in a manner that is pleasing to them and God" instead of in regimented group ceremonies.

6. Personal dress would be left to the discretion of each sister. Sisters engaged in varying occupations might wear habits suitable for their work.

7. Sisters would be free to pursue careers outside the church. "If one of the sisters has a special talent or interest, we will encourage her to pursue it. She might be a commercial artist, or a newspaperwoman, or a musician, or almost anything else. Whatever her talent, we will use it."

8. Within the community house, sisters would democratically choose their own form of government.

Reaction to the IHM nuns' new direction varied from high praise to accusations of doing the devil's handiwork. A great deal of support, as well as most of the criticism, came from within the Catholic world. Cardinal Francis McIntyre, one of the most conservative cardinals in the United States, who had no direct power over the nuns, threatened to prevent them from staffing the schools in the diocese.

Primarily a teaching order, IHM nuns had for many years taught in parochial schools with backgrounds less stringent than would have been required were they teaching in public schools. At the time, 39 percent of the nuns teaching in elementary schools and 9 percent of those teaching in the high schools had neither a college degree nor teaching credentials. It was not unusual for nuns to be teaching without degrees or credentials; what was unusual was their effort to change the arrangements. Sister Anita Caspary, mother general of the order, made the statement that where mutually satisfactory arrangements could not be made, the IHM nuns would withdraw from particular schools rather than do a disservice to their students.

A staunch supporter of the IHM nuns, Father Andrew Greeley, a sociologist and novelist, said about them, "At a time when Catholic liberals feel honor bound to take everything, especially themselves with the most solemn seriousness, the Sisters of the Immaculate Heart resolutely refuse to fit the pattern. They can laugh at themselves as casually as they laugh at anything else; they are . . . casual, happy, laughing liberals and this is a rare breed." Father Greeley also pointed out that although in most orders the average age of the nuns was increasing, one-third of the IHM nuns were under age 35. This meant that IHM was drawing new young people into their order.

See also Neal, Sister Marie Augusta; Plowshares Movement; Women's Movement

Reference Walt Anderson, ed. *The Age of Protest,* 1969.

Sit-ins

In Greensboro, North Carolina, on the afternoon of February 1, 1960, four black students from North Carolina A&T College walked into a Woolworth's, a chain "dime" store that sold low-cost items. After two students bought small toilet articles, the four sat down at a lunch counter reserved for whites only. In response to a request from one of the young men, Ezell Blair, Jr., the waitress said, "We don't serve Negroes here," a customary response during that era in places to eat across the South. Instead of leaving quietly, which blacks at that time usually did to avoid being jailed or worse, the four remained seated. Blair said, "I beg to disagree with you. You just finished serving me at a counter not two feet away from here. . . . This is a public place, isn't it?

Ronald Martin, Robert Patterson, and Mark Martin stage a sit-in at the F. W. Woolworth store in Greensboro, North Carolina, where they had previously been refused service.

If it isn't, then why don't you sell membership cards?"

For the remainder of the afternoon, until the store closed at 5:30 P.M., the waitress refused to serve the students. The students promised to return the next day with more students. News spread on campus about the "sit-in." The following day, thirty neatly dressed students returned. They sat for two hours at the counter, studying and occasionally trying to order. They ended the sit-in with a prayer. Within days, hundreds of students from nearby campuses had joined the four. Sit-ins spread to other sites—wherever food was served to whites only. Student participation was so great that teams took shifts. By occupying all the seats in a food establishment that would otherwise by occupied by paying customers, the students were costing the local merchants substantial income.

The city became tense. Woolworth's was visited by white youths who threatened the black students and attempted to hold seats for white customers. When a caller threatened to bomb the store, the manager closed. The mayor asked the black students to call off the protests for two weeks and meet with local business leaders to work out a solution. The request was an admission that the students had changed a local racist custom. A few weeks earlier the idea of blacks sitting at lunch counters would not have been a topic of discussion. The students had demonstrated that nonviolent protest could make a difference.

The Greensboro sit-ins were not the first. Others had preceded it. But it was the first that received substantial publicity and drew large numbers of other students as participants. The first sit-in was staged by the Congress of Racial Equality (CORE) in 1942 at a restaurant in the heart of Chicago's Loop district. Under the leadership of James Farmer, a series of sit-ins had the effect of opening the area's dime store and drugstore lunch counters to blacks. It did not attract the kind of national attention the sit-in in Greensboro had in the 1960s. World War II was in progress, and Chicago, unlike Greensboro, was not in the Deep South. Therefore, the Chicago sit-ins did not have much impact on the civil rights movement except to provide a model of a successful tactic.

See also Civil Rights Movement; Freedom Riders; Southern Christian Leadership Conference
Reference Terry Anderson. *The Movement and the Sixties: Protest in America from Greensboro to Wounded Knee*, 1995.

Social Movements

A social movement embodies attitudes and self-conscious actions of a collection of people aimed toward change in the structure of a society or in its ideology. The action takes place outside accepted channels or may use channels innovatively. Movements are distinguished from organized groups that make them up. The Student Nonviolent Coordinating Committee (SNCC) was a movement organization within the civil rights movement. Movements are also distinguished from changes in attitude that do not involve actions. For example, people who are sympathetic to the goals of a movement provide emotional and possibly financial support, but they are not participants in the movement.

Movements are not the same as rebellious acts. Movement participants are aware of the social structure against which they rebel. Street people of the 1960s were part of a movement. Street children of the 1990s, runaways and the abandoned, were not.

Changes brought into being by those in power are not generally classified as movements. For example, as part of the 1960s counterculture, the youth rebelled against dress codes because they made students feel like robots, cogs in mindless organizations. In the 1990s, however, dress codes were reinstituted by some parents and school administrators to protect students from violent attack by those who coveted articles of clothing, such as expensive jackets and sneakers. Widespread adoption of dress codes in the 1990s would not be considered a movement because the impetus came from those in charge, rather than from those affected or from outsiders trying to bring about change.

Why movements arise at a particular time is not well understood. The conditions of discrimination that precipitated the emergence of the civil rights movement in the late 1950s and the

1960s had prevailed since slavery. One theory to explain movement timing proposes that an improvement in conditions may generate hope that escalates faster than the rate of actual improvement. Movements also emerge among the advantaged whose lot in life is threatened.

The emergence of a social movement is not an automatic process arising from general conditions of dissatisfaction. Individuals must share their dissatisfaction and develop with others a collective sense of what they have in common. Besides objective factors that breed dissatisfaction, participants must share a perspective that makes action seem plausible and that makes concerted, collective action appear reasonable. Social movements generate a utopian mentality about the future. Anticipation of perceived future conditions enables participants to reach for seemingly impossible goals. Although the goals often cannot be attained, the effort to reach them often transforms a society.

See also Antiwar Movement; Civil Rights Movement; Hippies
Reference Roberta Ash. *Social Movements in America,* 1972.

Southern Christian Leadership Conference

The Southern Christian Leadership Conference (SCLC) was founded in January 1957, when the Reverend Martin Luther King, Jr., and the Reverend Ralph Abernathy, two black Montgomery, Alabama, ministers, met with black leaders from ten southern states at the Ebenezer Baptist Church in Atlanta, Georgia. King was elected president and Abernathy secretary-treasurer.

Prior to the 1957 meeting, King and Abernathy had led the Montgomery Improvement Association (MIA) to victory in the Montgomery, Alabama, bus boycott. The boycott had lasted from December 5, 1955, when seamstress Rosa Parks refused to give up her seat to a white passenger and was arrested, until December 21, 1956, when Montgomery buses became desegregated.

Under the leadership of King and Abernathy, SCLC waged a vigorous and far-reaching campaign of nonviolent resistance to segregation. With a small, dedicated staff, they organized sit-ins and other forms of civil disobedience of segregation laws. They also conducted widespread voter registration drives. The leaders and other SCLC members often found themselves in situations in which, according to Abernathy, "We really didn't know which were worst, the police or the angry mob."

King and Abernathy understood that the people who lived in the communities where they sought justice for blacks would continue to live in those communities after marches, sit-ins, and voter registration drives were concluded. For them, negotiation and reconciliation between blacks and whites were critical, but they were the least understood facets of SCLC's and King's philosophy.

Violence is a tempting and immediate solution, but it provides an easy excuse for maintaining the status quo. Even though King practiced nonviolence, he and SCLC were often accused of violence with words to this effect: "He claims to be for nonviolence, but it follows him wherever he goes." Despite constant provocation, SCLC adhered to the principle of nonviolence. In Abernathy's words, "Violence is the weapon of the weak. Nonviolence is the weapon of the strong. It's the job of the state troopers to use mace on us. It's our job to keep marching. It's their job to put us in jail. It's our job to be in jail."

SCLC extended its struggle from the South to the North by moving into Chicago in 1965. A small-scale effort to dramatize inadequate housing began when King rented an inner-city apartment. SCLC helped to organize tenants, who paid their rents to SCLC, which were put in an escrow account. The escrow account paid for heating fuels and repairs. The intent of the strategy was to force landlords to take SCLC to court to get their money. In court, the facts about the treatment of tenants by landlords could be made public. SCLC also applied for grants from the federal Housing and Urban Development (HUD) agency to buy structurally sound buildings from their owners, who in the wake of negative publicity were usually glad to sell.

SCLC mounted a successful "Operation Bread-basket" campaign in Atlanta in 1962. The objective was to encourage corporations and businesses located in inner-city neighborhoods to hire blacks and to buy products made by black companies. A similar campaign was mounted in Chicago in 1966. SCLC also developed a literacy and job placement program in Chicago and helped the participants find jobs. The program was undermined by Mayor Richard Daley, who controlled all city patronage. SCLC's efforts in Chicago are often cited as a failure. However, SCLC's work in Chicago focused attention on urban problems. It also created models of self-help that continue to be used by tenants in their struggles with landlords. Operation Breadbasket, under the leadership of Jesse Jackson, achieved substantial results.

The civil rights movement in the North faced different concerns than those encountered in the South. Southern issues often revolved around dignity and citizenship. In the North, the issues were more diffuse. Poor blacks feared their children would starve or freeze to death in unheated apartments. More affluent blacks wanted to sell their products. The politically educated longed to change the political system.

Chicago's problems forced King and other thinkers within SCLC to face directly the implications of poverty. During the years the civil rights movement was engaging in constant struggles to end segregation, the American economy had gradually displaced unskilled labor from the job market by replacing their work with automated machines. Victories in the field of constitutional rights alone would not be enough to bring freedom and equality to African Americans. Recognition of the roots of poverty plunged King into the nation's bitter debate about Vietnam. Although in time their supporters would cross over, in 1966 the civil rights movement and the peace/antiwar movement had distinctly different supporters. The leadership of the peace movement was made up of white radicals, a few black radicals, socialists, and leftists. The leadership of the traditional civil rights movement was made up of middle-class, religious blacks.

King's philosophy of nonviolence made it difficult for him to accept "the just war" theology that Christian churches had used to support World War II. Beginning in 1965, war, poverty, and racism were increasingly linked in King's speeches. However, because President Lyndon Johnson had done so much for the civil rights movement through passage and enforcement of the Civil Rights Act of 1964 and the Voting Rights Act of 1965, King was reluctant to criticize his handling of the Vietnam War. Eventually, he concluded that he could no longer condone the war. He condemned it in a speech on April 4, 1967, at the Riverside Church in New York and was severely criticized by the press.

By 1967, President Johnson, angered by King's stance against the war in Vietnam, was providing little federal support for the Voting Rights Act. Without federal support, campaigns in hundreds of small communities could not be mounted. SCLC had neither the staff nor the money necessary to help them. Sometimes money to bail people out of jail after a demonstration ran as high as $40,000. In facing its limitations in Chicago, SCLC recognized that poverty is profitable for some people. Slums exist because they make money for a few. A profound change would require a major redistribution of wealth. Even big labor unions in the mid-1960s were not interested in joining the struggle for equality. They failed to understand that huge numbers of unemployed people serve as a drag on union wages.

To address his concern about the pervasive effects of poverty, in December 1967 King decided to organize the Poor People's Campaign, a massive demonstration by poor people of all races from around the country to confront officials in Washington, D.C., with their grievances. The campaign was scheduled for March 1968, but the demonstration was postponed to permit King, at the end of March, to rally support for a Memphis, Tennessee, strike for higher wages by sanitation workers. He returned to Memphis April 4, 1968. While standing on his motel balcony on the evening of April 4, King was killed by a sniper's bullet. The strike was settled eight days later, and interest in the Poor People's Campaign, as well as financial support, mushroomed.

Abernathy, King's close friend and confidant, after a week of fasting and meditation, took command of SCLC. Abernathy vowed to lead "the most militant and aggressive nonviolent war ever waged by the civil rights movement." Following King's death, checks poured into SCLC, and a conflict arose between Abernathy and the SCLC staff and Coretta Scott King. Martin Luther King had made no provision for his wife and children. Many of the checks were made out to Coretta, and she needed the money to care for herself and her children. There was also conflict over the role Coretta would play. She had always perceived herself as a civil rights leader even though her husband had often treated her as just a wife. She had achieved skill and stature when she had represented her husband at rallies and demonstrations against the war in Vietnam. The SCLC staff wanted her to raise funds for them but to have no part in policy decisions.

Coretta King was committed to carrying on the legacy of her husband by training people in nonviolence. She tenaciously set out to establish the Martin Luther King Center for Nonviolent Social Change to preserve and share her husband's legacy with the world. The SCLC staff turned their attention to the Poor People's Campaign.

SCLC continued in its mission, but national attention shifted to more militant groups. Although seldom in the national news in the 1990s, SCLC continued its mission of nonviolent resistance to racial injustice. From its base in Atlanta, Georgia, SCLC conducts training programs in sixteen southern and border states in voter registration and the use of social protest techniques such as boycotts and picketing. Citizenship education schools teach reading and writing, help potential voters to pass literacy tests, and provide information about public resources. A goal of a program called "Crusade for the Ballot" is to double the black vote in the South through increased voter registration.

See also Abernathy, Reverend Ralph; King, Reverend Martin Luther, Jr.; Parks, Rosa; Poor People's Campaign; Young, Andrew

Reference Andrew Young. *An Easy Burden: The Civil Rights Movement and the Transformation of America,* 1996.

Southern Poverty Law Center

Attorney Morris Dees founded the Southern Poverty Law Center in 1971, based on the idea that winning a few important law cases could change the racism of the South. Julian Bond became the center's first president. One of the center's early cases resulted in reapportionment of the Alabama legislature to reflect the state's black population. Another early case led to the desegregation of the Montgomery, Alabama, YMCA.

In 1980, the center set up the Klanwatch Project to monitor the activities of the Ku Klux Klan. In late 1987, the center won a civil suit and was awarded a $7 million judgment against the United Klans of America (UKA) for the death of a young black man, Michael Donald, who was killed and hanged in a public street. The purpose of the hanging was to send a message to Alabama and the rest of the nation that the Klan did not want black people on juries. The judgment bankrupted the UKA for a period. By the 1990s, however, the Klan was making a comeback.

In a 1990 civil suit filed by the center against Tom Metzger and his son John, the center charged that the Metzgers were responsible for the death of Mulugeta Seraw, a 27-year-old Ethiopian student, at the hands of skinheads. The jury ordered a $12.5 million settlement against the Metzgers for inciting skinheads to commit violence against Jews and minorities.

See also Ku Klux Klan
Reference Morris Dees and Steve Fiffer. *A Season for Justice,* 1991.

Steinem, Gloria (b. 1934)

Tall, attractive, and articulate, a writer, lecturer, and spokesperson for the feminist movement, Gloria Steinem, to her chagrin, was often singled out for media attention. Her aura of success gave no hint about the struggle required to get where she was.

Steinem's childhood was chaotic. When her mother, Ruth Nunevillers Steinem, gave birth to her first daughter, Susanne, in 1925, she was a successful newspaperwoman and eventually became a Sunday editor for one of Toledo, Ohio's,

Women's rights activist Gloria Steinem.

major dailies. By the time Gloria was born in 1934, Ruth Steinem had stopped working, had become prey to bouts of depression, delusion, and fear, and had been hospitalized for a time. During her early childhood, for much of the year, Gloria's family lived a gypsy life, traveling in a trailer, while her father tried to make a living buying and selling antiques. Attendance at school for more than a week or two at a time was difficult. When Ruth Steinem was well enough, she taught the two girls herself. Susanne left for college when Gloria was eight. A couple of years later, her father left his family. For the next ten years, Gloria was responsible for her mother. Her father took over care of her mother for a year in order to enable Gloria to finish high school.

When Gloria was accepted for admission into Smith College, her mother sold their ramshackle home for $8,000 to finance her tuition. Gloria won a scholarship to help pay her tuition, graduated from Smith with high honors, and was offered a fellowship to study in India for two years. When she returned home from India in 1958, she had a mission to make Americans aware of life in Asia, but she found people were not interested. Her concern about Asians was just one of many lifelong passions to right injustices.

The election of John F. Kennedy as president renewed Steinem's optimism, and she moved to New York, where she hoped to forge a career in journalism. Her first job was with a humor magazine called *Help!* There Steinem not only learned how to put out a magazine but also made contacts with people who could help her find freelance writing assignments. *Esquire* published her first major article, entitled "The Moral Disarmament of Betty Coed." In it, Steinem proposed that although birth control pills and other contraceptives had changed sexual attitudes on major college campuses, thereby forcing a change in women's roles, it had not changed men's basic attitude toward women.

By the mid-1960s, she had a modest reputation as a magazine writer and was often seen with famous people. Despite her obvious ability as a writer, Steinem was typically assigned by editors to lightweight, frivolous topics. In 1968, she established her ability as a political and social critic when she began writing a lively column entitled "The City Politic" for *New York* magazine. Her commitment to feminism began in November 1968 with an assignment to attend a meeting of a radical feminist group called the Redstockings.

The topic under discussion in the church basement where the meeting was held was abortion. At the time, it was illegal in the United States. New York State had recently held hearings to consider relaxing its antiabortion laws. Fourteen men and only one woman, a nun, were invited to speak at the hearings. In protest, Redstockings held its own meeting in a church basement. Women talked about their experiences with illegal abortions. One woman's doctor agreed to perform an abortion only if she would agree to being sterilized. Another had been sexually attacked on the operating table. All who received so-called back-alley abortions had risked their lives, not knowing whether the abortionist had any skill or training.

The stories of danger and humiliation enraged Steinem, who, at age 22, had traveled to

England for an abortion, where the procedure was legal. All her life, Steinem had identified with minorities and second-class citizens. At the Redstockings meeting, she realized she herself was a second-class citizen. For the first time, Steinem understood that women as a group were discriminated against in the same way as blacks and other minorities. In the weeks and months that followed, she went to meetings held by a diverse range of feminist groups and read all the feminist books she could find, including those written by the founders of the feminist movement in the nineteenth century.

Steinem's first openly feminist article, "After Black Power, Women's Liberation," appeared in *New York* magazine in 1969. In the article, she made a prediction that if the younger, more radical groups would join forces with women in more conservative organizations, such as the National Organization for Women (NOW), then "an alliance with the second mass movement—poor women of all colors—should be no problem." The poor had already been targeted by several women's movement groups, who were working with them on issues they had in common, such as setting up day care centers and providing job training. The article won a prestigious Penney-Missouri Journalism Award a year after it was published.

Male colleagues warned Steinem against writing about "women's stuff" because it would ruin her reputation. She ignored them and wrote about feminist issues whenever she had an opportunity. In an essay for *Time*, Steinem pointed out that in many states women could not get credit, start a business, or even use their maiden name. *Time* paid Steinem less for the article than it would have paid a man for a comparable piece.

The feminist, or women's, movement was often referred to as "women's liberation" or "women's lib," often in a derogatory tone. In her piece for *Time*, Steinem wrote: "Women's Lib is not trying to destroy the American family; a look at the statistics on divorce—plus the way old people are farmed out to strangers and young people flee the home—shows the destruction that has already been done. Liberated women are just trying to point out the disaster, and build compassionate and practical alternatives from the ruins." She concluded with the words: "If Women's Lib wins, perhaps we all do."

From 1969 to 1974, Steinem spent much of her time traveling around the country on lecture tours. An article about her in *Esquire* magazine in 1971 called her "the intellectual's pinup" and hinted she owed her success to her shapely legs and powerful boyfriends, not to her talent or the importance of her ideas. The less caustic press treated her as the elected leader of all dissatisfied women, an assumption that embarrassed and angered her. The mainstream press did not take the women's movement seriously and did not think Americans wanted to read about it.

Steinem concluded that the only way to gain a forum for feminist ideas was to start a national magazine. She and her colleagues created the magazine and named it *Ms.*, a form of address that identifies a woman as an individual rather than by her marital status. Katharine Graham, the only woman among the nation's top newspaper publishers, contributed some money to cover start-up expenses for *Ms.* Clay Felker, editor and publisher of *New York* magazine, offered to insert a shortened sample of *Ms.*'s preview issue in the year-end issue of *New York*. The issue sold more copies than ever before in *New York*'s history. The preview issue of *Ms.*, distributed in January 1972, sold out in little over a week. Joyous letters from women across the country streamed into the *Ms.* office.

Throughout her life as a feminist leader and magazine editor, Steinem has continued to write about women's lives and to work on their behalf. In 1977, Steinem began a year-long fellowship at the Woodrow Wilson Center to begin work on a project called "Feminism and Its Impact on the Premises and Goals of Current Political Theory." The male-dominated center was ill prepared to give credence to her worldview. When she scheduled a talk and invited the women who worked at the center—the secretaries and cleaning women—to come, she upset the administration.

Steinem's fiftieth birthday in 1984, celebrated two months after her birthday, began a tradition of raising funds for the Ms. Foundation. A man with whom she had a long-time relationship believes Steinem put feminist principles over economic ones, which kept her tied up in an endless pattern of traveling around the country raising money.

The publication of *Revolution from Within* in 1992 represented time spent in therapy and obsessive reading on the topic of self-esteem. Reviews were mixed. One critic claimed she had written the book in order to connect internal authority to the overthrow of external authority. Some called it the expression of a "midlife crisis." The book stresses the importance of self-esteem to both personal well-being and political revolution and is a guide to reshaping patterns of childhood. The carping of critics had no effect on the impact the book made on women. Letters poured in and women camped out overnight to be admitted to one of her book signings.

By the time Steinem turned sixty in 1994, she had reduced her hectic schedule and was enjoying a new-found freedom.

> **See also** Black Feminist Organizations; Feminist Organizations; Friedan, Betty
> **References** Carolyn Heilbrun. *The Education of a Woman: The Life of Gloria Steinem*, 1995. Gloria Steinem. *It Changed My Life: Writings on the Women's Movement*, 1976; and *Outrageous Acts and Everyday Rebellions*, 1983.

Student Nonviolent Coordinating Committee

One of the more militant civil rights groups organized in the 1960s, the Student Nonviolent Coordinating Committee (SNCC, pronounced "Snick") coordinated the efforts in the South of black college students to desegregate lunch counters and other public accommodations, such as rest rooms. SNCC began as an adjunct to the Southern Christian Leadership Conference (SCLC), the organization started by the Reverend Martin Luther King, Jr., and the Reverend Ralph Abernathy. The membership became impatient with the nonviolent philosophy of SCLC and developed its own agenda.

Over time, SNCC became increasingly militant

as new leaders emerged. Following the death of Martin Luther King and a surge of riots, white students were asked to give up their membership and turn their efforts to racism in their own communities. Under Stokely Carmichael's leadership, SNCC became increasingly identified with Black Power, a term Carmichael was thought to have coined. Black Power referred to an ambiguous political position later defined by Carmichael and Charles Hamilton in their 1968 book, *Black Power: The Politics of Liberation*, as "a call for black people of this country to unite, to recognize their heritage, to build a sense of community ... to define their own goals."

The idea of Black Power alarmed conservative black leadership and white liberal supporters. So unsettling was the slogan that support for SNCC and organizations with which it was associated was swiftly withdrawn. By the end of the 1960s, the lack of a financial base and squabbles within the organization led to its demise.

SNCC's work to integrate public accommodations was augmented by an estimated 100,000 black and white college students across the country. Many were jailed; some were beaten; some were dismissed from the colleges they attended. SNCC members participated in most of the major activities and events of the civil rights movement. They were at the Greensboro, North Carolina, sit-ins, on the buses with the Freedom Riders, tramping along dusty roads locating potential voters to register, giving speeches at black churches, walking in marches, and spending time in jail.

> **See also** Albany Movement; Bloody Sunday; Bond, Julian; Carmichael, Stokely; Freedom Riders; Hamer, Fannie Lou; Hayden, Tom; March on Washington for Jobs and Freedom; Mississippi Freedom Democratic Party; Old Left and New Left; Port Huron Statement
> **Reference** Stokely Carmichael, with Charles Hamilton. *Black Power: The Politics of Liberation*, 1968.

Sweatshops

By targeting celebrities, American activists threw a spotlight in 1996 on sweatshops used by large clothing corporations. Celebrity television host Kathie Lee Gifford, basketball star Michael Jordan, and corporations like Nike, Walt Disney, The Gap, Levi's, Eddie Bauer, and Fruit of the Loom were publicly criticized. Some were easier to embarrass than others. Although responsibility for sweatshop labor conditions lies more with the corporations, celebrities make enormous sums for their endorsements. By targeting the celebrities, small organizations like the National Labor Committee (NLC) and Asian Immigrant Advocates (AIWA) have waged successful campaigns against large corporations, which typically have public relations staffs much larger than the staffs of the rights organizations.

A well-planned publicity campaign can sometimes do more than years in court. An article called "Sweatshops" by Larry Saloman in the September-October 1996 issue of *Third Force,* published by the Center for Third World Organizing in Oakland, California, described efforts by activists to bring attention to the plight of workers who labored under inhuman conditions. In testimony at a congressional hearing on labor abuse, Charles Kernaghan of the NLC, a small New York human rights organization, testified that Gifford's line of clothing sold by Wal-Mart stores was made by young Honduran girls working long days for as little as 31 cents an hour. In 1995, Wal-Mart made more than $300 million in sales, and Gifford was paid $9 million. When asked about labor conditions in Indonesian factories that make Nike shoes, Michael Jordan said, "I'm not really aware of that. My job with Nike is to endorse the product. Their job is to be up on that." Each year, Nike pays Michael Jordan more than the combined income of 30,000 workers who work for clothing suppliers in Indonesia.

In a campaign against The Gap, NLC secured independent monitoring of The Gap's Mandarin International factory in El Salvador. The factory also makes clothing under contract for other companies. The rights organization won by bringing two young women who work in the Mandarin International factory to the United States to talk about their daily working lives. The women often worked as long as twenty hours a day at pay levels that kept them in poverty. Supervisors frequently harassed the women sexu-

ally. Workers in Haitian sweatshops make Pocahontas Pajamas for the Walt Disney Company for as little as 11 cents an hour. In 1993 Disney's chief operating officer, Michael Eisner, earned $97,000 per hour for a yearly total of $203 million in salary and stock options.

However, a media strategy alone does not produce results. NLC spent months in research and planning. A cadre of organizers mobilized a network of supporters to attend demonstrations as needed.

Sweatshops are not confined to Third World countries. An August 1995 raid on a factory in El Monte, California, revealed seventy-two Thai immigrants whose low wages for long hours were turned over to smugglers to pay for the immigrants' passage to the United States. According to Sweatshop Watch, a California-based coalition of labor, immigrant, and civil rights organizations, two-thirds of Los Angeles sweatshops violate minimum wage and overtime regulations. While still the Clinton administration's labor secretary, Robert Reich estimated that more than one-half of the 22,000 garment contractors in the United States pay less than minimum wage. Among 350 garment factories that were investigated, more than half were in violation of federal labor laws.

Large companies contract with smaller factory owners. When factory owners are discovered to be in violation of labor laws, the large companies claim they are not responsible for the working conditions. To secure back wages owed twelve women when Lucky Sewing Company went out of business, AIWA ignored the bankrupt factory owner and targeted the well-known larger company of fashion designer and retailer Jessica McClintock. For more than three years, AIWA conducted a publicity and community pressure campaign to win justice for the women. Among the tactics AIWA used was a full-page ad in the *New York Times* that pictured a frilly gown against the setting of a sweatshop and an image of McClintock with a caption that read: "Let Them Eat Lace." It took three years before McClintock agreed to pay the back wages.

Nike is one of the largest corporations in the world. To secure cheap labor, between the 1970s and the 1990s, Nike moved its production out of the United States to Korea and Taiwan. When labor union organizing in Korea and Taiwan threatened to raise wages, Nike moved its operations to Indonesia, China, Pakistan, Vietnam, and Thailand, where organizing is repressed by the governments. Nike's competitors, Reebok, Adidas, Converse, and other shoe companies, followed suit.

In March 1996 twenty-four Indonesian workers were fired from a factory under contract with Nike for attempting to organize for better wages. A child who works all day stitching a Nike soccer ball that sells retail for $80 is paid 60 cents. The chairman of Nike's board defended his company's policy by saying that different populations have different needs. Nike's home office is located in Portland, Oregon.

In June 1996, a Portland public school board member, Joseph Tam, suggested to his fellow board members that they reject a six-figure Nike donation to the school district until the company improved its treatment of its workers. A Portland-based group called "An Oregon Coalition," made up of various groups—Press for Change, Jobs for Justice, and the East Timor Action Network— took advantage of the publicity that resulted from the Portland School Board member's suggestion. They demonstrated in Nike theme malls in four cities. In 1998 Nike had bigger problems than bad publicity—sales were dropping sharply as teenagers switched to other footwear styles.

See also Alinsky, Saul; Union Movement Rebirth
Reference Larry Saloman. "Sweatshops in the Spotlight," 1996.

Symbionese Liberation Army

Founded by a black former police informant, petty criminal, and escaped convict, Donald Defreeze, the Symbionese Liberation Army's (SLA's) original members consisted of Defreeze and nine radical white young people who had grown up in middle-class homes. Defreeze abandoned his "slave name" in favor of Cinque Mtume, which means "Fifth Prophet" in Swahili.

As the counterculture and the antiwar move-ment wound down in the early 1970s, there were some participants who could not endure integration back into the middle-class, white world they had repudiated. The SLA was a brutal caricature of the passions of the 1960s. The group came into being in the fall of 1973. SLA members Russell Little and Joseph Romero were captured after they killed Marcus Foster, the first black superintendent of the Oakland, California, school system, a charismatic man with a huge circle of friends and admirers. The murder gave the SLA local attention as a power to be feared. Otherwise, the murder was inexplicable. The murder gave the SLA national attention. While searching the belongings of Russell and Little, the police discovered an SLA "hit list." Patty Hearst, one of the people on the list, who was subsequently kidnapped by the SLA, was never notified that she was at risk.

As an action in the war the SLA had declared against "the fascist state of Amerikka," the SLA "arrested" Hearst, the granddaughter of William Randolph Hearst, the newspaper tycoon, and the daughter of Randolph Hearst, the head of a media conglomerate. In the opinion of the SLA, Randolph Hearst was a "reactionary corporate-military pig." The SLA originally planned to offer the heiress as an exchange for Russell and Little, who were in San Quentin prison. They changed their minds when the kidnapping generated enormous publicity. Holding her indefinitely became a route to fame. The SLA dangled the possibility of her release before the Hearst family in the form of a demand that the family set up a food program for California's poor. The Hearst Corporation spent several million dollars distributing food in San Francisco and Los Angeles, but Defreeze declared their effort a "mockery" and refused to release the young woman.

Patty Hearst was the SLA's most famous victim. Photographs show her transformation from a smiling, innocent face in February 1974 before capture to a transformed Patty, known as Tania, in April 1974. She was dressed in a beret and jumpsuit, her eyes black and her expression sour. She had been transformed from an heiress to a bank robber in two months. In May 1974, most of the SLA members were killed by Los Angeles police. Patty Hearst and two others escaped. She was captured in September 1975 and went on trial in February 1976. The SLA's revolution was over.

See also Hearst, Patricia
References Patricia Hearst. *Every Secret Thing,* 1982; Vin McLellan and Paul Avez. *The Voices of Guns,* 1977.

Teach-ins

In March 1965, University of Michigan students and faculty organized an all-night "teach-in." Faculty who were opposed to the Vietnam War debated as "truth teams." The event attracted thousands. Using similar formats, the idea was replicated on campuses around the nation. In May 1965, a mammoth teach-in was held at the University of California at Berkeley.

See also Antiwar Movement; Columbia University Campus Protest
Reference Terry Anderson. *The Movement and the Sixties: Protest from Greensboro to Wounded Knee,* 1995.

Terrorism

On April 19, 1995, a homemade bomb blew up the Alfred P. Murrah Federal Building in Oklahoma City. The explosion killed 168 people and injured more than 500 others. Law enforcement officials initially assumed that foreign terrorists were responsible. Middle Eastern terrorists had been responsible for the February 26, 1993, explosion at New York's World Trade Center that killed six people. On March 4, 1994, Islamic extremists Mohammed Salameh, Ahmad Ajaj, Nidal Ayyad, and Mahmud Abouhalima were convicted of the crime.

American experience with terrorism has been limited. Unlike Britain and Middle Eastern countries, Americans have not lived through frequent terrorist acts. The idea of homegrown terrorism being responsible for the Murrah Building explosion was unthinkable. But in short order federal officials were forced to give up their foreign terrorist theory. The primary suspect turned out to be an American, Timothy McVeigh, a former Gulf War veteran.

For years, McVeigh had read and listened to rhetoric espoused by hate groups. These groups are convinced that conspiracies to rob the American people of their freedom are regularly carried out by politicians and federal government employees. Hate groups number in the hundreds; among the best known are the Christian Identity Movement, the Ku Klux Klan, and the Neo-Nazis. Although hate groups preach violence, their vio-

lent actions tend to be against vulnerable individuals. A loner, McVeigh was not an active participant in any groups, but he absorbed their hate messages and feared the government would take guns away from Americans, leaving them unable to defend themselves against that same malevolent government.

McVeigh was particularly influenced by the 1978 novel *The Turner Diaries,* which has often been referred to as the bible of the racist right. The novel was written by former physics professor William Pierce under the pseudonym Andrew MacDonald Pierce. In the book, an underground resistance movement attacks Washington and bombs FBI headquarters.

Unlike hate groups, which mostly ranted, McVeigh decided to take decisive action. He apparently thought Americans would perceive the bombing as a signal to rise up against the government. In his trial, McVeigh's copy of *The Turner Diaries* became the prosecution's Exhibit No. 1. On June 13, 1997, McVeigh was sentenced to die for his crimes. An accomplice, in a separate trial, was found guilty of conspiring with McVeigh and of involuntary manslaughter.

Unlike an ordinary murderer, who kills someone because he or she wants that person dead, a terrorist like McVeigh kills people about whom he or she is indifferent. A 1988 U.S. government publication called *Terrorist Group Profiles* defined terrorism as "premeditated, politically motivated violence perpetrated against noncombatant targets by subnational groups or clandestine state agents, usually to influence an audience." McVeigh's crimes only partially fit the definition. He was not part of a subgroup or a clandestine state agent, but most of the people present in the Murrah Building that morning, including nineteen babies in day care, were noncombatants. And, like other terrorists, he hoped to force people not present at the scene of violence to take the action that he desired.

Terrorists seldom seize power. Probably, like McVeigh, they prefer not to have any responsibility that would prevent them from being nomads. Terrorists favor theatrical forms of violence. On occasion, they have provoked the overthrow of a democratic government by a military dictatorship. Paradoxically, the threat of terrorists has in some democratic societies melded a consensus that did not previously exist. The overall number of lives lost through terrorist acts is small, yet despite their limited threat, fear of terrorists promotes costly security systems and encourages curbs on civil liberties. Fear also affects business. The onset of the Persian Gulf War of 1990–1991 aroused such fear of terrorist retaliation among travelers around the world that ticket sales on airlines plummeted.

Rather than terrorists, many groups prefer to call themselves freedom fighters or urban guerrillas. Some groups even gain respectability. Perceptions of South Africa's African National Congress (ANC), once viewed by the South African government as a terrorist group, changed when ANC leader Nelson Mandela was released from jail in 1989 after almost three decades, and the ANC is now the governing party in that country.

Historically, terrorists are elitists, contemptuous of the masses. They do not believe in liberty, equality, or fraternity but in a historical mission for their tiny minority. A joke about the Tuparamos, a Uruguayan terrorist group, was that to be a member one had to have a Ph.D.

Reminders of McVeigh and America's hate groups can be found in an 1884 manual written by Johannes Most, a German Social Democrat turned anarchist. Most proposed the letter bomb and argued for the liquidation of "pigs" on the

grounds that the act would not be murder, since the police were not human.

Politics and religion, alone and in combination, play a significant role in terrorism. Religion is often the justification that terrorists use for their deeds. Between February 25, 1996, and March 4, 1996, four suicide bombings in Israel by two Islamic terrorist groups, Hamas and Islamic Jihad, jeopardized peace negotiations between Israel and the Palestinians.

Terrorism as a political concept emerged during the French Revolution (1789–1799), where it was used against the aristocracy—and anyone else perceived to be in opposition. Maximilien-François-Marie-Isidore de Robespierre and his followers, a faction of the Committee of Public Safety, carried out a "reign of terror." They accused people of treason and executed them on the guillotine. One scholar estimates that Robespierre's group was responsible for 40,000 deaths and 300,000 arrests. Using tactics of fear, a handful of men had coerced a nation of 27 million people. Robespierre's power was overturned when his own technique was used against him.

See also Christian Identity Movement; Ku Klux Klan; Mandela, Nelson; Militias
References Walter Laqueur. *The Age of Terrorism,* 1987; William Lineberry, ed. *The Struggle against Terrorism,* 1989; Richard Serrano. *One of Ours: Timothy McVeigh and the Oklahoma City Bombing,* 1998.

Till, Emmett

Several events in 1954 and 1955 were critical in hastening the slow evolution of the drive to give black Americans equal civil rights. The murder of Emmett Till was one of them. Southern backlash was set in motion in May 1954, when the U.S. Supreme Court handed down its decision in the case of *Brown v. Board of Education of Topeka,* which ended school segregation. The decision did not set a deadline for integration and instead asked for suggestions. On May 31, 1955, the Court issued guidelines that simply instructed local school boards to implement desegregation plans "with all deliberate speed." The ambiguous phrase "with all deliberate speed" encouraged school boards to delay implementation.

The *Brown* decision stimulated the formation of Citizens' Councils, often known as White Citizens' Councils. Critics called them the "uptown Ku Klux Klan." Lynchings, which had been on the decline, returned to the South. Three murders in Mississippi brought the glare of national publicity to the state. A National Association for the Advancement of Colored People (NAACP) organizer, the Reverend George W. Lee, was killed by a shotgun blast to the face on the streets of Belzoni, Mississippi, after he led a voter registration drive. His death was ruled a traffic accident by the local police. Another NAACP organizer, Lamar Smith, was killed on the courthouse lawn in Brookhaven, Mississippi, on a Saturday afternoon.

The most infamous case of 1955, sometimes cited as the incident that ignited the civil rights movement, was the murder of Emmett Louis Till, a 14-year-old boy from Chicago, who was vacationing with relatives in Leflore County. Emmett and his cousin, Curtis Jones, were staying with their great-uncle Mose "Preacher" Wright and his wife Elizabeth. Emmett attended an all-black school in Chicago and was familiar with segregation. His mother had warned him that in the South, "if you have to get on your knees and bow when a white person goes past, do it willingly." Nevertheless, Emmett had no sense of how rigid the rules of behavior were in Mississippi.

On August 24, 1955, he joined seven black teenage boys and girls, three of whom were visitors to the Delta, in a ride to Bryant's Grocery and Meat Market. The store was owned and operated by Roy Bryant, a 24-year-old former soldier, and his 21-year-old wife, Carolyn, a former beauty contest winner. Outside the store, Emmett showed off a picture of a white girl who he claimed was his girlfriend. A couple of the boys dared him to go inside the store and ask Carolyn Bryant for a date. Inside the store, Emmett bought 2 cents' worth of bubble gum. As he was leaving, he reportedly said, "Bye, baby," and wolf-whistled at her. A couple of the waiting boys rushed in, pulled him out of the store and into the car, and drove off. On August 28, after midnight, a car pulled up to Mose Wright's cabin. Roy Bryant and his brother-in-law, J. W. Milam, had come to get "that boy who had done the talkin'." A few hours later, Bryant and Milam were jailed, charged with kidnapping and suspicion of murder. When Emmett's body was found three days later, it was so badly battered and decomposed that Mose Wright could only identify it by a ring the boy had been wearing.

Emmett's mother demanded that her son's body be sent home. She insisted that his casket be open during his wake. Thousands lined the streets outside the funeral home on the first day of viewing. The viewing lasted four days. Two thousand people attended Emmett's funeral. *Jet* magazine published a photograph of Emmett's mutilated body. Contributions to the NAACP's "fight fund," money used to help victims of racial attacks, soared. The black newspaper *The Cleveland Call and Post,* polled black radio preachers throughout the United States and found that 80 percent were telling their listeners about Till's murder and half were demanding that "something be done in Mississippi" immediately.

On September 19, 1955, less than two weeks after Emmett was buried in Chicago, Bryant and Milam went on trial for murder in the courthouse in Sumner, Mississippi. No blacks were registered to vote in the county, nor had there been any since the turn of the century, and therefore no blacks were eligible to serve on the jury.

For a black to accuse a white of murder in Mississippi in 1955 was to risk being murdered. On the third day of the trial, Mose Wright took the stand. The 64-year-old sharecropper identified Bryant and Milam as the men who had taken Emmett away. Two other black witnesses also took the stand. Willis Reed testified he had seen Emmett in the back of Milam's pickup truck and heard a beating in Milam's barn. Reed's aunt, Amanda Bailey, had heard the victim cry out, "Momma, Lord have mercy. Lord have mercy." On Friday, September 23, 1955, after deliberating for one hour and seven minutes—part of that time had been spent in drinking a soft drink—the jury foreman, J. W. Shaw, read the verdict. "Not guilty." Shaw later told inquirers that the "state failed to prove the identity of the body."

The details of what happened to Emmett

emerged after the two men were acquitted of murdering the boy. They told their story to an Alabama journalist in exchange for $4,000. The two men claimed they had only meant to frighten Emmett, not to kill him. According to their account, Emmett had refused to repent even after being pistol-whipped. Milam told the journalist, "What else could we do. He was hopeless. I'm no bully; I never hurt a nigger in my life. I like niggers in their place. I know how to work 'em. But I just decided it was time a few people got put on notice." The two men drove Emmett to the Tallahatchie River and made him carry a 100-pound cotton-gin fan from the back of their truck to the river bank, where they made him undress. Milam fired a bullet into Emmett's head. The men tied the fan around the boy's neck with barbed wire and dumped his body into the river.

Blacks across the country staged major rallies. On the front page of *The Pittsburgh Courier*, a major black newspaper, a headline encircled by a half-inch black border proclaimed: "Sept. 23, 1955—BLACK FRIDAY!" Major white newspapers criticized the verdict. Southern newspapers reacted defensively to the criticism. The *Delta Democrat Times* in Greenville, Mississippi, wrote: "to blame two million Mississippians for the irresponsible act of two is about as illogical as one can become."

After Mose Wright testified before a jury on kidnapping charges against Bryant and Milam, he left Mississippi to live in Chicago. Bad publicity following the murder trial's acquittal did not prevent a jury from also acquitting the two men of kidnapping.

The only solace American blacks had was that black people had risked their lives by testifying against white people in a court of law. The example of Mose Wright, Willis Reed, and Amanda Bailey had a significant impact on young activists.

See also Baldwin, James; Civil Rights Movement; Evers, Medgar; Ku Klux Klan
References Sanford Wexler. *The Civil Rights Movement: An Eyewitness History*, 1993; Stephen J. Whitfield. *A Death in the Delta: The Story of Emmett Till*, 1988.

Title VII of the Civil Rights Act of 1964

Following the suffrage amendment that gave women the vote in 1920, they made no additional civil rights advances until 1962, when President John F. Kennedy established the Commission on the Status of Women. The president issued a directive in 1962 that prohibited federal agencies from discriminating against women in terms of appointments and promotions. In 1963, the Equal Pay Act, sponsored by Democratic representative Edith Green of Oregon, required employers to offer equal pay for equal work regardless of gender. Although severely limited in its scope, the Equal Pay Act set a precedent.

The most momentous change for women came from Title VII of the landmark 1964 Civil Rights Act. The act was intended primarily to alleviate injustices due to race. Title VII was the most controversial part of the bill. It barred discrimination in employment on the basis of race, color, religion, and national origin. Even people who firmly supported the rights of blacks were not convinced discrimination in employment could be abolished by law. Prior to the congressional debate on the Civil Rights Act, Democratic representative Martha Griffiths of Michigan polled colleagues and found she lacked sufficient support to add sex as an amendment. Small advocacy groups of women in Washington discussed the possibility of pushing for inclusion of sex among the protected groups. They decided against taking action for fear it might jeopardize opportunities the bill would give to blacks.

Southern representatives strongly opposed to the act sensed they were going to lose the battle. Nevertheless, they chipped away at the bill with amendments intended to ridicule it. Democratic representative Howard Smith of Virginia, a staunch conservative and vehement opponent of the Civil Rights Act, added sex to the list of protected categories as a cynical joke. Smith expected his colleagues to be so appalled at the idea of sex being included that they would get rid of Title VII. He rallied support for his amendment, and it passed. His ploy backfired. The presence of his amendment failed to prevent his fellow representatives from passing the bill. Although opposition developed in the Senate, Congresswoman Griffiths and Republican Senator Margaret Smith (R-ME) fought tenaciously to prevent the amendment's last-minute withdrawal. In July 1964, Congress enacted the Civil Rights Act with provisions for sex still in place.

Amended in 1972 and 1978, Title VII, in conjunction with the Civil Rights Act of 1991, forbids discrimination in all areas of the employer-employee relationship, from advertisements for new employees through termination or retirement.

The laws have had a significant impact on women in their childbearing years. Pregnancy is no longer grounds for termination. With some exceptions, women no longer have to fear being replaced permanently when they take leave to give birth.

Even though the workplace has shown improvement during the passage of three decades, equity has not yet been achieved. An affirmative action review requested by President Bill Clinton in March 1995 determined that the median female earnings compared with the median male earnings had risen from about 60 percent in the 1960s to 72 percent in 1993. Efforts to evade the law were on the increase in the 1990s. The National Organization for Women (NOW) launched a Women-Friendly Workplace campaign. A particular target has been securities dealers. A standard requirement for workers on Wall Street has been mandatory arbitration for employment discrimination complaints, a practice spreading rapidly to other companies. As a consequence, the securities industry remains dominated by white men because arbitration heavily weighted in favor of the employer made managers essentially immune to civil rights laws.

On May 13, 1998, the Ninth Circuit Court of Appeals, whose jurisdiction covers a large segment of the Northwest plus Hawaii, handed down a landmark decision prohibiting mandatory arbitration of Title VII employment discrimination claims. Patricia Ireland, president of NOW, said in response to the ruling, "We won't stop until the Ninth Circuit's opinion is the law of the land."

See also Black Feminist Organizations; Feminist Organizations; Women's Movement
References Caroline Bird. *Born Female: Source Book for the Women's Liberation Movement*, 1968; Miriam Schneir. *Feminism in Our Times*, 1994.

Union Movement Rebirth

Working conditions in the 1990s favored the rebirth of worker interest in unions. Purchasing power had declined by 28 percent since 1973, and 8 million jobs had been lost since 1980. In 1970, nearly 30 percent of all American workers employed in private industry belonged to unions. By 1996, the percentage had dropped to 11 percent, the lowest since the Depression years of the 1930s.

Poor working conditions for workers in the 1990s resulted from manufacturers' decisions to move operations in order to follow cheap labor. Companies shifted their operations from the North, where unions were strong, to the South, where unions were weak, or overseas, where unions were nonexistent. Another economic trend that hurt workers involved a shift from blue-collar manufacturing jobs to white-collar service ones. A large pool of blue-collar workers was left with only a small pool of jobs.

President Ronald Reagan contributed to the decline in union membership. In 1981, he fired 11,400 members of the Professional Air Traffic Controllers Union. His action encouraged companies across the nation to resist formation of unions. Union growth was also dampened by disclosures of corruption among some union officials.

To regain the power they once had, unions resurrected organizing techniques of the 1930s. The decision paid off. Almost half of the union organizing campaigns monitored in 1994 by the National Labor Relations Board resulted in union victories. Because being an organizer is so demanding—it leaves little time for family and friends—most organizers are young. Since research has shown that white male organizers have the least success, most organizer trainees are young, minority women recruited out of college. Although they come from a variety of socioeconomic backgrounds, the trainees all share a willingness to live in hotel rooms. Most have never worked in the industries they set out to organize.

Campaigns to organize unions are typically difficult for everyone involved. Deep-seated animosities between management and labor are unleashed. Both the organizers and the workers are

significantly changed by their participation in an organizing drive. Workers who participate in a drive to organize a union are taking risks. In 25 percent of the campaigns, some workers are demoted or fired, despite federal law prohibiting companies from taking retaliatory actions. Appeals take years, and the only penalty levied against an employer is reinstatement of the worker with back pay.

To fight the unions, companies hire outside consultants who specialize in anti-union campaigns. The consultants send out mailings and include leaflets in paycheck envelopes with messages that tell the workers a strike will mean that they will be ineligible for unemployment benefits, food stamps, or medical insurance. The consultants portray unions as outsiders who take the worker's money. Even though consultants are also outsiders, their presence is hidden behind the sophisticated mailings. It is true that a union organizer is generally an outsider—a drawback that must be dealt with immediately. Her or his first job is to become familiar with the social and emotional intricacies of the community. An organizer's job is to talk, to struggle for votes one person at a time. Organizers track each worker down, returning to his or her home repeatedly until the organizer catches the worker at home. One contact is generally not enough; the organizer must return for reinforcement visits. Organizing campaigns in which organizers visit workers in their own homes raise the expected level of worker participation from 37 percent to 61 percent.

In 1990, the Organizing Institute, a branch of the American Federation of Labor–Congress of Industrial Organizations (AFL-CIO), spent only $400,000 to recruit and train 25 organizers. In one of his first acts, John Sweeney, who became president of the AFL-CIO in October 1995, allocated substantial resources to the Organizing Institute. The Institute spent $4 million in 1996 to train 320 organizers.

See also Chavez, Cesar; Sweatshops
Reference Margot Hornblower. "Labor's Youth Brigade," 1996.

Urban Forestry

At a summer camp in the San Bernardino Mountains in 1970, 15-year-old Andy Lipkis and his friends were told by a naturalist that the forest around them would be killed by smog within the next twenty-five years. Andy questioned whether anything could be done. The naturalist, pessimistic about reducing fog, admitted there were some trees that resist smog. To Andy's question: "Why not plant them in place of the dying ones?" the naturalist responded, "You can't replant the whole forest." Andy's reaction sparked a national and international movement to plant trees, particularly in urban areas.

Before camp ended, Andy and his friends, with funds from the camp, planted twenty 4-foot-high Coulter pines and incense cedars in the camp's parking lot and ball field. He spent the next few years learning as much as he could about trees and smog. Then Andy wrote to the directors of twenty-five summer camps in the San Bernardino Mountains and asked them to participate in a tree-planting project. Twenty directors agreed. In April 1973, a California Division of Forestry expert on reforestation provided Andy with 40,000 tree seedlings. The fragile seedlings had to be potted in biodegradable containers within five days. With donated milk cartons and the help of scouts, schoolchildren, and college students, Andy beat the deadline. Then Andy and his friends needed money to finance the planting.

Two months of fund-raising followed. The fund-raising effort was the start of an organization, headed by Andy, called the California Conservation Project, better known as the Tree People. The California Air National Guard transported the donated trees to the mountains, and 3,000 campers planted them. Tree-planting became an annual event that renewed the forest at a rate of 150,000 trees every year.

Some years after the Tree People began their work, forest fires destroyed many Los Angeles trees. Research done by the Los Angeles Planning Department about the effect of the loss determined that the city needed 1 million additional trees to filter 200 tons of smog from the city's air each year. Such an undertaking would require twenty years of labor and cost $200 million. The planners asked the Tree People for advice. The Tree People devised a plan to expand their work with volunteers and plant 1 million trees before the start of the 1984 Summer Olympics, three and one-half years away. The one-millionth tree was planted four days before the games began.

Andy Lipkis and the Tree People inspired the formation of other groups around the country and around the world. Among them were Trees Atlanta in Georgia and Friends of the Urban Forest (FUF) in San Francisco. The Tree People, Trees Atlanta, and the FUF all provided substantial technical advice to tree-planting groups at the local level, and the American Forestry Association provided help on a national level.

See also Carson, Rachel; Earth Day; Hippies
Reference Stephen Diamond. *What the Trees Said: Life on a New Age Farm*, 1971.

Urban Renewal

With a few exceptions, protestors of the 1960s and 1970s failed to notice that urban renewal, which razed downtown neighborhoods, typically destroyed poor ethnic and black communities. Officials in American cities, beginning in the 1950s and extending through the 1970s, declared low-rent districts to be "urban blight" and used federal urban renewal funds to bulldoze them. Residents usually lacked the skills to protest. The destruction of black neighborhoods forced residents into already overcrowded segregated neighborhoods and probably contributed to subsequent riots.

One community that did get some attention from student protestors was Manilatown in San Francisco, where, by the end of the 1970s, businesses and organizations that served 10,000 Filipinos had disappeared. Four out of five residential hotels, home to mostly Filipino workers, had been razed, and more than 4,000 low-income units had been eliminated. High-rise buildings, among them the Bank of America headquarters, replaced the community. With the help of San Francisco State College professor Jovina Navarro and Asian-American college students, Manilatown residents made it difficult to remove the International Hotel (locally known as the I-Hotel). For half a century, the I-Hotel had been home to thousands of men who held low-paying jobs. By the end of the 1960s, most of the I-Hotel's residents, some of whom had lived there for twenty years, were elderly.

With plans to demolish it and build multilevel parking, magnate Walter Shorenstein bought the I-Hotel. Professor Navarro and the students staged demonstrations. The adverse publicity led to a lease agreement between Shorenstein and the United Filipino Association (UFA). The agreement had not yet been signed when a fire broke out in the building, killing three people and giving Shorenstein an excuse to cancel the agreement and schedule demolition. The community resisted, and the matter was tied up in the courts for years.

Shorenstein sold the building to the Four Seas Investment Corporation, which applied for a demolition permit. More protests and more years in court followed. Ultimately, Superior Court Judge Ira Brown, a former San Francisco landlord, ruled in favor of the Four Seas. Human barricades blocked police from posting eviction notices in the hotel. After the eviction notices were finally posted, approximately 5,000 people linked arms around the building to prevent the evictions. On August 4, 1977, at 3 A.M., a force of 400 police in full riot gear stormed a 2,000-person barricade to evict about 50 tenants. The brutal eviction, filmed by Curtis Choy, was made into a documentary called *The Fall of the I-Hotel*.

Boston's Italian-American West End, a cohesive, working-class neighborhood, was declared a "slum," which it was not. By the time West Enders emotionally acknowledged the danger to their community, it was too late to mobilize to save their homes. As the West End's buildings were torn down between 1958 and 1960, friendships and ties forged for generations in schools, clubs, stores, and churches disappeared. In January 1962, new West End residents moved into a luxury apartment complex. In his classic 1962 book *The Urban Villagers*, sociologist Herbert Gans said, "The West End was not really a slum, and although many of its inhabitants did have problems, these did not stem from the neighborhood." The same could be said for many other neighborhoods that fell victim to urban renewal dollars.

See also Asian-American Movement; Consumer Movement
Reference Herbert Gans. *The Urban Villagers*, 1962.

Volunteers in Service to America (VISTA)

After the first waves of Peace Corps volunteers returned to the United States, activists said, "If we are going to serve the poor abroad, why not serve them at home?" In response, VISTA was formed.

VISTA had none of the incentives offered by the Peace Corps: the lure of learning a new language, serving in a new culture, and traveling. During the Vietnam War, VISTA might be good for a one-year, possibly a two-year, deferment—provided the volunteer's draft board was amenable. Nevertheless, thousands volunteered. When Lyndon Johnson met with the first batch of volunteers at the White House on December 12, 1964, he said, "Your pay will be low; the conditions of your labor will often be difficult. But you will have the satisfaction of leading a great national effort, and you will have the ultimate reward which comes to those who serve their fellow man."

A representative action by VISTA volunteers took place in the summer of 1966. Laredo's Community Action Council lacked the one-third representation of the poor required to qualify for federal funds. VISTA volunteers were given three weeks to organize thirteen neighborhoods into councils that would elect two representatives to serve on the citywide board. The newly elected representatives were determined to do their job well. VISTA volunteers urged them at the first meeting of the council to cram the courthouse with the people they represented. The people decided to have a voter registration drive that resulted in registration of 14,000 people.

VISTA volunteers in Laredo were assigned to the sponsoring agency known as the Economic Opportunities Development Corporation of Laredo and Webb Counties. The corporation had been formed by local citizens and agencies to serve as an official group empowered to request the volunteers from Washington, establish the needs the volunteers would serve, and supervise the volunteers' activities.

From the outset, interest in VISTA mounted steadily. By mid-1968, requests had come into Washington for 22,750 volunteers to work on 1,896 projects. During the same period, 306,400 people inquired about VISTA and almost 70,000 sent in final applications for training. Because of the size of its budget, VISTA could accept fewer than 14,000.

In 1971, the government agency known as ACTION took over administration of the Peace Corps and VISTA. ACTION's supervision of the Peace Corps ended in 1981, but it continued as the parent organization of VISTA until 1994, when ACTION merged with the newly created AmeriCorps. In the 1990s, volunteers continued to live and work among the poor. They served in urban and rural areas and on Indian reservations. More than half of VISTA's programs were youth-oriented and addressed such problems as child abuse, drug prevention, runaways, illiteracy, and lack of job skills.

See also Peace Corps
Reference William Crook and Ross Thomas. *Warriors for the Poor: The Story of Vista, Volunteers in Service to America,* 1969.

War Resisters League (WRL)

During the antiwar movement of the 1960s and 1970s, many young men chose to avoid being drafted for military service in Vietnam. Guidance was available to draft resisters from existing pacifist organizations, such as the War Resisters League (WRL), founded in 1943 by pacifists who resisted participation in World War II. Many of WRL's most steadfast members joined after the United States dropped atomic bombs on the Japanese cities of Hiroshima and Nagasaki at the end of World War II.

A typical long-term activist member of WRL was Ralph DiGia, who refused to be inducted into the military in 1943 and served twenty-three months in jail for his refusal. After ten years of being a volunteer, DiGia became a staff member in 1955. He asked that his income taxes not be withheld from his pay because a portion of those taxes would be used to support the military. DiGia became WRL's in-house expert on war tax resistance. The kinds of chores DiGia and other staff and volunteers performed for WRL included clerical tasks, counseling draft resisters on their options, setting up literature tables at fairs, training young activists, and marching in innumerable marches in Washington, D.C. During the early days of the Cold War, DiGia rode a bike on behalf of pacifism into Eastern Europe.

In 1995, the Smithsonian Institution in Washington, D.C., put on an exhibition of the *Enola Gay*, the plane that had dropped the atomic bomb on Hiroshima. In protest, WRL put on an alternative exhibit called "Hiroshima, Nagasaki, and 50 Years of Nuclear Terror." Inside the Smithsonian, individual volunteers, staff, and board members of WRL joined in staging acts of civil disobedience Twenty-seven were arrested. WRL also put out a special issue of their publication *Nonviolent Activist* devoted to Hiroshima and Nagasaki.

In 1995, WRL launched Youth Peace, a campaign to promote nonviolence and justice and to protest the militarization of youth. On the third Saturday in May, Youth Peace staged actions using the slogan "Stop the Cycle; Break the Rifle."

See also Antiwar Movement; Child Warriors; Rustin, Bayard
Reference Milton Melzer. *Ain't Gonna Study War No More,* 1985.

Weathermen

The Weather Underground, also known as the Weathermen, was a small group of white, upper-middle-class radicals who felt guilty because of their privileged backgrounds. They persuaded each other to take up arms and a life of crime to support the black liberation movement.

In the 1960s, Kathy Boudin, the daughter of leftist lawyer Leonard Boudin, became a member of the Students for a Democratic Society (SDS). For a time, SDS worked on behalf of an interracial movement of the poor but never developed a coherent plan. In 1965, an Old Left critic said about the efforts of SDS activists to live among the poor: "These kids will have to decide whether they want to save their own souls, or change other people's lives." For Boudin, the two tasks were inseparable. The only way she could escape a sense of shame was to avoid privileges that came with her education and social class. Boudin joined the Weathermen faction of SDS in 1969. The Weathermen believed blacks would form the vanguard of a coming revolution.

In 1969, Boudin helped organize the Weathermen's October 8–11 National Action, known as "Four Days of Rage," a series of violent street protests in Chicago. In concept, the Days of Rage started out as an effort to re-create the disorder that dominated Chicago during the 1968 Democratic National Convention. Alarming rumors circulated out of the Weathermen's national office. There was talk of guerrilla warfare and an all-out assault on the city. As the summer wore on, efforts to recruit white, working-class young people to participate bore little fruit. On the first day of the four-day action, instead of 15,000 to 20,000 participants, just 200 hard-core Weathermen appeared. Twelve women, including Boudin, were arrested and released on bail. They did not appear for trial on March 16, 1970.

Ten days before their arrest, Boudin and others had been at a townhouse owned by member Cathy Wilkerson's father when bombs being made by member Terry Robbins had exploded. Three Weathermen died in the explosion. Most of the leaders went underground.

By 1971, the Weathermen consisted of a small group of radicals in hiding and a larger group operating in the open and providing support to those underground. Those aboveground were subjected to constant harassment by the Federal Bureau of Investigation (FBI) in its search for those still underground. Those underground seemed, to some, "to be living in the country growing organic vegetables and sewing patches on dungarees." In 1974, the government dropped two remaining indictments against the Weathermen. Nevertheless, a handful remained underground because they "believed in the necessity of building an underground."

Boudin was never a member of the ruling Weathermen's Central Committee (CC) made up of Bernadine Dohrn, Eleanor Raskin, Bill Ayers, and Jeff Jones. When the Central Committee was purged from the Weather Underground in 1976, Boudin was tainted by her relationship with them. The organization collapsed after the purge, and Boudin turned for support to hard-liners, who were mostly in jail by November 1977. The split in ideology helps explain what happened later to Boudin.

After the war in Vietnam was over, Jones and Ayers concluded that the Weather Underground

should surface and take a place of respect and influence on the Left by replacing its armed propaganda with an agenda of working-class values. They published a book and a magazine and produced a movie called *Underground,* in which Jones, Ayers, Dohrn, Wilkerson, and Boudin appeared to sanitize the public image of the Weathermen and return the group to public life. Boudin was a reluctant participant. The film was denounced by hard-liners as white-male supremacist and racist. The denunciation was engineered by Clayton Van Lydegraf, an ex-communist who had been trying to seize control for years. He advocated a return to armed struggle by bombing government buildings and annihilating police. Unfortunately for Van Lydegraf, his roommate was an FBI undercover agent.

In June 1979, Kathy Boudin, an employee of the Econo-Car rental company, rented a 1979 Ford Fairmont from the company's lot at New York City's LaGuardia Airport to members of a radical group known as the Family. The car was stolen and subsequently used in the robbery of two armored car guards. The Family was made up of disaffected radicals from the Black Panthers and the Weathermen. Under the guise of aiding blacks, the Family degenerated into bank robbers and murderers.

On October 20, 1981, Boudin was arrested following an armed robbery of a Brink's truck. During the botched robbery, a Brink's guard and two Nyack, New York, police officers were killed. Boudin had participated in the robbery as a member of a combined group of Weathermen and Black Panthers. The defense of Boudin for the Brink's robbery and murder financially and emotionally exhausted her attorney father, who was in ill health. Ultimately, he accepted a plea bargain. When Boudin pleaded guilty on April 26, 1984, she said, "I want my motivations understood. I was there out of a commitment to the black liberation struggle and its underground movement. I am a white woman who does not want the crimes committed against black people carried out in my name."

The author of *The Big Dance* summed up his opinion of the Family by saying, "The story as I see it is that a small band of fugitives banded together for a variety of purposes, and whose motives were hopelessly mixed. Because so many individuals were involved and their motivations and actions were so various, the only sweeping judgment that can be made is the obvious one: They committed crimes which cost three men their lives."

See also Old Left and New Left
Reference John Castellucci. *The Big Dance: The Untold Story of Kathy Boudin and the Terrorist Family That Committed the Brink's Robbery Murders,* 1986.

Women's Movement

Also known as the feminist movement and the women's liberation movement ("Women's Lib"), the women's movement that began in the 1960s was a reawakening of a nineteenth-century movement that lasted from 1848 until 1920, when women became eligible to vote across the nation. The seventy years of labor by nineteenth-century women made modern feminism possible.

In the village of Seneca Falls, New York, in 1848, Elizabeth Cady Stanton, age thirty-two, made her first public speech. She declared that the time had come for the "question of women's wrongs to be laid before the public." Only women could do this work, in Stanton's opinion, because only they knew the height, depth, length, and breadth of their degradation. The campaign on behalf of women's rights led by Stanton and her colleague, Susan B. Anthony, became a target of hostility and ridicule expressed by journalists, politicians, and clergy. The women persisted in holding conferences, giving speeches, passing out petitions, and traveling byroads throughout the country to carry their message. In 1850, two years after the Seneca Falls meeting, a national women's conference was held. At the Tenth Annual Women's Rights Convention held in New York City, Elizabeth Cady Stanton shocked the audience by recommending liberalized divorce laws. Through the remainder of their lives, Stanton and Anthony kept up a grueling schedule on behalf of women's rights.

By the time each pioneer died shortly after the turn of the century, women's property and legal rights had expanded, employment opportunities were more plentiful, and women had increased access to higher education. After the movement achieved women's suffrage in 1920, it lost momentum. Although some of women's rights diminished or disappeared, most gains did not, and these provided a base in the 1960s when the movement reawakened.

The first stirrings of a revived movement began following World War II. Various events contributed.

1. The United Nations, in its 1945 charter, affirmed "equal rights for women" and a few years later established the UN Commission on the Status of Women.
2. In several countries, women gained the right to vote.
3. Simone de Beauvoir's book, *The Second Sex*, was published in French in 1949 and in English in 1953. She proposed that women were forced to live in a world made up of institutions and ideas constructed by men. De Beauvoir's book was widely discussed by women around the world.
4. In honor of Eleanor Roosevelt, in 1962, President John F. Kennedy created a National Commission on the Status of Women.
5. Betty Friedan's book, *The Feminine Mystique*, published in 1963, although focusing on the discontent of middle-aged, middle-class white women, provoked discussion among women of all ages.
6. In 1966, the National Organization for Women (NOW) was formed.

For women who participated in the civil rights and the antiwar movements, a more direct influence came from their treatment by male colleagues. The avowed philosophy of such movements was based on principles of equality, especially among groups associated with the New Left and socialism/Marxism. After being relegated by men to typing, making coffee, and providing sex, the women broke away and formed their own groups to work on behalf of women's

Bella Abzug (second from left; continuing from left to right), Gloria Steinem, Dick Gregory, Betty Friedan, and others lead a march in support of the Equal Rights Amendment, July 9, 1978.

rights. Using techniques learned in the other movements, these leftist, socialist women were more radical in confrontations with male-dominated organizations than groups like NOW.

The divergence of the philosophy and tactics of the more radical groups from the more traditional-style organizations like NOW persisted for several years. NOW, structured with a hierarchy and made up mostly of business and professional women, campaigned for equality with men in employment, education, law, and politics. The young movement veterans, many of whom were college students or college dropouts, were reluctant to have formal structures that required designated leaders. They preferred "zap" actions to discussions and set out to liberate women from sex-role stereotypes and sexist limitations.

One of the radicals' media-attracting events took place in the fall of 1968, when approximately 200 demonstrators appeared at the annual Miss America pageant in Atlantic City, New Jersey. The

women carried picket signs with messages such as "Women are people, not livestock" and "Can makeup cover the wounds of our oppression?" During the protest, women were invited to toss "objects of female torture, such as hair curlers, bras, and high heels," into a "freedom trash can." Unfortunately, someone in the media created the impression that the protesters planned to burn bras in the trash barrel and labeled them "bra burners," an epithet that was used for years by opponents to ridicule all feminists.

The Atlantic City protest was organized by the New York Radical Women, one of the earliest of the radical women's groups, which was formed in 1967 by Pam Allen and Shulamith Firestone. Political differences within the group prompted members to form or join other radical feminist groups, among them Redstockings, WITCH, The Feminists, and New York Radical Feminists. From the New York collection of creative radical feminists emerged key ideas and a shorthand vocabulary that was lasting: "sisterhood is powerful"; "the personal is political"; and "consciousness raising."

The Redstockings, founded in 1969 by Shulamith Firestone and Ellen Willis, chose its name to call attention to the derogatory term "bluestocking," which was applied to highly intelligent women. Redstockings was committed to both consciousness raising and political action. One of the group's first actions was to interrupt a New York state legislative committee hearing on abortion reform. A protester confronted the committee with the question, "Why are fourteen men and only one woman on your list of speakers and she's a nun?" The confrontation with the legislature was followed by an "abortion speak-out" in the basement of a church. Women told the audience of their own harrowing experiences in obtaining an illegal abortion. In the audience was Gloria Steinem, a freelance reporter, who became instantly committed to the cause and one of the women's movement's best-known speakers.

The vitality and creativity of the radical groups gave feminism a style and brought attention to the movement. By contrast, they made the more conservative groups like NOW seem less threatening to traditional male customs. Eventually the divergent paths converged and lent strength to the movement.

From the vantage point of the 1990s, it is possible to see the many gains women have made. Professional schools such as medical, veterinary, and law schools that typically admitted no more than one or two women—if any—now have female enrollments of 50 percent or more. Laws have made it easier for a woman to have a child without losing her job. She can also choose not to have a child. Access to birth control information is easier to obtain and abortion is legal. The attitude of police toward women has changed—in part because there are women within their ranks. Where once police were typically skeptical when women reported rapes, many departments have rape units staffed by officers trained to treat victims with sensitivity. Some police departments have also changed their views about domestic violence. They are much more likely to arrest the abuser than they once were. Some departments have concluded that domestic violence is an area of crime in which they can make a difference by devoting time and resources to prevention.

Gains in the area of employment have been mixed. Many more women are in the workplace and they have seen some gains in income. Nevertheless, compared with men, women's incomes still lag behind. Women executives and academics often bump against a "glass ceiling," a level in their organization's hierarchy above which they are not allowed to rise. Day care for children remains a major stumbling block and women are still the parent most likely to take time off from work when the children are sick. The need for improvement continues to unite women.

See also Beauvoir, Simone de; Black Feminist Organizations; Feminist Organizations; Friedan, Betty; Hill, Anita; Steinem, Gloria
References Caroline Bird with Sara Welles Briller. *Born Female: The High Cost of Keeping Women Down,* 1973; Redstockings. *Feminist Revolution,* 1975; Miriam Schneir. *Feminism in Our Time,* 1994.

Women's Sex Workers Project

To stay alive, young Asian women immigrants in the United States with limited language and job skills often resort to prostitution. The residents of Asian communities in the United States typically criticize and shun prostitutes; nevertheless, Asian men use their services.

The summer 1996 issue of the newsletter of the Committee against Anti-Asian Violence (CAAV) reported the formation of the Women Workers' Project for Asian Sex Workers. The goal of the project was to organize women working in prostitution and secure rights from massage parlor and brothel owners in exchange for their labor. The rights the project sought were safer working conditions, health care in the form of physical examinations and treatment for job-related illness, and fair wages. Sex workers suffer from many work-related health problems that directly result from unsanitary, unsafe, often terrifying working conditions: anxiety related to their often illegal immigration status, depression as a consequence of the stigma attached to their work, and on-the-job injuries inflicted by violent customers.

Sex industries routinely spring up around military bases. The vast number of Asian women in America's sex industry can be linked to America's longtime presence in Asian countries, among them Korea, Thailand, the Philippines, and Vietnam. Many Asian women who make their living in prostitution came to the United States as the wives of American soldiers. Abandoned or forced to flee from violent husbands, they typically have no job skills and fear deportation. They end up working in massage parlors or brothels. Organized crime is another channel that forces Asian women into sex work. The false promise of a job lures poor women into immigrating. When they arrive in the new country, they are forced into prostitution. Some criminals don't even bother with promises but simply kidnap the women. Violence or a lack of options keeps them enslaved in the new country. Sweatshops, the only other work choice open to many unskilled Asian women, are not much better. A woman may work a seventy-two-hour week for less than $2. If she protests the working conditions, she loses her job. If her boss fails to pay her, she has no recourse. Nor does she have anywhere to turn if her boss physically or verbally harasses or assaults her.

CAAV used a variety of outreach methods to contact the young Asian women it hoped to organize. Among other things, it made regular visits to massage parlors and conducted workshops for women who had been arrested. CAAV's project worked in conjunction with the Foundation for Research in Sexually Transmitted Diseases (FROST'D). FROST'D ran several HIV/AIDS prevention programs in New York, which provided a free needle exchange; counseling; testing for hepatitis B, syphilis, and pregnancy; referrals to shelters, drug programs, and health care; and food, clothing, and sleeping bags. FROST'D also operated a mobile outreach project for street-based sex workers in New York City.

CAAV's program was not the only such organization. The North American Task Force on Prostitution (NTFP) is a network of sex workers' rights organizations in the United States and Canada and is affiliated with the International Network of Sex Workers. NTFP's goals include repeal of laws that prohibit prostitution or that force prostitutes to register and be tested regularly for sexually transmitted diseases. It also wants U.S. immigration restrictions against sex workers eliminated. NTFP's position is that a better way to regulate prostitution is to enforce occupational safety and health regulations. Its members also believe that criminal laws against rape, physical assault, kidnapping, fraud, extortion, and child labor should be enforced.

See also Sweatshops
Reference David Kaplan and Alec Dubro. *Yakuza: The Explosive Account of Japan's Criminal Underworld,* 1986.

Wounded Knee (February 28–May 8, 1973)

At the request of Oglala Sioux traditionalists, the American Indian Movement (AIM) took sides in a local dispute between the traditionalists and the Pine Ridge Reservation chairman, Richard Wilson. The traditionalists claimed that Wilson, backed by authoritarian tribal police and the Bureau of Indian Affairs (BIA), was denying them a voice in tribal government.

About 300 armed members of AIM occupied the small village of Wounded Knee, South Dakota, where, in 1890, the U.S. Seventh Cavalry had massacred about 350 (estimates of the number vary widely) Sioux, most of whom were women and children. The militants took eleven hostages, ransacked the trading post, and barricaded the church. Journalists rushed to the scene. AIM announced to reporters that it wanted an investigation of treaties between Indians and the federal government that had been broken; improvement of living conditions on the reservations; and Indian sovereignty over Indian affairs, by which it meant Indian tribes should be defined as independent nations.

When federal marshals tried to approach AIM members while they were talking to reporters, the marshals were fired upon. Russell Means declared: "We've got the whole Wounded Knee Valley

An American Indian Movement (AIM) poster, 1973.

and we definitely are going to hold it until death do us part." Means and Dennis Banks called for the resignation of Richard Wilson, whom they characterized as a puppet of the BIA and charged with corruption. Wilson, in turn, charged AIM members were outsiders interfering in local tribal affairs. Negotiations broke down with the government as the feud between the Indian factions increased. Gunfire on both sides went on sporadically until the seventh week, when the militants fired on a helicopter, wounding a federal agent. After more gunfire, a truce was called, and the government agreed to supply the militants with food and medicine. The government's offer enraged Wilson, who gathered together a group of Oglala and tried to block the road to prevent delivery.

AIM members began to slip away, including Dennis Banks, who went on a speaking tour, and Russell Means, who was arrested in Los Angeles. The occupation formally ended May 8, 1973. The Indians' surrender was in exchange for a promise of a White House investigation of their complaints. Although the hearings were held, Indians saw little improvement in their everyday lives. Wounded Knee faded away.

On June 26, 1975, there was a shoot-out at the Pine Ridge Reservation in South Dakota. Versions of the events differ depending on assessments of who is to blame. The FBI claims that two agents pursued a suspicious vehicle onto the reservation based on a belief that a fugitive was a passenger in the car. The occupants of the car being pursued opened fire when the agents stopped their car in a remote pasture, and Indians from a nearby American Indian Movement camp joined in the gunfire. The wounded officers were shot in the head at close range.

The Indians claimed the agents came on the reservation firing, as they had done often in the past. The Indians fired in self-defense, and one was killed. Two Indians were acquitted by a jury and the case for a third was dropped for lack of evidence. Leonard Peltier was tried and found guilty. Prior to sentencing, Peltier said to the judge, "You are a high-ranking member of the white racist American establishment which has consistently said, 'Oh God we tried,' while they went about the business of murdering my people and attempting to destroy our culture."

An ongoing Leonard Peltier defense committee has worked since his imprisonment to win his release. During the 1980s, Peltier's imprisonment served as a central issue around which to organize and lobby for other issues. Parole was denied at a May 4, 1998, hearing. The next hearing will be in 2008. Despite widespread support for Peltier's request for clemency, President Bill Clinton seemed disinclined to grant it.

See also Banks, Dennis; Bellecourt Brothers, Vernon and Clyde; Means, Russell

References Terry Anderson. *The Movement and the Sixties: Protest in America from Greensboro to Wounded Knee,* 1995; Peter Nabokov, ed. *Native American Testimony: A Chronicle of Indian-White Relations from Prophecy to the Present, 1492–1992,* 1991.

Year of the Woman (1992)

The revival of the women's movement in the 1960s inspired many women to run for office. The number of women holding local political offices rose at a modest pace, but on a national level the pace was much slower. The 1992 election brought dramatic change, caused for the most part by the Senate's confirmation hearings for Clarence Thomas. President George Bush nominated Appeals Court Judge Thomas to replace Justice Thurgood Marshall on the Supreme Court. Like Marshall, Thomas was black, the only characteristic the two men had in common. A conservative, Thomas's views on social issues were polar opposites of those held by Thurgood Marshall, who was the first black Supreme Court justice.

Despite public criticism of Thomas's limited experience on the bench and his antiabortion and anti–affirmative action viewpoints, his confirmation seemed assured. Then Anita Hill, a black law professor, came forward to charge Thomas with making unwelcome sexual advances when she worked for him in the early 1980s. National television carried Hill's testimony around the country and around the world. The Senate Judiciary Committee's panel of fourteen white, male senators listened impassively while Hill described graphic incidents of sexual harassment. Republican committee members cross-examined the professor rigorously, their skepticism evident. Democratic committee members said little. Pennsylvania Republican senator Arlen Specter declared one of Hill's statements to be "flat-out perjury." Viewers responded to the televised hearings with an avalanche of letters and phone calls. Opinions were divided, but the majority favored Hill. Nevertheless, Thomas was appointed by a slim margin, 52 in favor and 48 against, to a lifetime seat on the Supreme Court.

Discussions about the hearings and about the topic of sexual harassment continued for weeks on radio and television talk shows and in the newspapers. Personal reactions to the hearings prodded women into running for elective office in 1992. Outraged at the Senate's handling of the Thomas nomination, Patty Murray, in Washing-

ton state, decided to run against Senator Brock Adams in the Democratic primary. After Adam decided to retire, Murray defeated Representative Don Bonker in the primary. Although Murray had gained plenty of political experience on the local level, her Republican opponent called her a political neophyte. Murray put the perception of her as an outsider to use. As her campaign slogan, she adopted a criticism once made of her by a state lawmaker. He called her "a mom in tennis shoes." She won a seat in the Senate with 55 percent of the vote.

In Chicago, Carol Moseley Braun, a lawyer, perceived the Senate Judiciary Committee's insensitive handling of Hill as related to her being a woman. Her anger pushed her into a race against her fellow Democrat, Illinois senator Alan Dixon, who had voted to confirm Thomas's appointment. Moseley Braun defeated Dixon and another male candidate in the primary in an astonishing political upset and went on to win the general election and become the first black woman elected to the U.S. Senate.

Both of California's Senate seats were at stake in 1992. California Democratic senator Alan Cranston's six-year term was up, and Republican Pete Wilson had resigned after being elected governor of California in 1990. Governor Wilson appointed fellow Republican John Seymour to fill his own vacant seat until the general election in 1992.

Dianne Feinstein, who had narrowly lost to Wilson in the 1990 race for governor, ran against Seymour in the 1992 election. Feinstein had a long career in politics on a local level. First elected in 1969, she was regularly reelected to the San Francisco Board of Supervisors. Feinstein gained national attention in November 1978. She was serving her third term as board president when fellow supervisor Dan White killed Mayor George Moscone and Supervisor Harvey Milk. As board president, Feinstein inherited the office of the dead mayor, which she successfully held until 1989. In 1992, she won a seat in the U.S. Senate.

Barbara Boxer was already serving in Congress during the Thomas confirmation hearing. In the company of seven other women representatives from the House, Representative Boxer attempted to enter the U.S. Senate. The seven women were told by the Senate gatekeeper that no "strangers" could enter the Senate chambers. The rebuff convinced Boxer, who had served in the U.S. House of Representatives since 1983, that she should run for the Senate. She won the election, and when the 1992 race was over, California had two women senators.

The Senate Judiciary Committee, one of the most important committees in the Senate, was a white, male bastion. Chastened by the reaction to their treatment of Hill, the committee appointed freshman senators Dianne Feinstein and Carol Moseley Braun as members.

See also Hill, Anita
References Anita Hill. *Speaking Truth to Power,* 1997; Isobel Morin. *Women of the U.S. Congress,* 1994.

Yippies

According to Abbie Hoffman, the name "Yippie" was created in a New York City Lower East Side apartment in January 1968, when Paul Krassner, suffering from an acid hangover, staggered around asking, "Why? Why? Why?" He answered himself. "When you make the peace sign of the V the extension of your arms makes it a Y." Abbie Hoffman answered. "I, EYE! EYE! EYE! I love you very much." Jerry Rubin added, "PEE-PEE. You need a little pee-pee in every movement." Nancy

Kurshan proclaimed, "E is for everybody, energy." The group shouted "Yippie!"

The group decided that the press had created the term "hippie" and they had a right to coin "yippie," meaning a political hippie—a flower child who had been busted—a blending of pot and politics. In New York during March, when a few thousand yippies appeared at Grand Central Station to hold the first yip-in (blowing bubbles, singing, dancing, popping balloons, and removing the hands of a giant clock), the police charged into the crowd swinging their clubs. Throughout the whole spring, yippies were the target of the police and critical media articles that declared the movement had gone sour—the dark side of the hippie moon.

The yippies didn't mind. They reveled in the attention. To encourage young people to come to Chicago for the 1968 Democratic National Convention, they invented news. Among the made-up stories was a claim that yippie potheads had been growing weed in vacant lots for a giant August smoke-in. Another was that yippie men were getting in shape to seduce female Humphrey delegates and that luscious yippie females would pose as hookers and kidnap male delegates. Yippie cars, painted yellow, would pose as cabs and take delegates to Wisconsin. Yippies would put LSD (lysergic acid diethylamide) in Chicago's water supply and give snake-dancing lessons. Free cookies would be liberated from Nabisco's Chicago office and distributed. One hundred thousand yippies would float nude in Lake Michigan to protest the war. Those in authority did not see the absurdity of the stories. Mayor Richard Daley ordered his plainclothes police to infiltrate the movement organizations, and the federal government placed 1,000 agents in the city. The governor ordered troops to protect the water supply.

Most of the Chicago activist groups were not interested in participating with the yippies. Some saw them as "apolitical, irrational freaks" or "provocative New York radicals on an ego trip." Nevertheless, many activists and activist organizations from elsewhere began applying for various city permits. City officials stalled for weeks. Daley refused everything they asked. Despite being told they were not wanted, youth arrived in the summer of 1968 and pitched camp in Lincoln Park. There was little peace the entire week, either in the convention hall or outside in the streets.

Inside the hall, forces supporting Hubert Humphrey, who accepted Lyndon Johnson's policy of keeping U.S. troops in Vietnam, argued with forces supporting Eugene McCarthy, who called for their withdrawal and a halt to the bombing of North Vietnam. Unfortunately for the peace delegates, a few days earlier, the Soviet Union had invaded Czechoslovakia to crush a reformist government. Although the invasion ensured the nomination of Hubert Humphrey, the peace delegates felt they had a right to be heard. Nevertheless, the other delegates defeated the peace platform. The convention floor became rowdy as delegates continued to argue. A fistfight broke out in the Georgia delegation, and tempers soared as liberals and conservatives shouted at each other and threw ice. Additional scuffles broke out. When Columbia Broadcasting System (CBS) reporter Dan Rather rushed to the floor, policemen knocked him down.

Outside in the city, activists, hippies, yippies, and street people in Lincoln Park were ordered to leave by 11:00 P.M. Estimates of the number of people involved ranged from "about a thousand," to "probably five thousand," to "never more than ten thousand." When the crowd did not leave, the police launched tear gas. While chasing the activists, the police selectively pursued news photographers with cameras. The officers had removed their badges, nameplates, and unit patches to become a mob of unidentifiable club swingers. They chased people through the streets of Old Town, clubbing virtually anyone in the area. The next day, 2,000 young people gathered in both Lincoln and Grant Parks. At midnight, the police again launched tear gas and attacked.

The last siege took place on the day of Humphrey's nomination. The antiwar forces announced they would gather at Grant Park and march to the Amphitheatre, where the convention was being held. Daley refused a parade permit. About 10,000 people assembled for the march. They were joined by the police and the Illinois National Guard. During speeches at the park, a group of young men, including an undercover agent, took down the U.S. flag and replaced it with a red T-shirt. The police charged, batons swinging. At twilight, protestors assembled for the march to the Amphitheatre where the convention was being held. The Amphitheatre was across the street from the Conrad Hilton where the candidates were housed. Hotel and building lights illuminated the sky as television cameras recorded the events. Chanting, the marchers headed down Michigan Avenue. They approached the police line and stopped. A few began taunting the police. The police exploded into the crowd while an estimated 90 million viewers watched.

Singling out members of the media had an effect. For the first time, reports by the moderate establishment press agreed with those of underground reporters. National Broadcasting Company (NBC) news commentator Chet Huntley declared, "Chicago police are going out of their way to injure newsmen, and prevent them from filming or gathering information about what's going on."

In Chicago, the war between the viewpoints of the left and right had been declared. The silent majority, convinced the Democrats were out of control, elected Richard Nixon as president. Repressive governmental measures became commonplace. The House Un-American Activities Committee subpoenaed Tom Hayden, David Dellinger, and Rennie Davis in an effort to find evidence that communists helped plan the protest in Chicago. Federal Bureau of Investigation (FBI) director J. Edgar Hoover ordered his field agents to use all their resources to publicize the depraved nature and moral looseness of the left and "to destroy this insidious movement." Early in 1969, the new Nixon administration ordered agents to arrest the "Chicago Eight," the so-called leaders of the protests at the Democratic National Convention—Dave Dellinger, Tom Hayden, Rennie Davis, Abbie Hoffman, Jerry Rubin, Lee Weiner, John Froines, and Bobby Seale. The government kept the activists in and out of court until 1973, arresting them on questionable charges.

See also Daley, Richard; Hippies; Hoffman, Abbie; McCarthy, Eugene

Reference Terry Anderson. *The Movement and the Sixties: Protest in America from Greensboro to Wounded Knee,* 1995.

Young, Andrew (b. 1932)

Civil rights activist Andrew Young was born in New Orleans, Louisiana. He was educated at Dillard University in New Orleans, Howard University in Washington, D.C., and Hartford Theological Seminary in Connecticut. In 1957, Young joined the executive staff of the Youth Division of the National Council of Churches of Christ USA, where he remained until 1961, when he was asked to join the staff of the Highlander Folk School in Tennessee to run its leadership training program. To prepare them to implement a widespread voter registration drive, the Highlander program trained adults to read and write. Tennessee state officials brought charges of bootlegging against the school to block the Highlander's education efforts in the South. The state forced the school to close, and Young was out of a job before he even left New York.

The activist convinced the United Church to take over as a sponsor of the training program at an alternate site with Young as coordinator. The source of funding, the Field Foundation, agreed to the new arrangement and placed the administrative offices in the Reverend Martin Luther King, Jr.'s Southern Christian Leadership Conference (SCLC). From 1961 to 1966, more than 6,000 people were trained at the citizenship programs. Young relinquished leadership of the operation to become the executive vice president of the SCLC from 1967 to 1970, when he resigned to run for Atlanta's Fifth Congressional District and lost. In 1972 Young became the first black U.S. representative from Georgia since Reconstruction.

The Reverend Ralph Abernathy (center) and the Reverend Andrew Young (right) announced at a press conference in Los Angeles the plans to establish a "Poor People's Embassy" in Washington, D.C., 1968.

In 1977, President Jimmy Carter appointed Young as ambassador to the United Nations, a post he held until 1979. Young was elected mayor of Atlanta twice. He ran in the Democratic primary for governor of Alabama in 1990 and lost. In his 1996 book *An Easy Burden,* Young traced the inner workings of the civil rights movement.

See also Abernathy, Reverend Ralph; Horton, Myles; King, Reverend Martin Luther, Jr.; Southern Christian Leadership Conference

References Ralph Abernathy. *And the Walls Came Tumbling Down,* 1989; Andrew Young. *An Easy Burden: The Civil Rights Movement and the Transformation of America,* 1996.

Youth Rebellion Movies

In some cultures, the language has no word for teenager, and childhood extends from infancy through about age 6. Then children begin to work and are regarded as small adults. In many Western countries, in contrast, there is a period of transition between childhood and adulthood that begins about age 12 and ends about age 20. This transition period, referred to as adolescence or the teenage years, is perceived to be a period of rebellion when a young person makes a break with parental attitudes and values.

Prior to the 1950s, Hollywood films about young people depicted them in two ways. Youths were either delinquents from inner-city slums, or they were teenagers from happy homes whose most serious problem was to find a way to put on a musical. Most movies about juvenile delinquents portrayed them as a younger version of hardened gangsters. The story line usually blamed their antisocial behavior on weak authority figures, mostly parents, and offered as a solution a strong parent substitute, typically a judge or police officer and on occasion a priest.

The juvenile delinquency films of the 1930s hinted at the potential emergence of a youth culture. Hard economic times had left many young people on their own, and they turned to each other for support and friendship. During the 1940s, young people filled jobs left vacant by adult males who had been sent overseas to fight in World War II. With money to buy things they liked and without adult responsibilities, they developed a youth culture with distinctive customs, clothes, and opinions. Although dungarees (blue jeans) had been worn by college girls in the 1940s, they became standard wear for teenagers in the 1950s and were often worn with leather jackets.

Many social factors came together to foster a sense of alienation among young people. After World War II ended, young people and women lost their jobs to returning servicemen. The GI Bill provided returning servicemen with money to go to college. For several years, they invaded the college domain normally reserved for the young. Many veterans also took advantage of Veterans Housing Administration loans to move their families outside city limits and buy or build homes. The communities that sprang up—suburbs—tended to be populated with people who were similar in taste, customs, and income. The excitement and diversity of life in the city were lost. The suburbs were bland and typically lacked recreational facilities.

Not only did the post–World War II generation flee the cities, but also they produced a large number of babies from 1946 to 1964. As the "baby boom" babies grew up, they had many competitors for space, attention, and resources in the suburbs. By 1960, the first wave of boomers were in their teens and feeling alienated. A portent of a widespread sense of alienation among the young was the 1954 movie called *The Wild One,* starring Marlon Brando as the leader of a motorcycle gang. The movie suggested that young people were shut off from the rest of society. Both sides of the equation persisted in an almost willful lack of understanding of and appreciation for one another because to yield would have meant a loss of face. The director of *The Wild One* wanted young audiences to identify with the characters. They obviously identified with the outward appearance of rebellion. Motorcycles and fast cars became permanent symbols of youth culture.

Encouraged by *The Wild One*'s success, Hollywood seized the opportunity to mass-produce "teen flicks" about youth in rebellion. Most were badly done and disappeared quickly. The popularity of motorcycles among the young encouraged small studios to make dozens of biker movies every year. Violent stories, with no real message, they were hits at weekend drive-in movie theaters. An interruption in the chain of bad movies came when *Rebel without a Cause* was released in 1955. Audiences were astonished to find that the violent young rebels in the movie lived in middle-class homes—like those that had mushroomed in the suburbs. The role of Jim Stark, the major character, played by James Dean, made Dean a folk hero to the young. In addition, Dean's offscreen behavior contributed to his mythic rebel status. On September 30, 1955, Dean, with a friend, was on his way to an auto race in his Porsche Spider. Despite having received a speeding ticket earlier in the trip, Dean was traveling at 85 miles per hour. The driver of a car coming in the opposite direction failed to see him and tried to turn left. Dean's car slammed into the car turning left, and Dean died of a broken neck.

Another movie released in 1955, *Blackboard Jungle,* also had an enormous impact. Based on a book of the same name, it was the first movie to use a rock and roll song on the soundtrack. The movie's popularity increased rock and roll's audience. In the movie, a young, idealistic teacher, Richard Dadier, played by Glenn Ford, had just finished college and found a job in a school in which the students were poor and ethnic groups did not get along. An attempt to teach a class on racism created turmoil and earned Richard ridicule from both the students and the teachers. The movie blamed the whole society, not just the teachers, who were tired and discouraged by the overwhelming nature of the problems they faced each day.

Several later movies about youth in rebellion were particularly notable. The message of *The Young Stranger* (1957), directed by John Franken-

heimer, was that understanding between parents and teenagers must go in both directions. In *The Young Savages* (1961), Frankenheimer portrayed gangs in the 1950s. *Alice's Restaurant* (1969), based on a hit song by folksinger Arlo Guthrie, echoed the social movements going on outside the movies. It focused on resistance to the draft. Songwriters like Arlo Guthrie and Bob Dylan spread their antiwar sentiments via their songs, and the songs became rallying cries for the movement. *Easy Rider* (1969) strove to express the feelings of the youth culture. The lead characters, played by Peter Fonda and Dennis Hopper, viewed their motorcycles as symbols of individuality and freedom. The theme of the movie expressed adults' hatred for youth culture and youth's abandonment of any effort to fit into society.

The huge success of *Blackboard Jungle* encouraged filmmakers to offer other movies of youth rebellion in schools. *To Sir, with Love* (1967) starred Sidney Poitier as a teacher in a working-class London school. The movie addressed many of the issues dealt with in *Blackboard Jungle. My Bodyguard* (1980) and *Pump Up the Volume* (1990) explored teen suicide and peer pressure.

Teen movies helped to solidify the existence of a teenage culture. They also convinced teachers and parents that there was a youth culture, thus contributing to the continuance of that culture. The youth culture has become a major market for the producers of clothing, books, and entertainment.

See also Antiwar Movement; Guthrie, Arlo; Presley, Elvis; Rock and Roll
References David Considine. *The Cinema of Adolescence,* 1985; Marc Perlman. *Youth Rebellion Movies,* 1993.

Yuppies
See Baby Boomers

Abernathy, Ralph. *And the Walls Came Tumbling Down: An Autobiography*. New York: Harper and Row, 1989.

Ackerman, Peter, and Christopher Kruegler. *Strategic Nonviolent Conflict: The Dynamics of People Power in the Twentieth Century*. Westport, CT: Greenwood, 1993.

Adams, Frank, with Myles Horton. *Unearthing Seeds of Fire: The Idea of the Highlander*. Winston-Salem, NC: John Blair, 1975.

Alcorn, Randy. *ProLife Answers to ProChoice Arguments*. Sisters, OR: Multnomah Books, 1992.

Alexander, Shana. *Anyone's Daughter*. New York: Viking Press, 1979.

Alinsky, Saul. *Reveille for Radicals*. Chicago: University of Chicago Press, 1947.

———. *Rules for Radicals*. New York: Vintage Books, 1989.

Allen, Zita. *Black Women Leaders of the Civil Rights Movement*. New York: Franklin Watts, 1996.

Amado, Ana. "Women's Rights—No Buts about It." *UNESCO Sources,* November 1995.

American Psychiatric Association. *Diagnostic and Statistic Manual of Mental Disorders: DSM IV,* 4th ed. Washington, DC: American Psychiatric Association, 1994.

Anderson, Christopher. *Citizen Jane: The Turbulent Life of Jane Fonda*. New York: Henry Holt, 1990.

Anderson, Jervis. *Bayard Rustin: Troubles I've Seen: A Biography*. New York: HarperCollins, 1997.

Anderson, Terry. *The Movement and the Sixties: Protest in America from Greensboro to Wounded Knee*. New York: Oxford University Press, 1995.

Anderson, Walt, ed. *The Age of Protest*. Pacific Palisades, CA: Goodyear Publishing, 1969.

Antler, Joyce. *The Journey Home: Jewish Women and the American Century*. New York: Free Press, 1997.

Apple, R. W., Jr. "Ardor and Ambiguity." *New York Times,* October 17, 1995.

Asbell, Bernard. *The Pill: A Biography of the Drug That Changed the World*. New York: Random House, 1995.

Ash, Roberta. *Social Movements in America*. Chicago: Markham, 1972.

Ashby, LeRoy, and Bruce Stave. *The Discontented Society: Interpretations in Twentieth Century Protest*. Chicago: Rand McNally, 1972.

Associated Press. "Landmines Go About Their Sad Business." *Boston Globe,* October 12, 1997.

Auchincloss, Kenneth. "The Fire Next Time." *Newsweek,* September 2, 1996.

Bibliography

Baez, Joan. *And a Voice to Sing With*. New York: Summit Books, 1987.

Baraka, Imamu Amiri. *Eulogies.* New York: Marsilio Publishers, 1996.

Barkun, Michael. *Religion and the Racist Right: Origins of the Christian Identity Movement.* Chapel Hill: University of North Carolina, 1994.

Bates, Daisy. *The Long Shadow of Little Rock: A Memoir.* New York: David McKay, 1962.

Beauvoir, Simone de. *The Second Sex*. New York: Alfred A. Knopf, 1953; reprint, New York: Vintage Books, 1989.

Belcher, John, and Frederick DiBlasio. *Helping the Homeless: Where Do We Go from Here?* New York: Free Press, 1990.

Bender, David L. *The Vietnam War: Opposing Viewpoints*. San Diego: Greenhaven Press, 1990.

Bennett, Lerone. *What Manner of Man*. New York: Harper, 1964.

Berkmoes, Ryan Ver. "To Make a Difference: Physicians for Human Rights Monitor Medical Effects of Human Rights Abuse Worldwide." *American Medical News* (American Medical Association), May 26, 1989.

Berryman, Phillip. *Liberation Theology: Essential Facts about the Revolutionary Movement in Latin America and Beyond*. New York: Pantheon Books, 1987.

Bird, Caroline, with Sara Welles Briller. *Born Female: The High Cost of Keeping Women Down,* revised edition. New York: David McKay, 1968.

Blanchard, Dallas. *The Anti-Abortion Movement and the Rise of the Religious Right: From Polite to Fiery Protest.* New York: Macmillan, 1994.

Bradley, Robert. *Husband-Coached Childbirth.* New York: Bantam Books, 1996.

Brock, Peter. *A Brief History of Pacifism: From Jesus to Tolstoy.* N.p. Distributed by Syracuse University Press, 1992.

Brown, Michael, and John May. *The Greenpeace Story.* New York: Dorling Kindersley, 1991.

Buckley, Gail Lumet. "Left, Right, and Center." *America,* May 9, 1998.

Bullard, Sara. *Free at Last: A History of the Civil Rights Movement and Those Who Died in the Struggle.* New York: Oxford University Press, 1993.

Burkett, Elinor. *The Gravest Show on Earth: America in the Age of AIDS.* Boston: Houghton Mifflin, 1995.

Cade, Toni. *The Black Woman: An Anthology.* New York: New American Library, 1970.

Campbell, James. *Exiled in Paris.* New York: Scribner's, 1995.

———. *Talking at the Gate: A Life of James Baldwin.* New York: Viking, 1991.

Carmichael, Stokely, with Charles Hamilton. *Black Power: The Politics of Liberation.* New York: Random House, 1967.

Castañeda, Jorge. *Compañero: The Life and Death of Che Guevara.* New York: Knopf, 1997.

Castellucci, John. *The Big Dance: The Untold Story of Kathy Boudin and the Terrorist Family That Committed the Brink's Robbery Murders.* New York: Dodd, Mead, and Company, 1986.

Caute, David. *The Great Fear: The Anti-Communist Purge under Truman and Eisenhower.* New York: Simon and Schuster, 1978.

Chisholm, Shirley. *The Good Fight.* New York: Harper and Row, 1973.

———. *Unbought and Unbossed.* Boston: Houghton Mifflin, 1970.

Christopher, Joyce, and Eric Stover. *Witnesses from the Grave.* Boston: Little, Brown, 1991.

Clines, Francis X. "The Sting of Tear Gas and Regret." *New York Times,* August 26, 1996.

Clinton, Hillary Rodham. *It Takes a Village and Other Lessons Children Teach Us.* New York: Simon and Schuster.

Cohen, Marcia. *The Sisterhood: The Inside Story of the Women's Movement and the Leaders Who Made It Happen.* New York: Ballantine, 1988.

Collinge, William. *The American Holistic Health Association Complete Guide to Alternative Medicine.* New York: Warner Books, 1996.

Commoner, Barry. *Closing Circle: Nature, Man, and Technology.* New York: Alfred A. Knopf, 1971.

Cousteau, Jacques. *World without Sun.* New York: Harper and Row, 1965.

Cronkite, Kitty. *On the Edge of the Spotlight.* New York: Morrow, 1981.

David, Lester, and Irene David. *Bobby Kennedy: The Making of a Folk Hero.* New York: Dodd and Mead, 1986.

DeCurtis, Anthony, and James Henke, eds. *The Rolling Stone Illustrated History of Rock and Roll.* New York: Random House, 1992.

Dees, Morris, and Steve Fiffer. *A Season for Justice.* New York: Charles Scribner's Sons, 1991.

DeKeseredy, Walter, and Martin Schwartz. *Woman Abuse on Campus: Results from the Canadian National Survey.* Thousand Oaks, CA: Sage, 1997.

Deloria, Vine, Jr. *Custer Died for Your Sins: An Indian Manifesto.* New York: Macmillan, 1969.

Denenberg, Barry. *Nelson Mandela: No Easy Walk to Freedom.* New York: Scholastic, 1991.

Diamond, Stephen. *What the Trees Said: Life on a New Age Farm.* New York: Dell, 1971.

DiCanio, Margaret. *The Encyclopedia of Marriage, Divorce, and Family.* New York: Facts on File, 1989.

———. *The Encyclopedia of Violence: Origins, Attitudes, Consequences.* New York: Facts on File, 1993.

Dick-Read, Grantly. *The Original Approach to Natural Childbirth,* 4th ed. Revised and edited by Helen Wessel and Harlan Ellis. New York: Harper and Row, 1972.

Dolan, Edward. *America after Vietnam: Legacies of a Hated War.* New York: Franklin Watts, 1989.

Dooley, Thomas A. *Deliver Us from Evil: The Story of Vietnam's Flight to Freedom.* New York: Farrar, Straus, and Cudahy, 1956.

Edelman, Marian Wright. *Families in Peril: An Agenda for Social Change.* Cambridge, MA: Harvard University Press, 1987.

———. *The Measure of Our Success: A Letter to My Children and Yours.* Boston: Beacon Press, 1994.

Ehrlich, Paul. *The Population Bomb.* River City, MA: River City Press, 1968, 1975.

———. *The Population Explosion.* New York: Simon and Schuster, 1990.

Eisele, Albert. *Almost to the Presidency: A Biography of Two American Politicians.* Blue Earth, MN: Piper Company, 1972.

Ewing, Charles Patrick. *When Children Kill.* Lexington, MA: Lexington Books, 1990.

Faber, Doris. *Bella Abzug.* New York: Lothrop, Lee and Shepard, 1976.

Faludi, Susan. *Backlash: The Undeclared War against American Women.* New York: Doubleday, 1991.

Farber, David. *The Sixties: From Memory to History.* Chapel Hill: University of North Carolina Press, 1994.

Farley, Christopher John. "Rhyme or Reason?" *Time,* March 27, 1997.

Farmer, James. *Lay Bare the Heart: An Autobiography of the Civil Rights Movement.* New York: Simon and Schuster, 1988.

Feinberg, Barbara Silberdick. *Marx and Marxism.* New York: Franklin Watts, 1985.

Firestone, Shulamith, and Anne Koedt, eds. *Notes from a Second Year.* Anne Koedt, 1970.

Fisher, Robert. *Let the People Decide: Neighborhood Organizing in America.* New York: Twayne Publications, 1984.

Flader, Susan, and J. Baird Callicott, eds. *The River of the Mother of God and Other Essays by Aldo Leopold.* Madison: University of Wisconsin Press, 1991.

Folsom, Franklin, and Connie Fledderjohann. *The Great Peace March: An American Odyssey.* Santa Fe, NM: Ocean Tree Books, 1988.

Foner, Philip, ed. *The Black Panthers Speak.* Philadelphia: Lippincott, 1970.

Foster, Julian, and Durward Long, eds. *Protest! Student Activism in America.* New York: Morrow, 1970.

Fournier, Michael, ed. *Collected Poems of Louis Ginsberg.* Orono, ME: Northern Lights, 1992.

Frady, Marshall. *Jesse: The Life and Philosophy of Jesse Jackson.* New York: Random House, 1996.

Friedan, Betty. *Beyond Gender: The New Politics of Work and Family.* Washington, DC: Woodrow Wilson Center Press, 1997.

———. *The Feminine Mystique.* New York: Dell, 1963.

———. *Fountain of Age.* New York: Simon and Schuster, 1994.

———. *It Changed My Life: Writings on the Women's Movement.* New York: Random House, 1976.

———. *Second Stage.* New York: Simon and Schuster, 1981.

Friedman, Leon, ed. *Violence in America,* vols. 1–16. New York: Chelsea House, 1983.

Friedman, Myra. *Buried Alive: The Biography of Janis Joplin.* New York: Harmony Books, 1992.

Gan, Geraldine. *Lives of Notable Asian Americans: Arts, Entertainment, Sports.* New York: Chelsea House, 1995.

Gandhi, Mohandas. *Autobiography: The Story of My Experiments with Truth.* New York: Dover, 1963.

Gimlin, Hoyt, ed. *Youth Problems: Editorial Research Reports.* Washington, DC: Congressional Quarterly, 1982.

Ginsberg, Allen. *Collected Poems 1947–1980.* New York: Harper and Row, 1984.

Glaser, Elizabeth. *In the Absence of Angels.* New York: Berkley Books, 1991.

Glock, Charles, and Robert Bellah. *New Religious Consciousness.* Berkeley: University of California Press, 1976.

Goines, David Lance. *The Free Speech Movement: Coming of Age in the 1960s.* Berkeley, CA: Ten Speed Press, 1993.

Gonzales, Delores. *Cesar Chavez: Leader for Migrant Farm Workers.* Springfield, NJ: Enslow Publishers, 1996.

Goodman, Paul. *Growing Up Absurd.* New York: Random House, 1960.

Goodwin, Doris. *The Fitzgeralds and the Kennedys.* New York: Simon and Schuster, 1987.

Hampton, Willborn. "Allen Ginsberg, Major Poet of Beat Generation, Dies at 70." *New York Times,* April 6, 1997.

Harbury, Jennifer. *Searching for Everardo: A Story of Love, War, and the CIA in Guatemala.* New York: Warner Books, 1997.

Harrington, Michael. *The Long Distance Runner: An Autobiography.* New York: Holt, 1988.

———. *The Other America.* Markham, Ontario: Penguin Books, 1962.

———. *The Twilight of Capitalism.* New York: Simon and Schuster, 1976.

———. *A Vast Majority: A Journey to the World's Poor.* New York: Simon and Schuster, 1977.

Harrison, Barbara, and Daniel Terris. *A Ripple of Hope: The Life of Robert F. Kennedy.* New York: Lodestar Books, 1997.

———. *A Twilight Struggle: The Life of John Fitzgerald Kennedy.* New York: Lothrop, Lee and Shepard Books, 1992.

Haskins, James. *Freedom Rides: Journey for Justice.* New York: Hyperion, 1995.

Hayden, Tom. *Irish Hunger: Personal Reflections on the Legacy of the Famine.* Boulder, CO: Roberts Rinehart, 1997.

———. *Reunion: A Memoir.* New York: Random House, 1988.

Bibliography

———. *Trial*. New York: Holt, 1970.

Hearst, Patricia. *Every Secret Thing*. Garden City, NJ: Doubleday, 1982.

Hearst, Patricia, with Cordelia Frances Biddle. *Murder at San Simeon*. New York: Scribner, 1996.

Heilbrun, Carolyn G. *The Education of a Woman: The Life of Gloria Steinem*. New York: Dial Press, 1995.

Hill, Anita. *Speaking Truth to Power*. New York: Bantam Doubleday Dell, 1997.

Hoffman, Abbie. *Revolution for the Hell of It*. New York: Dial Press, 1968.

———. *Soon to Be a Motion Picture*. New York: Putnam, 1980.

Holmes, Ronald. *Profiling Violent Crime: An Investigative Tool*. Newbury Park, CA: Sage, 1989.

Hornblower, Margot. "Labor's Youth Brigade." *Time*, July 15, 1996.

Horowitz, Robert, and Howard Davidson, eds. *Legal Rights of Children* (Family Law Series). Colorado Springs, CO: Shepards/McGraw-Hill, 1984.

Horton, Myles, with Judith Kohl and Herbert Kohl. *The Long Haul: An Autobiography*. New York: Doubleday, 1990.

Hudson, Christopher. *Killing Fields*. New York: Dell, 1984.

Hull, Mary. *Rosa Parks*. New York: Chelsea House, 1994.

Isaac, Rael Jean, and Virginia Armat. *Madness in the Streets: How Psychiatry and the Law Abandoned the Mentally Ill*. New York: Free Press, 1990.

Isserman, Maurice. *If I Had a Hammer ... The Death of the Old Left and the Birth of the New Left*. New York: Basic Books, 1987.

Janofsky, Michael. "Debate on March, and Farrakhan, Persists as Black Men Converge on the Capital." *New York Times*, October 16, 1995.

Joint Commission on Mental Illness. *Action for Mental Illness and Mental Health: The Final Report on the Joint Commission on Mental Illness*. New York: Science Editions, 1961.

Johnson, A. M., et al. *Sexual Attitudes and Lifestyles*. Oxford: Blackwell Scientific, 1992.

Jones, LeRoi. *Autobiography of Leroi Jones/Amiri Baraka*. New York: Scribner, 1984.

Jones, Maxwell. *The Therapeutic Community: A Treatment Method in Psychiatry*. New York: Basic Books, 1953.

Kaplan, David, and Alec Dubro. *Yakuza: The Explosive Account of Japan's Criminal Underworld*. Reading, MA: Addison-Wesley, 1986.

Katz, Bobbi. *Nelson Mandela: A Champion of Freedom*. New York: Random House, 1995.

Katz, Jonathan. *Gay American History: Lesbians and Gay Men in the U.S.A.: A Documentary*. New York: Harper and Row, 1985.

Katz, Michael. *The Undeserving Poor: From the War on Poverty to the War on Welfare*. New York: Simon and Schuster, 1989.

Kellner, Douglas. *Ernesto "Che" Guevara*. New York: Chelsea House, 1989.

Kerr, Clark. *The Uses of the University*. Cambridge, MA: Harvard University Press, 1963.

Kesselus, Rev. Ken. "Former Presiding Bishop John E. Hines Dies after Leaving a Legacy of Social Action." *Episcopal News Service*, July 20, 1997.

Kherdian, David. *Beat Voices: An Anthology of Beat Poetry*. New York: Henry Holt, 1995.

King, Mary. *Freedom Song: A Personal Story of the 1960s Civil Rights Movement*. New York: Morrow, 1987.

King, Reverend Martin Luther, Jr. *Stride toward Freedom*. New York: Harper, 1958.

Kinoy, Arthur. *Rights on Trial: The Odyssey of a People's Lawyer*. Larchmont, NY: Bernel Books, 1983.

Kinsey, Alfred. *Sexual Behavior in the Human Female*. Philadelphia, PA: W. B. Saunders, 1953.

———. *Sexual Behavior in the Human Male*. Philadelphia, PA: W. B. Saunders, 1948.

Kismaric, Carole, ed. *Forced Out: The Agony of the Refugee in Our Time*. New York: Human Rights Watch and J.M. Kaplan Fund, in association with William Morrow, W. W. Norton, Penguin Books, and Random House, n.d. (ca. 1989).

Kitano, Harry, and Roger Daniels. *Asian Americans: An Emerging Minority after 1965*. New York: Chelsea House, 1995.

Klein, Aaron, and Cynthia Klein. *Mind Trips: The Story of Consciousness-Raising Movements*. Garden City, NY: Doubleday, 1979.

Kozol, Jonathan. *Rachel and Her Children*. New York: Crown, 1988.

Kriseova, Eda. *Vaclav Havel: The Authorized Biography*. New York: St. Martin's Press, 1993.

Kronenwetter, Michael. *The Peace Commandos: Nonviolent Heroes*. New York: New Discovery Books, 1994.

Laffin, Arthur, and Anne Montgomery. *Swords into Plowshares: Nonviolent Direct Action and Disarmament*. New York: Harper and Row, 1987.

Landau, Elaine. *The White Power Movement: America's Racist Hate Groups*. Brookfield, CT: Millbrook Press, 1993.

Lang, Susan. *Extremist Groups in America*. New York: Franklin Watts, 1990.

Laqueur, Walter. *The Age of Terrorism*. Boston: Little, Brown, 1987.

Lardiero, Carl. "Of Disproportionate Minority Confinement." *Corrections Today*, June 1997.

Larijani, L. Casey. *The Virtual Reality Primer*. New York: McGraw-Hill, 1994.

Lately, Thomas. *When Even Angels Wept: The Senator Joseph McCarthy Affair—A Story without a Hero*. New York: Morrow, 1973.

Lawless, Ray. *Folksingers and Folksongs in America*. New York: Duell, Sloan, Pearce, 1960.

Leary, Timothy. *Flashbacks: An Autobiography*. Boston: Houghton Mifflin, 1983.

———. *The Politics of Ecstasy*. New York: Putnam, 1968.

Leboyer, Frederick. *Birth without Violence*. New York: Knopf, 1975.

Leone, Daniel. *The Spread of AIDS*. San Diego, CA: Greenhaven Press, 1997.

Leopold, Aldo. *Sand County Almanac: Sketches Here and There*. New York: Oxford University Press, 1987.

Levy, Jacques. *Cesar Chavez: Autobiography of La Causa*. New York: W. W. Norton and Company, 1975.

Levy, Leonard. *Freedom of the Press from Zenger to Jefferson*. New York: Bobbs-Merrill, 1966.

Light, Donald. *Becoming Psychiatrists*. New York: W. W. Norton, 1980.

Light, Paul. *Baby Boomers*. New York: W. W. Norton, 1988.

Lincoln, C. Eric. *The Black Muslim in America*, 3d ed. Grand Rapids, MI: W. B. Eerdmans; Trenton, NJ: Africa World Press, 1965.

Lineberry, William, ed. *The Struggle against Terrorism*. New York: H. W. Wilson, 1989.

Loeb, Paul Rogat. *Hope and Hard Times: America's Peace Movement and the Reagan Era*. Lexington, MA: Lexington Books, 1987.

MacKinnon, Catharine. *Sexual Harassment of Working Women*. New Haven, CT: Yale University Press, 1979.

Madhubuti, Haki, and Maulana Karenga. *Million Man March/Day of Absence: A Commemorative Anthology*. Chicago: Third World Press, 1996.

Marcus, Eric. *Making History: The Struggle for Gay and Lesbian Equal Rights, 1945–1990: An Oral History*. New York: HarperCollins, 1993.

Marcuse, Herbert. *Eros and Civilization*. Boston: Beacon Press, 1955.

———. *One-Dimensional Man: Studies in Ideology of Advanced Industrial Society*. Boston: Beacon Press, 1964.

Marshall Cavendish Corp. *The Vietnam War: People and Politics*. New York: Marshall Cavendish, 1988.

Martinez, Demetria. "Time to Take a Stand against Deportation." *National Catholic Reporter*, April 18, 1997.

Marx, Doug. *The Homeless*. Ucro Beach, FL: The Rourke Corporation, 1990.

Massachusetts Coalition of Battered Women's Service Groups. *Shelter and Beyond*. Massachusetts Coalition of Battered Women's Services, 1993.

Massaquoi, Hans. "Rosa Parks: Still a Rebel with a Cause at 83." *Ebony*, March 1996.

McCarthy, Eugene. *The Year of the People*. Garden City, NY: Doubleday, 1969.

McGorvey, Norma, with Andy Mesler. *I Am Roe: My Life,* Roe v. Wade, *and Freedom of Choice*. New York: HarperCollins, 1994.

McGovern, George. *Grassroots: The Autobiography of George McGovern*. New York: Random House, 1977.

———. *Terry: My Daughter's Life and Death Struggle with Alcoholism*. New York: Villard Books, 1996.

———. *War against Want: America's Food for Peace Program*. New York: Walker, 1964.

McLellan, Vin, and Paul Avery. *The Voices of Guns*. New York: G. P. Putnam's Sons, 1977.

McLuhan, Marshall. *Gutenberg Galaxy: The Making of Typographic Man*. Toronto: University of Toronto Press, 1962.

———. *Mechanical Bride: Folklore of Industrial Man*. Boston: Beacon, 1962.

———. *The Medium Is the Massage: An Inventory of Effects*. New York: Random House, 1967.

———. *Understanding Media: The Extensions of Man*. New York: McGraw, 1964.

Means, Russell. *Road to Wounded Knee*. New York: Bantam, 1974.

———. *Where White Men Fear to Tread: The Autobiography of Russell Means*. New York: St. Martin's Press, 1995.

Michel, Virgil. *Christian Social Reconstruction: Some Fundamentals of the Quadragesimo Año*. Milwaukee, WI: Bruce Publishing Company, 1937.

Miles, Barry. *Ginsberg: A Biography*. New York: Simon and Schuster, 1989.

Miller, Timothy. *The Hippies and American Values*. Knoxville: University of Tennessee Press, 1991.

Mills, Kay. *The Little Life of Mine: The Life of Fannie Lou Hamer*. New York: Dutton, 1993.

Bibliography

Milton S. Eisenhower Foundation. *Youth Investment and Community Reconstruction: Street Lessons on Drugs and Crimes for the Nineties,* a Tenth Anniversary Report. Washington, DC: Milton Eisenhower Foundation, 1990.

Morgan, Robin. *Going Too Far: The Personal Chronicles of a Feminist.* New York: Vintage Books, 1977.

———. *Sisterhood Is Powerful: An Anthology from the Women's Liberation Movement.* New York: Random House, 1970.

Morin, Isobel. *Women of the U.S. Congress.* Minneapolis: Oliver Press, 1994.

Morrow, Lance. "The Whole World Was Watching." *Time,* August 26, 1996.

Muhammed, Elijah. *Message to the Black Man in America.* Chicago: Muhammed Mosque No. 2, 1965.

Nabokov, Peter, ed. *Native American Testimony: A Chronicle of Indian-White Relations from Prophecy to the Present, 1492–1992.* New York: Viking, 1991.

Nader, Ralph. *Unsafe at Any Speed.* New York: Grossman, 1965.

O'Ballance, Edgar. *Language of Violence.* San Rafael, CA: Presidio Press, 1979.

Othchet, Amy. "Muhammed Yunus: On Tour with Grameen Bank." *UNESCO Sources,* April 1995.

Parks, Rosa. *Rosa Parks, My Story.* New York: Dial Books, 1990.

Parks, Rosa, with Gregory Reed. *Quiet Strength: The Faith, the Hope, and the Heart of a Woman Who Changed a Nation.* Grand Rapids, MI: Sondervan Publishing House, 1994.

Pelka, Fred. *The ABC-CLIO Companion to the Disability Rights Movement.* Santa Barbara, CA: ABC-CLIO, 1997.

Podhoretz, Norman: "My War with Allen Ginsberg." *Commentary,* August 1997.

Powers, Richard Gid. *Secrecy and Power: The Life of J. Edgar Hoover.* New York: Free Press, 1987.

"A Protester with Politesse." *U.S. News and World Report,* November 18, 1996.

Prucha, Francis Paul. *The Great White Father: The United States Government and the American Indians.* Lincoln: University of Nebraska Press, 1984.

Rakove, Milton. *Don't Make No Waves—Don't Back No Losers.* Bloomington: Indiana University Press, 1974.

Reagan, Leslie. *When Abortion Was a Crime: Women, Medicine, and Law in the United States, 1867–1973.* Berkeley: University of California Press, 1997.

Redstockings. *Feminist Revolution.* N.p.: Redstockings, 1975.

Reef, Catherine. *Jacques Cousteau: Champion of the Sea.* New York: Harper and Row, 1965.

Reich, Charles. *The Greening of America.* New York: Random House, 1970.

———. *Opposing the System.* New York: Crown, 1995.

Ribadeneira, Diego. "Compassion in Action: Nun Honored for a Lifetime of Work." *Boston Globe,* 1997.

Rice, Gerard. *The Bold Experiment: JFK's Peace Corps.* Notre Dame, IN: University of Notre Dame Press, 1985.

"Riding the Che-Chic Route." *Economist,* October 11, 1997.

Roberts, Jack L. *Nelson Mandela: Determined to Be Free.* Brookfield, CT: Millbrook Press, 1995.

tone, June 29, 1995.

Rosenfeld, Isadore. *Doctor, What's My Alternative? An Establishment Doctor Looks at Complementary Medicine.* New York: Warner Books, 1996.

Royko, Mike. *Boss: Richard J. Daley of Chicago.* New York: Dutton.

Rubel, David. *Fannie Lou Hamer: From Sharecropping to Politics.* Englewood Cliffs, NJ: Silver Burdett Press, 1990.

Sale, Kirkpatrick. *SDS.* New York: Random House, 1973.

Scheidler, Joseph. *Closed: 99 Ways to Stop Abortion.* Rockford, IL: Tan Books and Pubs, 1993.

Schneir, Miriam. *Feminism in Our Time: The Essential Writings, World War II to the Present.* New York: Vintage Books, 1994.

Schwartz, Martin, and Walter DeKeseredy. *Sexual Assault on the College Campus.* Thousand Oaks, CA: Sage, 1997.

Scully, Rock, with David Dalton. *Living with the Dead: Twenty Years on the Bus with Garcia and the Grateful Dead.* Boston: Little, Brown, 1996.

Seeger, Pete. *Where Have All the Flowers Gone: A Musical Autobiography.* Bethlehem, PA: Sing Out, 1993.

Shapiro, Joseph. *No Pity.* New York: Random House, 1994.

———. "Others Saw a Victim, But Ed Roberts Didn't." *U. S. News and World Report,* March 27, 1995.

Sherrow, Victoria. *Mohandas Gandhi: The Power of the Spirit.* Brookfield, CT: Millbrook Press, 1994.

"Should Students with Disabilities Be Allowed to Try Out for and Compete on School Athletic Teams or

Should Schools Be Responsible for Providing Extracurricular Athletic Options for Those Students with Disabilities." *Journal of Physical Education, Recreation, and Dance,* March 1998.

Sleeper, James, and Alan Mintz, eds. *The New Jews.* New York: Vintage Books, 1971.

Small, Melvin, and William Hoover, eds. *Give Peace a Chance: Exploring the Vietnam Antiwar Movement.* Syracuse, NY: Syracuse University Press, 1992.

Solomon, Larry. "Sweatshops in the Spotlight." *Third Force,* September/October, 1996.

Stambler, Irwin. *The Encyclopedia of Pop, Rock, and Soul.* New York: St. Martin's Press, 1989.

Steinem, Gloria. *Outrageous Acts and Everyday Rebellions.* New York: Holt, Rinehart and Winston, 1983.

———. *Revolution from Within: A Book of Self-Esteem.* Boston: Little, Brown, 1992.

Steiner, Stan. *La Raza: The Mexican Americans.* New York: Harper Colophon, 1970.

———. *The New Indians.* New York: Harper and Row, 1968.

Stern, Kenneth S. *Loud Hawk: The United States versus the American Indian Movement.* Norman: University of Oklahoma Press, 1994.

Suro, Roberto. *Strangers among Us: How Latino Immigration Is Transforming America.* New York: Alfred A. Knopf, 1998.

Tackach, James. *The Importance of James Baldwin.* San Diego, CA: Lucent Books, 1997.

Takaki, Ronald. *Strangers at the Gate Again: Asian Immigration after 1965.* New York: Chelsea House, 1995.

Thomas, Norman. *The Great Dissenter.* New York: Norton, 1961.

Torey, E. Fuller. *Nowhere to Go: The Tragic Odyssey of the Homeless Mentally Ill.* New York: Harper and Row, 1988.

Tytell, John. *Naked Angels: The Lives and Literature of the Beat Generation.* New York: Grove-Atlantic, 1986.

Unger, Irwin. *The Best of Intentions: The Triumphs and Failures of the Great Society under Kennedy, Johnson and Nixon.* New York: Doubleday, 1996.

United Nations Educational, Scientific, and Cultural Organization (UNESCO) and the International Catholic Child Bureau. *Working with Street Children.* Paris: UNESCO/BICE, 1995.

Veglahn, Nancy. *Women Scientists.* New York: Facts on File, 1991.

Wallace, Jim. *Waging Peace: A Handbook for the Struggle to Abolish Nuclear Weapons.* San Francisco: Harper and Row, 1982.

Walters, Robert S., and David H. Blake. *The Politics of Global Economic Relations,* 4th ed. Paramus, NJ: Prentice-Hall, 1992.

Warren, James A. *Portrait of a Tragedy: America and the Vietnam War.* New York: Lothrop, Lee and Shepard Books, 1990.

Warrior, Betsy. *Battered Women's Directory.* Cambridge, MA: Betsy Warrior, 1982.

Watson, Steven. *The Birth of the Beat Generation: Visionaries, Rebels, and Hipsters, 1944–1960.* New York: Pantheon Books, 1995.

Wei, Willie. *The Asian American Movement.* Philadelphia, PA: Temple University Press, 1993.

Weitsman, Madeline. *The Peace Corps.* New York: Chelsea House, 1989.

Wellings, K., et al. *Sexual Behavior in Britain.* London: Penguin, 1994.

Wessells, Mike. "Child Soldiers." *Bulletin of the Atomic Scientists,* November/December 1997.

Westervelt, Eric. "Sisterly Love." *New Republic,* November 17, 1997.

Wexler, Sanford. *The Civil Rights Movement: An Eyewitness History.* New York: Facts on File, 1993.

White, Michael, and John Gribbin. *Stephen Hawking: A Life in Science.* New York: Dutton, 1992.

Whitfield, Stephen J. *A Death in the Delta: The Story of Emmett Till.* New York: Free Press, 1988.

Wilcox, Fred. *Uncommon Martyrs: The Berrigans, the Catholic Left, and the Plowshares Movement.* Reading, MA: Addison Wesley, 1991.

Williams, Juan, ed. *Eyes on the Prize: America's Civil Rights Years, 1954–1965.* New York: Viking Penguin, 1987.

Young, Andrew. *An Easy Burden: The Civil Rights Movement and the Transformation of America.* New York: HarperCollins, 1996.

Illustration
Credits

Index

Index

Index

Index

Index